LOLITA

Vladimir Nabokov was born in St Petersburg in 1899. He studied at Trinity College, Cambridge, before moving to Berlin in
1922. Between 1923 and 1940 he published novels, short stories,
plays, poems and translations in the Russian language and established himself as one of the most outstanding Russian *émigré*
writers. In 1940 he moved with his wife and son to America,
where he worked as a lecturer and professor until he retired from
teaching in 1959. Nabokov published his first novel in English,
The Real Life of Sebastian Knight, in 1941. His other books include
Ada; *Laughter in the Dark*; *Despair*; *Pnin*; *Nabokov's Dozen*;
Invitation to a Beheading; *Mary*; *Bend Sinister*; *Glory*; *Pale Fire*; *The
Gift*; *The Luzhin Defense* and *Lolita*, which brought him worldwide fame. In 1973 he was awarded the American National Medal
for Literature. Vladimir Nabokov died in 1977.

Kathryn Macnaughton is an illustrator and artist who lives and
works in Toronto. She is a graduate of Ontario College of Art and
Design whose work has appeared in magazines and on album covers.
Most recently her work was exhibited at Brooklynite Gallery in
New York. She was also accepted into the American Illustration
annual. Her website is www.kathrynmacnaughton.com.

Lolita

VLADIMIR NABOKOV

PENGUIN BOOKS

PENGUIN ESSENTIALS

Published by the Penguin Group
Penguin Books Ltd, 80 Strand, London WC2R ORL, England
Penguin Group (USA) Inc., 375 Hudson Street, New York, New York 10014, USA
Penguin Group (Canada), 90 Eglinton Avenue East, Suite 700, Toronto, Ontario, Canada M4P 2Y3
(a division of Pearson Penguin Canada Inc.)
Penguin Ireland, 25 St Stephen's Green, Dublin 2, Ireland (a division of Penguin Books Ltd)
Penguin Group (Australia), 250 Camberwell Road, Camberwell, Victoria 3124, Australia
(a division of Pearson Australia Group Pty Ltd)
Penguin Books India Pvt Ltd, 11 Community Centre, Panchsheel Park, New Delhi – 110 017, India
Penguin Group (NZ), 67 Apollo Drive, Rosedale, Auckland 0632, New Zealand
(a division of Pearson New Zealand Ltd)
Penguin Books (South Africa) (Pty) Ltd, 24 Sturdee Avenue, Rosebank, Johannesburg 2196, South Africa

Penguin Books Ltd, Registered Offices: 80 Strand, London WC2R ORL, England

www.penguin.com

First published in Great Britain by Weidenfeld & Nicolson 1959
Published in Penguin Books 1995
This Penguin Essentials edition published 2011

001

ISBN: 978-0-241-99649-2

www.greenpenguin.co.uk

to Véra

Foreword

"Lolita, or the Confession of a White Widowed Male," such were the two titles under which the writer of the present note received the strange pages it preambulates. "Humbert Humbert," their author, had died in legal captivity, of coronary thrombosis, on November 16, 1952, a few days before his trial was scheduled to start. His lawyer, my good friend and relation, Clarence Choate Clark, Esq., now of the District of Columbia bar, in asking me to edit the manuscript, based his request on a clause in his client's will which empowered my eminent cousin to use his discretion in all matters pertaining to the preparation of "Lolita" for print. Mr. Clark's decision may have been influenced by the fact that the editor of his choice had just been awarded the Poling Prize for a modest work ("Do the Senses make Sense?") wherein certain morbid states and perversions had been discussed.

My task proved simpler than either of us had anticipated. Save for the correction of obvious solecisms and a careful suppression of a few tenacious details that despite "H.H."'s own efforts still subsisted in his text as signposts and tombstones (indicative of places or persons that taste would conceal and compassion spare), this remarkable memoir is presented intact. Its author's bizarre cognomen is his own invention; and, of course, this mask—through which two hypnotic eyes seem to glow—had to remain unlifted in accordance with its wearer's wish. While "Haze" only rhymes with the heroine's real surname, her first name is too closely interwound with the inmost fiber of the book to allow one to alter it; nor (as the

I

reader will perceive for himself) is there any practical necessity to do so. References to "H.H."'s crime may be looked up by the inquisitive in the daily papers for September–October 1952; its cause and purpose would have continued to remain a complete mystery, had not this memoir been permitted to come under my reading lamp.

For the benefit of old-fashioned readers who wish to follow the destinies of the "real" people beyond the "true" story, a few details may be given as received from Mr. "Windmuller," of "Ramsdale," who desires his identity suppressed so that "the long shadow of this sorry and sordid business" should not reach the community to which he is proud to belong. His daughter, "Louise," is by now a college sophomore. "Mona Dahl" is a student in Paris. "Rita" has recently married the proprietor of a hotel in Florida. Mrs. "Richard F. Schiller" died in childbed, giving birth to a stillborn girl, on Christmas Day 1952, in Gray Star, a settlement in the remotest Northwest. "Vivian Darkbloom" has written a biography, "My Cue," to be published shortly, and critics who have perused the manuscript call it her best book. The caretakers of the various cemeteries involved report that no ghosts walk.

Viewed simply as a novel, "Lolita" deals with situations and emotions that would remain exasperatingly vague to the reader had their expression been etiolated by means of platitudinous evasions. True, not a single obscene term is to be found in the whole work; indeed, the robust philistine who is conditioned by modern conventions into accepting without qualms a lavish array of four-letter words in a banal novel, will be quite shocked by their absence here. If, however, for this paradoxical prude's comfort, an editor attempted to dilute or omit scenes that a certain type of mind might call "aphrodisiac" (see in this respect the monumental decision rendered December 6, 1933, by Hon. John M. Woolsey in regard to another, considerably more outspoken, book), one would have to forego the publication of "Lolita" altogether, since those very scenes that one might ineptly accuse of a sensuous existence of their own, are the most strictly functional ones in the development of a tragic tale tending unswervingly to nothing less than a moral apotheosis. The cynic may say that commercial pornography makes the same claim; the learned may counter by asserting that "H.H."'s impassioned confession is a tempest in a test tube; that at least 12% of American adult males—a "conservative" estimate according to Dr. Blanche Schwarzmann (verbal communication)—enjoy yearly, in one way or another, the special experience "H.H." describes with such despair; that had our demented diarist gone, in the fatal summer of 1947, to a competent psychopathologist, there would have been no disaster; but then, neither would there have been this book.

This commentator may be excused for repeating what he has stressed in his own books and lectures, namely that "offensive" is frequently but a synonym for "unusual"; and a great work of art is of course always original, and thus by its very nature should come as a more or less shocking surprise. I have no intention to glorify "H.H." No doubt, he is horrible, he is abject, he is a shining example of moral leprosy, a mixture of ferocity and jocularity that betrays supreme misery perhaps, but is not conducive to attractiveness. He is ponderously capricious. Many of his casual opinions on the people and scenery of this country are ludicrous. A desperate honesty that throbs through his confession does not absolve him from sins of diabolical cunning. He is abnormal. He is not a gentleman. But how magically his singing violin can conjure up a tendresse, a compassion for Lolita that makes us entranced with the book while abhorring its author!

As a case history, "Lolita" will become, no doubt, a classic in psychiatric circles. As a work of art, it transcends its expiatory aspects; and still more important to us than scientific significance and literary worth, is the ethical impact the book should have on the serious reader; for in this poignant personal study there lurks a general lesson; the wayward child, the egotistic mother, the panting maniac—these are not only vivid characters in a unique story: they warn us of dangerous trends; they point out potent evils. "Lolita" should make all of us—parents, social workers, educators—apply ourselves with still greater vigilance and vision to the task of bringing up a better generation in a safer world.

Widworth, Mass.   John Ray, Jr., Ph.D.
August 5, 1955

Part One

1

Lolita, light of my life, fire of my loins. My sin, my soul. Lo-lee-ta: the tip of the tongue taking a trip of three steps down the palate to tap, at three, on the teeth. Lo. Lee. Ta.

She was Lo, plain Lo, in the morning, standing four feet ten in one sock. She was Lola in slacks. She was Dolly at school. She was Dolores on the dotted line. But in my arms she was always Lolita.

Did she have a precursor? She did, indeed she did. In point of fact, there might have been no Lolita at all had I not loved, one summer, a certain initial girl-child. In a princedom by the sea. Oh when? About as many years before Lolita was born as my age was that summer. You can always count on a murderer for a fancy prose style.

Ladies and gentlemen of the jury, exhibit number one is what the seraphs, the misinformed, simple, noble-winged seraphs, envied. Look at this tangle of thorns.

2

I was born in 1910, in Paris. My father was a gentle, easy-going person, a salad of racial genes: a Swiss citizen, of mixed French and Austrian descent, with a dash of the Danube in his veins. I am going to pass around in a minute some lovely, glossy-blue picture-postcards. He owned a luxurious hotel on the Riviera. His father and two grand-fathers had sold wine, jewels and silk, respectively. At thirty he married an English girl, daughter of Jerome Dunn, the alpinist, and granddaughter of two Dorset parsons, experts in obscure subjects—paleopedology and Aeolian harps, respectively. My very photogenic mother died in a freak accident (picnic, lightning) when I was three, and, save for a pocket of warmth in the darkest past, nothing of her subsists within the hollows and dells of memory, over which, if you can still stand my style (I am writing under observation), the sun of my infancy had set: surely, you all know those redolent remnants of day suspended, with the midges, about some hedge in bloom or suddenly entered and traversed by the rambler, at the bottom of a hill, in the summer dusk; a furry warmth, golden midges.

My mother's elder sister, Sybil, whom a cousin of my father's had married and then neglected, served in my immediate family as a kind of unpaid governess and housekeeper. Somebody told me later that she had been in love with my father, and that he had lightheartedly taken advantage of it one rainy day and forgotten it by the time the weather cleared. I was extremely fond of her, despite the rigidity—the fatal rigidity—of some of her rules. Perhaps she wanted to make of me, in the fullness of time, a better widower than my father. Aunt Sybil had pink-rimmed azure eyes and a waxen complexion. She wrote poetry. She was poetically superstitious. She said she knew she would die soon after my sixteenth birthday, and did. Her husband, a great traveler in perfumes, spent most of his time in America, where eventually he founded a firm and acquired a bit of real estate.

I grew, a happy, healthy child in a bright world of illustrated books, clean sand, orange trees, friendly dogs, sea vistas and smiling faces. Around me the splendid Hotel Mirana revolved as a kind of private universe, a whitewashed cosmos within the blue greater one that blazed outside. From the aproned pot-scrubber to the flanneled potentate, everybody liked me, everybody petted me. Elderly American ladies leaning on their canes listed toward me like towers of Pisa. Ruined Russian princesses who could not pay my father, bought me expensive bonbons. He, *mon cher petit papa*, took me out boating and biking, taught me to swim and dive and water-ski, read to me *Don Quixote* and *Les Misérables*, and I adored and respected him and felt glad for him whenever I overheard the servants discuss his various lady-friends, beautiful and kind beings who made much of me and cooed and shed precious tears over my cheerful motherlessness.

I attended an English day school a few miles from home, and there I played rackets and fives, and got excellent marks, and was on perfect terms with schoolmates and teachers alike. The only definite sexual events that I can remember as having occurred before my thirteenth birthday (that is, before I first saw my little Annabel) were: a solemn, decorous and purely theoretical talk about pubertal surprises in the rose garden of the school with an American kid, the son of a then celebrated motion-picture actress whom he seldom saw in the three-dimensional world; and some interesting reactions on the part of my organism to certain photographs, pearl and umbra, with infinitely soft partings, in Pichon's sumptuous *La Beauté Humaine* that I had filched from under a mountain of marble-bound *Graphics* in the hotel library. Later, in his delightful debonair manner, my father gave me all the information he thought I needed about sex; this was just before sending me, in the autumn of 1923, to a *lycée* in Lyon (where we were to spend three winters); but alas, in the summer of that year, he was touring Italy with Mme de R. and her daughter, and I had nobody to complain to, nobody to consult.

3

Annabel was, like the writer, of mixed parentage: half-English, half-Dutch, in her case. I remember her features far less distinctly today than I did a few years ago, before I knew Lolita. There are two kinds of visual memory: one when you skillfully recreate an image in the laboratory of your mind, with your eyes open (and then I see Annabel in such general terms as: "honey-colored skin," "thin arms," "brown bobbed hair," "long lashes," "big bright mouth"); and the other when you instantly evoke, with shut eyes, on the dark innerside of your eyelids, the objective, absolutely optical replica of a beloved face, a little ghost in natural colors (and this is how I see Lolita).

Let me therefore primly limit myself, in describing Annabel, to saying she was a lovely child a few months my junior. Her parents were old friends of my aunt's, and as stuffy as she. They had rented a villa not far from Hotel Mirana. Bald brown Mr. Leigh and fat, powdered Mrs. Leigh (born Vanessa van Ness). How I loathed them! At first, Annabel and I talked of peripheral affairs. She kept lifting handfuls of fine sand and letting it pour through her fingers. Our brains were turned the way those of intelligent European preadolescents were in our day and set, and I doubt if much individual genius should be assigned to our interest in the plurality of inhabited worlds, competitive tennis, infinity, solipsism and so on. The softness and fragility of baby animals caused us the same intense pain. She wanted to be a nurse in some famished Asiatic country; I wanted to be a famous spy.

All at once we were madly, clumsily, shamelessly, agonizingly in love with each other; hopelessly, I should add, because that frenzy of mutual possession might have been assuaged only by our actually imbibing and assimilating every particle of each other's soul and flesh; but there we were, unable even to mate as slum children would have so easily found an opportunity to do. After one wild attempt we made to meet at night in her garden (of which more later), the only privacy we were allowed was to be out of earshot but not out of sight on the populous part of the *plage*. There, on the soft sand, a few feet away from our elders, we would sprawl all morning, in a petrified paroxysm of desire, and take advantage of every blessed quirk in space and time to touch each other: her hand, half-hidden in the sand, would creep toward me, its slender brown fingers sleepwalking nearer and nearer; then, her opalescent knee would start on a long cautious journey; sometimes a chance rampart built by younger children granted us sufficient concealment to graze each other's salty lips; these incomplete contacts drove our healthy and inexperienced young bodies to such a state of exasperation that not even the cold blue water, under which we still clawed at each other, could bring relief.

Among some treasures I lost during the wanderings of my adult years, there was a snapshot taken by my aunt which showed Annabel, her parents and the staid, elderly, lame gentleman, a Dr. Cooper, who that same summer courted my aunt, grouped around a table in a sidewalk café. Annabel did not come out well, caught as she was in the act of bending over her *chocolat glacé*, and her thin bare shoulders and the parting in her hair were about all that could be identified (as I remember that picture) amid the sunny blur into which her lost loveliness graded; but I, sitting somewhat apart from the rest, came out with a kind of dramatic conspicuousness: a moody, beetle-browed boy in a dark sport shirt and well-tailored white shorts, his legs crossed, sitting in profile, looking away. That photograph was taken on the last day of our fatal summer and just a few minutes before we made our second and final attempt to thwart fate. Under the flimsiest of pretexts (this was our very last chance, and nothing really mattered) we escaped from the café to the beach, and found a desolate stretch of sand, and there, in the violet shadow of some red rocks forming a kind of cave, had a brief session of avid caresses, with somebody's lost pair of sunglasses for only witness. I was on my knees, and on the point of possessing my darling, when two bearded bathers, the old man of the sea and his brother, came out of the sea with exclamations of ribald encouragement, and four months later she died of typhus in Corfu.

4

I leaf again and again through these miserable memories, and keep asking myself, was it then, in the glitter of that remote summer, that the rift in my life began; or was my excessive desire for that child only the first evidence of an inherent singularity? When I try to analyze my own cravings, motives, actions and so forth, I surrender to a sort of retrospective imagination which feeds the analytic faculty with boundless alternatives and which causes each visualized route to fork and re-fork without end in the maddeningly complex prospect of my past. I am convinced, however, that in a certain magic and fateful way Lolita began with Annabel.

I also know that the shock of Annabel's death consolidated the frustration of that nightmare summer, made of it a permanent obstacle to any further romance throughout the cold years of my youth. The spiritual and the physical had been blended in us with a perfection that must remain incomprehensible to the matter-of-fact, crude, standard-brained youngsters of today. Long after her death I felt her thoughts floating through mine. Long before we met we had had the same dreams. We compared notes. We found strange affinities. The same June of the same year (1919) a stray canary had fluttered into her house and mine, in two widely separated countries. Oh, Lolita, had *you* loved me thus!

I have reserved for the conclusion of my "Annabel" phase the account of our unsuccessful first tryst. One night, she managed to deceive the vicious vigilance of her family. In a nervous and slender-leaved mimosa grove at the back of their villa we found a perch on the ruins of a low stone wall. Through the darkness and the tender trees we could see the arabesques of lighted windows which, touched up by the colored inks of sensitive memory, appear to me now like playing cards—presumably because a bridge game was keeping the enemy busy. She trembled and twitched as I kissed the corner of her parted lips and the hot lobe of her ear. A cluster of stars palely glowed above us, between the silhouettes of long thin leaves; that vibrant sky seemed as naked as she was under her light frock. I saw her face in the sky, strangely distinct, as if it emitted a faint radiance of its own. Her legs, her lovely live legs, were not too close together, and when my hand located what it sought, a dreamy and eerie expression, half-pleasure, half-pain, came over those childish features. She sat a little higher than I, and whenever in her solitary ecstasy she was led to kiss me, her head would bend with a sleepy, soft, drooping movement that was almost woeful, and her bare knees caught and compressed my wrist, and slackened again; and her quivering mouth, distorted by the acridity of some mysterious potion, with a sibilant intake of breath came near to my face. She would try to relieve the pain of love by first roughly rubbing her dry lips against mine; then my darling would draw away with a nervous toss of her hair, and then again come darkly near and let me feed on her open mouth, while with a generosity that was ready to offer her everything, my heart, my throat, my entrails, I gave her to hold in her awkward fist the scepter of my passion.

I recall the scent of some kind of toilet powder—I believe she stole it from her mother's Spanish maid—a sweetish, lowly, musky perfume. It mingled with her own biscuity odor, and my senses were suddenly filled to the brim; a sudden commotion in a nearby bush prevented them from overflowing—and as we drew away from each other, and with aching veins attended to what was probably a prowling cat, there came from the house her mother's voice calling her, with a rising frantic note—and Dr. Cooper ponderously limped out into the garden. But that mimosa grove—the haze of stars, the tingle, the flame, the honeydew, and the ache remained with me, and that little girl with her seaside limbs and ardent tongue haunted me ever since—until at last, twenty-four years later, I broke her spell by incarnating her in another.

5

The days of my youth, as I look back on them, seem to fly away from me in a flurry of pale repetitive scraps like those morning snow storms of used tissue paper that a train passenger sees whirling in the wake of the observation car. In my sanitary relations with women I was practical, ironical and brisk. While a college student, in London and Paris, paid ladies sufficed me. My studies were meticulous and intense, although not particularly fruitful. At first, I planned to take a degree in psychiatry as many *manqué* talents do; but I was even more *manqué* than that; a peculiar exhaustion, I am so oppressed, doctor, set in; and I switched to English literature, where so many frustrated poets end as pipe-smoking teachers in tweeds. Paris suited me. I discussed Soviet movies with expatriates. I sat with uranists in the Deux Magots. I published tortuous essays in obscure journals. I composed pastiches:

> . . . Fräulein von Kulp
> may turn, her hand upon the door;
> I will not follow her. Nor Fresca. Nor
> that Gull.

A paper of mine entitled "The Proustian theme in a letter from Keats to Benjamin Bailey" was chuckled over by the six or seven scholars who read it. I launched upon an *"Histoire abrégée de la poésie anglaise"* for a prominent publishing firm, and then started to compile that manual of French literature for English-speaking students (with comparisons drawn from English writers) which was to occupy me throughout the forties—and the last volume of which was almost ready for press by the time of my arrest.

I found a job—teaching English to a group of adults in Auteuil. Then a school for boys employed me for a couple of winters. Now and then I took advantage of the acquaintances I had formed among social workers and psychotherapists to visit in their company various institutions, such as orphanages and reform schools, where pale pubescent girls with matted eyelashes could be stared at in perfect impunity remindful of that granted one in dreams.

Now I wish to introduce the following idea. Between the age limits of nine and fourteen there occur maidens who, to certain bewitched travelers, twice or many times older than they, reveal their true nature which is not human, but nymphic (that is, demoniac); and these chosen creatures I propose to designate as "nymphets."

It will be marked that I substitute time terms for spatial ones. In fact, I would have the reader see "nine" and "fourteen" as the boundaries—the mirrory beaches and rosy rocks—of an enchanted island haunted by those nymphets of mine and surrounded by a vast, misty sea. Between those age limits, are all girl-children nymphets? Of course not. Otherwise, we who are in the know, we lone voyagers, we nympholepts, would have long gone insane. Neither are good looks any criterion; and vulgarity, or at least what a given community terms so, does not necessarily impair certain mysterious characteristics, the fey grace, the elusive, shifty, soul-shattering, insidious charm that separates the nymphet from such coevals of hers as are incomparably more dependent on the spatial world of synchronous phenomena than on that intangible island of entranced time where Lolita plays with her likes. Within the same age limits the number of true nymphets is strikingly inferior to that of provisionally plain, or just nice, or "cute," or even "sweet" and "attractive," ordinary, plumpish, formless, cold-skinned, essentially human little girls, with tummies and pigtails, who may or may not turn into adults of great beauty (look at the ugly dumplings in black stockings and white hats that are metamorphosed into stunning stars of the screen). A normal man given a group photograph of school girls or Girl Scouts and asked to point out the comeliest one will not necessarily choose the nymphet among them. You have to be an artist and a madman, a creature of infinite melancholy, with a bubble of hot poison in your loins and a super-voluptuous flame permanently aglow in your subtle spine (oh, how you have to cringe and hide!), in order to discern at once, by ineffable signs—the slightly feline outline of a cheekbone, the slenderness of a downy limb, and other indices which despair and shame and tears of tenderness forbid me to tabulate—the little deadly demon among the wholesome children; *she* stands unrecognized by them and unconscious herself of her fantastic power.

Furthermore, since the idea of time plays such a magic part in the matter, the student should not be surprised to learn that there must be a gap of several years, never less than ten I should say, generally thirty or forty, and as many as ninety in a few known cases, between maiden and man to enable the latter to come under a nymphet's spell. It is a question of focal adjustment, of a certain distance that the inner eye thrills to surmount, and a certain contrast that the mind perceives with a gasp of perverse delight. When I was a child and she was a child, my little Annabel was no nymphet to me; I was her equal, a faunlet in my own right, on that same enchanted island of time; but today, in September 1952, after twenty-nine years have elapsed, I think I can distinguish in her the initial fateful elf in my life. We loved each other with a premature love, marked by a fierceness that so often destroys adult lives. I was a strong lad and survived; but the poison was in the wound, and the wound remained ever open, and soon I found myself maturing amid a civilization which allows a man of twenty-five to court a girl of sixteen but not a girl of twelve.

No wonder, then, that my adult life during the European period of my existence proved monstrously twofold. Overtly, I had so-called normal relationships with a number of terrestrial women having pumpkins or pears for breasts; inly, I was consumed by a hell furnace of localized lust for every passing nymphet whom as a law-abiding poltroon I never dared approach. The human females I was allowed to wield were but palliative agents. I am ready to believe that the sensations I derived from natural fornication were much the same as those known to normal big males consorting with their normal big mates in that routine rhythm which shakes the world. The trouble was that those gentlemen had not, and I *had*, caught glimpses of an incomparably more poignant bliss. The dimmest of my pollutive dreams was a thousand times more dazzling than all the adultery the most virile writer of genius or the most talented impotent might imagine. My world was split. I was aware of not one but two sexes, neither of which was mine; both would be termed female by the anatomist. But to me, through the prism of my senses, "they were as different as mist and mast." All this I rationalize now. In my twenties and early thirties, I did not understand my throes quite so clearly. While my body knew what it craved for, my mind rejected my body's every plea. One moment I was ashamed and frightened, another recklessly optimistic. Taboos strangulated me. Psychoanalysts wooed me with pseudoliberations of pseudolibidoes. The fact that to me the only objects of amorous tremor were sisters of Annabel's, her handmaids and girl-pages, appeared to me at times as a forerunner of insanity. At other times I would tell myself that it was all a question of attitude, that there was really nothing wrong in being moved to distraction by girl-children. Let me remind my reader that in England, with the passage of the Children and Young Person Act in 1933, the term "girl-child" is defined as "a girl who is over eight but under fourteen years" (after that, from fourteen to seventeen, the statutory definition is "young person"). In Massachusetts, U.S., on the other hand, a "wayward child" is, technically, one "between seven and seventeen years of age" (who, moreover, habitually associates with vicious or immoral persons). Hugh Broughton, a writer of controversy in the reign of James the First, has proved that Rahab was a harlot at ten years of age. This is all very interesting, and I daresay you see me already frothing at the mouth in a fit; but no, I am not; I am just winking happy thoughts into a little tiddle cup. Here are some more pictures. Here is Virgil who could the nymphet sing in single tone, but probably preferred a lad's perineum. Here are two of King Akhnaten's and Queen Nefertiti's pre-nubile Nile daughters (that royal couple had a litter of six), wearing nothing but many necklaces of bright beads, relaxed on cushions, intact after three thousand years, with their soft brown puppy-bodies, cropped hair and long ebony eyes. Here are some brides of ten compelled to seat themselves on the fascinum, the virile ivory in the temples of classical scholarship. Marriage and cohabitation before the age of puberty are still not uncommon in certain East Indian provinces. Lepcha old men of eighty copulate with girls of eight, and nobody minds. After all, Dante fell madly in love with his Beatrice when she was nine, a sparkling girleen, painted and lovely, and bejeweled, in a crimson frock, and this was in 1274, in Florence, at a private feast in the merry month of May. And when Petrarch fell madly in love with his Laureen, she was a fair-haired nymphet of twelve running in the wind, in the pollen and dust, a flower in flight, in the beautiful plain as descried from the hills of Vaucluse.

But let us be prim and civilized. Humbert Humbert tried hard to be good. Really and truly, he did. He had the utmost respect for ordinary children, with their purity and vulnerability, and under no circumstances would he have interfered with the innocence of a child, if there was the least risk of a row. But how his heart beat when, among the innocent throng, he espied a demon child, *"enfant charmante et fourbe,"* dim eyes, bright lips, ten years in jail if you only show her you are looking at her. So life went. Humbert was perfectly capable of intercourse with Eve, but it was Lilith he longed for. The bud-stage of breast development appears early (10.7 years) in the sequence of somatic changes accompanying pubescence. And the next maturational item available is the first appearance of pigmented pubic hair (11.2 years). My little cup brims with tiddles.

A shipwreck. An atoll. Alone with a drowned passenger's shivering child. Darling, this is only a game! How marvelous were my fancied adventures as I sat on a hard park bench pretending to be immersed in a trembling book. Around the quiet scholar, nymphets played freely, as if he were a familiar statue or part of an old tree's shadow and sheen. Once a perfect little beauty in a tartan frock, with a clatter put her heavily armed foot near me upon the bench to dip her slim bare arms into me and tighten the strap of her roller skate, and I dissolved in the sun, with my book for fig leaf, as her auburn ringlets fell all over her skinned knee, and the shadow of leaves I shared pulsated and melted on her radiant limb next to my chameleonic cheek. Another time a red-haired school girl hung over me in the *métro*, and a revelation of axillary russet I obtained remained in my blood for weeks. I could list a great number of these one-sided diminutive romances. Some of them ended in a rich flavor of hell. It happened for instance that from my balcony I would notice a lighted window across the street and what looked like a nymphet in the act of undressing before a co-operative mirror. Thus isolated, thus removed, the vision acquired an especially keen charm that made me race with all speed toward my lone gratification. But abruptly, fiendishly, the tender pattern of nudity I had adored would be transformed into the disgusting lamp-lit bare arm of a man in his underclothes reading his paper by the open window in the hot, damp, hopeless summer night.

Rope-skipping, hopscotch. That old woman in black who sat down next to me on my bench, on my rack of joy (a nymphet was groping under me for a lost marble), and asked if I had stomachache, the insolent hag. Ah, leave me alone in my pubescent park, in my mossy garden. Let them play around me forever. Never grow up.

6

A propos: I have often wondered what became of those nymphets later? In this wrought-iron world of criss-cross cause and effect, could it be that the hidden throb I stole from them did not affect *their* future? I had possessed her—and she never knew it. All right. But would it not tell some-time later? Had I not somehow tampered with her fate by involving her image in my voluptas? Oh, it was, and remains, a source of great and terrible wonder.

I learned, however, what they looked like, those lovely, maddening, thin-armed nymphets, when they grew up. I remember walking along an animated street on a gray spring afternoon somewhere near the Madeleine. A short slim girl passed me at a rapid, high-heeled, tripping step, we glanced back at the same moment, she stopped and I accosted her. She came hardly up to my chest hair and had the kind of dimpled round little face French girls so often have, and I liked her long lashes and tight-fitting tailored dress sheathing in pearl-gray her young body which still retained—and that was the nymphic echo, the chill of delight, the leap in my loins—a childish something mingling with the professional *frétillement* of her small agile rump. I asked her price, and she promptly replied with melodious silvery precision (a bird, a very bird!) *"Cent."* I tried to haggle but she saw the awful lone longing in my lowered eyes, directed so far down at her round forehead and rudimen-tary hat (a band, a posy); and with one beat of her lashes: *"Tant pis,"* she said, and made as if to move away. Perhaps only three years earlier I might have seen her coming home from school! That evocation settled the matter. She led me up the usual steep stairs, with the usual bell clearing the way for the *monsieur* who might not care to meet another *monsieur*, on the mournful climb to the abject room, all bed and *bidet*. As usual, she asked at once for her *petit cadeau*, and as usual I asked her name (Monique) and her age (eighteen). I was pretty well acquainted with the banal way of streetwalkers. They all answer *"dix-huit"*—a trim twitter, a note of finality and wistful deceit which they emit up to

21

ten times per day, the poor little creatures. But in Monique's case there could be no doubt she was, if anything, adding one or two years to her age. This I deduced from many details of her compact, neat, curiously immature body. Having shed her clothes with fascinating rapidity, she stood for a moment partly wrapped in the dingy gauze of the window curtain listening with infantile pleasure, as pat as pat could be, to an organ-grinder in the dust-brimming courtyard below. When I examined her small hands and drew her attention to their grubby fingernails, she said with a naïve frown *"Oui, ce n'est pas bien,"* and went to the wash-basin, but I said it did not matter, did not matter at all. With her brown bobbed hair, luminous gray eyes and pale skin, she looked perfectly charming. Her hips were no bigger than those of a squatting lad; in fact, I do not hesitate to say (and indeed this is the reason why I linger gratefully in that gauze-gray room of memory with little Monique) that among the eighty or so *grues* I had had operate upon me, she was the only one that gave me a pang of genuine pleasure. *"Il était malin, celui qui a inventé ce truc-là,"* she commented amiably, and got back into her clothes with the same high-style speed.

I asked for another, more elaborate, assignment later the same evening, and she said she would meet me at the corner café at nine, and swore she had never *posé un lapin* in all her young life. We returned to the same room, and I could not help saying how very pretty she was to which she answered demurely: *"Tu es bien gentil de dire ça"* and then, noticing what I noticed too in the mirror reflecting our small Eden—the dreadful grimace of clenched-teeth tenderness that distorted my mouth—dutiful little Monique (oh, she had been a nymphet all right!) wanted to know if she should remove the layer of red from her lips *avant qu'on se couche* in case I planned to kiss her. Of course, I planned it. I let myself go with her more completely than I had with any young lady before, and my last vision that night of long-lashed Monique is touched up with a gaiety that I find seldom associated with any event in my humiliating, sordid, taciturn love life. She looked tremendously pleased with the bonus of fifty I gave her as she trotted out into the April night drizzle with Humbert Humbert lumbering in her narrow wake. Stopping before a window display she said with great gusto: *"Je vais m'acheter des bas!"* and never may I forget the way her Parisian childish lips exploded on *"bas,"* pronouncing it with an appetite that all but changed the "a" into a brief buoyant bursting "o" as in *"bot."*

I had a date with her next day at 2.15 P.M. in my own rooms, but it was less successful, she seemed to have grown less juvenile, more of a woman overnight. A cold I caught from her led me to cancel a fourth assignment, nor was I sorry to break an emotional series that threatened to burden me with heart-rending fantasies and peter out in dull disappointment. So let her remain, sleek, slender Monique, as she was for a minute or two: a delinquent nymphet shining through the matter-of-fact young whore.

My brief acquaintance with her started a train of thought that may seem pretty obvious to the reader who knows the ropes. An advertisement in a lewd magazine landed me, one brave day, in the office of a Mlle Edith who began by offering me to choose a kindred soul from a collection of rather formal photographs in a rather soiled album (*"Regardez-moi cette belle brune!"*). When I pushed the album away and somehow managed to blurt out my criminal craving, she looked as if about to show me the door; however, after asking me what price I was prepared to disburse, she condescended to put me in touch with a person *qui pourrait arranger la chose.* Next day, an asthmatic woman, coarsely painted, garrulous, garlicky, with an almost farcical Provençal accent and a black mustache above a purple lip, took me to what was apparently her own domicile, and there, after explosively kissing the bunched tips of her fat fingers to signify the delectable rosebud quality of her merchandise, she theatrically drew aside a curtain to reveal what I judged was that part of the room where a large and unfastidious family usually slept. It was now empty save for a monstrously plump, sallow, repulsively plain girl of at least fifteen with red-ribboned thick black braids who sat on a chair perfunctorily nursing a bald doll. When I shook my head and tried to shuffle out of the trap, the woman, talking fast, began removing the dingy woolen jersey from the young giantess' torso; then, seeing my determination to leave, she demanded *son argent*. A door at the end of the room was opened, and two men who had been dining in the kitchen joined in the squabble. They were misshapen, bare-necked, very swarthy and one of them wore dark glasses. A small boy and a begrimed, bowlegged toddler lurked behind them. With the insolent logic of a nightmare, the enraged procuress, indicating the man in glasses, said he had served in the police, *lui*, so that I had better do as I was told. I went up to Marie—for that was her stellar name—who by then had quietly transferred her heavy haunches to a stool at the kitchen table and resumed her interrupted soup while the toddler picked up the doll. With a surge of pity dramatizing my idiotic gesture, I thrust a banknote into her indifferent hand. She surrendered my gift to the ex-detective, whereupon I was suffered to leave.

7

I do not know if the pimp's album may not have been another link in the daisy-chain; but soon after, for my own safety, I decided to marry. It occurred to me that regular

24

hours, home-cooked meals, all the conventions of marriage, the prophylactic routine of its bedroom activities and, who knows, the eventual flowering of certain moral values, of certain spiritual substitutes, might help me, if not to purge myself of my degrading and dangerous desires, at least to keep them under pacific control. A little money that had come my way after my father's death (nothing very grand—the Mirana had been sold long before), in addition to my striking if somewhat brutal good looks, allowed me to enter upon my quest with equanimity. After considerable deliberation, my choice fell on the daughter of a Polish doctor: the good man happened to be treating me for spells of dizziness and tachycardia. We played chess: his daughter watched me from behind her easel, and inserted eyes or knuckles borrowed from me into the cubistic trash that accomplished misses then painted instead of lilacs and lambs. Let me repeat with quiet force: I was, and still am, despite *mes malheurs*, an exceptionally handsome male; slow-moving, tall, with soft dark hair and a gloomy but all the more seductive cast of demeanor. Exceptional virility often reflects in the subject's displayable features a sullen and congested something that pertains to what he has to conceal. And this was my case. Well did I know, alas, that I could obtain at the snap of my fingers any adult female I chose; in fact, it had become quite a habit with me of not being too attentive to women lest they come toppling, bloodripe, into my cold lap. Had I been a *français moyen* with a taste for flashy ladies, I might have easily found, among the many crazed beauties that lashed my grim rock, creatures far more fascinating than Valeria. My choice, however, was prompted by considerations whose essence was, as I realized too late, a piteous compromise. All of which goes to show how dreadfully stupid poor Humbert always was in matters of sex.

8

Although I told myself I was looking merely for a soothing presence, a glorified *pot-au-feu*, an animated merkin, what really attracted me to Valeria was the imitation she gave of a little girl. She gave it not because she had divined something about me; it was just her style—and I fell for it. Actually, she was at least in her late twenties (I never established her exact age for even her passport lied) and had mislaid her virginity under circumstances that changed with her reminiscent moods. I, on my part, was as naïve as only a pervert can be. She looked fluffy and frolicsome, dressed *à la gamine*, showed a generous amount of smooth leg, knew how to stress the white of a bare instep by the black of a velvet slipper, and pouted, and dimpled, and romped, and dirndled, and shook her short curly blond hair in the cutest and tritest fashion imaginable.

After a brief ceremony at the *mairie*, I took her to the new apartment I had rented and, somewhat to her surprise, had her wear, before I touched her, a girl's plain nightshirt that I had managed to filch from the linen closet of an orphanage. I derived some fun from that nuptial night and had the idiot in hysterics by sunrise. But reality soon asserted itself. The bleached curl revealed its melanic root; the down turned to prickles on a shaved shin; the mobile moist mouth, no matter how I stuffed it with love, disclosed ignominiously its resemblance to the corresponding part in a treasured portrait of her toadlike dead mama; and presently, instead of a pale little gutter girl, Humbert Humbert had on his hands a large, puffy, short-legged, big-breasted and practically brainless *baba*.

This state of affairs lasted from 1935 to 1939. Her only asset was a muted nature which did help to produce an odd sense of comfort in our small squalid flat: two rooms, a hazy view in one window, a brick wall in the other, a tiny kitchen, a shoe-shaped bath tub, within which I felt like Marat but with no white-necked maiden to stab me. We had quite a few cozy evenings together, she deep in her *Paris-Soir*, I working at a rickety table. We went to movies, bicycle races and boxing matches. I appealed to her stale flesh very seldom, only in cases of great urgency and despair. The grocer opposite had a little daughter whose shadow drove me mad; but with Valeria's help I did find after all some legal outlets to my fantastic predicament. As to cooking, we tacitly dismissed the *pot-au-feu* and had most of our meals at a crowded place in rue Bonaparte where there were wine stains on the table cloth and a good deal of foreign babble. And next door, an art dealer displayed in his cluttered window a splendid, flamboyant, green, red, golden and inky blue, ancient American *estampe*—a loco-motive with a gigantic smokestack, great baroque lamps and a tremendous cowcatcher, hauling its mauve coaches through the stormy prairie night and mixing a lot of spark-studded black smoke with the furry thunder clouds.

These burst. In the summer of 1939 *mon oncle d'Amérique* died bequeathing me an annual income of a few thousand dollars on condition I came to live in the States and showed some interest in his business. This prospect was most welcome to me. I felt my life needed a shake-up. There was another thing, too: moth holes had appeared in the plush of matrimonial comfort. During the last weeks I had kept noticing that my fat Valeria was not her usual self; had acquired a queer restlessness; even showed something like irritation at times, which was quite out of keeping with the stock character she was supposed to impersonate. When I informed her we were shortly to sail for New York, she looked distressed and bewildered. There were some tedious difficulties with her papers. She had a Nansen, or better say

Nonsense, passport which for some reason a share in her husband's solid Swiss citizenship could not easily transcend; and I decided it was the necessity of queuing in the *préfecture*, and other formalities, that had made her so listless, despite my patiently describing to her America, the country of rosy children and great trees, where life would be such an improvement on dull dingy Paris.

We were coming out of some office building one morning, with her papers almost in order, when Valeria, as she waddled by my side, began to shake her poodle head vigorously without saying a word. I let her go on for a while and then asked if she thought she had something inside. She answered (I translate from her French which was, I imagine, a translation in its turn of some Slavic platitude): "There is another man in my life."

Now, these are ugly words for a husband to hear. They dazed me, I confess. To beat her up in the street, there and then, as an honest vulgarian might have done, was not feasible. Years of secret sufferings had taught me superhuman self-control. So I ushered her into a taxi which had been invitingly creeping along the curb for some time, and in this comparative privacy I quietly suggested she comment her wild talk. A mounting fury was suffocating me—not because I had any particular fondness for that figure of fun, *Mme Humbert*, but because matters of legal and illegal conjunction were for me alone to decide, and here she was, Valeria, the comedy wife, brazenly preparing to dispose in her own way of my comfort and fate. I demanded her lover's name. I repeated my question; but she kept up a burlesque babble, discoursing on her unhappiness with me and announcing plans for an immediate divorce. "*Mais qui est-ce?*" I shouted at last, striking her on the knee with my fist; and she, without even wincing, stared at me as if the answer were too simple for words, then gave a quick shrug and pointed at the thick neck of the taxi driver. He pulled up at a small café and introduced himself. I do not remember his ridiculous name but after all those years I still see him quite clearly—a stocky White Russian ex-colonel with a bushy mustache and a crew cut; there were thousands of them plying that fool's trade in Paris. We sat down at a table; the Tsarist ordered wine; and Valeria, after applying a wet napkin to her knee, went on talking—*into* me rather than to me; she poured words into this dignified receptacle with a volubility I had never suspected she had in her. And every now and then she would volley a burst of Slavic at her stolid lover. The situation was preposterous and became even more so when the taxi-colonel, stopping Valeria with a possessive smile, began to unfold *his* views and plans. With an atrocious accent to his careful French, he delineated the world of love and work into which he proposed to enter hand in hand with his child-wife Valeria. She by now was preening herself, between him and me, rouging her pursed lips, tripling her chin to pick at her blouse-bosom and so forth, and he spoke of her as if she were absent, and also as if she were a kind of little ward that was in the act of being transferred, for her own good, from one wise guardian to another even wiser one; and although my helpless wrath may have exaggerated and disfigured certain impressions, I can swear that he actually consulted me on such things as her diet, her periods, her wardrobe and the books she had read or should read. "I think," he said, "she will like *Jean Christophe*?" Oh, he was quite a scholar, Mr. Taxovich.

I put an end to this gibberish by suggesting Valeria pack up her few belongings immediately, upon which the platitudinous colonel gallantly offered to carry them into the car. Reverting to his professional state, he drove the Humberts to their residence and all the way Valeria talked, and Humbert the Terrible deliberated with Humbert the Small whether Humbert Humbert should kill her or her lover, or both, or neither. I remember once handling an automatic belonging to a fellow student, in the days (I have not spoken of them, I think, but never mind) when I toyed with the idea of enjoying his little sister, a most diaphanous nymphet with a black hair bow, and then shooting myself. I now wondered if Valechka (as the colonel called her) was really worth shooting, or strangling, or drowning. She had very vulnerable legs, and I decided I would limit myself to hurting her very horribly as soon as we were alone.

But we never were. Valechka—by now shedding torrents of tears tinged with the mess of her rainbow make-up,—started to fill anyhow a trunk, and two suit-cases, and a bursting carton, and visions of putting on my mountain boots and taking a running kick at her rump were of course impossible to put into execution with the cursed colonel hovering around all the time. I cannot say he behaved insolently or anything like that; on the contrary, he displayed, as a small sideshow in the theatricals I had been inveigled in, a discreet old-world civility, punctuating his movements with all sorts of mispronounced apologies (*j'ai demannde pardonne*—excuse me—*est-ce que j'ai puis*— may I—and so forth), and turning away tactfully when Valechka took down with a flourish her pink panties from the clothesline above the tub; but he seemed to be all over the place at once, *le gredin*, agreeing his frame with the anatomy of the flat, reading in my chair my newspaper, untying a knotted string, rolling a cigarette, counting the teaspoons, visiting the bathroom, helping his moll to wrap up the electric fan her father had given her, and carrying streetward her luggage. I sat with arms folded, one hip on the window sill, dying of hate and boredom. At last both were out of the quivering apartment—the vibration of the door I had slammed after them still rang in my every nerve, a poor substitute for the backhand slap with which I ought to have hit her across the cheekbone according to the rules of the movies. Clumsily playing my part, I stomped to the bathroom to check if they had taken my English toilet water; they had not; but I noticed with a spasm of fierce disgust that the former Counselor of the Tsar, after thoroughly easing his bladder, had not flushed the toilet. That solemn pool of alien urine with a soggy, tawny cigarette butt disintegrating in it struck me as a crowning insult, and I wildly looked around for a weapon. Actually I daresay it was nothing but middle-class Russian courtesy (with an oriental tang, perhaps) that had prompted the good colonel (Maximovich! his name suddenly taxies back to me), a very formal person as they all are, to muffle his private need in decorous silence so as not to underscore the small size of his host's domicile with the rush of a gross cascade on top of his own hushed trickle. But this did not enter my mind at the moment, as groaning with rage I ransacked the kitchen for something better than a broom. Then, canceling my search, I dashed out of the house with the heroic decision of attacking him barefisted; despite my natural vigor, I am no pugilist, while the short but broad-shouldered Maximovich seemed made of pig iron. The void of the street, revealing nothing of my wife's departure except a rhinestone button that she had dropped in the mud after preserving it for three unnecessary years in a broken box, may have spared me a bloody nose. But no matter. I had my little revenge in due time. A man from Pasadena told me one day that Mrs. Maximovich née Zborovski had died in childbirth around 1945; the couple had somehow got over to California and had been used there, for an excellent salary, in a year-long experiment conducted by a distinguished American ethnologist. The experiment dealt with human and racial reactions to a diet of bananas and dates in a constant position on all fours. My informant, a doctor, swore he had seen with his own eyes obese Valechka and her colonel, by then gray-haired and also quite corpulent, diligently crawling about the well-swept floors of a brightly lit set of rooms (fruit in one, water in another, mats in a third and so on) in the company of several other hired quadrupeds, selected from indigent and helpless groups. I tried to find the results of these tests in the *Review of Anthropology*; but they appear not to have been published yet. These scientific products take of course some time to fructuate. I hope they will be illustrated with good photographs when they do get printed, although it is not very likely that a prison library will harbor such erudite works. The one to which I am restricted these days, despite my lawyer's favors, is a good example of the inane eclecticism governing the selection of books in prison libraries. They have the Bible, of course, and Dickens (an ancient set, N. Y., G. W., Dillingham, Publisher, MDCCCLXXXVII); and the *Children's Encyclopedia* (with some nice photographs of sunshine-haired Girl Scouts in shorts), and *A Murder Is Announced* by Agatha Christie; but they also have such coruscating trifles as *A Vagabond in Italy* by Percy Elphinstone, author of *Venice Revisited*, Boston, 1868, and a comparatively recent (1946) *Who's Who in the Limelight*—actors, producers, playwrights, and shots of static scenes. In looking through the latter volume, I was treated last night to one of those dazzling coincidences that logicians loathe and poets love. I transcribe most of the page:

Pym, Roland. Born in Lundy, Mass., 1922. Received stage training at Elsinore Playhouse, Derby, N.Y. Made debut in *Sunburst*. Among his many appearances are *Two Blocks from Here, The Girl in Green, Scrambled Husbands, The Strange Mushroom, Touch and Go, John Lovely, I Was Dreaming of You*.

Quilty, Clare, American dramatist. Born in Ocean City, N.J., 1911. Educated at Columbia University. Started on a commercial career but turned to play-writing. Author of *The Little Nymph, The Lady Who Loved Lightning* (in collaboration with Vivian Darkbloom), *Dark Age, The Strange Mushroom, Fatherly Love*, and others. His many plays for children are notable. *Little Nymph* (1940) traveled 14,000 miles and played 280 performances on the road during the winter before ending in New York. Hobbies: fast cars, photography, pets.

Quine, Dolores. Born in 1882, in Dayton, Ohio. Studied for stage at American Academy. First played in Ottawa in 1900. Made New York debut in 1904 in *Never Talk to Strangers*. Has disappeared since in [a list of some thirty plays follows].

How the look of my dear love's name even affixed to some old hag of an actress, still makes me rock with helpless pain! Perhaps, she might have been an actress too. Born 1935. Appeared (I notice the slip of my pen in the preceding paragraph, but please do not correct it, Clarence) in *The Murdered Playwright*. Quine the Swine. Guilty of killing Quilty. Oh, my Lolita, I have only words to play with!

9

Divorce proceedings delayed my voyage, and the gloom of yet another World War had settled upon the globe when, after a winter of ennui and pneumonia in Portugal, I at last reached the States. In New York I eagerly accepted the soft job fate offered me: it consisted mainly of thinking up and editing perfume ads. I welcomed its desultory character and pseudoliterary aspects, attending to it whenever I had nothing better to do. On the other hand, I was urged by a war-time university in New York to complete my comparative history of French literature for English-speaking students. The first volume took me a couple of years during which I put in seldom less than fifteen hours of work daily. As I look back on those days, I see them divided tidily into ample light and narrow shade: the light pertaining to the solace of research in palatial libraries, the shade to my excruciating desires and insomnias of which enough has been said. Knowing me by now, the reader can easily imagine how dusty and hot I got, trying to catch a glimpse of nymphets (alas, always remote) playing in Central Park, and how repulsed I was by the glitter of deodorized career girls that a gay dog in one of the offices kept unloading upon me. Let us skip all that. A dreadful breakdown sent me to a sanatorium for more than a year; I went back to my work—only to be hospitalized again.

Robust outdoor life seemed to promise me some relief. One of my favorite doctors, a charming cynical chap with a little brown beard, had a brother, and this brother was about to lead an expedition into arctic Canada. I was attached to it as a "recorder of psychic reactions." With two young botanists and an old carpenter I shared now and then (never very successfully) the favors of one of our nutritionists, a Dr. Anita Johnson—who was soon flown back, I am glad to say. I had little notion of what object the expedition was pursuing. Judging by the number of meteorologists upon it, we may have been tracking to its lair (somewhere on Prince of Wales' Island, I understand) the wandering and wobbly north magnetic pole. One group, jointly with the Canadians, established a weather station on Pierre Point in Melville Sound. Another group, equally misguided, collected plankton. A third studied tuberculosis in the tundra. Bert, a film photographer—an insecure fellow with whom at one time I was made to partake in a good deal of menial work (he, too, had some psychic troubles)—maintained that the big men on our team, the real leaders we never saw, were mainly engaged in checking the influence of climatic amelioration on the coats of the arctic fox.

We lived in prefabricated timber cabins amid a Pre-Cambrian world of granite. We had heaps of supplies—the *Reader's Digest*, an ice cream mixer, chemical toilets, paper caps for Christmas. My health improved wonderfully in spite or because of all the fantastic blankness and boredom. Surrounded by such dejected vegetation as willow scrub and lichens; permeated, and, I suppose, cleansed by a whistling gale; seated on a boulder under a completely translucent sky (through which, however, nothing of importance showed), I felt curiously aloof from my own self. No temptations maddened me. The plump, glossy little Eskimo girls with their fish smell, hideous raven hair and guinea pig faces, evoked even less desire in me than Dr. Johnson had. Nymphets do not occur in polar regions.

I left my betters the task of analyzing glacial drifts, drumlins, and gremlins, and kremlins, and for a time tried to jot down what I fondly thought were "reactions" (I noticed, for instance, that dreams under the midnight sun tended to be highly colored, and this my friend the photographer confirmed). I was also supposed to quiz my various companions on a number of important matters, such as nostalgia, fear of unknown animals, food-fantasies, nocturnal emissions, hobbies, choice of radio programs, changes in outlook and so forth. Everybody got so fed up with this that I soon dropped the project completely, and only toward the end of my twenty months of cold labor (as one of the botanists jocosely put it) concocted a perfectly spurious and very racy report that the reader will find published in the *Annals of Adult Psychophysics* for 1945 or 1946, as well as in the issue of *Arctic Explorations* devoted to that particular expedition; which, in conclusion, was not really concerned with Victoria Island copper or anything like that, as I learned later from my genial doctor; for the nature of its real purpose was what is termed "hush-hush," and so let me add merely that whatever it was, that purpose was admirably achieved.

The reader will regret to learn that soon after my return to civilization I had another bout with insanity (if to melancholia and a sense of insufferable oppression that cruel term must be applied). I owe my complete restoration to a discovery I made while being treated at that particular very expensive sanatorium. I discovered there was an endless source of robust enjoyment in trifling with psychiatrists: cunningly leading them on; never letting them see that you know all the tricks of the trade; inventing for them elaborate dreams, pure classics in style (which make *them*, the dream-extortionists, dream and wake up shrieking); teasing them with fake "primal scenes"; and never allowing them the slightest glimpse of one's real sexual predicament. By bribing a nurse I won access to some files and discovered, with glee, cards calling me "potentially homosexual" and "totally impotent." The sport was so excellent, its results—in *my* case—so ruddy that I stayed on for a whole month after I was quite well (sleeping admirably and eating like a schoolgirl). And then I added another week just for the pleasure of taking on a powerful newcomer, a displaced (and, surely, deranged) celebrity, known for his knack of making patients believe they had witnessed their own conception.

10

Upon signing out, I cast around for some place in the New England countryside or sleepy small town (elms, white church) where I could spend a studious summer subsisting on a compact boxful of notes I had accumulated and bathing in some nearby lake. My work had begun to interest me again—I mean my scholarly exertions; the other thing, my active participation in my uncle's posthumous perfumes, had by then been cut down to a minimum.

One of his former employees, the scion of a distinguished family, suggested I spend a few months in the residence of his impoverished cousins, a Mr. McCoo, retired, and his wife, who wanted to let their upper story where a late aunt had delicately dwelt. He said they had two little daughters, one a baby, the other a girl of twelve, and a beautiful garden, not far from a beautiful lake, and I said it sounded perfectly perfect.

I exchanged letters with these people, satisfying them I was housebroken, and spent a fantastic night on the train, imagining in all possible detail the enigmatic nymphet I would coach in French and fondle in Humbertish. Nobody met me at the toy station where I alighted with my new expensive bag, and nobody answered the telephone; eventually, however, a distraught McCoo in wet clothes turned up at the only hotel of green-and-pink Ramsdale with the news that his house had just burned down—possibly, owing to the synchronous conflagration that had been raging all night in my veins. His family, he said, had fled to a farm he owned, and had taken the car, but a friend of his wife's, a grand person, Mrs. Haze of 342 Lawn Street, offered to accommodate me. A lady who lived opposite Mrs. Haze's had lent McCoo her limousine, a marvelously old-fashioned, square-topped affair, manned by a cheerful

Negro. Now, since the only reason for my coming at all had vanished, the aforesaid arrangement seemed preposterous. All right, his house would have to be completely rebuilt, so what? Had he not insured it sufficiently? I was angry, disappointed and bored, but being a polite European, could not refuse to be sent off to Lawn Street in that funeral car, feeling that otherwise McCoo would devise an even more elaborate means of getting rid of me. I saw him scamper away, and my chauffeur shook his head with a soft chuckle. En route, I swore to myself I would not dream of staying in Ramsdale under any circumstance but would fly that very day to the Bermudas or the Bahamas or the Blazes. Possibilities of sweetness on technicolor beaches had been trickling through my spine for some time before, and McCoo's cousin had, in fact, sharply diverted that train of thought with his well-meaning but as it transpired now absolutely inane suggestion.

Speaking of sharp turns: we almost ran over a meddlesome suburban dog (one of those who lie in wait for cars) as we swerved into Lawn Street. A little further, the Haze house, a white-frame horror, appeared, looking dingy and old, more gray than white—the kind of place you know will have a rubber tube affixable to the tub faucet in lieu of shower. I tipped the chauffeur and hoped he would immediately drive away so that I might double back unnoticed to my hotel and bag; but the man merely crossed to the other side of the street where an old lady was calling to him from her porch. What could I do? I pressed the bell button.

A colored maid let me in—and left me standing on the mat while she rushed back to the kitchen where something was burning that ought not to burn.

The front hall was graced with door chimes, a white-eyed wooden thingamabob of commercial Mexican origin, and that banal darling of the arty middle class, van Gogh's "Arlésienne." A door ajar to the right afforded a glimpse of a living room, with some more Mexican trash in a corner cabinet and a striped sofa along the wall. There was a staircase at the end of the hallway, and as I stood mopping my brow (only now did I realize how hot it had been out-of-doors) and staring, to stare at something, at an old gray tennis ball that lay on an oak chest, there came from the upper landing the contralto voice of Mrs. Haze, who leaning over the banisters inquired melodiously, "Is that Monsieur Humbert?" A bit of cigarette ash dropped from there in addition. Presently, the lady herself—sandals, maroon slacks, yellow silk blouse, squarish face, in that order—came down the steps, her index finger still tapping upon her cigarette.

I think I had better describe her right away, to get it over with. The poor lady was in her middle thirties, she had a shiny forehead, plucked eyebrows and quite simple but not unattractive features of a type that may be defined as a weak solution of Marlene Dietrich. Patting her bronze-brown bun, she led me into the parlor and we talked for a minute about the McCoo fire and the privilege of living in Ramsdale. Her very wide-set sea-green eyes had a funny way of traveling all over you, carefully avoiding your own eyes. Her smile was but a quizzical jerk of one eyebrow; and uncoiling herself from the sofa as she talked, she kept making spasmodic dashes at three ashtrays and the near fender (where lay the brown core of an apple); whereupon she would sink back again, one leg folded under her. She was, obviously, one of those women whose polished words may reflect a book club or bridge club, or any other deadly conventionality, but never her soul; women who are completely devoid of humor; women utterly indifferent at heart to the dozen or so possible subjects of a parlor conversation, but very particular about the rules of such conversations, through the sunny cellophane of which not very appetizing frustrations can be readily distinguished. I was perfectly aware that if by any wild chance I became her lodger, she would methodically proceed to do in regard to me what taking a lodger probably meant to her all along, and I would again be enmeshed in one of those tedious affairs I knew so well.

But there was no question of my settling there. I could not be happy in that type of household with bedraggled magazines on every chair and a kind of horrible hybridization between the comedy of so-called "functional modern furniture" and the tragedy of decrepit rockers and rickety lamp tables with dead lamps. I was led upstairs, and to the left—into "my" room. I inspected it through the mist of my utter rejection of it; but I did discern above "my" bed René Prinet's "Kreutzer Sonata." And she called that servant maid's room a "semi-studio"! Let's get out of here at once, I firmly said to myself as I pretended to deliberate over the absurdly, and ominously, low price that my wistful hostess was asking for board and bed.

Old-world politeness, however, obliged me to go on with the ordeal. We crossed the landing to the right side of the house (where "I and Lo have our rooms"—Lo being presumably the maid), and the lodger-lover could hardly conceal a shudder when he, a very fastidious male, was granted a preview of the only bathroom, a tiny oblong between the landing and "Lo's" room, with limp wet things overhanging the dubious tub (the question mark of a hair inside); and there were the expected coils of the rubber snake, and its complement—a pinkish cozy, coyly covering the toilet lid.

"I see you are not too favorably impressed," said the lady letting her hand rest for a moment upon my sleeve: she combined a cool forwardness—the overflow of what

I think is called "poise"—with a shyness and sadness that caused her detached way of selecting her words to seem as unnatural as the intonation of a professor of "speech." "This is not a neat household, I confess," the doomed dear continued, "but I assure you [she looked at my lips], you will be very comfortable, very comfortable, indeed. Let me show you the garden" (the last more brightly, with a kind of winsome toss of the voice).

Reluctantly I followed her downstairs again; then through the kitchen at the end of the hall, on the right side of the house—the side where also the dining room and the parlor were (under "my" room, on the left, there was nothing but a garage). In the kitchen, the Negro maid, a plump youngish woman, said, as she took her large glossy black purse from the knob of the door leading to the back porch: "I'll go now, Mrs. Haze." "Yes, Louise," answered Mrs. Haze with a sigh. "I'll settle with you Friday." We passed on to a small pantry and entered the dining room, parallel to the parlor we had already admired. I noticed a white sock on the floor. With a deprecatory grunt, Mrs. Haze stooped without stopping and threw it into a closet next to the pantry. We cursorily inspected a mahogany table with a fruit vase in the middle, containing nothing but the still glistening stone of one plum. I groped for the timetable I had in my pocket and surreptitiously fished it out to look as soon as possible for a train. I was still walking behind Mrs. Haze through the dining room when, beyond it, there came a sudden burst of greenery—"the piazza," sang out my leader, and then, without the least warning, a blue sea-wave swelled under my heart and, from a mat in a pool of sun, half-naked, kneeling, turning about on her knees, there was my Riviera love peering at me over dark glasses.

It was the same child—the same frail, honey-hued shoulders, the same silky supple bare back, the same

41

chestnut head of hair. A polka-dotted black kerchief tied around her chest hid from my aging ape eyes, but not from the gaze of young memory, the juvenile breasts I had fondled one immortal day. And, as if I were the fairy-tale nurse of some little princess (lost, kidnaped, discovered in gypsy rags through which her nakedness smiled at the king and his hounds), I recognized the tiny dark-brown mole on her side. With awe and delight (the king crying for joy, the trumpets blaring, the nurse drunk) I saw again her lovely in-drawn abdomen where my southbound mouth had briefly paused; and those puerile hips on which I had kissed the crenulated imprint left by the band of her shorts—that last mad immortal day behind the "Roches Roses." The twenty-five years I had lived since then, tapered to a palpitating point, and vanished.

I find it most difficult to express with adequate force that flash, that shiver, that impact of passionate recognition. In the course of the sun-shot moment that my glance slithered over the kneeling child (her eyes blinking over those stern dark spectacles—the little Herr Doktor who was to cure me of all my aches) while I passed by her in my adult disguise (a great big handsome hunk of movieland manhood), the vacuum of my soul managed to suck in every detail of her bright beauty, and these I checked against the features of my dead bride. A little later, of course, she, this *nouvelle*, this Lolita, *my* Lolita, was to eclipse completely her prototype. All I want to stress is that my discovery of her was a fatal consequence of that "princedom by the sea" in my tortured past. Everything between the two events was but a series of gropings and blunders, and false rudiments of joy. Everything they shared made one of them.

I have no illusions, however. My judges will regard all this as a piece of mummery on the part of a madman with a gross liking for the *fruit vert*. *Au fond, ça m'est bien égal.*

All I know is that while the Haze woman and I went down the steps into the breathless garden, my knees were like reflections of knees in rippling water, and my lips were like sand, and—

"That was my Lo," she said, "and these are my lilies."

"Yes," I said, "yes. They are beautiful, beautiful, beautiful!"

11

Exhibit number two is a pocket diary bound in black imitation leather, with a golden year, 1947, *en escalier*, in its upper left-hand corner. I speak of this neat product of the Blank Blank Co., Blankton, Mass., as if it were really before me. Actually, it was destroyed five years ago and what we examine now (by courtesy of a photographic memory) is but its brief materialization, a puny unfledged phœnix.

I remember the thing so exactly because I wrote it really twice. First I jotted down each entry in pencil (with many erasures and corrections) on the leaves of what is commercially known as a "typewriter tablet"; then, I copied it out with obvious abbreviations in my smallest, most satanic, hand in the little black book just mentioned.

May 30 is a Fast Day by Proclamation in New Hampshire but not in the Carolinas. That day an epidemic of "abdominal flu" (whatever that is) forced Ramsdale to close its schools for the summer. The reader may check the weather data in the Ramsdale *Journal* for 1947. A few days before that I moved into the Haze house, and the little diary which I now propose to reel off (much as a spy delivers by heart the contents of the note he swallowed) covers most of June.

Thursday. Very warm day. From a vantage point (bathroom window) saw Dolores taking things off a clothesline in the apple-green light behind the house. Strolled out. She wore a plaid shirt, blue jeans and sneakers. Every movement she made in the dappled sun plucked at the most secret and sensitive chord of my abject body. After a while she sat down next to me on the lower step of the back porch and began to pick up the pebbles between her feet—pebbles, my God, then a curled bit of milk-bottle glass resembling a snarling lip—and chuck them at a can. *Ping*. You can't a second time—you can't hit it—this is agony—a second time. *Ping*. Marvelous skin—oh, marvelous: tender and tanned, not the least blemish. Sundaes cause acne. The excess of the oily substance called sebum which nourishes the hair follicles of the skin creates, when too profuse, an irritation that opens the way to infection. But nymphets do not have acne although they gorge themselves on rich food. God, what agony, that silky shimmer above her temple grading into bright brown hair. And the little bone twitching at the side of her dust-powdered ankle. "The McCoo girl? Ginny McCoo? Oh, she's a fright. And mean. And lame. Nearly died of polio." Ping. The glistening tracery of down on her forearm. When she got up to take in the wash, I had a chance of adoring from afar the faded seat of her rolled-up jeans. Out of the lawn, bland Mrs. Haze, complete with camera, grew up like a fakir's fake tree and after some heliotropic fussing—sad eyes up, glad eyes down—had the cheek of taking my picture as I sat blinking on the steps, Humbert le Bel.

Friday. Saw her going somewhere with a dark girl called Rose. Why does the way she walks—a child, mind you, a mere child!—excite me so abominably? Analyze it. A faint suggestion of turned in toes. A kind of wiggly looseness below the knee prolonged to the end of each footfall. The ghost of a drag. Very infantile, infinitely meretricious. Humbert Humbert is also infinitely moved by the little one's slangy speech, by her harsh high voice. Later heard her volley crude nonsense at Rose across the fence.

Twanging through me in a rising rhythm. Pause. "I must go now, kiddo."

Saturday. (Beginning perhaps amended.) I know it is madness to keep this journal but it gives me a strange thrill to do so; and only a loving wife could decipher my microscopic script. Let me state with a sob that today my L. was sun-bathing on the so-called "piazza," but her mother and some other woman were around all the time. Of course, I might have sat there in the rocker and pretended to read. Playing safe, I kept away, for I was afraid that the horrible, insane, ridiculous and pitiful tremor that palsied me might prevent me from making my *entrée* with any semblance of casualness.

Sunday. Heat ripple still with us; a most favonian week. This time I took up a strategic position, with obese newspaper and new pipe, in the piazza rocker *before* L. arrived. To my intense disappointment she came with her mother, both in two-piece bathing suits, black, as new as my pipe. My darling, my sweetheart stood for a moment near me— wanted the funnies—and she smelt almost exactly like the other one, the Riviera one, but more intensely so, with rougher overtones—a torrid odor that at once set my manhood astir—but she had already yanked out of me the coveted section and retreated to her mat near her phocine mamma. There my beauty lay down on her stomach, showing me, showing the thousand eyes wide open in my eyed blood, her slightly raised shoulder blades, and the bloom along the incurvation of her spine, and the swellings of her tense narrow nates clothed in black, and the seaside of her schoolgirl thighs. Silently, the seventh-grader enjoyed her green-red-blue comics. She was the loveliest nymphet green-red-blue Priap himself could think up. As I looked on, through prismatic layers of light, dry-lipped, focusing my lust and rocking slightly under my newspaper, I felt

45

that my perception of her, if properly concentrated upon, might be sufficient to have me attain a beggar's bliss immediately; but, like some predator that prefers a moving prey to a motionless one, I planned to have this pitiful attainment coincide with one of the various girlish movements she made now and then as she read, such as trying to scratch the middle of her back and revealing a stippled armpit—but fat Haze suddenly spoiled everything by turning to me and asking me for a light, and starting a make-believe conversation about a fake book by some popular fraud.

Monday. Delectatio morosa. I spend my doleful days in dumps and dolors. We (mother Haze, Dolores and I) were to go to Our Glass Lake this afternoon, and bathe, and bask; but a nacreous morn degenerated at noon into rain, and Lo made a scene.

The median age of pubescence for girls has been found to be thirteen years and nine months in New York and Chicago. The age varies for individuals from ten, or earlier, to seventeen. Virginia was not quite fourteen when Harry Edgar possessed her. He gave her lessons in algebra. *Je m'imagine cela.* They spent their honeymoon at Petersburg, Fla. "Monsieur Poe-poe," as that boy in one of Monsieur Humbert Humbert's classes in Paris called the poet-poet.

I have all the characteristics which, according to writers on the sex interests of children, start the responses stirring in a little girl: clean-cut jaw, muscular hand, deep sonorous voice, broad shoulder. Moreover, I am said to resemble some crooner or actor chap on whom Lo has a crush.

Tuesday. Rain. Lake of the Rains. Mamma out shopping. L., I knew, was somewhere quite near. In result of some stealthy maneuvering, I came across her in her mother's bedroom. Prying her left eye open to get rid of a speck of something. Checked frock. Although I do love that intoxicating brown fragrance of hers, I really think she should wash her hair once in a while. For a moment, we were both in the same warm green bath of the mirror that reflected the top of a poplar with us in the sky. Held her roughly by the shoulders, then tenderly by the temples, and turned her about. "It's right there," she said, "I can feel it." "Swiss peasant would use the tip of her tongue." "Lick it out?" "Yeth. Shly try?" "Sure," she said. Gently I pressed my quivering sting along her rolling salty eyeball. "Goody-goody," she said nictating. "It *is* gone" "Now the other?" "You dope," she began, "there is noth—" but here she noticed the pucker of my approaching lips. "Okay," she said co-operatively, and bending toward her warm upturned russet face somber Humbert pressed his mouth to her fluttering eyelid. She laughed, and brushed past me out of the room. My heart seemed everywhere at once. Never in my life—not even when fondling my child-love in France—never—

Night. Never have I experienced such agony. I would like to describe her face, her ways—and I cannot, because my own desire for her blinds me when she is near. I am not used to being with nymphets, damn it. If I close my eyes I see but an immobilized fraction of her, a cinematographic still, a sudden smooth nether loveliness, as with one knee up under her tartan skirt she sits tying her shoe. "Dolores Haze, *ne montrez pas vos zhambes*" (this is her mother who thinks she knows French).

A poet *à mes heures*, I composed a madrigal to the soot-black lashes of her pale-gray vacant eyes, to the five asymmetrical freckles of her bobbed nose, to the blond down of her brown limbs; but I tore it up and cannot recall it today. Only in the tritest of terms (diary resumed) can I describe Lo's features: I might say her hair is auburn, and her lips as red as licked red candy, the lower one prettily plump— oh, that I were a lady writer who could have her pose naked in a naked light! But instead I am lanky, big-boned, wooly-chested Humbert Humbert, with thick black eyebrows and a queer accent, and a cesspoolful of rotting monsters behind his slow boyish smile. And neither is she the fragile child of a feminine novel. What drives me insane is the twofold nature of this nymphet—of every nymphet, perhaps; this mixture in my Lolita of tender dreamy child-ishness and a kind of eerie vulgarity, stemming from the snub-nosed cuteness of ads and magazine pictures, from the blurry pinkness of adolescent maidservants in the Old Country (smelling of crushed daisies and sweat); and from very young harlots disguised as children in provincial brothels; and then again, all this gets mixed up with the exquisite stainless tenderness seeping through the musk and the mud, through the dirt and the death, oh God, oh God. And what is most singular is that she, *this* Lolita, *my* Lolita, has individualized the writer's ancient lust, so that above and over everything there is—Lolita.

Wednesday. "Look, make Mother take you and me to Our Glass Lake tomorrow." These were the textual words said to me by my twelve-year-old flame in a voluptuous whisper, as we happened to bump into one another on the front porch, I out, she in. The reflection of the afternoon sun, a dazzling white diamond with innumerable irides-cent spikes quivered on the round back of a parked car. The leafage of a voluminous elm played its mellow shadows upon the clapboard wall of the house. Two poplars shivered and shook. You could make out the form-less sounds of remote traffic; a child calling "Nancy, Nan-cy!" In the house, Lolita had put on her favorite "Little Carmen" record which I used to call "Dwarf Conductors," making her snort with mock derision at my mock wit.

Thursday. Last night we sat on the piazza, the Haze woman, Lolita and I. Warm dusk had deepened into amorous darkness. The old girl had finished relating in great detail the plot of a movie she and L. had seen sometime in the winter. The boxer had fallen extremely low when he met the good old priest (who had been a boxer himself in his robust youth and could still slug a sinner). We sat on cushions heaped on the floor, and L. was between the woman and me (she had squeezed herself in, the pet). In my turn, I launched upon a hilarious account of my arctic adventures. The muse of invention handed me a rifle and I shot a white bear who sat down and said: Ah! All the while I was acutely aware of L.'s nearness and as I spoke I gestured in the merciful dark and took advantage of those invisible gestures of mine to touch her hand, her shoulder and a ballerina of wool and gauze which she played with and kept sticking into my lap; and finally, when I had completely enmeshed my glowing darling in this weave of ethereal caresses, I dared stroke her bare leg along the gooseberry fuzz of her shin, and I chuckled at my own jokes, and trembled, and concealed my tremors, and once or twice felt with my rapid lips the warmth of her hair as I treated her to a quick nuzzling, humorous aside and caressed her plaything. She, too, fidgeted a good deal so that finally her mother told her sharply to quit it and sent the doll flying into the dark, and I laughed and addressed myself to Haze across Lo's legs to let my hand creep up my nymphet's thin back and feel her skin through her boy's shirt.

But I knew it was all hopeless, and was sick with longing, and my clothes felt miserably tight, and I was almost glad when her mother's quiet voice announced in the dark: "And now we all think that Lo should go to bed." "I think you stink," said Lo. "Which means there will be no picnic tomorrow," said Haze. "This is a free country," said Lo. When angry Lo with a Bronx cheer had gone, I stayed on from sheer inertia, while Haze smoked her tenth cigarette of the evening and complained of Lo.

She had been spiteful, if you please, at the age of one, when she used to throw her toys out of her crib so that her poor mother should keep picking them up, the villainous infant! Now, at twelve, she was a regular pest, said Haze. All she wanted from life was to be one day a strutting and prancing baton twirler or a jitterbug. Her grades were poor, but she was better adjusted in her new school than in Pisky (Pisky was the Haze home town in the Middle West. The Ramsdale house was her late mother-in-law's. They had moved to Ramsdale less than two years ago). "Why was she unhappy there?" "Oh," said Haze, "poor me should know, I went through that when *I* was a kid: boys twisting one's arm, banging into one with loads of books, pulling one's hair, hurting one's breasts, flipping one's skirt. Of course, moodiness is a common concomitant of growing up, but Lo exaggerates. Sullen and evasive. Rude and defiant. Stuck Viola, an Italian schoolmate, in the seat with a fountain pen. Know what I would like? If you, monsieur, happened to be still here in the fall, I'd ask you to help her with her home-work—you seem to know everything, geography, mathematics, French." "Oh, everything," answered monsieur. "That means," said Haze quickly, "you'll *be* here!" I wanted to shout that I would stay on eternally if only I could hope to caress now and then my incipient pupil. But I was wary of Haze. So I just grunted and stretched my limbs nonconcomitantly (*le mot juste*) and presently went up to my room. The woman, however, was evidently not prepared to call it a day. I was already lying upon my cold bed both hands pressing to my face Lolita's fragrant ghost when I heard my indefatigable landlady creeping stealthily up to my door to whisper through it—just to make sure, she said, I was through with the Glance and Gulp magazine I had borrowed the other day. From her room Lo yelled *she* had it. We are quite a lending library in this house, thunder of God.

Friday. I wonder what my academic publishers would say if I were to quote in my textbook Ronsard's *"la vermeillette fente"* or Remy Belleau's *"un petit mont feutré de mousse délicate, tracé sur le milieu d'un fillet escarlatte"* and so forth. I shall probably have another breakdown if I stay any longer in this house, under the strain of this intolerable temptation, by the side of my darling—my darling—my life and my bride. Has she already been initiated by mother nature to the Mystery of the Menarche? Bloated feeling. The Curse of the Irish. Falling from the roof. Grandma is visiting. "Mr. Uterus [I quote from a girls' magazine] starts to build a thick soft wall on the chance a possible baby may have to be bedded down there." The tiny madman in his padded cell.

Incidentally: if I ever commit a serious murder . . . Mark the "if." The urge should be something more than the kind of thing that happened to me with Valeria. Carefully mark that *then* I was rather inept. If and when you wish to sizzle me to death, remember that only a spell of insanity could ever give me the simple energy to be a brute (all this amended, perhaps). Sometimes I attempt to kill in my dreams. But do you know what happens? For instance I hold a gun. For instance I aim at a bland, quietly interested enemy. Oh, I press the trigger all right, but one bullet after another feebly drops on the floor from the sheepish muzzle. In those dreams, my only thought is to conceal the fiasco from my foe, who is slowly growing annoyed.

At dinner tonight the old cat said to me with a sidelong gleam of motherly mockery directed at Lo (I had just been describing, in a flippant vein, the delightful little toothbrush mustache I had not quite decided to grow): "Better don't, if somebody is not to go absolutely dotty." Instantly Lo pushed her plate of boiled fish away, all but knocking her milk over, and bounced out of the dining room. "Would it bore you very much," quoth Haze, "to come with us tomorrow for a swim in Our Glass Lake if Lo apologizes for her manners?"

Later, I heard a great banging of doors and other sounds coming from quaking caverns where the two rivals were having a ripping row.

She has not apologized. The lake is out. It might have been fun.

Saturday. For some days already I had been leaving the door ajar, while I wrote in my room; but only today did the trap work. With a good deal of additional fidgeting, shuffling, scraping—to disguise her embarrassment at visiting me without having been called—Lo came in and after pottering around, became interested in the nightmare curlicues I had penned on a sheet of paper. Oh no: they were not the outcome of a belle-lettrist's inspired pause between two paragraphs; they were the hideous hieroglyphics (which she could not decipher) of my fatal lust. As she bent her brown curls over the desk at which I was sitting, Humbert the Hoarse put his arm around her in a miserable imitation of blood-relationship; and still studying, somewhat shortsightedly, the piece of paper she held, my innocent little visitor slowly sank to a half-sitting position upon my knee. Her adorable profile, parted lips, warm hair were some three inches from my bared eyetooth; and I felt the heat of her limbs through her rough tomboy clothes. All at once I knew I could kiss her throat or the wick of her mouth with perfect impunity. I knew she would let me do so, and even close her eyes as Hollywood teaches. A double vanilla with hot fudge— hardly more unusual than that. I cannot tell my learned reader (whose eyebrows, I suspect, have by now traveled all the way to the back of his bald head), I cannot tell him how the knowledge came to me; perhaps my ape-ear had unconsciously caught some slight change in the rhythm of her respiration—for now she was not really looking at my scribble, but waiting with curiosity and composure—oh, my limpid nymphet!—for the glamorous lodger to do what he was dying to do. A modern child, an avid reader of movie magazines, an expert in dream-slow close-ups, might not think it too strange, I guessed, if a handsome, intensely virile grown-up friend—too late. The house was suddenly vibrating with voluble Louise's voice telling Mrs. Haze who had just come home about a dead something she and Leslie Tomson had found in the basement, and little Lolita was not one to miss such a tale.

Sunday. Changeful, bad-tempered, cheerful, awkward, graceful with the tart grace of her coltish subteens, excruciatingly desirable from head to foot (all New England for a lady-writer's pen!), from the black ready-made bow and bobby pins holding her hair in place to the little scar on the lower part of her neat calf (where a roller-skater kicked her in Pisky), a couple of inches above her rough white sock. Gone with her mother to the Hamiltons—a birthday party or something. Full-skirted gingham frock. Her little doves seem well formed already. Precocious pet!

Monday. Rainy morning. "*Ces matins gris si doux . . .*" My white pajamas have a lilac design on the back. I am like one of those inflated pale spiders you see in old gardens. Sitting in the middle of a luminous web and giving little jerks to this or that strand. *My* web is spread all over the house as I listen from my chair where I sit like a wily wizard. Is Lo in her room? Gently I tug on the silk. She is not. Just heard the toilet paper cylinder make its staccato sound as it is turned; and no footfalls has my outflung filament traced from the bathroom back to her room. Is she still brushing her teeth (the only sanitary act Lo performs with real zest)? No. The bathroom door has just slammed, so one has to feel elsewhere about the house for the beautiful warm-colored prey. Let us have a strand of silk descend the stairs. I satisfy myself by this means that she is not in the kitchen—not banging the refrigerator door or screeching at her detested mamma (who, I suppose, is enjoying her third, cooing and subduedly mirthful, telephone conversation of the morning). Well, let us grope and hope. Ray-like, I glide in thought to the parlor and find the radio silent (and mamma still talking to Mrs. Chatfield or Mrs. Hamilton, very softly, flushed, smiling, cupping the telephone with her free hand, denying by implication that she denies those amusing rumors, rumor, roomer, whispering intimately, as she never does, the clear-cut lady, in face to face talk). So my nymphet is not in the house at all! Gone! What I thought was a prismatic weave turns out to be but an old gray cobweb, the house is empty, is dead. And then comes Lolita's soft sweet chuckle through my half-open door "Don't tell Mother but I've eaten *all* your bacon." Gone when I scuttle out of my room. Lolita, where are you? My breakfast tray, lovingly prepared by my landlady, leers at me toothlessly, ready to be taken in. Lola, Lolita!

Tuesday. Clouds again interfered with that picnic on that unattainable lake. Is it Fate scheming? Yesterday I tried on before the mirror a new pair of bathing trunks.

Wednesday. In the afternoon, Haze (common-sensical shoes, tailor-made dress), said she was driving downtown to buy a present for a friend of a friend of hers, and would I please come too because I have such a wonderful taste in textures and perfumes. "Choose your favorite seduction," she purred. What could Humbert, being in the perfume business, do? She had me cornered between the front porch and her car. "Hurry up," she said as I laboriously doubled up my large body in order to crawl in (still desperately devising a means of escape). She had started the engine, and was genteelly swearing at a backing and turning truck in front that had just brought old invalid Miss Opposite a brand new wheel chair, when my Lolita's sharp voice came from the parlor window: "You! Where are you going? I'm coming too! Wait!" "Ignore her," yelped Haze (killing the motor); alas for my fair driver; Lo was already pulling at the door on my side. "This is intolerable," began Haze; but Lo had scrambled in, shivering with glee. "Move your bottom, you," said Lo. "Lo!" cried Haze (sideglancing at me, hoping I would throw rude Lo out). "And behold," said Lo (not for the first time), as she jerked back, as I jerked back, as the car leapt forward. "It is intolerable," said Haze, violently getting into second, "that a child should be so ill-mannered. And so very persevering. When she knows she is unwanted. And needs a bath."

My knuckles lay against the child's blue jeans. She was barefooted; her toenails showed remnants of cherry-red polish and there was a bit of adhesive tape across her big toe; and, God, what would I not have given to kiss then and there those delicate-boned, long-toed, monkeyish feet! Suddenly her hand slipped into mine and without our chaperon's seeing, I held, and stroked, and squeezed that little hot paw, all the way to the store. The wings of the driver's Marlenesque nose shone, having shed or burned up their ration of powder, and she kept up an elegant monologue anent the local traffic, and smiled in profile, and pouted in profile, and beat her painted lashes in profile, while I prayed we would never get to that store, but we did.

I have nothing else to report, save, *primo:* that big Haze had little Haze sit behind on our way home, and *secundo:* that the lady decided to keep Humbert's Choice for the backs of her own shapely ears.

Thursday. We are paying with hail and gale for the tropical beginning of the month. In a volume of the *Young*

People's Encyclopedia, I found a map of the States that a child's pencil had started copying out on a sheet of lightweight paper, upon the other side of which, counter to the unfinished outline of Florida and the Gulf, there was a mimeographed list of names referring, evidently, to her class at the Ramsdale school. It is a poem I know already by heart.

Angel, Grace
Austin, Floyd
Beale, Jack
Beale, Mary
Buck, Daniel
Byron, Marguerite
Campbell, Alice
Carmine, Rose
Chatfield, Phyllis
Clarke, Gordon
Cowan, John
Cowan, Marion
Duncan, Walter
Falter, Ted
Fantasia, Stella
Flashman, Irving
Fox, George
Glave, Mabel
Goodale, Donald
Green, Lucinda
Hamilton, Mary Rose
Haze, Dolores
Honeck, Rosaline
Knight, Kenneth
McCoo, Virginia
McCrystal, Vivian
McFate, Aubrey

Miranda, Anthony
Miranda, Viola
Rosato, Emil
Schlenker, Lena
Scott, Donald
Sheridan, Agnes
Sherva, Oleg
Smith, Hazel
Talbot, Edgar
Talbot, Edwin
Wain, Lull
Williams, Ralph
Windmuller, Louise

A poem, a poem, forsooth! So strange and sweet was it to discover this "Haze, Dolores" (she!) in its special bower of names, with its bodyguard of roses—a fairy princess between her two maids of honor. I am trying to analyze the spine-thrill of delight it gives me, this name among all those others. What is it that excites me almost to tears (hot, opalescent, thick tears that poets and lovers shed)? What is it? The tender anonymity of this name with its formal veil ("Dolores") and that abstract transposition of first name and surname, which is like a pair of new pale gloves or a mask? Is "mask" the keyword? Is it because there is always delight in the semitranslucent mystery, the flowing charshaf, through which the flesh and the eye you alone are elected to know smile in passing at you alone? Or is it because I can imagine so well the rest of the colorful classroom around my dolorous and hazy darling: Grace and her ripe pimples; Ginny and her lagging leg; Gordon, the haggard masturbator; Duncan, the foul-smelling clown; nail-biting Agnes; Viola, of the blackheads and the bouncing bust; pretty Rosaline; dark Mary Rose; adorable

Stella, who has let strangers touch her; Ralph, who bullies and steals; Irving, for whom I am sorry. And there she is there, lost in the middle, gnawing a pencil, detested by teachers, all the boys' eyes on her hair and neck, *my* Lolita.

Friday. I long for some terrific disaster. Earthquake. Spectacular explosion. Her mother is messily but instantly and permanently eliminated, along with everybody else for miles around. Lolita whimpers in my arms. A free man, I enjoy her among the ruins. Her surprise, my explanations, demonstrations, ullulations. Idle and idiotic fancies! A brave Humbert would have played with her most disgustingly (yesterday, for instance, when she was again in my room to show me her drawings, school-artware); he might have bribed her—and got away with it. A simpler and more practical fellow would have soberly stuck to various commercial substitutes—if you know where to go, I don't. Despite my manly looks, I am horribly timid. My romantic soul gets all clammy and shivery at the thought of running into some awful indecent unpleasantness. Those ribald sea monsters. *"Mais allez-y, allez-y!"* Annabel skipping on one foot to get into her shorts, I seasick with rage, trying to screen her.

Same date, later, quite late. I have turned on the light to take down a dream. It had an evident antecedent. Haze at dinner had benevolently proclaimed that since the weather bureau promised a sunny weekend we would go to the lake Sunday after church. As I lay in bed, erotically musing before trying to go to sleep, I thought of a final scheme how to profit by the picnic to come. I was aware that mother Haze hated my darling for her being sweet on me. So I planned my lake day with a view to satisfying the mother. To her alone would I talk; but at some appropriate moment I would say I had left my wrist watch or my sunglasses in that glade yonder—and plunge with my nymphet into the wood. Reality at this juncture withdrew, and the Quest for the

Glasses turned into a quiet little orgy with a singularly knowing, cheerful, corrupt and compliant Lolita behaving as reason knew she could not possibly behave. At 3 A.M. I swallowed a sleeping pill, and presently, a dream that was not a sequel but a parody revealed to me, with a kind of meaningful clarity, the lake I had never yet visited: it was glazed over with a sheet of emerald ice, and a pockmarked Eskimo was trying in vain to break it with a pickaxe, although imported mimosas and oleanders flowered on its gravelly banks. I am sure Dr. Blanche Schwarzmann would have paid me a sack of schillings for adding such a libidream to her files. Unfortunately, the rest of it was frankly eclectic. Big Haze and little Haze rode on horseback around the lake, and I rode too, dutifully bobbing up and down, bowlegs astraddle although there was no horse between them, only elastic air—one of those little omissions due to the absent-mindedness of the dream agent.

Saturday. My heart is still thumping. I still squirm and emit low moans of remembered embarrassment.

Dorsal view. Glimpse of shiny skin between T-shirt and white gym shorts. Bending, over a window sill, in the act of tearing off leaves from a poplar outside while engrossed in torrential talk with a newspaper boy below (Kenneth Knight, I suspect) who had just propelled the Ramsdale *Journal* with a very precise thud onto the porch. I began creeping up to her—"crippling" up to her, as pantomimists say. My arms and legs were convex surfaces between which—rather than upon which—I slowly progressed by some neutral means of locomotion: Humbert the Wounded Spider. I must have taken hours to reach her: I seemed to see her through the wrong end of a telescope, and toward her taut little rear I moved like some paralytic, on soft distorted limbs, in terrible concentration. At last I was right behind her when I had the unfortunate idea of blustering a trifle—shaking her by the scruff of the neck and that sort of thing to cover my real *manège*, and she said in a shrill brief whine: "Cut it out!"—most coarsely, the little wench, and with a ghastly grin Humbert the Humble beat a gloomy retreat while she went on wisecracking streetward.

But now listen to what happened next. After lunch I was reclining in a low chair trying to read. Suddenly two deft little hands were over my eyes: she had crept up from behind as if re-enacting, in a ballet sequence, my morning maneuver. Her fingers were a luminous crimson as they tried to blot out the sun, and she uttered hiccups of laughter and jerked this way and that as I stretched my arm sideways and backwards without otherwise changing my recumbent position. My hand swept over her agile giggling legs, and the book like a sleigh left my lap, and Mrs. Haze strolled up and said indulgently: "Just slap her hard if she interferes with your scholarly meditations. How I love this garden [no exclamation mark in her tone]. Isn't it divine in the sun [no question mark either]." And with a sign of feigned content, the obnoxious lady sank down on the grass and looked up at the sky as she leaned back on her splayed-out hands, and presently an old gray tennis ball bounced over her, and Lo's voice came from the house haughtily: "*Pardonnez*, Mother. I was not aiming at *you*." Of course not, my hot downy darling.

12

This proved to be the last of twenty entries or so. It will be seen from them that for all the devil's inventiveness, the scheme remained daily the same. First he would tempt me—and then thwart me, leaving me with a dull pain in the very root of my being. I knew exactly what I wanted to do, and how to do it, without impinging on a child's chastity; after all, I had had *some* experience in my life of pederosis; had visually possessed dappled nymphets in parks; had wedged my wary and bestial way into the hottest, most crowded corner of a city bus full of strap-hanging school children. But for almost three weeks I had been interrupted in all my pathetic machinations. The agent of these interruptions was usually the Haze woman (who, as the reader will mark, was more afraid of Lo's deriving some pleasure from me than of my enjoying Lo). The passion I had developed for that nymphet—for the first nymphet in my life that could be reached at last by my awkward, aching, timid claws—would have certainly landed me again in a sanatorium, had not the devil realized that I was to be granted some relief if he wanted to have me as a plaything for some time longer.

The reader has also marked the curious Mirage of the Lake. It would have been logical on the part of Aubrey McFate (as I would like to dub that devil of mine) to arrange a small treat for me on the promised beach, in the presumed forest. Actually, the promise Mrs. Haze had made was a fraudulent one: she had not told me that Mary Rose Hamilton (a dark little beauty in her own right) was to come too, and that the two nymphets would be whis-pering apart, and playing apart, and having a good time all by themselves, while Mrs. Haze and her handsome lodger conversed sedately in the seminude, far from prying eyes. Incidentally, eyes did pry and tongues did wag. How queer life is! We hasten to alienate the very fates we intended to woo. Before my actual arrival, my landlady had planned to have an old spinster, a Miss Phalen, whose mother had been cook in Mrs. Haze's family, come to stay in the house with Lolita and me, while Mrs. Haze, a career girl at heart, sought some suitable job in the nearest city. Mrs. Haze had seen the whole situation very clearly: the bespectacled, round-backed Herr Humbert coming with his Central-European trunks to gather dust in his corner behind a heap of old books; the unloved ugly little daughter firmly supervised by Miss Phalen who had already once had my Lo under her buzzard wing (Lo recalled that 1944 summer with an indignant shudder); and Mrs. Haze herself engaged as a receptionist in a great elegant city. But a not too complicated event interfered with that program. Miss Phalen broke her hip in Savannah, Ga., on the very day I arrived in Ramsdale.

13

The Sunday after the Saturday already described proved to be as bright as the weatherman had predicted. When putting the breakfast things back on the chair outside my room for my good landlady to remove at her convenience, I gleaned the following situation by listening from the landing across which I had softly crept to the bannisters in my old bedroom slippers—the only old things about me.

There had been another row. Mrs. Hamilton had tele-phoned that her daughter "was running a temperature." Mrs. Haze informed *her* daughter that the picnic would have to be postponed. Hot little Haze informed big cold Haze that, if so, she would not go with her to church. Mother said very well and left.

I had come out on the landing straight after shaving, soapy-earlobed, still in my white pajamas with the corn-flower blue (not the lilac) design on the back; I now wiped off the soap, perfumed my hair and armpits, slipped on a purple silk dressing gown, and, humming nervously, went down the stairs in quest of Lo.

I want my learned readers to participate in the scene I am about to replay; I want them to examine its every detail and see for themselves how careful, how chaste, the whole wine-sweet event is if viewed with what my lawyer has called, in a private talk we have had, "impartial sympathy." So let us get started. I have a difficult job before me.

Main character: Humbert the Hummer. Time: Sunday morning in June. Place: sunlit living room. Props: old, candy-striped davenport, magazines, phonograph, Mexican knick-knacks (the late Mr. Harold E. Haze—God bless the good man—had engendered my darling at the siesta hour in a blue-washed room, on a honeymoon trip to Vera Cruz, and mementoes, among these Dolores, were all over the place). She wore that day a pretty print dress that I had seen on her once before, ample in the skirt, tight in the bodice, short-sleeved, pink, checkered with darker pink, and, to complete the color scheme, she had painted her lips and was holding in her hollowed hands a beautiful, banal, Eden-red apple. She was not shod, however, for church. And her white Sunday purse lay discarded near the phonograph.

My heart beat like a drum as she sat down, cool skirt ballooning, subsiding, on the sofa next to me, and played with her glossy fruit. She tossed it up into the sun-dusted air, and caught it—it made a cupped polished *plop*.

Humbert Humbert intercepted the apple.

"Give it back," she pleaded, showing the marbled flush of her palms. I produced Delicious. She grasped it and bit into it, and my heart was like snow under thin crimson skin, and with the monkeyish nimbleness that was so typical of that American nymphet, she snatched out of my abstract grip the magazine I had opened (pity no film had recorded the curious pattern, the monogrammic linkage of our simultaneous or overlapping moves). Rapidly, hardly hampered by the disfigured apple she held, Lo flipped violently through the pages in search of something she wished Humbert to see. Found it at last. I faked interest by bringing my head so close that her hair touched my temple and her arm brushed my cheek as she wiped her lips with her wrist.

Because of the burnished mist through which I peered at the picture, I was slow in reacting to it, and her bare knees rubbed and knocked impatiently against each other. Dimly there came into view: a surrealist painter relaxing, supine, on a beach, and near him, likewise supine, a plaster replica of the Venus di Milo, half-buried in sand. Picture of the Week, said the legend. I whisked the whole obscene thing away. Next moment, in a sham effort to retrieve it, she was all over me. Caught her by her thin knobby wrist. The magazine escaped to the floor like a flustered fowl. She twisted herself free, recoiled, and lay back in the right-hand corner of the davenport. Then, with perfect simplicity, the impudent child extended her legs across my lap.

By this time I was in a state of excitement bordering on insanity; but I also had the cunning of the insane. Sitting there, on the sofa, I managed to attune, by a series of stealthy movements, my masked lust to her guileless limbs. It was no easy matter to divert the little maiden's attention while I performed the obscure adjustments necessary for the success of the trick. Talking fast, lagging behind my own breath, catching up with it, mimicking a sudden toothache to explain the breaks in my patter—and all the while keeping a maniac's inner eye on my distant golden goal, I cautiously increased the magic friction that was doing away, in an illusional, if not factual, sense, with the physically irremovable, but psychologically very friable texture of the material divide (pajamas and robe) between the weight of two sunburnt legs, resting athwart my lap, and the hidden tumor of an unspeakable passion. Having, in the course of my patter, hit upon something nicely mechanical, I recited, garbling them slightly, the words of a foolish song that was then popular—O my Carmen, my little Carmen, something, something, those something nights, and the stars, and the cars, and the bars, and the barmen; I kept repeating this automatic stuff and holding her under its special spell (spell because of the garbling), and all the while I was mortally afraid that some act of God might interrupt me, might remove the golden load in the sensation of which all my being seemed concentrated, and this anxiety forced me to work, for the first minute or so, more hastily than was consensual with deliberately modulated enjoyment. The stars that sparkled, and the cars that parkled, and the bars, and the barmen, were presently taken over by her; her voice stole and corrected the tune I had been mutilating. She was musical and apple-sweet. Her legs twitched a little as they lay across my live lap; I stroked them; there she lolled in the right-hand corner, almost asprawl, Lola the bobby-soxer, devouring her immemorial fruit, singing through its juice, losing her slipper, rubbing the heel of her slipperless foot in its sloppy anklet, against the pile of old magazines heaped on my left on the sofa—and every movement she made, every shuffle and ripple, helped me to conceal and to improve the secret system of tactile correspondence between beast and beauty—between my gagged, bursting beast and the beauty of her dimpled body in its innocent cotton frock.

Under my glancing finger tips I felt the minute hairs bristle ever so slightly along her shins. I lost myself in the pungent but healthy heat which like summer haze hung about little Haze. Let her stay, let her stay . . . As she strained to chuck the core of her abolished apple into the fender, her young weight, her shameless innocent shanks and round bottom, shifted in my tense, tortured, surreptitiously laboring lap; and all of a sudden a mysterious change came over my senses. I entered a plane of being where nothing mattered, save the infusion of joy brewed within my body. What had begun as a delicious distension of my innermost roots became a glowing tingle which *now* had reached that state of absolute security, confidence and reliance not found elsewhere in conscious life. With the deep hot sweetness thus established and well on its way to the ultimate convulsion, I felt I could slow down in order to prolong the glow. Lolita had been safely solipsized. The implied sun pulsated in the supplied poplars; we were fantastically and divinely alone; I watched her, rosy, gold-dusted, beyond the veil of my controlled delight, unaware of it, alien to it, and the sun was on her lips, and her lips were apparently still forming the words of the Carmen-barmen ditty that no longer reached my consciousness. Everything was now ready. The nerves of pleasure had been laid bare. The corpuscles of Krause were entering the phase of frenzy. The least pressure would suffice to set all paradise loose. I had ceased to be Humbert the Hound, the sad-eyed degenerate cur clasping the boot that would presently kick him away. I was above the tribulations of ridicule, beyond the possibilities of retribution. In my self-made seraglio, I was a radiant and robust Turk, deliberately, in the full consciousness of his freedom, postponing the moment of actually enjoying the youngest and frailest of his slaves. Suspended on the brink of that voluptuous abyss (a nicety of physiological equipoise comparable to certain techniques in the arts) I kept repeating chance words after her—barmen, alarmin', my charmin', my carmen, ahmen, ahahamen—as one talking and laughing in his sleep while my happy hand crept up her sunny leg as far as the shadow of decency allowed. The day before she had collided with the heavy chest in the hall and— "Look, look!"—I gasped—"look what you've done, what you've done to yourself, ah, look"; for there was, I swear, a yellowish-violet bruise on her lovely nymphet thigh which my huge hairy hand massaged and slowly enveloped—and because of her very perfunctory underthings, there seemed to be nothing to prevent my muscular thumb from reaching the hot hollow of her groin—just as you might tickle and caress a giggling child—just that— and: "Oh it's nothing at all," she cried with a sudden shrill note in her voice, and she wiggled, and squirmed, and threw her head back, and her teeth rested on her glistening underlip as she half-turned away, and my moaning mouth, gentlemen of the jury, almost reached her bare neck, while I crushed out against her left buttock the last throb of the longest ecstasy man or monster had ever known.

Immediately afterward (as if we had been struggling and now my grip had eased) she rolled off the sofa and jumped to her feet—to her foot, rather—in order to attend to the formidably loud telephone that may have been ringing for ages as far as I was concerned. There she stood and blinked, cheeks aflame, hair awry, her eyes passing over me as lightly as they did over the furniture, and as she listened or spoke (to her mother who was telling her to come to lunch with her at the Chatfields—neither Lo nor Hum knew yet what busybody Haze was plotting), she kept tapping the edge of the table with the slipper she held in her hand. Blessed be the Lord, she had noticed nothing!

With a handkerchief of multicolored silk, on which her listening eyes rested in passing, I wiped the sweat off my forehead, and, immersed in a euphoria of release, rearranged my royal robes. She was still at the telephone, haggling with her mother (wanted to be fetched by car, my little Carmen) when, singing louder and louder, I swept up the stairs and set a deluge of steaming water roaring into the tub.

At this point I may as well give the words of that song hit in full—to the best of my recollection at least—I don't think I ever had it right. Here goes:

O my Carmen, my little Carmen!
Something, something those something nights,
And the stars, and the cars, and the bars, and the [barmen—
And, O my charmin', our dreadful fights.

And the something town where so gaily, arm in
Arm, we went, and our final row,
And the gun I killed you with, O my Carmen,
The gun I am holding now.

(Drew his .32 automatic, I guess, and put a bullet through his moll's eye.)

14

I had lunch in town—had not been so hungry for years. The house was still Lo-less when I strolled back. I spent the afternoon musing, scheming, blissfully digesting my experience of the morning.

I felt proud of myself. I had stolen the honey of a spasm without impairing the morals of a minor. Absolutely no harm done. The conjurer had poured milk, molasses, foaming champagne into a young lady's new white purse; and lo, the purse was intact. Thus had I delicately constructed my ignoble, ardent, sinful dream; and still Lolita was safe—and I was safe. What I had madly possessed was not she, but my own creation, another, fanciful Lolita—perhaps, more real than Lolita; overlapping, encasing her; floating between me and her, and having no will, no consciousness—indeed, no life of her own.

The child knew nothing. I had done nothing to her. And nothing prevented me from repeating a performance that affected her as little as if she were a photographic image rippling upon a screen and I humble hunchback abusing myself in the dark. The afternoon drifted on and on, in ripe silence, and the sappy tall trees seemed to be in the know; and desire, even stronger than before, began to afflict me again. Let her come soon, I prayed, addressing a loan God, and while mamma is in the kitchen, let a repetition of the davenport scene be staged, please, I adore her so horribly.

No: "horribly" is the wrong word. The elation with which the vision of new delights filled me was not horrible but pathetic. I qualify it as pathetic. Pathetic—because despite the insatiable fire of my venereal appetite, I intended, with the most fervent force and foresight, to protect the purity of that twelve-year-old child.

And now see how I was repaid for my pains. No Lolita came home—she had gone with the Chatfields to a movie. The table was laid with more elegance than usual: candlelight, if you please. In this mawkish aura, Mrs. Haze gently touched the silver on both sides of her plate as if touching piano keys, and smiled down on her empty plate (was on a diet), and said she hoped I liked the salad (recipe lifted from a woman's magazine). She hoped I liked the cold cuts, too. It had been a perfect day. Mrs. Chatfield was a lovely person. Phyllis, her daughter, was going to a summer camp tomorrow. For three weeks. Lolita, it was decided, would go Thursday. Instead of waiting till July, as had been initially planned. And stay there after Phyllis had left. Till school began. A pretty prospect, my heart.

Oh, how I was taken aback—for did it not mean I was losing my darling, just when I had secretly made her mine? To explain my grim mood, I had to use the same toothache I had already simulated in the morning. Must have been an enormous molar, with an abscess as big as a maraschino cherry.

"We have," said Haze, "an excellent dentist. Our neighbor, in fact. Dr. Quilty. Uncle or cousin, I think, of the playwright. Think it will pass? Well, just as you wish. In the fall I shall have him 'brace' her, as my mother used to say. It may curb Lo a little. I am afraid she has been bothering you frightfully all these days. And we are in for a couple of stormy ones before she goes. She has flatly refused to go, and I confess I left her with the Chatfields because I dreaded to face her alone just yet. The movie may mollify her. Phyllis is a very sweet girl, and there is no earthly reason for Lo to dislike her. Really, monsieur, I am very sorry about that tooth of yours. It would be so much more reasonable to let me contact Ivor Quilty first thing tomorrow morning if it still hurts. And, you know, I think a summer camp is so much healthier, and—well, it is all so much more *reasonable* as I say than to mope on a suburban lawn and use mamma's lipstick, and pursue shy studious gentlemen, and go into tantrums at the least provocation."

"Are you sure," I said at last, "that she will be happy there?" (lame, lamentably lame!)

"She'd better," said Haze. "And it won't be all play either. The camp is run by Shirley Holmes—you know, the woman who wrote *Campfire Girl*. Camp will teach Dolores Haze to grow in many things—health, knowledge, temper. And particularly in a sense of responsibility toward other people. Shall we take these candles with us and sit for a while on the piazza, or do you want to go to bed and nurse that tooth?"

Nurse that tooth.

15

Next day they drove downtown to buy things needed for the camp: any wearable purchase worked wonders with Lo. She seemed her usual sarcastic self at dinner. Immediately afterwards, she went up to her room to plunge into the comic books acquired for rainy days at Camp Q (they were so thoroughly sampled by Thursday that she left them behind). I too retired to my lair, and wrote letters. My plan now was to leave for the seaside and then, when school began, resume my existence in the Haze household; for I knew already that I could not live without the child. On Tuesday they went shopping again, and I was asked to answer the phone if the camp mistress rang up during their absence. She did; and a month or so later we had occasion to recall our pleasant chat. That Tuesday, Lo had her dinner in her room. She had been crying after a routine row with her mother and, as had happened on former occasions, had not wished me to see her swollen eyes: she had one of those tender complexions that after a good cry get all blurred and inflamed, and morbidly alluring. I regretted keenly her mistake about my private aesthetics, for I simply love that tinge of Botticellian pink, that raw rose about the lips, those wet, matted eyelashes; and, naturally, her bashful whim deprived me of many opportunities of specious consolation. There was, however, more to it than I thought. As we sat in the darkness of the veranda (a rude wind had put out her red candles), Haze, with a dreary laugh, said she had told Lo that her beloved Humbert thoroughly approved of the whole camp idea "and now," added Haze, "the child throws a fit; pretext: you and I want to get rid of her; actual reason: I told her we would exchange tomorrow for plainer stuff some much too cute night things that she bullied me into buying for her. You see, *she* sees herself as a starlet; *I* see her as a sturdy, healthy, but decidedly homely kid. This, I guess, is at the root of our troubles."

On Wednesday I managed to waylay Lo for a few seconds: she was on the landing, in sweatshirt and green-stained white shorts, rummaging in a trunk. I said something meant to be friendly and funny but she only emitted a snort without looking at me. Desperate, dying Humbert patted her clumsily on her coccyx, and she struck him, quite painfully, with one of the late Mr. Haze's shoetrees. "Doublecrosser," she said as I crawled downstairs rubbing my arm with a great show of rue. She did not condescend to have dinner with Hum and mum: washed her hair and went to bed with her ridiculous books. And on Thursday quiet Mrs. Haze drove her to Camp Q.

As greater authors than I have put it: "Let readers imagine" etc. On second thought, I may as well give those imaginations a kick in the pants. I knew I had fallen in love with Lolita forever; but I also knew she would not be forever Lolita. She would be thirteen on January 1. In two years or so she would cease being a nymphet and would turn into a "young girl," and then, into a "college girl"—that horror of horrors. The word "forever" referred only to my own passion, to the eternal Lolita as reflected in my blood. The Lolita whose iliac crests had not yet flared, the Lolita that today I could touch and smell and hear and see, the Lolita of the strident voice and the rich brown hair—of the bangs and the swirls at the sides and the curls at the back, and the sticky hot neck, and the vulgar vocabulary—"revolting," "super," "luscious," "goon," "drip"—*that* Lolita, *my* Lolita, poor Catullus would lose forever. So how could I afford not to see her for two months of summer insomnias? Two whole months out of the two years of her remaining nymphage! Should I disguise myself as a somber old-fashioned girl, gawky Mlle Humbert, and put up my tent on the outskirts of Camp Q, in the hope that its russet nymphets would clamor: "Let us adopt that deep-voiced D.P.," and drag the sad, shyly smiling Berthe *au Grand Pied* to their rustic hearth. Berthe will sleep with Dolores Haze!

Idle dry dreams. Two months of beauty, two months of tenderness, would be squandered forever, and I could do nothing about it, but nothing, *mais rien*.

One drop of rare honey, however, that Thursday did hold in its acorn cup. Haze was to drive her to the camp in the early morning. Upon sundry sounds of departure reaching me, I rolled out of bed and leaned out of the window. Under the poplars, the car was already athrob. On the sidewalk, Louise stood shading her eyes with her hand, as if the little traveler were already riding into the low morning sun. The gesture proved to be premature. "Hurry up!" shouted Haze. My Lolita, who was half in and about to slam the car door, wind down the glass, wave to Louise and the poplars (whom and which she was never to see again), interrupted the motion of fate: she looked up—and dashed back into the house (Haze furiously calling after her). A moment later I heard my sweetheart running up the stairs. My heart expanded with such force that it almost blotted me out. I hitched up the pants of my pajamas, flung the door open: and simultaneously Lolita arrived, in her Sunday frock, stamping, panting, and then she was in my arms, her innocent mouth melting under the ferocious pressure of dark male jaws, my palpitating darling! The next instant I heard her—alive, unraped— clatter downstairs. The motion of fate was resumed. The blond leg was pulled in, the car door was slammed—was re-slammed—and driver Haze at the violent wheel, rubber-red lips writhing in angry, inaudible speech, swung my darling away, while unnoticed by them or Louise, old Miss Opposite, an invalid, feebly but rhythmically waved from her vined veranda.

16

The hollow of my hand was still ivory-full of Lolita—full of the feel of her pre-adolescently incurved back, that ivory-smooth, sliding sensation of her skin through the thin frock that I had worked up and down while I held her. I marched into her tumbled room, threw open the door of the closet and plunged into a heap of crumpled things that had touched her. There was particularly one pink texture, sleazy, torn, with a faintly acrid odor in the seam. I wrapped in it Humbert's huge engorged heart. A poignant chaos was welling within me—but I had to drop those things and hurriedly regain my composure, as I became aware of the maid's velvety voice calling me softly from the stairs. She had a message for me, she said; and, topping my automatic thanks with a kindly "you're welcome," good Louise left an unstamped, curiously clean-looking letter in my shaking hand.

This is a confession: I love you [so the letter began; and for a distorted moment I mistook its hysterical scrawl for a schoolgirl's scribble]. Last Sunday in church—bad you, who refused to come to see our beautiful new windows!—only last Sunday, my dear one, when I asked the Lord what to do about it, I was told to act as I am acting now. You see, there is no alternative. I have loved you from the minute I saw you. I am a passionate and lonely woman and you are the love of my life.

Now, my dearest, dearest, mon cher, cher monsieur, you have read this; now you know. So, will you please, at once, pack and leave. This is a landlady's order. I am dismissing a lodger. I am kicking you out. Go! Scram! Departez! I shall be back by dinnertime, if I do eighty both ways and don't have an accident (but what would it matter?), and I do not wish to find you in the house. Please, please, leave at once, now, do not even read this absurd note to the end. Go. Adieu.

The situation, chéri, is quite simple. Of course, I know with absolute certainty that I am nothing to you, nothing at all. Oh yes, you enjoy talking to me (and kidding poor me), you have grown fond of our friendly house, of the books I like, of my lovely garden, even of Lo's noisy ways—but I am nothing to you. Right? Right. Nothing to you whatever. But if, after reading my "confession," you decided, in your dark romantic European way, that I am attractive enough for you to take advantage of my letter and make a pass at me, then you would be a criminal— worse than a kidnaper who rapes a child. You see, chéri. If you decided to stay, if I found you at home (which I know I won't—and that's why I am able to go on like this), the fact of your remaining would only mean one thing: that you want me as much as I do you: as a lifelong mate; and that you are ready to link up your life with mine forever and ever and be a father to my little girl.

Let me rave and ramble on for a teeny while more, my dearest, since I know this letter has been by now torn by you, and its pieces (illegible) in the vortex of the toilet. My dearest, mon très, très cher, what a world of love I have built up for you during this miraculous June! I know how reserved you are, how "British." Your old-world reticence, your sense of decorum may be shocked by the boldness of an American girl! You who conceal your strongest feelings must think me a shameless little idiot for throwing open my poor bruised heart like this. In years gone by, many disappointments came my way. Mr. Haze was a splendid person, a sterling soul, but he happened to be twenty years my senior, and—well, let us not gossip about the past. My dearest, your curiosity must be well satisfied if you have ignored my request and read this letter to the bitter end. Never mind. Destroy it and go. Do not forget to leave the key on the desk in your

room. And some scrap of address so that I could refund
the twelve dollars I owe you till the end of the month.
Good-bye, dear one. Pray for me—if you ever pray.

C.H.

What I present here is what I remember of the letter,
and what I remember of the letter I remember verbatim
(including that awful French). It was at least twice longer.
I have left out a lyrical passage which I more or less skipped
at the time, concerning Lolita's brother who died at 2 when
she was 4, and how much I would have liked him. Let me
see what else can I say? Yes. There is just a chance that
"the vortex of the toilet" (where the letter did go) is my
own matter-of-fact contribution. She probably begged me
to make a special fire to consume it.

My first movement was one of repulsion and retreat.
My second was like a friend's calm hand falling upon my
shoulder and bidding me take my time. I did. I came out
of my daze and found myself still in Lo's room. A full-
page ad ripped out of a slick magazine was affixed to the
wall above the bed, between a crooner's mug and the lashes
of a movie actress. It represented a dark-haired young
husband with a kind of drained look in his Irish eyes. He
was modeling a robe by So-and-So and holding a bridge-
like tray by So-and-So, with breakfast for two. The legend,
by the Rev. Thomas Morell, called him a "conquering
hero." The thoroughly conquered lady (not shown) was
presumably propping herself up to receive her half of the
tray. How her bed-fellow was to get under the bridge
without some messy mishap was not clear. Lo had drawn
a jocose arrow to the haggard lover's face and had put, in
block letters: H.H. And indeed, despite a difference of a
few years, the resemblance was striking. Under this was

another picture, also a colored ad. A distinguished play-wright was solemnly smoking a Drome. He always smoked Dromes. The resemblance was slight. Under this was Lo's chaste bed, littered with "comics." The enamel had come off the bedstead, leaving black, more or less rounded, marks on the white. Having convinced myself that Louise had left, I got into Lo's bed and reread the letter.

17

Gentlemen of the jury! I cannot swear that certain motions pertaining to the business in hand—if I may coin an expression—had not drifted across my mind before. My mind had not retained them in any logical form or in any relation to definitely recollected occasions; but I cannot swear—let me repeat—that I had not toyed with them (to rig up yet another expression), in my dimness of thought, in my darkness of passion. There may have been times—there must have been times, if I know my Humbert—when I had brought up for detached inspection the idea of marrying a mature widow (say, Charlotte Haze) with not one relative left in the wide gray world, merely in order to have my way with her child (Lo, Lola, Lolita). I am even prepared to tell my tormentors that perhaps once or twice I had cast an appraiser's cold eye at Charlotte's coral lips and bronze hair and dangerously low neckline, and had vaguely tried to fit her into a plausible daydream. This I confess under torture. Imaginary torture, perhaps, but all the more horrible. I wish I might digress and tell you more of the *pavor nocturnus* that would rack me at night hideously after a chance term had struck me in the random readings of my boyhood, such as *peine forte et dure* (what a Genius of Pain must have invented that!) or the dreadful, mysterious, insidious words "trauma," "traumatic event," and "transom." But my tale is sufficiently incondite already.

After a while I destroyed the letter and went to my room, and ruminated, and rumpled my hair, and modeled my purple robe, and moaned through clenched teeth and suddenly—Suddenly, gentlemen of the jury, I felt a Dostoevskian grin dawning (through the very grimace that twisted my lips) like a distant and terrible sun. I imagined (under conditions of new and perfect visibility) all the casual caresses her mother's husband would be able to lavish on his Lolita. I would hold her against me three times a day, every day. All my troubles would be expelled, I would be a healthy man. "To hold thee lightly on a gentle knee and print on thy soft cheek a parent's kiss . . ." Well-read Humbert!

Then, with all possible caution, on mental tiptoe so to speak, I conjured up Charlotte as a possible mate. By God, I could make myself bring her that economically halved grapefruit, that sugarless breakfast.

Humbert Humbert sweating in the fierce white light, and howled at, and trodden upon by sweating policemen, is now ready to make a further "statement" (*quel mot!*) as he turns his conscience inside out and rips off its innermost lining. I did not plan to marry poor Charlotte in order to eliminate her in some vulgar, gruesome and dangerous manner such as killing her by placing five bichloride-of-mercury tablets in her preprandial sherry or anything like that; but a delicately allied, pharmacopoeial thought did tinkle in my sonorous and clouded brain. Why limit myself to the modest masked caress I had tried already? Other visions of venery presented themselves to me swaying and smiling. I saw myself administering a powerful sleeping potion to both mother and daughter so as to fondle the latter through the night with perfect impunity. The house was full of Charlotte's snore, while Lolita hardly breathed in her sleep, as still as a painted girl-child. "Mother, I swear Kenny never even *touched* me." "You either lie, Dolores

Haze, or it was an incubus." No, I would not go that far.

So Humbert the Cubus schemed and dreamed—and the red sun of desire and decision (the two things that create a live world) rose higher and higher, while upon a succession of balconies a succession of libertines, sparkling glass in hand, toasted the bliss of past and future nights. Then, figuratively speaking, I shattered the glass, and boldly imagined (for I was drunk on those visions by then and underrated the gentleness of my nature) how eventually I might blackmail—no, that is too strong a word—mauvemail big Haze into letting me consort with little Haze by gently threatening the poor doting Big Dove with desertion if she tried to bar me from playing with my legal step-daughter. In a word, before such an Amazing Offer, before such a vastness and variety of vistas, I was as helpless as Adam at the preview of early oriental history, miraged in his apple orchard.

And now take down the following important remark: the artist in me has been given the upper hand over the gentleman. It is with a great effort of will that in this memoir I have managed to tune my style to the tone of the journal that I kept when Mrs. Haze was to me but an obstacle. That journal of mine is no more; but I have considered it my artistic duty to preserve its intonations no matter how false and brutal they may seem to me now. Fortunately, my story has reached a point where I can cease insulting poor Charlotte for the sake of retrospective verisimilitude.

Wishing to spare poor Charlotte two or three hours of suspense on a winding road (and avoid, perhaps, a head-on collision that would shatter our different dreams), I made a thoughtful but abortive attempt to reach her at the camp by telephone. She had left half an hour before, and getting Lo instead, I told her—trembling and brimming with my mastery over fate—that I was going to marry her mother. I had to repeat it twice because something was preventing her from giving me her attention. "Gee, that's swell," she said laughing. "When is the wedding? Hold on a sec, the pup—That pup here has got hold of my sock. Listen—" and she added she guessed she was going to have loads of fun . . . and I realized as I hung up that a couple of hours at that camp had been sufficient to blot out with new impressions the image of handsome Humbert Humbert from little Lolita's mind. But what did it matter now? I would get her back as soon as a decent amount of time after the wedding had elapsed. "The orange blossom would have scarcely withered on the grave," as a poet might have said. But I am no poet. I am only a very conscientious recorder.

After Louise had gone, I inspected the icebox, and finding it much too puritanic, walked to town and bought the richest foods available. I also bought some good liquor and two or three kinds of vitamins. I was pretty sure that with the aid of these stimulants and my natural resources, I would avert any embarrassment that my indifference might incur when called upon to display a strong and impatient flame. Again and again resourceful Humbert evoked Charlotte as seen in the raree-show of a manly imgination. She was well groomed and shapely, this I could say for her, and she was my Lolita's big sister—this notion, perhaps, I could keep up if only I did not visualize too realistically her heavy hips, round knees, ripe bust, the coarse pink skin of her neck ("coarse" by comparison with silk and honey) and all the rest of that sorry and dull thing: a handsome woman.

The sun made its usual round of the house as the afternoon ripened into evening. I had a drink. And another. And yet another. Gin and pineapple juice, my favorite mixture, always double my energy. I decided to busy myself with our unkempt lawn. *Une petite attention*. It was crowded with dandelions, and a cursed dog—I loathe dogs—had defiled the flat stones where a sundial had once stood. Most of the dandelions had changed from suns to moons. The gin and Lolita were dancing in me, and I almost fell over the folding chairs that I attempted to dislodge. Incarnadine zebras! There are some eructations that sound like cheers—at least, mine did. An old fence at the back of the garden separated us from the neighbor's garbage receptacles and lilacs; but there was nothing between the front end of our lawn (where it sloped along one side of the house) and the street. Therefore I was able to watch (with the smirk of one about to perform a good action) for the return of Charlotte: that tooth should be extracted at once. As I lurched and lunged with the hand mower, bits of grass optically twittering in the low sun, I kept an eye on that section of suburban street. It curved in from under an archway of huge shade trees, then sped towards us down, down, quite sharply, past old Miss Opposite's ivied brick house and high-sloping lawn (much trimmer than ours) and disappeared behind our own front porch which I could not see from where I happily belched and labored. The dandelions perished. A reek of sap mingled with the pineapple. Two little girls, Marion and Mabel, whose comings and goings I had mechanically followed of late (but who could replace my Lolita?) went toward the avenue (from which our Lawn Street cascaded), one pushing a bicycle, the other feeding from a paper bag, both talking at the top of their sunny voices. Leslie, old Miss Opposite's gardener and chauffeur, a very amiable and athletic Negro, grinned at me from afar and shouted, re-shouted, commented by gesture, that I was mighty energetic to-day. The fool dog of the prosperous junk dealer next door ran after a blue car—not Charlotte's. The prettier of the two little girls (Mabel, I think), shorts, halter with little to halt, bright hair—a nymphet, by Pan!—ran back down the street crumpling her paper bag and was hidden from this Green Goat by the frontage of Mr. and Mrs. Humbert's residence. A station wagon popped out of the leafy shade of the avenue, dragging some of it on its roof before the shadows snapped, and swung by at an idiotic pace, the sweatshirted driver roof-holding with his left hand and the junkman's dog tearing alongside. There was a smiling pause—and then, with a flutter in my breast, I witnessed the return of the Blue Sedan. I saw it glide downhill and disappear behind the corner of the house. I had a glimpse of her calm pale profile. It occurred to me that until she went upstairs she would not know whether I had gone or not. A minute later, with an expression of great anguish on her face, she looked down at me from the window of Lo's room. By sprinting upstairs, I managed to reach that room before she left it.

18

When the bride is a widow and the groom is a widower; when the former has lived in Our Great Little Town for hardly two years, and the latter for hardly a month; when Monsieur wants to get the whole damned thing over with as quickly as possible, and Madame gives in with a tolerant smile; then, my reader, the wedding is generally a "quiet" affair. The bride may dispense with a tiara of orange blossoms securing her finger-tip veil, nor does she carry a white orchid in a prayer book. The bride's little daughter might have added to the ceremonies uniting H. and H. a touch of vivid vermeil; but I knew I would not dare be too tender with cornered Lolita yet, and therefore agreed it was not worth while tearing the child away from her beloved Camp Q.

My *soi-disant* passionate and lonely Charlotte was in everyday life matter-of-fact and gregarious. Moreover, I discovered that although she could not control her heart or her cries, she was a woman of principle. Immediately after she had become more or less my mistress (despite the stimulants, her "nervous, eager *chéri*"—a heroic *chéri!*—had some initial trouble, for which, however, he amply compensated her by a fantastic display of old-world endearments), good Charlotte interviewed me about my relations with God. I could have answered that on that score my mind was open; I said, instead—paying my tribute to a pious platitude—that I believed in a cosmic spirit. Looking down at her fingernails, she also asked me had I not in my family a certain strange strain. I countered by inquiring whether she would still want to marry me if my father's maternal grandfather had been, say, a Turk. She said it did not matter a bit; but that, if she ever found out I did not believe in Our Christian God, she would commit suicide. She said it so solemnly that it gave me the creeps. It was then I knew she was a woman of principle.

Oh, she was very genteel: she said "excuse me" whenever a slight burp interrupted her flowing speech, called an envelope an ahnvelope, and when talking to her lady-friends referred to me as Mr. Humbert. I thought it would please her if I entered the community trailing some glamor after me. On the day of our wedding a little interview with me appeared in the Society Column of the Ramsdale *Journal*, with a photograph of Charlotte, one eyebrow up and a misprint in her name ("Hazer"). Despite this contretemps, the publicity warmed the porcelain cockles of her heart—and made my rattles shake with awful glee. By engaging in church work as well as by getting to know the better mothers of Lo's schoolmates, Charlotte in the course of twenty months or so had managed to become if not a prominent, at least an acceptable citizen, but never before had she come under that thrilling *rubrique*, and it was I who put her there, Mr. Edgar H. Humbert (I threw in the "Edgar" just for the heck of it), "writer and explorer." McCoo's brother, when taking it down, asked me what I had written. Whatever I told him came out as "several books on Peacock, Rainbow and other poets." It was also noted that Charlotte and I had known each other for several years and that I was a distant relation of her first husband. I hinted I had had an affair with her thirteen years ago but this was not mentioned in print. To Charlotte I said that society columns *should* contain a shimmer of errors.

Let us go on with this curious tale. When called upon to enjoy my promotion from lodger to lover, did I experience only bitterness and distaste? No. Mr. Humbert confesses to a certain titillation of his vanity, to some faint tenderness, even to a pattern of remorse daintily running along the steel of his conspiratorial dagger. Never had I thought that the rather ridiculous, though rather handsome Mrs. Haze, with her blind faith in the wisdom of her church and book club, her mannerisms of elocution, her harsh, cold, contemptuous attitude toward an adorable, downy-armed child of twelve, could turn into such a touching, helpless creature as soon as I laid my hands upon her which happened on the threshold of Lolita's room whither she tremulously backed repeating "no, no, please no."

The transformation improved her looks. Her smile that had been such a contrived thing, thenceforth became the radiance of utter adoration—a radiance having something soft and moist about it, in which, with wonder, I recognized a resemblance to the lovely, inane, lost look that Lo had when gloating over a new kind of concoction at the soda fountain or mutely admiring my expensive, always tailor-fresh clothes. Deeply fascinated, I would watch Charlotte while she swapped parental woes with some other lady and made that national grimace of feminine resignation (eyes rolling up, mouth drooping sideways) which, in an infantile form, I had seen Lo making herself. We had highballs before turning in, and with their help, I would manage to evoke the child while caressing the mother. This was the white stomach within which my nymphet had been a little curved fish in 1934. This carefully dyed hair, so sterile to my sense of smell and touch, acquired at certain lamplit moments in the poster bed the tinge, if not the texture, of Lolita's curls. I kept telling myself, as I wielded my brand-new large-as-life wife, that biologically this was the nearest I could get to Lolita; that at Lolita's age, Lotte had been as desirable a schoolgirl as her daughter was, and as Lolita's daughter would be some day. I had my wife unearth from under a collection of shoes (Mr. Haze had a passion for them, it appears) a thirty-year-old album, so that I might see how Lotte had looked as a child; and even though the light was wrong and the dresses graceless, I was able to make out a dim first version of Lolita's outline, legs, cheekbones, bobbed nose. Lottelita, Lolitchen.

So I tom-peeped across the hedges of years, into wan little windows. And when, by means of pitifully ardent, naïvely lascivious caresses, she of the noble nipple and massive thigh prepared me for the performance of my nightly duty, it was still a nymphet's scent that in despair I tried to pick up, as I bayed through the undergrowth of dark decaying forests.

I simply can't tell you how gentle, how touching my poor wife was. At breakfast, in the depressingly bright kitchen, with its chrome glitter and Hardware and Co. Calendar and cute breakfast nook (simulating that Coffee Shoppe where in their college days Charlotte and Humbert used to coo together), she would sit, robed in red, her elbow on the plastic-topped table, her cheek propped on her fist, and stare at me with intolerable tenderness as I consumed my ham and eggs. Humbert's face might twitch with neuralgia, but in her eyes it vied in beauty and animation with the sun and shadows of leaves rippling on the white refrigerator. My solemn exasperation was to her the silence of love. My small income added to her even smaller one impressed her as a brilliant fortune; not because the resulting sum now sufficed for most middle-class needs, but because even my money shone in her eyes with the magic of my manliness, and she saw our joint account as one of those southern boulevards at midday that have solid shade on one side and smooth sunshine on the other, all the way to the end of a prospect, where pink mountains loom.

Into the fifty days of our cohabitation Charlotte crammed the activities of as many years. The poor woman busied herself with a number of things she had foregone long before or had never been much interested in, as if (to prolong these Proustian intonations) by my marrying the mother of the child I loved I had enabled my wife to regain an abundance of youth by proxy. With the zest of a banal young bride, she started to "glorify the home." Knowing as I did its every cranny by heart—since those days when from my chair I mentally mapped out Lolita's course through the house—I had long entered into a sort of emotional relationship with it, with its very ugliness and dirt, and now I could almost feel the wretched thing cower in its reluctance to endure the bath of ecru and ocher and putty-buff-and-snuff that Charlotte planned to give it. She never got as far as that, thank God, but she did use up a tremendous amount of energy in washing window shades, waxing the slats of Venetian blinds, purchasing new shades and new blinds, returning them to the store, replacing them by others, and so on, in a constant chiaroscuro of smiles and frowns, doubts and pouts. She dabbled in cretonnes and chintzes; she changed the colors of the sofa—the sacred sofa where a bubble of paradise had once burst in slow motion within me. She rearranged the furniture—and was pleased when she found, in a household treatise, that "it is permissible to separate a pair of sofa commodes and their companion lamps." With the authoress of *Your Home Is You*, she developed a hatred for little lean chairs and spindle tables. She believed that a room having a generous expanse of glass, and lots of rich wood paneling was an example of the masculine type of room, whereas the feminine type was characterized by lighter-looking windows and frailer woodwork. The novels I had found her reading when I moved in were now replaced by illustrated catalogues and homemaking guides. From a firm located at 4640 Roosevelt Blvd., Philadelphia, she ordered for our double bed a "damask covered 312 coil mattress"—although the old one seemed to me resilient and durable enough for whatever it had to support.

A Midwesterner, as her late husband had also been, she had lived in coy Ramsdale, the gem of an eastern state, not long enough to know all the nice people. She knew slightly the jovial dentist who lived in a kind of ramshackle wooden chateau behind our lawn. She had met at a church tea the "snooty" wife of the local junk dealer who owned the "colonial" white horror at the corner of the avenue. Now and then she "visited with" old Miss Opposite; but the more patrician matrons among those she called upon, or met at lawn functions, or had telephone chats with—such dainty ladies as Mrs. Glave, Mrs. Sheridan, Mrs. McCrystal, Mrs. Knight and others, seldom seemed to call on my neglected Charlotte. Indeed, the only couple with whom she had relations of real cordiality, devoid of any *arrière-pensée* or practical foresight, were the Farlows who had just come back from a business trip to Chile in time to attend our wedding, with the Chatfields, McCoos, and a few others (but not Mrs. Junk or the even prouder Mrs. Talbot). John Farlow was a middle-aged, quiet, quietly athletic, quietly successful dealer in sporting goods, who had an office at Parkington, forty miles away: it was he who got me the cartridges for that Colt and showed me how to use it, during a walk in the woods one Sunday; he was also what he called with a smile a part-time lawyer and had handled some of Charlotte's affairs. Jean, his youngish wife (and first cousin), was a long-limbed girl in harlequin glasses with two boxer dogs, two pointed breasts and a big red mouth. She painted—landscapes and portraits—and vividly do I remember praising, over cocktails, the picture she had made of a niece of hers, little Rosaline Honeck, a rosy honey in a Girl Scout uniform, beret of green worsted, belt of green webbing, charming shoulder-long curls—and John removed his pipe and said it was a pity Dolly (my Dolita) and Rosaline were so critical of each other at school, but he hoped they would get on better when they returned from their respective camps. We talked of the school. It had its drawbacks, and it had its virtues. "Of course, too many of the tradespeople here are Italians," said John, "but on the other hand we are still spared—" "I wish," interrupted Jean with a laugh, "Dolly and Rosaline were spending the summer together." Suddenly I imagined Lo returning from camp—brown, warm, drowsy, drugged—and was ready to weep with passion and impatience.

19

A few words more about Mrs. Humbert while the going is good (a bad accident is to happen quite soon). I had been always aware of the possessive streak in her, but I never thought she would be so crazily jealous of anything in my life that had not been she. She showed a fierce insatiable curiosity for my past. She desired me to resuscitate all my loves so that she might make me insult them, and trample upon them, and revoke them apostately and totally, thus destroying my past. She made me tell her about my marriage to Valeria, who was of course a scream; but I also had to invent, or to pad atrociously, a long series of mistresses for Charlotte's morbid delectation. To keep her happy, I had to present her with an illustrated catalogue of them, all nicely differentiated, according to the rules of those American ads where schoolchildren are pictured in a subtle ratio of races, with one—only one, but as cute as they make them—chocolate-colored round-eyed little lad, almost in the very middle of the front row. So I presented my women, and had them smile and sway—the languorous blond, the fiery brunette, the sensual copper-head—as if on parade in a bordello. The more popular and platitudinous I made them, the more Mrs. Humbert was pleased with the show.

Never in my life had I confessed so much or received so many confessions. The sincerity and artlessness with which she discussed what she called her "love-life," from first necking to connubial catch-as-catch-can, were, ethic-ally, in striking contrast with my glib compositions, but technically the two sets were congeneric since both were affected by the same stuff (soap operas, psychoanalysis and cheap novelettes) upon which I drew for my characters and she for her mode of expression. I was considerably amused by certain remarkable sexual habits that the good Harold Haze had had according to Charlotte who thought my mirth improper; but otherwise her autobiography was as devoid of interests as her autopsy would have been. I never saw a healthier woman than she, despite thinning diets.

Of my Lolita she seldom spoke—more seldom, in fact, than she did of the blurred, blond male baby whose photograph to the exclusion of all others adorned our bleak bedroom. In one of her tasteless reveries, she predicted that the dead infant's soul would return to earth in the form of the child she would bear in her present wedlock. And although I felt no special urge to supply the Humbert line with a replica of Harold's production (Lolita, with an incestuous thrill, I had grown to regard as *my* child), it occurred to me that a prolonged confinement, with a nice Caesarean operation and other complications in a safe maternity ward sometime next spring, would give me a chance to be alone with my Lolita for weeks, perhaps— and gorge the limp nymphet with sleeping pills.

Oh, she simply hated her daughter! What I thought especially vicious was that she had gone out of her way to answer with great diligence the questionnaires in a fool's book she had (*A Guide to Your Child's Development*), published in Chicago. The rigmarole went year by year, and Mom was supposed to fill out a kind of inventory at each of her child's birthdays. On Lo's twelfth, January 1, 1947, Charlotte Haze, née Becker, had underlined the following epithets, ten out of forty, under "Your Child's Personality": aggressive, boisterous, critical, distrustful, impatient, irritable, inquisitive, listless, negativistic (underlined twice) and obstinate. She had ignored the thirty remaining adjectives, among which were cheerful, co-operative, energetic, and so forth. It was really maddening. With a brutality that otherwise never appeared in my loving wife's mild nature, she attacked and routed such of Lo's little belongings that had wandered to various parts of the house to freeze there like so many hypnotized bunnies. Little did the good lady dream that one morning when an upset stomach (the result of my trying to improve on her sauces) had prevented me from accompanying her to church, I deceived her with one of Lolita's anklets. And then, her attitude toward my saporous darling's letters!

DEAR MUMMY AND HUMMY,

Hope you are fine. Thank you very much for the candy. I [crossed out and re-written again] I lost my new sweater in the woods. It has been cold here for the last few days. I'm having a time. Love.

DOLLY

"The dumb child," said Mrs. Humbert, "has left out a word before 'time.' That sweater was all-wool, and I wish you would not send her candy without consulting me."

20

There was a woodlake (Hourglass Lake—not as I had thought it was spelled) a few miles from Ramsdale, and there was one week of great heat at the end of July when we drove there daily. I am now obliged to describe in some tedious detail our last swim there together, one tropical Tuesday morning.

We had left the car in a parking area not far from the road and were making our way down a path cut through the pine forest to the lake, when Charlotte remarked that Jean Farlow, in quest of rare light effects (Jean belonged to the old school of painting), had seen Leslie taking a dip "in the ebony" (as John had quipped) at five o'clock in the morning last Sunday.

"The water," I said, "must have been quite cold."

"That is not the point," said the logical doomed dear. "He is subnormal, you see. And," she continued (in that carefully phrased way of hers that was beginning to tell on my health), "I have a very definite feeling our Louise is in love with that moron."

Feeling. "We feel Dolly is not doing as well" etc. (from an old school report).

The Humberts walked on, sandaled and robed.

"Do you know, Hum: I have one most ambitious dream," pronounced Lady Hum, lowering her head—shy of that dream—and communing with the tawny ground. "I would love to get hold of a real trained servant maid like that German girl the Talbots spoke of; and have her live in the house."

"No room," I said.

"Come," she said with her quizzical smile, "surely, chéri, you underestimate the possibilities of the Humbert home. We would put her in Lo's room. I intended to make a guestroom of that hole anyway. It's the coldest and meanest in the whole house."

"What are you talking about?" I asked, the skin of my cheekbones tensing up (this I take the trouble to note only because my daughter's skin did the same when she felt that way: disbelief, disgust, irritation).

"Are you bothered by Romantic Associations?" queried my wife—in allusion to her first surrender.

"Hell no," said I. "I just wonder where will you put your daughter when you get your guest or your maid."

"Ah," said Mrs. Humbert, dreaming, smiling, drawing out the "Ah" simultaneously with the raise of one eyebrow and a soft exhalation of breath. "Little Lo, I'm afraid, does not enter the picture at all, at all. Little Lo goes straight from camp to a good boarding school with strict discipline and some sound religious training. And then—Beardsley College. I have it all mapped out, you need not worry."

She went on to say that she, Mrs. Humbert, would have to overcome her habitual sloth and write to Miss Phalen's sister who taught at St. Algebra. The dazzling lake emerged. I said I had forgotten my sunglasses in the car and would catch up with her.

I had always thought that wringing one's hands was a fictional gesture—the obscure outcome, perhaps, of some medieval ritual; but as I took to the woods, for a spell of despair and desperate meditation, this was the gesture ("look, Lord, at these chains!") that would have come nearest to the mute expression of my mood.

Had Charlotte been Valeria, I would have known how to handle the situation; and "handle" is the word I want. In the good old days, by merely twisting fat Valechka's brittle wrist (the one she had fallen upon from a bicycle) I could make her change her mind instantly; but anything of the sort in regard to Charlotte was unthinkable. Bland American Charlotte frightened me. My lighthearted dream of controlling her through her passion for me was all wrong. I dared not do anything to spoil the image of me she had set up to adore. I had toadied to her when she was the awesome duenna of my darling, and a groveling something still persisted in my attitude toward her. The only ace I held was her ignorance of my monstrous love for her Lo. She had been annoyed by Lo's liking me; but *my* feelings she could not divine. To Valeria I might have said: "Look here, you fat fool, *c'est moi qui décide* what is good for Dolores Humbert." To Charlotte, I could not even say (with ingratiating calm): "Excuse me, my dear, I disagree. Let us give the child one more chance. Let me be her private tutor for a year or so. You once told me yourself—" In fact, I could not say anything at all to Charlotte about the child without giving myself away. Oh, you cannot imagine (as I had never imagined) what these women of principle are! Charlotte, who did not notice the falsity of all the everyday conventions and rules of behavior, and foods, and books, and people she doted upon, would distinguish at once a false intonation in anything I might say with a view to keeping Lo near. She was like a musician who may be an odious vulgarian in ordinary life, devoid of tact and taste; but who will hear a false note in music with diabolical accuracy of judgment. To break Charlotte's will, I would have to break her heart. If I broke her heart, her image of me would break too. If I said: "Either I have my way with Lolita, and you help me to keep the matter quiet, or we part at once," she would have turned as pale as a woman of clouded glass and slowly replied: "All right, whatever you add or retract, this is the end." And the end it would be.

Such, then, was the mess. I remember reaching the parking area and pumping a handful of rust-tasting water, and drinking it as avidly as if it could give me magic wisdom, youth, freedom, a tiny concubine. For a while, purple-robed, heel-dangling, I sat on the edge of one of the rude tables, under the wooshing pines. In the middle distance, two little maidens in shorts and halters came out of a sun-dappled privy marked "Women." Gum-chewing Mabel (or Mabel's understudy) laboriously, absent-mindedly, straddled a bicycle, and Marion, shaking her hair because of the flies, settled behind, legs wide apart; and, wobbling, they slowly, absently, merged with the light and shade. Lolita! Father and daughter melting into these woods! The natural solution was to destroy Mrs. Humbert. But how?

No man can bring about the perfect murder; chance, however, can do it. There was the famous dispatch of a Mme Lacour in Arles, southern France, at the close of last century. An unidentified bearded six-footer, who, it was later conjectured, had been the lady's secret lover, walked up to her in a crowded street, soon after her marriage to Colonel Lacour, and mortally stabbed her in the back, three times, while the Colonel, a small bulldog of a man, hung onto the murderer's arm. By a miraculous and beautiful coincidence, right at the moment when the operator was in the act of loosening the angry little husband's jaws (while several onlookers were closing in upon the group), a cranky Italian in the house nearest to the scene set off by sheer accident some kind of explosive he was tinkering with, and immediately the street was turned into a pandemonium of smoke, falling bricks and running people. The explosion hurt no one (except that it knocked out game Colonel Lacour); but the lady's vengeful lover ran when the others ran—and lived happily ever after.

Now look what happens when the operator himself plans a perfect removal.

I walked down to Hourglass Lake. The spot from which we and a few other "nice" couples (the Farlows, the Chatfields) bathed was a kind of small cove; my Charlotte liked it because it was almost "a private beach." The main bathing facilities (or "drowning facilities" as the Ramsdale *Journal* had had occasion to say) were in the left (eastern) part of the hourglass, and could not be seen from our covelet. To our right, the pines soon gave way to a curve of marshland which turned again into forest on the opposite side.

I sat down beside my wife so noiselessly that she started.

"Shall we go in?" she asked.

"We shall in a minute. Let me follow a train of thought."

I thought. More than a minute passed.

"All right. Come on."

"Was I on that train?"

"You certainly were."

"I hope so," said Charlotte entering the water. It soon reached the gooseflesh of her thick thighs; and then, joining her outstretched hands, shutting her mouth tight, very plain-faced in her black rubber headgear, Charlotte flung herself forward with a great splash.

Slowly we swam out into the shimmer of the lake.

On the opposite bank, at least a thousand paces away (if one could walk across water), I could make out the tiny figures of two men working like beavers on their stretch of shore. I knew exactly who they were: a retired policeman of Polish descent and the retired plumber who owned most of the timber on that side of the lake. And I also knew they were engaged in building, just for the dismal fun of the thing, a wharf. The knocks that reached us seemed so much bigger than what could be distinguished of those dwarfs' arms and tools; indeed, one suspected the director of those acrosonic effects to have been at odds with the puppet-master, especially since the hefty crack of each diminutive blow lagged behind its visual version.

The short white-sand strip of "our" beach—from which by now we had gone a little way to reach deep water—was empty on weekday mornings. There was nobody around except those two tiny very busy figures on the opposite side, and a dark-red private plane that droned overhead, and then disappeared in the blue. The setting was really perfect for a brisk bubbling murder, and here was the subtle point: the man of law and the man of water were just near enough to witness an accident and just far enough not to observe a crime. They were near enough to hear a distracted bather thrashing about and bellowing for somebody to come and help him save his drowning wife; and they were too far to distinguish (if they happened to look too soon) that the anything but distracted swimmer was finishing to tread his wife underfoot. I was not yet at that stage; I merely want to convey the ease of the act, the nicety of the setting! So there was Charlotte swimming on with dutiful awkwardness (she was a very mediocre mermaid), but not without a certain solemn pleasure (for was not her merman by her side?); and as I watched, with the stark lucidity of a future recollection (you know— trying to see things as you will remember having seen them), the glossy whiteness of her wet face so little tanned despite all her endeavors, and her pale lips, and her naked convex forehead, and the tight black cap, and the plump wet neck, I knew that all I had to do was to drop back, take a deep breath, then grab her by the ankle and rapidly dive with my captive corpse. I say corpse because surprise, panic and inexperience would cause her to inhale at once a lethal gallon of lake, while I would be able to hold on for at least a full minute, open-eyed under water. The fatal gesture passed like the tail of a falling star across the black-ness of the contemplated crime. It was like some dreadful silent ballet, the male dancer holding the ballerina by her foot and streaking down through watery twilight. I might come up for a mouthful of air while still holding her down, and then would dive again as many times as would be necessary, and only when the curtain came down on her for good, would I permit myself to yell for help. And when some twenty minutes later the two puppets steadily growing arrived in a rowboat, one half newly painted, poor Mrs. Humbert Humbert, the victim of a cramp or coron-ary occlusion, or both, would be standing on her head in the inky ooze, some thirty feet below the smiling surface of Hourglass Lake.

Simple, was it not? But what d'ye know, folks—I just could not make myself do it!

She swam beside me, a trustful and clumsy seal, and all the logic of passion screamed in my ear: Now is the time! And, folks, I just couldn't! In silence I turned shoreward and gravely, dutifully, she also turned, and still hell screamed its counsel, and still I could not make myself drown the poor, slippery, big-bodied creature. The scream grew more and more remote as I realized the melancholy fact that neither tomorrow, nor Friday, nor any other day or night, could I make myself put her to death. Oh, I could visualize myself slapping Valeria's breasts out of alignment, or otherwise hurting her—and I could see myself, no less clearly, shooting her lover in the underbelly and making him say "akh!" and sit down. But I could not kill Charlotte—especially when things were on the whole not quite as hopeless, perhaps, as they seemed at first wince on that miserable morning. Were I to catch her by her strong kicking foot; were I to see her amazed look, hear her awful voice; were I still to go through with the ordeal, her ghost would haunt me all my life. Perhaps if the year were 1447 instead of 1947 I might have hoodwinked my gentle nature by administering her some classical poison from a hollow agate, some tender philter of death. But in our middle-class nosy era it would not have come off the way it used to in the brocaded palaces of the past. Nowadays you have to be a scientist if you want to be a killer. No, no, I was neither. Ladies and gentlemen of the jury, the majority of sex offenders that hanker for some throbbing, sweet-moaning, physical but not necessarily coital, relation with a girl-child, are innocuous, inadequate, passive, timid strangers who merely ask the community to allow them to pursue their practically harmless, so-called aberrant behavior, their little hot wet private acts of sexual deviation without the police and society cracking down upon them. We are not sex fiends! We do not rape as good soldiers do. We are unhappy, mild, dog-eyed gentlemen, sufficiently well integrated to control our urge in the presence of adults, but ready to give years and years of life for one chance to touch a nymphet. Emphatically, no killers are we. Poets never kill. Oh, my poor Charlotte, do not hate me in your eternal heaven among an eternal alchemy of asphalt and rubber and metal and stone—but thank God, not water, not water!

Nonetheless it was a very close shave, speaking quite objectively. And now comes the point of my perfect-crime parable.

We sat down on our towels in the thirsty sun. She looked around, loosened her bra, and turned over on her stomach to give her back a chance to be feasted upon. She said she loved me. She sighed deeply. She extended one arm and groped in the pocket of her robe for her cigarettes. She sat up and smoked. She examined her right shoulder. She kissed me heavily with open smoky mouth. Suddenly, down the sand bank behind us, from under the bushes and pines, a stone rolled, then another.

"Those disgusting prying kids," said Charlotte, holding up her big bra to her breast and turning prone again. "I shall have to speak about that to Peter Krestovski."

From the debouchment of the trail came a rustle, a footfall, and Jean Farlow marched down with her easel and things.

"You scared us," said Charlotte.

Jean said she had been up there, in a place of green concealment, spying on nature (spies are generally shot), trying to finish a lakescape, but it was no good, she had no talent whatever (which was quite true)—"And have *you* ever tried painting, Humbert?" Charlotte, who was a little jealous of Jean, wanted to know if John was coming.

He was. He was coming home for lunch today. He had dropped her on the way to Parkington and should be picking her up any time now. It was a grand morning. She always felt a traitor to Cavall and Melampus for leaving them roped on such gorgeous days. She sat down on the white sand between Charlotte and me. She wore shorts. Her long brown legs were about as attractive to me as those of a chestnut mare. She showed her gums when she smiled.

"I almost put both of you into my lake," she said. "I even noticed something you overlooked. You [addressing Humbert] had your wrist.watch on in, yes, sir, you had."

"Waterproof," said Charlotte softly, making a fish mouth.

Jean took my wrist upon her knee and examined Charlotte's gift, then put back Humbert's hand on the sand, palm up.

"You could see anything that way," remarked Charlotte coquettishly.

Jean sighed. "I once saw," she said, "two children, male and female, at sunset, right here, making love. Their shadows were giants. And I told you about Mr. Tomson at daybreak. Next time I expect to see fat old Ivor in the ivory. He is really a freak, that man. Last time he told me a completely indecent story about his nephew. It appears—"

"Hullo there," said John's voice.

21

My habit of being silent when displeased, or, more exactly, the cold and scaly quality of my displeased silence, used to frighten Valeria out of her wits. She used to whimper and wail, saying *"Ce qui me rend folle, c'est que je ne sais à quoi tu penses quand tu es comme ça."* I tried being silent with Charlotte—and she just chirped on, or chucked my silence under the chin. An astonishing woman! I would retire to my former room, now a regular "studio," mumbling I had after all a learned opus to write, and cheerfully Charlotte went on beautifying the home, warbling on the telephone and writing letters. From my window, through the lacquered shiver of poplar leaves, I could see her crossing the street and contentedly mailing her letter to Miss Phalen's sister.

The week of scattered showers and shadows which

elapsed after our last visit to the motionless sands of Hourglass Lake was one of the gloomiest I can recall. Then came two or three dim rays of hope—before the ultimate sunburst.

It occurred to me that I had a fine brain in beautiful working order and that I might as well use it. If I dared not meddle with my wife's plans for her daughter (getting warmer and browner every day in the fair weather of hopeless distance), I could surely devise some general means to assert myself in a general way that might be later directed toward a particular occasion. One evening, Charlotte herself provided me with an opening.

"I have a surprise for you," she said looking at me with fond eyes over a spoonful of soup. "In the fall we two are going to England."

I swallowed *my* spoonful, wiped my lips with pink paper (Oh, the cool rich linens of Mirana Hotel!) and said:

"I have also a surprise for you, my dear. We two are not going to England."

"Why, what's the matter?" she said, looking—with more surprise than I had counted upon—at my hands (I was involuntarily folding and tearing and crushing and tearing again the innocent pink napkin). My smiling face set her somewhat at ease, however.

"The matter is quite simple," I replied. "Even in the most harmonious of households, as ours is, not all decisions are taken by the female partner. There are certain things that the husband is there to decide. I can well imagine the thrill that you, a healthy American gal, must experience at crossing the Atlantic on the same ocean liner with Lady Bumble—or Sam Bumble, the Frozen Meat King, or a Hollywood harlot. And I doubt not that you and I would make a pretty ad for the Traveling Agency when portrayed looking—you, frankly starry-eyed, I, controlling my envious admiration—at the Palace Sentries, or Scarlet Guards, or Beaver Eaters, or whatever they are called. But I happen to be allergic to Europe, including merry old England. As you well know, I have nothing but very sad associations with the Old and rotting World. No colored ads in your magazines will change the situation."

"My darling," said Charlotte. "I really—"

"No, wait a minute. The present matter is only incidental. I am concerned with a general trend. When you wanted me to spend my afternoons sunbathing on the Lake instead of doing my work, I gladly gave in and became a bronzed glamor boy for your sake, instead of remaining a scholar and, well, an educator. When you lead me to bridge and bourbon with the charming Farlows, I meekly follow. No, please, wait. When you decorate your home, I do not interfere with your schemes. When you decide—when you decide all kinds of matters, I may be in complete, or in partial, let us say, disagreement—but I say nothing. I ignore the particular. I cannot ignore the general. I love being bossed by you, but every game has its rules. I am not cross. I am not cross at all. Don't do that. But I am one half of this household, and have a small but distinct voice."

She had come to my side and had fallen on her knees and was slowly, but very vehemently, shaking her head and clawing at my trousers. She said she had never realized. She said I was her ruler and her god. She said Louise had gone, and let us make love right away. She said I must forgive her or she would die.

This little incident filled me with considerable elation. I told her quietly that it was a matter not of asking forgiveness, but of changing one's ways; and I resolved to press my advantage and spend a good deal of time, aloof and moody, working at my book—or at least pretending to work.

The "studio bed" in my former room had long been converted into the sofa it had always been at heart, and Charlotte had warned me since the very beginning of our cohabitation that gradually the room would be turned into a regular "writer's den." A couple of days after the British Incident, I was sitting in a new and very comfortable easy chair, with a large volume in my lap, when Charlotte rapped with her ring finger and sauntered in. How different were her movements from those of my Lolita, when *she* used to visit me in her dear dirty blue jeans, smelling of orchards in nymphetland; awkward and fey, and dimly depraved, the lower buttons of her shirt unfastened. Let me tell you, however, something. Behind the brashness of little Haze, and the poise of big Haze, a trickle of shy life ran that tasted the same, that murmured the same. A great French doctor once told my father that in near relatives the faintest gastric gurgle has the same "voice."

So Charlotte sauntered in. She felt all was not well between us. I had pretended to fall asleep the night before, and the night before that, as soon as we had gone to bed, and had risen at dawn.

Tenderly, she inquired if she were not "interrupting."

"Not at the moment," I said, turning volume C of the *Girls' Encyclopedia* around to examine a picture printed "bottom-edge" as printers say.

Charlotte went up to a little table of imitation mahogany with a drawer. She put her hand upon it. The little table was ugly, no doubt, but it had done nothing to her.

"I have always wanted to ask you," she said (businesslike, not coquettish), "why is this thing locked up? Do you want it in this room? It's so abominably uncouth."

"Leave it alone," I said. I was Camping in Scandinavia. "Is there a key?"

"Hidden."

"Oh, Hum . . ."

"Locked up love letters."

She gave me one of those wounded-doe looks that irritated me so much, and then, not quite knowing if I was serious, or how to keep up the conversation, stood for several slow pages (Campus, Canada, Candid Camera, Candy) peering at the windowpane rather than through it, drumming upon it with sharp almond-and-rose fingernails.

Presently (at Canoeing or Canvasback) she strolled up to my chair and sank down, tweedily, weightily, on its arm, inundating me with the perfume my first wife had used. "Would his lordship like to spend the fall *here?*" she asked, pointing with her little finger at an autumn view in a conservative Eastern State. "Why?" (very distinctly and slowly). She shrugged. (Probably Harold used to take a vacation at that time. Open season. Conditional reflex on her part.)

"I think I know where that is," she said, still pointing. "There is a hotel I remember, Enchanted Hunters, quaint, isn't it? And the food is a dream. And nobody bothers anybody."

She rubbed her cheek against my temple. Valeria soon got over that.

"Is there anything special you would like for dinner, dear? John and Jean will drop in later."

I answered with a grunt. She kissed me on my underlip, and, brightly saying she would bake a cake (a tradition subsisted from my lodging days that I adored her cakes), left me to my idleness.

Carefully putting down the open book where she had sat (it attempted to send forth a rotation of waves, but an inserted pencil stopped the pages), I checked the hiding place of the key: rather self-consciously it lay under the old expensive safety razor I had used before she bought me a much better and cheaper one. Was it the perfect hiding place—there, under that razor, in the groove of its velvet-lined case? The case lay in a small trunk where I kept various business papers. Could I improve upon this? Remarkable how difficult it is to conceal things—especially when one's wife keeps monkeying with the furniture.

22

I think it was exactly a week after our last swim that the noon mail brought a reply from the second Miss Phalen. The lady wrote she had just returned to St. Algebra from her sister's funeral. "Euphemia had never been the same after breaking that hip." As to the matter of Mrs. Humbert's daughter, she wished to report that it was too late to enroll her this year; but that she, the surviving Phalen, was practically certain that if Mr. and Mrs. Humbert brought Dolores over in January, her admittance might be arranged.

Next day, after lunch, I went to see "our" doctor, a friendly fellow whose perfect bedside manner and complete reliance on a few patented drugs adequately masked his ignorance of, and indifference to, medical science. The fact that Lo would have to come back to Ramsdale was a treasure of anticipation. For this event I wanted to be fully prepared. I had in fact begun my campaign earlier, before Charlotte made that cruel decision of hers. I had to be sure when my lovely child arrived, that very night, and then night after night, until St. Algebra took her away from me, I would possess the means of putting two creatures to sleep so thoroughly that neither sound nor touch should rouse them. Throughout most of July I had been experimenting with various sleeping powders, trying them out on Charlotte, a great taker of pills. The last dose I had given her (she thought it was a tablet of mild bromides— to anoint her nerves) had knocked her out for four solid hours. I had put the radio at full blast. I had blazed in her face an olisbos-like flashlight. I had pushed her, pinched her, prodded her—and nothing had disturbed the rhythm of her calm and powerful breathing. However, when I had done such a simple thing as kiss her, she had awakened at once, as fresh and strong as an octopus (I barely escaped). This would not do, I thought; had to get something still safer. At first, Dr. Byron did not seem to believe me when I said his last prescription was no match for my insomnia. He suggested I try again, and for a moment diverted my attention by showing me photographs of his family. He had a fascinating child of Dolly's age; but I saw through his tricks and insisted he prescribe the mightiest pill extant. He suggested I play golf, but finally agreed to give me something that, he said, "would really work"; and going to a cabinet, he produced a vial of violet-blue capsules banded with dark purple at one end, which, he said, had just been placed on the market and were intended not for neurotics whom a draft of water could calm if properly administered, but only for great sleepless artists who had to die for a few hours in order to live for centuries. I love to fool doctors, and though inwardly rejoicing, pocketed the pills with a skeptical shrug. Incidentally, I had had to be careful with him. Once, in another connection, a stupid lapse on my part made me mention my last sanatorium, and I thought I saw the tips of his ears twitch. Being not at all keen for Charlotte or anybody else to know that period of my past, I had hastily explained that I had once done some research among the insane for a novel. But no matter; the old rogue certainly had a sweet girleen.

I left in great spirits. Steering my wife's car with one finger, I contentedly rolled homeward. Ramsdale had, after all, lots of charm. The cicadas whirred; the avenue had been freshly watered. Smoothly, almost silkily, I turned down into our steep little street. Everything was somehow so right that day. So blue and green. I knew the sun shone because my ignition key was reflected in the windshield; and I knew it was exactly half past three because the nurse who came to massage Miss Opposite every afternoon was tripping down the narrow sidewalk in her white stockings and shoes. As usual, Junk's hysterical setter attacked me as I rolled downhill, and as usual, the local paper was lying on the porch where it had just been hurled by Kenny.

The day before I had ended the regime of aloofness I had imposed upon myself, and now uttered a cheerful homecoming call as I opened the door of the living room. With her cream-white nape and bronze bun to me, wearing the yellow blouse and maroon slacks she had on when I first met her, Charlotte sat at the corner bureau writing a letter. My hand still on the doorknob, I repeated my hearty cry. Her writing hand stopped. She sat still for a moment; then she slowly turned in her chair and rested her elbow on its curved back. Her face, disfigured by her emotion, was not a pretty sight as she stared at my legs and said:

"The Haze woman, the big bitch, the old cat, the obnoxious mamma, the—the old stupid Haze is no longer your dupe. She has—she has . . ."

My fair accuser stopped, swallowing her venom and her tears. Whatever Humbert Humbert said—or attempted to say—is inessential. She went on:

"You're a monster. You're a detestable, abominable, criminal fraud. If you come near—I'll scream out the window. Get back!"

Again, whatever H.H. murmured may be omitted, I think.

"I am leaving tonight. This is all yours. Only you'll never, never see that miserable brat again. Get out of this room."

Reader, I did. I went up to the ex-semi-studio. Arms akimbo, I stood for a moment quite still and self-composed, surveying from the threshold the raped little table with its open drawer, a key hanging from the lock, four other household keys on the table top. I walked across the landing into the Humberts' bedroom, and calmly removed my diary from under her pillow into my pocket. Then I started to walk downstairs, but stopped halfway: she was talking on the telephone which happened to be plugged just outside the door of the living room. I wanted to hear what she was saying: she canceled an order for something or other, and returned to the parlor. I rearranged my respiration and went through the hallway to the kitchen. There, I opened a bottle of Scotch. She could never resist Scotch. Then I walked into the dining room and from there, through the half-open door, contemplated Charlotte's broad back.

"You are ruining my life and yours," I said quietly. "Let us be civilized people. It is all your hallucination. You are crazy, Charlotte. The notes you found were fragments of a novel. Your name and hers were put in by mere chance. Just because they came handy. Think it over. I shall bring you a drink."

She neither answered nor turned, but went on writing in a scorching scrawl whatever she was writing. A third letter, presumably (two in stamped envelopes were already laid out on the desk). I went back to the kitchen.

I set out two glasses (to St. Algebra? to Lo?) and opened the refrigerator. It roared at me viciously while I removed the ice from its heart. Rewrite. Let her read it again. She will not recall details. Change, forge. Write a fragment and show it to her or leave it lying around. Why do faucets sometimes whine so horribly? A horrible situation, really. The little pillow-shaped blocks of ice—pillows for polar teddy bear, Lo—emitted rasping, crackling, tortured sounds as the warm water loosened them in their cells. I bumped down the glasses side by side. I poured in the whiskey and a dram of soda. She had tabooed my pin.

Bark and bang went the icebox. Carrying the glasses, I walked through the dining room and spoke through the parlor door which was a fraction ajar, not quite space enough for my elbow.

"I have made you a drink," I said.

She did not answer, the mad bitch, and I placed the glasses on the sideboard near the telephone, which had started to ring.

"Leslie speaking. Leslie Tomson," said Leslie Tomson who favored a dip at dawn. "Mrs. Humbert, sir, has been run over and you'd better come quick."

I answered, perhaps a bit testily, that my wife was safe and sound, and still holding the receiver, I pushed open the door and said:

"There's this man saying you've been killed, Charlotte."

But there was no Charlotte in the living room.

23

I rushed out. The far side of our steep little street presented a peculiar sight. A big black glossy Packard had climbed Miss Opposite's sloping lawn at an angle from the sidewalk (where a tartan laprobe had dropped in a heap), and stood there, shining in the sun, its doors open like wings, its front wheels deep in evergreen shrubbery. To the anatomical right of this car, on the trim turf of the lawn-slope, an old gentleman with a white mustache, well-dressed—double-breasted gray suit, polka-dotted bow-tie—lay supine, his long legs together, like a death-size wax figure. I have to put the impact of an instantaneous vision into a sequence of words; their physical accumulation in the page impairs the actual flash, the sharp unity of impression: Rug-heap, car, old man-doll, Miss O.'s nurse running with a rustle, a half-empty tumbler in her hand, back to the screened porch—where the propped-up, imprisoned, decrepit lady herself may be imagined screeching, but not loud enough to drown the rhythmical yaps of the Junk setter walking from group to group—from a bunch of neighbors already collected on the sidewalk, near the bit of checked stuff, and back to the car which he had finally run to earth, and then to another group on the lawn, consisting of Leslie, two policemen and a sturdy man with tortoise shell glasses. At this point, I should explain that the prompt appearance of the patrolmen, hardly more than a minute after the accident, was due to their having been ticketing the illegally parked cars in a cross lane two blocks down the grade; that the fellow with the glasses was Frederick Beale, Jr., driver of the Packard; that his 79-year-old father, whom the nurse had just watered on the green bank where he lay—a banked banker so to speak—was not in a dead faint, but was comfortably and methodically recovering from a mild heart attack or its possibility; and, finally, that the laprobe on the sidewalk (where she had so often pointed out to me with disapproval the crooked green cracks) concealed the mangled remains of Charlotte Humbert who had been knocked down and dragged several feet by the Beale car as she was hurrying across the street to drop three letters in the mailbox, at the corner of Miss Opposite's lawn. These were picked up and handed to me by a pretty child in a dirty pink frock, and I got rid of them by clawing them to fragments in my trouser pocket.

Three doctors and the Farlows presently arrived on the scene and took over. The widower, a man of exceptional self-control, neither wept nor raved. He staggered a bit, that he did; but he opened his mouth only to impart such information or issue such directions as were strictly necessary in connection with the identification, examination and disposal of a dead woman, the top of her head a porridge of bone, brains, bronze hair and blood. The sun was still a blinding red when he was put to bed in Dolly's room by his two friends, gentle John and dewy-eyed Jean; who, to be near, retired to the Humberts' bedroom for the night; which, for all I know, they may not have spent as innocently as the solemnity of the occasion required.

I have no reason to dwell, in this very special memoir, on the pre-funeral formalities that had to be attended to, or on the funeral itself, which was as quiet as the marriage had been. But a few incidents pertaining to those four or five days after Charlotte's simple death, have to be noted.

My first night of widowhood I was so drunk that I slept as soundly as the child who had slept in that bed. Next morning I hastened to inspect the fragments of letters in my pocket. They had got too thoroughly mixed up to be sorted into three complete sets. I assumed that ". . . and you had better find it because I cannot buy . . ." came from a letter to Lo; and other fragments seemed to point to Charlotte's intention of fleeing with Lo to Parkington, or even back to Pisky, lest the vulture snatch her precious lamb. Other tatters and shreds (never had I thought I had such strong talons) obviously referred to an application not to St. A. but to another boarding school which was said to be so harsh and gray and gaunt in its methods (although supplying croquet under the elms) as to have earned the nickname of "Reformatory for Young Ladies." Finally, the third epistle was obviously addressed to me. I made out such items as ". . . after a year of separation we may . . ." ". . . oh, my dearest, oh my . . ." ". . . worse than if it had been a woman you kept . . ." ". . . or, maybe, I shall die . . ." But on the whole my gleanings made little sense; the various fragments of those three hasty missives were as jumbled in the palms of my hands as their elements had been in poor Charlotte's head.

That day John had to see a customer, and Jean had to

feed her dogs, and so I was to be deprived temporarily of my friends' company. The dear people were afraid I might commit suicide if left alone, and since no other friends were available (Miss Opposite was incommunicado, the McCoos were busy building a new house miles away, and the Chatfields had been recently called to Maine by some family trouble of their own), Leslie and Louise were commissioned to keep me company under the pretense of helping me to sort out and pack a multitude of orphaned things. In a moment of superb inspiration I showed the kind and credulous Farlows (we were waiting for Leslie to come for his paid tryst with Louise) a little photograph of Charlotte I had found among her affairs. From a boulder she smiled through blown hair. It had been taken in April 1934, a memorable spring. While on a business visit to the States, I had had occasion to spend several months in Pisky. We met— and had a mad love affair. I was married, alas, and she was engaged to Haze, but after I returned to Europe, we corresponded through a friend, now dead. Jean whispered she had heard some rumors and looked at the snapshot, and, still looking, handed it to John, and John removed his pipe and looked at lovely and fast Charlotte Becker, and handed it back to me. Then they left for a few hours. Happy Louise was gurgling and scolding her swain in the basement.

Hardly had the Farlows gone than a blue-chinned cleric called—and I tried to make the interview as brief as was consistent with neither hurting his feelings nor arousing his doubts. Yes, I would devote all my life to the child's welfare. Here, incidentally, was a little cross that Charlotte Becker had given me when we were both young. I had a female cousin, a respectable spinster in New York. There we would find a good private school for Dolly. Oh, what a crafty Humbert!

For the benefit of Leslie and Louise who might (and

did) report it to John and Jean I made a tremendously loud and beautifully enacted long-distance call and simulated a conversation with Shirley Holmes. When John and Jean returned, I completely took them in by telling them, in a deliberately wild and confused mutter, that Lo had gone with the intermediate group on a five-day hike and could not be reached.

"Good Lord," said Jean, "what shall we do?"

John said it was perfectly simple—he would get the Climax police to find the hikers—it would not take them an hour. In fact, he knew the country and—

"Look," he continued, "why don't I drive there right now, and you may sleep with Jean"—(he did not really add that but Jean supported his offer so passionately that it might be implied).

I broke down. I pleaded with John to let things remain the way they were. I said I could not bear to have the child all around me, sobbing, clinging to me, she was so high-strung, the experience might react on her future, psychiatrists have analyzed such cases. There was a sudden pause.

"Well, you are the doctor," said John a little bluntly. "But after all I was Charlotte's friend and adviser. One would like to know what you are going to do about the child anyway."

"John," cried Jean, "she is his child, not Harold Haze's. Don't you understand? Humbert is Dolly's real father."

"I see," said John. "I am sorry. Yes, I see. I did not realize that. It simplifies matters, of course. And whatever you feel is right."

The distraught father went on to say he would go and fetch his delicate daughter immediately after the funeral, and would do his best to give her a good time in totally different surroundings, perhaps a trip to New Mexico or California—granted, of course, he lived.

So artistically did I impersonate the calm of ultimate despair, the hush before some crazy outburst, that the perfect Farlows removed me to their house. They had a good cellar, as cellars go in this country; and that was helpful, for I feared insomnia and a ghost.

Now I must explain *my* reasons for keeping Dolores away. Naturally, at first, when Charlotte had just been eliminated and I re-entered the house a free father, and gulped down the two whiskey-and-sodas I had prepared, and topped them with a pint or two of my "pin," and went to the bathroom to get away from neighbors and friends, there was but one thing in my mind and pulse—namely, the awareness that a few hours hence, warm, brown-haired, and mine, mine, mine, Lolita would be in my arms, shedding tears that I would kiss away faster than they could well. But as I stood wide-eyed and flushed before the mirror, John Farlow tenderly tapped to inquire if I was okay—and I immediately realized it would be madness on my part to have her in the house with all those busybodies milling around and scheming to take her away from me. Indeed, unpredictable Lo herself might—who knows?— show some foolish distrust of me, a sudden repugnance, vague fear and the like—and gone would be the magic prize at the very instant of triumph.

Speaking of busybodies, I had another visitor—friend Beale, the fellow who eliminated my wife. Stodgy and solemn, looking like a kind of assistant executioner, with his bulldog jowls, small black eyes, thickly rimmed glasses and conspicuous nostrils, he was ushered in by John who then left us, closing the door upon us, with the utmost tact. Suavely saying he had twins in my stepdaughter's class, my grotesque visitor unrolled a large diagram he had made of the accident. It was, as my stepdaughter would have put it, "a beaut," with all kinds of impressive arrows and dotted lines in varicolored inks. Mrs. H. H.'s trajectory was illustrated at several points by a series of those little outline figures—doll-like wee career girl or WAC—used in statistics as visual aids. Very clearly and conclusively, this route came into contact with a boldly traced sinuous line representing two consecutive swerves—one which the Beale car made to avoid the Junk dog (dog not shown), and the second, a kind of exaggerated continuation of the first, meant to avert the tragedy. A very black cross indicated the spot where the trim little outline figure had at last come to rest on the sidewalk. I looked for some similar mark to denote the place on the embankment where my visitor's huge wax father had reclined, but there was none. That gentleman, however, had signed the document as a witness underneath the name of Leslie Tomson, Miss Opposite and a few other people.

With his hummingbird pencil deftly and delicately flying from one point to another, Frederick demonstrated his absolute innocence and the recklessness of my wife: while he was in the act of avoiding the dog, *she* had slipped on the freshly watered asphalt and plunged forward whereas she should have flung herself not forward but backward (Fred showed how by a jerk of his padded shoulder). I said it was certainly not his fault, and the inquest upheld my view.

Breathing violently through jet-black tense nostrils, he shook his head and my hand; then, with an air of perfect *savoir vivre* and gentlemanly generosity, he offered to pay the funeral-home expenses. He expected me to refuse his offer. With a drunken sob of gratitude I accepted it. This took him aback. Slowly, incredulously, he repeated what he had said. I thanked him again, even more profusely than before.

In result of that weird interview, the numbness of my soul was for a moment resolved. And no wonder! I had actually seen the agent of fate. I had palpated the very flesh of fate—and its padded shoulder. A brilliant and monstrous mutation had suddenly taken place, and here was the instrument. Within the intricacies of the pattern (hurrying housewife, slippery pavement, a pest of a dog, steep grade, big car, baboon at its wheel), I could dimly distinguish my own vile contribution. Had I not been such a fool—or such an intuitive genius—to preserve that journal, fluids produced by vindictive anger and hot shame would not have blinded Charlotte in her dash to the mailbox. But even had they blinded her, still nothing might have happened, had not precise fate, that synchronizing phantom, mixed within its alembic the car and the dog and the sun and the shade and the wet and the weak and the strong and the stone. Adieu, Marlene! Fat fate's formal handshake (as reproduced by Beale before leaving the room) brought me out of my torpor; and I wept. Ladies and gentlemen of the jury—I wept.

24

The elms and the poplars were turning their ruffled backs to a sudden onslaught of wind, and a black thunderhead loomed above Ramsdale's white church tower when I looked around me for the last time. For unknown adventures I was leaving the livid house where I had rented a room only ten weeks before. The shades—thrifty, practical bamboo shades—were already down. On porches or in the house their rich textures lend modern drama. The house of heaven must seem pretty bare after that. A raindrop fell on my knuckles. I went back into the house for something or other while John was putting my bags into the car, and then a funny thing happened. I do not know if in these tragic notes I have sufficiently stressed the peculiar "sending" effect that the writer's good looks—pseudo-Celtic, attractively simian, boyishly manly—had on women of every age and environment. Of course, such announcements made in the first person may sound ridiculous. But every once in a while I have to remind the reader of my appearance much as a professional novelist, who has given a character of his some mannerism or a dog, has to go on producing that dog or that mannerism every time the character crops up in the course of the book. There may be more to it in the present case. My gloomy good looks should be kept in the mind's eye if my story is to be properly understood. Pubescent Lo swooned to Humbert's charm as she did to hiccuppy music; adult Lotte loved me with a mature, possessive passion that I now deplore and respect more than I care to say. Jean Farlow, who was thirty-one and absolutely neurotic, had also apparently developed a strong liking for me. She was handsome in a carved-Indian sort of way, with a burnt sienna complexion. Her lips were like large crimson polyps, and when she emitted her special barking laugh, she showed large dull teeth and pale gums.

She was very tall, wore either slacks with sandals or billowing skirts with ballet slippers, drank any strong liquor in any amount, had had two miscarriages, wrote stories about animals, painted, as the reader knows, lakescapes, was already nursing the cancer that was to kill her at thirty-three, and was hopelessly unattractive to me. Judge then of my alarm when a few seconds before I left (she and I stood in the hallway) Jean, with her always trembling fingers, took me by the temples, and, tears in her bright blue eyes, attempted, unsuccessfully, to glue herself to my lips.

"Take care of yourself," she said, "kiss your daughter for me."

A clap of thunder reverberated throughout the house, and she added:

"Perhaps, somewhere, some day, at a less miserable time, we may see each other again" (Jean, whatever, wherever you are, in minus time-space or plus soul-time, forgive me all this, parenthesis included).

And presently I was shaking hands with both of them in the street, the sloping street, and everything was whirling and flying before the approaching white deluge, and a truck with a mattress from Philadelphia was confidently rolling down to an empty house, and dust was running and writhing over the exact slab of stone where Charlotte, when they lifted the laprobe for me, had been revealed, curled up, her eyes intact, their black lashes still wet, matted, like yours, Lolita.

25

One might suppose that with all blocks removed and a prospect of delirious and unlimited delights before me, I would have mentally sunk back, heaving a sigh of delicious relief. *Eh bien, pas du tout!* Instead of basking in the beams of smiling Chance, I was obsessed by all sorts of purely ethical doubts and fears. For instance: might it not surprise people that Lo was so consistently debarred from attending festive and funeral functions in her immediate family? You remember—we had not had her at our wedding. Or another thing: granted it was the long hairy arm of Coincidence that had reached out to remove an innocent woman, might Coincidence not ignore in a heathen moment what its twin lamb had done and hand Lo a premature note of commiseration? True, the accident had been reported only by the Ramsdale *Journal*—not by the Parkington *Recorder* or the Climax *Herald*, Camp Q being in another state, and local deaths having no federal news interest; but I could not help fancying that somehow Dolly Haze had been informed already, and that at the very time I was on my way to fetch her, she was being driven to Ramsdale by friends unknown to me. Still more disquieting than all these conjectures and worries, was the fact that Humbert Humbert, a brand-new American citizen of obscure European origin, had taken no steps toward becoming the legal guardian of his dead wife's daughter (twelve years and seven months old). Would I ever dare take those steps? I could not repress a shiver whenever I imagined my nudity hemmed in by mysterious statutes in the merciless glare of the Common Law.

My scheme was a marvel of primitive art: I would whizz over to Camp Q, tell Lolita her mother was about to undergo a major operation at an invented hospital, and then keep moving with my sleepy nymphet from inn to inn while her mother got better and better and finally died. But as I traveled campward my anxiety grew. I could not bear to think I might not find Lolita there—or find, instead, another, scared, Lolita clamoring for some family friend: not the Farlows, thank God—she hardly knew them—but might there not be other people I had not reckoned with? Finally, I decided to make the long-distance call I had simulated so well a few days before. It was raining hard when I pulled up in a muddy suburb of Parkington, just before the Fork, one prong of which bypassed the city and led to the highway which crossed the hills to Lake Climax and Camp Q. I flipped off the ignition and for quite a minute sat in the car bracing myself for that telephone call, and staring at the rain, at the inundated sidewalk, at a hydrant: a hideous thing, really, painted a thick silver and red, extending the red stumps of its arms to be varnished by the rain which like stylized blood dripped upon its argent chains. No wonder that stopping beside those nightmare cripples is taboo. I drove up to a gasoline station. A surprise awaited me when at last the coins had satisfactorily clanked down and a voice was allowed to answer mine.

Holmes, the camp mistress, informed me that Dolly

had gone Monday (this was Wednesday) on a hike in the hills with her group and was expected to return rather late today. Would I care to come tomorrow, and what was exactly—Without going into details, I said that her mother was hospitalized, that the situation was grave, that the child should not be told it was grave and that she should be ready to leave with me tomorrow afternoon. The two voices parted in an explosion of warmth and good will, and through some freak mechanical flaw all my coins came tumbling back to me with a hitting-the-jackpot clatter that almost made me laugh despite the disappointment at having to postpone bliss. One wonders if this sudden discharge, this spasmodic refund, was not correlated somehow, in the mind of McFate, with my having invented that little expedition before ever learning of it as I did now.

What next? I proceeded to the business center of Parkington and devoted the whole afternoon (the weather had cleared, the wet town was like silver-and-glass) to buying beautiful things for Lo. Goodness, what crazy purchases were prompted by the poignant predilection Humbert had in those days for check weaves, bright cottons, frills, puffed-out short sleeves, soft pleats, snug-fitting bodices and generously full skirts! Oh Lolita, you are my girl, as Vee was Poe's and Bea Dante's, and what little girl would not like to whirl in a circular skirt and scanties? Did I have something special in mind? coaxing voices asked me. Swimming suits? We have them in all shades. Dream pink, frosted aqua, glans mauve, tulip red, oolala black. What about playsuits? Slips? No slips. Lo and I loathed slips.

One of my guides in these matters was an anthropometric entry made by her mother on Lo's twelfth birthday (the reader remembers that Know-Your-Child book). I had the feeling that Charlotte, moved by obscure motives of envy and dislike, had added an inch here, a pound there;

but since the nymphet had no doubt grown somewhat in the last seven months, I thought I could safely accept most of those January measurements: hip girth, twenty-nine inches; thigh girth (just below the gluteal sulcus), seventeen; calf girth and neck circumference, eleven; chest circumference, twenty-seven; upper arm girth, eight; waist, twenty-three; stature, fifty-seven inches; weight, seventy-eight pounds; figure, linear; intelligence quotient, 121; vermiform appendix present, thank God.

Apart from measurements, I could of course visualize Lolita with hallucinational lucidity; and nursing as I did a tingle on my breastbone at the exact spot her silky top had come level once or twice with my heart; and feeling as I did her warm weight in my lap (so that, in a sense, I was always "with Lolita" as a woman is "with child"), I was not surprised to discover later that my computation had been more or less correct. Having moreover studied a midsummer sale book, it was with a very knowing air that I examined various pretty articles, sport shoes, sneakers, pumps of crushed kid for crushed kids. The painted girl in black who attended to all these poignant needs of mine turned parental scholarship and precise description into commercial euphemisms, such as *"petite."* Another, much older woman, in a white dress, with a pancake make-up, seemed to be oddly impressed by my knowledge of junior fashions; perhaps I had a midget for mistress; so, when shown a skirt with two "cute" pockets in front, I intentionally put a naïve male question and was rewarded by a smiling demonstration of the way the zipper worked in the back of the skirt. I had next great fun with all kinds of shorts and briefs—phantom little Lolitas dancing, falling, daisying all over the counter. We rounded up the deal with some prim cotton pajamas in popular butcher-boy style. Humbert, the popular butcher.

There is a touch of the mythological and the enchanted

in those large stores where according to ads a career girl can get a complete desk-to-date wardrobe, and where little sister can dream of the day when her wool jersey will make the boys in the back row of the classroom drool. Lifesize plastic figures of snubbed-nosed children with dun-colored, greenish, brown-dotted, faunish faces floated around me. I realized I was the only shopper in that rather eerie place where I moved about fish-like, in a glaucous aquarium. I sensed strange thoughts form in the minds of the languid ladies that escorted me from counter to counter, from rock ledge to seaweed, and the belts and the bracelets I chose seemed to fall from siren hands into transparent water. I bought an elegant valise, had my purchases put into it, and repaired to the nearest hotel, well pleased with my day.

Somehow, in connection with that quiet poetical afternoon of fastidious shopping, I recalled the hotel or inn with the seductive name of The Enchanted Hunters which Charlotte had happened to mention shortly before my liberation. With the help of a guidebook I located it in the secluded town of Briceland, a four-hour drive from Lo's camp. I could have telephoned but fearing my voice might go out of control and lapse into coy croaks of broken English, I decided to send a wire ordering a room with twin beds for the next night. What a comic, clumsy, wavering Prince Charming I was! How some of my readers will laugh at me when I tell them the trouble I had with the wording of my telegram! What should I put: Humbert and daughter? Humberg and small daughter? Homberg and immature girl? Homburg and child? The droll mistake— the "g" at the end—which eventually came through may have been a telepathic echo of these hesitations of mine.

And then, in the velvet of a summer night, my broodings over the philter I had with me! Oh miserly Hamburg! Was he not a very Enchanted Hunter as he deliberated with himself over his boxful of magic ammunition? To rout the monster of insomnia should he try himself one of those amethyst capsules? There were forty of them, all told—forty nights with a frail little sleeper at my throbbing side; could I rob myself of one such night in order to sleep? Certainly not: much too precious was each tiny plum, each microscopic planetarium with its live stardust. Oh, let me be mawkish for the nonce! I am so tired of being cynical.

26

This daily headache in the opaque air of this tombal jail is disturbing, but I must persevere. Have written more than a hundred pages and not got anywhere yet. My calendar is getting confused. That must have been around August 15, 1947. Don't think I can go on. Heart, head—everything. Lolita, Lolita, Lolita, Lolita, Lolita, Lolita, Lolita, Lolita, Lolita. Repeat till the page is full, printer.

27

Still in Parkington. Finally, I did achieve an hour's slumber—from which I was aroused by gratuitous and horribly exhausting congress with a small hairy hermaphrodite, a total stranger. By then it was six in the morning, and it suddenly occurred to me it might be a good thing to arrive at the camp earlier than I had said. From Parkington I had still a hundred miles to go, and there would be more than that to the Hazy Hills and Briceland. If I had said I would come for Dolly in the afternoon, it was only because my fancy insisted on merciful night falling as soon as possible upon my impatience. But now I foresaw all kinds of misunderstandings and was all a-jitter lest delay might give her the opportunity of some idle telephone call to Ramsdale. However, when at 9.30 A.M. I attempted to start, I was confronted by a dead battery, and noon was nigh when at last I left Parkington.

I reached my destination around half past two; parked my car in a pine grove where a green-shirted, redheaded impish lad stood throwing horseshoes in sullen solitude; was laconically directed by him to an office in a stucco cottage; in a dying state, had to endure for several minutes the inquisitive commiseration of the camp mistress, a sluttish worn out female with rusty hair. Dolly she said was all packed and ready to go. She knew her mother was sick but not critically. Would Mr. Haze, I mean, Mr. Humbert, care to meet the camp counsellors? Or look at the cabins where the girls live? Each dedicated to a Disney creature? Or visit the Lodge? Or should Charlie be sent over to fetch her? The girls were just finishing fixing the Dining Room for a dance. (And perhaps afterwards she would say to somebody or other: "The poor guy looked like his own ghost.")

Let me retain for a moment that scene in all its trivial and fateful detail: hag Holmes writing out a receipt, scratching her head, pulling a drawer out of her desk, pouring change into my impatient palm, then neatly spreading a banknote over it with a bright ". . . and five!"; photographs of girl-children; some gaudy moth or butterfly, still alive, safely pinned to the wall ("nature study"); the framed diploma of the camp's dietitian; my trembling hands; a card produced by efficient Holmes with a report of Dolly Haze's behavior for July ("fair to good; keen on swimming and boating"); a sound of trees and birds, and my pounding heart . . . I was standing with my back to the open door, and then I felt the blood rush to my head as I heard her respiration and voice behind me. She arrived dragging and bumping her heavy suitcase. "Hi!" she said, and stood still, looking at me with sly, glad eyes, her soft lips parted in a slightly foolish but wonderfully endearing smile.

She was thinner and taller, and for a second it seemed to me her face was less pretty than the mental imprint I had cherished for more than a month: her cheeks looked hollowed and too much lentigo camouflaged her rosy rustic features; and that first impression (a very narrow human interval between two tiger heartbeats) carried the clear implication that all widower Humbert had to do, wanted to do, or would do, was to give this wan-looking though sun-colored little orphan *aux yeux battus* (and even those plumbaceous umbrae under her eyes bore freckles) a sound education, a healthy and happy girlhood, a clean home, nice girl-friends of her age among whom (if the fates deigned to repay me) I might find, perhaps, a pretty little *Mägdlein* for Herr Doktor Humbert alone. But "in a wink," as the Germans say, the angelic line of conduct was erased, and I overtook my prey (time moves ahead of our fancies!), and she was my Lolita again—in fact, more of my Lolita than ever. I let my hand rest on her warm auburn head and took up her bag. She was all rose and honey, dressed in her brightest gingham, with a pattern of little red apples, and her arms and legs were of a deep golden brown, with scratches like tiny dotted lines of coagulated rubies, and the ribbed cuffs of her white socks were turned down at the remembered level, and because of her childish gait, or because I had memorized her as always wearing heelless shoes, her saddle oxfords looked somehow too large and too high-heeled for her. Good-bye, Camp Q, merry Camp Q. Good-bye, plain unwholesome food, good-bye Charlie boy. In the hot car she settled down beside me, slapped a prompt fly on her lovely knee; then, her mouth working violently on a piece of chewing gum, she rapidly cranked down the window on her side and settled back again. We sped through the striped and speckled forest.

"How's Mother?" she asked dutifully.

I said the doctors did not quite know yet what the trouble was. Anyway, something abdominal. Abominable? No, abdominal. We would have to hang around for a while. The hospital was in the country, near the gay town of Lepingville, where a great poet had resided in the early nineteenth century and where we would take in all the shows. She thought it a peachy idea and wondered if we could make Lepingville before nine P.M.

"We should be at Briceland by dinner time," I said, "and tomorrow we'll visit Lepingville. How was the hike? Did you have a marvelous time at the camp?"

"Uh-huh."

"Sorry to leave?"

"Un-un."

"Talk, Lo—don't grunt. Tell me something."

"What thing, Dad?" (she let the word expand with ironic deliberation).

"Any old thing."

"Okay, if I call you that?" (eyes slit at the road).

"Quite."

"It's a sketch, you know. When did you fall for my mummy?"

"Some day, Lo, you will understand many emotions and situations, such as for example the harmony, the beauty of spiritual relationship."

"Bah!" said the cynical nymphet.

Shallow lull in the dialogue, filled with some landscape.

"Look, Lo, at all those cows on that hillside."

"I think I'll vomit if I look at a cow again."

"You know, I missed you terribly, Lo."

"*I* did not. Fact I've been revoltingly unfaithful to you, but it does not matter one bit, because you've stopped caring for me, anyway. You drive much faster than my mummy, mister."

I slowed down from a blind seventy to a purblind fifty.

"Why do you think I have ceased caring for you, Lo?"

"Well, you haven't kissed me yet, have you?"

Inly dying, inly moaning, I glimpsed a reasonably wide shoulder of road ahead, and bumped and wobbled into the weeds. Remember she is only a child, remember she is only—

Hardly had the car come to a standstill than Lolita positively flowed into my arms. Not daring, not daring let myself go—not even daring let myself realize that *this* (sweet wetness and trembling fire) was the beginning of the ineffable life which, ably assisted by fate, I had finally willed into being—not daring really kiss her, I touched her hot, opening lips with the utmost piety, tiny sips, nothing salacious; but she, with an impatient wriggle, pressed her mouth to mine so hard that I felt her big front teeth and shared in the peppermint taste of her saliva. I knew, of course, it was but an innocent game on her part, a bit of backfisch foolery in imitation of some simulacrum of fake romance, and since (as the psychotherapist, as well as the rapist, will tell you) the limits and rules of such girlish games are fluid, or at least too childishly subtle for the senior partner to grasp—I was dreadfully afraid I might go too far and cause her to start back in revulsion and terror. And, as above all I was agonizingly anxious to smuggle her into the hermetic seclusion of The Enchanted Hunters, and we had still eighty miles to go, blessed intuition broke our embrace—a split second before a highway patrol car drew up alongside.

Florid and beetle-browed, its driver stared at me:

"Happen to see a blue sedan, same make as yours, pass you before the junction?"

"Why, no."

"We didn't," said Lo, eagerly leaning across me, her

innocent hand on my legs, "but are you sure it was blue, because—"

The cop (what shadow of us was he after?) gave the little colleen his best smile and went into a U-turn.

We drove on.

"The fruithead!" remarked Lo. "He should have nabbed *you*."

"Why me for heaven's sake?"

"Well, the speed in this bum state is fifty, and—No, don't slow down, you, dull bulb. He's gone now."

"We have still quite a stretch," I said, "and I want to get there before dark. So be a good girl."

"Bad, bad girl," said Lo comfortably. "Juvenile delick-went, but frank and fetching. That light was red. I've never seen such driving."

We rolled silently through a silent townlet.

"Say, wouldn't Mother be absolutely mad if she found out we were lovers?"

"Good Lord, Lo, let us not talk that way."

"But we *are* lovers, aren't we?"

"Not that I know of. I think we are going to have some more rain. Don't you want to tell me of those little pranks of yours in camp?"

"You talk like a book, *Dad*."

"What have you been up to? I insist you tell me."

"Are you easily shocked?"

"No. Go on."

"Let us turn into a secluded lane and I'll tell you."

"Lo, I must seriously ask you not to play the fool. Well?"

"Well—I joined in all the activities that were offered."

"*Ensuite?*"

"Ansooit, I was taught to live happily and richly with others and to develop a wholesome personality. Be a cake, in fact."

"Yes. I saw something of the sort in the booklet."

"We loved the sings around the fire in the big stone fire-place or under the darned stars, where every girl merged her own spirit of happiness with the voice of the group."

"Your memory is excellent, Lo, but I must trouble you to leave out the swear words. Anything else?"

"The Girl Scout's motto," said Lo rhapsodically, "is also mine. I fill my life with worthwhile deeds such as—well, never mind what. My duty is—to be useful. I am a friend to male animals. I obey orders. I am cheerful. That was another police car. I am thrifty and I am absolutely filthy in thought, word and deed."

"Now I do hope that's all, you witty child."

"Yep. That's all. No—wait a sec. We baked in a reflector oven. Isn't that terrific?"

"Well, that's better."

"We washed zillions of dishes. 'Zillions' you know is schoolmarm's slang for many-many-many-many. Oh yes, last but not least, as Mother says—Now let me see—what was it? I know: We made shadowgraphs. Gee, what fun."

"C'est bien tout?"

"C'est. Except for one little thing, something I simply can't tell you without blushing all over."

"Will you tell it me later?"

"If we sit in the dark and you let me whisper, I will. Do you sleep in your old room or in a heap with Mother?"

"Old room. Your mother may have to undergo a very serious operation, Lo."

"Stop at that candy bar, will you," said Lo.

Sitting on a high stool, a band of sunlight crossing her bare brown forearm, Lolita was served an elaborate ice-cream concoction topped with synthetic syrup. It was erected and brought her by a pimply brute of a boy in a greasy bow-tie who eyed my fragile child in her thin cotton frock with carnal deliberation. My impatience to reach Briceland and The Enchanted Hunters was becoming more than I could endure. Fortunately she dispatched the stuff with her usual alacrity.

"How much cash do you have?" I asked.

"Not a cent," she said sadly, lifting her eyebrows, showing me the empty inside of her money purse.

"This is a matter that will be mended in due time," I rejoined archly. "Are you coming?"

"Say, I wonder if they have a washroom."

"You are not going there," I said firmly. "It is sure to be a vile place. Do come on."

She was on the whole an obedient little girl and I kissed her in the neck when we got back into the car.

"*Don't* do that," she said looking at me with unfeigned surprise. "Don't drool on me. You dirty man."

She rubbed the spot against her raised shoulder.

"Sorry," I murmured. "I'm rather fond of you, that's all."

We drove under a gloomy sky, up a winding road, then down again.

"Well, I'm also sort of fond of you," said Lolita in a delayed soft voice, with a sort of sigh, and sort of settled closer to me.

(Oh, my Lolita, we shall never get there!)

Dusk was beginning to saturate pretty little Briceland, its phony colonial architecture, curiosity shops and imported shade trees, when we drove through the weakly lighted streets in search of The Enchanted Hunters. The air, despite a steady drizzle beading it, was warm and green, and a queue of people, mainly children and old men, had already formed before the box office of a movie house, dripping with jewel-fires.

"Oh, I want to see that picture. Let's go right after dinner. Oh, let's!"

"We might," chanted Humbert—knowing perfectly well, the sly tumescent devil, that by nine, when *his* show began, she would be dead in his arms.

"Easy!" cried Lo, lurching forward, as an accursed truck in front of us, its backside carbuncles pulsating, stopped at a crossing.

If we did not get to the hotel soon, immediately, miraculously, in the very next block, I felt I would lose all control over the Haze jalopy with its ineffectual wipers and whimsical brakes; but the passers-by I applied to for directions were either strangers themselves or asked with a frown "Enchanted what?" as if I were a madman; or else they went into such complicated explanations, with geometrical gestures, geographical generalities and strictly local clues (. . . then bear south after you hit the courthouse . . .) that I could not help losing my way in the maze of their well-meaning gibberish. Lo, whose lovely prismatic entrails had already digested the sweetmeat, was looking forward to a big meal and had begun to fidget. As to me, although I had long become used to a kind of secondary fate (McFate's inept secretary, so to speak) pettily interfering with the boss's generous magnificent plan—to grind and grope through the avenues of Briceland was perhaps the most exasperating ordeal I had yet faced. In later months I could laugh at my inexperience when recalling the obstinate boyish way in which I had concentrated upon that particular inn with its fancy name; for all along our route countless motor courts proclaimed their vacancy in neon lights, ready to accommodate salesmen, escaped convicts, impotents, family groups, as well as the most corrupt and vigorous couples. Ah, gentle drivers gliding through summer's black nights, what frolics, what twists of lust, you might see from your impeccable highways if Kumfy Kabins were suddenly drained of their pigments and became as transparent as boxes of glass!

The miracle I hankered for did happen after all. A man and a girl, more or less conjoined in a dark car under dripping trees, told us we were in the heart of The Park, but had only to turn left at the next traffic light and there we would be. We did not see any next traffic light—in fact, The Park was as black as the sins it concealed—but soon after falling under the smooth spell of a nicely graded curve, the travelers became aware of a diamond glow through the mist, then a gleam of lakewater appeared— and there it was, marvelously and inexorably, under spectral trees, at the top of a graveled drive—the pale palace of The Enchanted Hunters.

A row of parked cars, like pigs at a trough, seemed at first sight to forbid access; but then, by magic, a formidable convertible, resplendent, rubious in the lighted rain, came into motion—was energetically backed out by a broad-shouldered driver—and we gratefully slipped into the gap it had left. I immediately regretted my haste for I noticed that my predecessor had now taken advantage of a garage-like shelter nearby where there was ample space for another car; but I was too impatient to follow his example.

"Wow! Looks swank," remarked my vulgar darling squinting at the stucco as she crept out into the audible drizzle and with a childish hand tweaked loose the frock-fold that had stuck in the peach-cleft—to quote Robert Browning. Under the arclights enlarged replicas of chestnut leaves plunged and played on white pillars. I unlocked the trunk compartment. A hunchbacked and hoary Negro in a uniform of sorts took our bags and wheeled them slowly into the lobby. It was full of old ladies and clergymen. Lolita sank down on her haunches to caress a pale-faced, blue-freckled, black-eared cocker spaniel swooning on the floral carpet under her hand—as who would not, my heart— while I cleared my throat through the throng to the desk.

There a bald porcine old man—everybody was old in that old hotel—examined my features with a polite smile, then leisurely produced my (garbled) telegram, wrestled with some dark doubts, turned his head to look at the clock, and finally said he was very sorry, he had held the room with the twin beds till half past six, and now it was gone. A religious convention, he said, had clashed with a flower show in Briceland, and—"The name," I said coldly, "is not Humberg and not Humbug, but Herbert, I mean Humbert, and any room will do, just put in a cot for my little daughter. She is ten and very tired."

The pink old fellow peered good-naturedly at Lo—still squatting, listening in profile, lips parted, to what the dog's mistress, an ancient lady swathed in violet veils, was telling her from the depths of a cretonne easy chair.

Whatever doubts the obscene fellow had, they were dispelled by that blossom-like vision. He said, he might still have a room, had one, in fact—with a double bed. As to the cot—

"Mr. Potts, do we have any cots left?" Potts, also pink and bald, with white hairs growing out of his ears and other holes, would see what could be done. He came and spoke while I unscrewed my fountain pen. Impatient Humbert!

"Our double beds are really triple," Potts cozily said tucking me and my kid in. "One crowded night we had three ladies and a child like yours sleep together. I believe one of the ladies was a disguised man [my static]. However—would there be a spare cot in 49, Mr. Swine?"

"I think it went to the Swoons," said Swine, the initial old clown.

"We'll manage somehow," I said. "My wife may join us later—but even then, I suppose, we'll manage."

The two pink pigs were now among my best friends. In the slow clear hand of crime I wrote: Dr. Edgar H. Humbert and daughter, 342 Lawn Street, Ramsdale. A key (342!) was half-shown to me (magician showing object he is about to palm)—and handed over to Uncle Tom. Lo, leaving the dog as she would leave me some day, rose from her haunches; a raindrop fell on Charlotte's grave; a handsome young Negress slipped open the elevator door, and the doomed child went in followed by her throat-clearing father and crayfish Tom with the bags.

Parody of a hotel corridor. Parody of silence and death.

"Say, it's our house number," said cheerful Lo.

There was a double bed, a mirror, a double bed in the mirror, a closet door with mirror, a bathroom door ditto, a blue-dark window, a reflected bed there, the same in the closet mirror, two chairs, a glass-topped table, two bed-tables, a double bed: a big panel bed, to be exact, with a Tuscan rose chenille spread, and two frilled, pink-shaded nightlamps, left and right.

I was tempted to place a five-dollar bill in that sepia palm, but thought the largesse might be misconstrued, so I placed a quarter. Added another. He withdrew. Click. *Enfin seuls.*

"Are we to sleep in *one* room?" said Lo, her features working in that dynamic way they did—not cross or disgusted (though plain on the brink of it) but just dynamic—when she wanted to load a question with violent significance.

"I've asked them to put in a cot. Which I'll use if you like."

"You are crazy," said Lo.

"Why, my darling?"

"Because, my dahrling, when dahrling Mother finds out she'll divorce you and strangle me."

Just dynamic. Not really taking the matter too seriously.

"Now look here," I said, sitting down, while she stood,

a few feet from me, and stared at herself contentedly, not unpleasantly surprised at her own appearance, filling with her own rosy sunshine the surprised and pleased closet-door mirror.

"Look here, Lo. Let's settle this once for all. For all practical purposes I am your father. I have a feeling of great tenderness for you. In your mother's absence I am responsible for your welfare. We are not rich, and while we travel, we shall be obliged—we shall be thrown a good deal together. Two people sharing one room, inevitably enter into a kind—how shall I say—a kind—"

"The word is incest," said Lo—and walked into the closet, walked out again with a young golden giggle, opened the adjoining door, and after carefully peering inside with her strange smoky eyes lest she make another mistake, retired to the bathroom.

I opened the window, tore off my sweat-drenched shirt, changed, checked the pill vial in my coat pocket, unlocked the—

She drifted out. I tried to embrace her: casually, a bit of controlled tenderness before dinner.

She said: "Look, let's cut out the kissing game and get something to eat."

It was then that I sprang my surprise.

Oh, what a dreamy pet! She walked up to the open suit-case as if stalking it from afar, at a kind of slow-motion walk, peering at that distant treasure box on the luggage support. (Was there something wrong, I wondered, with those great gray eyes of hers, or were we both plunged in the same enchanted mist?) She stepped up to it, lifting her rather high-heeled feet rather high, and bending her beautiful boy-knees while she walked through dilating space with the lentor of one walking under water or in a flight dream. Then she raised by the armlets a copper-colored,

135

charming and quite expensive vest, very slowly stretching it between her silent hands as if she were a bemused bird-hunter holding his breath over the incredible bird he spreads out by the tips of its flaming wings. Then (while I stood waiting for her) she pulled out the slow snake of a brilliant belt and tried it on.

Then she crept into my waiting arms, radiant, relaxed, caressing me with her tender, mysterious, impure, indifferent, twilight eyes—for all the world, like the cheapest of cheap cuties. For that is what nymphets imitate—while we moan and die.

"What's the katter with misses?" I muttered (word-control gone) into her hair.

"If you must know," she said, "you do it the wrong way."

"Show, wight ray."

"All in good time," responded the spoonerette.

Seva ascendes, pulsata, brulans, kitzelans, dementissima. Elevator clatterans, pausa, clatterans, populus in corridoro. Hanc nisi mors mihi adimet nemo! Juncea puellula, jo pensavo fondissime, nobserva nihil quidquam; but, of course, in another moment I might have committed some dreadful blunder; fortunately, she returned to the treasure box.

From the bathroom, where it took me quite a time to shift back into normal gear for a humdrum purpose, I heard, standing, drumming, retaining my breath, my Lolita's "oo's" and "gee's" of girlish delight.

She had used the soap only because it was sample soap.

"Well, come on, my dear, if you are as hungry as I am."

And so to the elevator, daughter swinging her old white purse, father walking in front (nota bene: never behind, she is not a lady). As we stood (now side by side) waiting to be taken down, she threw back her head, yawned without restraint and shook her curls.

"When did they make you get up at that camp?"

"Half-past—" she stifled another yawn—"six"—yawn in full with a shiver of all her frame. "Half-past," she repeated, her throat filling up again.

The dining room met us with a smell of fried fat and a faded smile. It was a spacious and pretentious place with maudlin murals depicting enchanted hunters in various postures and states of enchantment amid a medley of pallid animals, dryads and trees. A few scattered old ladies, two clergymen, and a man in a sports coat were finishing their meals in silence. The dining room closed at nine, and the green-clad, poker-faced serving girls were, happily, in a desperate hurry to get rid of us.

"Does not he look exactly, but exactly, like Quilty?" said Lo in a soft voice, her sharp brown elbow not pointing, but visibly burning to point, at the lone diner in the loud checks, in the far corner of the room.

"Like our fat Ramsdale dentist?"

Lo arrested the mouthful of water she had just taken, and put down her dancing glass.

"Course not," she said with a splutter of mirth. "I meant the writer fellow in the Dromes ad."

Oh, Fame! Oh, Femina!

When the dessert was plunked down—a huge wedge of cherry pie for the young lady and vanilla ice cream for her protector, most of which she expeditiously added to her pie—I produced a small vial containing Papa's Purple Pills. As I look back at those seasick murals, at that strange and monstrous moment, I can only explain my behavior then by the mechanism of that dream vacuum wherein revolves a deranged mind; but at the time, it all seemed quite simple and inevitable to me. I glanced around, satisfied myself that the last diner had left, removed the stopper, and with the utmost deliberation tipped the philter into my palm. I had carefully rehearsed before a mirror the gesture of clapping my empty hand to my open mouth and swallowing a (fictitious) pill. As I expected, she pounced upon the vial with its plump, beautifully colored capsules loaded with Beauty's Sleep.

"Blue!" she exclaimed. "Violet blue. What are they made of?"

"Summer skies," I said, "and plums and figs, and the grapeblood of emperors."

"No, seriously—please."

"Oh, just Purpills. Vitamin X. Makes one strong as an ox or an ax. Want to try one?"

Lolita stretched out her hand, nodding vigorously.

I had hoped the drug would work fast. It certainly did. She had had a long long day, she had gone rowing in the morning with Barbara whose sister was Waterfront Director, as the adorable accessible nymphet now started to tell me in between suppressed palate-humping yawns, growing in volume—oh, how fast the magic potion worked!—and had been active in other ways too. The movie that had vaguely loomed in her mind was, of course, by the time we watertreaded out of the dining room, forgotten. As we stood in the elevator, she leaned against me, faintly smiling—wouldn't you like me to tell you?— half closing her dark-lidded eyes. "Sleepy, huh?" said Uncle Tom who was bringing up the quiet Franco-Irish gentleman and his daughter as well as two withered women, experts in roses. They looked with sympathy at my frail, tanned, tottering, dazed rosedarling. I had almost to carry her into our room. There, she sat down on the edge of the bed, swaying a little, speaking in dove-dull, long-drawn tones.

"If I tell you—if I tell you, will you promise [sleepy, so sleepy—head lolling, eyes going out], promise you won't make complaints?"

"Later, Lo. Now go to bed. I'll leave you here, and you go to bed. Give you ten minutes."

"Oh, I've been such a disgusting girl," she went on, shaking her hair, removing with slow fingers a velvet hair ribbon. "Lemme tell you—"

"Tomorrow, Lo. Go to bed, go to bed—for goodness sake, to bed."

I pocketed the key and walked downstairs.

28

Gentlewomen of the jury! Bear with me! Allow me to take just a tiny bit of your precious time! So this was *le grand moment*. I had left my Lolita still sitting on the edge of the abysmal bed, drowsily raising her foot, fumbling at the shoelaces and showing as she did so the nether side of her thigh up to the crotch of her panties—she had always been singularly absentminded, or shameless, or both, in matters of legshow. This, then, was the hermetic vision of her which I had locked in—after satisfying myself that the door carried no inside bolt. The key, with its numbered dangler of carved wood, became forthwith the weighty sesame to a rapturous and formidable future. It was mine, it was part of my hot hairy fist. In a few minutes—say, twenty, say half-an-hour, *sicher ist sicher* as my uncle Gustave used to say—I would let myself into that "342" and find my nymphet, my beauty and bride, emprisoned in her crystal sleep. Jurors! If my happiness could have talked, it would have filled that genteel hotel with a deafening roar. And my only regret today is that I did not quietly deposit key "342" at the office, and leave the town, the country, the continent, the hemisphere,—indeed, the globe—that very same night.

Let me explain. I was not unduly disturbed by her self-accusatory innuendoes. I was still firmly resolved to pursue my policy of sparing her purity by operating only in the stealth of night, only upon a completely anesthetized little nude. Restraint and reverence were still my motto—even if that "purity" (incidentally, thoroughly debunked by modern science) had been slightly damaged through some juvenile erotic experience, no doubt homosexual, at that accursed camp of hers. Of course, in my old-fashioned, old-world way, I, Jean-Jacques Humbert, had taken for granted, when I first met her, that she was as unravished as the stereotypical notion of "normal child" had been since the lamented end of the Ancient World B.C. and its fascinating practices. We are not surrounded in our enlighted era by little slave flowers that can be casually plucked between business and bath as they used to be in the days of the Romans; and we do not, as dignified Orientals did in still more luxurious times, use tiny entertainers fore and aft between the mutton and the rose sherbet. The whole point is that the old link between the adult world and the child world has been completely severed nowadays by new customs and new laws. Despite my having dabbled in psychiatry and social work, I really knew very little about children. After all, Lolita was only twelve, and no matter what concessions I made to time and place—even bearing in mind the crude behavior of American schoolchildren—I still was under the impression that whatever went on among those brash brats, went on at a later age, and in a different environment. Therefore (to retrieve the thread of this explanation) the moralist in me by-passed the issue by clinging to conventional notions of what twelve-year-old girls should be. The child therapist in me (a fake, as most of them are—but no matter) regurgitated neo-Freudian hash and conjured up a dreaming and exaggerating Dolly in the "latency" period of girlhood. Finally, the sensualist in me (a great and insane monster) had no objection to some depravity in his prey.

But somewhere behind the raging bliss, bewildered shadows conferred—and not to have heeded them, this is what I regret! Human beings, attend! I should have understood that Lolita had *already* proved to be something quite different from innocent Annabel, and that the nymphean evil breathing through every pore of the fey child that I had prepared for my secret delectation, would make the secrecy impossible, and the delectation lethal. I should have known (by the signs made to me by something in Lolita— the real child Lolita or some haggard angel behind her back) that nothing but pain and horror would result from the expected rapture. Oh, winged gentlemen of the jury!

And she was mine, she was mine, the key was in my fist, my fist was in my pocket, she was mine. In the course of the evocations and schemes to which I had dedicated so many insomnias, I had gradually eliminated all the superfluous blur, and by stacking level upon level of translucent vision, had evolved a final picture. Naked, except for one sock and her charm bracelet, spread-eagled on the bed where my philter had felled her—so I foreglimpsed her; a velvet hair ribbon was still clutched in her hand; her honey-brown body, with the white negative image of a rudimentary swimsuit patterned against her tan, presented to me its pale breastbuds; in the rosy lamplight, a little pubic floss glistened on its plump hillock. The cold key with its warm wooden addendum was in my pocket.

I wandered through various public rooms, glory below, gloom above: for the look of lust always is gloomy; lust is never quite sure—even when the velvety victim is locked up in one's dungeon—that some rival devil or influential god may still not abolish one's prepared triumph. In common parlance, I needed a drink; but there was no barroom in that venerable place full of perspiring philistines and period objects.

I drifted to the Men's Room. There, a person in clerical black—a "hearty party" *comme on dit*—checking with the assistance of Vienna, if it was still there, inquired of me how I had liked Dr. Boyd's talk, and looked puzzled when I (King Sigmund the Second) said Boyd was quite a boy. Upon which, I neatly chucked the tissue paper I had been wiping my sensitive finger tips with into the receptacle provided for it, and sallied lobbyward. Comfortably resting my elbows on the counter, I asked Mr. Potts was he quite sure my wife had not telephoned, and what about that cot? He answered she had not (she was dead, of course) and the cot would be installed tomorrow if we decided to stay on. From a big crowded place called The Hunters' Hall came a sound of many voices discussing horticulture or eternity. Another room, called The Raspberry Room, all bathed in light, with bright little tables and a large one with "refreshments," was still empty except for a hostess (that type of worn woman with a glassy smile and Charlotte's manner of speaking); she floated up to me to ask if I was Mr. Braddock, because if so, Miss Beard had been looking for me. "What a name for a woman," I said and strolled away.

In and out of my heart flowed my rainbow blood. I would give her till half-past-nine. Going back to the lobby, I found there a change: a number of people in floral dresses or black cloth had formed little groups here and there, and some elfish chance offered me the sight of a delightful child of Lolita's age, in Lolita's type of frock, but pure white, and there was a white ribbon in her black hair. She was not pretty, but she was a nymphet, and her ivory pale legs and lily neck formed for one memorable moment a most pleasurable antiphony (in terms of spinal music) to my desire for Lolita, brown and pink, flushed and fouled. The pale child noticed my gaze (which was really quite casual and debonair), and being ridiculously self-conscious, lost countenance completely, rolling her eyes and putting the back of her hand to her cheek, and pulling at the hem of her skirt, and finally turning her thin mobile shoulder blades to me in specious chat with her cow-like mother.

I left the loud lobby and stood outside, on the white steps, looking at the hundreds of powdered bugs wheeling around the lamps in the soggy black night, full of ripple and stir. All I would do—all I would dare to do—would amount to such a trifle . . .

Suddenly I was aware that in the darkness next to me there was somebody sitting in a chair on the pillared porch. I could not really see him but what gave him away was the rasp of a screwing off, then a discreet gurgle, then the final note of a placid screwing on. I was about to move away when his voice addressed me:

"Where the devil did you get her?"

"I beg your pardon?"

"I said: the weather is getting better."

"Seems so."

"Who's the lassie?"

"My daughter."

"You lie—she's not."

"I beg your pardon?"

"I said: July was hot. Where's her mother?"

"Dead."

"I see. Sorry. By the way, why don't you two lunch with me tomorrow. That dreadful crowd will be gone by then."

"We'll be gone too. Good night."

"Sorry. I'm pretty drunk. Good night. That child of yours needs a lot of sleep. Sleep is a rose, as the Persians say. Smoke?"

"Not now."

He struck a light, but because he was drunk, or because the wind was, the flame illumined not him but another person, a very old man, one of those permanent guests of old hotels—and his white rocker. Nobody said anything and the darkness returned to its initial place. Then I heard the old-timer cough and deliver himself of some sepulchral mucus.

I left the porch. At least half an hour in all had elapsed. I ought to have asked for a sip. The strain was beginning to tell. If a violin string can ache, then I was that string. But it would have been unseemly to display any hurry. As I made my way through a constellation of fixed people in one corner of the lobby, there came a blinding flash—and beaming Dr. Braddock, two orchid-ornamentalized matrons, the small girl in white, and presumably the bared teeth of Humbert Humbert sidling between the bridelike lassie and the enchanted cleric, were immortalized—insofar as the texture and print of small-town newspapers can be deemed immortal. A twittering group had gathered near the elevator. I again chose the stairs. 342 was near the fire escape. One could still—but the key was already in the lock, and then I was in the room.

29

The door of the lighted bathroom stood ajar; in addition to that, a skeleton glow came through the Venetian blind from the outside arclights; these intercrossed rays penetrated the darkness of the bedroom and revealed the following situation.

Clothed in one of her old nightgowns, my Lolita lay on her side with her back to me, in the middle of the bed. Her lightly veiled body and bare limbs formed a Z. She had put both pillows under her dark tousled head; a band of pale light crossed her top vertebrae.

I seemed to have shed my clothes and slipped into pajamas with the kind of fantastic instantaneousness which is implied when in a cinematographic scene the process of changing is cut; and I had already placed my knee on the edge of the bed when Lolita turned her head and stared at me through the striped shadows.

Now this was something the intruder had not expected. The whole pill-spiel (a rather sordid affair, *entre nous soit dit*) had had for object a fastness of sleep that a whole regiment would not have disturbed, and here she was staring at me, and thickly calling me "Barbara." Barbara, wearing my pajamas which were much too tight for her, remained poised motionless over the little sleep-talker. Softly, with a hopeless sigh, Dolly turned away, resuming her initial position. For at least two minutes I waited and strained on the brink, like that tailor with his homemade parachute forty years ago when about to jump from the Eiffel Tower. Her faint breathing had the rhythm of sleep. Finally I heaved myself onto my narrow margin of bed, stealthily pulled at the odds and ends of sheets piled up to the south of my stone-cold heels—and Lolita lifted her head and gaped at me.

As I learned later from a helpful pharmaceutist, the purple pill did not even belong to the big and noble family of barbiturates, and though it might have induced sleep in a neurotic who believed it to be a potent drug, it was too mild a sedative to affect for any length of time a wary, albeit weary, nymphet. Whether the Ramsdale doctor was a charlatan or a shrewd old rogue, does not, and did not, really matter. What mattered, was that I had been deceived. When Lolita opened her eyes again, I realized that whether or not the drug might work later in the night, the security I had relied upon was a sham one. Slowly her head turned away and dropped onto her unfair amount of pillow. I lay quite still on my brink, peering at her rumpled hair, at the glimmer of nymphet flesh, where half a haunch and half a shoulder dimly showed, and trying to gauge the depth of her sleep by the rate of her respiration. Some time passed, nothing changed, and I decided I might risk getting a little closer to that lovely and maddening glimmer; but hardly had I moved into its warm purlieus than her breathing was suspended, and I had the odious feeling that little Dolores was wide awake and would explode in screams if I touched her with any part of my wretchedness. Please, reader: no matter your exasperation with the tenderhearted, morbidly sensitive, infinitely circumspect hero of my book, do not skip these essential pages! Imagine me; I shall not exist if you do not imagine me; try to discern the doe in me, trembling in the forest of my own iniquity; let's even smile a little. After all, there is no harm in smiling. For instance (I almost wrote "frinstance"), I had no place to rest my head, and a fit of heartburn (they call those fries "French," *grand Dieu!*) was added to my discomfort.

She was again fast asleep, my nymphet, but still I did not dare to launch upon my enchanted voyage. *La Petite Dormeuse ou l'Amant Ridicule.* Tomorrow I would stuff her with those earlier pills that had so thoroughly numbed her mummy. In the glove compartment—or in the Gladstone bag? Should I wait a solid hour and then creep up again? The science of nympholepsy is a precise science. Actual contact would do it in one second flat. An interspace of a millimeter would do it in ten. Let us wait.

There is nothing louder than an American hotel; and, mind you, this was supposed to be a quiet, cozy, old-fashioned, homey place—"gracious living" and all that stuff. The clatter of the elevator's gate—some twenty yards northeast of my head but as clearly perceived as if it were inside my left temple—alternated with the banging and booming of the machine's various evolutions and lasted well beyond midnight. Every now and then, immediately east of my left ear (always assuming I lay on my back, not daring to direct my viler side toward the nebulous haunch of my bed-mate), the corridor would brim with cheerful, resonant and inept exclamations ending in a volley of good-nights. When *that* stopped, a toilet immediately north of my cerebellum took over. It was a manly, energetic, deep-throated toilet, and it was used many times. Its gurgle and gush and long afterflow shook the wall behind me. Then someone in a southern direction was extravagantly sick, almost coughing out his life with his liquor, and his toilet descended like a veritable Niagara, immediately beyond our bathroom. And when finally all the waterfalls had stopped, and the enchanted hunters were sound asleep, the avenue under the window of my insomnia, to the west of my wake—a staid, eminently residential, dignified alley of huge trees—degenerated into the despicable haunt of gigantic trucks roaring through the wet and windy night.

And less than six inches from me and my burning life, was nebulous Lolita! After a long stirless vigil, my tentacles moved towards her again, and this time the creak of the mattress did not awake her. I managed to bring my ravenous bulk so close to her that I felt the aura of her bare shoulder like a warm breath upon my cheek. And then, she sat up, gasped, muttered with insane rapidity something about boats, tugged at the sheets and lapsed back into her rich, dark, young unconsciousness. As she tossed, within that abundant flow of sleep, recently auburn, at present lunar, her arm struck me across the face. For a second I held her. She freed herself from the shadow of my embrace—doing this not consciously, not violently, not with any personal distaste, but with the neutral plaintive murmur of a child demanding its natural rest. And again the situation remained the same: Lolita with her curved spine to Humbert, Humbert resting his head on his hand and burning with desire and dyspepsia.

The latter necessitated a trip to the bathroom for a draft of water which is the best medicine I know in my case, except perhaps milk with radishes; and when I re-entered the strange pale-striped fastness where Lolita's old and new clothes reclined in various attitudes of enchantment on pieces of furniture that seemed vaguely afloat, my impossible daughter sat up and in clear tones demanded a drink, too. She took the resilient and cold paper cup in her shadowy hand and gulped down its contents gratefully, her long eyelashes pointing cupward, and then, with an infantile gesture that carried more charm than any carnal caress, little Lolita wiped her lips against my shoulder. She fell back on her pillow (I had subtracted mine while she drank) and was instantly asleep again.

I had not dared offer her a second helping of the drug, and had not abandoned hope that the first might still consolidate her sleep. I started to move toward her, ready for any disappointment, knowing I had better wait but incapable of waiting. My pillow smelled of her hair. I moved toward my glimmering darling, stopping or retreating every time I thought she stirred or was about to stir. A breeze from wonderland had begun to affect my thoughts, and now they seemed couched in italics, as if the surface reflecting them were wrinkled by the phantasm of that breeze. Time and again my consciousness folded the wrong way, my shuffling body entered the sphere of sleep, shuffled out again, and once or twice I caught myself drifting into a melancholy snore. Mists of tenderness enfolded mountains of longing. Now and then it seemed to me that the enchanted prey was about to meet halfway the enchanted hunter, that her haunch was working its way toward me under the soft sand of a remote and fabulous beach; and then her dimpled dimness would stir, and I would know she was farther away from me than ever.

If I dwell at some length on the tremors and gropings of that distant night, it is because I insist upon proving that I am not, and never was, and never could have been, a brutal scoundrel. The gentle and dreamy regions through which I crept were the patrimonies of poets—*not* crime's prowling ground. Had I reached my goal, my ecstasy would have been all softness, a case of internal combustion of which she would hardly have felt the heat, even if she were wide awake. But I still hoped she might gradually be engulfed in a completeness of stupor that would allow me to taste more than a glimmer of her. And so, in between tentative approximations, with a confusion of perception metamorphosing her into eyespots of moonlight or a fluffy flowering bush, I would dream I regained consciousness, dream I lay in wait.

In the first antemeridian hours there was a lull in the restless hotel night. Then around four the corridor toilet cascaded and its door banged. A little after five a reverberating monologue began to arrive, in several installments, from some courtyard or parking place. It was not really a monologue, since the speaker stopped every few seconds to listen (presumably) to another fellow, but that other voice did not reach me, and so no real meaning could be derived from the part heard. Its matter-of-fact intonations, however, helped to bring in the dawn, and the room was already suffused with lilac gray, when several industrious toilets went to work, one after the other, and the clattering and whining elevator began to rise and take down early risers and downers, and for some minutes I miserably dozed, and Charlotte was a mermaid in a greenish tank, and somewhere in the passage Dr. Boyd said "Good morning to you" in a fruity voice, and birds were busy in the trees, and then Lolita yawned.

Frigid gentlewomen of the jury! I had thought that months, perhaps years, would elapse before I dared to reveal myself to Dolores Haze; but by six she was wide awake, and by six fifteen we were technically lovers. I am going to tell you something very strange: it was she who seduced me.

Upon hearing her first morning yawn, I feigned handsome profiled sleep. I just did not know what to do. Would she be shocked at finding me by her side, and not in some spare bed? Would she collect her clothes and lock herself up in the bathroom? Would she demand to be taken at once to Ramsdale—to her mother's bedside—back to camp? But my Lo was a sportive lassie. I felt her eyes on me, and when she uttered at last that beloved chortling note of hers, I knew her eyes had been laughing. She rolled over to my side, and her warm brown hair came against my collarbone. I gave a mediocre imitation of waking up. We lay quietly. I gently caressed her hair, and we gently kissed. Her kiss, to my delirious embarrassment, had some rather comical refinements of flutter and probe which made me conclude she had been coached at an early age by a little Lesbian. No Charlie boy could have taught her *that*. As if to see whether I had my fill and learned the lesson, she drew away and surveyed me. Her cheekbones were flushed, her full underlip glistened, my dissolution was near. All at once, with a burst of rough glee (the sign of the nymphet!), she put her mouth to my ear—but for quite a while my mind could not separate into words the hot thunder of her whisper, and she laughed, and brushed the hair off her face, and tried again, and gradually the odd sense of living in a brand new, mad new dream world, where everything was permissible, came over me as I realized what she was suggesting. I answered I did not know what game she and Charlie had played. "You mean you have never—?"—her features twisted into a stare of disgusted incredulity. "You have never—" she started again. I took time out by nuzzling her a little. "Lay off, will you," she said with a twangy whine, hastily removing her brown shoulder from my lips. (It was very curious the way she considered—and kept doing so for a long time—all caresses except kisses on the mouth or the stark act of love either "romantic slosh" or "abnormal".)

"You mean," she persisted, now kneeling above me, "you never did it when you were a kid?"

"Never," I answered quite truthfully.

"Okay," said Lolita, "here is where we start."

However, I shall not bore my learned readers with a detailed account of Lolita's presumption. Suffice it to say that not a trace of modesty did I perceive in this beautiful hardly formed young girl whom modern co-education, juvenile mores, the campfire racket and so forth had utterly and hopelessly depraved. She saw the stark act merely as part of a youngster's furtive world, unknown to adults. What adults did for purposes of procreation was no business of hers. My life was handled by little Lo in an energetic, matter-of-fact manner as if it were an insensate gadget unconnected with me. While eager to impress me with the world of tough kids, she was not quite prepared for certain discrepancies between a kid's life and mine. Pride alone prevented her from giving up; for, in my strange predicament, I feigned supreme stupidity and had her have her way—at least while I could still bear it. But really these are irrelevant matters; I am not concerned with so-called "sex" at all. Anybody can imagine those elements of animality. A greater endeavor lures me on: to fix once for all the perilous magic of nymphets.

30

I have to tread carefully. I have to speak in a whisper. Oh you, veteran crime reporter, you grave old usher, you once popular policeman, now in solitary confinement after gracing that school crossing for years, you wretched emeritus read to by a boy! It would never do, would it, to have you fellows fall madly in love with my Lolita! Had I been a painter, had the management of The Enchanted Hunters lost its mind one summer day and commissioned me to redecorate their dining room with murals of my own making, this is what I might have thought up, let me list some fragments:

There would have been a lake. There would have been an arbor in flame-flower. There would have been nature studies—a tiger pursuing a bird of paradise, a choking snake sheathing whole the flayed trunk of a shoat. There would have been a sultan, his face expressing great agony (belied, as it were, by his molding caress), helping a callypygean slave child to climb a column of onyx. There would have been those luminous globules of gonadal glow that travel up the opalescent sides of juke boxes. There would have been all kinds of camp activities on the part of the intermediate group, Canoeing, Coranting, Combing Curls in the lakeside sun. There would have been poplars, apples, a suburban Sunday. There would have been a fire opal dissolving within a ripple-ringed pool, a last throb, a last dab of color, stinging red, smarting pink, a sigh, a wincing child.

31

I am trying to describe these things not to relive them in my present boundless misery, but to sort out the portion of hell and the portion of heaven in that strange, awful, maddening world—nymphet love. The beastly and beautiful merged at one point, and it is that borderline I would like to fix, and I feel I fail to do so utterly. Why?

The stipulation of the Roman law, according to which a girl may marry at twelve, was adopted by the Church, and is still preserved, rather tacitly, in some of the United

States. And fifteen is lawful everywhere. There is nothing wrong, say both hemispheres, when a brute of forty, blessed by the local priest and bloated with drink, sheds his sweat-drenched finery and thrusts himself up to the hilt into his youthful bride. "In such stimulating temperate climates [says an old magazine in this prison library] as St. Louis, Chicago and Cincinnati, girls mature about the end of their twelfth year." Dolores Haze was born less than three hundred miles from stimulating Cincinnati. I have but followed nature. I am nature's faithful hound. Why then this horror that I cannot shake off? Did I deprive her of her flower? Sensitive gentlewomen of the jury, I was not even her first lover.

32

She told me the way she had been debauched. We ate flavorless mealy bananas, bruised peaches and very palatable potato chips, and *die Kleine* told me everything. Her voluble but disjointed account was accompanied by many a droll *moue*. As I think I have already observed, I especially remember one wry face on an "ugh!" basis: jelly-mouth distended sideways and eyes rolled up in a routine blend of comic disgust, resignation and tolerance for young frailty.

Her astounding tale started with an introductory mention of her tent-mate of the previous summer, at another camp, a "very select" one as she put it. That tent-mate ("quite a derelict character," "half-crazy," but a "swell kid") instructed her in various manipulations. At first, loyal Lo refused to tell me her name.

"Was it Grace Angel?" I asked.

She shook her head. No, it wasn't, it was the daughter of a big shot. He—

"Was it perhaps Rose Carmine?"

"No, of course not. Her father—"

"Was it, then, Agnes Sheridan perchance?"

She swallowed and shook her head—and then did a double take.

"Say, how come you know all those kids?"

I explained.

"Well," she said. "They are pretty bad, some of that school bunch, but not that bad. If you have to know, her name was Elizabeth Talbot, she goes now to a swanky private school, her father is an executive."

I recalled with a funny pang the frequency with which poor Charlotte used to introduce into party chat such elegant tidbits as "when my daughter was out hiking last year with the Talbot girl."

I wanted to know if either mother learned of those sapphic diversions?

"Gosh no," exhaled limp Lo mimicking dread and relief, pressing a falsely fluttering hand to her chest.

I was more interested, however, in heterosexual experience. She had entered the sixth grade at eleven, soon after moving to Ramsdale from the Middle West. What did she mean by "pretty bad"?

Well, the Miranda twins had shared the same bed for years, and Donald Scott, who was the dumbest boy in the school, had done it with Hazel Smith in his uncle's garage, and Kenneth Knight—who was the brightest—used to exhibit himself wherever and whenever he had a chance, and—

"Let us switch to Camp Q," I said. And presently I got the whole story.

Barbara Burke, a sturdy blond, two years older than Lo and by far the camp's best swimmer, had a very special canoe which she shared with Lo "because I was the only other girl who could make Willow Island" (some swimming test, I imagine). Through July, every morning—mark, reader, every blessed morning—Barbara and Lo would be helped to carry the boat to Onyx or Eryx (two small lakes in the wood) by Charlie Holmes, the camp mistress' son, aged thirteen—and the only human male for a couple of miles around (excepting an old meek stone-deaf handyman, and a farmer in an old Ford who sometimes sold the campers eggs as farmers will); every morning, oh my reader, the three children would take a short cut through the beautiful innocent forest brimming with all the emblems of youth, dew, birdsongs, and at one point, among the luxuriant undergrowth, Lo would be left as sentinel, while Barbara and the boy copulated behind a bush.

At first, Lo had refused "to try what it was like," but curiosity and camaraderie prevailed, and soon she and Barbara were doing it by turns with the silent, coarse and surly but indefatigable Charlie, who had as much sex appeal as a raw carrot but sported a fascinating collection of contraceptives which he used to fish out of a third nearby lake, a considerably larger and more populous one, called Lake Climax, after the booming young factory town of that name. Although conceding it was "sort of fun" and "fine for the complexion," Lolita, I am glad to say, held Charlie's mind and manners in the greatest contempt. Nor had her temperament been roused by that filthy fiend. In fact, I think he had rather stunned it, despite the "fun."

By that time it was close to ten. With the ebb of lust, an ashen sense of awfulness, abetted by the realistic drabness of a gray neuralgic day, crept over me and hummed within my temples. Brown, naked, frail Lo, her narrow white buttocks to me, her sulky face to a door mirror, stood, arms akimbo, feet (in new slippers with pussy-fur tops) wide apart, and through a forehanging lock tritely mugged at herself in the glass. From the corridor came the cooing voices of colored maids at work, and presently there was a mild attempt to open the door of our room. I had Lo go to the bathroom and take a much-needed soap shower. The bed was a frightful mess with overtones of potato chips. She tried on a two-piece navy wool, then a sleeveless blouse with a swirly clathrate skirt, but the first was too tight and the second too ample, and when I begged her to hurry up (the situation was beginning to frighten me), Lo viciously sent those nice presents of mine hurtling into a corner, and put on yesterday's dress. When she was ready at last, I gave her a lovely new purse of simulated calf (in which I had slipped quite a few pennies and two mint-bright dimes) and told her to buy herself a magazine in the lobby.

"I'll be down in a minute," I said. "And if I were you, my dear, I would not talk to strangers."

Except for my poor little gifts, there was not much to pack; but I was forced to devote a dangerous amount of time (was she up to something downstairs?) to arranging the bed in such a way as to suggest the abandoned nest of a restless father and his tomboy daughter, instead of an ex-convict's saturnalia with a couple of fat old whores. Then I finished dressing and had the hoary bellboy come up for the bags.

Everything was fine. There, in the lobby, she sat, deep in an overstuffed blood-red armchair, deep in a lurid movie magazine. A fellow of my age in tweeds (the genre of the place had changed overnight to a spurious country-squire atmosphere) was staring at my Lolita over his dead cigar and stale newspaper. She wore her professional white socks and saddle oxfords, and that bright print frock with the square throat; a splash of jaded lamplight brought out the golden down on her warm brown limbs. There she sat, her legs carelessly highcrossed, and her pale eyes skimming along the lines with every now and then a blink. Bill's wife had worshiped him from afar long before they ever met: in fact, she used to secretly admire the famous young actor as he ate sundaes in Schwab's drugstore. Nothing could have been more childish than her snubbed nose, freckled face or the purplish spot on her naked neck where a fairytale vampire had feasted, or the unconscious movement of her tongue exploring a touch of rosy rash around her swollen lips; nothing could be more harmless than to read about Jill, an energetic starlet who made her own clothes and was a student of serious literature; nothing could be more innocent than the part in that glossy brown hair with that silky sheen on the temple; nothing could be more naïve—But what sickening envy the lecherous fellow whoever he was— come to think of it, he resembled a little my Swiss uncle Gustave, also a great admirer of *le découvert*—would have experienced had he known that every nerve in me was still anointed and ringed with the feel of her body—the body of some immortal daemon disguised as a female child.

Was pink pig Mr. Swoon absolutely sure my wife had not telephoned? He was. If she did, would he tell her we had gone on to Aunt Clare's place? He would, indeedie. I settled the bill and roused Lo from her chair. She read to the car. Still reading, she was driven to a so-called coffee shop a few blocks south. Oh, she ate all right. She even laid aside her magazine to eat, but a queer dullness had replaced her usual cheerfulness. I knew little Lo could be very nasty, so I braced myself and grinned, and waited for a squall. I was unbathed, unshaven, and had had no bowel movement. My nerves were a-jangle. I did not like the way my little mistress shrugged her shoulders and distended her nostrils when I attempted casual small talk. Had Phyllis been in the know before she joined her parents in Maine? I asked with a smile. "Look," said Lo making a weeping grimace, "let us get off the subject." I then tried—also unsuccessfully, no matter how I smacked my lips—to interest her in the road map. Our destination was, let me remind my patient reader whose meek temper Lo ought to have copied, the gay town of Lepingville, somewhere near a hypothetical hospital. That destination was in itself a perfectly arbitrary one (as, alas, so many were to be), and I shook in my shoes as I wondered how to keep the whole arrangement plausible, and what other plausible objectives to invent after we had taken in all the movies in Lepingville. More and more uncomfortable did Humbert feel. It was something quite special, that feeling: an oppressive, hideous constraint as if I were sitting with the small ghost of somebody I had just killed.

As she was in the act of getting back into the car, an expression of pain flitted across Lo's face. It flitted again, more meaningfully, as she settled down beside me. No doubt, she reproduced it that second time for my benefit. Foolishly, I asked her what was the matter. "Nothing, you brute," she replied. "You what?" I asked. She was silent. Leaving Briceland. Loquacious Lo was silent. Cold spiders of panic crawled down my back. This was an orphan. This was a lone child, an absolute waif, with whom a heavy-limbed, foul-smelling adult had had strenuous intercourse three times that very morning. Whether or not the real-ization of a lifelong dream had surpassed all expectation, it had, in a sense, overshot its mark—and plunged into a nightmare. I had been careless, stupid, and ignoble. And let me be quite frank: somewhere at the bottom of that dark turmoil I felt the writhing of desire again, so monstrous was my appetite for that miserable nymphet. Mingled with the pangs of guilt was the agonizing thought that her mood might prevent me from making love to her again as soon as I found a nice country road where to park in peace. In other words, poor Humbert Humbert was dreadfully unhappy, and while steadily and inanely driving toward Lepingville, he kept racking his brains for some quip, under the bright wing of which he might dare turn to his seatmate. It was she, however, who broke the silence:

"Oh, a squashed squirrel," she said. "What a shame."

"Yes, isn't it?" (eager, hopeful Hum).

"Let us stop at the next gas station," Lo continued. "I want to go to the washroom."

"We shall stop wherever you want," I said. And then as a lovely, lonely, supercilious grove (oaks, I thought; American trees at that stage were beyond me) started to echo greenly the rush of our car, a red and ferny road on our right turned its head before slanting into the woodland, and I suggested we might perhaps—

"Drive on," my Lo cried shrilly.

"Righto. Take it easy." (Down, poor beast, down.)

I glanced at her. Thank God, the child was smiling.

"You chump," she said, sweetly smiling at me. "You revolting creature. I was a daisy-fresh girl, and look what you've done to me. I ought to call the police and tell them you raped me. Oh, you dirty, dirty old man."

Was she just joking? An ominous hysterical note rang through her silly words. Presently, making a sizzling sound with her lips, she started complaining of pains, said she could not sit, said I had torn something inside her. The sweat rolled down my neck, and we almost ran over some little animal or other that was crossing the road with tail erect, and again my vile-tempered companion called me an ugly name. When we stopped at the filling station, she scrambled out without a word and was a long time away. Slowly, lovingly, an elderly friend with a broken nose wiped my windshield—they do it differently at every place, from chamois cloth to soapy brush, this fellow used a pink sponge.

She appeared at last. "Look," she said in that neutral

voice that hurt me so, "give me some dimes and nickels. I want to call mother in that hospital. What's the number?"

"Get in," I said. "You can't call that number."

"Why?"

"Get in and slam the door."

She got in and slammed the door. The old garage man beamed at her. I swung onto the highway.

"Why can't I call my mother if I want to?"

"Because," I answered, "your mother is dead."

33

In the gay town of Lepingville I bought her four books of comics, a box of candy, a box of sanitary pads, two cokes, a manicure set, a travel clock with a luminous dial, a ring with a real topaz, a tennis racket, roller skates with white high shoes, field glasses, a portable radio set, chewing gum, a transparent raincoat, sunglasses, some more garments—swooners, shorts, all kinds of summer frocks. At the hotel we had separate rooms, but in the middle of the night she came sobbing into mine, and we made it up very gently. You see, she had absolutely nowhere else to go.

Part Two

It was then that began our extensive travels all over the States. To any other type of tourist accommodation I soon grew to prefer the Functional Motel—clean, neat, safe nooks, ideal places for sleep, argument, reconciliation, insatiable illicit love. At first, in my dread of arousing suspicion, I would eagerly pay for both sections of one double unit, each containing a double bed. I wondered what type of foursome this arrangement was ever intended for, since only a pharisaic parody of privacy could be attained by means of the incomplete partition dividing the cabin or room into two communicating love nests. By and by, the very possibilities that such honest promiscuity suggested (two young couples merrily swapping mates or a child shamming sleep to earwitness primal sonorities) made me bolder, and every now and then I would take a bed-and-cot or twin-bed cabin, a prison cell of paradise, with yellow window shades pulled down to create a morning illusion of Venice and sunshine when actually it was Pennsylvania and rain.

We came to know—*nous connûmes*, to use a Flaubertian intonation—the stone cottages under enormous Chateaubriandesque trees, the brick unit, the adobe unit, the stucco court, on what the Tour Book of the Automobile Association describes as "shaded" or "spacious" or "landscaped" grounds. The log kind, finished in knotty pine, reminded Lo, by its golden-brown glaze, of fried-chicken bones. We held in contempt the plain whitewashed clapboard Kabins, with their faint sewerish smell or some other gloomy self-conscious stench and nothing to boast of (except "good beds"), and an unsmiling landlady always prepared to have her gift (". . . well, I could give you . . .") turned down.

Nous connûmes (this is royal fun) the would-be enticements of their repetitious names—all those Sunset Motels, U-Beam Cottages, Hillcrest Courts, Pine View Courts, Mountain View Courts, Skyline Courts, Park Plaza Courts, Green Acres, Mac's Courts. There was sometimes a special line in the write-up, such as "Children welcome, pets allowed" (*You* are welcome, *you* are allowed). The baths were mostly tiled showers, with an endless variety of spouting mechanisms, but with one definitely non-Laodicean characteristic in common, a propensity, while in use, to turn instantly beastly hot or blindingly cold upon you, depending on whether your neighbor turned on his cold or his hot to deprive you of a necessary complement in the shower you had so carefully blended. Some motels had instructions pasted above the toilet (on whose tank the towels were unhygienically heaped) asking guests not to throw into its bowl garbage, beer cans, cartons, still-born babies; others had special notices under glass, such as Things to Do (Riding: *You will often see riders coming down Main Street on their way back from a romantic moonlight ride.* "Often at 3 A.M.," sneered unromantic Lo).

Nous connûmes the various types of motor court operators, the reformed criminal, the retired teacher and the business flop, among the males; and the motherly, pseudo-ladylike and madamic variants among the females. And sometimes trains would cry in the monstrously hot and humid night with heartrending and ominous plangency, mingling power and hysteria in one desperate scream.

We avoided Tourist Homes, country cousins of Funeral ones, old-fashioned, genteel and showerless, with elaborate dressing tables in depressingly white-and-pink little bedrooms, and photographs of the landlady's children in all their instars. But I did surrender, now and then, to Lo's predilection for "real" hotels. She would pick out in the book, while I petted her in the parked car in the silence of a dusk-mellowed, mysterious side-road, some highly recommended lake lodge which offered all sorts of things magnified by the flashlight she moved over them, such as congenial company, between-meals snacks, outdoor barbe-cues—but which in my mind conjured up odious visions of stinking high school boys in sweatshirts and an ember-red cheek pressing against hers, while poor Dr. Humbert, embracing nothing but two masculine knees, would cold-humor his piles on the damp turf. Most tempting to her, too, were those "Colonial" Inns, which apart from "gracious atmosphere" and picture windows, promised "unlimited quantities of M-m-m food." Treasured recollec-tions of my father's palatial hotel sometimes led me to seek for its like in the strange country we traveled through. I was soon discouraged; but Lo kept following the scent of rich food ads, while I derived a not exclusively economic kick from such roadside signs as TIMBER HOTEL, *Children under 14 Free*. On the other hand, I shudder when recalling that *soi-disant* "high-class" resort in a Midwestern state, which advertised "raid-the-icebox" midnight snacks and, intrigued by my accent, wanted to know my dead wife's and dead mother's maiden names. A two-days' stay there cost me a hundred and twenty-four dollars! And do you remember, Miranda, that other "ultrasmart" robbers' den with complimentary morning coffee and circulating ice water, and no children under sixteen (no Lolitas, of course)?

Immediately upon arrival at one of the plainer motor courts which became our habitual haunts, she would set the electric fan a-whirr, or induce me to drop a quarter into the radio, or she would read all the signs and inquire with a whine why she could not go riding up some advertised trail or swimming in that local pool of warm mineral water. Most often, in the slouching, bored way she cultivated, Lo would fall prostrate and abominably desirable into a red springchair or a green chaise longue, or a steamer chair of striped canvas with footrest and canopy, or a sling chair, or any other lawn chair under a garden umbrella on the patio, and it would take hours of blandishments, threats and promises to make her lend me for a few seconds her brown limbs in the seclusion of the five-dollar room before undertaking anything she might prefer to my poor joy.

A combination of naïveté and deception, of charm and vulgarity, of blue sulks and rosy mirth, Lolita, when she chose, could be a most exasperating brat. I was not really quite prepared for her fits of disorganized boredom, intense and vehement griping, her sprawling, droopy, dopey-eyed style, and what is called goofing off—a kind of diffused clowning which she thought was tough in a boyish hoodlum way. Mentally, I found her to be a disgustingly conventional little girl. Sweet hot jazz, square dancing, gooey fudge sundaes, musicals, movie magazines and so forth—these were the obvious items in her list of beloved things. The Lord knows how many nickels I fed to the gorgeous music boxes that came with every meal we had! I still hear the nasal voices of those invisibles serenading her, people with names like Sammy and Jo and Eddy and Tony and Peggy and Guy and Patty and Rex, and sentimental song hits, all of them as similar to my ear as her various candies were to my palate. She believed, with a kind of celestial trust, any advertisement or advice that appeared in *Movie Love* or *Screen Land*—Starasil Starves Pimples, or "You better watch out if you're wearing your shirttails outside your jeans, gals, because Jill says you

shouldn't." If a roadside sign said: VISIT OUR GIFT SHOP—
we *had* to visit it, *had* to buy its Indian curios, dolls, copper
jewelry, cactus candy. The words "novelties and souvenirs"
simply entranced her by their trochaic lilt. If some café sign
proclaimed Icecold Drinks, she was automatically stirred,
although all drinks everywhere were ice-cold. She it was to
whom ads were dedicated: the ideal consumer, the subject
and object of every foul poster. And she attempted—unsuccessfully—to patronize only those restaurants where the
holy spirit of Huncan Dines had descended upon the cute
paper napkins and cottage-cheese-crested salads.

In those days, neither she nor I had thought up yet the
system of monetary bribes which was to work such havoc
with my nerves and her morals somewhat later. I relied on
three other methods to keep my pubescent concubine in
submission and passable temper. A few years before, she
had spent a rainy summer under Miss Phalen's bleary eye
in a dilapidated Appalachian farmhouse that had belonged
to some gnarled Haze or other in the dead past. It still
stood among its rank acres of golden rod on the edge of
a flowerless forest, at the end of a permanently muddy
road, twenty miles from the nearest hamlet. Lo recalled
that scarecrow of a house, the solitude, the soggy old
pastures, the wind, the bloated wilderness, with an energy
of disgust that distorted her mouth and fattened her half-
revealed tongue. And it was there that I warned her she
would dwell with me in exile for months and years if need
be, studying under me French and Latin, unless her "present
attitude" changed. Charlotte, I began to understand you!

A simple child, Lo would scream no! and frantically
clutch at my driving hand whenever I put a stop to her
tornadoes of temper by turning in the middle of a highway
with the implication that I was about to take her straight
to that dark and dismal abode. The farther, however, we

traveled away from it west, the less tangible that menace became, and I had to adopt other methods of persuasion.

Among these, the reformatory threat is the one I recall with the deepest moan of shame. From the very beginning of our concourse, I was clever enough to realize that I must secure her complete co-operation in keeping our relations secret, that it should become a second nature with her, no matter what grudge she might bear me, no matter what other pleasures she might seek.

"Come and kiss your old man," I would say, "and drop that moody nonsense. In former times, when I was still your dream male [the reader will notice what pains I took to speak Lo's tongue], you swooned to records of the number one throb-and-sob idol of your coevals [Lo: "Of my what? Speak English"]. That idol of your pals sounded, you thought, like friend Humbert. But now, I am just your *old man*, a dream dad protecting his dream daughter.

"My *chère Dolorès!* I want to protect you, dear, from all the horrors that happen to little girls in coal sheds and alley ways, and, alas, *comme vous le savez trop bien, ma gentille*, in the blueberry woods during the bluest of summers. Through thick and thin I will still stay your guardian, and if you are good, I hope a court may legalize that guardianship before long. Let us, however, forget, Dolores Haze, so-called legal terminology, terminology that accepts as rational the term 'lewd and lascivious cohabitation.' I am not a criminal sexual psychopath taking indecent liberties with a child. The rapist was Charlie Holmes; I am the therapist—a matter of nice spacing in the way of distinction. I am your daddum, Lo. Look, I've a learned book here about young girls. Look, darling, what it says. I quote: the normal girl—normal, mark you—the normal girl is usually extremely anxious to please her father. She feels in him the forerunner of the desired elusive male ('elusive' is good, by Polonius!). The wise mother (and your poor mother would have been wise, had she lived) will encourage a companionship between father and daughter, realizing—excuse the corny style—that the girl forms her ideals of romance and of men from her association with her father. Now, what association does this cheery book mean—and recommend? I quote again: Among Sicilians sexual relations between a father and his daughter are accepted as a matter of course, and the girl who participates in such relationship is not looked upon with disapproval by the society of which she is part. I'm a great admirer of Sicilians, fine athletes, fine musicians, fine upright people, Lo, and great lovers. But let's not digress. Only the other day we read in the newspapers some bunkum about a middle-aged morals offender who pleaded guilty to the violation of the Mann Act and to transporting a nine-year-old girl across state lines for immoral purposes, whatever these are. Dolores darling! You are not nine but almost thirteen, and I would not advise you to consider yourself my cross-country slave, and I deplore the Mann Act as lending itself to a dreadful pun, the revenge that the Gods of Semantics take against tight-zippered Philistines. I am your father, and I *am* speaking English, and I love you.

"Finally, let us see what happens if you, a minor, accused of having impaired the morals of an adult in a respectable inn, what happens if you complain to the police of my having kidnaped and raped you? Let us suppose they believe you. A minor female, who allows a person over twenty-one to know her carnally, involves her victim into statutory rape, or second-degree sodomy, depending on the technique; and the maximum penalty is ten years. So I go to jail. Okay. I go to jail. But what happens to you, my orphan? Well, you are luckier. You become the ward of the Department of Public Welfare—which I am afraid sounds a little bleak. A nice grim matron of the Miss Phalen type, but more rigid and not a drinking woman, will take away your lipstick and fancy clothes. No more gadding about! I don't know if you have ever heard of the laws relating to dependent, neglected, incorrigible and delinquent children. While I stand gripping the bars, you, happy neglected child, will be given a choice of various dwelling places, all more or less the same, the correctional school, the reformatory, the juvenile detention home, or one of those admirable girls' protectories where you knit things, and sing hymns, and have rancid pancakes on Sundays. You will go there, Lolita—*my* Lolita, *this* Lolita will leave her Catullus and go there, as the wayward girl you are. In plainer words, if we two are found out, you will be analyzed and institutional- ized, my pet, *c'est tout*. You will dwell, my Lolita will dwell (come here, my brown flower) with thirty-nine other dopes in a dirty dormitory (no, allow me, please) under the super- vision of hideous matrons. This is the situation, this is the choice. Don't you think that under the circumstances Dolores Haze had better stick to her old man?"

By rubbing all this in, I succeeded in terrorizing Lo, who despite a certain brash alertness of manner and spurts of wit was not as intelligent a child as her I.Q. might suggest. But if I managed to establish that background of shared secrecy and shared guilt, I was much less successful in keeping her in good humor. Every morning during our yearlong travels I had to devise some expectation, some special point in space and time for her to look forward to, for her to survive till bedtime. Otherwise, deprived of a shaping and sustaining purpose, the skeleton of her day sagged and collapsed. The object in view might be anything—a lighthouse in Virginia, a natural cave in Arkansas converted to a café, a collection of guns and violins some- where in Oklahoma, a replica of the Grotto of Lourdes in

Louisiana, shabby photographs of the bonanza mining period in the local museum of a Rocky Mountains resort, anything whatsoever—but it had to be there, in front of us, like a fixed star, although as likely as not Lo would feign gagging as soon as we got to it.

By putting the geography of the United States into motion, I did my best for hours on end to give her the impression of "going places," of rolling on to some definite destination, to some unusual delight. I have never seen such smooth amiable roads as those that now radiated before us, across the crazy quilt of forty-eight states. Voraciously we consumed those long highways, in rapt silence we glided over their glossy black dance floors. Not only had Lo no eye for scenery but she furiously resented my calling her attention to this or that enchanting detail of landscape; which I myself learned to discern only after being exposed for quite a time to the delicate beauty ever present in the margin of our undeserving journey. By a paradox of pictorial thought, the average lowland North-American countryside had at first seemed to me something I accepted with a shock of amused recognition because of those painted oilcloths which were imported from America in the old days to be hung above washstands in Central-European nurseries, and which fascinated a drowsy child at bed time with the rustic green views they depicted—opaque curly trees, a barn, cattle, a brook, the dull white of vague orchards in bloom, and perhaps a stone fence or hills of greenish gouache. But gradually the models of those elementary rusticities became stranger and stranger to the eye, the nearer I came to know them. Beyond the tilled plain, beyond the toy roofs, there would be a slow suffusion of inutile loveliness, a low sun in a platinum haze with a warm, peeled-peach tinge pervading the upper edge of a two-dimensional, dove-gray cloud fusing with the distant amorous mist. There might be a line of spaced trees silhouetted against the horizon, and hot still noons above a wilderness of clover, and Claude Lorrain clouds inscribed remotely into misty azure with only their cumulus part conspicuous against the neutral swoon of the background. Or again, it might be a stern El Greco horizon, pregnant with inky rain, and a passing glimpse of some mummy-necked farmer, and all around alternating strips of quick-silverish water and harsh green corn, the whole arrangement opening like a fan, somewhere in Kansas.

Now and then, in the vastness of those plains, huge trees would advance toward us to cluster self-consciously by the roadside and provide a bit of humanitarian shade above a picnic table, with sun flecks, flattened paper cups, samaras and discarded ice-cream sticks littering the brown ground. A great user of roadside facilities, my unfastidious Lo would be charmed by toilet signs—Guys-Gals, John-Jane, Jack-Jill and even Buck's-Doe's; while lost in an artist's dream, I would stare at the honest brightness of the gasoline paraphernalia against the splendid green of oaks, or at a distant hill scrambling out—scarred but still untamed—from the wilderness of agriculture that was trying to swallow it.

At night, tall trucks studded with colored lights, like dreadful giant Christmas trees, loomed in the darkness and thundered by the belated little sedan. And again next day a thinly populated sky, losing its blue to the heat, would melt overhead, and Lo would clamor for a drink, and her cheeks would hollow vigorously over the straw, and the car inside would be a furnace when we got in again, and the road shimmered ahead, with a remote car changing its shape mirage-like in the surface glare, and seeming to hang for a moment, old-fashionedly square and high, in the hot haze. And as we pushed westward, patches of what the garageman called "sage brush" appeared, and then the mysterious outlines of table-like hills, and then red bluffs ink-blotted with junipers, and then a mountain range, dun grading into blue, and blue into dream, and the desert would meet us with a steady gale, dust, gray thorn bushes, and hideous bits of tissue paper mimicking pale flowers among the prickles of wind-tortured withered stalks all along the highway; in the middle of which there sometimes stood simple cows, immobilized in a position (tail left, white eyelashes right) cutting across all human rules of traffic.

My lawyer has suggested I give a clear, frank account of the itinerary we followed, and I suppose I have reached here a point where I cannot avoid that chore. Roughly, during that mad year (August 1947 to August 1948), our route began with a series of wiggles and whorls in New England, then meandered south, up and down, east and west; dipped deep into *ce qu'on appelle* Dixieland, avoided Florida because the Farlows were there, veered west, zigzagged through corn belts and cotton belts (this is not *too* clear I am afraid, Clarence, but I did not keep any notes, and have at my disposal only an atrociously crippled tour book in three volumes, almost a symbol of my torn and tattered past, in which to check these recollections); crossed and recrossed the Rockies, straggled through southern deserts where we wintered; reached the Pacific, turned north through the pale lilac fluff of flowering shrubs along forest roads; almost reached the Canadian border; and proceeded east, across good lands and bad lands, back to agriculture on a grand scale, avoiding, despite little Lo's strident remonstrations, little Lo's birth-place, in a corn, coal and hog producing area; and finally returned to the fold of the East, petering out in the college town of Beardsley.

2

Now, in perusing what follows, the reader should bear in mind not only the general circuit as adumbrated above, with its many sidetrips and tourist traps, secondary circles and skittish deviations, but also the fact that far from being an indolent *partie de plaisir*, our tour was a hard, twisted, teleological growth, whose sole *raison d'être* (these French clichés are symptomatic) was to keep my companion in passable humor from kiss to kiss.

Thumbing through that battered tour book, I dimly evoke that Magnolia Garden in a southern state which cost me four bucks and which, according to the ad in the book, you must visit for three reasons: because John Galsworthy (a stone-dead writer of sorts) acclaimed it as the world's fairest garden; because in 1900 Baedeker's Guide had marked it with a star; and finally, because . . . O, Reader, My Reader, guess! . . . because children (and by Jingo was not my Lolita a child!) will "walk starry-eyed and reverently through this foretaste of Heaven, drinking in beauty that can influence a life." "Not mine," said grim Lo, and settled down on a bench with the fillings of two Sunday papers in her lovely lap.

We passed and re-passed through the whole gamut of American roadside restaurants, from the lowly Eat with its deer head (dark trace of long tear at inner canthus), "humorous" picture post cards of the posterior "Kurort" type, impaled guest checks, life savers, sunglasses, adman visions of celestial sundaes, one half of a chocolate cake under glass, and several horribly experienced flies zigzagging over the sticky sugar-pour on the ignoble counter; and all the way to the expensive place with the subdued lights, preposterously poor table linen, inept waiters (ex-convicts or college boys), the roan back of a screen actress, the sable eyebrows of her male of the moment, and an orchestra of zoot-suiters with trumpets.

We inspected the world's largest stalagmite in a cave where three southeastern states have a family reunion; admission by age; adults one dollar, pubescents sixty cents. A granite obelisk commemorating the Battle of Blue Licks, with old bones and Indian pottery in the museum nearby, Lo a dime, very reasonable. The present log cabin boldly simulating the past log cabin where Lincoln was born. A boulder, with a plaque, in memory of the author of "Trees" (by now we are in Poplar Cove, N.C., reached by what my kind, tolerant, usually so restrained tour book angrily calls "a very narrow road, poorly maintained," to which, though no Kilmerite, I subscribe). From a hired motorboat operated by an elderly, but still repulsively handsome White Russian, a baron they said (Lo's palms were damp, the little fool), who had known in California good old Maximovich and Valeria, we could distinguish the inaccessible "millionaires' colony" on an island, somewhere off the Georgia coast. We inspected further: a collection of European hotel picture post cards in a museum devoted to hobbies at a Mississippi resort, where with a hot wave of pride I discovered a colored photo of my father's Mirana, its striped awnings, its flag flying above the retouched palm trees. "So what?" said Lo, squinting at the bronzed owner of an expensive car who had followed us into the Hobby House. Relics of the cotton era. A forest in Arkansas and, on her brown shoulder, a raised purple-pink swelling (the work of some gnat) which I eased of its beautiful transparent poison between my long thumbnails and then sucked till I was gorged on her spicy blood. Bourbon Street (in a town named New Orleans) whose sidewalks, said the tour book, "may [I liked the "may"] feature entertainment by pickaninnies who will [I liked the "will" even better] tap-dance for pennies" (what fun), while "its numerous small and intimate night clubs are thronged with visitors" (naughty). Collections of frontier lore. Ante-bellum homes with iron-trellis balconies and hand-worked stairs, the kind down which movie ladies with sun-kissed shoulders run in rich Technicolor, holding up the fronts of their flounced skirts with both little hands in that special way, and the devoted Negress shaking her head òn the upper landing. The Menninger Foundation, a psychiatric clinic, just for the heck of it. A patch of beautifully eroded clay; and yucca blossoms, so pure, so waxy, but lousy with creeping white flies. Independence, Missouri, the starting point of the Old Oregon Trail; and Abilene, Kansas, the home of the Wild Bill Something Rodeo. Distant mountains. Near mountains. More mountains; bluish beauties never attainable, or ever turning into inhabited hill after hill; south-eastern ranges, altitudinal failures as alps go; heart and sky-piercing snow-veined gray colossi of stone, relentless peaks appearing from nowhere at a turn of the highway; timbered enormities, with a system of neatly overlapping dark firs, interrupted in places by pale puffs of aspen; pink and lilac formations, Pharaonic, phallic, "too prehistoric for words" (blasé Lo); buttes of black lava; early spring mountains with young-elephant lanugo along their spines; end-of-the-summer mountains, all hunched up, their heavy Egyptian limbs folded under folds of tawny moth-eaten plush; oatmeal hills, flecked with green round oaks; a last rufous mountain with a rich rug of lucerne at its foot.

Moreover, we inspected: Little Iceberg Lake, somewhere in Colorado, and the snow banks, and the cushionets of tiny alpine flowers, and more snow; down which Lo in red-peaked cap tried to slide, and squealed, and was snowballed by some youngsters, and retaliated in kind *comme on dit*. Skeletons of burned aspens, patches of spired blue flowers.

The various items of a scenic drive. Hundreds of scenic drives, thousands of Bear Creeks, Soda Springs, Painted Canyons. Texas, a drought-struck plain. Crystal Chamber in the longest cave in the world, children under 12 free, Lo a young captive. A collection of a local lady's homemade sculptures, closed on a miserable Monday morning, dust, wind, witherland. Conception Park, in a town on the Mexican border which I dared not cross. There and else-where, hundreds of gray hummingbirds in the dusk, probing the throats of dim flowers. Shakespeare, a ghost town in New Mexico, where bad man Russian Bill was colorfully hanged seventy years ago. Fish hatcheries. Cliff dwellings. The mummy of a child (Florentine Bea's Indian contempor-ary). Our twentieth Hell's Canyon. Our fiftieth Gateway to something or other *fide* that tour book, the cover of which had been lost by that time. A tick in my groin. Always the same three old men, in hats and suspenders, idling away the summer afternoon under the trees near the public foun-tain. A hazy blue view beyond railings on a mountain pass, and the backs of a family enjoying it (with Lo, in a hot, happy, wild, intense, hopeful, hopeless whisper—"Look, the McCrystals, please, let's talk to them, please"—let's talk to them, reader!—"please! I'll do anything you want, oh, please . . ."). Indian ceremonial dances, strictly commercial. ART: American Refrigerator Transit Company. Obvious Arizona, pueblo dwellings, aboriginal pictographs, a dinosaur track in a desert canyon, printed there thirty million years ago, when I was a child. A lanky, six-foot, pale boy with an active Adam's apple, ogling Lo and her orange-brown bare midriff, which I kissed five minutes later, Jack. Winter in the desert, spring in the foothills, almonds in bloom. Reno, a dreary town in Nevada, with a nightlife said to be "cosmopolitan and mature." A winery in California, with a church built in the shape of a wine barrel. Death

Valley. Scotty's Castle. Works of Art collected by one Rogers over a period of years. The ugly villas of handsome actresses. R. L. Stevenson's footprint on an extinct volcano. Mission Dolores: good title for book. Surf-carved sandstone festoons. A man having a lavish epileptic fit on the ground in Russian Gulch State Park. Blue, blue Crater Lake. A fish hatchery in Idaho and the State Penitentiary. Somber Yellowstone Park and its colored hot springs, baby geysers, rainbows of bubbling mud—symbols of my passion. A herd of antelopes in a wildlife refuge. Our hundredth cavern, adults one dollar, Lolita fifty cents. A chateau built by a French marquess in N.D. The Corn Palace in S.D.; and the huge heads of presidents carved in towering granite. The Bearded Woman read our jingle and now she is no longer single. A zoo in Indiana where a large troop of monkeys lived on concrete replica of Christopher Columbus' flagship. Billions of dead, or halfdead, fish-smelling May flies in every window of every eating place all along a dreary sandy shore. Fat gulls on big stones as seen from the ferry *City of Cheboygan*, whose brown woolly smoke arched and dipped over the green shadow it cast on the aquamarine lake. A motel whose ventilator pipe passed under the city sewer. Lincoln's home, largely spurious, with parlor books and period furniture that most visitors reverently accepted as personal belongings.

We had rows, minor and major. The biggest ones we had took place: at Lacework Cabins, Virginia; on Park Avenue, Little Rock, near a school; on Milner Pass, 10,759 feet high, in Colorado; at the corner of Seventh Street and Central Avenue in Phoenix, Arizona; on Third Street, Los Angeles, because the tickets to some studio or other were sold out; at a motel called Poplar Shade in Utah, where six pubescent trees were scarcely taller than my Lolita, and where she asked, *à propos de rien*, how long did I think we were going to live in stuffy cabins, doing filthy things together and never behaving like ordinary people? On N. Broadway, Burns, Oregon, corner of W. Washington, facing Safeway, a grocery. In some little town in the Sun Valley of Idaho, before a brick hotel, pale and flushed bricks nicely mixed, with, opposite, a poplar playing its liquid shadows all over the local Honor Roll. In a sage brush wilderness, between Pinedale and Farson. Somewhere in Nebraska, on Main Street, near the First National Bank, established 1889, with a view of a railway crossing in the vista of the street, and beyond that the white organ pipes of a multiple silo. And on McEwen St., corner of Wheaton Ave., in a Michigan town bearing his first name.

We came to know the curious roadside species, Hitchhiking Man, *Homo pollex* of science, with all its many sub-species and forms: the modest soldier, spic and span, quietly waiting, quietly conscious of khaki's viatic appeal; the schoolboy wishing to go two blocks; the killer wishing to go two thousand miles; the mysterious, nervous, elderly gent, with brand-new suitcase and clipped mustache; a trio of optimistic Mexicans; the college student displaying the grime of vacational outdoor work as proudly as the name of the famous college arching across the front of his sweat-shirt; the desperate lady whose battery has just died on her; the clean-cut, glossy-haired, shifty-eyed, white-faced young beasts in loud shirts and coats, vigorously, almost priapically thrusting out tense thumbs to tempt lone women or sadsack salesmen with fancy cravings.

"Let's take him," Lo would often plead, rubbing her knees together in a way she had, as some particularly disgusting *pollex*, some man of my age and shoulder breadth, with the *face à claques* of an unemployed actor, walked backwards, practically in the path of our car.

Oh, I had to keep a very sharp eye on Lo, little limp Lo! Owing perhaps to constant amorous exercise, she radiated, despite her very childish appearance, some special languorous glow which threw garage fellows, hotel pages, vacationists, goons in luxurious cars, maroon morons near blued pools, into fits of concupiscence which might have tickled my pride, had it not incensed my jealousy. For little Lo was aware of that glow of hers, and I would often catch her *coulant un regard* in the direction of some amiable male, some grease monkey, with a sinewy golden-brown forearm and watch-braceleted wrist, and hardly had I turned my back to go and buy this very Lo a lollipop, than I would hear her and the fair mechanic burst into a perfect love song of wisecracks.

When, during our longer stops, I would relax after a particularly violent morning in bed, and out of the goodness of my lulled heart allow her—indulgent Hum!—to visit the rose garden or children's library across the street with a motor court neighbor's plain little Mary and Mary's eight-year-old brother, Lo would come back an hour late, with barefoot Mary trailing far behind, and the little boy metamorphosed into two gangling, golden-haired high school uglies, all muscles and gonorrhea. The reader may well imagine what I answered my pet when—rather uncertainly, I admit—she would ask me if she could go with Carl and Al here to the roller-skating rink.

I remember the first time, a dusty windy afternoon, I did let her go to one such rink. Cruelly she said it would be no fun if I accompanied her, since that time of day was reserved for teenagers. We wrangled out a compromise: I remained in the car, among other (empty) cars with their noses to the canvas-topped open-air rink, where some fifty young people, many in pairs, were endlessly rolling round and round to mechanical music, and the wind silvered the trees. Dolly wore blue jeans and white high shoes, as most of the other girls did. I kept counting the revolutions of the rolling crowd—and suddenly she was missing. When she rolled past again, she was together with three hoodlums whom I had heard analyze a moment before the girl skaters from the outside—and jeer at a lovely leggy young thing who had arrived clad in red shorts instead of those jeans or slacks.

At inspection stations on highways entering Arizona or California, a policeman's cousin would peer with such intensity at us that my poor heart wobbled. "Any honey?" he would inquire, and every time my sweet fool giggled. I still have, vibrating all along my optic nerve, visions of Lo on horseback, a link in the chain of a guided trip along a bridle trail: Lo bobbing at a walking pace, with an old woman rider in front and a lecherous red-necked dude-rancher behind; and I behind him, hating his fat flowery-shirted back even more fervently than a motorist does a slow truck on a mountain road. Or else, at a ski lodge, I would see her floating away from me, celestial and solitary, in an ethereal chairlift, up and up, to a glittering summit where laughing athletes stripped to the waist were waiting for her, for her.

In whatever town we stopped I would inquire, in my polite European way, anent the whereabouts of natatoriums, museums, local schools, the number of children in the nearest school and so forth; and at school bus time, smiling and twitching a little (I discovered this *tic nerveux* because cruel Lo was the first to mimic it), I would park at a strategic point, with my vagrant schoolgirl beside me in the car, to watch the children leave school—always a pretty sight. This sort of thing soon began to bore my so easily bored Lolita, and, having a childish lack of sympathy for other people's whims, she would insult me and my desire to have her caress me while blue-eyed little brunettes in blue shorts, copperheads in green boleros, and blurred boyish blondes in faded slacks passed by in the sun.

As a sort of compromise, I freely advocated whenever

and wherever possible the use of swimming pools with other girl-children. She adored brilliant water and was a remarkably smart diver. Comfortably robed, I would settle down in the rich postmeridian shade after my own demure dip, and there I would sit, with a dummy book or a bag of bonbons, or both, or nothing but my tingling glands, and watch her gambol, rubber-capped, bepearled, smoothly tanned, as glad as an ad, in her trim-fitted satin pants and shirred bra. Pubescent sweetheart! How smugly would I marvel that she was mine, mine, mine, and revise the recent matitudinal swoon to the moan of the mourning doves, and devise the late afternoon one, and slitting my sun-speared eyes, compare Lolita to whatever other nymphets parsimonious chance collected around her for my antho-logical delectation and judgment; and today, putting my hand on my ailing heart, I really do not think that any of them ever surpassed her in desirability, or if they did, it was so two or three times at the most, in a certain light, with certain perfumes blended in the air—once in the hope-less case of a pale Spanish child, the daughter of a heavy-jawed nobleman, and another time—*mais je divague*.

Naturally, I had to be always wary, fully realizing, in my lucid jealousy, the danger of those dazzling romps. I had only to turn away for a moment—to walk, say, a few steps in order to see if our cabin was at last ready after the morning change of linen—and Lo and Behold, upon returning, I would find the former, *les yeux perdus*, dipping and kicking her long-toed feet in the water on the stone edge of which she lolled, while, on either side of her, there crouched a *brun adolescent* whom her russet beauty and the quicksilver in the baby folds of her stomach were sure to cause to *se tordre*—oh Baudelaire!—in recurrent dreams for months to come.

I tried to teach her to play tennis so we might have

more amusements in common; but although I had been a good player in my prime, I proved to be hopeless as a teacher; and so, in California, I got her to take a number of very expensive lessons with a famous coach, a husky, wrinkled old-timer, with a harem of ball boys; he looked an awful wreck off the court, but now and then, when, in the course of a lesson, to keep up the exchange, he would put out as it were an exquisite spring blossom of a stroke and twang the ball back to his pupil, that divine delicacy of absolute power made me recall that, thirty years before, I had seen *him* in Cannes demolish the great Gobbert! Until she began taking those lessons, I thought she would never learn the game. On this or that hotel court I would drill Lo, and try to relive the days when in a hot gale, a daze of dust, and queer lassitude, I fed ball after ball to gay, innocent, elegant Annabel (gleam of bracelet, pleated white skirt, black velvet hair band). With every word of persistent advice I would only augment Lo's sullen fury. To our games, oddly enough, she preferred—at least, before we reached California—formless pat ball approximations—more ball hunting than actual play—with a wispy, weak, wonderfully pretty in an *ange gauche* way coeval. A helpful spectator, I would go up to that other child, and inhale her faint musky fragrance as I touched her forearm and held her knobby wrist, and push this way or that her cool thigh to show her the back-hand stance. In the meantime, Lo, bending forward, would let her sunny-brown curls hang forward as she stuck her racket, like a cripple's stick, into the ground and emitted a tremendous ugh of disgust at my intrusion. I would leave them to their game and look on, comparing their bodies in motion, a silk scarf round my throat; this was in south Arizona, I think—and the days had a lazy lining of warmth, and awkward Lo would slash at the ball and miss it, and curse, and send a simulacrum of a serve into the net, and show the wet glistening young down of her armpit as she brandished her racket in despair, and her even more insipid partner would dutifully rush out after every ball, and retrieve none; but both were enjoying themselves beautifully, and in clear ringing tones kept the exact score of their ineptitudes all the time.

One day, I remember, I offered to bring them cold drinks from the hotel, and went up the gravel path, and came back with two tall glasses of pineapple juice, soda and ice; and then a sudden void within my chest made me stop as I saw that the tennis court was deserted. I stooped to set down the glasses on a bench and for some reason, with a kind of icy vividness, saw Charlotte's face in death, and I glanced around, and noticed Lo in white shorts receding through the speckled shadow of a garden path in the company of a tall man who carried two tennis rackets. I sprang after them, but as I was crashing through the shrubbery, I saw, in an alternate vision, as if life's course constantly branched, Lo, in slacks, and her companion, in shorts, trudging up and down a small weedy area, and beating bushes with their rackets in listless search for their last lost ball.

I itemize these sunny nothings mainly to prove to my judges that I did everything in my power to give my Lolita a really good time. How charming it was to see her, a child herself, showing another child some of her few accomplishments, such as for example a special way of jumping rope. With her right hand holding her left arm behind her untanned back, the lesser nymphet, a diaphanous darling, would be all eyes, as the pavonine sun was all eyes on the gravel under the flowering trees, while in the midst of that oculate paradise, my freckled and raffish lass skipped, repeating the movements of so many others I had gloated over on the sun-shot, watered, damp-smelling sidewalks and ramparts of ancient Europe. Presently, she would hand the rope back to her little Spanish friend, and watch in her turn the repeated lesson, and brush away the hair from her brow, and fold her arms, and step on one toe with the other, or drop her hands loosely upon her still unflared hips, and I would satisfy myself that the damned staff had at last finished cleaning up our cottage; whereupon, flashing a smile to the shy, dark-haired page girl of my princess and thrusting my fatherly fingers deep into Lo's hair from behind, and then gently but firmly clasping them around the nape of her neck, I would lead my reluctant pet to our small home for a quick connection before dinner.

"Whose cat has scratched poor you?" a full-blown fleshy handsome woman of the repulsive type to which I was particularly attractive might ask me at the "lodge," during a table d'hôte dinner followed by dancing promised to Lo. This was one of the reasons why I tried to keep as far away from people as possible, while Lo, on the other hand, would do her utmost to draw as many potential witnesses into her orbit as she could.

She would be, figuratively speaking, wagging her tiny tail, her whole behind in fact as little bitches do—while some grinning stranger accosted us and began a bright conversation with a comparative study of license plates. "Long way from home!" Inquisitive parents, in order to pump Lo about me, would suggest her going to a movie with their children. We had some close shaves. The waterfall nuisance pursued me of course in all our caravansaries. But I never realized how wafery their wall substance was until one evening, after I had loved too loudly, a neighbor's masculine cough filled the pause as clearly as mine would have done; and next morning as I was having breakfast at the milk bar (Lo was a late sleeper, and I liked to bring her a pot of hot coffee in bed), my neighbor of the eve, an elderly fool wearing plain glasses on his long virtuous nose and a convention badge on his lapel, somehow managed to rig up a conversation with me, in the course of which he inquired, if my missus was like his missus a rather reluctant get-upper when not on the farm; and had not the hideous danger I was skirting almost suffocated me, I might have enjoyed the odd look of surprise on his thin-lipped weather-beaten face when I drily answered, as I slithered off my stool, that I was thank God a widower.

How sweet it was to bring that coffee to her, and then deny it until she had done her morning duty. And I was such a thoughtful friend, such a passionate father, such a good pediatrician, attending to all the wants of my little auburn brunette's body! My only grudge against nature was that I could not turn my Lolita inside out and apply voracious lips to her young matrix, her unknown heart, her nacreous liver, the sea-grapes of her lungs, her comely twin kidneys. On especially tropical afternoons, in the sticky closeness of the siesta, I liked the cool feel of armchair leather against my massive nakedness as I held her in my lap. There she would be, a typical kid picking her nose while engrossed in the lighter sections of a newspaper, as indifferent to my ecstasy as if it were something she had sat upon, a shoe, a doll, the handle of a tennis racket, and was too indolent to remove. Her eyes would follow the adventures of her favorite strip characters: there was one well-drawn sloppy bobby-soxer, with high cheekbones and angular gestures, that I was not above enjoying myself; she studied the photographic results of head-on collisions; she never doubted the reality of place, time and circumstance alleged to match the publicity pictures of naked-thighed beauties; and she was curiously fascinated by the photographs of local brides, some in full wedding apparel, holding bouquets and wearing glasses.

A fly would settle and walk in the vicinity of her navel or explore her tender pale areolas. She tried to catch it in her fist (Charlotte's method) and then would turn to the column Let's Explore Your Mind.

"Let's explore your mind. Would sex crimes be reduced if children obeyed a few don'ts? Don't play around public toilets. Don't take candy or rides from strangers. If picked up, mark down the license of the car."

". . . and the brand of the candy," I volunteered.

She went on, her cheek (recedent) against mine (pursuant); and this was a good day, mark, O reader!

"If you don't have a pencil, but are old enough to read—"

"We," I quip-quoted, "medieval mariners, have placed in this bottle—"

"If," she repeated, "you don't have a pencil, but are old enough to read and write—this is what the guy means, isn't it, you dope—scratch the number somehow on the roadside."

"With your little claws, Lolita."

3

She had entered my world, umber and black Humberland, with rash curiosity; she surveyed it with a shrug of amused distaste; and it seemed to me now that she was ready to turn away from it with something akin to plain repulsion. Never did she vibrate under my touch, and a strident "what d'you think you are doing?" was all I got for my pains. To the wonderland I had to offer, my fool preferred the corniest movies, the most cloying fudge. To think that between a Hamburger and a Humburger, she would—invariably, with icy precision—plump for the former. There is nothing more atrociously cruel than an adored child. Did I mention the name of that milk bar I visited a moment ago? It was, of all things, The Frigid Queen. Smiling a little sadly, I dubbed her My Frigid Princess. She did not see the wistful joke.

Oh, do not scowl at me, reader, I do not intend to convey the impression that I did not manage to be happy. Reader must understand that in the possession and thralldom of a nymphet the enchanted traveler stands, as it were, *beyond happiness*. For there is no other bliss on earth comparable to that of fondling a nymphet. It is *hors concours*, that bliss, it belongs to another class, another plane of sensitivity. Despite our tiffs, despite her nastiness, despite all the fuss and faces she made, and the vulgarity, and the danger, and the horrible hopelessness of it all, I still dwelled deep in my elected paradise—a paradise whose skies were the color of hell-flames—but still a paradise.

The able psychiatrist who studies my case—and whom by now Dr. Humbert has plunged, I trust, into a state of leporine fascination—is no doubt anxious to have me take my Lolita to the seaside and have me find there, at last, the "gratification" of a lifetime urge, and release from the "subconscious" obsession of an incomplete childhood romance with the initial little Miss Lee.

Well, comrade, let me tell you that I *did* look for a beach, though I also have to confess that by the time we reached its mirage of gray water, so many delights had already been granted me by my traveling companion that the search for a Kingdom by the Sea, a Sublimated Riviera, or whatnot, far from being the impulse of the subconscious, had become the rational pursuit of a purely theoretical thrill. The angels knew it, and arranged things accordingly. A visit to a plausible cove on the Atlantic side was completely messed up by foul weather. A thick damp sky, muddy waves, a sense of boundless but somehow matter-of-fact mist— what could be further removed from the crisp charm, the sapphire occasion and rosy contingency of my Riviera romance? A couple of semitropical beaches on the Gulf, though bright enough, were starred and spattered by venomous beasties and swept by hurricane winds. Finally, on a Californian beach, facing the phantom of the Pacific, I hit upon some rather perverse privacy in a kind of cave whence you could hear the shrieks of a lot of girl scouts taking their first surf bath on a separate part of the beach, behind rotting trees; but the fog was like a wet blanket, and the sand was gritty and clammy, and Lo was all goose-flesh and grit, and for the first time in my life I had as little desire for her as for a manatee. Perhaps, my learned readers may perk up if I tell them that even had we discovered a piece of sympathetic seaside somewhere, it would have come too late, since my real liberation had occurred much earlier: at the moment, in point of fact, when Annabel Haze, alias Dolores Lee, alias Loleeta, had appeared to me, golden and brown, kneeling, looking up, on that shoddy veranda, in a kind of fictitious, dishonest, but eminently satisfactory seaside arrangement (although there was nothing but a second-rate lake in the neighborhood).

So much for those special sensations, influenced, if not actually brought about, by the tenets of modern psychiatry. Consequently, I turned away—I headed my Lolita away—from beaches which were either too bleak when lone, or too populous when ablaze. However, in recollection, I suppose, of my hopeless hauntings of public parks in Europe, I was still keenly interested in outdoor activities and desirous of finding suitable playgrounds in the open where I had suffered such shameful privations. Here, too, I was to be thwarted. The disappointment I must now register (as I gently grade my story into an expression of the continuous risk and dread that ran through my bliss) should in no wise reflect on the lyrical, epic, tragic but never Arcadian American wilds. They are beautiful, heart-rendingly beautiful, those wilds, with a quality of wide-eyed, unsung, innocent surrender that my lacquered, toy-bright Swiss villages and exhaustively lauded Alps no longer possess. Innumerable lovers have clipped and kissed on the trim turf of old-world mountainsides, on the inner-spring moss, by a handy, hygienic rill, on rustic benches under the initialed oaks, and in so many *cabanes* in so many beech forests. But in the Wilds of America the open-air lover will not find it easy to indulge in the most ancient of all crimes and pastimes. Poisonous plants burn his sweetheart's buttocks, nameless insects sting his; sharp items of the forest floor prick his knees, insects hers; and all around there abides a sustained rustle of potential snakes—*que dis-je*, of semi-extinct dragons!—while the crablike seeds of ferocious flowers cling, in a hideous green crust, to gartered black sock and sloppy white sock alike.

I am exaggerating a little. One summer noon, just below timberline, where heavenly-hued blossoms that I would fain call larkspur crowded all along a purly mountain brook, we did find, Lolita and I, a secluded romantic spot, a hundred feet or so above the pass where we had left our car. The slope seemed untrodden. A last panting pine was taking a well-earned breather on the rock it had reached. A marmot whistled at us and withdrew. Beneath the lap-robe I had spread for Lo, dry flowers crepitated softly. Venus came and went. The jagged cliff crowning the upper talus and a tangle of shrubs growing below us seemed to offer us protection from sun and man alike. Alas, I had not reckoned with a faint side trail that curled up in cagey fashion among the shrubs and rocks a few feet from us.

It was then that we came closer to detection than ever before, and no wonder the experience curbed forever my yearning for rural amours.

I remember the operation was over, all over, and she was weeping in my arms;—a salutory storm of sobs after one of the fits of moodiness that had become so frequent with her in the course of that otherwise admirable year! I had just retracted some silly promise she had forced me to make in a moment of blind impatient passion, and there she was sprawling and sobbing, and pinching my caressing hand, and I was laughing happily, and the atrocious, unbelievable, unbearable, and, I suspect, eternal horror that I know *now* was still but a dot of blackness in the blue of my bliss; and so we lay, when with one of those jolts that have ended by knocking my poor heart out of its groove, I met the unblinking dark eyes of two strange and beautiful children, faunlet and nymphet, whom their identical flat dark hair and bloodless cheeks proclaimed siblings if not twins. They stood crouching and gaping at us, both in blue play-suits, blending with the mountain blossoms. I plucked at the lap-robe for desperate concealment—and within the same instant, something that looked like a polka-dotted pushball among the undergrowth a few paces away, went into a turning motion which was transformed into the gradually rising figure of a stout lady with a raven-black bob, who automatically added a wild lily to her bouquet, while staring over her shoulder at us from behind her lovely carved bluestone children.

Now that I have an altogether different mess on my conscience, I know that I am a courageous man, but in those days I was not aware of it, and I remember being surprised by my own coolness. With the quiet murmured order one gives a sweat-stained distracted cringing trained animal even in the worst of plights (what mad hope or hate makes the young beast's flanks pulsate, what black stars pierce the heart of the tamer!), I made Lo get up, and we decorously walked, and then indecorously scuttled down to the car. Behind it a nifty station wagon was parked, and a handsome Assyrian with a little blue-black beard, *un monsieur très bien*, in silk shirt and magenta slacks, presumably the corpulent botanist's husband, was gravely taking the picture of a signboard giving the altitude of the pass. It was well over 10,000 feet and I was quite out of breath; and with a scrunch and a skid we drove off, Lo still struggling with her clothes and swearing at me in language that I never dreamed little girls could know, let alone use.

There were other unpleasant incidents. There was the movie theatre once, for example. Lo at the time still had for the cinema a veritable passion (it was to decline into tepid condescension during her second high school year). We took in, voluptuously and indiscriminately, oh, I don't know, one hundred and fifty or two hundred programs during that one year, and during some of the denser periods of movie-going we saw many of the newsreels up to half-a-dozen times since the same weekly one went with different main pictures and pursued us from town to town. Her favorite kinds were, in this order: musicals, underworlders, westerners. In the first, real singers and dancers had unreal stage careers in an essentially grief-proof sphere of existence wherefrom death and truth were banned, and where, at the end, white-haired, dewy-eyed, technically deathless, the initially reluctant father of a show-crazy girl always finished by applauding her apotheosis on fabulous Broadway. The underworld was a world apart: there, heroic newspapermen were tortured, telephone bills ran to billions, and, in a robust atmosphere of incompetent marksmanship, villains were chased through sewers and storehouses by pathologically fearless cops (I was to give them less exercise). Finally there was the mahogany landscape, the florid-faced, blue-eyed roughriders, the prim pretty schoolteacher arriving in Roaring Gulch, the rearing horse, the spectacular stampede, the pistol thrust through the shivered windowpane, the stupendous fist fight, the crashing mountain of dusty old-fashioned furniture, the table used as a weapon, the timely somersault, the pinned hand still groping for the dropped bowie knife, the grunt, the sweet crash of fist against chin, the kick in the belly, the flying tackle; and immediately after a plethora of pain that would have hospitalized a Hercules (I should know by now), nothing to show but the rather becoming bruise on the bronzed cheek of the warmed-up hero embracing his gorgeous frontier bride. I remember one matinee in a small airless theatre crammed with children and reeking with the hot breath of popcorn. The moon was yellow above the neckerchiefed crooner, and his finger was on his strumstring, and his foot was on a pine log, and I had innocently encircled Lo's shoulder and approached my jawbone to her temple, when two harpies behind us started muttering the queerest things—I do not know if I understood aright, but what I thought I did, made me withdraw my gentle hand, and of course the rest of the show was fog to me.

Another jolt I remember is connected with a little burg we were traversing at night, during our return journey. Some twenty miles earlier I had happened to tell her that the day school she would attend at Beardsley was a rather high-class, non-coeducational one, with no modern nonsense, whereupon Lo treated me to one of those furious harangues of hers where entreaty and insult, self-assertion and double talk, vicious vulgarity and childish despair, were interwoven in an exasperating semblance of logic which prompted a semblance of explanation from me. Enmeshed in her wild words (swell chance . . . I'd be a sap if I took your opinion seriously . . . Stinker . . . You can't boss me . . . I despise you . . . and so forth), I drove through the slumbering town at a fifty-mile-per-hour pace in continuance of my smooth highway swoosh, and a twosome of patrolmen put their spotlight on the car, and told me to pull over. I shushed Lo who was automatically raving on. The men peered at her and me with malevolent curiosity. Suddenly all dimples, she beamed sweetly at them, as she never did at my orchideous masculinity; for, in a sense, my Lo was even more scared of the law than I—and when the kind officers pardoned us and servilely we crawled on, her eyelids closed and fluttered as she mimicked limp prostration.

At this point I have a curious confession to make. You will laugh—but really and truly I somehow never managed to find out quite exactly what the legal situation was. I do not know it yet. Oh, I have learned a few odds and ends. Alabama prohibits a guardian from changing the ward's residence without an order of the court; Minnesota, to whom I take off my hat, provides that when a relative assumes permanent care and custody of any child under fourteen, the authority of a court does not come into play. Query: is the stepfather of a gaspingly adorable pubescent pet, a stepfather of only one month's standing, a neurotic widower of mature years and small but independent means, with the parapets of Europe, a divorce and a few madhouses behind him, is he to be considered a relative, and thus a natural guardian? And if not, must I, and could I reasonably dare notify some Welfare Board and file a petition (how do you file a petition?), and have a court's agent investigate meek, fishy me and dangerous Dolores Haze? The many books on marriage, rape, adoption and so on, that I guiltily consulted at the public libraries of big and small towns, told me nothing beyond darkly insinuating that the state is the super-guardian of minor children. Pilvin and Zapel, if I remember their names right, in an impressive volume on the legal side of marriage, completely ignored stepfathers with motherless girls on their hands and knees. My best friend, a social service monograph (Chicago, 1936), which was dug out for me at great pains from a dusty storage recess by an innocent old spinster, said "There is no principle that every minor must have a guardian; the court is passive and enters the fray only when the child's situation becomes conspicuously perilous." A guardian, I concluded, was appointed only when he expressed his solemn and formal desire; but months might elapse before he was given notice to appear at a hearing and grow his pair of gray wings, and in the meantime the fair daemon child was legally left to her own devices which, after all, was the case of Dolores Haze. Then came the hearing. A few questions from the bench, a few reassuring answers from the attorney, a smile, a nod, a light drizzle outside, and the appointment was made. And still I dared not. Keep away, be a mouse, curl up in your hole. Courts became extravagantly active only when there was some monetary question involved: two greedy guardians, a robbed orphan, a third, still greedier, party. But here all was in perfect order, an inventory had been made, and her mother's small property was waiting untouched for Dolores Haze to grow up. The best policy seemed to be to refrain from any application. Or would some busybody, some Humane Society, butt in if I kept *too* quiet?

Friend Farlow, who was a lawyer of sorts and ought to have been able to give me some solid advice, was too much occupied with Jean's cancer to do anything more than what he had promised—namely, to look after Charlotte's meager estate while I recovered very gradually from the shock of her death. I had conditioned him into believing Dolores was my natural child, and so could not expect him to bother his head about the situation. I am, as the reader must have gathered by now, a poor businessman; but neither ignorance nor indolence should have prevented me from seeking professional advice elsewhere. What stopped me was the awful feeling that if I meddled with fate in any way and tried to rationalize her fantastic gift, that gift would be snatched away like that palace on the mountain top in the Oriental tale which vanished whenever a prospective owner asked its custodian how come a strip of sunset sky was clearly visible from afar between black rock and foundation.

I decided that at Beardsley (the site of Beardsley College for Women) I would have access to works of reference that I had not yet been able to study, such as Woerner's Treatise "On the American Law of Guardianship" and certain United States Children's Bureau Publications. I also decided that anything was better for Lo than the demoralizing idleness in which she lived. I could persuade her to do so many things—their list might stupefy a professional educator; but no matter how I pleaded or stormed, I could never make her read any other book than the so-called comic books or stories in magazines for American females. Any literature a peg higher smacked to her of school, and though theoretically willing to enjoy *A Girl of the Limberlost* or the *Arabian Nights*, or *Little Women*, she was quite sure she would not fritter away her "vacation" on such highbrow reading matter.

I now think it was a great mistake to move east again and have her go to that private school in Beardsley, instead of somehow scrambling across the Mexican border while the scrambling was good so as to lie low for a couple of years in subtropical bliss until I could safely marry my little Creole for I must confess that depending on the condition of my glands and ganglia, I could switch in the course of the same day from one pole of insanity to the other—from the thought that around 1950 I would have to get rid somehow of a difficult adolescent whose magic nymphage had evaporated—to the thought that with patience and luck

I might have her produce eventually a nymphet with my blood in her exquisite veins, a Lolita the Second, who would be eight or nine around 1960, when I would still be *dans la force de l'âge*; indeed, the telescopy of my mind, or un-mind, was strong enough to distinguish in the remoteness of time a *vieillard encore vert*—or was it green rot?—bizarre, tender, salivating Dr. Humbert, practicing on supremely lovely Lolita the Third the art of being a granddad.

In the days of that wild journey of ours, I doubted not that as father to Lolita the First I was a ridiculous failure. I did my best; I read and reread a book with the unintentionally biblical title *Know Your Own Daughter*, which I got at the same store where I bought Lo, for her thirteenth birthday, a de luxe volume with commercially "beautiful" illustrations, of Andersen's *The Little Mermaid*. But even at our very best moments, when we sat reading on a rainy day (Lo's glance skipping from the window to her wrist watch and back again), or had a quiet hearty meal in a crowded diner, or played a childish game of cards, or went shopping, or silently stared, with other motorists and their children, at some smashed, blood-bespattered car with a young woman's shoe in the ditch (Lo, as we drove on: "That was the exact type of moccasin I was trying to describe to that jerk in the store"); on all those random occasions, I seemed to myself as implausible a father as she seemed to be a daughter. Was, perhaps, guilty locomotion instrumental in vitiating our powers of impersonation? Would improvement be forthcoming with a fixed domicile and a routine schoolgirl's day?

In my choice of Beardsley I was guided not only by the fact of there being a comparatively sedate school for girls located there, but also by the presence of the women's college. In my desire to get myself *casé*, to attach myself somehow to some patterned surface which my stripes would blend with, I thought of a man I knew in the department of French at Beardsley College; he was good enough to use my textbook in his classes and had attempted to get me over once to deliver a lecture. I had no intention of doing so, since, as I have once remarked in the course of these confessions, there are few physiques I loathe more than the heavy low-slung pelvis, thick calves and deplorable complexion of the average coed (in whom I see, maybe, the coffin of coarse female flesh within which my nymphets are buried alive); but I did crave for a label, a background, and a simulacrum, and, as presently will become clear, there was a reason, a rather zany reason, why old Gaston Godin's company would be particularly safe.

Finally, there was the money question. My income was cracking under the strain of our joy-ride. True, I clung to the cheaper motor courts; but every now and then, there would be a loud hotel de luxe, or a pretentious dude ranch, to mutilate our budget; staggering sums, moreover, were expended on sightseeing and Lo's clothes, and the old Haze bus, although a still vigorous and very devoted machine, necessitated numerous minor and major repairs. In one of our strip maps that has happened to survive among the papers which the authorities have so kindly allowed me to use for the purpose of writing my statement, I find some jottings that help me compute the following. During that extravagant year 1947–1948, August to August, lodgings and food cost us around 5,500 dollars; gas, oil and repairs, 1,234, and various extras almost as much; so that during about 150 days of actual motion (we covered about 27,000 miles!) plus some 200 days of interpolated standstills, this modest *rentier* spent around 8,000 dollars, or better say 10,000 because, unpractical as I am, I have surely forgotten a number of items.

And so we rolled East, I more devastated than braced

with the satisfaction of my passion, and she glowing with health, her bi-iliac garland still as brief as a lad's, although she had added two inches to her stature and eight pounds to her weight. We had been everywhere. We had really seen nothing. And I catch myself thinking today that our long journey had only defiled with a sinuous trail of slime the lovely, trustful, dreamy, enormous country that by then, in retrospect, was no more to us than a collection of dog-eared maps, ruined tour books, old tires, and her sobs in the night— every night, every night—the moment I feigned sleep.

4

When, through decorations of light and shade, we drove up to 14 Thayer Street, a grave little lad met us with the keys and a note from Gaston who had rented the house for us. My Lo, without granting her new surroundings one glance, unseeingly turned on the radio to which instinct led her and lay down on the living room sofa with a batch of old magazines which in the same precise and blind manner she landed by dipping her hand into the nether anatomy of a lamp table.

I really did not mind where to dwell provided I could lock my Lolita up somewhere; but I had, I suppose, in the course of my correspondence with vague Gaston, vaguely visualized a house of ivied brick. Actually the place bore a dejected resemblance to the Haze home (a mere 400 miles distant): it was the same sort of dull gray frame affair with a shingled roof and dull green drill awnings; and the rooms, though smaller and furnished in a more consistent plush-and-plate style, were arranged in much the same order. My study turned out to be, however, a much larger room, lined from floor to ceiling with some two thousand books on chemistry which my landlord (on sabbatical leave for the time being) taught at Beardsley College.

I had hoped Beardsley School for girls, an expensive day school, with lunch thrown in and a glamorous gymnasium, would, while cultivating all those young bodies, provide some formal education for their minds as well. Gaston Godin, who was seldom right in his judgment of American habitus, had warned me that the institution might turn out to be one of those where girls are taught, as he put it with a foreigner's love for such things: "not to spell very well, but to smell very well." I don't think they achieved even that.

At my first interview with headmistress Pratt, she approved of my child's "nice blue eyes" (blue! Lolita!) and of my own friendship with that "French genius" (a genius! Gaston!)—and then, having turned Dolly over to a Miss Cormorant, she wrinkled her brow in a kind of *recueillement* and said:

"We are not so much concerned, Mr. Humbird, with having our students become bookworms or be able to reel off all the capitals of Europe which nobody knows anyway, or learn by heart the dates of forgotten battles. What we are concerned with is the adjustment of the child to group life. This is why we stress the four D's: Dramatics, Dance, Debating and Dating. We are confronted by certain facts. Your delightful Dolly will presently enter an age group where dates, dating, date dress, date book, date etiquette, mean as much to her as, say, business, business connections, business success, mean to you, or as much as [smiling] the happiness of my girls means to me. Dorothy Humbird is already involved in a whole system of social life which consists, whether we like it or not, of hot-dog stands, corner drugstores, malts and cokes, movies, square-dancing, blanket parties on beaches, and even hair-fixing parties! Naturally at Beardsley School we disapprove of some of these activities; and we rechannel others into more constructive directions. But we do try to turn our backs on the fog and squarely face the sunshine. To put it briefly, while adopting certain teaching techniques, we are more interested in communication than in composition. That is, with due respect to Shakespeare and others, we want our girls to *communicate* freely with the live world around them rather than plunge into musty old books. We are still groping perhaps, but we grope intelligently, like a gynecologist feeling a tumor. We think, Dr. Humburg, in organismal and organizational terms. We have done away with the mass of irrelevant topics that have traditionally been presented to young girls, leaving no place, in former days, for the knowledges and the skills, and the attitudes they will need in managing their lives and—as the cynic might add—the lives of their husbands. Mr. Humberson, let us put it this way: the position of a star is important, but the most practical spot for an icebox in the kitchen may be even more important to the budding housewife. You say that all you expect a child to obtain from school is a sound education. But what do we mean by education? In the old days it was in the main a verbal phenomenon; I mean, you could have a child learn by heart a good encyclopedia and he or she would know as much as or more than a school could offer. Dr. Hummer, do you realize that for the modern pre-adolescent child, medieval dates are of less vital value than weekend ones [twinkle]?—to repeat a pun that I heard the Beardsley college psychoanalyst permit herself the other day. We live not only in a world of thoughts, but also in a world of things. Words without experience are meaningless. What on earth can Dorothy Hummerson care for Greece and the Orient with their harems and slaves?"

This program rather appalled me, but I spoke to two intelligent ladies who had been connected with the school, and they affirmed that the girls did quite a bit of sound reading and that the "communication" line was more or less ballyhoo aimed at giving old-fashioned Beardsley School a financially remunerative modern touch, though actually it remained as prim as a prawn.

Another reason attracting me to that particular school may seem funny to some readers, but it was very important to me, for that is the way I am made. Across our street, exactly in front of our house, there was, I noticed, a gap of weedy wasteland, with some colorful bushes and a pile of bricks and a few scattered planks, and the foam of shabby mauve and chrome autumn roadside flowers; and through that gap you could see a shimmery section of School Rd., running parallel to our Thayer St., and immediately beyond that, the playground of the school. Apart from the psychological comfort this general arrangement should afford me by keeping Dolly's day adjacent to mine, I immediately foresaw the pleasure I would have in distinguishing from my study-bedroom, by means of powerful binoculars, the statistically inevitable percentage of nymphets among the other girl-children playing around Dolly during recess; unfortunately, on the very first day of school, workmen arrived and put up a fence some way down the gap, and in no time a construction of tawny wood maliciously arose beyond that fence utterly blocking my magic vista; and as soon as they had erected a sufficient amount of material to spoil everything, those absurd builders suspended their work and never appeared again.

5

In a street called Thayer Street, in the residential green, fawn, and golden of a mellow academic townlet, one was bound to have a few amiable fine-dayers yelping at you. I prided myself on the exact temperature of my relations with them: never rude, always aloof. My west-door neighbor, who might have been a businessman or a college teacher, or both, would speak to me once in a while as he barbered some late garden blooms or watered his car, or, at a later date, defrosted his driveway (I don't mind if these verbs are all wrong), but my brief grunts, just sufficiently articulate to sound like conventional assents or interrogative pause-fillers, precluded any evolution toward chumminess. Of the two houses flanking the bit of scrubby waste opposite, one was closed, and the other contained two professors of English, tweedy and short-haired Miss Lester and fadedly feminine Miss Fabian, whose only subject of brief sidewalk conversation with me was (God bless their tact!) the young loveliness of my daughter and the naïve charm of Gaston Godin. My east-door neighbor was by far the most dangerous one, a sharp-nosed character whose late brother had been attached to the College as Superintendent of Buildings and Grounds. I remember her waylaying Dolly, while I stood at the living-room window, feverishly awaiting my darling's return from school. The odious spinster, trying to conceal her morbid inquisitiveness under a mask of dulcet goodwill, stood leaning on her slim umbrella (the sleet had just stopped, a cold wet sun had sidled out), and Dolly, her brown coat open despite the raw weather, her structural heap of books pressed against her stomach, her knees showing pink above her clumsy wellingtons, a sheepish frightened little smile flitting over and off her snubnosed face, which—owing perhaps to the pale wintry light—looked almost plain, in a rustic, German, *Mägdlein*-like way, as she stood there and dealt with Miss East's questions "And where is your mother, my dear? And what is your poor father's occupation? And where did you live before?" Another time the loathsome creature accosted me with a welcoming whine—but I evaded her; and a few days later there came from her a note in a blue-margined envelope, a nice mixture of poison and treacle, suggesting

Dolly come over on a Sunday and curl up in a chair to look through the "loads of beautiful books my dear mother gave me when I was a child, instead of having the radio on at full blast till all hours of the night."

I had also to be careful in regard to a Mrs. Holigan, a charwoman and cook of sorts whom I had inherited with the vacuum cleaner from the previous tenants. Dolly got lunch at school, so that this was no trouble, and I had become adept at providing her with a big breakfast and warming up the dinner that Mrs. Holigan prepared before leaving. That kindly and harmless woman had, thank God, a rather bleary eye that missed details, and I had become a great expert in bedmaking; but still I was continuously obsessed by the feeling that some fatal stain had been left somewhere, or that, on the rare occasions where Holigan's presence happened to coincide with Lo's, simple Lo might succumb to buxom sympathy in the course of a cozy kitchen chat. I often felt we lived in a lighted house of glass, and that any moment some thin-lipped parchment face would peer through a carelessly unshaded window to obtain a free glimpse of things that the most jaded *voyeur* would have paid a small fortune to watch.

6

A word about Gaston Godin. The main reason why I enjoyed—or at least tolerated with relief—his company was the spell of absolute security that his ample person cast on my secret. Not that he knew it; I had no special reason to confide in him, and he was much too self-centered and abstract to notice or suspect anything that might lead to a frank question on his part and a frank answer on mine. He spoke well of me to Beardsleyans, he was my good herald. Had he discovered *mes goûts* and Lolita's status, it would have interested him only insofar as throwing some light on the simplicity of my attitude toward *him*, which attitude was as free of polite strain as it was of ribald allusions; for despite his colorless mind and dim memory, he was perhaps aware that I knew more about him than the burghers of Beardsley did. He was a flabby, dough-faced, melancholy bachelor tapering upward to a pair of narrow, not quite level shoulders and a conical pear-head which had sleek black hair on one side and only a few plastered wisps on the other. But the lower part of his body was enormous, and he ambulated with a curious elephantine stealth by means of phenomenally stout legs. He always wore black, even his tie was black; he seldom bathed; his English was a burlesque. And, nonetheless, everybody considered him to be a supremely lovable, lovably freakish fellow! Neighbors pampered him; he knew by name all the small boys in our vicinity (he lived a few blocks away from me) and had some of them clean his sidewalk and burn leaves in his back yard, and bring wood from his shed, and even perform simple chores about the house, and he would feed them fancy chocolates, with *real* liqueurs inside—in the privacy of an orientally furnished den in his basement, with amusing daggers and pistols arrayed on the moldy, rug-adorned walls among the camouflaged hot-water pipes. Upstairs he had a studio—he painted a little, the old fraud. He had decorated its sloping wall (it was really not more than a garret) with large photographs of pensive André Gide, Tchaïkovsky, Norman Douglas, two other well-known English writers, Nijinsky (all thighs and fig leaves), Harold D. Doublename (a misty-eyed left-wing professor at a Midwestern university) and Marcel Proust. All these poor people seemed about to fall on you from their inclined plane. He had also an album with snapshots of all the Jackies and Dickies of the neighborhood, and when I happened to thumb through it and make some casual remark, Gaston would purse his fat lips and murmur with a wistful pout *"Oui, ils sont gentils."* His brown eyes would roam around the various sentimental and artistic bric-a-brac present, and his own banal *toiles* (the conventionally primitive eyes, sliced guitars, blue nipples and geometrical designs of the day), and with a vague gesture toward a painted wooden bowl or veined vase, he would say *"Prenez donc une de ces poires. La bonne dame d'en face m'en offre plus que je n'en peux savourer."* Or: *"Missise Taille Lore vient de me donner ces dahlias, belles fleurs que j'exècre."* (Somber, sad, full of world-weariness.)

For obvious reasons, I preferred my house to his for the games of chess we had two or three times weekly. He looked like some old battered idol as he sat with his pudgy hands in his lap and stared at the board as if it were a corpse. Wheezing he would meditate for ten minutes— then make a losing move. Or the good man, after even more thought, might utter: *Au roi!* with a slow old-dog woof that had a gargling sound at the back of it which made his jowls wabble; and then he would lift his circumflex eyebrows with a deep sigh as I pointed out to him that he was in check himself.

Sometimes, from where we sat in my cold study I could hear Lo's bare feet practicing dance techniques in the living room downstairs; but Gaston's outgoing senses were comfortably dulled, and he remained unaware of those naked rhythms—and-one, and-two, and-one, and-two, weight transferred on a straight right leg, leg up and out to the side, and-one, and-two, and only when she started jumping, opening her legs at the height of the jump, and flexing one leg, and extending the other, and flying, and landing on her toes—only then did my pale, pompous, morose opponent rub his head or cheek as if confusing those distant thuds with the awful stabs of my formidable Queen.

Sometimes Lola would slouch in while we pondered the board—and it was every time a treat to see Gaston, his elephant eye still fixed on his pieces, ceremoniously rise to shake hands with her, and forthwith release her limp fingers, and without looking once at her, descend again into his chair to topple into the trap I had laid for him. One day around Christmas, after I had not seen him for a fortnight or so, he asked me *"Et toutes vos fillettes, elles vont bien?"* from which it became evident to me that he had multiplied my unique Lolita by the number of sartorial categories his downcast moody eye had glimpsed during a whole series of her appearances: blue jeans, a skirt, shorts, a quilted robe.

I am loath to dwell so long on the poor fellow (sadly enough, a year later, during a voyage to Europe, from which he did not return, he got involved in a *sale histoire*, in Naples of all places!). I would have hardly alluded to him at all had not his Beardsley existence had such a queer bearing on my case. I need him for my defense. There he was, devoid of any talent whatsoever, a mediocre teacher, a worthless scholar, a glum repulsive fat old invert, highly contemptuous of the American way of life, triumphantly ignorant of the English language—there he was in priggish New England, crooned over by the old and caressed by the young—oh, having a grand time and fooling everybody; and here was I.

7

I am now faced with the distasteful task of recording a definite drop in Lolita's morals. If her share in the ardors she kindled had never amounted to much, neither had pure lucre ever come to the fore. But I was weak, I was not wise, my schoolgirl nymphet had me in thrall. With the human element dwindling, the passion, the tenderness, and the torture only increased; and of this she took advantage.

Her weekly allowance, paid to her under condition she fulfill her basic obligations, was twenty-one cents at the start of the Beardsley era—and went up to one dollar five before its end. This was a more than generous arrangement seeing she constantly received from me all kinds of small presents and had for the asking any sweetmeat or movie under the moon—although, of course, I might fondly demand an additional kiss, or even a whole collection of assorted caresses, when I knew she coveted very badly some item of juvenile amusement. She was, however, not easy to deal with. Only very listlessly did she earn her three pennies—or three nickels—per day; and she proved to be a cruel negotiator whenever it was in her power to deny me certain life-wrecking, strange, slow paradisal philters without which I could not live more than a few days in a row, and which, because of the very nature of love's languor, I could not obtain by force. Knowing the magic and might of her own soft mouth, she managed— during one schoolyear!—to raise the bonus price of a fancy embrace to three, and even four bucks. O Reader! Laugh not, as you imagine me, on the very rack of joy noisily emitting dimes and quarters, and great big silver dollars like some sonorous, jingly and wholly demented machine vomiting riches; and in the margin of that leaping epilepsy she would firmly clutch a handful of coins in her little fist, which, anyway, I used to pry open afterwards unless she gave me the slip, scrambling away to hide her loot. And just as every other day I would cruise all around the school area and on comatose feet visit drugstores, and peer into foggy lanes, and listen to receding girl laughter in between my heart throbs and the falling leaves, so every now and then I would burgle her room and scrutinize torn papers in the wastebasket with the painted roses, and look under the pillow of the virginal bed I had just made myself. Once I found eight one-dollar notes in one of her books (fittingly—*Treasure Island*), and once a hole in the wall behind Whistler's Mother yielded as much as twenty-four dollars and some change—say twenty-four sixty—which I quietly removed, upon which, next day, she accused, to my face, honest Mrs. Holigan of being a filthy thief. Eventually, she lived up to her I.Q. by finding a safer hoarding place which I never discovered; but by that time I had brought prices down drastically by having her earn the hard and nauseous way permission to participate in the school's theatrical program; because what I feared most was not that she might ruin me, but that she might accumulate sufficient cash to run away. I believe the poor fierce-eyed child had figured out that with a mere fifty dollars in her purse she might somehow reach Broadway or Hollywood—or the foul kitchen of a diner (Help Wanted) in a dismal ex-prairie state, with the wind blowing, and the stars blinking, and the cars, and the bars, and the barmen, and everything soiled, torn, dead.

8

I did my best, your Honor, to tackle the problem of boys. Oh, I used even to read in the Beardsley *Star* a so-called Column for Teens, to find out how to behave!

A word to fathers. Don't frighten away daughter's friend. Maybe it is a bit hard for you to realize that now the boys are finding her attractive. To you she is still a little girl. To the boys she's charming and fun, lovely and gay. They like her. Today you clinch big deals in an executive's office, but yesterday you were just highschool Jim carrying Jane's school books. Remember? Don't you want your daughter, now that her turn has come, to be happy in the admiration and company of boys she likes? Don't you want them to have wholesome fun together?

Wholesome fun? Good Lord!

Why not treat the young fellows as guests in your house? Why not make conversation with them? Draw them out, make them laugh and feel at ease?

Welcome, fellow, to this bordello.

If she breaks the rules don't explode out loud in front of her partner in crime. Let her take the brunt of your displeasure in private. And stop making the boys feel she's the daughter of an old ogre.

First of all the old ogre drew up a list under "absolutely forbidden" and another under "reluctantly allowed." Absolutely forbidden were dates, single or double or triple—the next step being of course mass orgy. She might visit a candy bar with her girl friends, and there giggle-chat with occasional young males, while I waited in the car at a discreet distance; and I promised her that if her group were invited by a socially acceptable group in Butler's Academy for Boys for their annual ball (heavily chaperoned, of course), I might consider the question whether a girl of fourteen can don her first "formal" (a kind of gown that makes thin-armed teen-agers look like flamingoes). Moreover, I promised her to throw a party at our house to which she would be allowed to invite her prettier girl friends and the nicer boys she would have met by that time at the Butler dance. But I was quite positive that as long as my regime lasted she would never, never be permitted to go with a youngster in rut to a movie, or neck in a car, or go to boy-girl parties at the houses of schoolmates, or indulge out of my earshot in boy-girl telephone conversations, even if "only discussing his relations with a friend of mine."

Lo was enraged by all this—called me a lousy crook and worse—and I would probably have lost my temper had I not soon discovered, to my sweetest relief, that what really angered her was my depriving her not of a specific satisfaction but of a general right. I was impinging, you see, on the conventional program, the stock pastimes, the "things that are done," the routine of youth; for there is nothing more conservative than a child, especially a girl-child, be she the most auburn and russet, the most mythopoeic nymphet in October's orchard-haze.

Do not misunderstand me. I cannot be absolutely certain that in the course of the winter she did not manage to have, in a casual way, improper contacts with unknown young fellows; of course, no matter how closely I controlled her leisure, there would constantly occur unaccounted-for time leaks with overelaborate explanations to stop them up in retrospect; of course, my jealousy would constantly catch its jagged claw in the fine fabrics of nymphet falsity; but I did definitely feel—and can now vouchsafe for the accuracy of my feeling—that there was no reason for serious alarm. I felt that way not because I never once discovered any palpable hard young throat to crush among the masculine mutes that flickered somewhere in the background; but because it was to me "overwhelmingly obvious" (a favorite expression with my aunt Sybil) that all varieties of high school boys—from the perspiring nincompoop whom "holding hands" thrills, to the self-sufficient rapist with pustules and a souped-up car—equally bored my sophisticated young mistress. "All this noise about boys gags me," she had scrawled on the inside of a schoolbook, and underneath, in Mona's hand (Mona is due any minute now), there was the sly quip: "What about Rigger?" (due too).

Faceless, then, are the chappies I happened to see in her company. There was for instance Red Sweater who one day, the day we had the first snow—saw her home; from the parlor window I observed them talking near our porch. She wore her first cloth coat with a fur collar; there was a small brown cap on my favorite hairdo—the fringe in front and the swirl at the sides and the natural curls at the back—and her damp-dark moccasins and white socks were more sloppy than ever. She pressed as usual her books to her chest while speaking or listening, and her feet gestured all the time: she would stand on her left instep with her right toe, remove it backward, cross her feet, rock slightly, sketch a few steps, and then start the series all over again. There was Windbreaker who talked to her in front of a restaurant one Sunday afternoon while his mother and sister attempted to walk me away for a chat; I dragged along and looked back at my only love. She had developed more than one conventional mannerism, such as the polite adolescent way of showing one is literally "doubled up" with laughter by inclining one's head, and so (as she sensed my call), still feigning helpless merriment, she walked backward a couple of steps, and then faced about, and walked toward me with a fading smile. On the other hand, I greatly liked—perhaps because it reminded me of her first unforgettable confession—her trick of sighing "oh dear!" in humorous wistful submission to fate, or emitting a long "no-o" in a deep almost growling undertone when the blow of fate had actually fallen. Above all—since we are speaking of movement and youth—I liked to see her spinning up and down Thayer Street on her beautiful young bicycle: rising on the pedals to work on them lustily, then sinking back in a languid posture while the speed wore itself off; and then she would stop at our mailbox and, still astride, would flip through a magazine she found there, and put it back, and press her tongue to one side of her upperlip and push off with her foot, and again sprint through pale shade and sun.

On the whole she seemed to me better adapted to her surroundings than I had hoped she would be when considering my spoiled slave-child and the bangles of demeanor she naïvely affected the winter before in California. Although I could never get used to the constant state of anxiety in which the guilty, the great, the tenderhearted live, I felt I was doing my best in the way of mimicry. As I lay on my narrow studio bed after a session of adoration and despair in Lolita's cold bedroom, I used to review the concluded day by checking my own image as it prowled rather than passed before the mind's red eye. I watched dark-and-handsome, not un-Celtic, probably high-church, possibly very high-church, Dr. Humbert see his daughter off to school. I watched him greet with his slow smile and pleasantly arched thick black ad-eyebrows good Mrs. Holigan, who smelled of the plague (and would head, I knew, for master's gin at the first opportunity). With Mr. West, retired executioner or writer of religious tracts—who cared?—I saw neighbor what's his name, I think they are French or Swiss, meditate in his frank-windowed study over a typewriter, rather gaunt-profiled, an almost Hitlerian cowlick on his pale brow. Weekends, wearing a well-tailored overcoat and brown gloves, Professor H. might be seen with his daughter strolling to Walton Inn (famous for its violet-ribboned china bunnies and chocolate boxes among which you sit and wait for a "table for two" still filthy with your predecessor's crumbs). Seen on weekdays, around one P.M., saluting with dignity Argus-eyed East while maneuvering the car out of the garage and around the damned evergreens, and down onto the slippery road. Raising a cold eye from book to clock in the positively sultry Beardsley College library, among bulky young women caught and petrified in the overflow of human knowledge. Walking across the campus with the college clergyman, the Rev. Rigger (who also taught Bible in Beardsley School). "Somebody told me her mother was a celebrated actress killed in an airplane accident. Oh? My mistake, I presume. Is that so? I see. How sad." (Sublimating her mother, eh?) Slowly pushing my little pram through the labyrinth of the supermarket, in the wake of Professor W., also a slow-moving and gentle widower with the eyes of a goat. Shoveling the snow in my shirt-sleeves, a voluminous black and white muffler around my neck. Following with no show of rapacious haste (even taking time to wipe my feet on the mat) my schoolgirl daughter into the house. Taking Dolly to the dentist—pretty nurse beaming at her—old magazines—*ne montrez pas vos zhambes*. At dinner with Dolly in town, Mr. Edgar H. Humbert was seen eating his steak in the conti-nental knife-and-fork manner. Enjoying, in duplicate, a concert: two marble-faced, becalmed Frenchmen sitting side by side, with Monsieur H. H.'s musical little girl on her father's right, and the musical little boy of Professor W. (father spending a hygienic evening in Providence) on Monsieur G. G.'s left. Opening the garage, a square of light that engulfs the car and is extinguished. Brightly pajamaed, jerking down the window shade in Dolly's bedroom. Saturday morning, unseen, solemnly weighing the winter-bleached lassie in the bathroom. Seen and heard Sunday morning, no churchgoer after all, saying don't be too late, to Dolly who is bound for the covered court. Letting in a queerly observant schoolmate of Dolly's: "First time I've seen a man wearing a smoking jacket, sir—except in movies, of course."

<h1 style="text-align:center">9</h1>

Her girl friends, whom I had looked forward to meet, proved on the whole disappointing. There was Opal Something, and Linda Hall, and Avis Chapman, and Eva Rosen, and Mona Dahl (save one, all these names are approximations, of course). Opal was a bashful, formless, bespectacled, bepimpled creature who doted on Dolly who bullied her. With Linda Hall the school tennis champion, Dolly played singles at least twice a week: I suspect Linda was a true nymphet, but for some unknown reason she did not come— was perhaps not allowed to come—to our house; so I recall her only as a flash of natural sunshine on an indoor court. Of the rest, none had any claims to nymphetry except Eva Rosen. Avis was a plump lateral child with hairy legs, while Mona, though handsome in a coarse sensual way and only a year older than my aging mistress, had obviously long ceased to be a nymphet, if she ever had been one. Eva Rosen, a displaced little person from France, was on the other hand a good example of a not strikingly beautiful child revealing to the perspicacious amateur some of the basic elements of nymphet charm, such as a perfect pubescent figure and lingering eyes and high cheekbones. Her glossy copper hair had Lolita's silkiness, and the features of her delicate milky-white face with pink lips and silverfish eyelashes were less foxy than those of her likes—the great clan of intra-racial redheads; nor did she sport their green uniform but wore, as I remember her, a lot of black or cherry dark—a very smart black pullover, for instance, and high-heeled black shoes, and garnet-red fingernail polish. I spoke French to her (much to Lo's disgust). The child's tonalities were still admirably pure, but for school words and play words she resorted to current American and then a slight Brooklyn accent would crop up in her speech, which was amusing in a little Parisian who went to a select New England school with phoney British aspirations. Unfortunately, despite "that French kid's uncle" being "a millionaire," Lo dropped Eva for some reason before I had had time to enjoy in my modest way her fragrant presence in the Humbert open house. The reader knows what importance I attached to having a bevy of page girls, consolation prize nymphets, around my Lolita. For a while, I endeavored to interest my senses in Mona Dahl who was a good deal around, especially during the spring term when Lo and she got so enthusiastic about dramatics. I have often wondered what secrets outrageously treacherous Dolores Haze had imparted to Mona while blurting out to me by urgent and well-paid request various really incredible details concerning an affair that Mona had had with a marine at the seaside. It was characteristic of Lo that she chose for her closest chum that elegant, cold, lascivious, experienced young female whom I once heard (misheard, Lo swore) cheerfully say in the hallway to Lo— who had remarked that her (Lo's) sweater was of virgin wool: "The only thing about you that is, kiddo . . ." She had a curiously husky voice, artificially waved dull dark hair, earrings, amber-brown prominent eyes and luscious lips. Lo said teachers had remonstrated with her on her loading herself with so much costume jewelry. Her hands trembled. She was burdened with a 150 I.Q. And I also know she had a tremendous chocolate-brown mole on her womanish back which I inspected the night Lo and she had worn low-cut pastel-colored, vaporous dresses for a dance at the Butler Academy.

I am anticipating a little, but I cannot help running my memory all over the keyboard of that school year. In meeting my attempts to find out what kind of boys Lo knew, Miss Dahl was elegantly evasive. Lo who had gone to play tennis at Linda's country club had telephoned she might be a full half hour late, and so, would I entertain Mona who was coming to practice with her a scene from *The Taming of the Shrew*. Using all the modulations, all the allure of manner and voice she was capable of and staring at me with perhaps—could I be mistaken?—a faint gleam of crystalline irony, beautiful Mona replied: "Well, sir, the fact is Dolly is not much concerned with mere boys. Fact is, we are rivals. She and I have a crush on the Reverend Rigger." (This was a joke—I have already mentioned that gloomy giant of a man, with the jaw of a horse: he was to bore me to near murder with his impressions of Switzerland at a tea party for parents that I am unable to place correctly in terms of time.)

How had the ball been? Oh, it had been a riot. A what? A panic. Terrific, in a word. Had Lo danced a lot? Oh, not a frightful lot, just as much as she could stand. What did she, languorous Mona, think of Lo? Sir? Did she think Lo was doing well at school? Gosh, she certainly was quite a kid. But her general behavior was—? Oh, she was a swell kid. But still? "Oh, she's a doll," concluded Mona, and sighed abruptly, and picked up a book that happened to lie at hand, and with a change of expression, falsely furrowing her brow, inquired: "Do tell me about Ball Zack, sir. Is he really that good?" She moved up so close to my chair that I made out through lotions and creams her uninteresting skin scent. A sudden odd thought stabbed me: was my Lo playing the pimp? If so, she had found the wrong substitute. Avoiding Mona's cool gaze, I talked literature for a minute. Then Dolly arrived—and slit her pale eyes at us. I left the two friends to their own devices. One of the latticed squares in a small cobwebby casement window at the turn of the staircase was glazed with ruby, and that raw wound among the unstained rectangles and its asymmetrical position—a knight's move from the top—always strangely disturbed me.

10

Sometimes . . . Come on, how often exactly, Bert? Can you recall four, five, more such occasions? Or would no human heart have survived two or three? Sometimes (I have nothing to say in reply to your question), while Lolita would be haphazardly preparing her homework, sucking a pencil, lolling sideways in an easy chair with both legs over its arm, I would shed all my pedagogic restraint, dismiss all our quarrels, forget all my masculine pride—and literally crawl on my knees to your chair, my Lolita! You would give me one look—a gray furry question mark of a look: "Oh no, not again" (incredulity, exasperation); for you never deigned to believe that I could, without any specific designs, ever crave to bury my face in your plaid skirt, my darling! The fragility of those bare arms of yours—how I longed to enfold them, all your four limpid lovely limbs, a folded colt, and take your head between my unworthy hands, and pull the temple-skin back on both sides, and kiss your chinesed eyes, and—"Pulease, leave me alone, will you," you would say, "for Christ's sake leave me alone." And I would get up from the floor while you looked on, your face deliberately twitching in imitation of my *tic nerveux*. But never mind, never mind, I am only a brute, never mind, let us go on with my miserable story.

11

One Monday forenoon, in December I think, Pratt asked me to come over for a talk. Dolly's last report had been poor, I knew. But instead of contenting myself with some such plausible explanation of this summons, I imagined all sorts of horrors, and had to fortify myself with a pint of my "pin" before I could face the interview. Slowly, all Adam's apple and heart, I went up the steps of the scaffold.

A huge woman, gray-haired, frowsy, with a broad flat nose and small eyes behind black-rimmed glasses—"Sit down," she said, pointing to an informal and humiliating hassock, while she perched with ponderous spryness on the arm of an oak chair. For a moment or two, she peered at me with smiling curiosity. She had done it at our first meeting, I recalled, but I could afford then to scowl back. Her eye left me. She lapsed into thought—probably assumed. Making up her mind she rubbed, fold on fold, her dark gray flannel skirt at the knee, dispelling a trace of chalk or something. Then she said, still rubbing, not looking up:

"Let me ask a blunt question, Mr. Haze. You are an old-fashioned Continental father, aren't you?"

"Why, no," I said, "conservative, perhaps, but not what you would call old-fashioned."

She sighed, frowned, then clapped her big plump hands together in a let's-get-down-to-business manner, and again fixed her beady eyes upon me.

"Dolly Haze," she said, "is a lovely child, but the onset of sexual maturing seems to give her trouble."

I bowed slightly. What else could I do?

"She is still shuttling," said Miss Pratt, showing how with her liver-spotted hands, "between the anal and genital zones of development. Basically she is a lovely—"

"I beg your pardon," I said, "what zones?"

"That's the old-fashioned European in you!" cried Pratt delivering a slight tap on my wrist watch and suddenly disclosing her dentures. "All I mean is that biologic and psychologic drives—do you smoke?—are not fused in Dolly, do not fall so to speak into a—into a rounded pattern." Her hands held for a moment an invisible melon.

"She is attractive, bright though careless" (breathing heavily, without leaving her perch, the woman took time out to look at the lovely child's report sheet on the desk at her right). "Her marks are getting worse and worse. Now I wonder, Mr. Haze—" Again the false meditation.

"Well," she went on with zest, "as for me, I do smoke, and, as dear Dr. Pierce used to say: I'm not proud of it but I jeest love it." She lit up and the smoke she exhaled from her nostrils was like a pair of tusks.

"Let me give you a few details, it won't take a moment. Now let me see [rummaging among her papers]. She is defiant toward Miss Redcock and impossibly rude to Miss Cormorant. Now here is one of our special research reports: Enjoys singing with group in class though mind seems to wander. Crosses her knees and wags left leg to rhythm. Type of by-words: a two-hundred-forty-two word area of the commonest pubescent slang fenced in by a number of obviously European polysyllabics. Sighs a good deal in class. Let me see. Yes. Now comes the last week in November. Sighs a good deal in class. Chews gum vehemently. Does not bite her nails though if she did, this would conform better to her general pattern—scientifically speaking, of course. Menstruation, according to the subject, well established. Belongs at present to no church organization. By the way, Mr. Haze, her mother was—? Oh, I see. And you are—? Nobody's business is, I suppose, God's business. Something else we wanted to know. She has no regular home duties, I understand. Making a princess of your Dolly, Mr. Haze, eh? Well, what else have we got here? Handles books gracefully. Voice pleasant. Giggles rather often. A littly dreamy. Has private jokes of her own, transposing for instance the first letters of some of her teacher's names. Hair light and dark brown, lustrous—well [laughing] you are aware of *that*, I suppose. Nose unobstructed, feet high-arched, eyes—let me see, I had here somewhere a still more recent report. Aha, here we are. Miss Gold says Dolly's tennis form is excellent to superb, even better than Linda Hall's, but concentration and point-accumulation are just "poor to fair." Miss Cormorant cannot decide whether Dolly has exceptional emotional control or none at all. Miss Horn reports she— I mean, Dolly—cannot verbalize her emotions, while according to Miss Cole Dolly's metabolic efficiency is superfine. Miss Molar thinks Dolly is myopic and should see a good ophthalmologist, but Miss Redcock insists that the girl simulates eye-strain to get away with scholastic incompetence. And to conclude, Mr. Haze, our researchers are wondering about something really crucial. Now I want to ask you something. I want to know if your poor wife, or yourself, or anyone else in the family—I understand she has several aunts and a maternal grandfather in California?—oh, *had!*—I'm sorry—well, we all wonder if anybody in the family has instructed Dolly in the process of mammalian reproduction. The general impression is that fifteen-year-old Dolly remains morbidly uninterested in sexual matters, or to be exact, represses her curiosity in order to save her ignorance and self-dignity. All right— fourteen. You see, Mr. Haze, Beardsley School does not believe in bees and blossoms, and storks and love birds, but it does believe very strongly in preparing its students for mutually satisfactory mating and successful child rearing. We feel Dolly could make excellent progress if only she would put her mind to her work. Miss Cormorant's report is significant in that respect. Dolly is inclined to be, mildly speaking, impudent. But all feel that *primo*, you should have your family doctor tell her the facts of life and, *secundo*, that you allow her to enjoy the company of her schoolmates' brothers at the Junior Club or in Dr. Rigger's organization, or in the lovely homes of our parents."

"She may meet boys at her own lovely home," I said.

"I hope she will," said Pratt buoyantly. "When we questioned her about her troubles, Dolly refused to discuss the home situation, but we have spoken to some of her friends and really—well, for example, we insist you un-veto her nonparticipation in the dramatic group. You just must allow her to take part in *The Hunted Enchanters*. She was such a perfect little nymph in the try-out, and sometime in spring the author will stay for a few days at Beardsley College and may attend a rehearsal or two in our new auditorium. I mean it is all part of the fun of being young and alive and beautiful. You must understand—"

"I always thought of myself," I said, "as a very understanding father."

"Oh no doubt, no doubt, but Miss Cormorant thinks, and I am inclined to agree with her, that Dolly is obsessed by sexual thoughts for which she finds no outlet, and will tease and martyrize other girls, or even our younger instructors because *they* do have innocent dates with boys."

Shrugged my shoulders. A shabby émigré.

"Let us put our two heads together, Mr. Haze. What on earth is wrong with that child?"

"She seems quite normal and happy to me," I said (disaster coming at last? was I found out? had they got some hypnotist?).

"What worries me," said Miss Pratt looking at her watch and starting to go over the whole subject again, "is that both teachers and schoolmates find Dolly antagonistic, dissatisfied, cagey—and everybody wonders why you are so firmly opposed to all the natural recreations of a normal child."

"Do you mean sex play?" I asked jauntily, in despair, a cornered old rat.

"Well, I certainly welcome this civilized terminology," said Pratt with a grin. "But this is not quite the point. Under the auspices of Beardsley School, dramatics, dances and other natural activities are not technically sex play, though girls do meet boys, if that is what you object to."

"All right," I said, my hassock exhaling a weary sigh. "You win. She can take part in that play. Provided male parts are taken by female parts."

"I am always fascinated," said Pratt, "by the admirable way foreigners—or at least naturalized Americans—use our rich language. I'm sure Miss Gold, who conducts the play group, will be overjoyed. I notice she is one of the few teachers that seem to like—I mean who seem to find Dolly manageable. This takes care of general topics, I guess; now comes a special matter. We are in trouble again."

Pratt paused truculently, then rubbed her index finger under her nostrils with such vigor that her nose performed a kind of war dance.

"I'm a frank person," she said, "but conventions are conventions, and I find it difficult . . . Let me put it this way . . . The Walkers, who live in what we call around here the Duke's Manor, you know the great gray house on the hill—they send their two girls to our school, and we have the niece of President Moore with us, a really gracious child, not to speak of a number of other prominent children. Well, under the circumstances, it is rather a jolt when Dolly, who looks like a little lady, uses words which you as a foreigner probably simply do not know or do not understand. Perhaps it might be better—Would you like me to have Dolly come up here right away to discuss things? No? You see—oh well, let's have it out. Dolly has written a most obscéne four-letter word which our Dr.

Cutler tells me is low-Mexican for urinal with her lipstick on some health pamphlets which Miss Redcock, who is getting married in June, distributed among the girls, and we thought she should stay after hours—another half hour at least. But if you like—"

"No," I said, "I don't want to interfere with rules. I shall talk to her later. I shall thrash it out."

"Do," said the woman rising from her chair arm. "And perhaps we can get together again soon, and if things do not improve we might have Dr. Cutler analyze her."

Should I marry Pratt and strangle her?

". . . And perhaps your family doctor might like to examine her physically—just a routine check-up. She is in Mushroom—the last classroom along that passage."

Beardsley School, it may be explained, copied a famous girls' school in England by having "traditional" nicknames for its various classrooms: Mushroom, Room-In 8, B-room, Room-BA and so on. Mushroom was smelly, with a sepia print of Reynolds' "Age of Innocence" above the chalkboard, and several rows of clumsy-looking pupil desks. At one of these, my Lolita was reading the chapter on "Dialogue" in Baker's *Dramatic Technique*, and all was very quiet, and there was another girl with a very naked, porcelain-white neck and wonderful platinum hair, who sat in front reading too, absolutely lost to the world and interminably winding a soft curl around one finger, and I sat beside Dolly just behind that neck and that hair, and unbuttoned my overcoat and for sixty-five cents plus the permission to participate in the school play, had Dolly put her inky, chalky, red-knuckled hand under the desk. Oh, stupid and reckless of me, no doubt, but after the torture I had been subjected to, I simply had to take advantage of a combination that I knew would never occur again.

12

Around Christmas she caught a bad chill and was examined by a friend of Miss Lester, a Dr. Ilse Tristramson (hi, Ilse, you were a dear, uninquisitive soul, and you touched my dove very gently). She diagnosed bronchitis, patted Lo on the back (all its bloom erect because of the fever) and put her to bed for a week or longer. At first she "ran a temperature" in American parlance, and I could not resist the exquisite caloricity of unexpected delights—Venus febriculosa—though it was a very languid Lolita that moaned and coughed and shivered in my embrace. And as soon as she was well again, I threw a Party with Boys.

Perhaps I had drunk a little too much in preparation for the ordeal. Perhaps I made a fool of myself. The girls had decorated and plugged in a small fir tree—German custom, except that colored bulbs had superseded wax candles. Records were chosen and fed into my landlord's phonograph. Chic Dolly wore a nice gray dress with fitted bodice and flared skirt. Humming, I retired to my study upstairs—and then every ten or twenty minutes I would come down like an idiot just for a few seconds; to pick up ostensibly my pipe from the mantelpiece or hunt for the newspaper; and with every new visit these simple actions became harder to perform, and I was reminded of the dreadfully distant days when I used to brace myself to casually enter a room in the Ramsdale house where Little Carmen was on.

The party was not a success. Of the three girls invited, one did not come at all, and one of the boys brought his cousin Roy, so there was a superfluity of two boys, and the cousins knew all the steps, and the other fellows could hardly dance at all, and most of the evening was spent in messing up the kitchen, and then endlessly jabbering about what card game to play, and sometime later, two girls and four boys sat on the floor of the living room, with all windows open, and played a word game which Opal could not be made to understand, while Mona and Roy, a lean handsome lad, drank ginger ale in the kitchen, sitting on the table and dangling their legs, and hotly discussing Predestination and the Law of Averages. After they had all gone my Lo said ugh, closed her eyes, and dropped into a chair with all four limbs starfished to express the utmost disgust and exhaustion and swore it was the most revolting bunch of boys she had ever seen. I bought her a new tennis racket for that remark.

January was humid and warm, and February fooled the forsythia: none of the townspeople had ever *seen* such weather. Other presents came tumbling in. For her birthday I bought her a bicycle, the doe-like and altogether charming machine already mentioned—and added to this a *History of Modern American Painting*: her bicycle manner, I mean her approach to it, the hip movement in mounting, the grace and so on, afforded me supreme pleasure; but my attempt to refine her pictorial taste was a failure; she wanted to know if the guy noon-napping on Doris Lee's hay was the father of the pseudo-voluptuous hoyden in the foreground, and could not understand why I said Grant Wood or Peter Hurd was good, and Reginald Marsh or Frederick Waugh awful.

13

By the time spring had touched up Thayer Street with yellow and green and pink, Lolita was irrevocably stage-struck. Pratt, whom I chanced to notice one Sunday lunching with some people at Walton Inn, caught my eye from afar and went through the motion of sympathetically and discreetly clapping her hands while Lo was not looking. I detest the theatre as being a primitive and putrid form, historically speaking; a form that smacks of stone-age rites and communal nonsense despite those individual injections of genius, such as, say, Elizabethan poetry which a closeted reader automatically pumps out of the stuff. Being much occupied at the time with my own literary labors, I did not bother to read the complete text of *The Enchanted Hunters*, the playlet in which Dolores Haze was assigned the part of a farmer's daughter who imagines herself to be a wood-land witch, or Diana, or something, and who, having got hold of a book on hypnotism, plunges a number of lost hunters into various entertaining trances before falling in her turn under the spell of a vagabond poet (Mona Dahl). That much I gleaned from bits of crumpled and poorly typed script that Lo sowed all over the house. The coinci-dence of the title with the name of an unforgettable inn was pleasant in a sad little way: I wearily thought I had better not bring it to my own enchantress's notice, lest a brazen accusation of mawkishness hurt me even more than her failure to notice it for herself had done. I assumed the playlet was just another, practically anonymous, version of some banal legend. Nothing prevented one, of course, from supposing that in quest of an attractive name the founder of the hotel had been immediately and solely influenced by the chance fantasy of the second-rate muralist he had hired, and that subsequently the hotel's name had suggested the play's title. But in my credulous, simple, benevolent mind I happened to twist it the other way round, and without giving the whole matter much thought really, supposed that mural, name and title had all been derived from a common source, from some local tradition, which I, an alien unversed in New England lore, would not be supposed to know. In consequence I was under the impression (all this quite casu-ally, you understand, quite outside any orbit of importance) that the accursed playlet belonged to the type of whimsey for juvenile consumption, arranged and rearranged many times, such as *Hansel and Gretel* by Richard Roe, or *The Sleeping Beauty* by Dorothy Doe, or *The Emperor's New Clothes* by Maurice Vermont and Marion Rumpelmeyer—all this to be found in any *Plays for School Actors* or *Let's Have a Play!* In other words, I did not know—and would not have cared, if I did—that actually *The Enchanted Hunters* was a quite recent and technically original composition which had been produced for the first time only three or four months ago by a highbrow group in New York. To me—inasmuch as I could judge from my charmer's part—it seemed to be a pretty dismal kind of fancy work, with echoes from Lenormand and Maeterlinck and various quiet British dreamers. The red-capped, uniformly attired hunters, of which one was a banker, another a plumber, a third a policeman, a fourth an undertaker, a fifth an underwriter, a sixth an escaped convict (you see the possibilities!), went through a complete change of mind in Dolly's Dell, and remembered their real lives only as dreams or nightmares from which little Diana had aroused them; but a seventh Hunter (in a *green* cap, the fool) was a Young Poet, and he insisted, much to Diana's annoyance, that she and the entertainment provided (dancing nymphs, and elves, and monsters) were his, the Poet's, invention. I understand that finally, in utter disgust at this cocksureness, barefooted Dolores was to lead check-trousered Mona to the paternal farm behind the Perilous Forest to prove to the braggard she was not a poet's fancy, but a rustic, down-to-brown-earth lass—and a last-minute kiss was to enforce the play's profound message, namely, that mirage and reality merge in love. I considered it wiser not to criticize the thing in front of Lo: she was so healthily engrossed in "problems of expression," and so charmingly did she put her narrow Florentine hands together, batting her eyelashes and pleading with me not to come to rehearsals as some ridiculous parents did because she wanted to dazzle me with a perfect First Night—and because I was, anyway, always butting in and saying the wrong thing, and cramping her style in the presence of other people.

There was one very special rehearsal . . . my heart, my heart . . . there was one day in May marked by a lot of gay flurry—it all rolled past, beyond my ken, immune to my memory, and when I saw Lo next, in the late afternoon, balancing on her bike, pressing the palm of her hand to the damp bark of a young birch tree on the edge of our lawn, I was so struck by the radiant tenderness of her smile that for an instant I believed all our troubles gone. "Can you remember," she said, "what was the name of that hotel, *you* know [nose puckered], come on, you know—with those white columns and the marble swan in the lobby? Oh, you know [noisy exhalation of breath]—the hotel where you raped me. Okay, skip it. I mean, was it [almost in a whisper] The Enchanted Hunters? Oh, it was? [musingly] Was it?"—and with a yelp of amorous vernal laughter she slapped the glossy bole and tore uphill, to the end of the street, and then rode back, feet at rest on stopped pedals, posture relaxed, one hand dreaming in her print-flowered lap.

14

Because it supposedly tied up with her interest in dance and dramatics, I had permitted Lo to take piano lessons with a Miss Emperor (as we French scholars may conveniently call her) to whose blue-shuttered little white house a mile or so beyond Beardsley Lo would spin off twice a week. One Friday night toward the end of May (and a week or so after the very special rehearsal Lo had not had me attend) the telephone in my study, where I was in the act of mopping up Gustave's—I mean Gaston's—king's side,

229

rang and Miss Emperor asked if Lo was coming next Tuesday because she had missed last Tuesday's and today's lessons. I said she would by all means—and went on with the game. As the reader may well imagine, my faculties were now impaired, and a move or two later, with Gaston to play, I noticed through the film of my general distress that he could collect my queen; he noticed it too, but thinking it might be a trap on the part of his tricky opponent, he demurred for quite a minute, and puffed and wheezed, and shook his jowls, and even shot furtive glances at me, and made hesitating half-thrusts with his pudgily bunched fingers—dying to take that juicy queen and not daring—and all of a sudden he swooped down upon it (who knows if it did not teach him certain later audacities?), and I spent a dreary hour in achieving a draw. He finished his brandy and presently lumbered away, quite satisfied with this result (*mon pauvre ami, je ne vous ai jamais revu et quoiqu'il y ait bien peu de chance que vous voyiez mon livre, permettez-moi de vous dire que je vous serre la main bien cordialement, et que toutes mes fillettes vous saluent*). I found Dolores Haze at the kitchen table, consuming a wedge of pie, with her eyes fixed on her script. They rose to meet mine with a kind of celestial vapidity. She remained singularly unruffled when confronted with my discovery, and said *d'un petit air faussement contrit* that she knew she was a very wicked kid, but simply had not been able to resist the enchantment, and had used up those music hours—O Reader, My Reader!—in a nearby public park rehearsing the magic forest scene with Mona. I said "fine"—and stalked to the telephone. Mona's mother answered: "Oh yes, she's in" and retreated with a mother's neutral laugh of polite pleasure to shout off stage "Roy calling!" and the very next moment Mona rustled up, and forthwith, in a low monotonous not untender voice started berating Roy for something he had said or done and I interrupted her, and presently Mona was saying in her humblest, sexiest contralto, "yes, sir," "surely, sir," "I am alone to blame, sir, in this unfortunate business," (what elocution! what poise!) "honest, I feel very bad about it"—and so on and so forth as those little harlots say.

So downstairs I went clearing my throat and holding my heart. Lo was now in the living room, in her favorite over-stuffed chair. As she sprawled there, biting at a hangnail and mocking me with her heartless vaporous eyes, and all the time rocking a stool upon which she had placed the heel of an outstretched shoeless foot, I perceived all at once with a sickening qualm how much she had changed since I first met her two years ago. Or had this happened during those last two weeks? *Tendresse*? Surely that was an exploded myth. She sat right in the focus of my incandescent anger. The fog of all lust had been swept away leaving nothing but this dreadful lucidity. Oh, she had changed! Her complexion was now that of any vulgar untidy highschool girl who applies shared cosmetics with grubby fingers to an unwashed face and does not mind what soiled texture, what pustulate epidermis comes in contact with her skin. Its smooth tender bloom had been so lovely in former days, so bright with tears, when I used to roll, in play, her tousled head on my knee. A coarse flush had now replaced that innocent fluorescence. What was locally known as a "rabbit cold" had painted with flaming pink the edges of her contemptuous nostrils. As in terror I lowered my gaze, it mechanically slid along the underside of her tensely stretched bare thigh—how polished and muscular her legs had grown! She kept her wide-set eyes, clouded-glass gray and slightly bloodshot, fixed upon me, and I saw the stealthy thought showing through them that perhaps after all Mona was right, and she, orphan Lo, could expose me without getting penalized herself. How wrong I was. How mad I was! Everything about her was of the same exasperating impenetrable order—the strength of her shapely legs, the dirty sole of her white sock, the thick sweater she wore despite the closeness of the room, her wenchy smell, and especially the dead end of her face with its strange flush and freshly made-up lips. Some of the red had left stains on her front teeth, and I was struck by a ghastly recollection—the evoked image not of Monique, but of another young prostitute in a bell-house, ages ago, who had been snapped up by somebody else before I had time to decide whether her mere youth warranted my risking some appalling disease, and who had just such flushed prominent *pommettes* and a dead *maman*, and big front teeth, and a bit of dingy red ribbon in her country-brown hair.

"Well, speak," said Lo. "Was the corroboration satisfactory?"

"Oh, yes," I said. "Perfect. Yes. And I do not doubt you two made it up. As a matter of fact, I do not doubt you have told her everything about us."

"Oh, yah?"

I controlled my breath and said: "Dolores, this must stop right away. I am ready to yank you out of Beardsley and lock you up you know where, but this must stop. I am ready to take you away the time it takes to pack a suitcase. This must stop or else anything may happen."

"Anything may happen, huh?"

I snatched away the stool she was rocking with her heel and her foot fell with a thud on the floor.

"Hey," she cried, "take it easy."

"First of all you go upstairs," I cried in my turn,—and simulataneously grabbed at her and pulled her up. From that moment, I stopped restraining my voice, and we continued yelling at each other, and she said unprintable things. She said she loathed me. She made monstrous faces

at me, inflating her cheeks and producing a diabolical plop-
ping sound. She said I had attempted to violate her several
times when I was her mother's roomer. She said she was
sure I had murdered her mother. She said she would sleep
with the very first fellow who asked her and I could do
nothing about it. I said she was to go upstairs and show
me all her hiding places. It was a strident and hateful scene.
I held her by her knobby wrist and she kept turning and
twisting it this way and that, surreptitiously trying to find
a weak point so as to wrench herself free at a favorable
moment, but I held her quite hard and in fact hurt her
rather badly for which I hope my heart may rot, and once
or twice she jerked her arm so violently that I feared her
wrist might snap, and all the while she stared at me with
those unforgettable eyes where cold anger and hot tears
struggled, and our voices were drowning the telephone,
and when I grew aware of its ringing she instantly escaped.

With people in movies I seem to share the services of
the machina telephonica and its sudden god. This time it
was an irate neighbor. The east window happened to be
agape in the living room, with the blind mercifully down,
however; and behind it the damp black night of a sour
New England spring had been breathlessly listening to us.
I had always thought that type of haddocky spinster with
the obscene mind was the result of considerable literary
inbreeding in modern fiction; but now I am convinced that
prude and prurient Miss East—or to explode her incog-
nito, Miss Fenton Lebone—had been probably protruding
three-quarter-way from her bedroom window as she strove
to catch the gist of our quarrel.

". . . This racket . . . lacks all sense of . . ." quacked
the receiver, "we do not live in a tenement here. I must
emphatically . . ."

I apologized for my daughter's friends being so loud.

Young people, you know—and cradled the next quack and a half.

Downstairs the screen door banged. Lo? Escaped?

Through the casement on the stairs I saw a small impetuous ghost slip through the shrubs; a silvery dot in the dark—hub of bicycle wheel—moved, shivered, and she was gone.

It so happened that the car was spending the night in a repair shop downtown. I had no other alternative than to pursue on foot the winged fugitive. Even now, after more than three years have heaved and elapsed, I cannot visualize that spring-night street, that already so leafy street, without a gasp of panic. Before their lighted porch Miss Lester was promenading Miss Fabian's dropsical dackel. Mr. Hyde almost knocked it over. Walk three steps and run three. A tepid rain started to drum on the chestnut leaves. At the next corner, pressing Lolita against an iron railing, a blurred youth held and kissed—no, not her, mistake. My talons still tingling, I flew on.

Half a mile or so east of number fourteen, Thayer Street tangles with a private lane and a cross street; the latter leads to the town proper; in front of the first drugstore, I saw—with what melody of relief!—Lolita's fair bicycle waiting for her. I pushed instead of pulling, pulled, pushed, pulled, and entered. Look out! Some ten paces away Lolita, through the glass of a telephone booth (membranous god still with us), cupping the tube, confidentially hunched over it, slit her eyes at me, turned away with her treasure, hurriedly hung up, and walked out with a flourish.

"Tried to reach you at home," she said brightly. "A great decision has been made. But first buy me a drink, dad."

She watched the listless pale fountain girl put in the ice, pour in the coke, add the cherry syrup—and my heart was bursting with love-ache. That childish wrist. My lovely child. You have a lovely child, Mr. Humbert. We always admire her as she passes by. Mr. Pim watched Pippa suck in the concoction.

J'ai toujours admiré l'œuvre ormonde du sublime Dublinois. And in the meantime the rain had become a voluptuous shower.

"Look," she said as she rode the bike beside me, one foot scraping the darkly glistening sidewalk, "look, I've decided something. I want to leave school. I hate that school. I hate the play, I really do! Never go back. Find another. Leave at once. Go for a long trip again. But *this* time we'll go wherever *I* want, won't we?"

I nodded. My Lolita.

"I choose? *C'est entendu?*" she asked wobbling a little beside me. Used French only when she was a very good little girl.

"Okay. *Entendu.* Now hop-hop-hop, Lenore, or you'll get soaked." (A storm of sobs was filling my chest.)

She bared her teeth and after her adorable school-girl fashion, leaned forward, and away she sped, my bird.

Miss Lester's finely groomed hand held a porch-door open for a waddling old dog *qui prenait son temps*.

Lo was waiting for me near the ghostly birch tree.

"I am drenched," she declared at the top of her voice. "Are you glad? To hell with the play! See what I mean?"

An invisible hag's claw slammed down an upper-floor window.

In our hallway, ablaze with welcoming lights, my Lolita peeled off her sweater, shook her gemmed hair, stretched towards me two bare arms, raised one knee:

"Carry me upstairs, please. I feel sort of romantic to-night."

It may interest physiologists to learn, at this point, that

I have the ability—a most singular case, I presume—of shedding torrents of tears throughout the other tempest.

15

The brakes were relined, the waterpipes unclogged, the valves ground, and a number of other repairs and improvements were paid for by not very mechanically-minded but prudent papa Humbert, so that the late Mrs. Humbert's car was in respectable shape when ready to undertake a new journey.

We had promised Beardsley School, good old Beardsley School, that we would be back as soon as my Hollywood engagement came to an end (inventive Humbert was to be, I hinted, chief consultant in the production of a film dealing with "existentialism," still a hot thing at the time). Actually I was toying with the idea of gently trickling across the Mexican border—I was braver now than last year—and there deciding what to do with my little concubine who was now sixty inches tall and weighed ninety pounds. We had dug out our tour books and maps. She had traced our route with immense zest. Was it thanks to those theatricals that she had now outgrown her juvenile jaded airs and was so adorably keen to explore rich reality? I experienced the queer lightness of dreams that pale but warm Sunday morning when we abandoned Professor Chem's puzzled house and sped along Main Street toward the four-lane highway. My Love's striped, black-and-white, cotton frock, jaunty blue cap, white socks and brown moccasins were not quite in keeping with the large beautifully cut aquamarine on a silver chainlet, which gemmed her throat: a spring rain gift from me. We passed the New Hotel, and she laughed. "A penny for your thoughts," I said and she stretched out her palm at once, but at that moment I had to apply the brakes rather abruptly at a red light. As we pulled up, another car came to a gliding stop alongside, and a very striking looking, athletically lean young woman (where had I seen her?) with a high complexion and shoulder-length brilliant bronze hair, greeted Lo with a ringing "Hi!"—and then, addressing me, effusively, edusively (placed!), stressing certain words, said: "What a *shame* it was to *tear* Dolly away from the play— you should have *heard* the author *raving* about her after that rehearsal—" "Green light, you dope," said Lo under her breath, and simultaneously, waving in bright adieu a bangled arm, Joan of Arc (in a performance we saw at the local theatre) violently outdistanced us to swerve into Campus Avenue.

"Who was it exactly? Vermont or Rumpelmeyer?"

"No—Edusa Gold—the gal who coaches us."

"I was not referring to her. Who exactly concocted that play?"

"Oh! Yes, of course. Some old woman, Clare Something, I guess. There was quite a crowd of them there."

"So she complimented you?"

"Complimented my eye—she kissed me on my pure brow"—and my darling emitted that new yelp of merriment which—perhaps in connection with her theatrical mannerisms—she had lately begun to affect.

"You are a funny creature, Lolita," I said—or some such words. "Naturally, I am overjoyed you gave up that absurd stage business. But what is curious is that you dropped the whole thing only a week before its natural climax. Oh, Lolita, you should be careful of those surrenders of yours. I remember you gave up Ramsdale for camp, and camp for a joyride, and I could list other abrupt changes in your disposition. You must be careful. There are things that should never be given up. You must persevere. You should try to be a little nicer to me, Lolita. You should also watch your diet. The tour of your thigh, you know, should not

237

exceed seventeen and a half inches. More might be fatal (I was kidding, of course). We are now setting out on a long happy journey. I remember—"

16

I remember as a child in Europe gloating over a map of North America that had "Appalachian Mountains" boldly running from Alabama up to New Brunswick, so that the whole region they spanned—Tennessee, the Virginias, Pennsylvania, New York, Vermont, New Hampshire and Maine, appeared to my imagination as a gigantic Switzerland or even Tibet, all mountain, glorious diamond peak upon peak, giant conifers, *le montagnard émigré* in his bear skin glory, and *Felis tigris goldsmithi*, and Red Indians under the catalpas. That it all boiled down to a measly suburban lawn and a smoking garbage incinerator, was appalling. Farewell, Appalachia! Leaving it, we crossed Ohio, the three states beginning with "I," and Nebraska— ah, that first whiff of the West! We travelled very leisurely, having more than a week to reach Wace, Continental Divide, where she passionately desired to see the Ceremonial Dances marking the seasonal opening of Magic Cave, and at least three weeks to reach Elphinstone, gem of a western State where she yearned to climb Red Rock from which a mature screen star had recently jumped to her death after a drunken row with her gigolo.

Again we were welcomed to wary motels by means of inscriptions that read:

"We wish you to feel at home while here. *All* equipment was carefully checked upon your arrival. Your license number is on record here. Use hot water sparingly. We reserve the right to eject without notice any objectionable person. Do not throw waste material of *any* kind in the toilet bowl. Thank you. Call again. The Management. P.S.

238

We consider our guests the Finest People of the World."

In these frightening places we paid ten for twins, flies queued outside at the screenless door and successfully scrambled in, the ashes of our predecessors still lingered in the ashtrays, a woman's hair lay on the pillow, one heard one's neighbor hanging his coat in his closet, the hangers were ingeniously fixed to their bars by coils of wire so as to thwart theft, and, in crowning insult, the pictures above the twin beds were identical twins. I also noticed that commercial fashion was changing. There was a tendency for cabins to fuse and gradually form the caravansary, and, lo (she was not interested but the reader may be), a second story was added, and a lobby grew in, and cars were removed to a communal garage, and the motel reverted to the good old hotel.

I now warn the reader not to mock me and my mental daze. It is easy for him and me to decipher *now* a past destiny; but a destiny in the making is, believe me, not one of those honest mystery stories where all you have to do is keep an eye on the clues. In my youth I once read a French detective tale where the clues were actually in italics; but that is not McFate's way—even if one does learn to recognize certain obscure indications.

For instance: I would not swear that there was not at least one occasion, prior to, or at the very beginning of, the Midwest lap of our journey, when she managed to convey some information to, or otherwise get into contact with, a person or persons unknown. We had stopped at a gas station, under the sign of Pegasus, and she had slipped out of her seat and escaped to the rear of the premises while the raised hood, under which I had bent to watch the mechanic's manipulations, hid her for a moment from my sight. Being inclined to be lenient, I only shook my benign head though strictly speaking such visits were taboo, since I felt instinctively that toilets—as also telephones—happened to be, for reasons unfathomable, the points where my destiny was liable to catch. We all have such fateful objects—it may be a recurrent landscape in one case, a number in another—carefully chosen by the gods to attract events of special significance for us: here shall John always stumble; there shall Jane's heart always break.

Well—my car had been attended to, and I had moved it away from the pumps to let a pickup truck be serviced—when the growing volume of her absence began to weigh upon me in the windy grayness. Not for the first time, and not for the last, had I stared in such dull discomfort of mind at those stationary trivialities that look almost surprised, like staring rustics, to find themselves in the stranded traveller's field of vision: that green garbage can, those very black, very whitewalled tires for sale, those bright cans of motor oil, that red icebox with assorted drinks, the four, five, seven discarded bottles within the incompleted crossword puzzle of their wooden cells, that bug patiently walking up the inside of the window of the office. Radio music was coming from its open door, and because the rhythm was not synchronized with the heave and flutter and other gestures of wind-animated vegetation, one had the impression of an old scenic film living its own life while piano or fiddle followed a line of music quite outside the shivering flower, the swaying branch. The sound of Charlotte's last sob incongruously vibrated through me as, with her dress fluttering athwart the rhythm, Lolita veered from a totally unexpected direction. She had found the toilet occupied and had crossed over to the sign of the Conche in the next block. They said there they were proud of their home-clean restrooms. These prepaid postcards, they said, had been provided for your comments. No postcards. No soap. Nothing. No comments.

That day or the next, after a tedious drive through a land

of food crops, we reached a pleasant little burg and put up at Chestnut Court—nice cabins, damp green grounds, apple trees, an old swing—and a tremendous sunset which the tired child ignored. She had wanted to go through Kasbeam because it was only thirty miles north from her home town but on the following morning I found her quite listless, with no desire to see again the sidewalk where she had played hopscotch some five years before. For obvious reasons I had rather dreaded that side trip, even though we had agreed not to make ourselves conspicuous in any way—to remain in the car and not look up old friends. My relief at her abandoning the project was spoiled by the thought that had she felt I were totally against the nostalgic possibilities of Pisky, as I had been last year, she would not have given up so easily. On my mentioning this with a sigh, she sighed too and complained of being out of sorts. She wanted to remain in bed till teatime at least, with lots of magazines, and then if she felt better she suggested we just continue westward. I must say she was very sweet and languid, and craved for fresh fruits, and I decided to go and fetch her a toothsome picnic lunch in Kasbeam. Our cabin stood on the timbered crest of a hill, and from our window you could see the road winding down, and then running as straight as a hair parting between two rows of chestnut trees, towards the pretty town, which looked singularly distinct and toylike in the pure morning distance. One could make out an elf-like girl on an insect-like bicycle, and a dog, a bit too large proportionately, all as clear as those pilgrims and mules winding up wax-pale roads in old paintings with blue hills and red little people. I have the European urge to use my feet when a drive can be dispensed with, so I leisurely walked down, eventually meeting the cyclist—a plain plump girl with pigtails, followed by a huge St. Bernard dog with orbits like pansies. In Kasbeam a very old barber gave me a very mediocre haircut: he babbled of a baseball-playing son of his, and, at every explodent, spat into my neck, and every now and then wiped his glasses on my sheet-wrap, or interrupted his tremulous scissor work to produce faded newspaper clippings, and so inattentive was I that it came as a shock to realize as he pointed to an easeled photograph among the ancient gray lotions, that the mustached young ball player had been dead for the last thirty years.

I had a cup of hot flavorless coffee, bought a bunch of bananas for my monkey, and spent another ten minutes or so in a delicatessen store. At least an hour and a half must have elapsed when this homeward-bound little pilgrim appeared on the winding road leading to Chestnut Castle.

The girl I had seen on my way to town was now loaded with linen and engaged in helping a misshapen man whose big head and coarse features reminded me of the "Bertoldo" character in low Italian comedy. They were cleaning the cabins of which there was a dozen or so on Chestnut Crest, all pleasantly spaced amid the copious verdure. It was noon, and most of them, with a final bang of their screen doors, had already got rid of their occupants. A very elderly, almost mummy-like couple in a very new model were in the act of creeping out of one of the contiguous garages; from another a red hood protruded in somewhat cod-piece fashion; and nearer to our cabin, a strong and handsome young man with a shock of black hair and blue eyes was putting a portable refrigerator into a station wagon. For some reason he gave me a sheepish grin as I passed. On the grass expanse opposite, in the many-limbed shade of luxuriant trees, the familiar St. Bernard dog was guarding his mistress' bicycle, and nearby a young woman, far gone in the family way, had seated a rapt baby on a swing and was rocking it gently, while a jealous boy of two or three was making a nuisance of himself by trying to push or pull the swing board; he finally succeeded in getting himself knocked down by it, and bawled loudly as he lay supine on the grass while his mother continued to smile gently at neither of her present children. I recall so clearly these minutiae probably because I was to check my impressions so thoroughly only a few minutes later; and besides, something in me had been on guard ever since that awful night in Beardsley. I now refused to be diverted by the feeling of well-being that my walk had engendered—by the young summer breeze that enveloped the nape of my neck, the giving crunch of the damp gravel, the juicy tidbit I had sucked out at last from a hollow tooth, and even the comfortable weight of my provisions which the general condition of my heart should not have allowed me to carry; but even that miserable pump of mine seemed to be working sweetly, and I felt *adolori d'amoureuse langueur*, to quote dear old Ronsard, as I reached the cottage where I had left my Dolores.

To my surprise I found her dressed. She was sitting on the edge of the bed in slacks and T-shirt, and was looking at me as if she could not quite place me. The frank soft shape of her small breasts was brought out rather than blurred by the limpness of her thin shirt, and this frankness irritated me. She had not washed; yet her mouth was freshly though smudgily painted, and her broad teeth glistened like wine-tinged ivory, or pinkish poker chips. And there she sat, hands clasped in her lap, and dreamily brimmed with a diabolical glow that had no relation to me whatever.

I plumped down my heavy paper bag and stood staring at the bare ankles of her sandaled feet, then at her silly face, then again at her sinful feet. "You've been out," I said (the sandals were filthy with gravel).

"I just got up," she replied, and added upon intercepting my downward glance: "Went out for a sec. Wanted to see if you were coming back."

She became aware of the bananas and uncoiled herself tableward.

What special suspicion could I have? None indeed—but those muddy, moony eyes of hers, that singular warmth emanating from her! I said nothing. I looked at the road meandering so distinctly within the frame of the window . . . Anybody wishing to betray my trust would have found it a splendid lookout. With rising appetite, Lo applied herself to the fruit. All at once I remembered the ingratiating grin of the Johnny nextdoor. I stepped out quickly. All cars had disappeared except his station wagon; his pregnant young wife was now getting into it with her baby and the other, more or less cancelled, child.

"What's the matter, where are you going?" cried Lo from the porch.

I said nothing. I pushed her softness back into the room and went in after her. I ripped her shirt off. I unzipped the rest of her. I tore off her sandals. Wildly, I pursued the shadow of her infidelity; but the scent I travelled upon was so slight as to be practically undistinguishable from a madman's fancy.

17

Gros Gaston, in his prissy way, had liked to make presents—presents just a prissy wee bit out of the ordinary, or so he prissily thought. Noticing one night that my box of chessmen was broken, he sent me next morning, with a little lad of his, a copper case: it had an elaborate Oriental design over the lid and could be securely locked. One glance sufficed to assure me that it was one of those cheap money boxes called for some reason "luizettas" that you buy in Algiers and elsewhere, and wonder what to do with afterwards. It turned out to be much too flat for holding my bulky chessmen, but I kept it—using it for a totally different purpose.

244

In order to break some pattern of fate in which I obscurely felt myself being enmeshed, I had decided—despite Lo's visible annoyance—to spend another night at Chestnut Court; definitely waking up at four in the morning, I ascertained that Lo was still sound asleep (mouth open, in a kind of dull amazement at the curiously inane life we all had rigged up for her) and satisfied myself that the precious contents of the "luizetta" were safe. There, snugly wrapped in a white woollen scarf, lay a pocket automatic: caliber .32, capacity of magazine 8 cartridges, length a little under one ninth of Lolita's length, stock checked walnut, finish full blued. I had inherited it from the late Harold Haze, with a 1938 catalog which cheerily said in part: "Particularly well adapted for use in the home and car as well as on the person." There it lay, ready for instant service on the person or persons, loaded and fully cocked with the slide lock in safety position, thus precluding any accidental discharge. We must remember that a pistol is the Freudian symbol of the Ur-father's central forelimb.

I was now glad I had it with me—and even more glad that I had learned to use it two years before, in the pine forest around my and Charlotte's glass lake. Farlow, with whom I had roamed those remote woods, was an admirable marksman, and with his .38 actually managed to hit a hummingbird, though I must say not much of it could be retrieved for proof—only a little iridescent fluff. A burley ex-policeman called Krestovski, who in the twenties had shot and killed two escaped convicts, joined us and bagged a tiny woodpecker—completely out of season, incidentally. Between those two sportsmen I of course was a novice and kept missing everything, though I did wound a squirrel on a later occasion when I went out alone. "You lie here," I whispered to my light-weight compact little chum, and then toasted it with a dram of gin.

18

The reader must now forget Chestnuts and Colts, and accompany us further west. The following days were marked by a number of great thunderstorms—or perhaps, there was but one single storm which progressed across country in ponderous frogleaps and which we could not shake off just as we could not shake off detective Trapp: for it was during those days that the problem of the Aztec Red Convertible presented itself to me, and quite overshadowed the theme of Lo's lovers.

Queer! I who was jealous of every male we met—queer, how I misinterpreted the designations of doom. Perhaps I had been lulled by Lo's modest behavior in winter, and anyway it would have been too foolish even for a lunatic to suppose another Humbert was avidly following Humbert and Humbert's nymphet with Jovian fireworks, over the great and ugly plains. I surmised, *donc*, that the Red Yak keeping behind us at a discreet distance mile after mile was operated by a detective whom some busybody had hired to see what exactly Humbert Humbert was doing with that minor stepdaughter of his. As happens with me at periods of electrical disturbance and crepitating lightnings, I had hallucinations. Maybe they were more than hallucinations. I do not know what she or he, or both had put into my liquor but one night I felt sure somebody was tapping on the door of our cabin, and I flung it open, and noticed two things—that I was stark naked and that, white-glistening in the rain-dripping darkness, there stood a man holding before his face the mask of Jutting Chin, a grotesque sleuth in the funnies. He emitted a muffled guffaw and scurried away, and I reeled back into the room, and fell asleep again, and am not sure even to this day that the visit was not a drug-provoked dream: I have thoroughly studied Trapp's type of humor, and this might have been a plausible sample. Oh, crude and absolutely ruthless! Somebody, I imagined, was making money on those masks of popular monsters and morons. Did I see next morning two urchins rummaging in a garbage can and trying on Jutting Chin? I wonder. It may all have been a coincidence—due to atmospheric conditions, I suppose.

Being a murderer with a sensational but incomplete and unorthodox memory, I cannot tell you, ladies and gentlemen, the exact day when I first knew with utter certainty that the red convertible was following us. I do remember, however, the first time I saw its driver quite clearly. I was proceeding slowly one afternoon through torrents of rain and kept seeing that red ghost swimming and shivering with lust in my mirror, when presently the deluge dwindled to a patter, and then was suspended altogether. With a swishing sound a sunburst swept the highway, and needing a pair of new sunglasses, I pulled up at a filling station. What was happening was a sickness, a cancer, that could not be helped, so I simply ignored the fact that our quiet pursuer, in his converted state, stopped a little behind us at a café or bar bearing the idiotic sign: The Bustle: A Deceitful Seatful. Having seen to the needs of my car, I walked into the office to get those glasses and pay for the gas. As I was in the act of signing a traveller's check and wondered about my exact whereabouts, I happened to glance through a side window, and saw a terrible thing. A broad-backed man, baldish, in an oatmeal coat and dark-brown trousers, was listening to Lo who was leaning out of the car and talking to him very rapidly, her hand with outspread fingers going up and down as it did when she was very serious and emphatic. What struck me with sickening force was—how should I put it?—the voluble familiarity of her way, as if they had known each other—

oh, for weeks and weeks. I saw him scratch his cheek and nod, and turn, and walk back to his convertible, a broad and thickish man of my age, somewhat resembling Gustave Trapp, a cousin of my father's in Switzerland—same smoothly tanned face, fuller than mine, with a small dark mustache and a rosebud degenerate mouth. Lolita was studying a road map when I got back into the car.

"What did that man ask you, Lo?"

"Man? Oh, that man. Oh yes. Oh, I don't know. He wondered if I had a map. Lost his way, I guess."

We drove on, and I said:

"Now listen, Lo. I do not know whether you are lying or not, and I do not know whether you are insane or not, and I do not care for the moment; but that person has been following us all day, and his car was at the motel yesterday, and I think he is a cop. You know perfectly well what will happen and where you will go if the police find out about things. Now I want to know exactly what he said to you and what you told him."

She laughed.

"If he's really a cop," she said shrilly but not illogically, "the worst thing we could do, would be to show him we are scared. Ignore him, *Dad*."

"Did he ask where we were going?"

"Oh, he knows *that*" (mocking me).

"Anyway," I said, giving up, "I have seen his face now. He is not pretty. He looks exactly like a relative of mine called Trapp."

"Perhaps he is Trapp. If I were you—Oh, look, all the nines are changing into the next thousand. When I was a little kid," she continued unexpectedly, "I used to think they'd stop and go back to nines, if only my mother agreed to put the car in reverse."

It was the first time, I think, she spoke spontaneously

of her pre-Humbertian childhood; perhaps, the theatre had taught her that trick; and silently we travelled on, unpursued.

But next day, like pain in a fatal disease that comes back as the drug and hope wear off, there it was again behind us, that glossy red beast. The traffic on the highway was light that day; nobody passed anybody; and nobody attempted to get in between our humble blue car and its imperious red shadow—as if there were some spell cast on that interspace, a zone of evil mirth and magic, a zone whose very precision and stability had a glass-like virtue that was almost artistic. The driver behind me, with his stuffed shoulders and Trappish mustache, looked like a display dummy, and his convertible seemed to move only because an invisible rope of silent silk connected it with our shabby vehicle. We were many times weaker than his splendid, lacquered machine, so that I did not even attempt to outspeed him. *O lente currite noctis equi!* O softly run, nightmares! We climbed long grades and rolled downhill again, and heeded speed limits, and spared slow children, and reproduced in sweeping terms the black wiggles of curves on their yellow shields, and no matter how and where we drove, the enchanted interspace slid on intact, mathematical, mirage-like, the viatic counterpart of a magic carpet. And all the time I was aware of a private blaze on my right: her joyful eye, her flaming cheek.

A traffic policeman, deep in the nightmare of crisscross streets—at half-past-four P.M. in a factory town—was the hand of chance that interrupted the spell. He beckoned me on, and then with the same hand cut off my shadow. A score of cars were launched in between us, and I sped on, and deftly turned into a narrow lane. A sparrow alighted with a jumbo bread crumb, was tackled by another, and lost the crumb.

When after a few grim stoppages and a bit of deliberate

meandering, I returned to the highway, our shadow had disappeared.

Lola snorted and said: "If he is what you think he is, how silly to give him the slip."

"I have other notions by now," I said.

"You should—ah—check them by—ah—keeping in touch with him, father deah," said Lo, writhing in the coils of her own sarcasm. "Gee, you *are* mean," she added in her ordinary voice.

We spent a grim night in a very foul cabin, under a sonorous amplitude of rain, and with a kind of prehistorically loud thunder incessantly rolling above us.

"I am not a lady and do not like lightning," said Lo, whose dread of electric storms gave me some pathetic solace.

We had breakfast in the township of Soda, pop. 1001.

"Judging by the terminal figure," I remarked, "Fatface is already here."

"Your humor," said Lo, "is sidesplitting, deah fahther."

We were in sage-brush country by that time, and there was a day or two of lovely release (I had been a fool, all was well, that discomfort was merely a trapped flatus), and presently the mesas gave way to real mountains, and, on time, we drove into Wace.

Oh, disaster. Some confusion had occurred, she had misread a date in the Tour Book, and the Magic Cave ceremonies were over! She took it bravely, I must admit—and, when we discovered there was in kurortish Wace a summer theatre in full swing, we naturally drifted toward it one fair mid-June evening. I really could not tell you the plot of the play we saw. A trivial affair, no doubt, with self-conscious light effects and a mediocre leading lady. The only detail that pleased me was a garland of seven little graces, more or less immobile, prettily painted, bare-limbed—seven bemused pubescent girls in colored gauze that had been recruited locally (judging by the partisan flurry here and there among the audience) and were supposed to represent a living rainbow, which lingered throughout the last act, and rather teasingly faded behind a series of multiplied veils. I remember thinking that this idea of children-colors had been lifted by authors Clare Quilty and Vivian Darkbloom from a passage in James Joyce, and that two of the colors were quite exasperatingly lovely—Orange who kept fidgeting all the time, and Emerald who, when her eyes got used to the pitch-black pit where we all heavily sat, suddenly smiled at her mother or her protector.

As soon as the thing was over, and manual applause—a sound my nerves cannot stand—began to crash all around me, I started to pull and push Lo toward the exit, in my so natural amorous impatience to get her back to our neon-blue cottage in the stunned, starry night: I always say nature is stunned by the sights she sees. Dolly-Lo, however, lagged behind, in a rosy daze, her pleased eyes narrowed, her sense of vision swamping the rest of her senses to such an extent that her limp hands hardly came together at all in the mechanical action of clapping they still went through. I had seen that kind of thing in children before but, by God, this was a special child, myopically beaming at the already remote stage where I glimpsed something of the joint authors—a man's tuxedo and the bare shoulders of a hawk-like, black-haired, strikingly tall woman.

"You've again hurt my wrist, you brute," said Lolita in a small voice as she slipped into her car seat.

"I am dreadfully sorry, my darling, my own ultraviolet darling," I said, unsuccessfully trying to catch her elbow, and I added, to change the conversation—to change the direction of fate, oh God, oh God: "Vivian is quite a woman. I am sure we saw her yesterday in that restaurant, in Soda pop."

"Sometimes," said Lo, "you are quite revoltingly dumb. First, Vivian is the male author, the gal author is Clare; and second, she is forty, married and has Negro blood."

"I thought," I said kidding her, "Quilty was an ancient flame of yours, in the days when you loved me, in sweet old Ramsdale."

"What?" countered Lo, her features working. "That fat dentist? You must be confusing me with some other fast little article."

And I thought to myself how those fast little articles forget everything, everything, while we, old lovers, treasure every inch of their nymphancy.

19

With Lo's knowledge and assent, the two post offices given to the Beardsley postmaster as forwarding addresses were P.O. Wace and P.O. Elphinstone. Next morning we visited the former and had to wait in a short but slow queue. Serene Lo studied the rogues' gallery. Handsome Bryan Bryanski, alias Anthony Bryan, alias Tony Brown, eyes hazel, complexion fair, was wanted for kidnaping. A sad-eyed old gentleman's faux-pas was mail fraud, and, as if that were not enough, he was cursed with deformed arches. Sullen Sullivan came with a caution: Is believed armed, and should be considered extremely dangerous. If you want to make a movie out of my book, have one of these faces gently melt into my own, while I look. And moreover there was a smudgy snapshot of a Missing Girl, age fourteen, wearing brown shoes when last seen, rhymes. Please notify Sheriff Buller.

I forget my letters; as to Dolly's, there was her report and a very special-looking envelope. This I deliberately opened and perused its contents. I concluded I was doing the foreseen since she did not seem to mind and drifted toward the newsstand near the exit.

"Dolly-Lo: Well, the play was a grand success. All three hounds lay quiet having been slightly drugged by Cutler, I suspect, and Linda knew all your lines. She was fine, she had alertness and control, but lacked somehow the *responsiveness*, the *relaxed vitality*, the charm of *my*—and the author's—Diana; but there was no author to applaud us as last time, and the terrific electric storm outside interfered with our own modest offstage thunder. Oh dear, life does fly. Now that everything is over, school, play, the Roy mess, mother's confinement (our baby, alas, did not live!), it all seems such a long time ago, though practically I still bear traces of the paint.

"We are going to New York after to-morrow, and I guess I can't manage to wriggle out of accompanying my parents to Europe. I have even worse news for you. Dolly-Lo! I may not be back at Beardsley if and when you return. With one thing and another, one being you know who, and the other not being who you think you know, Dad wants me to go to school in Paris for one year while he and Fullbright are around.

"As expected, poor Poet stumbled in Scene III when arriving at the bit of French nonsense. Remember? *Ne manque pas de dire à ton amant, Chimène, comme le lac est beau car il faut qu'il t'y mène.* Lucky beau! *Qu'il t'y*—What a tongue-twister! Well, be good, Lollikins. Best love from your Poet, and best regards to the Governor. Your Mona. P.S. Because of one thing and another, my correspondence happens to be rigidly controlled. So better wait till I write you from Europe." (She never did as far as I know. The letter contained an element of mysterious nastiness that I am too tired to-day to analyze. I found it later preserved in one of the Tour Books, and give it here *à titre documentaire*. I read it twice.)

I looked up from the letter and was about to—There

was no Lo to behold. While I was engrossed in Mona's witchery, Lo had shrugged her shoulders and vanished. "Did you happen to see—" I asked of a hunchback sweeping the floor near the entrance. He had, the old lecherer. He guessed she had seen a friend and had hurried out. I hurried out too. I stopped—she had not. I hurried on. I stopped again. It had happened at last. She had gone for ever.

In later years I have often wondered why she did *not* go for ever that day. Was it the retentive quality of her new summer clothes in my locked car? Was it some unripe particle in some general plan? Was it simply because, all things considered, I might as well be used to convey her to Elphinstone—the secret terminus, anyway? I only know I was quite certain she had left me for ever. The noncommittal mauve mountains half encircling the town seemed to me to swarm with panting, scrambling, laughing, panting Lolitas who dissolved in their haze. A big W made of white stones on a steep talus in the far vista of a cross street seemed the very initial of woe.

The new and beautiful post office I had just emerged from stood between a dormant movie house and a conspiracy of poplars. The time was 9 A.M. mountain time. The street was Main Street. I paced its blue side peering at the opposite one: charming it into beauty, was one of those fragile young summer mornings with flashes of glass here and there and a general air of faltering and almost fainting at the prospect of an intolerably torrid noon. Crossing over, I loafed and leafed, as it were, through one long block: Drugs, Real Estate, Fashions, Auto Parts, Cafe, Sporting Goods, Real Estate, Furniture, Appliances, Western Union, Cleaners, Grocery. Officer, officer, my daughter has run away. In collusion with a detective; in love with a blackmailer. Took advantage of my utter helplessness. I peered into all the stores. I deliberated inly if I should talk to any of the sparse foot-passengers. I did not. I sat for a while in the parked car. I inspected the public garden on the east side. I went back to Fashions and Auto Parts. I told myself with a burst of furious sarcasm—*un ricanement*—that I was crazy to suspect her, that she would turn up in a minute.

She did.

I wheeled around and shook off the hand she had placed on my sleeve with a timid and imbecile smile.

"Get into the car," I said.

She obeyed, and I went on pacing up and down, struggling with nameless thoughts, trying to plan some way of tackling her duplicity.

Presently she left the car and was at my side again. My sense of hearing gradually got tuned in to station Lo again, and I became aware she was telling me that she had met a former girl friend.

"Yes? Whom?"

"A Beardsley girl."

"Good. I know every name in your group. Alice Adams?"

"This girl was not in my group."

"Good. I have a complete student list with me. Her name please."

"She was not in my school. She is just a town girl in Beardsley."

"Good. I have the Beardsley directory with me too. We'll look up all the Browns."

"I only know her first name."

"Mary or Jane?"

"No—Dolly, like me."

"So that's the dead end" (the mirror you break your nose against). "Good. Let us try another angle. You have been absent twenty-eight minutes. What did the two Dollys do?"

"We went to a drugstore."

"And you had there—?"

"Oh, just a couple of Cokes."

"Careful, Dolly. We can check that, you know."

"At least, she had. I had a glass of water."

"Good. Was it that place there?"

"Sure."

"Good, come on, we'll grill the soda jerk."

"Wait a sec. Come to think it might have been further down—just around the corner."

"Come on all the same. Go in please. Well, let's see." (Opening a chained telephone book.) "Dignified Funeral Service. No, not yet. Here we are: Druggists-Retail. Hill Drug Store. Larkin's Pharmacy. And two more. That's all Wace seems to have in the way of soda fountains—at least in the business section. Well, we will check them all."

"Go to hell," she said.

"Lo, rudeness will get you nowhere."

"Okay," she said. "But you're not going to trap me. Okay, so we did not have a pop. We just talked and looked at dresses in show windows."

"Which? That window there for example?"

"Yes, that one there, for example."

"Oh Lo! Let's look closer at it."

It was indeed a pretty sight. A dapper young fellow was vacuum-cleaning a carpet of sorts upon which stood two figures that looked as if some blast had just worked havoc with them. One figure was stark naked, wigless and armless. Its comparatively small stature and smirking pose suggested that when clothed it had represented, and would represent when clothed again, a girl-child of Lolita's size. But in its present state it was sexless. Next to it, stood a much taller veiled bride, quite perfect and *intacta* except for the lack of one arm. On the floor, at the feet of these damsels, where the man crawled about laboriously with his cleaner, there lay a cluster of three slender arms, and a blond wig. Two of the arms happened to be twisted and seemed to suggest a clasping gesture of horror and supplication.

"Look, Lo," I said quietly. "Look well. Is not that a rather good symbol of something or other? However"—I went on as we got back in to the car—"I have taken certain precautions. Here (delicately opening the glove compartment), on this pad, I have our boy friend's car number."

As the ass I was I had not memorized it. What remained of it in my mind were the initial letter and the closing figure as if the whole amphitheatre of six signs receded concavely behind a tinted glass too opaque to allow the central series to be deciphered, but just translucent enough to make out its extreme edges—a capital P and a 6. I have to go into those details (which in themselves can interest only a professional psychologue) because otherwise the reader (ah, if I could visualize him as a blond-bearded scholar with rosy lips sucking *la pomme de sa canne* as he quaffs my manuscript!) might not understand the quality of the shock I experienced upon noticing that the P had acquired the bustle of a B and that the 6 had been deleted altogether. The rest, with erasures revealing the hurried shuttle smear of a pencil's rubber end, and with parts of numbers obliterated or reconstructed in a child's hand, presented a tangle of barbed wire to any logical interpretation. All I knew was the state—one adjacent to the state Beardsley was in.

I said nothing. I put the pad back, closed the compartment, and drove out of Wace. Lo had grabbed some comics from the back seat and, mobile-white-bloused, one brown elbow out of the window, was deep in the current adventure of some clout or clown. Three or four miles out of Wace, I turned into the shadow of a picnic ground where the morning had dumped its litter of light on an empty table; Lo looked up with a semi-smile of surprise and without a word I delivered a tremendous backhand cut that caught her smack on her hot hard little cheekbone.

And then the remorse, the poignant sweetness of sobbing atonement, groveling love, the hopelessness of sensual reconciliation. In the velvet night, at Mirana Motel (Mirana!) I kissed the yellowish soles of her long-toed feet, I immolated myself . . . But it was all of no avail. Both doomed were we. And soon I was to enter a new cycle of persecution.

In a street of Wace, on its outskirts . . . Oh, I am quite sure it was not a delusion. In a street of Wace, I had glimpsed the Aztec Red convertible, or its identical twin. Instead of Trapp, it contained four or five loud young people of several sexes—but I said nothing. After Wace a totally new situation arose. For a day or two, I enjoyed the mental emphasis with which I told myself that we were not, and never had been followed; and then I became sickeningly conscious that Trapp had changed his tactics and was still with us, in this or that rented car.

A veritable Proteus of the highway, with bewildering ease he switched from one vehicle to another. This technique implied the existence of garages specializing in "stage-automobile" operations, but I never could discover the remises he used. He seemed to patronize at first the Chevrolet genus, beginning with a Campus Cream convertible, then going on to a small Horizon Blue sedan, and thenceforth fading into Surf Gray and Driftwood Gray. Then he turned to other makes and passed through a pale dull rainbow of paint shades, and one day I found myself attempting to cope with the subtle distinction between our own Dream Blue Melmoth and the Crest Blue Oldsmobile he had rented; grays, however, remained his favorite cryptochromism, and, in agonizing nightmares, I tried in vain to sort out properly such ghosts as Chrysler's Shell Gray,

Chevrolet's Thistle Gray, Dodge's French Gray . . .

The necessity of being constantly on the lookout for his little moustache and open shirt—or for his baldish pate and broad shoulders—led me to a profound study of all cars on the road—behind, before, alongside, coming, going, every vehicle under the dancing sun: the quiet vacationist's automobile with the box of Tender-Touch tissues in the back window; the recklessly speeding jalopy full of pale children with a shaggy dog's head protruding, and a crumpled mudguard; the bachelor's tudor sedan crowded with suits on hangers; the huge fat house trailer weaving in front, immune to the Indian file of fury boiling behind it; the car with the young female passenger politely perched in the middle of the front seat to be closer to the young male driver; the car carrying on its roof a red boat bottom up . . . The gray car slowing up before us, the gray car catching up with us.

We were in mountain country, somewhere between Snow and Champion, and rolling down an almost imperceptible grade, when I had my next distinct view of Detective Paramour Trapp. The gray mist behind us had deepened and concentrated into the compactness of a Dominion Blue sedan. All of a sudden, as if the car I drove responded to my poor heart's pangs, we were slithering from side to side, with something making a helpless plap-plap-plap under us.

"You got a flat, mister," said cheerful Lo.

I pulled up—near a precipice. She folded her arms and put her foot on the dashboard. I got out and examined the right rear wheel. The base of its tire was sheepishly and hideously square. Trapp had stopped some fifty yards behind us. His distant face formed a grease spot of mirth. This was my chance. I started to walk towards him—with the brilliant idea of asking him for a jack though I had one. He backed a little. I stubbed my toe against a stone—and there was a sense of general laughter. Then a tremendous truck loomed from behind Trapp and thundered by me—and immediately after, I heard it utter a convulsive honk. Instinctively I looked back—and saw my own car gently creeping away. I could make out Lo ludicrously at the wheel, and the engine was certainly running—though I remembered I had cut it but had not applied the emergency brake; and during the brief space of throb-time that it took me to reach the croaking machine which came to a standstill at last, it dawned upon me that during the last two years little Lo had had ample time to pick up the rudiments of driving. As I wrenched the door open, I was goddam sure she had started the car to prevent me from walking up to Trapp. Her trick proved useless, however, for even while I was pursuing her he had made an energetic U-turn and was gone. I rested for a while. Lo asked wasn't I going to thank her—the car had started to move by itself and—Getting no answer, she immersed herself in a study of the map. I got out again and commenced the "ordeal of the orb," as Charlotte used to say. Perhaps, I was losing my mind.

We continued our grotesque journey. After a forlorn and useless dip, we went up and up. On a steep grade I found myself behind the gigantic truck that had overtaken us. It was now groaning up a winding road and was impossible to pass. Out of its front part a small oblong of smooth silver—the inner wrapping of chewing gum—escaped and flew back into our windshield. It occurred to me that if I were really losing my mind, I might end by murdering somebody. In fact—said high-and-dry Humbert to floundering Humbert—it might be quite clever to prepare things—to transfer the weapon from box to pocket—so as to be ready to take advantage of the spell of insanity when it does come.

20

By permitting Lolita to study acting I had, fond fool, suffered her to cultivate deceit. It now appeared that it had not been merely a matter of learning the answers to such questions as what is the basic conflict in "Hedda Gabler," or where are the climaxes in "Love Under the Lindens," or analyze the prevailing mood of "Cherry Orchard"; it was really a matter of learning to betray me. How I deplored now the exercises in sensual simulation that I had so often seen her go through in our Beardsley parlor when I would observe her from some strategic point while she, like a hypnotic subject or a performer in a mystic rite, produced sophisticated versions of infantile make-believe by going through the mimetic actions of hearing a moan in the dark, seeing for the first time a brand new young stepmother, tasting something she hated, such as buttermilk, smelling crushed grass in a lush orchard, or touching mirages of objects with her sly, slender, girl-child hands. Among my papers I still have a mimeographed sheet suggesting:

Tactile drill. Imagine yourself picking up and holding: a pingpong ball, an apple, a sticky date, a new flannel-fluffed tennis ball, a hot potato, an ice cube, a kitten, a puppy, a horseshoe, a feather, a flashlight.

Knead with your fingers the following imaginary things: a piece of bread, india rubber, a friend's aching temple, a sample of velvet, a rose petal.

You are a blind girl. Palpate the face of: a Greek youth, Cyrano, Santa Claus, a baby, a laughing faun, a sleeping stranger, your father.

But she had been so pretty in the weaving of those delicate spells, in the dreamy performance of her enchantments and duties! On certain adventurous evenings, in Beardsley, I also had her dance for me with the promise of some treat or gift, and although these routine leg-parted leaps of hers were more like those of a football cheerleader than like the languorous and jerky motions of a Parisian *petit rat*, the rhythms of her not quite nubile limbs had given me pleasure. But all that was nothing, absolutely nothing, to the indescribable itch of rapture that her tennis game produced in me—the teasing delirious feeling of teetering on the very brink of unearthly order and splendor.

Despite her advanced age, she was more of a nymphet than ever, with her apricot-colored limbs, in her sub-teen tennis togs! Winged gentlemen! No hereafter is acceptable if it does not produce her as she was then, in that Colorado resort between Snow and Elphinstone, with everything right: the white wide little-boy shorts, the slender waist, the apricot midriff, the white breast-kerchief whose ribbons went up and encircled her neck to end behind in a dangling knot leaving bare her gaspingly young and adorable apricot shoulder blades with that pubescence and those lovely gentle bones, and the smooth, downward-tapering back. Her cap had a white peak. Her racket had cost me a small fortune. Idiot, triple idiot! I could have filmed her! I would have had her now with me, before my eyes, in the projection room of my pain and despair!

She would wait and relax for a bar or two of white-lined time before going into the act of serving, and often bounced the ball once or twice, or pawed the ground a little, always at ease, always rather vague about the score, always cheerful as she so seldom was in the dark life she led at home. Her tennis was the highest point to which I can imagine a young creature bringing the art of make-believe, although I daresay, for her it was the very geometry of basic reality.

The exquisite clarity of all her movements had its auditory counterpart in the pure ringing sound of her every stroke. The ball when it entered her aura of control became somehow whiter, its resilience somehow richer, and the instrument of precision she used upon it seemed inordinately prehensile and deliberate at the moment of clinging contact. Her form was, indeed, an absolutely perfect imitation of absolutely top-notch tennis—without any utilitarian results. As Edusa's sister, Electra Gold, a marvelous young coach, said to me once while I sat on a pulsating hard bench watching Dolores Haze toying with Linda Hall (and being beaten by her): "Dolly has a magnet in the center of her racket guts, but why the heck is she so polite?" Ah, Electra, what did it matter, with such grace! I remember at the very first game I watched being drenched with an almost painful convulsion of beauty assimilation. My Lolita had a way of raising her bent left knee at the ample and springy start of the service cycle when there would develop and hang in the sun for a second a vital web of balance between toed foot, pristine armpit, burnished arm and far back-flung racket, as she smiled up with gleaming teeth at the small globe suspended so high in the zenith of the powerful and graceful cosmos she had created for the express purpose of falling upon it with a clean resounding crack of her golden whip.

It had, that serve of hers, beauty, directness, youth, a classical purity of trajectory, and was, despite its spanking pace, fairly easy to return, having as it did no twist or sting to its long elegant hop.

That I could have had all her strokes, all her enchantments, immortalized in segments of celluloid, makes me moan to-day with frustration. They would have been so much more than the snapshots I burned! Her overhead volley was related to her service as the envoy is to the ballade; for she had been trained, my pet, to patter up at once to the net on her nimble, vivid, white-shod feet. There was nothing to choose between her forehand and backhand drives: they were mirror images of one another— my very loins still tingle with those pistol reports repeated by crisp echoes and Electra's cries. One of the pearls of Dolly's game was a short half-volley that Ned Litam had taught her in California.

She preferred acting to swimming, and swimming to tennis; yet I insist that had not something within her been broken by me—not that I realized it then!—she would have had on the top of her perfect form the will to win, and would have become a real girl champion. Dolores, with two rackets under her arm, in Wimbledon. Dolores endorsing a Dromedary. Dolores turning professional. Dolores acting a girl champion in a movie. Dolores and her gray, humble, hushed husband-coach, old Humbert.

There was nothing wrong or deceitful in the spirit of her game—unless one considered her cheerful indifference toward its outcome as the feint of a nymphet. She who was so cruel and crafty in everyday life, revealed an innocence, a frankness, a kindness of ball-placing, that permitted a second-rate but determined player, no matter how uncouth and incompetent, to poke and cut his way to victory. Despite her small stature, she covered the one thousand and fifty-three square feet of her half of the court with wonderful ease, once she had entered into the rhythm of a rally and as long as she could direct that rhythm; but any abrupt attack, or sudden change of tactics on her adversary's part, left her helpless. At match point, her second serve, which— rather typically—was even stronger and more stylish than her first (for she had none of the inhibitions that cautious winners have), would strike vibrantly the harp-cord of the net—and ricochet out of court. The polished gem of her dropshot was snapped up and put away by an opponent who seemed four-legged and wielded a crooked paddle. Her dramatic drives and lovely volleys would candidly fall at his feet. Over and over again she would land an easy one into the net—and merrily mimic dismay by drooping in a ballet attitude, with her forelocks hanging. So sterile were her grace and whipper that she could not even win from panting me and my old-fashioned lifting drive.

I suppose I am especially susceptible to the magic of games. In my chess sessions with Gaston I saw the board as a square pool of limpid water with rare shells and stratagems rosily visible upon the smooth tessellated bottom, which to my confused adversary was all ooze and squid-cloud. Similarly, the initial tennis coaching I had inflicted on Lolita—prior to the revelations that came to her through the great Californian's lessons—remained in my mind as oppressive and distressful memories—not only because she had been so hopelessly and irritatingly irritated by every suggestion of mine—but because the precious symmetry of the court instead of reflecting the harmonies latent in her was utterly jumbled by the clumsiness and lassitude of the resentful child I mistaught. Now things were different, and on that particular day, in the pure air of Champion, Colorado, on that admirable court at the foot of steep stone stairs leading up to Champion Hotel where we had spent the night, I felt I could rest from the nightmare of unknown betrayals within the innocence of her style, of her soul, of her essential grace.

She was hitting hard and flat, with her usual effortless sweep, feeding me deep skimming balls—all so rhythmically coordinated and overt as to reduce my footwork to, practically, a swinging stroll—crack players will understand what I mean. My rather heavily cut serve that I had been taught by my father who had learned it from Decugis or

Borman, old friends of his and great champions, would have seriously troubled my Lo, had I really tried to trouble her. But who would upset such a lucid dear? Did I ever mention that her bare arm bore the 8 of vaccination? That I loved her hopelessly? That she was only fourteen?

An inquisitive butterfly passed, dipping, between us.

Two people in tennis shorts, a red-haired fellow only about eight years my junior, with sunburnt bright pink shins, and an indolent dark girl with a moody mouth and hard eyes, about two years Lolita's senior, appeared from nowhere. As is common with dutiful tyros, their rackets were sheathed and framed, and they carried them not as if they were the natural and comfortable extensions of certain specialized muscles, but hammers or blunderbusses or wimbles, or my own dreadful cumbersome sins. Rather unceremoniously seating themselves near my precious coat, on a bench adjacent to the court, they fell to admiring very vocally a rally of some fifty exchanges that Lo innocently helped me to foster and uphold—until there occurred a syncope in the series causing her to gasp as her overhead smash went out of court, whereupon she melted into winsome merriment, my golden pet.

I felt thirsty by then, and walked to the drinking fountain; there Red approached me and in all humility suggested a mixed double. "I am Bill Mead," he said. "And that's Fay Page, actress. Maffy On Say"—he added (pointing with his ridiculously hooded racket at polished Fay who was already talking to Dolly). I was about to reply "Sorry, but—" (for I hate to have my filly involved in the chops and jabs of cheap bunglers), when a remarkably melodious cry diverted my attention: a bellboy was tripping down the steps from the hotel to our court and making me signs. I was wanted, if you please, on an urgent long distance call—so urgent in fact that the line was being held for me. Certainly. I got into my coat (inside pocket heavy with pistol) and told Lo I would be back in a minute. She was picking up a ball—in the continental foot-racket way which was one of the few nice things I had taught her,—and smiled—she smiled at me!

An awful calm kept my heart afloat as I followed the boy up to the hotel. This, to use an American term, in which discovery, retribution, torture, death, eternity appear in the shape of a singularly repulsive nutshell, was *it*. I had left her in mediocre hands, but it hardly mattered now. I would fight, of course. Oh, I would fight. Better destroy everything than surrender her. Yes, quite a climb.

At the desk, a dignified, Roman-nosed man, with, I suggest, a very obscure past that might reward investigation, handed me a message in his own hand. The line had not been held after all. The note said:

"Mr. Humbert. The head of Birdsley (sic!) School called. Summer residence—Birdsley 2–8282. Please call back immediately. Highly important."

I folded myself into a booth, took a little pill, and for about twenty minutes tussled with space-spooks. A quartet of propositions gradually became audible: soprano, there was no such number in Beardsley; alto, Miss Pratt was on her way to England; tenor, Beardsley School had not telephoned; bass, they could not have done so, since nobody knew I was, that particular day, in Champion, Colo. Upon my stinging him, the Roman took the trouble to find out if there had been a long distance call. There had been none. A fake call from some local dial was not excluded. I thanked him. He said: You bet. After a visit to the purling men's room and a stiff drink at the bar, I started on my return march. From the very first terrace I saw, far below, on the tennis court which seemed the size of a school child's ill-wiped slate, golden Lolita playing in a double.

She moved like a fair angel among three horrible Boschian cripples. One of these, her partner, while changing sides, jocosely slapped her on her behind with his racket. He had a remarkably round head and wore incongruous brown trousers. There was a momentary flurry—he saw me, and throwing away his racket—mine!—scuttled up the slope. He waved his wrists and elbows in would-be comical imitation of rudimentary wings, as he climbed, bow-legged, to the street, where his gray car awaited him. Next moment he and the grayness were gone. When I came down, the remaining trio were collecting and sorting out the balls.

"Mr. Mead, who was that person?"

Bill and Fay, both looking very solemn, shook their heads.

That absurd intruder had butted in to make up a double, hadn't he, Dolly?

Dolly. The handle of my racket was still disgustingly warm. Before returning to the hotel, I ushered her into a little alley half-smothered in fragrant shrubs, with flowers like smoke, and was about to burst into ripe sobs and plead with her imperturbed dream in the most abject manner for clarification, no matter how meretricious, of the slow awfulness enveloping me, when we found ourselves behind the convulsed Mead twosome—assorted people, you know, meeting among idyllic settings in old comedies. Bill and Fay were both weak with laughter—we had come at the end of their private joke. It did not really matter.

Speaking as if it really did not really matter, and assuming, apparently, that life was automatically rolling on with all its routine pleasures, Lolita said she would like to change into her bathing things, and spend the rest of the afternoon at the swimming pool. It was a gorgeous day. Lolita!

21

"Lo! Lola! Lolita!" I hear myself crying from a doorway into the sun, with the acoustics of time, domed time, endowing my call and its tell-tale hoarseness with such a wealth of anxiety, passion and pain that really it would have been instrumental in wrenching open the zipper of her nylon shroud had she been dead. Lolita! In the middle of a trim turfed terrace I found her at last—she had run out before I was ready. Oh Lolita! There she was playing with a damned dog, not me. The animal, a terrier of sorts, was losing and snapping up again and adjusting between his jaws a wet little red ball; he took rapid chords with his front paws on the resilient turf, and then would bounce away. I had only wanted to see where she was, I could not swim with my heart in that state, but who cared—and there she was, and there was I, in my robe—and so I stopped calling; but suddenly something in the pattern of her motions, as she dashed this way and that in her Aztec Red bathing briefs and bra, struck me . . . there was an ecstasy, a madness about her frolics that was too much of a glad thing. Even the dog seemed puzzled by the extravagance of her reactions. I put a gentle hand to my chest as I surveyed the situation. The turquoise blue swimming pool some distance behind the lawn was no longer behind that lawn, but within my thorax, and my organs swam in it like excrements in the blue sea water in Nice. One of the bathers had left the pool and, half-concealed by the peacocked shade of trees, stood quite still, holding the ends of the towel around his neck and following Lolita with his amber eyes. There he stood, in the camouflage of sun and shade, disfigured by them and masked by his own nakedness, his damp black hair or what was left of it, glued to his round head, his little mustache a humid smear, the wool on his chest spread like a symmetrical trophy, his naval pulsating, his hirsute thighs dripping with bright droplets, his tight wet black bathing trunks bloated and bursting with vigor where his great fat bullybag was pulled up and back like a padded shield over his reversed beasthood. And as I looked at his oval nut-brown face, it dawned upon me that what I had recognized him by was the reflection of my daughter's countenance—the same beatitude and grimace but made hideous by his maleness. And I also knew that the child, my child, knew he was looking, enjoyed the lechery of his look and was putting on a show of gambol and glee, the vile and beloved slut. As she made for the ball and missed it, she fell on her back, with her obscene young legs madly pedalling in the air; I could sense the musk of her excitement from where I stood, and then I saw (petrified with a kind of sacred disgust) the man close his eyes and bare his small, horribly small and even, teeth as he leaned against a tree in which a multitude of dappled Priaps shivered. Immediately afterwards a marvelous transformation took place. He was no longer the satyr but a very good-natured and foolish Swiss cousin, the Gustave Trapp I have mentioned more than once, who used to counteract his "sprees" (he drank beer with milk, the good swine) by feats of weight-lifting—tottering and grunting on a lake beach with his otherwise very complete bathing suit jauntily stripped from one shoulder. *This* Trapp noticed me from afar and working the towel on his nape walked back with false insouciance to the pool. And as if the sun had gone out of the game, Lo slackened and slowly got up ignoring the ball that the terrier placed before her. Who can say what heartbreaks are caused in a dog by our discontinuing a romp? I started to say something, and then sat down on the grass with a quite monstrous pain in my chest and vomited a torrent of browns and greens that I had never remembered eating.

I saw Lolita's eyes, and they seemed to be more calculating than frightened. I heard her saying to a kind lady that her father was having a fit. Then for a long time I lay in a lounge chair swallowing pony upon pony of gin. And next morning I felt strong enough to drive on (which in later years no doctor believed).

22

The two-room cabin we had ordered at Silver Spur Court, Elphinstone, turned out to belong to the glossily browned pinelog kind that Lolita used to be so fond of in the days of our carefree first journey; oh, how different things were now! I am not referring to Trapp or Trapps. After all— well, really . . . After all, gentlemen, it was becoming abundantly clear that all those identical detectives in prismatically changing cars were figments of my persecution mania, recurrent images based on coincidence and chance resemblance. *Soyons logiques*, crowed the cocky Gallic part of my brain—and proceeded to rout the notion of a Lolita-maddened salesman or comedy gangster, with stooges, persecuting me, and hoaxing me, and otherwise taking riotous advantage of my strange relations with the law. I remember humming my panic away. I remember evolving even an explanation of the "Birdsley" telephone call . . . But if I could dismiss Trapp, as I had dismissed my convulsions on the lawn at Champion, I could do nothing with the anguish of knowing Lolita to be so tantalizingly, so miserably unattainable and beloved on the very eve of a new era, when my alembics told me she should stop being a nymphet, stop torturing me.

An additional, abominable, and perfectly gratuitous worry was lovingly prepared for me in Elphinstone. Lo had been dull and silent during the last lap—two hundred mountainous miles uncontaminated by smoke-gray sleuths or zigzagging zanies. She hardly glanced at the famous, oddly shaped, splendidly flushed rock which jutted above the mountains and had been the take-off for nirvana on the part of a temperamental show girl. The town was newly built, or rebuilt, on the flat floor of a seven-thousand-foot-high valley; it would soon bore Lo, I hoped, and we would spin on to California, to the Mexican border, to mythical bays, saguaro deserts, fatamorganas. José Lizzarrabengoa, as you remember, planned to take his Carmen to the *Etats Unis*. I conjured up a Central American tennis competition in which Dolores Haze and various Californian schoolgirl champions would dazzlingly participate. Good-will tours on that smiling level eliminate the distinction between passport and sport. Why did I hope we would be happy abroad? A change of environment is the traditional fallacy upon which doomed loves, and lungs, rely.

Mrs. Hays, the brisk, brickly rouged, blue-eyed widow who ran the motor court, asked me if I were Swiss perchance, because her sister had married a Swiss ski instructor. I was, whereas my daughter happened to be half Irish. I registered, Hays gave me the key and a twinkling smile, and, still twinkling, showed me where to park the car; Lo crawled out and shivered a little: the luminous evening air was decidedly crisp. Upon entering the cabin, she sat down on a chair at a card table, buried her face in the crook of her arm and said she felt awful. Shamming, I thought, shamming, no doubt, to evade my caresses; I was passionately parched; but she began to whimper in an unusually dreary way when I attempted to fondle her. Lolita ill. Lolita dying. Her skin was scalding hot! I took her temperature, orally, then looked up a scribbled formula I fortunately had in a jotter and after laboriously reducing the, meaningless to me, degrees Fahrenheit to the intimate centrigrade of my childhood, found she had 40.4, which at least made sense. Hysterical little nymphs might, I knew, run up all kinds of temperature—even exceeding a fatal count. And I would have given her a sip of hot spiced wine, and two aspirins, and kissed the fever away, if, upon an examination of her lovely uvula, one of the gems of her body, I had not seen that it was a burning red. I undressed her. Her breath was bittersweet. Her brown rose tasted of blood. She was shaking from head to toe. She complained of a painful stiffness in the upper vertebrae—and I thought of poliomyelitis as any American parent would. Giving up all hope of intercourse, I wrapped her up in a laprobe and carried her into the car. Kind Mrs. Hays in the meantime had alerted the local doctor. "You are lucky it happened here," she said; for not only was Blue the best man in the district, but the Elphinstone hospital was as modern as modern could be, despite its limited capacity. With a hetero-sexual Erlkönig in pursuit, thither I drove, half-blinded by a royal sunset on the lowland side and guided by a little old woman, a portable witch, perhaps his daughter, whom Mrs. Hays had lent me, and whom I was never to see again. Dr. Blue, whose learning, no doubt, was infinitely inferior to his reputation, assured me it was a virus infection, and when I alluded to her comparatively recent flu, curtly said this was another bug, he had forty such cases on his hands; all of which sounded like the "ague" of the ancients. I wondered if I should mention, with a casual chuckle, that my fifteen-year-old daughter had had a minor accident while climbing an awkward fence with her boy friend, but knowing I was drunk, I decided to withhold the informa-tion till later if necessary. To an unsmiling blond bitch of a secretary I gave my daughter's age as "practically sixteen." While I was not looking, my child was taken away from me! In vain I insisted I be allowed to spend the night on a "welcome" mat in a corner of their damned hospital. I ran up constructivistic flights of stairs, I tried to trace my darling so as to tell her she had better not babble, especially if she felt as lightheaded as we all did. At one point, I was rather dreadfully rude to a very young and very cheeky nurse with overdeveloped gluteal parts and blazing black eyes—of Basque descent, as I learned. Her father was an imported shepherd, a trainer of sheep dogs. Finally, I returned to the car and remained in it for I do not know how many hours, hunched up in the dark, stunned by my new solitude, looking out open-mouthed now at the dimly illumed, very square and low hospital building squatting in the middle of its lawny block, now up at the wash of stars and the jagged silvery ramparts of the *haute montagne* where at the moment Mary's father, lonely Joseph Lore, was dreaming of Oloron, Lagore, Rolas—*que sais-je!*—or seducing a ewe. Such-like fragrant vagabond thoughts have been always a solace to me in times of unusual stress, and only when, despite liberal libations, I felt fairly numbed by the endless night, did I think of driving back to the motel. The old woman had disappeared, and I was not quite sure of my way. Wide gravel roads criss-crossed drowsy rectangular shadows. I made out what looked like the silhouette of gallows on what was probably a school playground; and in another wastelike block there rose in domed silence the pale temple of some local sect. I found the highway at last, and then the motel, where millions of so-called "millers," a kind of insect, were swarming around the neon contours of "No Vacancy"; and, when, at 3 A.M., after one of those untimely hot showers which like some mordant only help to fix a man's despair and weariness, I lay on her bed that smelled of chestnuts and roses, and peppermint, and the very delicate, very special French perfume I latterly allowed her to use, I found myself unable to assimilate the simple fact that for the first time in two years I was separated from my Lolita. All at once it occurred to me that her illness was somehow the development of a theme—that it had the same taste and tone as the series of linked impressions which had puzzled and tormented me during our journey; I imagined that secret agent, or secret lover, or prankster, or hallucination, or whatever he was, prowling around the hospital—and Aurora had hardly "warmed her hands," as the pickers of lavender say in the country of my birth, when I found myself trying to get into that dungeon again, knocking upon its green doors, breakfast-less, stool-less, in despair.

This was Tuesday, and Wednesday or Thursday, splendidly reacting like the darling she was to some "serum" (sparrow's sperm or dugong's dung), she was much better, and the doctor said that in a couple of days she would be "skipping" again.

Of the eight times I visited her, the last one alone remains sharply engraved on my mind. It had been a great feat to come for I felt all hollowed out by the infection that by then was at work on me too. None will know the strain it was to carry that bouquet, that load of love, those books that I had traveled sixty miles to buy: Browning's *Dramatic Works*, *The History of Dancing*, *Clowns and Columbines*, *The Russian Ballet*, *Flowers of the Rockies*, *The Theatre Guild Anthology*, *Tennis* by Helen Wills, who had won the National Junior Girl Singles at the age of fifteen. As I was staggering up to the door of my daughter's thirteen-dollar-a-day private room, Mary Lore, the beastly young part-time nurse who had taken an unconcealed dislike to me, emerged with a finished breakfast tray, placed it with a quick crash on a chair in the corridor, and, fundament jigging, shot back into the room—probably to warn her poor little Dolores that the tyrannic old father was creeping up on crepe soles, with books and bouquet: the latter I had composed of wild flowers and beautiful leaves gathered with my own gloved hands on a mountain pass at sunrise (I hardly slept at all that fateful week).

Feeding my Carmencita well? Idly I glanced at the tray. On a yolk-stained plate there was a crumpled envelope. It had contained something, since one edge was torn, but there was no address on it—nothing at all, save a phony armorial design with "Ponderosa Lodge" in green letters; thereupon I performed a *chassé-croisé* with Mary, who was in the act of bustling out again—wonderful how fast they move and how little they do, those rumpy young nurses. She glowered at the envelope I had put back, uncrumpled.

"You better not touch," she said, nodding directionally. "Could burn your fingers."

Below my dignity to rejoin. All I said was:

"Je croyais que c'était un bill—not a *billet doux."* Then, entering the sunny room, to Lolita: *"Bonjour, mon petit."*

"Dolores," said Mary Lore, entering with me, past me, through me, the plump whore, and blinking, and starting to fold very rapidly a white flannel blanket as she blinked: "Dolores, your pappy thinks you are getting letters from my boy friend. It's me (smugly tapping herself on the small gilt cross she wore) gets them. And my pappy can parlay-voo as well as yours."

She left the room. Dolores, so rosy and russet, lips freshly painted, hair brilliantly brushed, bare arms straightened out on neat coverlet, lay innocently beaming at me or nothing. On the bed table, next to a paper napkin and a pencil, her topaz ring burned in the sun.

"What gruesome funeral flowers," she said. "Thanks all the same. But do you mind very much cutting out the French? It annoys everybody."

Back at the usual rush came the ripe young hussy,

reeking of urine and garlic, with the *Deseret News*, which her fair patient eagerly accepted, ignoring the sumptuously illustrated volumes I had brought.

"My sister Ann," said Mary (topping information with after-thought), "works at the Ponderosa place."

Poor Bluebeard. Those brutal brothers. *Est-ce que tu ne m'aimes plus, ma Carmen?* She never had. At the moment I knew my love was as hopeless as ever—and I also knew the two girls were conspirators, plotting in Basque, or Zemfirian, against my hopeless love. I shall go further and say that Lo was playing a double game since she was also fooling sentimental Mary whom she had told, I suppose, that she wanted to dwell with her fun-loving young uncle and not with cruel melancholy me. And another nurse whom I never identified, and the village idiot who carted cots and coffins into the elevator, and the idiotic green love birds in a cage in the waiting room—all were in the plot, the sordid plot. I suppose Mary thought comedy father Professor Humbertoldi was interfering with the romance between Dolores and her father-substitute, roly-poly Romeo (for you *were* rather lardy, you know, Rom, despite all that "snow" and "joy juice").

My throat hurt. I stood, swallowing, at the window and stared at the mountains, at the romantic rock high up in the smiling plotting sky.

"My Carmen," I said (I used to call her that sometimes), "we shall leave this raw sore town as soon as you get out of bed."

"Incidentally, I want all my clothes," said the gitanilla, humping up her knees and turning to another page.

". . . Because, really," I continued, "there is no point in staying here."

"There is no point in staying anywhere," said Lolita.

I lowered myself into a cretonne chair and, opening the

attractive botanical work, attempted, in the fever-humming hush of the room, to identify my flowers. This proved impossible. Presently a musical bell softly sounded somewhere in the passage.

I do not think they had more than a dozen patients (three or four were lunatics, as Lo had cheerfully informed me earlier) in that show place of a hospital, and the staff had too much leisure. However—likewise for reasons of show—regulations were rigid. It is also true that I kept coming at the wrong hours. Not without a secret flow of dreamy *malice*, visionary Mary (next time it will be *une belle dame toute en bleu* floating through Roaring Gulch) plucked me by the sleeve to lead me out. I looked at her hand; it dropped. As I was leaving, leaving voluntarily, Dolores Haze reminded me to bring her next morning . . . She did not remember where the various things she wanted were . . . "Bring me," she cried (out of sight already, door on the move, closing, closed), "the new gray suitcase and Mother's trunk"; but by next morning I was shivering, and boozing, and dying in the motel bed she had used for just a few minutes, and the best I could do under the circular and dilating circumstances was to send the two bags over with the widow's beau, a robust and kindly trucker. I imagined Lo displaying her treasures to Mary . . . No doubt, I was a little delirious—and on the following day I was still a vibration rather than a solid, for when I looked out of the bathroom window at the adjacent lawn, I saw Dolly's beautiful young bicycle propped up there on its support, the graceful front wheel looking away from me, as it always did, and a sparrow perched on the saddle—but it was the landlady's bike, and smiling a little, and shaking my poor head over my fond fancies, I tottered back to my bed, and lay as quiet as a saint—

Saint, forsooth! While brown Dolores,
On a patch of sunny green
With Sanchicha reading stories
In a movie magazine—

—which was represented by numerous specimens wherever Dolores landed, and there was some great national
celebration in town judging by the firecrackers, veritable
bombs, that exploded all the time, and at five minutes to
two P.M. I heard the sound of whistling lips nearing the
half-opened door of my cabin, and then a thump upon it.

It was big Frank. He remained framed in the opened
door, one hand on its jamb, leaning forward a little.

Howdy. Nurse Lore was on the telephone. She wanted
to know was I better and would I come today?

At twenty paces Frank used to look a mountain of
health; at five, as now, he was a ruddy mosaic of scars—
had been blown through a wall overseas; but despite
nameless injuries he was able to man a tremendous truck,
fish, hunt, drink, and buoyantly dally with roadside ladies.
That day, either because it was such a great holiday, or
simply because he wanted to divert a sick man, he had
taken off the glove he usually wore on his left hand (the
one pressing against the side of the door) and revealed to
the fascinated sufferer not only an entire lack of fourth
and fifth fingers, but also a naked girl, with cinnabar
nipples and indigo delta, charmingly tattooed on the back
of his crippled hand, its index and middle digit making
her legs while his wrist bore her flower-crowned head.
Oh, delicious . . . reclining against the woodwork, like
some sly fairy.

I asked him to tell Mary Lore I would stay in bed all
day and would get into touch with my daughter sometime tomorrow if I felt probably Polynesian.

He noticed the direction of my gaze and made her right hip twitch amorously.

"Okey-dokey," big Frank sang out, slapped the jamb, and whistling, carried my message away, and I went on drinking, and by morning the fever was gone, and although I was as limp as a toad, I put on the purple dressing gown over my maize yellow pajamas, and walked over to the office telephone. Everything was fine. A bright voice informed me that yes, everything was fine, my daughter had checked out the day before, around two, her uncle, Mr. Gustave, had called for her with a cocker spaniel pup and a smile for everyone, and a black Caddy Lack, and had paid Dolly's bill in cash, and told them to tell me I should not worry, and keep warm, they were at Grandpa's ranch as agreed.

Elphinstone was, and I hope still is, a very cute little town. It was spread like a maquette, you know, with its neat green-wool trees and red-roofed houses over the valley floor and I think I have alluded earlier to its model school and temple and spacious rectangular blocks, some of which were, curiously enough, just unconventional pastures with a mule or a unicorn grazing in the young July morning mist. Very amusing: at one gravel-groaning sharp turn I sideswiped a parked car but said to myself telestically—and, telephathically (I hoped), to its gesticulating owner—that I would return later, address Bird School, Bird, New Bird, the gin kept my heart alive but bemazed my brain, and after some lapses and losses common to dream sequences, I found myself in the reception room, trying to beat up the doctor, and roaring at people under chairs, and clamoring for Mary who luckily for her was not there; rough hands plucked at my dressing gown, ripping off a pocket, and somehow I seem to have been sitting on a bald brown-headed patient, whom I had mistaken for Dr. Blue, and who eventually stood up, remarking with a preposterous accent: "Now, who is nevrotic, I ask?"—and then a gaunt unsmiling nurse presented me with seven beautiful, *beautiful* books and the exquisitely folded tartan lap robe, and demanded a receipt; and in the sudden silence I became aware of a policeman in the hallway, to whom my fellow motorist was pointing me out, and meekly I signed the very symbolic receipt, thus surrendering my Lolita to all those apes. But what else could I do? One simple and stark thought stood out and this was: "Freedom for the moment is everything." One false move—and I might have been made to explain a life of crime. So I simulated a coming out of a daze. To my fellow motorist I paid what he thought was fair. To Dr. Blue, who by then was stroking my hand, I spoke in tears of the liquor I bolstered too freely a tricky but not necessarily diseased heart with. To the hospital in general I apologized with a flourish that almost bowled me over, adding however that I was not on particularly good terms with the rest of the Humbert clan. To myself I whispered that I still had my gun, and was still a free man—free to trace the fugitive, free to destroy my brother.

23

A thousand-mile stretch of silk-smooth road separated Kasbeam, where, to the best of my belief, the red fiend had been scheduled to appear for the first time, and fateful Elphinstone which we had reached about a week before Independence Day. The journey had taken up most of June for we had seldom made more than a hundred and fifty miles per traveling day, spending the rest of the time, up to five days in one case, at various stopping places, all of them also prearranged, no doubt. It was that stretch, then, along which the fiend's spoor should be sought; and to this I devoted myself, after several unmentionable days of dashing up and down the relentlessly radiating roads in the vicinity of Elphinstone.

Imagine me, reader, with my shyness, my distaste for any ostentation, my inherent sense of the *comme il faut*, imagine me masking the frenzy of my grief with a trembling ingratiating smile while devising some casual pretext to flip through the hotel register: "Oh," I would say, "I am almost positive that I stayed here once—let me look up the entries for mid-June—no, I see I'm wrong after all—what a very quaint name for a home town, Kawtagain. Thanks very much." Or: "I had a customer staying here—I mislaid his address—may I . . . ?" And every once in a while, especially if the operator of the place happened to be a certain type of gloomy male, personal inspection of the books was denied me.

I have a memo here: between July 5 and November 18, when I returned to Beardsley for a few days, I registered, if not actually stayed, at 342 hotels, motels and tourist homes. This figure includes a few registrations between Chestnut and Beardsley, one of which yielded a shadow of the fiend ("N. Petit, Larousse, Ill."); I had to space and time my inquiries carefully so as not to attract undue attention; and there must have been at least fifty places where I merely inquired at the desk—but that was a futile quest, and I preferred building up a foundation of verisimilitude and good will by first paying for an unneeded room. My survey showed that of the 300 or so books inspected, at least 20 provided me with a clue: the loitering fiend had stopped even more often than we, or else—he was quite capable of that—he had thrown in additional registrations in order to keep me well furnished with derisive hints. Only in one case had he actually stayed at the same motor court as we, a few paces from Lolita's pillow. In some instances he had taken up quarters in the same or in a neighboring block; not infrequently he had lain in wait at an intermediate spot between two bespoken points. How vividly I recalled Lolita, just before our departure from Beardsley, prone on the parlor rug, studying tour books and maps, and marking laps and stops with her lipstick!

I discovered at once that he had foreseen my investigations and had planted insulting pseudonyms for my special benefit. At the very first motel office I visited, Ponderosa Lodge, his entry, among a dozen obviously human ones, read: Dr. Gratiano Forbeson, Mirandola, NY. Its Italian Comedy connotations could not fail to strike me, of course. The landlady deigned to inform me that the gentleman had been laid up for five days with a bad cold, that he had left his car for repairs in some garage or other and that he had checked out on the 4th of July. Yes, a girl called Ann Lore had worked formerly at the Lodge, but was now married to a grocer in Cedar City. One moonlit night I waylaid white-shoed Mary on a solitary street; an automaton, she was about to shriek, but I managed to humanize her by the simple act of falling on my knees and with pious yelps imploring her to help. She did not know a thing, she swore. Who was this Gratiano Forbeson? She seemed to waver. I whipped out a hundred-dollar bill. She lifted it to the light of the moon. "He is your brother," she whispered at last. I plucked the bill out of her moon-cold hand, and spitting out a French curse turned and ran away. This taught me to rely on myself alone. No detective could discover the clues Trapp had tuned to my mind and manner. I could not hope, of course, he would ever leave his correct name and address; but I did hope he might slip on the glaze of his own subtlety, by daring, say, to introduce a richer and more personal shot of color than was strictly necessary, or by revealing too much through a qualitative sum of quantitative parts which revealed too little. In one thing he succeeded: he succeeded in thoroughly enmeshing me and my thrashing anguish in his demoniacal game. With infinite skill, he swayed and staggered, and regained an impossible balance, always leaving me with the sportive hope—if I may use such a term in speaking of betrayal, fury, desolation, horror and hate—that he might give himself away next time. He never did—though coming damn close to it. We all admire the spangled acrobat with classical grace meticulously walking his tight rope in the talcum light; but how much rarer art there is in the sagging rope expert wearing scarecrow clothes and impersonating a grotesque drunk! *I* should know.

The clues he left did not establish his identity but they reflected his personality, or at least a certain homogenous and striking personality; his genre, his type of humor—at its best at least—the tone of his brain, had affinities with my own. He mimed and mocked me. His allusions were definitely highbrow. He was well-read. He knew French. He was versed in logodaedaly and logomancy. He was an amateur of sex lore. He had a feminine handwriting. He would change his name but he could not disguise, no matter how he slanted them, his very peculiar t's, w's and l's. Quelquepart Island was one of his favorite residences. He did not use a fountain pen which fact, as any psychoanalyst will tell you, meant that the patient was a repressed undinist. One mercifully hopes there are water nymphs in the Styx.

His main trait was his passion for tantalization. Goodness, what a tease the poor fellow was! He challenged my scholarship. I am sufficiently proud of my knowing something to be modest about my not knowing all; and I daresay I missed some elements in that cryptogrammic paper chase. What a shiver of triumph and loathing shook my frail frame when, among the plain innocent names in the hotel recorder, his fiendish conundrum would ejaculate in my face! I noticed that whenever he felt his enigmas were becoming too recondite, even for such a solver as I, he would lure me back with an easy one. "Arsène Lupin" was obvious to a Frenchman who remembered the detective stories of his youth; and one hardly had to be a Coleridgian to appreciate the trite poke of "A. Person, Porlock, England." In horrible taste but basically suggestive of a cultured man—not a policeman, not a common goon, not a lewd salesman—were such assumed names as "Arthur Rainbow"— plainly the travestied author of *Le Bateau Bleu*—let me laugh a little too, gentlemen—and "Morris Schmetterling," of *L'Oiseau Ivre* fame (*touché*, reader!). The silly but funny "D. Orgon, Elmira, NY," was from Molière, of course, and because I had quite recently tried to interest Lolita in a famous 18th-century play, I welcomed as an old friend "Harry Bumper, Sheridan, Wyo." An ordinary encyclopedia informed me who the peculiar looking "Phineas Quimby, Lebanon, NH" was; and any good Freudian, with a German name and some interest in religious prostitution, should recognize at a glance the implication of "Dr. Kitzler, Eryx, Miss." So far so good. That sort of fun was shoddy but on the whole imper-sonal and thus innocuous. Among entries that arrested my attention as undoubtable clues *per se* but baffled me in respect to their finer points I do not care to mention many since I feel I am groping in a border-land mist with verbal phantoms turning, perhaps, into living vacationists. Who was "Johnny Randall, Ramble, Ohio"? Or was he a real person who just happened to write a hand similar to "N.S. Aristoff, Catagela, NY"? What was the sting in "Catagela"? And what about "James Mavor Morell, Hoaxton, England"? "Aristophanes," "hoax"—fine, but what was I missing?

There was one strain running through all that pseudo-nymity which caused me especially painful palpitations when I came across it. Such things as "G. Trapp, Geneva,

285

NY." was the sign of treachery on Lolita's part. "Aubrey Beardsley, Quelquepart Island" suggested more lucidly than the garbled telephone message had that the starting point of the affair should be looked for in the East. "Lucas Picador, Merrymay, Pa." insinuated that my Carmen had betrayed my pathetic endearments to the impostor. Horribly cruel, forsooth, was "Will Brown, Dolores, Colo." The gruesome "Harold Haze, Tombstone, Arizona" (which at another time would have appealed to my sense of humor) implied a familiarity with the girl's past that in nightmare fashion suggested for a moment that my quarry was an old friend of the family, maybe an old flame of Charlotte's, maybe a redresser of wrongs ("Donald Quix, Sierra, Nev."). But the most penetrating bodkin was the anagramtailed entry in the register of Chestnut Lodge "Ted Hunter, Cane, NH.".

The garbled license numbers left by all these Persons and Orgons and Morells and Trapps only told me that motel keepers omit to check if guests' cars are accurately listed. References—incompletely or incorrectly indicated— to the cars the fiend had hired for short laps between Wace and Elphinstone were of course useless; the license of the initial Aztec was a shimmer of shifting numerals, some transposed, others altered or omitted, but somehow forming interrelated combinations (such as "WS 1564" and "SH 1616," and "Q32888" or "CU 88322") which however were so cunningly contrived as to never reveal a common denominator.

It occurred to me that after he had turned that convertible over to accomplices at Wace and switched to the stage-motor car system, his successors might have been less careful and might have inscribed at some hotel office the archtype of those interrelated figures. But if looking for the fiend along a road I knew he had taken was such a complicated vague and unprofitable business, what could I expect from any attempt to trace unknown motorists traveling along unknown routes?

24

By the time I reached Beardsley, in the course of the harrowing recapitulation I have now discussed at sufficient length, a complete image had formed in my mind; and through the—always risky—process of elimination I had reduced this image to the only concrete source that morbid cerebration and torpid memory could give it.

Except for the Rev. Rigor Mortis (as the girls called him), and an old gentleman who taught non-obligatory German and Latin, there were no regular male teachers at Beardsley School. But on two occasions an art instructor on the Beardsley College faculty had come over to show the schoolgirls magic lantern pictures of French castles and nineteenth-century paintings. I had wanted to attend those projections and talks, but Dolly, as was her wont, had asked me not to, period. I also remembered that Gaston had referred to that particular lecturer as a brilliant *garçon*; but that was all; memory refused to supply me with the name of the chateau-lover.

On the day fixed for the execution, I walked through the sleet across the campus to the information desk in Maker Hall, Beardsley College. There I learned that the fellow's name was Riggs (rather like that of the minister), that he was a bachelor, and that in ten minutes he would issue from the "Museum" where he was having a class. In the passage leading to the auditorium I sat on a marble bench of sorts donated by Cecilia Dalrymple Ramble. As I waited there, in prostatic discomfort, drunk, sleep-starved, with my gun in my fist in my raincoat pocket, it suddenly occurred to me that I was demented and was about to do something stupid. There was not one chance in a million that Albert Riggs, Ass. Prof., was hiding my Lolita at his Beardsley home, 24 Pritchard Road. He could not be the villain. It was absolutely preposterous. I was losing my time and my wits. He and she were in California and not here at all.

Presently, I noticed a vague commotion behind some white statues; a door—not the one I had been staring at—opened briskly, and amid a bevy of women students a baldish head and two bright brown eyes bobbed, advanced.

He was a total stranger to me but insisted we had met at a lawn party at Beardsley School. How was my delightful tennis-playing daughter? He had another class. He would be seeing me.

Another attempt at identification was less speedily resolved: through an advertisement in one of Lo's magazines I dared to get in touch with a private detective, an ex-pugilist, and merely to give him some idea of the *method* adopted by the fiend, I acquainted him with the kind of names and address I had collected. He demanded a goodish deposit and for two years—two years, reader!—that imbecile busied himself with checking those nonsense data. I had long severed all monetary relations with him when he turned up one day with the triumphant information that an eighty-year-old Indian by the name of Bill Brown lived near Dolores, Colo.

25

This book is about Lolita; and now that I have reached the part which (had I not been forestalled by another internal combustion martyr) might be called *"Dolorès Disparue,"* there would be little sense in analyzing the three empty years that followed. While a few pertinent points have to be marked, the general impression I desire to convey is of a side door crashing open in life's full flight, and a rush of roaring black time drowning with its whipping wind the cry of lone disaster.

Singularly enough, I seldom if ever dreamed of Lolita as I remembered her—as I saw her constantly and obsessively in my conscious mind during my daymares and insomnias. More precisely: she did haunt my sleep but she appeared there in strange and ludicrous disguises as Valeria or Charlotte, or a cross between them. That complex ghost would come to me, shedding shift after shift, in an atmosphere of great melancholy and disgust, and would recline in dull invitation on some narrow board or hard settee, with flesh ajar like the rubber valve of a soccer ball's bladder. I would find myself, dentures fractured or hopelessly mislaid, in horrible *chambres garnies* where I would be entertained at tedious vivisecting parties that generally ended with Charlotte or Valeria weeping in my bleeding arms and being tenderly kissed by my brotherly lips in a dream disorder of auctioneered Viennese bric-à-brac, pity, impotence and the brown wigs of tragic old women who had just been gassed.

One day I removed from the car and destroyed an accumulation of teen-magazines. You know the sort. Stone age at heart; up to date, or at least Mycenaean, as to hygiene. A handsome, very ripe actress with huge lashes and a pulpy red underlip, endorsing a shampoo. Ads and fads. Young scholars dote on plenty of pleats—*que c'était loin, tout cela!* It is your hostess' duty to provide robes. Unattached details take all the sparkle out of your conversation. All of us have known "pickers"—one who picks her cuticle at the office party. Unless he is very elderly or very important, a man should remove his gloves before shaking hands with a woman. Invite Romance by wearing the Exciting New Tummy Flattener. Trims tums, nips hips. Tristram in Movielove. Yessir! The Joe-Roe marital enigma is making yaps flap. Glamourize yourself quickly and inexpensively.

Comics. Bad girl dark hair fat father cigar; good girl red hair handsome daddums clipped mustache. Or that repulsive strip with the big gagoon and his wife, a kiddoid gnomide. *Et moi qui t'offrais mon génie* . . . I recalled the rather charming nonsense verse I used to write her when she was a child: "nonsense," she used to say mockingly, "is correct."

The Squirl and his Squirrel, the Rabs and their Rabbits
Have certain obscure and peculiar habits.
Male hummingbirds make the most exquisite rockets.
The snake when he walks holds his hands in his pockets . . .

Other things of hers were harder to relinquish. Up to the end of 1949, I cherished and adored, and stained with my kisses and merman tears, a pair of old sneakers, a boy's shirt she had worn, some ancient blue jeans I found in the trunk compartment, a crumpled school cap, suchlike wanton treasures. Then, when I understood my mind was cracking, I collected these sundry belongings, added to them what had been stored in Beardsley—a box of books, her bicycle, old coats, galoshes—and on her fifteenth birthday mailed everything as an anonymous gift to a home for orphaned girls on a windy lake, on the Canadian border.

It is just possible that had I gone to a strong hypnotist he might have extracted from me and arrayed in a logical pattern certain chance memories that I have threaded through my book with considerably more ostentation than they present themselves with to my mind even now when I know what to seek in the past. At the time I felt I was merely losing contact with reality; and after spending the rest of the winter and most of the following spring in a Quebec sanatorium where I had stayed before, I resolved first to settle some affairs of mine in New York and then to proceed to California for a thorough search there.

Here is something I composed in my retreat:

Wanted, wanted: Dolores Haze.
Hair: brown. Lips: scarlet.
Age: five thousand three hundred days.
Profession: none, or "starlet."

Where are you hiding, Dolores Haze?
Why are you hiding, darling?
(I talk in a daze, I walk in a maze,
I cannot get out, said the starling).

Where are you riding, Dolores Haze?
What make is the magic carpet?
Is a Cream Cougar the present craze?
And where are you parked, my car pet?

Who is your hero, Dolores Haze?
Still one of those blue-caped star-men?
Oh the balmy days and the palmy bays,
And the cars, and the bars, my Carmen!

Oh Dolores, that juke-box hurts!
Are you still dancin', darlin'?
(Both in worn levis, both in torn T-shirts,
And I, in my corner, snarlin').

Happy, happy is gnarled McFate
Touring the States with a child wife,
Plowing his Molly in every State
Among the protected wild life.

My Dolly, my folly! Her eyes were *vair*,

And never closed when I kissed her.
Know an old perfume called *Soleil Vert?*
Are you from Paris, mister?

L'autre soir un air froid d'opéra m'alita:
Son fêlé—bien fol est qui s'y fie!
Il neige, le décor s'écroule, Lolita!
Lolita, qu'ai-je fait de ta vie?

Dying, dying, Lolita Haze,
Of hate and remorse, I'm dying.
And again my hairy fist I raise,
And again I hear you crying.

Officer, officer, there they go—
In the rain, where that lighted store is!
And her socks are white, and I love her so,
And her name is Haze, Dolores.

Officer, officer, there they are—
Dolores Haze and her lover!
Whip out your gun and follow that car.
Now tumble out, and take cover.

Wanted, wanted: Dolores Haze.
Her dream-gray gaze never flinches.
Ninety pounds is all she weighs
With a height of sixty inches.

My car is limping, Dolores Haze,
And the last long lap is the hardest,
And I shall be dumped where the weed decays,
And the rest is rust and stardust.

By psychoanalyzing this poem, I notice it is really a maniac's masterpiece. The stark, stiff, lurid rhymes correspond very exactly to certain perspectiveless and terrible landscapes and figures, and magnified parts of landscapes and figures, as drawn by psychopaths in tests devised by their astute trainers. I wrote many more poems. I immersed myself in the poetry of others. But not for a second did I forget the load of revenge.

I would be a knave to say, and the reader a fool to believe, that the shock of losing Lolita cured me of pederosis. My accursed nature could not change, no matter how my love for her did. On playgrounds and beaches, my sullen and stealthy eye, against my will, still sought out the flash of a nymphet's limbs, the sly tokens of Lolita's handmaids and rosegirls. But one essential vision in me had withered: never did I dwell now on possibilities of bliss with a little maiden, specific or synthetic, in some out-of-the-way place; never did my fancy sink its fangs into Lolita's sisters, far far away, in the coves of evoked islands. *That* was all over, for the time being at least. On the other hand, alas, two years of monstrous indulgence had left me with certain habits of lust: I feared lest the void I lived in might drive me to plunge into the freedom of sudden insanity when confronted with a chance temptation in some lane between school and supper. Solitude was corrupting me. I needed company and care. My heart was a hysterical unreliable organ. This is how Rita enters the picture.

26

She was twice Lolita's age and three quarters of mine: a very slight, dark-haired, pale-skinned adult, weighing a hundred and five pounds, with charmingly asymmetrical eyes, an angular, rapidly sketched profile, and a most appealing *ensellure* to her supple back—I think she had some

Spanish or Babylonian blood. I picked her up one depraved May evening somewhere between Montreal and New York, or more narrowly, between Toylestown and Blake, at a darkishly burning bar under the sign of the Tigermoth, where she was amiably drunk: she insisted we had gone to school together, and she placed her trembling little hand on my ape paw. My senses were very slightly stirred but I decided to give her a try; I did—and adopted her as a constant companion. She was so kind, was Rita, such a good sport, that I daresay she would have given herself to any pathetic creature or fallacy, an old broken tree or a bereaved porcupine, out of sheer chumminess and compassion.

When I first met her she had but recently divorced her third husband—and a little more recently had been abandoned by her seventh *cavalier servant*—the others, the mutables, were too numerous and mobile to tabulate. Her brother was—and no doubt still is—a prominent, pasty-faced, suspenders-and-painted-tie-wearing politician, mayor and booster of his ball-playing Bible-reading, grain-handling home town. For the last eight years he had been paying his great little sister several hundred dollars per month under the stringent condition that she would never never enter great little Grainball City. She told me, with wails of wonder, that for some God-damn reason every new boy friend of hers would first of all take her Grainball-ward: it was a fatal attraction; and before she knew what was what, she would find herself sucked into the lunar orbit of the town, and would be following the flood-lit drive that encircled it—"going round and round," as she phrased it, "like a God-damn mulberry moth."

She had a natty little coupé; and in it we traveled to California so as to give my venerable vehicle a rest. Her natural speed was ninety. Dear Rita! We cruised together for two dim years, from summer 1950 to summer 1952, and she was the sweetest, simplest, gentlest, dumbest Rita imaginable. In comparison to her, Valechka was a Schlegel, and Charlotte a Hegel. There is no earthly reason why I should dally with her in the margin of this sinister memoir, but let me say (hi, Rita—wherever you are, drunk or hangoverish, Rita, hi!) that she was the most soothing, the most comprehending companion that I ever had, and certainly saved me from the madhouse. I told her I was trying to trace a girl and plug that girl's bully. Rita solemnly approved of the plan—and in the course of some investigation she undertook on her own (without really knowing a thing), around San Humbertino, got entangled with a pretty awful crook herself; I had the devil of a time retrieving her—used and bruised but still cocky. Then one day she proposed playing Russian roulette with my sacred automatic; I said you couldn't, it was not a revolver, and we struggled for it, until at last it went off, touching off a very thin and very comical spurt of hot water from the hole it made in the wall of the cabin room; I remember her shrieks of laughter.

The oddly prepubescent curve of her back, her ricey skin, her slow languorous columbine kisses kept me from mischief. It is not the artistic aptitudes that are secondary sexual characters as some shams and shamans have said; it is the other way around: sex is but the ancilla of art. One rather mysterious spree that had interesting repercussions I must notice. I had abandoned the search: the fiend was either in Tartary or burning away in my cerebellum (the flames fanned by my fancy and grief) but certainly not having Dolores Haze play champion tennis on the Pacific Coast. One afternoon, on our way back East, in a hideous hotel, the kind where they hold conventions and where labeled, fat, pink men stagger around, all first names and business and booze—dear Rita and I awoke to find a third in our room, a blond, almost albino, young fellow with white eyelashes and large transparent ears, whom neither Rita nor I recalled having ever seen in our sad lives. Sweating in thick dirty underwear, and with old army boots on, he lay snoring on the double bed beyond my chaste Rita. One of his front teeth was gone, amber pustules grew on his forehead. Ritochka enveloped her sinuous nudity in my rain-coat—the first thing at hand; I slipped on a pair of candy-striped drawers; and we took stock of the situation. Five glasses had been used, which, in the way of clues, was an embarrassment of riches. The door was not properly closed. A sweater and a pair of shapeless tan pants lay on the floor. We shook their owner into miserable consciousness. He was completely amnesic. In an accent that Rita recognized as pure Brooklynese, he peevishly insinuated that somehow we had purloined his (worthless) identity. We rushed him into his clothes and left him at the nearest hospital, real-izing on the way that somehow or other after forgotten gyrations, we were in Grainball. Half a year later Rita wrote the doctor for news. Jack Humbertson as he had been taste-lessly dubbed was still isolated from his personal past. Oh Mnemosyne, sweetest and most mischievous of muses!

I would not have mentioned this incident had it not started a chain of ideas that resulted in my publishing in the *Cantrip Review* an essay on "Mimir and Memory," in which I suggested among other things that seemed orig-inal and important to that splendid review's benevolent readers, a theory of perceptual time based on the circula-tion of the blood and conceptually depending (to fill up this nutshell) on the mind's being conscious not only of matter but also of its own self, thus creating a continuous spanning of two points (the storable future and the stored past). In result of this venture—and in culmination of the impression made by my previous *travaux*—I was called from New York, where Rita and I were living in a little flat with a view of gleaming children taking shower baths far below in a fountainous arbor of Central Park, to Cantrip College, four hundred miles away, for one year. I lodged there, in special apartments for poets and philosophers, from September 1951 to June 1952, while Rita whom I preferred not to display vegetated—somewhat indecorously, I am afraid—in a roadside inn where I visited her twice a week. Then she vanished—more humanly than her predecessor had done: a month later I found her in the local jail. She was *très digne*, had had her appendix removed, and managed to convince me that the beautiful bluish furs she had been accused of stealing from a Mrs. Roland MacCrum had really been a spontaneous, if somewhat alcoholic, gift from Roland himself. I succeeded in getting her out without appealing to her touchy brother, and soon afterwards we drove back to Central Park West, by way of Briceland, where we had stopped for a few hours the year before.

A curious urge to relive my stay there with Lolita had got hold of me. I was entering a phase of existence where I had given up all hope of tracing her kidnaper and her. I now attempted to fall back on old settings in order to save what still could be saved in the way of *souvenir, souvenir que me veux-tu?* Autumn was ringing in the air. To a post card requesting twin beds Professor Hamburg got a prompt expression of regret in reply. They were full up. They had one bathless basement room with four beds which they thought I would not want. Their note paper was headed:

THE ENCHANTED HUNTERS

NEAR CHURCHES   NO DOGS
All legal beverages

I wondered if the last statement was true. All? Did they have for instance sidewalk grenadine? I also wondered if a

297

hunter, enchanted or otherwise, would not need a pointer more than a pew, and with a spasm of pain I recalled a scene worthy of a great artist: *petite nymphe accroupie*; but that silky cocker spaniel had perhaps been a baptized one. No—I felt I could not endure the throes of revisiting that lobby. There was a much better possibility of retrievable time elsewhere in soft, rich-colored, autumnal Briceland. Leaving Rita in a bar, I made for the town library. A twittering spinster was only too glad to help me disinter mid-August 1947 from the bound *Briceland Gazette*, and presently, in a secluded nook under a naked light, I was turning the enormous and fragile pages of a coffin-black volume almost as big as Lolita.

Reader! *Bruder!* What a foolish Hamburg that Hamburg was! Since his supersensitive system was loath to face the actual scene, he thought he could at least enjoy a secret part of it—which reminds one of the tenth or twentieth soldier in the raping queue who throws the girl's black shawl over her white face so as not to see those impossible eyes while taking his military pleasure in the sad, sacked village. What *I* lusted to get was the printed picture that had chanced to absorb my trespassing image while the *Gazette's* photographer was concentrating on Dr. Braddock and his group. Passionately I hoped to find preserved the portrait of the artist as a younger brute. An innocent camera catching me on my dark way to Lolita's bed—what a magnet for Mnemosyne! I cannot well explain the true nature of that urge of mine. It was allied, I suppose, to that swooning curiosity which impels one to examine with a magnifying glass bleak little figures—still life practically, and everybody about to throw up—at an early morning execution, and the patient's expression impossible to make out in the print. Anyway, I was literally gasping for breath, and one corner of the book of doom kept stabbing me in the stomach while I scanned and skimmed . . . *Brute Force* and *Possessed* were coming on Sunday, the 24th, to both theatres. Mr. Purdom, independent tobacco auctioneer, said that ever since 1925 he had been an Omen Faustum smoker. Husky Hank and his petite bride were to be the guests of Mr. and Mrs. Reginald G. Gore, 58 Inchkeith Ave. The size of certain parasites is one sixth of the host. Dunkerque was fortified in the tenth century. Misses' socks, 39 c. Saddle Oxfords 3.98. Wine, wine, wine, quipped the author of *Dark Age* who refused to be photographed, may suit a Persian bubble bird, but I say give me rain, rain, rain on the shingle roof for roses and inspiration every time. Dimples are caused by the adherence of the skin to the deeper tissues. Greeks repulse a heavy guerilla assault—and, ah, at last, a little figure in white, and Dr. Braddock in black, but whatever spectral shoulder was brushing against his ample form—nothing of myself could I make out.

I went to find Rita who introduced me with her *vin triste* smile to a pocket-sized wizened truculently tight old man saying this was—what was the name again, son?—a former schoolmate of hers. He tried to retain her, and in the slight scuffle that followed I hurt my thumb against his hard head. In the silent painted park where I walked her and aired her a little, she sobbed and said I would soon, soon leave her as everybody had, and I sang her a wistful French ballad, and strung together some fugitive rhymes to amuse her:

> The place was called *Enchanted Hunters*. Query:
> What Indian dyes, Diana, did thy dell
> endorse to make of Picture Lake a very
> blood bath of trees before the blue hotel?

She said: "Why blue when it is white, why blue for heaven's sake?" and started to cry again, and I marched her to the car, and we drove on to New York, and soon she was reasonably happy again high up in the haze on the little terrace of our flat. I notice I have somehow mixed up two events, my visit with Rita to Briceland on our way to Cantrip, and our passing through Briceland again on our way back to New York, but such suffusions of swimming colors are not to be disdained by the artist in recollection.

27

My letterbox in the entrance hall belonged to the type that allows one to glimpse something of its contents through a glassed slit. Several times already, a trick of harlequin light that fell through the glass upon an alien handwriting had twisted it into a semblance of Lolita's script causing me almost to collapse as I leant against an adjacent urn, almost my own. Whenever that happened—whenever her lovely, loopy, childish scrawl was horribly transformed into the dull hand of one of my few correspondents—I used to recollect, with anguished amusement, the times in my trustful, pre-dolorian past when I would be misled by a jewel-bright window opposite wherein my lurking eye, the ever alert periscope of my shameful vice, would make out from afar a half-naked nymphet stilled in the act of combing her Alice-in-Wonderland hair. There was in the fiery phantasm a perfection which made my wild delight also perfect, just because the vision was out of reach, with no possibility of attainment to spoil it by the awareness of an appended taboo; indeed, it may well be that the very attraction immaturity has for me lies not so much in the limpidity of pure young forbidden fairy child beauty as in the security of a situation where infinite perfections fill the gap between the little given and the great promised—the great rosegray never-to-be-had. *Mes fenêtres!* Hanging above blotched sunset and welling night, grinding my

300

teeth, I would crowd all the demons of my desire against the railing of a throbbing balcony: it would be ready to take off in the apricot and black humid evening; did take off—whereupon the lighted image would move and Eve would revert to a rib, and there would be nothing in the window but an obese partly clad man reading the paper.

Since I sometimes won the race between my fancy and nature's reality, the deception was bearable. Unbearable pain began when chance entered the fray and deprived me of the smile meant for me. *"Savez-vous qu'à dix ans ma petite était folle de vous?"* said a woman I talked to at a tea in Paris, and the *petite* had just married, miles away, and I could not even remember if I had ever noticed her in that garden, next to those tennis courts, a dozen years before. And now likewise, the radiant foreglimpse, the promise of reality, a promise not only to be simulated seductively but also to be nobly held—all this, chance denied me—chance and a change to smaller characters on the pale beloved writer's part. My fancy was both Proustianized and Procrusteanized; for that particular morning, late in September 1952, as I had come down to grope for my mail, the dapper and bilious janitor with whom I was on execrable terms started to complain that a man who had seen Rita home recently had been "sick like a dog" on the front steps. In the process of listening to him and tipping him, and then listening to a revised and politer version of the incident, I had the impression that one of the two letters which that blessed mail brought was from Rita's mother, a crazy little woman, whom we had once visited on Cape Cod and who kept writing me to my various addresses, saying how wonderfully well matched her daughter and I were, and how wonderful it would be if we married; the other letter which I opened and scanned rapidly in the elevator was from John Farlow.

I have often noticed that we are inclined to endow our friends with the stability of type that literary characters acquire in the reader's mind. No matter how many times we reopen "King Lear," never shall we find the good king banging his tankard in high revelry, all woes forgotten, at a jolly reunion with all three daughters and their lapdogs. Never will Emma rally, revived by the sympathetic salts in Flaubert's father's timely tear. Whatever evolution this or that popular character has gone through between the book covers, his fate is fixed in our minds, and, similarly, we expect our friends to follow this or that logical and conventional pattern we have fixed for them. Thus X will never compose the immortal music that would clash with the secondrate symphonies he has accustomed us to. Y will never commit murder. Under no circumstances can Z ever betray us. We have it all arranged in our minds, and the less often we see a particular person the more satisfying it is to check how obediently he conforms to our notion of him every time we hear of him. Any deviation in the fates we have ordained would strike us as not only anomalous but unethical. We would prefer not to have known at all our neighbor, the retired hot-dog stand operator, if it turns out he has just produced the greatest book of poetry his age has seen.

I am saying all this in order to explain how bewildered I was by Farlow's hysterical letter. I knew his wife had died but I certainly expected him to remain, throughout a devout widowhood, the dull, sedate and reliable person he had always been. Now he wrote that after a brief visit to the U.S. he had returned to South America and had decided that whatever affairs he had controlled at Ramsdale he would hand over to Jack Windmuller of that town, a lawyer whom we both knew. He seemed particularly relieved to get rid of the Haze "complications." He had married a

Spanish girl. He had stopped smoking and had gained thirty pounds. She was very young and a ski champion. They were going to India for their honeymonsoon. Since he was "building a family" as he put it, he would have no time henceforth for my affairs which he termed "very strange and very aggravating." Busybodies—a whole committee of them, it appeared—had informed him that the whereabouts of little Dolly Haze were unknown, and that I was living with a notorious divorcee in California. His father-in-law was a count, and exceedingly wealthy. The people who had been renting the Haze house for some years now wished to buy it. He suggested that I better produce Dolly quick. He had broken his leg. He enclosed a snapshot of himself and a brunette in white wool beaming at each other among the snows of Chile.

I remember letting myself into my flat and starting to say: Well, at least we shall now track them down—when the other letter began talking to me in a small matter-of-fact voice:

DEAR DAD:

How's everything? I'm married. I'm going to have a baby. I guess he's going to be a big one. I guess he'll come right for Christmas. This is a hard letter to write. I'm going nuts because we don't have enough to pay our debts and get out of here. Dick is promised a big job in Alaska in his very specialized corner of the mechanical field, that's all I know about it but it's really grand. Pardon me for withholding our home address but you may still be mad at me, and Dick must not know. This town is something. You can't see the morons for the smog. Please do send us a check, Dad. We could manage with three or four hundred or even less, anything is welcome, you might sell my old things, because once we

get there the dough will just start rolling in. Write,
please. I have gone through much sadness and hardship.
    Yours expecting,
        DOLLY (MRS. RICHARD F. SCHILLER)

28

I was again on the road, again at the wheel of the old blue
sedan, again alone. Rita had still been dead to the world
when I read that letter and fought the mountains of agony
it raised within me. I had glanced at her as she smiled in
her sleep and had kissed her on her moist brow, and had
left her forever, with a note of tender adieu which I taped
to her navel—otherwise she might not have found it.

"Alone" did I say? *Pas tout à fait.* I had my little black
chum with me, and as soon as I reached a secluded spot,
I rehearsed Mr. Richard F. Schiller's violent death. I had
found a very old and very dirty gray sweater of mine in
the back of the car, and this I hung up on a branch, in a
speechless glade, which I had reached by a wood road from
the now remote highway. The carrying out of the sentence
was a little marred by what seemed to me a certain stiffness in the play of the trigger, and I wondered if I should
get some oil for the mysterious thing but decided I had
no time to spare. Back into the car went the old dead
sweater, now with additional perforations, and having
reloaded warm Chum, I continued my journey.

The letter was dated September 18, 1952 (this was
September 22), and the address she gave was "General
Delivery, Coalmont" (not "Va.," not "Pa.," not "Tenn."—
and not Coalmont, anyway—I have camouflaged everything, my love). Inquiries showed this to be a small industrial
community some eight hundred miles from New York City.
At first I planned to drive all day and all night, but then
thought better of it and rested for a couple of hours around

dawn in a motor court room, a few miles before reaching the town. I had made up my mind that the fiend, this Schiller, had been a car salesman who had perhaps got to know my Lolita by giving her a ride in Beardsley—the day her bike blew a tire on the way to Miss Emperor—and that he had got into some trouble since then. The corpse of the executed sweater, no matter how I changed its contours as it lay on the back seat of the car, had kept revealing various outlines pertaining to Trapp-Schiller—the grossness and obscene bonhommie of his body, and to counteract this taste of coarse corruption I resolved to make myself especially handsome and smart as I pressed home the nipple of my alarm clock before it exploded at the set hour of six A.M. Then, with the stern and romantic care of a gentleman about to fight a duel, I checked the arrangement of my papers, bathed and perfumed my delicate body, shaved my face and chest, selected a silk shirt and clean drawers, pulled on transparent taupe socks, and congratulated myself for having with me in my trunk some very exquisite clothes—a waistcoat with nacreous buttons, for instance, a pale cashmere tie and so on.

I was not able, alas, to hold my breakfast, but dismissed that physicality as a trivial contretemps, wiped my mouth with a gossamer handkerchief produced from my sleeve, and, with a blue block of ice for heart, a pill on my tongue and solid death in my hip pocket, I stepped neatly into a telephone booth in Coalmont (Ah-ah-ah, said its little door) and rang up the only Schiller—Paul, Furniture—to be found in the battered book. Hoarse Paul told me he did know a Richard, the son of a cousin of his, and his address was, let me see, 10 Killer Street (I am not going very far for my pseudonyms). Ah-ah-ah, said the little door.

At 10 Killer Street, a tenement house, I interviewed a number of dejected old people and two long-haired strawberry-blond incredibly grubby nymphets (rather abstractly, just for the heck of it, the ancient beast in me was casting about for some lightly clad child I might hold against me for a minute, after the killing was over and nothing mattered any more, and everything was allowed). Yes, Dick Skiller had lived there, but had moved when he married. Nobody knew his address. "They might know at the store," said a bass voice from an open manhole near which I happened to be standing with the two thin-armed, barefoot little girls and their dim grandmothers. I entered the wrong store and a wary old negro shook his head even before I could ask anything. I crossed over to a bleak grocery and there, summoned by a customer at my request, a woman's voice from some wooden abyss in the floor, the manhole's counterpart, cried out: Hunter Road, last house.

Hunter Road was miles away, in an even more dismal district, all dump and ditch, and wormy vegetable garden, and shack, and gray drizzle, and red mud, and several smoking stacks in the distance. I stopped at the last "house"—a clapboard shack, with two or three similar ones farther away from the road and a waste of withered weeds all around. Sounds of hammering came from behind the house, and for several minutes I sat quite still in my old car, old and frail, at the end of my journey, at my gray goal, *finis*, my friends, *finis*, my fiends. The time was around two. My pulse was 40 one minute and 100 the next. The drizzle crepitated against the hood of the car. My gun had migrated to my right trouser pocket. A nondescript cur came out from behind the house, stopped in surprise, and started good-naturedly woof-woofing at me, his eyes slit, his shaggy belly all muddy, and then walked about a little and woofed once more.

I got out of the car and slammed its door. How matter-of-fact, how square that slam sounded in the void of the sunless day! *Woof*, commented the dog perfunctorily. I pressed the bell button, it vibrated through my whole system. *Personne. Je resonne. Repersonne.* From what depth this re-nonsense? Woof, said the dog. A rush and a shuffle, and woosh-woof went the door.

Couple of inches taller. Pink-rimmed glasses. New, heaped-up hairdo, new ears. How simple! The moment, the death I had kept conjuring up for three years was as simple as a bit of dry wood. She was frankly and hugely pregnant. Her head looked smaller (only two seconds had passed really, but let me give them as much wooden dura-tion as life can stand), and her pale-freckled cheeks were hollowed, and her bare shins and arms had lost all their tan, so that the little hairs showed. She wore a brown, sleeveless cotton dress and sloppy felt slippers.

"We—e—ell!" she exhaled after a pause with all the emphasis of wonder and welcome.

"Husband at home?" I croaked, fist in pocket.

I could not kill *her*, of course, as some have thought. You see, I loved her. It was love at first sight, at last sight, at ever and ever sight.

"Come in," she said with a vehement cheerful note. Against the splintery deadwood of the door, Dolly Schiller flattened herself as best she could (even rising on tiptoe a little) to let me pass, and was crucified for a moment, looking down, smiling down at the threshold, hollow-cheeked with round *pommettes*, her watered-milk-white arms outspread on the wood. I passed without touching her bulging babe. Dolly-smell, with a faint fried addition. My teeth chattered like an idiot's. "No, you stay out" (to the dog). She closed the door and followed me and her belly into the dollhouse parlor.

"Dick's down there," she said pointing with an invisible tennis racket, inviting my gaze to travel from the drab parlor-bedroom where we stood, right across the kitchen, and through the back-doorway where, in a rather primitive vista, a dark-haired young stranger in overalls, instantaneously reprieved, was perched with his back to me on a ladder fixing something near or upon the shack of his neighbor, a plumper fellow with only one arm, who stood looking up.

This pattern she explained from afar, apologetically ("Men will be men"); should she call him in?

No.

Standing in the middle of the slanting room and emitting questioning "hm's," she made familiar Javanese gestures with her wrists and hands, offering me, in a brief display of humorous courtesy, to choose between a rocker and the divan (their bed after ten P.M.). I say "familiar" because one day she had welcomed me with the same wrist dance to her party in Beardsley. We both sat down on the divan. Curious: although actually her looks had faded, I definitely realized, so hopelessly late in the day, how much she looked—had always looked—like Botticelli's russet Venus—the same soft nose, the same blurred beauty. In my pocket my fingers gently let go and repacked a little at the tip, within the handkerchief it was nested in, my unused weapon.

"That's not the fellow I want," I said.

The diffuse look of welcome left her eyes. Her forehead puckered as in the old bitter days:

"Not *who?*"

"Where is he? Quick!"

"Look," she said, inclining her head to one side and shaking it in that position. "Look, you are not going to bring that up."

"I certainly am," I said, and for a moment—strangely enough the only merciful, endurable one in the whole interview—we were bristling at each other as if she were still mine.

A wise girl, she controlled herself.

Dick did not know a thing of the whole mess. He thought I was her father. He thought she had run away from an upperclass home just to wash dishes in a diner. He believed anything. Why should I want to make things harder than they were by raking up all that muck?

But, I said, she must be sensible, she must be a sensible girl (with her bare drum under that thin brown stuff), she must understand that if she expected the help I had come to give, I must have at least a clear comprehension of the situation.

"Come, his name!"

She thought I had guessed long ago. It was (with a mischievous and melancholy smile) such a sensational name. I would never believe it. She could hardly believe it herself.

His name, my fall nymph.

It was so unimportant, she said. She suggested I skip it. Would I like a cigarette?

No. His name.

She shook her head with great resolution. She guessed it was too late to raise hell and I would never believe the unbelievably unbelievable—

I said I had better go, regards, nice to have seen her.

She said really it was useless, she would never tell, but on the other hand, after all—"Do you really want to know who it was? Well, it was—"

And softly, confidentially, arching her thin eyebrows and puckering her parched lips, she emitted, a little mockingly, somewhat fastidiously, not untenderly, in a kind of muted whistle, the name that the astute reader has guessed long ago.

Waterproof. Why did a flash from Hourglass Lake cross my consciousness? I, too, had known it, without knowing it, all along. There was no shock, no surprise. Quietly the fusion took place, and everything fell into order, into the pattern of branches that I have woven throughout this memoir with the express purpose of having the ripe fruit fall at the right moment; yes, with the express and perverse purpose of rendering—she was talking but I sat melting in my golden peace—of rendering that golden and monstrous peace through the satisfaction of logical recognition, which my most inimical reader should experience now.

She was, as I say, talking. It now came in a relaxed flow. He was the only man she had ever been crazy about. What about Dick? Oh, Dick was a lamb, they were quite happy together, but she meant something different. And *I* had never counted, of course?

She considered me as if grasping all at once the incredible—and somehow tedious, confusing and unnecessary—fact that the distant, elegant, slender, forty-year-old valetudinarian in velvet coat sitting beside her had known and adored every pore and follicle of her pubescent body. In her washed-out gray eyes, strangely spectacled, our poor romance was for a moment reflected, pondered upon, and dismissed like a dull party, like a rainy picnic to which only the dullest bores had come, like a humdrum exercise, like a bit of dry mud caking her childhood.

I just managed to jerk my knee out of the range of a sketchy tap—one of her acquired gestures.

She asked me not to be dense. The past was the past. I had been a good father, she guessed—granting me *that*. Proceed, Dolly Schiller.

Well, did I know that he had known her mother? That

he was practically an old friend? That he had visited with his uncle in Ramsdale?—oh, years ago—and spoken at Mother's club, and had tugged and pulled her, Dolly, by her bare arm onto his lap in front of everybody, and kissed her face, she was ten and furious with him? Did I know he had seen me and her at the inn where he was writing the very play she was to rehearse in Beardsley, two years later? Did I know—It had been horrid of her to sidetrack me into believing that Clare was an old female, maybe a relative of his or a sometime lifemate—and oh, what a close shave it had been when the Wace *Journal* carried his picture.

The *Briceland Gazette* had not. Yes, very amusing.

Yes, she said, this world was just one gag after another, if somebody wrote up her life nobody would ever believe it.

At this point, there came brisk homey sounds from the kitchen into which Dick and Bill had lumbered in quest of beer. Through the doorway they noticed the visitor, and Dick entered the parlor.

"Dick, this is my Dad!" cried Dolly in a resounding violent voice that struck me as totally strange, and new, and cheerful, and old, and sad, because the young fellow, veteran of a remote war, was hard of hearing.

Arctic blue eyes, black hair, ruddy cheeks, unshaven chin. We shook hands. Discreet Bill, who evidently took pride in working wonders with one hand, brought in the beer cans he had opened. Wanted to withdraw. The exquisite courtesy of simple folks. Was made to stay. A beer ad. In point of fact, I preferred it that way, and so did the Schillers. I switched to the jittery rocker. Avidly munching, Dolly plied me with marshmallows and potato chips. The men looked at her fragile, *frileux*, diminutive, old-world, youngish but sickly, father in velvet coat and beige vest, maybe a viscount. They were under the impression I had come to stay, and

Dick with a great wrinkling of brows that denoted difficult thought, suggested Dolly and he might sleep in the kitchen on a spare mattress. I waved a light hand and told Dolly who transmitted it by means of a special shout to Dick that I had merely dropped in on my way to Readsburg where I was to be entertained by some friends and admirers. It was then noticed that one of the few thumbs remaining to Bill was bleeding (not such a wonder-worker after all). How womanish and somehow never seen that way before was the shadowy division between her pale breasts when she bent down over the man's hand! She took him for repairs to the kitchen. For a few minutes, three or four little eternities which positively welled with artificial warmth, Dick and I remained alone. He sat on a hard chair rubbing his forelimbs and frowning. I had an idle urge to squeeze out the blackheads on the wings of his perspiring nose with my long agate claws. He had nice sad eyes with beautiful lashes, and very white teeth. His Adam's apple was large and hairy. Why don't they shave better, those young brawny chaps? He and his Dolly had had unrestrained intercourse on that couch there, at least a hundred and eighty times, probably much more; and before that—how long had she known him? No grudge. Funny—no grudge at all, nothing except grief and nausea. He was now rubbing his nose. I was sure that when finally he would open his mouth, he would say (slightly shaking his head): "Aw, she's a swell kid, Mr. Haze. She sure is. And she's going to make a swell mother." He opened his mouth—and took a sip of beer. This gave him countenance—and he went on sipping till he frothed at the mouth. He was a lamb. He had cupped her Florentine breasts. His fingernails were black and broken, but the phalanges, the whole carpus, the strong shapely wrist were far, far finer than mine: I have hurt too much too many bodies with my twisted poor hands to be proud of them.

French epithets, a Dorset yokel's knuckles, an Austrian tailor's flat finger tips—that's Humbert Humbert.

Good. If he was silent I could be silent too. Indeed, I could very well do with a little rest in this subdued, frightened-to-death rocking chair, before I drove to wherever the beast's lair was—and then pulled the pistol's foreskin back, and then enjoyed the orgasm of the crushed trigger: I was always a good little follower of the Viennese medicine man. But presently I became sorry for poor Dick whom, in some hypnotoid way, I was horribly preventing from making the only remark he could think up ("She's a swell kid . . .").

"And so," I said, "you are going to Canada?"

In the kitchen, Dolly was laughing at something Bill had said or done.

"And so," I shouted, "you are going to Canada? Not Canada—I re-shouted—"I mean Alaska, of course."

He nursed his glass and, nodding sagely, replied: "Well, he cut it on a jagger, I guess. Lost his right arm in Italy."

Lovely mauve almond trees in bloom. A blown-off surrealistic arm hanging up there in the pointillistic mauve. A flowergirl tattoo on the hand. Dolly and band-aided Bill reappeared. It occurred to me that her ambiguous, brown and pale beauty excited the cripple. Dick, with a grin of relief stood up. He guessed Bill and he would be going back to fix those wires. He guessed Mr. Haze and Dolly had loads of things to say to each other. He guessed he would be seeing me before I left. Why do those people guess so much and shave so little, and are so disdainful of hearing aids?

"Sit down," she said, audibly striking her flanks with her palms. I relapsed into the black rocker.

"So you betrayed me? Where did you go? Where is he now?"

She took from the mantelpiece a concave glossy

snapshot. Old woman in white, stout, beaming, bowlegged, very short dress; old man in his shirtsleeves, drooping mustache, watch chain. Her in-laws. Living with Dick's brother's family in Juneau.

"Sure you don't want to smoke?"

She was smoking herself. First time I saw her doing it. *Streng verboten* under Humbert the Terrible. Gracefully, in a blue mist, Charlotte Haze rose from her grave. I would find him through Uncle Ivory if she refused.

"Betrayed you? No." She directed the dart of her cigarette, index rapidly tapping upon it, toward the hearth exactly as her mother used to do, and then, like her mother, oh my God, with her fingernail scratched and removed a fragment of cigarette paper from her underlip. No. She had not betrayed me. I was among friends. Edusa had warned her that Cue liked little girls, had been almost jailed once, in fact (nice fact), and he knew she knew. Yes . . . Elbow in palm, puff, smile, exhaled smoke, darting gesture. Waxing reminiscent. He saw—smiling—through everything and everybody, because he was not like me and her but a genius. A great guy. Full of fun. Had rocked with laughter when she confessed about me and her, and said he had thought so. It was quite safe, under the circumstances, to tell him . . .

Well, Cue—they all called him Cue—

Her camp five years ago. Curious coincidence— . . . took her to a dude ranch about a day's drive from Elephant (Elphinstone). Named? Oh, some silly name—Duk Duk Ranch—*you* know just plain silly—but it did not matter now, anyway, because the place had vanished and disintegrated. Really, she meant, I could not imagine how utterly lush that ranch was, she meant it had everything but everything, even an indoor waterfall. Did I remember the redhaired guy we ("we" was good) had once had some

314

tennis with? Well, the place really belonged to Red's brother, but he had turned it over to Cue for the summer. When Cue and she came, the others had them actually go through a coronation ceremony and then—a terrific ducking, as when you cross the Equator. *You* know.

Her eyes rolled in synthetic resignation.

"Go on, please."

Well. The idea was he would take her in September to Hollywood and arrange a tryout for her, a bit part in the tennis-match scene of a movie picture based on a play of his—*Golden Guts*—and perhaps even have her double one of its sensational starlets on the Klieg-struck tennis court. Alas, it never came to that.

"Where is the hog now?"

He was not a hog. He was a great guy in many respects. But it was all drink and drugs. And, of course, he was a complete freak in sex matters, and his friends were his slaves. I just could not imagine (I, Humbert, could not imagine!) what they all did at Duk Duk Ranch. She refused to take part because she loved him, and he threw her out.

"What things?"

"Oh, weird, filthy, fancy things. I mean, he had two girls and two boys, and three or four men, and the idea was for all of us to tangle in the nude while an old woman took movie pictures." (Sade's Justine was twelve at the start.)

"What things exactly?"

"Oh, things . . . Oh, I—really I"—she uttered the "I" as a subdued cry while she listened to the source of the ache, and for lack of words spread the five fingers of her angularly up-and-down-moving hand. No, she gave it up, she refused to go into particulars with that baby inside her.

That made sense.

"It is of no importance now," she said pounding a gray cushion with her fist and then lying back, belly up, on the divan. "Crazy things, filthy things. I said no, I'm just not going to [she used, in all insouciance really, a disgusting slang term which, in a literal French translation, would be *souffler*] your beastly boys, because I want only you. Well, he kicked me out."

There was not much else to tell. That winter 1949, Fay and she had found jobs. For almost two years she had—oh, just drifted, oh, doing some restaurant work in small places, and then she had met Dick. No, she did not know where the other was. In New York, she guessed. Of course, he was so famous she would have found him at once if she had wanted. Fay had tried to get back to the Ranch—and it just was not there any more—it had burned to the ground, *nothing* remained, just a charred heap of rubbish. It was so *strange*, so *strange*—

She closed her eyes and opened her mouth, leaning back on the cushion, one felted foot on the floor. The wooden floor slanted, a little steel ball would have rolled into the kitchen. I knew all I wanted to know. I had no intention of torturing my darling. Somewhere beyond Bill's shack an afterwork radio had begun singing of folly and fate, and there she was with her ruined looks and her adult, rope-veined narrow hands and her gooseflesh white arms, and her shallow ears, and her unkempt armpits, there she was (my Lolita!), hopelessly worn at seventeen, with that baby, dreaming already in her of becoming a big shot and retiring around 2020 A.D.—and I looked and looked at her, and knew as clearly as I know I am to die, that I loved her more than anything I had ever seen or imagined on earth, or hoped for anywhere else. She was only the faint violet whiff and dead leaf echo of the nymphet I had rolled myself upon with such cries in the past; an echo on the brink of a russet ravine, with a far wood under a white sky, and brown leaves choking the brook, and one last cricket in the crisp weeds . . . but thank God it was not that echo alone that I worshipped. What I used to pamper among the tangled vines of my heart, *mon grand péché radieux*, had dwindled to its essence: sterile and selfish vice, all *that* I canceled and cursed. You may jeer at me, and threaten to clear the court, but until I am gagged and half-throttled, I will shout my poor truth. I insist the world know how much I loved my Lolita, *this* Lolita, pale and polluted, and big with another's child, but still gray-eyed, still sooty-lashed, still auburn and almond, still Carmencita, still mine; *Changeons de vie, ma Carmen, allons vivre quelque part où nous ne serons jamais séparés*; Ohio? The wilds of Massachusetts? No matter, even if those eyes of hers would fade to myopic fish, and her nipples swell and crack, and her lovely young velvety delicate delta be tainted and torn—even then I would go mad with tenderness at the mere sight of your dear wan face, at the mere sound of your raucous young voice, my Lolita.

"Lolita," I said, "this may be neither here nor there but I have to say it. Life is very short. From here to that old car you know so well there is a stretch of twenty, twenty-five paces. It is a very short walk. Make those twenty-five steps. Now. Right now. Come just as you are. And we shall live happily ever after."

Carmen, voulez-vous venir avec moi?

"You mean," she said opening her eyes and raising herself slightly, the snake that may strike, "you mean you will give us [us] that money only if I go with you to a motel. Is *that* what you mean?"

"No," I said, "you got it all wrong. I want you to leave your incidental Dick, and this awful hole, and come to live with me, and die with me, and everything with me" (words to that effect).

"You're crazy," she said, her features working.

"Think it over, Lolita. There are no strings attached.

Except, perhaps—well, no matter." (A reprieve, I wanted to say but did not.) "Anyway, if you refuse you will still get your . . . *trousseau*."

"No kidding?" asked Dolly.

I handed her an envelope with four hundred dollars in cash and a check for three thousand six hundred more.

Gingerly, uncertainly, she received *mon petit cadeau*; and then her forehead became a beautiful pink. "You mean," she said, with agonized emphasis, "you are giving us *four thousand bucks*?" I covered my face with my hand and broke into the hottest tears I had ever shed. I felt them winding through my fingers and down my chin, and burning me, and my nose got clogged, and I could not stop, and then she touched my wrist.

"I'll die if you touch me," I said. "You are sure you are not coming with me? Is there no hope of your coming? Tell me only this."

"No," she said. "No, honey, no."

She had never called me honey before.

"No," she said, "it is quite out of the question. I would sooner go back to Cue. I mean—"

She groped for words. I supplied them mentally ("*He* broke my heart. *You* merely broke my life").

"I think," she went on—"oops"—the envelope skidded to the floor—she picked it up—"I think it's oh utterly *grand* of you to give us all that dough. It settles everything, we can start next week. Stop crying, please. You should understand. Let me get you some more beer. Oh, don't cry, I'm so sorry I cheated so much, but that's the way things are."

I wiped my face and my fingers. She smiled at the *cadeau*. She exulted. She wanted to call Dick. I said I would have to leave in a moment, did not want to see him at all, at all. We tried to think of some subject of conversation. For some reason, I kept seeing—it trembled and silkily glowed on my damp retina—a radiant child of twelve, sitting on a threshold, "pinging" pebbles at an empty can. I almost said—trying to find some casual remark—"I wonder sometimes what has become of the little McCoo girl, did she ever get better?"—but stopped in time lest she rejoin: "I wonder sometimes what has become of the little Haze girl . . ." Finally, I reverted to money matters. That sum, I said, represented more or less the net rent from her mother's house; she said: "Had it not been sold years ago?" No (I admit I *had* told her this in order to sever all connections with R.); a lawyer would send a full account of the financial situation later; it was rosy; some of the small securities her mother had owned had gone up and up. Yes, I was quite sure I had to go. I had to go, and find him, and destroy him.

Since I would not have survived the touch of her lips, I kept retreating in a mincing dance, at every step she and her belly made toward me.

She and the dog saw me off. I was surprised (this a rhetorical figure, I was not) that the sight of the old car in which she had ridden as a child and a nymphet, left her so very indifferent. All she remarked was it was getting sort of purplish about the gills. I said it was hers, I could go by bus. She said don't be silly, they would fly to Jupiter and buy a car there. I said I would buy this one from her for five hundred dollars.

"At this rate we'll be millionnaires next," she said to the ecstatic dog.

Carmencita, lui demandais-je . . . "One last word," I said in my horrible careful English, "are you quite, quite sure that—well, not tomorrow, of course, and not after tomorrow, but—well—some day, any day, you will not come to live with me? I will create a brand new God and thank him with piercing cries, if you give me that microscopic hope" (to that effect).

"No," she said smiling, "no."

"It would have made all the difference," said Humbert Humbert.

Then I pulled out my automatic—I mean, this is the kind of fool thing a reader might suppose I did. It never even occurred to me to do it.

"Good by-aye!" she chanted, my American sweet immortal dead love; for she is dead and immortal if you are reading this. I mean, such is the formal agreement with the so-called authorities.

Then, as I drove away, I heard her shout in a vibrant voice to her Dick; and the dog started to lope alongside my car like a fat dolphin, but he was too heavy and old, and very soon gave up.

And presently I was driving through the drizzle of the dying day, with the windshield wipers in full action but unable to cope with my tears.

30

Leaving as I did Coalmont around four in the afternoon (by Route X—I do not remember the number), I might have made Ramsdale by dawn had not a short-cut tempted me. I had to get onto Highway Y. My map showed quite blandly that just beyond Woodbine, which I reached at nightfall, I could leave paved X and reach paved Y by means of a transverse dirt road. It was only some forty miles long according to my map. Otherwise I would have to follow X for another hundred miles and then use leisurely looping Z to get to Y and my destination. However, the short-cut in question got worse and worse, bumpier and bumpier, muddier and muddier, and when I attempted to turn back after some ten miles of purblind, tortuous and tortoise-slow progress, my old and weak Melmoth got stuck in deep clay. All was dark and muggy, and hopeless. My headlights hung over a broad ditch full of water. The surrounding country, if any, was a black wilderness. I sought to extricate myself but my rear wheels only whined in slosh and anguish. Cursing my plight, I took off my fancy clothes, changed into slacks, pulled on the bullet-riddled sweater, and waded four miles back to a roadside farm. It started to rain on the way but I had not the strength to go back for a mackintosh. Such incidents have convinced me that my heart is basically sound despite recent diagnoses. Around midnight, a wrecker dragged my car out. I navigated back to Highway X and traveled on. Utter weariness overtook me an hour later, in an anonymous little town. I pulled up at the curb and in darkness drank deep from a friendly flask.

The rain had been cancelled miles before. It was a black warm night, somewhere in Appalachia. Now and then cars passed me, red tail-lights receding, white headlights advancing, but the town was dead. Nobody strolled and laughed on the sidewalks as relaxing burghers would in sweet, mellow, rotting Europe. I was alone to enjoy the innocent night and my terrible thoughts. A wire receptacle on the curb was very particular about acceptable contents: Sweepings. Paper. No Garbage. Sherry-red letters of light marked a Camera Shop. A large thermometer with the name of a laxative quietly dwelt on the front of a drugstore. Rubinov's Jewelry Company had a display of artificial diamonds reflected in a red mirror. A lighted green clock swam in the linenish depths of Jiffy Jeff Laundry. On the other side of the street a garage said in its sleep—genuflexion lubricity; and corrected itself to Gulflex Lubrication. An airplane, also gemmed by Rubinov, passed, droning, in the velvet heavens. How many small dead-of-night towns I had seen! This was not yet the last.

Let me dally a little, he is as good as destroyed. Some way further across the street, neon lights flickered twice slower than my heart: the outline of a restaurant sign, a large coffee-pot, kept bursting, every full second or so, into emerald life, and every time it went out, pink letters saying Fine Foods relayed it, but the pot could still be made out as a latent shadow teasing the eye before its next emerald resurrection. We made shadowgraphs. This furtive burg was not far from The Enchanted Hunters. I was weeping again, drunk on the impossible past.

31

At this solitary stop for refreshments between Coalmont and Ramsdale (between innocent Dolly Schiller and jovial Uncle Ivor), I reviewed my case. With the utmost simplicity and clarity I now saw myself and my love. Previous attempts seemed out of focus in comparison. A couple of years before, under the guidance of an intelligent French-speaking confessor, to whom, in a moment of metaphysical curiosity, I had turned over a Protestant's drab atheism for an old-fashioned popish cure, I had hoped to deduce from my sense of sin the existence of a Supreme Being. On those frosty mornings in rime-laced Quebec, the good priest worked on me with the finest tenderness and understanding. I am infinitely obliged to him and the great Institution he represented. Alas, I was unable to transcend the simple human fact that whatever spiritual solace I might find, whatever lithophanic eternities might be provided for me, nothing could make my Lolita forget the foul lust I had inflicted upon her. Unless it can be proven to me—to me as I am now, today, with my heart and my beard, and my putrefaction—that in the infinite run it does not matter a jot that a North American girl-child named Dolores Haze had been deprived of her childhood by a maniac, unless this can be proven (and if it can, then life is a joke), I see nothing for the treatment of my misery but the melancholy and very local palliative of articulate art. To quote an old poet:

> The moral sense in mortals is the duty
> We have to pay on mortal sense of beauty.

32

There was the day, during our first trip—our first circle of paradise—when in order to enjoy my phantasms in peace I firmly decided to ignore what I could not help perceiving, the fact that I was to her not a boy friend, not a glamour man, not a pal, not even a person at all, but just two eyes and a foot of engorged brawn—to mention only mentionable matters. There was the day when having withdrawn the functional promise I had made her on the eve (whatever she had set her funny little heart on—a roller rink with some special plastic floor or a movie matinee to which she wanted to go alone), I happened to glimpse from the bathroom, through a chance combination of mirror aslant and door ajar, a look on her face . . . that look I cannot exactly describe . . . an expression of helplessness so perfect that it seemed to grade into one of rather comfortable inanity just because this was the very limit of injustice and frustration—and every limit presupposes something beyond it—hence the neutral illumination. And when you bear in mind that these were the raised eyebrows and parted lips of a child, you may better appreciate what depths of calculated carnality, what reflected despair, restrained me from falling at her dear feet and dissolving in human tears, and sacrificing my jealousy to whatever pleasure Lolita might hope to derive from mixing with dirty and dangerous children in an outside world that was real to her.

And I have still other smothered memories, now unfolding themselves into limbless monsters of pain. Once, in a sunset-ending street of Beardsley, she turned to little Eva Rosen (I was taking both nymphets to a concert and walking behind them so close as almost to touch them with my person), she turned to Eva, and so very serenely and seriously, in answer to something the other had said about its being better to die than hear Milton Pinski, some local schoolboy she knew, talk about music, my Lolita remarked:

"You know, what's so dreadful about dying is that you are completely on your own"; and it struck me, as my automaton knees went up and down, that I simply did not know a thing about my darling's mind and that quite possibly, behind the awful juvenile clichés, there was in her a garden and a twilight, and a palace gate—dim and adorable regions which happened to be lucidly and absolutely forbidden to me, in my polluted rags and miserable convulsions; for I often noticed that living as we did, she and I, in a world of total evil, we would become strangely embarrassed whenever I tried to discuss something she and an older friend, she and a parent, she and a real healthy sweetheart, I and Annabel, Lolita and a sublime, purified, analyzed, deified Harold Haze, might have discussed—an abstract idea, a painting, stippled Hopkins or shorn Baudelaire, God or Shakespeare, anything of a genuine kind. Good will! She would mail her vulnerability in trite brashness and boredom, whereas I, using for my desperately detached comments an artificial tone of voice that set my own last teeth on edge, provoked my audience to such outbursts of rudeness as made any further conversation impossible, oh my poor, bruised child.

I loved you. I was a pentapod monster, but I loved you. I was despicable and brutal, and turpid, and everything, *mais je t'aimais, je t'aimais!* And there were times when I knew how you felt, and it was hell to know it, my little one. Lolita girl, brave Dolly Schiller.

I recall certain moments, let us call them icebergs in paradise, when after having had my fill of her—after fabulous, insane exertions that left me limp and azure-barred—I would gather her in my arms with, at last, a mute moan of human tenderness (her skin glistening in the neon light coming from the paved court through the slits in the blind, her soot-black lashes matted, her grave gray eyes more vacant than ever—for all the world a little patient still in the confusion of a drug after a major operation)—and the tenderness would deepen to shame and despair, and I would lull and rock my lone light Lolita in my marble arms, and moan in her warm hair, and caress her at random and mutely ask her blessing, and at the peak of this human agonized selfless tenderness (with my soul actually hanging around her naked body and ready to repent), all at once, ironically, horribly, lust would swell again—and "oh, *no*," Lolita would say with a sigh to heaven, and the next moment the tenderness and the azure—all would be shattered.

Mid-twentieth century ideas concerning child-parent relationship have been considerably tainted by the scholastic rigmarole and standardized symbols of the psychoanalytic racket, but I hope I am addressing myself to unbiased readers. Once when Avis's father had honked outside to signal papa had come to take his pet home, I felt obliged to invite him into the parlor, and he sat down for a minute, and while we conversed, Avis, a heavy, unattractive, affectionate child, drew up to him and eventually perched plumply on his knee. Now, I do not remember if I have mentioned that Lolita always had an absolutely enchanting smile for strangers, a tender furry slitting of the eyes, a dreamy sweet radiance of all her features which did not mean a thing of course, but was so beautiful, so endearing that one found it hard to reduce such sweetness to but a magic gene automatically lighting up her face in atavistic token of some ancient rite of welcome—

hospitable prostitution, the coarse reader may say. Well, there she stood while Mr. Byrd twirled his hat and talked, and— yes, look how stupid of me, I have left out the main characteristic of the famous Lolita smile, namely: while the tender, nectared, dimpled brightness played, it was never directed at the stranger in the room but hung in its own remote flowered void, so to speak, or wandered with myopic softness over chance objects—and this is what was happening now: while fat Avis sidled up to her papa, Lolita gently beamed at a fruit knife that she fingered on the edge of the table, whereon she leaned, many miles away from me. Suddenly, as Avis clung to her father's neck and ear while, with a casual arm, the man enveloped his lumpy and large offspring, I saw Lolita's smile lose all its light and become a frozen little shadow of itself, and the fruit knife slipped off the table and struck her with its silver handle a freak blow on the ankle which made her gasp, and crouch head forward, and then, jumping on one leg, her face awful with the preparatory grimace which children hold till the tears gush, she was gone—to be followed at once and consoled in the kitchen by Avis who had such a wonderful fat pink dad and a small chubby brother, and a brand-new baby sister, and a home, and two grinning dogs, and Lolita had nothing. And I have a neat pendant to that little scene—also in a Beardsley setting. Lolita, who had been reading near the fire, stretched herself, and then inquired, her elbow up, with a grunt: "Where is she buried anyway?" "Who?" "Oh, you know, my murdered mummy." "And *you* know where her grave is," I said controlling myself, whereupon I named the cemetery— just outside Ramsdale, between the railway tracks and Lakeview Hill. "Moreover," I added, "the tragedy of such an accident is somewhat cheapened by the epithet you saw fit to apply to it. If you really wish to triumph in your mind over the idea of death—" "Ray," said Lo for hurray, and languidly left the room, and for a long while I stared with smarting eyes into the fire. Then I picked up her book. It was some trash for young people. There was a gloomy girl Marion, and there was her stepmother who turned out to be, against all expectations, a young, gay, understanding redhead who explained to Marion that Marion's dead mother had really been a heroic woman since she had deliberately dissimulated her great love for Marion because she was dying, and did not want her child to miss her. I did not rush up to her room with cries. I always preferred the mental hygiene of noninterference. Now, squirming and pleading with my own memory, I recall that on this and similar occasions, it was always my habit and method to ignore Lolita's states of mind while comforting my own base self. When my mother, in a livid wet dress, under the tumbling mist (so I vividly imagined her), had run panting ecstatically up that ridge above Moulinet to be felled there by a thunderbolt, I was but an infant, and in retrospect no yearnings of the accepted kind could I ever graft upon any moment of my youth, no matter how savagely psychotherapists heckled me in my later periods of depression. But I admit that a man of my power of imagination cannot plead personal ignorance of universal emotions. I may also have relied too much on the abnormally chill relations between Charlotte and her daughter. But the awful point of the whole argument is this. It had become gradually clear to my conventional Lolita during our singular and bestial cohabitation that even the most miserable of family lives was better than the parody of incest, which, in the long run, was the best I could offer the waif.

33

Ramsdale revisited. I approached it from the side of the lake. The sunny noon was all eyes. As I rode by in my mud-flecked car, I could distinguish scintillas of diamond water between the far pines. I turned into the cemetery and walked among the long and short stone monuments. *Bonzhur*, Charlotte. On some of the graves there were pale, transparent little national flags slumped in the windless air under the evergreens. Gee, Ed, that was bad luck—referring to G. Edward Grammar, a thirty-five-year-old New York office manager who had just been arrayed on a charge of murdering his thirty-three-year-old wife, Dorothy. Bidding for the perfect crime, Ed had bludgeoned his wife and put her into a car. The case came to light when two county policemen on patrol saw Mrs. Grammar's new big blue Chrysler, an anniversary present from her husband, speeding crazily down a hill, just inside their jurisdiction (God bless our good cops!). The car sideswiped a pole, ran up an embankment covered with beard grass, wild strawberry and cinquefoil, and overturned. The wheels were still gently spinning in the mellow sunlight when the officers removed Mrs. G's body. It appeared to be a routine highway accident at first. Alas, the woman's battered body did not match up with only minor damage suffered by the car. I did better.

I rolled on. It was funny to see again the slender white church and the enormous elms. Forgetting that in an American suburban street a lone pedestrian is more conspicuous than a lone motorist, I left the car in the avenue to walk unobtrusively past 342 Lawn Street. Before the great bloodshed, I was entitled to a little relief, to a cathartic spasm of mental regurgitation. Closed were the white shutters of the Junk mansion, and somebody had attached a found black velvet hair ribbon to the white FOR SALE sign which was leaning toward the sidewalk. No dog barked. No gardener telephoned. No Miss Opposite sat on the vined porch—where to the lone pedestrian's annoyance two pony-tailed young women in identical polka-dotted pinafores stopped doing whatever they were doing to stare at him: she was long dead, no doubt, these might be her twin nieces from Philadelphia.

Should I enter my old house? As in a Turgenev story, a torrent of Italian music came from an open window— that of the living room: what romantic soul was playing the piano where no piano had plunged and plashed on that bewitched Sunday with the sun on her beloved legs? All at once I noticed that from the lawn I had mown a golden-skinned, brown-haired nymphet of nine or ten, in white shorts, was looking at me with wild fascination in her large blue-black eyes. I said something pleasant to her, meaning no harm, an old-world compliment, what nice eyes you have, but she retreated in haste and the music stopped abruptly, and a violent-looking dark man, glistening with sweat, came out and glared at me. I was on the point of identifying myself when, with a pang of dream-embarrassment, I became aware of my mud-caked dungarees, my filthy and torn sweater, my bristly chin, my bum's bloodshot eyes. Without saying a word, I turned and plodded back the way I had come. An aster-like anemic flower grew out of a remembered chink in the sidewalk. Quietly resurrected, Miss Opposite was being wheeled out by her nieces, onto her porch, as if it were a stage and I the star performer. Praying she would not call to me, I hurried to my car. What a steep little street. What a profound avenue. A red ticket showed between wiper and windshield; I carefully tore it into two, four, eight pieces.

Feeling I was losing my time, I drove energetically to the downtown hotel where I had arrived with a new bag more than five years before. I took a room, made two appointments by telephone, shaved, bathed, put on black clothes and went down for a drink in the bar. Nothing had changed. The barroom was suffused with the same dim, impossible garnet-red light that in Europe years ago went with low haunts, but here meant a bit of atmosphere in a family hotel. I sat at the same little table where at the very start of my stay, immediately after becoming Charlotte's lodger, I had thought fit to celebrate the occasion by suavely sharing with her half a bottle of champagne, which had fatally conquered her poor brimming heart. As then, a moon-faced waiter was arranging with stellar care fifty sherries on a round tray for a wedding party. Murphy-Fantasia, this time. It was eight minutes to three. As I walked through the lobby, I had to skirt a group of ladies who with *mille grâces* were taking leave of each other after a luncheon party. With a harsh cry of recognition, one pounced upon me. She was a stout, short woman in pearl-gray, with a long, gray, slim plume to her small hat. It was Mrs. Chatfield. She attacked me with a fake smile, all aglow with evil curiosity. (Had I done to Dolly, perhaps, what Frank Lasalle, a fifty-year-old mechanic, had done to eleven-year-old Sally Horner in 1948?) Very soon I had that avid glee well under control. She thought I was in California. How was—? With exquisite pleasure I informed her that my stepdaughter had just married a brilliant young mining engineer with a hush-hush job in the Northwest. She said she disapproved of such early marriages, she would never let her Phyllis, who was now eighteen—

"Oh yes, of course," I said quietly. "I remember Phyllis. Phyllis and Camp Q. Yes, of course. By the way, did she ever tell you how Charlie Holmes debauched there his mother's little charges?"

Mrs. Chatfield's already broken smile now disintegrated completely.

"For shame," she cried, "for shame, Mr. Humbert! The poor boy has just been killed in Korea."

I said didn't she think *"vient de,"* with the infinitive, expressed recent events so much more neatly than the English "just," with the past? But I had to be trotting off, I said.

There were only two blocks to Windmuller's office. He greeted me with a very slow, very enveloping, strong, searching grip. He thought I was in California. Had I not lived at one time at Beardsley? His daughter had just entered Beardsley College. And how was—? I gave all necessary information about Mrs. Schiller. We had a pleasant business conference. I walked out into the hot September sunshine a contented pauper.

Now that everything had been put out of the way, I could dedicate myself freely to the main object of my visit to Ramsdale. In the methodical manner on which I have always prided myself, I had been keeping Clare Quilty's face masked in my dark dungeon, where he was waiting for me to come with barber and priest: *"Réveillez-vous, Laqueue, il est temps de mourir!"* I have no time right now to discuss the mnemonics of physiognomization—I am on my way to his uncle and walking fast—but let me jot down this: I had preserved in the alcohol of a clouded memory the toad of a face. In the course of a few glimpses, I had noticed its slight resemblance to a cheery and rather repulsive wine dealer, a relative of mine in Switzerland. With his dumbbells and stinking tricot, and fat hairy arms, and bald patch, and pig-faced servant-concubine, he was on the whole a harmless old rascal. Too harmless, in fact, to be confused with my prey. In the state of mind I now found myself, I had lost contact with Trapp's image. It had become completely engulfed by the face of Clare Quilty—as represented, with artistic precision, by an easeled photograph of him that stood on his uncle's desk.

In Beardsley, at the hands of charming Dr. Molnar, I had undergone a rather serious dental operation, retaining only a few upper and lower front teeth. The substitutes were dependent on a system of plates with an inconspicuous wire affair running along my upper gums. The whole arrangement was a masterpiece of comfort, and my canines were in perfect health. However, to garnish my secret purpose with a plausible pretext, I told Dr. Quilty that, in hope of alleviating facial neuralgia, I had decided to have all my teeth removed. What would a complete set of dentures cost? How long would the process take, assuming we fixed our first appointment for some time in November? Where was his famous nephew now? Would it be possible to have them all out in one dramatic session?

A white-smocked, gray-haired man, with a crew cut and the big flat cheeks of a politician, Dr. Quilty perched on the corner of his desk, one foot dreamily and seductively rocking as he launched on a glorious long-range plan. He would first provide me with provisional plates until the gums settled. Then he would make me a permanent set. He would like to have a look at that mouth of mine. He wore perforated pied shoes. He had not visited with the rascal since 1946, but supposed he could be found at his ancestral home, Grimm Road, not far from Parkington. It was a noble dream. His foot rocked, his gaze was inspired. It would cost me around six hundred. He suggested he take measurements right away, and make the first set before starting operations. My mouth was to him a splendid cave full of priceless treasures, but I denied him entrance.

"No," I said. "On second thoughts, I shall have it all done by Dr. Molnar. His price is higher, but he is of course a much better dentist than you."

I do not know if any of my readers will ever have a chance to say that. It is a delicious dream feeling. Clare's uncle remained sitting on the desk, still looking dreamy, but his foot had stopped push-rocking the cradle of rosy antici-pation. On the other hand, his nurse, a skeleton-thin, faded girl, with the tragic eyes of unsuccessful blondes, rushed after me so as to be able to slam the door in my wake.

Push the magazine into the butt. Press home until you hear or feel the magazine catch engage. Delightfully snug. Capacity: eight cartridges. Full Blued. Aching to be discharged.

34

A gas station attendant in Parkington explained to me very clearly how to get to Grimm Road. Wishing to be sure Quilty would be at home, I attempted to ring him up but learned that his private telephone had recently been disconnected. Did that mean he was gone? I started to drive to Grimm Road, twelve miles north of the town. By that time night had eliminated most of the landscape and as I followed the narrow winding highway, a series of short posts, ghostly white, with reflectors, borrowed my own lights to indicate this or that curve. I could make out a dark valley on one side of the road and wooded slopes on the other, and in front of me, like derelict snowflakes, moths drifted out of the blackness into my probing aura. At the twelfth mile, as foretold, a curiously hooded bridge sheathed me for a moment and, beyond it, a white-washed rock loomed on the right, and a few car lengths further, on the same side, I turned off the highway up gravelly Grimm Road. For a couple of minutes all was dank, dark, dense forest. Then, Pavor Manor, a wooden house with a turret, arose in a circular clearing. Its windows glowed yellow and red; its drive was cluttered with half a dozen cars. I stopped in the shelter of the trees and abolished my lights to ponder the next move quietly. He would be surrounded by his henchmen and whores. I could not help seeing the inside of that festive and ramshackle castle in terms of "Troubled Teens," a story in one of her magazines, vague "orgies," a sinister adult with penele cigar, drugs, bodyguards. At least, he was there. I would return in the torpid morning.

Gently I rolled back to town, in that old faithful car of mine which was serenely, almost cheerfully working for me. My Lolita! There was still a three-year-old bobby pin of hers in the depths of the glove compartment. There was still that stream of pale moths siphoned out of the night by my head-lights. Dark barns still propped themselves up here and there by the roadside. People were still going to the movies. While searching for night lodgings, I passed a drive-in. In a selenian glow, truly mystical in its contrast with the moonless and massive night, on a gigantic screen slanting away among dark drowsy fields, a thin phantom raised a gun, both he and his arm reduced to tremulous dishwater by the oblique angle of that receding world,—and the next moment a row of trees shut off the gesticulation.

35

I left Insomnia Lodge next morning around eight and spent some time in Parkington. Visions of bungling the execu-tion kept obsessing me. Thinking that perhaps the cartridges in the automatic had gone stale during a week of inactivity, I removed them and inserted a fresh batch. Such a thorough oil bath did I give Chum that now I could not get rid of the stuff. I bandaged him up with a rag, like a maimed limb, and used another rag to wrap up a handful of spare bullets.

A thunderstorm accompanied me most of the way back to Grimm Road, but when I reached Pavor Manor, the sun was visible again, burning like a man, and the birds screamed in the drenched and steaming trees. The elabor-ate and decrepit house seemed to stand in a kind of daze, reflecting as it were my own state, for I could not help real-izing, as my feet touched the springy and insecure ground, that I had overdone the alcoholic stimulation business.

A guardedly ironic silence answered my bell. The garage, however, was loaded with his car, a black convertible for the nonce. I tried the knocker. Re-nobody. With a petulant snarl, I pushed the front door—and, how nice, it swung open as in a medieval fairy tale. Having softly closed it behind me, I made my way across a spacious and very ugly hall; peered into an adjacent drawing room; noticed a number of used glasses growing out of the carpet; decided that master was still asleep in the master bedroom.

So I trudged upstairs. My right hand clutched muffled Chum in my pocket, my left patted the sticky banisters. Of the three bedrooms I inspected, one had obviously been slept in that night. There was a library full of flowers. There was a rather bare room with ample and deep mirrors and a polar bear skin on the slippery floor. There were still other rooms. A happy thought struck me. If and when master returned from his constitutional in the woods, or emerged from some secret lair, it might be wise for an unsteady gunman with a long job before him to prevent his playmate from locking himself up in a room. Consequently, for at least five minutes I went about—lucidly insane, crazily calm, an enchanted and very tight hunter—turning whatever keys in whatever locks there were and pocketing them with my free left hand. The house, being an old one, had more planned privacy than have modern glamour-boxes, where the bathroom, the only lockable locus, has to be used for the furtive needs of planned parenthood.

Speaking of bathrooms—I was about to visit a third one when master came out of it, leaving a brief waterfall behind him. The corner of a passage did not quite conceal me. Gray-faced, baggy-eyed, fluffily disheveled in a scanty balding way, but still perfectly recognizable, he swept by me in a purple bathrobe, very like one I had. He either did not notice me, or else dismissed me as some familiar and innocuous hallu-cination—and, showing me his hairy calves, he proceeded, sleepwalker-wise, downstairs. I pocketed my last key and followed him into the entrance hall. He had half opened his mouth and the front door, to peer out through a sunny chink as one who thinks he has heard a half-hearted visitor ring and recede. Then, still ignoring the raincoated phantasm that had stopped in midstairs, master walked into a cozy boudoir across the hall from the drawing room, through which— taking it easy, knowing he was safe—I now went away from him, and in a bar-adorned kitchen gingerly unwrapped dirty Chum, taking care not to leave any oil stains on the chrome— I think I got the wrong product, it was black and awfully messy. In my usual meticulous way, I transferred naked Chum to a clean recess about me and made for the little boudoir. My step, as I say, was springy—too springy perhaps for success. But my heart pounded with tiger joy, and I crunched a cocktail glass underfoot.

Master met me in the Oriental parlor.

"Now who are you?" he asked in a high hoarse voice, his hands thrust into his dressing-gown pockets, his eyes fixing a point to the northeast of my head. "Are you by any chance Brewster?"

By now it was evident to everybody that he was in a fog and completely at my so-called mercy. I could enjoy myself.

"That's right," I answered suavely. "*Je suis Monsieur Brustère*. Let us chat for a moment before we start."

He looked pleased. His smudgy mustache twitched. I removed my raincoat. I was wearing a black suit, a black shirt, no tie. We sat down in two easy chairs.

"You know," he said, scratching loudly his fleshy and gritty gray cheek and showing his small pearly teeth in a crooked grin, "you don't *look* like Jack Brewster. I mean, the resemblance is not particularly striking. Somebody told me he had a brother with the same telephone company."

To have him trapped, after those years of repentance and rage . . . To look at the black hairs on the back of his pudgy hands . . . To wander with a hundred eyes over his purple silks and hirsute chest foreglimpsing the punctures, and mess, and music of pain . . . To know that this semi-animated, subhuman trickster who had sodomized my darling—oh, my darling, this was intolerable bliss!

"No, I am afraid I am neither of the Brewsters."

He cocked his head, looking more pleased than ever.

"Guess again, Punch."

"Ah," said Punch, "so you have not come to bother me about those long-distance calls?"

"You do make them once in a while, don't you?"

"Excuse me?"

I said I had said I thought he had said he had never—

"People," he said, "people in general, I'm not accusing you, Brewster, but you know it's absurd the way people invade this damned house without even knocking. They use the *vaterre*, they use the kitchen, they use the telephone. Phil calls Philadelphia. Pat calls Patagonia. I refuse to pay. You have a funny accent, Captain."

"Quilty," I said, "do you recall a little girl called Dolores Haze, Dolly Haze? Dolly called Dolores, Colo.?"

"Sure, she may have made those calls, sure. Any place. Paradise, Wash., Hell Canyon. Who cares?"

"I do, Quilty. You see, I am her father."

"Nonsense," he said. "You are not. You are some foreign literary agent. A Frenchman once translated my *Proud Flesh* as *La Fierté de la Chair*. Absurd."

"She was my child, Quilty."

In the state he was in he could not really be taken aback by anything, but his blustering manner was not quite convincing. A sort of wary inkling kindled his eyes into a semblance of life. They were immediately dulled again.

"I'm very fond of children myself," he said, "and fathers are among my best friends."

He turned his head away, looking for something. He beat his pockets. He attempted to rise from his seat.

"Down!" I said—apparently much louder than I intended.

"You need not roar at me," he complained in his strange feminine manner. "I just wanted a smoke. I'm dying for a smoke."

"You're dying anyway."

"Oh, chucks," he said. "You begin to bore me. What do you want? Are you French, mister? Woolly-woo-boo-are? Let's go to the barroomette and have a stiff—"

He saw the little dark weapon lying in my palm as if I were offering it to him.

"Say!" he drawled (now imitating the underworld numbskull of movies), "that's a swell little gun you've got there. What d'you want for her?"

I slapped down his outstretched hand and he managed to knock over a box on a low table near him. It ejected a handful of cigarettes.

"Here they are," he said cheerfully. "You recall Kipling: *une femme est une femme, mais un Caporal est une cigarette?* Now we need matches."

"Quilty," I said. "I want you to concentrate. You are going to die in a moment. The hereafter for all we know may be an eternal state of excruciating insanity. You smoked your last cigarette yesterday. Concentrate. Try to understand what is happening to you."

He kept taking the Drome cigarette apart and munching bits of it.

"I am willing to try," he said. "You are either Australian, or a German refugee. Must you talk to me? This is a Gentile's house, you know. Maybe, you'd better run along.

And do stop demonstrating that gun. I've an old Stern-Luger in the music room."

I pointed Chum at his slippered foot and crushed the trigger. It clicked. He looked at his foot, at the pistol, again at his foot. I made another awful effort, and, with a ridiculously feeble and juvenile sound, it went off. The bullet entered the thick pink rug, and I had the paralyzing impression that it had merely trickled in and might come out again.

"See what I mean?" said Quilty. "You should be a little more careful. Give me that thing for Christ's sake."

He reached for it. I pushed him back into the chair. The rich joy was waning. It was high time I destroyed him, but he must understand why he was being destroyed. His condition infected me, the weapon felt limp and clumsy in my hand.

"Concentrate," I said, "on the thought of Dolly Haze whom you kidnaped—"

"I did not!" he cried. "You're all wet. I saved her from a beastly pervert. Show me your badge instead of shooting at my foot, you ape, you. Where is that badge? I'm not responsible for the rapes of others. Absurd! That joy ride, I grant you, was a silly stunt but you got her back, didn't you? Come, let's have a drink."

I asked him whether he wanted to be executed sitting or standing.

"Ah, let me think," he said. "It is not an easy question. Incidentally—I made a mistake. Which I sincerely regret. You see, I had no fun with your Dolly. I am practically impotent, to tell the melancholy truth. And I gave her a splendid vacation. She met some remarkable people. Do you happen to know—"

And with a tremendous lurch he fell all over me, sending the pistol hurtling under a chest of drawers. Fortunately he was more impetuous than vigorous, and I had little difficulty in shoving him back into his chair.

He puffed a little and folded his arms on his chest.

"Now you've done it," he said. "*Vous voilà dans de beaux draps, mon vieux.*"

His French was improving.

I looked around. Perhaps, if—Perhaps I could—On my hands and knees? Risk it?

"*Alors, que fait-on?*" he asked watching me closely.

I stooped. He did not move. I stooped lower.

"My dear sir," he said, "stop trifling with life and death. I am a playwright. I have written tragedies, comedies, fantasies. I have made private movies out of *Justine* and other eighteenth-century sexcapades. I'm the author of fifty-two successful scenarios. I know all the ropes. Let me handle this. There should be a poker somewhere, why don't I fetch it, and then we'll fish out your property."

Fussily, busybodily, cunningly, he had risen again while he talked. I groped under the chest trying at the same time to keep an eye on him. All of a sudden I noticed that he had noticed that I did not seem to have noticed Chum protruding from beneath the other corner of the chest. We fell to wrestling again. We rolled all over the floor, in each other's arms, like two huge helpless children. He was naked and goatish under his robe, and I felt suffocated as he rolled over me. I rolled over him. We rolled over me. They rolled over him. We rolled over us.

In its published form, this book is being read, I assume, in the first years of 2000 A.D. (1935 plus eighty or ninety, live long, my love); and elderly readers will surely recall at this point the obligatory scene in the Westerns of their childhood. Our tussle, however, lacked the ox-stunning fisticuffs, the flying furniture. He and I were two large dummies, stuffed with dirty cotton and rags. It was a silent, soft, formless tussle on the part of two literati, one of whom was utterly disorganized by a drug while the other was handicapped by a heart condition and too much gin. When at last I had possessed myself of my precious weapon, and the scenario writer had been reinstalled in his low chair, both of us were panting as the cowman and the sheepman never do after their battle.

I decided to inspect the pistol—our sweat might have spoiled something—and regain my wind before proceeding to the main item in the program. To fill in the pause, I proposed he read his own sentence—in the poetical form I had given it. The term "poetical justice" is one that may be most happily used in this respect. I handed him a neat typescript.

"Yes," he said, "splendid idea. Let me fetch my reading glasses" (he attempted to rise).

"No."

"Just as you say. Shall I read out loud?"

"Yes."

"Here goes. I see it's in verse.

> Because you took advantage of a sinner
> because you took advantage
> because you took
> because you took advantage of my disadvantage . . .

"That's good, you know. That's damned good."

> . . . when I stood Adam-naked
> before a federal law and all its stinging stars

"Oh, grand stuff!"

> . . . Because you took advantage of a sin
> when I was helpless moulting moist and tender

hoping for the best
dreaming of marriage in a mountain state
aye of a litter of Lolitas . . .

"Didn't get that."

Because you took advantage of my inner
essential innocence
because you cheated me—

"A little repetitious, what? Where was I?"

Because you cheated me of my redemption
because you took
her at the age when lads
play with erector sets

"Getting smutty, eh?"

a little downy girl still wearing poppies
still eating popcorn in the colored gloom
where tawny Indians took paid croppers
because you stole her
from her wax-browed and dignified protector
spitting into his heavy-lidded eye
ripping his flavid toga and at dawn
leaving the hog to roll upon his new discomfort
the awfulness of love and violets
remorse despair while you
took a dull doll to pieces
and threw its head away
because of all you did
because of all I did not
you have to die

"Well, sir, this is certainly a fine poem. Your best as far as I am concerned."

He folded and handed it back to me.

I asked him if he had anything serious to say before dying. The automatic was again ready for use on the person. He looked at it and heaved a big sigh.

"Now look here, Mac," he said. "You are drunk and I am a sick man. Let us postpone the matter. I need quiet. I have to nurse my impotence. Friends are coming in the afternoon to take me to a game. This pistol-packing farce is becoming a frightful nuisance. We are men of the world, in everything—sex, free verse, marksmanship. If you bear me a grudge, I am ready to make unusual amends. Even an old-fashioned *rencontre*, sword or pistol, in Rio or else-where—is not excluded. My memory and my eloquence are not at their best today but really, my dear Mr. Humbert, you were not an ideal stepfather, and I did not force your little protégée to join me. It was she made me remove her to a happier home. This house is not as modern as that ranch we shared with dear friends. But it is roomy, cool in summer and winter, and in a word comfortable, so, since I intend retiring to England or Florence forever, I suggest you move in. It is yours, gratis. Under the condition you stop pointing at me that [he swore disgustingly] gun. By the way, I do not know if you care for the bizarre, but if you do, I can offer you, also gratis, as house pet, a rather exciting little freak, a young lady with three breasts, one a dandy, this is a rare and delightful marvel of nature. Now, *soyons raisonnables*. You will only wound me hideously and then rot in jail while I recuperate in a tropical setting. I promise you, Brewster, you will be happy here, with a magnificent cellar, and all the royalties from my next play— I have not much at the bank right now but I propose to borrow—you know, as the Bard said, with that cold in his head, to borrow and to borrow and to borrow. There are other advantages. We have here a most reliable and bribable charwoman, a Mrs. Vibrissa—curious name—who comes from the village twice a week, alas not today, she has daughters, granddaughters, a thing or two I know about the chief of police makes him my slave. I am a playwright. I have been called the American Maeterlinck. Maeterlinck-Schmetterling, says I. Come on! All this is very humiliating, and I am not sure I am doing the right thing. Never use herculanita with rum. Now drop that pistol like a good fellow. I knew your dear wife slightly. You may use my wardrobe. Oh, another thing—you are going to like this. I have an absolutely unique collection of erotica upstairs. Just to mention one item: the in folio de-luxe *Bagration Island* by the explorer and psychoanalyst Melanie Weiss, a remarkable lady, a remarkable work—drop that gun—with photographs of eight hundred and something male organs she examined and measured in 1932 on Bagration, in the Barda Sea, very illuminating graphs, plotted with love under pleasant skies—drop that gun— and moreover I can arrange for you to attend executions, not everybody knows that the chair is painted yellow—"

Feu. This time I hit something hard. I hit the back of a black rocking chair, not unlike Dolly Schiller's—my bullet hit the inside surface of its back whereupon it immediately went into a rocking act, so fast and with such zest that any one coming into the room might have been flabbergasted by the double miracle: that chair rocking in a panic all by itself, and the armchair, where my purple target had just been, now void of all live content. Wiggling his fingers in the air, with a rapid heave of his rump, he flashed into the music room and the next second we were tugging and gasping on both sides of the door which had a key I had overlooked. I won again, and with another abrupt movement Clare the Impredictable sat down before the piano and played several atrociously vigorous, fundamentally hysterical, plangent chords, his jowls quivering, his spread hands tensely plunging, and his nostrils emitting the soundtrack snorts which had been absent from our fight. Still singing those impossible sonorities, he made a futile attempt to open with his foot a kind of seaman's chest near the piano. My next bullet caught him somewhere in the side, and he rose from his chair higher and higher, like old, gray, mad Nijinski, like Old Faithful, like some old nightmare of mine, to a phenomenal altitude, or so it seemed, as he rent the air—still shaking with the rich black music—head thrown back in a howl, hand pressed to his brow, and with his other hand clutching his armpit as if stung by a hornet, down he came on his heels and, again a normal robed man, scurried out into the hall.

I see myself following him through the hall, with a kind of double, triple, kangaroo jump, remaining quite straight on straight legs while bouncing up twice in his wake, and then bouncing between him and the front door in a ballet-like stiff bounce, with the purpose of heading him off, since the door was not properly closed.

Suddenly dignified, and somewhat morose, he started to walk up the broad stairs, and, shifting my position, but not actually following him up the steps, I fired three or four times in quick succession, wounding him at every blaze; and every time I did it to him, that horrible thing to him, his face would twitch in an absurd clownish manner, as if he were exaggerating the pain; he slowed down, rolled his eyes half closing them and made a feminine "ah!" and he shivered every time a bullet hit him as if I were tickling him, and every time I got him with those slow, clumsy, blind bullets of mine, he would say under his breath, with a phoney British accent—all the while

345

dreadfully twitching, shivering, smirking, but withal talking in a curiously detached and even amiable manner: "Ah, that hurts, sir, enough! Ah, that hurts atrociously, my dear fellow. I pray you, desist. Ah—very painful, very painful, indeed . . . God! Hah! This is abominable, you should really not—" His voice trailed off as he reached the landing, but he steadily walked on despite all the lead I had lodged in his bloated body—and in distress, in dismay, I understood that far from killing him I was injecting spurts of energy into the poor fellow, as if the bullets had been capsules wherein a heady elixir danced.

I reloaded the thing with hands that were black and bloody—I had touched something he had anointed with his thick gore. Then I rejoined him upstairs, the keys jangling in my pockets like gold.

He was trudging from room to room, bleeding majestically, trying to find an open window, shaking his head, and still trying to talk me out of murder. I took aim at his head, and he retired to the master bedroom with a burst of royal purple where his ear had been.

"Get out, get out of here," he said coughing and spitting; and in a nightmare of wonder, I saw this blood-spattered but still buoyant person get into his bed and wrap himself up in the chaotic bedclothes. I hit him at very close range through the blankets, and then he lay back, and a big pink bubble with juvenile connotations formed on his lips, grew to the size of a toy balloon, and vanished.

I may have lost contact with reality for a second or two—oh, nothing of the I-just-blacked-out sort that your common criminal enacts; on the contrary, I want to stress the fact that I was responsible for every shed drop of his bubbleblood; but a kind of momentary shift occurred as if I were in the connubial bedroom, and Charlotte were sick in bed. Quilty was a very sick man. I held one of his slippers instead of the pistol—I was sitting on the pistol. Then I made myself a little more comfortable in the chair near the bed, and consulted my wrist watch. The crystal was gone but it ticked. The whole sad business had taken more than an hour. He was quiet at last. Far from feeling any relief, a burden even weightier than the one I had hoped to get rid of was with me, upon me, over me. I could not bring myself to touch him in order to make sure he was really dead. He looked it: a quarter of his face gone, and two flies beside themselves with a dawning sense of unbelievable luck. My hands were hardly in better condition than his. I washed up as best I could in the adjacent bathroom. Now I could leave. As I emerged on the landing, I was amazed to discover that a vivacious buzz I had just been dismissing as a mere singing in my ears was really a medley of voices and radio music coming from the down-stairs drawing room.

I found there a number of people who apparently had just arrived and were cheerfully drinking Quilty's liquor. There was a fat man in an easy chair; and two dark-haired pale young beauties, sisters no doubt, big one and small one (almost a child), demurely sat side by side on a daven-port. A florid-faced fellow with sapphire-blue eyes was in the act of bringing two glasses out of the bar-like kitchen, where two or three women were chatting and chinking ice. I stopped in the doorway and said: "I have just killed Clare Quilty." "Good for you," said the florid fellow as he offered one of the drinks to the elder girl. "Somebody ought to have done it long ago," remarked the fat man. "What does he say, Tony?" asked a faded blonde from the bar. "He says," answered the florid fellow, "he has killed Cue." "Well," said another unidentified man rising in a corner where he had been crouching to inspect some records, "I guess we all should do it to him some day." "Anyway," said Tony, "he'd better come down. We can't wait for him much longer if we want to go to that game." "Give this man a drink somebody," said the fat person. "Want a beer?" said a woman in slacks, showing it to me from afar.

Only the two girls on the davenport, both wearing black, the younger fingering a bright something about her white neck, only they said nothing, but just smiled on, so young, so lewd. As the music paused for a moment, there was a sudden noise on the stairs. Tony and I stepped out into the hall. Quilty of all people had managed to crawl out onto the landing, and there we could see him, flapping and heaving, and then subsiding, forever this time, in a purple heap.

"Hurry up, Cue," said Tony with a laugh. "I believe, he's still—" He returned to the drawing room, music drowned the rest of the sentence.

This, I said to myself, was the end of the ingenious play staged for me by Quilty. With a heavy heart I left the house and walked through the spotted blaze of the sun to my car. Two other cars were parked on both sides of it, and I had some trouble squeezing out.

36

The rest is a little flattish and faded. Slowly I drove downhill, and presently found myself going at the same lazy pace in a direction opposite to Parkington. I had left my raincoat in the boudoir and Chum in the bathroom. No, it was not a house I would have liked to live in. I wondered idly if some surgeon of genius might not alter his own career, and perhaps the whole destiny of mankind, by reviving quilted Quilty, Clare Obscure. Not that I cared; on the whole I wished to forget the whole mess—and when I did learn he was dead, the only satisfaction it gave me, was the relief of knowing I need not mentally accompany

for months a painful and disgusting convalescence interrupted by all kinds of unmentionable operations and
relapses, and perhaps an actual visit from him, with trouble
on my part to rationalize him as not being a ghost. Thomas
had something. It is strange that the tactile sense, which
is so infinitely less precious to men than sight, becomes at
critical moments our main, if not only, handle to reality. I
was all covered with Quilty—with the feel of that tumble
before the bleeding.

The road now stretched across open country, and it
occurred to me—not by way of protest, not as a symbol, or
anything like that, but merely as a novel experience—that
since I had disregarded all laws of humanity, I might as well
disregard the rules of traffic. So I crossed to the left side of
the highway and checked the feeling, and the feeling was
good. It was a pleasant diaphragmal melting, with elements
of diffused tactility, all this enhanced by the thought that
nothing could be nearer to the elimination of basic physical
laws than deliberately driving on the wrong side of the road.
In a way, it was a very spiritual itch. Gently, dreamily, not
exceeding twenty miles an hour, I drove on that queer mirror
side. Traffic was light. Cars that now and then passed me on
the side I had abandoned to them, honked at me brutally.
Cars coming towards me wobbled, swerved, and cried out
in fear. Presently I found myself approaching populated
places. Passing through a red light was like a sip of forbidden
Burgundy when I was a child. Meanwhile complications were
arising. I was being followed and escorted. Then in front of
me I saw two cars placing themselves in such a manner as
to completely block my way. With a graceful movement I
turned off the road, and after two or three big bounces, rode
up a grassy slope, among surprised cows, and there I came
to a gentle rocking stop. A kind of thoughtful Hegelian
synthesis linking up two dead women.

I was soon to be taken out of the car (Hi, Melmoth, thanks a lot, old fellow)—and was, indeed, looking forward to surrender myself to many hands, without doing anything to cooperate, while they moved and carried me, relaxed, comfortable, surrendering myself lazily, like a patient, and deriving an eerie enjoyment from my limpness and the absolutely reliable support given me by the police and the ambulance people. And while I was waiting for them to run up to me on the high slope, I evoked a last mirage of wonder and hopelessness. One day, soon after her disappearance, an attack of abominable nausea forced me to pull up on the ghost of an old mountain road that now accompanied, now traversed a brand new highway, with its population of asters bathing in the detached warmth of a pale-blue afternoon in late summer. After coughing myself inside out, I rested a while on a boulder, and then, thinking the sweet air might do me good, walked a little way toward a low stone parapet on the precipice side of the highway. Small grasshoppers spurted out of the withered roadside weeds. A very light cloud was opening its arms and moving toward a slightly more substantial one belonging to another, more sluggish, heavenlogged system. As I approached the friendly abyss, I grew aware of a melodious unity of sounds rising like vapor from a small mining town that lay at my feet, in a fold of the valley. One could make out the geometry of the streets between blocks of red and gray roofs, and green puffs of trees, and a serpentine stream, and the rich, ore-like glitter of the city dump, and beyond the town, roads crisscrossing the crazy quilt of dark and pale fields, and behind it all, great timbered mountains. But even brighter than those quietly rejoicing colors—for there are colors and shades that seem to enjoy themselves in good company—both brighter and dreamier to the ear than they were to the eye, was that vapory vibration of accumulated sounds that never ceased for a moment, as it rose to the lip of granite where I stood wiping my foul mouth. And soon I realized that all these sounds were of one nature, that no other sounds but these came from the streets of the transparent town, with the women at home and the men away. Reader! What I heard was but the melody of children at play, nothing but that, and so limpid was the air that within this vapor of blended voices, majestic and minute, remote and magically near, frank and divinely enigmatic—one could hear now and then, as if released, an almost articulate spurt of vivid laughter, or the crack of a bat, or the clatter of a toy wagon, but it was all really too far for the eye to distinguish any movement in the lightly etched streets. I stood listening to that musical vibration from my lofty slope, to those flashes of separate cries with a kind of demure murmur for background, and then I knew that the hopelessly poignant thing was not Lolita's absence from my side, but the absence of her voice from that concord.

This then is my story. I have reread it. It has bits of marrow sticking to it, and blood, and beautiful bright-green flies. At this or that twist of it I feel my slippery self eluding me, gliding into deeper and darker waters than I care to probe. I have camouflaged what I could so as not to hurt people. And I have toyed with many pseudonyms for myself before I hit on a particularly apt one. There are in my notes "Otto Otto" and "Mesmer Mesmer" and "Lambert Lambert," but for some reason I think my choice expresses the nastiness best.

When I started, fifty-six days ago, to write *Lolita*, first in the psychopathic ward for observation, and then in this well-heated, albeit tombal, seclusion, I thought I would use these notes in toto at my trial, to save not my head, of course, but my soul. In mid-composition, however, I realized that I could not parade living Lolita. I still may use parts of this memoir in hermetic sessions, but publication is to be deferred.

For reasons that may appear more obvious than they really are, I am opposed to capital punishment; this attitude will be, I trust, shared by the sentencing judge. Had I come before myself, I would have given Humbert at least thirty-five years for rape, and dismissed the rest of the charges. But even so, Dolly Schiller will probably survive me by many years. The following decision I make with all the legal impact and support of a signed testament: I wish this memoir to be published only when Lolita is no longer alive.

Thus, neither of us is alive when the reader opens this book. But while the blood still throbs through my writing hand, you are still as much part of blessed matter as I am, and I can still talk to you from here to Alaska. Be true to your Dick. Do not let other fellows touch you. Do not talk to strangers. I hope you will love your baby. I hope it will be a boy. That husband of yours, I hope, will always treat you well, because otherwise my specter shall come at him, like black smoke, like a demented giant, and pull him apart nerve by nerve. And do not pity C. Q. One had to choose between him and H. H., and one wanted H. H. to exist at least a couple of months longer, so as to have him make you live in the minds of later generations. I am thinking of aurochs and angels, the secret of durable pigments, prophetic sonnets, the refuge of art. And this is the only immortality you and I may share, my Lolita.

Vladimir Nabokov
On a Book Entitled Lolita

After doing my impersonation of suave John Ray, the character in *Lolita* who pens the Foreword, any comments coming straight from me may strike one—may strike me, in fact—as an impersonation of Vladimir Nabokov talking about his own book. A few points, however, have to be discussed; and the autobiographic device may induce mimic and model to blend.

Teachers of Literature are apt to think up such problems as "What is the author's purpose?" or still worse "What is the guy trying to say?" Now, I happen to be the kind of author who in starting to work on a book has no other purpose than to get rid of that book and who, when asked to explain its origin and growth, has to rely on such ancient terms as Interreaction of Inspiration and Combination—which, I admit, sounds like a conjurer explaining one trick by performing another.

The first little throb of *Lolita* went through me late in 1939 or early in 1940, in Paris, at a time when I was laid up with a severe attack of intercostal neuralgia. As far as I can recall, the initial shiver of inspiration was somehow prompted by a newspaper story about an ape in the Jardin des Plantes, who, after months of coaxing by a scientist, produced the first drawing ever charcoaled by an animal: this sketch showed the bars of the poor creature's cage.

The impulse I record had no textual connection with the ensuing train of thought, which resulted, however, in a prototype of my present novel, a short story some thirty pages long. I wrote it in Russian, the language in which I had been writing novels since 1924 (the best of these are not translated into English, and all are prohibited for political reasons in Russia). The man was a Central European, the anonymous nymphet was French, and the loci were Paris and Provence. I had him marry the little girl's sick mother who soon died, and after a thwarted attempt to take advantage of the orphan in a hotel room, Arthur (for that was his name) threw himself under the wheels of a truck. I read the story one blue-papered wartime night to a group of friends—Mark Aldanov, two social revolutionaries, and a woman doctor; but I was not pleased with the thing and destroyed it sometime after moving to America in 1940.

Around 1949, in Ithaca, upstate New York, the throbbing, which had never quite ceased, began to plague me again. Combination joined inspiration with fresh zest and involved me in a new treatment of the theme, this time in English—the language of my first governess in St. Petersburg, circa 1903, a Miss Rachel Home. The nymphet, now with a dash of Irish blood, was really much the same lass, and the basic marrying-her-mother idea also subsisted; but otherwise the thing was new and had grown in secret the claws and wings of a novel.

The book developed slowly, with many interruptions and asides. It had taken me some forty years to invent Russia and Western Europe, and now I was faced by the task of inventing America. The obtaining of such local ingredients as would allow me to inject a modicum of average "reality" (one of the few words which mean nothing without quotes) into the brew of individual fancy, proved at fifty a much more difficult process than it had been in the Europe of my youth when receptiveness and retention were at their automatic best. Other books intervened. Once or twice I was on the point of burning the unfinished draft and had carried my Juanita Dark as far as the shadow of the leaning incinerator on the innocent lawn, when I was stopped by the thought that the ghost of the destroyed book would haunt my files for the rest of my life.

Every summer my wife and I go butterfly hunting. The specimens are deposited at scientific institutions, such as the Museum of Comparative Zoology at Harvard or the Cornell University collection. The locality labels pinned under these butterflies will be a boon to some twenty-first-century scholar with a taste for recondite biography. It was at such of our headquarters as Telluride, Colorado; Afton, Wyoming; Portal, Arizona; and Ashland, Oregon, that Lolita was energetically resumed in the evenings or on cloudy days. I finished copying the thing out in longhand in the spring of 1954, and at once began casting around for a publisher.

At first, on the advice of a wary old friend, I was meek enough to stipulate that the book be brought out anonymously. I doubt that I shall ever regret that soon afterwards, realizing how likely a mask was to betray my own cause, I decided to sign Lolita. The four American publishers, W, X, Y, Z, who in turn were offered the typescript and had their readers glance at it, were shocked by Lolita to a degree that even my wary old friend F.P. had not expected.

While it is true that in ancient Europe, and well into the eighteenth century (obvious examples come from France), deliberate lewdness was not inconsistent with flashes of comedy, or vigorous satire, or even the verve of a fine poet in a wanton mood, it is also true that in modern times the term "pornography" connotes mediocrity, commercialism, and certain strict rules of narration. Obscenity must be mated with banality because every kind of aesthetic enjoyment has to be entirely replaced by simple sexual stimulation which demands the traditional word for direct action upon the patient. Old rigid rules must be followed by the pornographer in order to have his patient feel the same security of satisfaction as, for example, fans of detective stories feel—stories where, if you do not watch out, the real murderer may turn out to be, to the fan's disgust, artistic originality (who for instance would want a detective story without a single dialogue in it?). Thus, in pornographic novels, action has to be limited to the copulation of clichés. Style, structure, imagery should never distract the reader from his tepid lust. The novel must consist of an alternation of sexual scenes. The passages in between must be reduced to sutures of sense, logical bridges of the simplest design, brief expositions and explanations, which the reader will probably skip but must know they exist in order not to feel cheated (a mentality stemming from the routine of "true" fairy tales in childhood). Moreover, the sexual scenes in the book must follow a crescendo line, with new variations, new combinations, new sexes, and a steady increase in the number of participants (in a Sade play they call the gardener in), and therefore the end of the book must be more replete with lewd lore than the first chapters.

Certain techniques in the beginnig of *Lolita* (Humbert's Journal, for example) misled some of my first readers into assuming that this was going to be a lewd book. They expected the rising succession of erotic scenes; when these stopped, the readers stopped, too, and felt bored and let down. This, I suspect, is one of the reasons why not all the four firms read the typescript to the end. Whether they found it pornographic or not did not interest me. Their refusal to buy the book was based not on my treatment of the theme but on the theme itself, for there are at least three themes which are utterly taboo as far as most American publishers are concerned. The two others are: a Negro-White marriage which is a complete and glorious success resulting in lots of children and grandchildren; and the total atheist who lives a happy and useful life, and dies in his sleep at the age of 106.

Some of the reactions were very amusing: one reader suggested that his firm might consider publication if I turned my Lolita into a twelve-year-old lad and had him seduced by Humbert, a farmer, in a barn, amidst gaunt and arid surroundings, all this set forth in short, strong, "realistic" sentences ("He acts crazy. We all act crazy, I guess. I guess God acts crazy." Etc.). Although everybody should know that I detest symbols and allegories (which is due partly to my old feud with Freudian voodooism and partly to my loathing of generalizations devised by literary mythists and sociologists), an otherwise intelligent reader who flipped through the first part described Lolita as "Old Europe debauching young America," while another flipper saw in it "Young America debauching old Europe." Publisher X, whose advisers got so bored with Humbert that they never got beyond page 188, had the naïveté to write me that Part Two was too long. Publisher Y, on the other hand, regretted there were no good people in the book. Publisher Z said if he printed Lolita, he and I would go to jail.

No writer in a free country should be expected to bother about the exact demarcation between the sensuous and the sensual; this is preposterous; I can only admire but cannot emulate the accuracy of judgment of those who pose the fair young mammals photographed in magazines where the general neckline is just low enough to provoke a past master's chuckle and just high enough not to make a postmaster frown. I presume there exist readers who find titillating the display of mural words in those hopelessly banal and enormous novels which are typed out by the thumbs of tense mediocrities and called "powerful" and "stark" by the reviewing hack. There are gentle souls who would pronounce *Lolita* meaningless because it does not teach them anything. I am neither a reader nor a writer of didactic fiction, and, despite John Ray's assertion, *Lolita* has no moral in tow. For me a work of fiction exists only insofar as it affords me what I shall bluntly call aesthetic bliss, that is a sense of being somehow, somewhere, connected with other states of being where art (curiosity, tenderness, kindness, ecstasy) is the norm. There are not many such books. All the rest is either topical trash or what some call the Literature of Ideas, which very often is topical trash coming in huge blocks of plaster that are carefully transmitted from age to age until somebody comes along with a hammer and takes a good crack at Balzac, at Gorki, at Mann.

Another charge which some readers have made is that *Lolita* is anti-American. This is something that pains me considerably more than the idiotic accusation of immorality. Considerations of depth and perspective (a suburban lawn, a mountain meadow) led me to build a number of North American sets. I needed a certain exhilarating milieu. Nothing is more exhilarating than philistine vulgarity. But in regard to philistine vulgarity there is no intrinsic difference between Palearctic manners and Nearctic manners. Any proletarian from Chicago can be as bourgeois (in the Flaubertian sense) as a duke. I chose American motels instead of Swiss hotels or English inns only because I am trying to be an American writer and claim only the same rights that other American writers enjoy. On the other hand, my creature Humbert is a foreigner and an anarchist, and there are many things, besides nymphets, in which I disagree with him. And all my Russian readers know that my old worlds—Russian, British, German, French—are just as fantastic and personal as my new one is.

Lest the little statement I am making here seem an airing of grudges, I must hasten to add that besides the lambs who read the typescript of *Lolita* or its Olympia Press edition in a spirit of "Why did he have to write it?" or "Why should I read about maniacs?" there have been a number of wise, sensitive, and staunch people who understood my book much better than I can explain its mechanism here.

Every serious writer, I dare say, is aware of this or that published book of his as of a constant comforting presence. Its pilot light is steadily burning somewhere in the basement and a mere touch applied to one's private thermostat instantly results in a quiet little explosion of familiar warmth. This presence, this glow of the book in an ever accessible remoteness is a most companionable feeling, and the better the book has conformed to its prefigured contour and color the ampler and smoother it glows. But even so, there are certain points, byroads, favorite hollows that one evokes more eagerly and enjoys more tenderly than the rest of one's book. I have not reread *Lolita* since I went through the proofs in the spring of 1955 but I find it to be a delightful presence now that it quietly hangs about the house like a summer day which one knows to be bright behind the haze. And when I thus think of *Lolita*, I seem always to pick out for special delectation such images as Mr. Taxovich, or that class list of Ramsdale School, or

Charlotte saying "waterproof," or Lolita in slow motion advancing toward Humbert's gifts, or the pictures decorating the stylized garret of Gaston Godin, or the Kasbeam barber (who cost me a month of work), or Lolita playing tennis, or the hospital at Elphinstone, or pale, pregnant, beloved, irretrievable Dolly Schiller dying in Gray Star (the capital town of the book), or the tinkling sounds of the valley town coming up the mountain trail (on which I caught the first known female of *Lycaeides sublivens* Nabokov). These are the nerves of the novel. These are the secret points, the subliminal co-ordinates by means of which the book is plotted—although I realize very clearly that these and other scenes will be skimmed over or not noticed, or never even reached, by those who begin reading the book under the impression that it is something on the lines of *Memoirs of a Woman of Pleasure* or *Les Amours de Milord Grosvit*. That my novel does contain various allusions to the physiological urges of a pervert is quite true. But after all we are not children, not illiterate juvenile delinquents, not English public school boys who after a night of homosexual romps have to endure the paradox of reading the Ancients in expurgated versions.

It is childish to study a work of fiction in order to gain information about a country or about a social class or about the author. And yet one of my very few intimate friends, after reading *Lolita*, was sincerely worried that I (I!) should be living "among such depressing people"—when the only discomfort I really experienced was to live in my workshop among discarded limbs and unfinished torsos.

After Olympia Press, in Paris, published the book, an American critic suggested that *Lolita* was the record of my love affair with the romantic novel. The substitution "English language" for "romantic novel" would make this elegant formula more correct. But here I feel my voice rising to a much too strident pitch. None of my American friends have read my Russian books and thus every appraisal on the strength of my English ones is bound to be out of focus. My private tragedy, which cannot, and indeed should not, be anybody's concern, is that I had to abandon my natural idiom, my untrammeled, rich, and infinitely docile Russian tongue for a second-rate brand of English, devoid of any of those apparatuses—the baffling mirror, the black velvet backdrop, the implied associations and traditions—which the native illusionist, frac-tails flying, can magically use to transcend the heritage in his own way.

November 12, 1956

PENGUIN ESSENTIALS

The Penguin Essentials are some of the twentieth-century's most important books. When they were first published they changed the way we thought about literature and about life. And they have remained vital reading ever since. These new, stylish editions remind readers that once upon a time each book in the Essentials series was the only book worth being seen with.

Eva Luna by Isabel Allende

Out of Africa by Karen Blixen

A Clockwork Orange by Anthony Burgess

Breakfast at Tiffany's by Truman Capote

My Family and Other Animals by Gerald Durrell

The Great Gatsby by F. Scott Fitzgerald

A Room with a View by E.M. Forster

Cold Comfort Farm by Stella Gibbons

Goodbye to All That by Robert Graves

Steppenwolf by Hermann Hesse

On the Road by Jack Kerouac

Lady Chatterley's Lover by D.H. Lawrence

Lolita by Vladimir Nabokov

Wide Sargasso Sea by Jean Rhys

Bonjour Tristesse by Françoise Sagan

Hell's Angels by Hunter S. Thompson

A Confederacy of Dunces by John Kennedy Toole

Cat's Cradle by Kurt Vonnegut

Brideshead Revisited by Evelyn Waugh

To Wilf,
Lovely meeting you!

GOD'S
GOLDEN
ACRE

The inspirational story of one woman's fight
for some of the world's most vulnerable AIDS orphans

A biography of
Heather Reynolds
by **Dale le Vack**

With love!
Heather 13/7/2007

MONARCH
B O O K S
Oxford, UK, and Grand Rapids, Michigan, USA

Copyright © Heather Reynolds and Dale le Vack 2005.
The right of Heather Reynolds and Dale le Vack to be identified
as authors of this work has been asserted by them in
accordance with the Copyright, Designs
and Patents Act 1988.

First published in the UK in 2005 by Monarch Books
(a publishing imprint of Lion Hudson plc),
Mayfield House, 256 Banbury Road, Oxford OX2 7DH
Tel: +44 (0) 1865 302750   Fax: +44 (0) 1865 302757
Email: monarch@lionhudson.com
www.lionhudson.com

Distributed by:
UK: Marston Book Services Ltd, PO Box 269,
Abingdon, Oxon OX14 4YN
USA: Kregel Publications, PO Box 2607,
Grand Rapids, Michigan 49501

ISBN 1 85424 706 9 (UK)
ISBN 0 8254 6085 9 (USA)

Unless otherwise stated, Scripture quotations are
taken from the Holy Bible, New International Version,
copyright © 1973, 1978, 1984 by the International Bible Society.
Used by permission of Hodder and Stoughton Ltd.
All rights reserved.

British Library Cataloguing Data
A catalogue record for this book is available
from the British Library.

Book design and production for the publishers by Lion Hudson plc.
Printed in Great Britain.

AUTHOR'S
ACKNOWLEDGEMENTS

The idea for a biography of Heather Reynolds was first discussed not in South Africa, but thousands of miles away in Stratford-upon-Avon, England, one summer evening in June 2002. Heather and the Young Zulu Warriors were on a UK tour and we met at the Croft Preparatory School where both the children and adults were staying before their one-night performance in the town.

I was on an assignment for the Stratford Herald to report on both the visit and concert of this unusual party of adults and children from South Africa. They were travelling the country in an old school bus and delighting audiences with their blend of traditional Zulu song and dance. We reckoned in the newsroom at the Herald that the performance of the Young Zulu Warriors would certainly be a change for Stratford audiences from the world of William Shakespeare at the Royal Shakespeare Theatre.

Heather appeared in the garden of the school as the dancers were being lined up in Zulu costume for a photograph. I listened in astonishment as this plump and loquacious woman told me about her life and extraordinary adventures among the thousands of AIDS orphans in the Valley of a Thousand Hills, KwaZulu-Natal. She described how she and her husband Patrick had risked bankruptcy – sacrificing their business and virtually all their worldly material possessions and savings – to bring some form of sanctuary to thousands of needy children. Death and danger had stalked them at every step for more than ten years.

Heather did not consider her story to be of interest to the world and made it clear she would never have the time to write her autobiography. Having just heard a brief account of her life I realised it was certainly a story that should be told, and also one that could help to finance God's Golden Acre and its vital work, as the AIDS pandemic continued to demolish the foundations of rural Zulu society.

"You should find a journalist, a writer, in South Africa and get to work on your story," I told her. A reflective expression came over her face and she beamed the warm smile that is her hallmark. A few days later, after reading my report about the Young Zulu Warriors in the newspaper, she asked me over the telephone to write her life story.

I did not consider the proposition to be practical because of the great distance that separated us. However, a number of factors came into play over the next two years that made our project possible.

Heather and Patrick enjoy coming to England and Europe at least twice a year to recharge their batteries and also to talk to the God's Golden Acre funding organisations and people who run them. Their favourite haunt during these times is Marriage Hill Farm in the Warwickshire village of Bidford-on-Avon.

This is the home of Ann and Brian Smith who are members of a Warwickshire family that has dedicated itself to the cause of God's Golden Acre. In addition to Ann and Brian, prominent among the family are their daughter Angela Foster, granddaughter Lucy Foster, Brian's sister Angela Hands and his brother-in-law Jeff Hands. All have served God's Golden Acre in some way, both in KwaZulu-Natal and in the United Kingdom, and one of them, Rebecca Hands, is currently general manager of God's Golden Acre on a two-year assignment at Cato Ridge with her partner Tom Ward-Jackson.

Over a period of two years Heather and I recorded many hours of conversation at Marriage Hill Farm about her life. Once the early drafts were written, having culminated in a visit by myself to God's Golden Acre at Christmas 2003, Ann Smith played a key support role in helping me to bring the project to fruition. The book could not have been written without that support.

The other great support of the project was literary agent Robert Dudley who expressed great enthusiasm for the proposed book from an early stage and whose wise counsel ensured it emerged as an acceptable piece of work for our publisher, Monarch Books of Oxford, to consider. I must thank my old school friend Andrew Trotman for the introduction to Robert.

Many contributors to the book have enhanced its perspective – both of Heather, and of her inspirational work as founder of God's Golden Acre. Paramount among these is Susan Balfour. Her journals have been quoted in this book and have added perception and sensitivity to the manuscript. Susan Balfour was an early volunteer at God's Golden Acre at Cato Ridge and her vivid accounts of life there through the eyes of a volunteer nurse have been complemented by those from Hugh Evans, Lucy Foster, Vibeke Blaker, Marianne Jenum, Sophie Wong, Helen Beresford and Esther Perenyi. I should also like to thank Orin Wilson for his original thoughts about Heather and her family, and Gael Tremaux for a long conversation about God's Golden Acre that extended into the early hours of one morning while on a game park weekend with the children.

Others who have helped to provide a deep and personal insight into Heather and her work as a leading humanitarian include her husband Patrick Reynolds, daughter Bronwen Reynolds, and Heather's sister Myrtle Venter.

Outside the family Alan McCarthy, the chairman of God's Golden Acre, and Dr Gerrit Ter Haar, the deputy chairman, also made meaningful contributions, as did the benefactors Gerrit and Anneke Mons. On the staff at God's Golden Acre, Mary Van der Leeuw, Rosetta Heunis, Cheryl Harris and Alta Collins all went out of their way to help me collect background information about how things are run under Heather's management of the children's sanctuary and the rural outreach projects.

A highly readable account of his visit to God's Golden Acre was provided by my former colleague, BBC producer Bill Hamilton, and I am also grateful to Oprah Winfrey, Heather's great friend, in allowing me to use extracts from her published works on her altruistic and humanitarian work in South Africa, and in particular her visits to God's Golden Acre where she is "mother" to a number of children.

Among Heather's African "children" I owe thanks to Zanele Jila. She is a young woman of great beauty and intelligence who I believe will be among the first whose childhood spent at God's Golden Acre, and also higher education, will be repaid through a lifetime of achievement and dedication among her Zulu people.

From the valley, Nkosi Mlaba of KwaXimba was most generous in the help he gave me in providing vital information about Zulu culture, and the political and economic structure of rural life in KwaZulu-Natal. I should also like to thank an old friend, Clive Bromilow of Howick, for his hospitality and introductions to the farming communities in the region – and also for allowing me to draw information from his book, *Problem Plants of South Africa*, published by Bayer. Another old friend, Martin Edwards, President of Manchester United, was tireless in helping Heather to have the ear of other very important men in the world of professional football. These include Dave Richards, chairman of the Premier League, who has become one of Heather's major advocates, and David Davies, Executive Director of the Football Association. Finally, my thanks to Chris Towner, Editor of the Stratford Herald, for his support during the two demanding years when the book was in its gestation period.

Dale le Vack
March 2005

CONTENTS

Introduction 9

Part One 15
1. Easter 1965 16
2. Many Years Later... a Miracle at Mpolweni 21
3. Football, Funerals, Miracles – *Over the Rainbow* 26
4. Christmas Week 35
5. Christmas Eve 49
6. Christmas Morning 55

Part Two 61
7. Life on the Trading Station 62
8. Children in the Wilderness 65
9. The Family History 71
10. The Odd One Out 77
11. Love at First Sight 84
12. Betrayal and Divorce 89
13. A Foolish Decision 96
14. A New Life with Patrick 110
15. Heather Returns to God 116
16. The Deep Valley Years 124
17. A Life-changing Journey 141

Part Three   151

18. The Establishment of God's Golden Acre   152
19. The Horrors of the Valley   165
20. Local Hostility to God's Golden Acre   173
21. The Norwegian Volunteers Arrive   179
22. Bankruptcy Looms   184
23. The Street Protest   188
24. Heather's Desperate Gamble   199
25. Hatred and Resentment Grows   203
26. Buying McPherson Farm   207
27. A Man She Could do Business with   213
28. More Miracles Follow   220
29. More Volunteers Arrive   226
30. The Death of Thulani and the Inspiration of Ellie   233
31. Volunteers and Visitors in the Valley   235
32. Practical Hands Arrive... and More Miracles   243
33. The Young Zulu Warriors Tour the UK   247
34. Oprah Winfrey Comes to God's Golden Acre   254
35. The Children of God's Golden Acre   263
36. Symbols of Reconciliation   269
37. "I Feel Like Crying till I Die..."   278
38. A Treat for the Orphans   287
39. The Little Boy from Uppington   292
40. A Prophet in Her Own Land   296
41. Over the Rainbow   301
42. The Football Miracle   308
43. The Parable of the Good Samaritan   315

INTRODUCTION

In 1993 on a trip to Uganda, South African Heather Reynolds turned a corner that would change her life for ever. Heather was visiting a remote part of the country, and she encountered by chance the human and social devastation the AIDS pandemic leaves in its wake. She came face to face with the worst scourge to afflict humankind since the medieval plagues, and one that has destroyed the lives of millions of children. As she got out of her car at a small settlement to get water from a spring, she met a group of children, the orphaned victims of AIDS. Here she witnessed their misery and terror as they awaited death by starvation, uncared for by adults.

Some years before that day, Heather Reynolds had given her life to God but was waiting for the call to serve him. At that moment she knew this was his call. Slowly, she knelt down in the native hut and looked upon a little boy covered by a dirty sack. His parents had either abandoned him, or they themselves had died. He was spending his last hours alone and uncared for. The African child and the white woman could not communicate because of the barrier of language. The boy lay still, waiting for death, and the look in his eyes stills haunts Heather, even though, in later years, she has encountered many more young AIDS victims, some of whom have died in her arms.

She promised God she would live, for the rest of her life if necessary, by serving him in the cause of caring for, and nursing, babies and children orphaned by the AIDS pandemic. Heather decided she would use her life savings to provide shelter for orphaned children. Earlier, she had taken in pregnant girls to work in her pottery in the 1980s, and also provided sanctuary for youngsters left homeless as a result of the civil disorder in KwaZulu-Natal during the decade of transition to majority rule in 1994.

Now, believing they were answering God's call, Heather and her husband Patrick Reynolds, a well-known sculptor, filled their home at Wartburg, in KwaZulu-Natal, with sick and abandoned children. They called their little community "God's Golden Acre". From there, in 1999, God's Golden Acre moved on to become a cluster of foster homes at Cato Ridge, a few miles away. Built on the top of a hill, it is near to the Valley of a Thousand Hills, a vast rural area between Durban and Pietermaritzburg. Approximately 95 children, between the ages of a few months and 16 years, live in the community.

Most of Heather's children are healthy. Many HIV-positive babies die before their first birthday; few make it beyond their fourth. God's Golden Acre is designed as a sanctuary to allow this small minority to die with dignity in a loving environment, and as a family home for the surviving children, who are well fed, cheerful, confident, and attend the best local state schools. Then there is a series of rural outreach programmes for thousands of orphans who are living in extended families in the Valley of a Thousand Hills. Heather's teams of staff and volunteers distribute basic food supplies to the *ad hoc* families she has helped to create, many headed by an elderly "granny" figure, or a teenage girl. The teams supply rice, salt, mealie-meal, samp beans, and other basic foodstuffs.

Each day they rub shoulders with death, gaze upon the expressionless faces of the abused, and sometimes encounter both hostility and resentment. Heather drives her familiar

Land Rover alone into remote countryside to visit the sick and dying, offering comfort and prayer, and rescuing children. To many of the Zulus in the Valley of a Thousand Hills, Heather has become known as Mawethu, which means "our mother", or Gogo, our "gran".

Within the whole of Southern Africa, KwaZulu-Natal has the greatest number of HIV/AIDS cases. In 2000, 36 percent of its people were recorded as infected, eight percent higher than in the capital province of Gauteng. Among TB cases in KwaZulu-Natal, 55 percent were infected with HIV/AIDS, as were 37 percent of its pregnant women, and 80 percent of its prostitutes.

Many believe this tragic situation is an appalling legacy from the country's advanced motorway network – unique in Africa – that opened up the vast rural hinterland 30 years ago. Initially these new road networks brought greater prosperity to a land blessed with natural resources and a diversity of climates for producing food and wine. Later they became the arteries through which the virus multiplied itself. The drivers of the great juggernauts, away from home sometimes for weeks, travelling into and out of South Africa, use the services of the army of sex workers who can be found waiting for them at gas stations or walking along the verges of the highways. The men become infected with the HIV virus and then bring it home with them to the rural areas – with deadly consequences.

Similarly, young men from areas such as the Valley of a Thousand Hills can only find work in the towns and cities, and migrate there – returning occasionally to infect those that they love. It is an endless cycle fuelled by ignorance, and sometimes indifference. In these stricken lands of the AIDS pandemic, where murder, hijack and robbery are common, it is mostly grandmothers and older siblings who are left to cope with the responsibility of bringing up the family's children. Their own deceased offspring, the working adult generation, have disappeared, victims of the virus.

These extended families are impoverished, and the *gogos* (grandmothers) who run them find it increasingly difficult to provide for their young ones. Only a few have piped water to their home, electricity, fuel or opportunities for employment – factors which make it more difficult for the small groups to survive. Failing health and almost non-existent medical facilities further add to the seriousness of the situation. Adolescent girls are vulnerable to rape and abuse by adults. The South African state is making grants available to the needy child-led families in the valleys, but the bureaucracy that supports their distribution to genuine claimants tries in vain to process a huge backlog. In the end the grants seem inaccessible to the largely uneducated people in the remote areas.

Much of the help the children receive is dependent upon individuals like Heather, working with the support of other non-government organizations and a patchwork of charities that include the Rockefeller Brothers Foundation, Rotary clubs, HopeHIV and a London-based network of South Africans called Starfish, founded by Anthony Farr, who spent nine months at God's Golden Acre. His charity draws on the donations of expatriates working in London, who are being paid in sterling. Many Dutch charitable foundations have also been extremely supportive of God's Golden Acre.

However, until recently Heather has been alone in her task. It is only because of her total commitment to her work that she has been able to establish sufficient trust and respect within these desperate communities to bring relief to the needy. As she has continued walking her lonely path in the Valley of a Thousand Hills, it is the world that has come to find her. Heather has received growing news media coverage in all of South Africa's major papers, in British newspapers like the *Guardian*, and in television broadcasts in South Africa and on the BBC, ABC, CNN and Norwegian TV news.

The scale of what Heather has achieved over a number of years has come to the attention of both Nelson Mandela and

Archbishop Desmond Tutu. The international press is now becoming aware of the significance of Heather's work. She is a mother figure to thousands of children. In 2002 the American broadcasting star Oprah Winfrey visited God's Golden Acre and brought film crews to the valley. Deeply moved by what she found, Oprah Winfrey arranged for her private Foundation to fund projects, at God's Golden Acre and a rural outreach project.

Lucy Foster was one of the first European volunteer workers to arrive at God's Golden Acre in 2000 when she was 19 years old. She writes:

You will find 97 happy children – Heather is responsible for most of them being alive and for them being well-adjusted children with strong hopes for the future. Many of the orphans now go to very good schools thanks to sponsorship. In the valley there are thousands more people whose lives have been touched by her through the rural outreach programmes.

Heather now has pilot projects – such as the Strategic National Action Plan (SNAP) and the Child Sponsorship Programme – that could make a major contribution to fighting the effects of the AIDS pandemic in South Africa. We all pray that those who have the power politically will help her to make it happen, and that the general public in all countries will get to hear about what she is doing, and give her support.

Her faith in God, and her journey through the years with him, is part of the story of an amazing life that will surely appeal to people of all religions throughout the world, whether Muslim, Jew, Hindu or Buddhist. She is the personification, in our era, of the Good Samaritan.

Alan McCarthy, chairman of God's Golden Acre, shares Heather's strength of faith, conviction and belief in miracles: "I know many people who walk closely with God – and wonderful miracles happen because God can use them as a channel. It's not their own power, and they will be the first to say that. So they are not performing the miracles. Heather is no better or worse than most average people – but she is allowing God to use her, trying to let God guide her. When she prays she allows God's power to flow into the situation – so it's not Heather, it's God."

On a special episode of "The Oprah Winfrey Show" that highlighted her ChristmasKindness South Africa 2002 initiative and also included information on the AIDS pandemic in South Africa, Oprah Winfrey pledged to devote the rest of her life to the cause and interests of its orphans. The influential American TV talk show host, whose programme is distributed to more than 100 countries, told millions of her viewers that a child is orphaned through AIDS in South Africa every fourteen seconds – during the hour-long programme 257 children would be orphaned. She said: "Many of us are really just not aware of the challenges so many children face… My life was changed when I saw firsthand the devastation that AIDS is having on the lives of children and families in South Africa, as well as other parts of the world. [The] AIDS [pandemic] has become, as my friend Bono says, the defining moral issue of our time. For children, many of them already devastatingly poor, who are now left motherless, there is no question, no question at all, that we have to help them right now. We are human beings sharing the planet with other human beings, and we cannot continue to ignore one of the greatest crises facing humanity in our lifetime."

Part One

1
EASTER 1965

For years afterwards, the Xhosa herdsman talked about the night he saw the ghost truck in the hills on the Flagstaff road to the Wild Coast. It made him famous locally and he would take pleasure from terrifying his children with the story. By the time the herdsman's children had their own offspring, the tale had passed into local legend. To this day the Xhosa regard it as a haunted stretch of road.

It was Easter 1965. The fog was thick and the herdsman could hear the noise of an approaching truck. Then he could see headlights, yellow eyes in a wall of mist. It did not sound normal and he felt fear gripping him. The labouring engine was rising and then falling back, as the accelerator was applied and then released.

The apparition approached at a slow speed – not much greater than the jogging pace of a man. As the Xhosa stepped aside, a horse that had been hidden in the mist reared in fright and the cream-coloured Dodge truck swerved to avoid it. The herdsman peered through the windscreen and muttered an oath, his heart beating faster, his feet welded to the spot. He wanted to run away.

The truck had no driver. All he could see was a small pair of white hands gripping the steering wheel. The man's gasp of alarm went unheeded in the wilderness. He ran terrified to his kraal. The Xhosa had witnessed the supernatural, and this was not a good omen for his family.

What the Xhosa didn't see at the wheel of the Dodge was a diminutive girl of less than five feet, in her early teens with cropped blonde hair, wearing yellow shorts, and a hand-me-down white T-shirt belonging to an older brother. She was slightly chubby with sad brown eyes, and a determined jaw. Fourteen-year-old Heather McLellan had never driven any vehicle in her life, but she was at the wheel of one now, on one of the Transkei's most dangerous roads. It connects Kokstad with Flagstaff in Pondoland and has claimed the lives of many people over the years with its sheer drops and unguarded sharp bends. Its worst hazard, the 5,285-feet Brooks Nek Pass, is well known.

Heather could hardly reach the pedals of the truck from the driving position; her head was level with the bottom of the windscreen. After the Flagstaff turning to the Wild Coast, the road becomes a dust track and is much narrower. There are hairpin bends and sloping drops. Untended cattle, horses, donkeys, wander the mountain passes at night, creating further sudden hazards for the unprepared. As she drove, Heather prayed for guidance and protection. She was praying when the horse reared as she passed the Xhosa, but never noticed his presence. Her eyes were fixed on the dangers ahead. Beside her, asleep on the seat, was eleven-year-old Basil. Next to him sprawled John McLellan, drunk and oblivious to anything going on around him. The constant pleading of the engine for release into a higher gear filled Heather's ears.

Twelve hours earlier, the two youngsters had broken up for their Easter holidays from Kokstad High School, where they were boarders. They should have been home hours before. For years the McLellan children had dreaded the end of term. They feared it because their father regarded the occasion as an opportunity to meet up with his old comrades at the bars of various hotels. By the time he arrived at the school he was more boisterous — and much louder — than the sober adults who had also come to collect their children.

The McLellans were never teased about their father, but his behaviour was an embarrassment to his daughter. It had always been the same at the end of term over a period of seven years. In daylight it should have been a two-hour journey. The route would take the truck about fifteen miles through the tarmac mountain road from Kokstad, a further 22 miles after turning left at the Flagstaff turn onto the dirt road towards the Wild Coast, and then a further 16 miles along a narrow track to a dead end at the remote trading post at Madada.

Under normal circumstances, the youngsters should have been eagerly anticipating the delights of home and a welcome cuddle from Mum. But it never turned out like that. Once John McLellan had driven away from the school in late afternoon, he never had any intention of getting back home as soon as he could. Without exception the war veteran would want to play snooker with his old comrades — usually winning round after round. He would find old pals in the hotel bars of Kokstad, then he'd insist upon driving to another small town called Mt Ayliffe, and there join a second group of snooker-playing veterans to drink until one or two in the morning. He would leave the depressed children in the front cabin of the Dodge to await his drunken return, returning only occasionally with some money to send them to a tea room, or enable them to buy a glass of lemonade and a packet of chips.

The problem at Easter 1965 was that Heather's older brother and sister, who had usually shared her misery and long hours of waiting, and who always took over the responsibility of driving home, had now left the school. This time Heather was shouldering the responsibility for getting young Basil and herself safely back to the Madada trading post. Her father had promised their mother he would not go drinking, but he had forgotten that promise many hours before the Xhosa herdsman saw them. After drinking until eleven o'clock that night in Kokstad, he was drunk but wanted more.

"Please, Dad, let's go home. Please, Dad, please, Dad, don't drink any more," Heather pleaded – but he ignored the Flagstaff turn and began the long and dangerous ascent through the mountains to Mt Ayliffe. The children waited outside the small town hotel for a further two hours while their father drank with the other customers inside. At one stage a young policeman wandered out of the hotel and stood on the veranda, looking with interest at the teenager in the Dodge. For a moment the girl thought she could ask him to help her extract her father from the bar. Perhaps he might issue a stiff warning to him about the dangers of drinking and driving.

"Hey, could you tell Uncle Mac we want to go home now?" she asked him. However, as he sauntered back towards the bar with a grin on his face, Heather was old enough to sense that the policeman's motives had more to do with sexual opportunism than the call of duty. She became more frightened as he pestered her on several occasions. "Just go away and leave us alone, please," she eventually snapped. He lost interest and wandered back to the bar.

At last, John McLellan staggered out of the hotel. He slumped inside the cabin of the Dodge, stupefied by alcohol, and was soon losing consciousness. Heather shunted the big man to the edge of the bench and got behind the wheel herself. She knew where the pedals were, and what they were for, but couldn't reach them. She was too small to shift the gears in a normal way. The girl at length managed to start the vehicle and moved off, lurching forward in second gear, where the truck stayed for the rest of the journey.

At five o'clock in the morning, after more than four hours at the wheel of the Dodge, Heather finally arrived back at Madada trading station. Brenda McLellan was waiting by the gate as it pulled up. She opened the door and gasped with astonishment when she saw her daughter at the wheel. "Good

God!" she said. "We're going to have to give you some driving lessons! I think we'll start tomorrow."

The children walked with their mother into the house. John McLellan was left to snore the rest of his night out in the Dodge. The following day he didn't ask how he'd got home, and the subject was never mentioned afterwards.

2
MANY YEARS LATER... A MIRACLE AT MPOLWENI

Patrick Reynolds sat in silence in his studio and pondered over what he had heard from his wife at breakfast. It had not pleased him. He never intervened in Heather's pastoral work, but he objected strongly when she told him she wanted to go to Mpolweni to find out what she could do to help distressed people living there. Heather Reynolds has never been renowned for taking the advice of others – and that morning she had chosen not to heed her husband.

"Why do you *have* to go Mpolweni? It is not safe for white people. You will be taking an unacceptable risk. Don't do it. There are so many people that need you in the valley areas where you are a familiar figure," he warned her. But Heather decided to go anyway.

Mpolweni is an informal settlement, 20 miles from Pietermaritzburg, where the Church of Scotland once established a mission. Several thousand Zulus live there. Many of the Africans living there still had a deep hatred for anyone connected with the former white government. White people did not go there alone unless they had to. A popular slogan among the Zulus in Mpolweni in the 1990s was "One bullet, one Boer".

Heather had been working without serious mishap in Swayimane and the neighbouring Trust Feed, but for several years she had been too scared to venture into Mpolweni, with its network of narrow tracks that seemed to lead nowhere. This day, however, she felt the call that she must go there – despite the risk, and regardless of Patrick's advice. She recalls: "First I drove over to a minister who lived close to, but not actually in Mpolweni, and asked him if he would help me to find where the *nkosi* (chief) actually lived. It was Zulu protocol for me to first ask the *nkosi* if he would give permission for me to help the people of Mpolweni. The *nkosi* would then consult with his councillors and headmen before committing himself. The minister agreed to help me. I had brought with me some of my own little children from God's Golden Acre, and he said some of his children could also ride with us.

"So we drove into Mpolweni, but I soon got confused. This was unfamiliar territory without tarmac roads and signposts – and we got horribly, horribly lost. Then my truck got stuck in a ditch as I tried to do a U-turn on a narrow track. A Zulu boy of about 16 who said his name was Eric Zondi came walking past and offered to help. I was grateful for the offer from this lad and sent him with a small group of the older girls up the road to ask local people to come and help push us out.

"Suddenly I heard my girls screaming – some were as young as eight years old – and I raced up the track to find that a group of drunken men were accosting them. For a moment it looked as if they would assault me too. Fortunately, Eric had the presence of mind to tell the drunks: 'She's going to see the *nkosi*. She is a friend of the *nkosi*.' It worked. The men released the girls, backed off, and went away. With Eric's help we managed to release the truck, but we spent the rest of the afternoon going this way, and that way, in confusion and mounting anxiety as Eric asked people if they knew where the *nkosi* lived. It was dusk when we eventually arrived at his house.

"Then I remembered that I should not be asking for a meeting with the *nkosi* at this time of day. In Zulu culture you never visit a family at dusk – for this is the time when both good and bad spirits move around. People often sweep their houses just before dusk to ward off evil spirits. However, having taken so long to get there, I decided to take the risk and asked a woman at the house if I could speak to the *nkosi*. She told us to wait, went inside the house, and consulted with him. When she returned some time later she said: 'Yes, Nkosi Mgadi will see you but he is not feeling well, so you will have to wait for him.'

"We stayed outside the house probably for about an hour and by now it was pitch-dark. Night had descended. So there we were, in the night, in an area where many Africans hated white people – and I was alone with my children. I had no idea how we would find our way out of Mpolweni and it scared me. Eventually we were asked to go into the house, and as I led the children up the steps and into the living room, they sang a Zulu song.

"I gasped inwardly when I saw the *nkosi* sitting in a chair against the wall. He was very sick, and I thought, *This man is dying. He can hardly breathe. Everything about him looks bad – the pallor, the sweating, the gasping for breath, the high fever. He is dreadfully ill.* I apologized for coming without invitation so late in the day and when he was unwell, and explained I had tried to telephone him several times but the lines were not working. Then I told him briefly who we were, why we had come, and what we wanted. There was a silence as he scrutinized me and fought for breath, his fever mounting. Then he nodded to indicate that he would consult with his headmen and let me know the outcome. He seemed positive about me, despite his condition.

"The meeting was over, but I heard myself asking him if he wanted me to pray for him. I could see from the way he was breathing and sweating that he was very, very ill. It was a dilemma for me – if I prayed for the *nkosi* and he died, or didn't survive, they would probably say I had brought a bad spirit with me, pointing to the fact that I had come in the dark. They might also say that I was not a good minister, that my power was weak. This could have negative consequences for God's Golden Acre.

"As I stood before him with my little children, a voice within me was warning that I should not pray for him. For a moment I had doubts about the power of prayer. I knew that I would not be praying for someone who was sick, but for someone who was dying. The tiny voice, from deep within, whispered, *What if God does not heal him?* but I knew I had to do it. Then, as I began to pray, my faith came flooding back. I realized that I could not walk away from this *nkosi*. I remembered what Jesus said about faith, the mustard seed, and the mountain: 'With the faith of a mustard seed you can move a mountain; what you ask in my name will be done; these things you will do and greater things.'

"When somebody is really sick, it is beholden upon us – as Christians – to pray. So I prayed with fervour and intensity – a greater intensity in fact than at any time in my life. I also laid my hands on his head, which I later discovered is contrary to Zulu custom. I finished praying, and as I turned around in the dim light I felt a shock go right through my body as I looked straight up into the faces of three Zulu men. They were standing behind my back. I had to control myself not to scream out loud. They looked down at me with expressionless eyes, but I had nothing to fear. Nkosi Mgadi introduced his son, and his friends. They were not hostile and we were allowed to leave in peace.

"For ten days I could not get back to the *nkosi* because the telephones were not working. Thieves had stolen all the copper wire. Eventually, however, I did get through and suddenly a man answered. It was a young-sounding voice.

" 'I'm trying to get hold of Nkosi Mgadi, old Nkosi Mgadi,' I said.

" 'This is old Nkosi Mgadi,' he replied.

"The tears poured down my face. 'Have you recovered?' I asked, incredulous.

" 'Yes, I'm well,' he replied.

"A few months later I asked an African teacher I knew, and who lived in Mpolweni, whether Chief Mgadi was still in a good state of health. 'Oh, yes, it's wonderful,' she said. 'He went on the radio and told everybody how he was healed one night by a white woman who came and prayed in his house.'"

3
FOOTBALL, FUNERALS, MIRACLES – OVER THE RAINBOW

Sipho and Thando, two Zulu brothers, not yet teenagers, squat on their haunches beside the potholed track in the midday sun. They screw up their eyes in a competition to get the first glimpse of the lorry approaching in the dust along the mountain road.

There is tranquillity in their valley, KwaXimba, which might persuade the traveller that he has stumbled into paradise. As the sun rises, children fish with hand-lines in a river that tumbles through the boulders into swirling pools, women wash their clothes in chattering groups, cattle and goats graze on the bush grasses. But Sipho and Thando often go hungry, and soon their clothes will be little better than rags. Both boys are orphans of the AIDS pandemic, although no one has told them so. They only know that their mother, and then their father, died of what they were told was tuberculosis, leaving an older sister in charge of four younger siblings. Some uncles buried their mother in the garden, and a few months later their father joined her.

For Sipho and Thando it is a time recalled through horrendous nightmares – visions from the subconscious that feature repulsive skeletal demons arisen from graveyards, stalking them from the shadows of the dark. The boys wake up screaming in the night. Their last memories of those funerals are the coffins, the ritual Zulu burial, the singing at the graveside, and the putting to rest, with customary respect, of the bodies of the dead. Two mounds of red earth, close to the hut where Sipho and Thando live, reveal where their parents were interred side by side beneath a mound of stones.

The boys cannot go to school now, because their sisters do not earn enough money to pay the school fees. Relatives bring mealie-meal to the mud hut, which is rapidly deteriorating, and the men who come to see their sisters sometimes bring cabbages and potatoes. The child-headed family survives — just — but the younger ones can only hope their sisters don't get sick too. The garden is untended, nothing has been planted, and the fowls have been killed. Both boys are unwell and suffer constant pain. The brothers experience debilitation through tapeworm. They are emaciated, yet their bellies are distended. Skin irritations, including ringworm and scabies, itch on their arms and legs, and everywhere they are covered in sores.

Today, however, hunger and pain are not in the thoughts of Sipho and Thando. They are excited. Today is special, like no other Saturday they can remember, and it makes them feel happy. For once, there is a fluttering sensation inside their bellies. They grin at each other. The boys are waiting for a four-ton truck to pick them up and take them, along with 50 other Zulu boys, to a football ground.

Most of the lads that Sipho and Thando will travel with in the lorry cannot read or write. A few have only basic schooling. But ask them questions about football! The demi-gods of the world in which they exist are African football players like Mbulelo Mabizela, Siyabonga Nomvete, Arthur Zwane and John Moshhoeu. Football offers them hope, and it feeds their dreams.

Nkosi Mlaba, councillors like Simon Ngubane, and important people from as far away as Durban, including the mayor, and some soccer stars, are also going to the football ground today. There will be singing, dancing and food — and maybe, just maybe, a chance for the boys to fulfil a dream. They might play in a real game of football, and kick a proper ball. The youngsters know it is all something to do with the white *gogo* they call Mawethu, from Cato Ridge, who owns the truck upon which they are about to climb. She has started a boys' soccer league, which is all they have heard. They are not sure. However, Sipho and Thando are certain they want to be part of it – whatever it is.

There are thousands of children like Sipho and Thando, who have lost their parents. The other orphan boys want to play football too, but there is no money in the valleys where they live. Community life, as the Zulus in the rural areas have known it for hundreds of years, is in decay. There are funerals every Friday, Saturday and Sunday. Children are dying. The impact is devastating.

A generation of young people has gone absent from school in the valley, because no one can afford to pay the fees. The children are turning towards each other to find comfort. A false sense of security comes from being in gangs. It leads to drug taking, violence and crime. Marijuana grows everywhere. Then there is the temptation of glue sniffing to alleviate the hunger, the pain and the misery.

The white *gogo* has met Nkosi Mlaba and the local councillor. She told them: "We must get these children into some sort of organized sport. They love soccer. They are soccer fanatics. The easiest thing to do is just give them an opportunity to become part of a football team. It's the biggest gift you could give any of them. All we need to do is get it started. These are our leaders of tomorrow. They are wonderful children, let's give them an opportunity, but we will need a miracle. I must find someone with influence in the world of professional football, perhaps in England, who can help us."

A few miles from the dilapidated hut where Sipho and Thando live, an old African woman is sitting on a mat in the shadows and staring across the hills through an open door. The room is cleared of its meagre furniture in preparation for a funeral. A Xhosa, this woman came to the valley many years before to marry a Zulu. Like many African mothers, she carried the burden of bringing up her children alone. The nearest work was in Durban, nearly 30 miles away. To keep them alive she had to leave them in the house alone. *Leave them behind, leave them behind. Don't look back.* When it was dark, they sometimes experienced deprivation and terror — but it was the only way to protect them.

The Xhosa woman was torn, her emotions in turmoil. Some of the children did not get a proper schooling and one of these was Sibongile, her eldest daughter. The children grew to become young adults but gradually began to die in the late 1990s. Now four of the eight are gone. In a few hours Sibongile will return in her coffin from the undertaker for the funeral. The African woman feels the presence of spirits.

Soon the white visitors will come to pay their respects and this reminds her of the day when she walked in desperation from her valley to the orphan settlement run by a white *gogo* at Cato Ridge. She had heard about this woman, and the orphaned children who lived with her. She had begged the woman for a job. The white woman told her she was too old. She begged some more. The white woman gave her work helping out in the kitchen. It was the turning point in the long and hard life of Gogo Beauty, who was to become a much-loved caregiver at God's Golden Acre.

Sibongile was discharged from the local hospital because they said they could no longer help her. She was admitted to the hospice at God's Golden Acre for palliative care. Soon Gogo Beauty and her younger daughter Zani were told that infection had spread to Sibongile's brain. She would die within the next few days, they said. Gogo Beauty insisted Sibongile be taken home and within days she passed away, surrounded by her family. She was 29 years old and left two surviving children, aged eight and twelve.

During the days following the death of her daughter, Gogo Beauty remains on a mat on the floor of her living room and is attended to, day and night, by neighbours. In Zulu culture, the bereaved mother or wife should not be left alone until after the funeral. People come to offer comfort and practical support. They sing and pray together. Sibongile's body is there, having been returned from the undertaker that afternoon.

The funeral next day is long and emotional. All the mourners are seated under a tarpaulin erected at the side of the mud-and-stick hut. "KZNFC" is painted in bright yellow on all the benches provided; it is not the provincial football team, but KwaZulu-Natal Funeral Club. Grannies contribute a regular sum so that they can bury their children, or grandchildren, with dignity. The service over, the coffin is carried along the dirt track down the slope to a prepared grave in the garden. The coffin is lowered – more singing – then the grave is filled, the mound covered with large stones, and a crucifix planted. The mourners' memory of Sibongile will live on.

Now the group of orphans whom Gogo Beauty is supporting on her small income is growing, but she does not complain. The phone rings at God's Golden Acre. It is the hospital in Pietermaritzburg. An eight-year-old girl called Thandi, who has been physically abused and abandoned, needs a home. On arrival, her sunken eyes and her swollen yet frail body tell the inevitable story of neglect and starvation. She is so withdrawn and timid that Gogo Heather cannot reach into her mind and get her to respond to the new surroundings, even though she tries hard to counsel, stimulate and care for her. Thandi won't sing or join in any of the games. Her tiny body makes her look strange; she feels the difference between herself and the other strong, more robust children.

At night Gogo Heather and the African caregivers sit beside her bed for hours, comforting Thandi as nightmares rack her mind. She cries out in anguish. Gogo Heather writes in her diary: "I can still hear her strangled cries. I can still feel the hopelessness and pain as I stroke her tiny little body helplessly, trying to reassure her, wishing I could in some way take away some of the fear and terror that rack her little mind. Thandi's nightmares continue for several hours until finally she falls into a deep exhausted sleep."

Time passes and Thandi starts to gain weight. Her sores begin to heal. New clothes improve her outward appearance but her mind is still locked away and communication is difficult. Gogo cannot take her to a male doctor for examination, as her fear will escalate into panic within seconds. She is terrified of men. Natascha, a Dutch missionary girl, and Gogo Heather are the only ones with whom she will relax.

Gogo still cannot find the secret of how to get her to smile and laugh — no matter how hard she tries. Thandi's tiny pointed face remains serious and sombre. During December, Natascha and Gogo Heather take all the toddlers to Durban. Thandi comes along too. She is still fragile and only feels secure when she is close to Gogo.

There are problems on the journey. The old Mercedes that Dorcas South Africa has donated to God's Golden Acre breaks down, and the party are forced to spend an extra two days in Durban. While they wait for the repairs to be done, Gogo takes the children to the beach. She wades into the shallow waves, holding Thandi's hand. All the toddlers are shrieking with laughter and trepidation. Suddenly, very close to her, Gogo Heather hears the strangest cackling sound. She turns around to see what is making this strange noise. It is coming from Thandi and she is laughing. Gogo Heather writes:

Her face is beaming with an expression I'll never forget, as the waves swirl around her. We all just stare at her, totally dumbstruck, and then we all join in laughing and splashing, tears of joy and seawater mingling together. We watch as this miracle is taking place. It is as though the water is washing away all the memories that have frozen her mind. The healing has begun.

Today Thandi is a well-adjusted little girl; she sleeps soundly and plays happily with all the other children. My son Brendan, who is six feet two and very athletic, loves teasing and playing with her and it is such a blessing to hear her squeal with laughter as he pretends to chase and catch her. I thank our Father for this miracle and we continue to see the miracle of his wondrous love as we take care daily of the little ones he has entrusted to our care.

In another valley fourteen-year-old Andile collects what wood he can find in the dry scrubland. He bundles it up before making the three-mile trip back to his grandmother's rondavel. He has already collected water from the well that is 20 minutes walk from the hut. Andile has plenty of time to do these daily tasks, for he no longer goes to school.

The boy has a limp but walks home painfully to find his grandmother pouring water into a pot. She looks at the bundle of sticks carried by Andile and mentally calculates there will be just enough fire to heat the mealie-meal. A small child, a girl of about four, runs out of the rondavel to Andile. She is dressed in rags and her legs are no thicker than most of the sticks that Andile has collected. Her hair is matted and her elfin face is creased in a smile.

"I saw my mummy today," she announces in excitement, whispering the words in his ear as if revealing a secret. Andile shakes his head and says nothing. There is nothing to say. His mother and father are buried in the garden. His older teenage sister is dead too. Now there are just the two of them and their grandmother – who is nearly blind. He walks with the girl into the hut and says quietly to his grandmother: "I must go now."

Some miles away at God's Golden Acre great excitement is afoot. The Golden Acre Singers, a new choir that Gogo has put into place, drawn from the youngsters who live with her as well as others from the nearby rural areas, are all taking part in a talent contest to identify talented performers. A music producer from England has arrived to record vocal and backing tracks. He will then return to Birmingham to edit the music, with other tracks already recorded in England, into a CD album.

There are more than 40 people, including children and young adults up to the age of 23, in the new community theatre at God's Golden Acre, all of whom are overwhelmed with excitement at this opportunity. The music producer and the choir work hard all day, recording tracks and rehearsing for each of the nine titles. Late in the afternoon the producer notices an adolescent boy standing quietly apart from the choir. He is not part of it and does not sing. He looks at the floor to avoid eye contact. The music producer ignores the boy — he has much work to do in the four remaining days he has in South Africa.

The boy is there again the following day in the late afternoon and his appearance this time evokes a response from the producer. He speaks to Gogo Heather, who is helping to direct the choir. "Who is that boy?" he asks.

"He wants to be in the choir," she replies.

"Then why doesn't he show up with everyone else at nine o'clock?" asks the record producer.

"Andile is an orphan from the valley. He has to collect water and wood for his grandmother. It takes several hours, and then he has to walk three miles to get here from his home. So he always misses the choir practice. But he hopes to be a singer one day and he is talented," she explains.

The music producer looks at the Zulu lad and feels a knot in his throat. The boy is still avoiding eye contact.

The producer speaks with his companions, two Rotarians from England who masterminded the CD album. The record producer says to Gogo Heather, "We want to help this boy — ask him if he would like a bicycle." She suggests it might be better to buy the boy a musical instrument so that he could learn to play it and earn money as a street performer. However, she confers in Zulu with the lad, who listens to her question and shakes his head before replying.

She turns to the three Englishmen. "He says he would rather have a school uniform because without one he cannot go to school."

Now Andile has both a bicycle and a school uniform. He is one of the lucky ones.

4
CHRISTMAS WEEK

The woman spoke. "We call it the silent killer. Someone is lying there dying in about every third dwelling, in the darkness and cold. You don't see it… somebody in a bed, just dying quietly. It's not noticeable, not visible – and that's why it's very hard to get the world to react to it. It's not like a disaster where there's a flood and things are visible – where the houses are floating away and there are bodies being washed down the river. Here every night, people are just dying, and every few days there are dozens of people being buried."

A white Land Rover, driven by a small blonde woman of heavy build, turns off the tarmac road at the bottom of Sankontshe valley in KwaZulu-Natal, and begins the tortuous ascent of a slope along a potholed track. Her hands grasp the steering wheel of the vehicle as she continues talking, while looking intently into the mist and driving rain, through the arc created by the windscreen wipers. Streaks of lightning illuminate the misty horizon in the Valley of a Thousand Hills, the rural hinterland that lies between Durban and Pietermaritzburg.

White people keep away from places like Sankontshe, especially after dusk. Indeed danger lurks here for any stranger, whether black or white. Three years before, two nuns were butchered in a neighbouring valley. The journalist from the United Kingdom, who is travelling in the Land Rover, feels uneasy, but Heather Reynolds of God's Golden Acre, as she drives through the gloom towards her remote destination, is preoccupied by other thoughts. Has she brought sufficient food and presents? This is her only concern. She is thinking about the Zulu families, and their children, waiting for her Christmas visit. The vehicle is loaded with food parcels and presents for the unfortunates who live in poverty at the bottom of the social scale in this rural African community.

"Sankontshe is just one area in the Valley of a Thousand Hills, and we refer to them collectively as 'the valleys'. We'll go to a few of the most remote homes and give out food and presents to people we know are desperately poor," she says.

The rondavels, and larger settlements known as *umuzis*, are scattered in profusion around the valley, some as close as a few yards apart, others in solitude on the higher reaches of the hillside. Traditionally the Zulus do not live in village communities, but the members of an extended family might live in close proximity to one another. The smaller, poorer family groups, those without the benefit of support from an extended family such as uncles, aunts or cousins, or those born out of wedlock, were hit hardest when the HIV virus first manifested itself in the mid-1990s. In the years following the millennium, the mortality rate impoverished those further up the social scale, as the productivity of the working generation diminished. There are freshly dug graves all around the track, and many abandoned Zulu rondavels, some in a state of collapse. It is like driving onto the set of a horror movie – only this is real life.

"There is poverty, hunger and deprivation here," Heather explains. She drives the Land Rover through the potholes at a crawl, and points out a succession of huts, most without glass in the windows. Many of the dilapidated shacks have just one thin layer of rusting corrugated iron roofing – and many of those have gaping holes where the rain is pouring through.

"The HIV virus is unique and devastating because it is

selective, transmitted through sexual activity and therefore targeting the sexually active members of society, between the ages of 16 and 50. These are the income generators, leaving behind the most vulnerable members of our society, the old and the very young. There is no one left to repair the rondavels or tend the gardens, or to provide financially for the family."

"Look over there!" she exclaims. She points to a traditional round Zulu hut built of mud and fronted by a small garden, planted with maize, in which there are four small burial mounds. A gravestone marks the oldest grave, and two more have wooden crosses. The newest and smallest is signified by nothing but the red earth and rocks that cover it. "By the time they buried the child, there was probably no money left for a burial stone, or even a wooden cross," Heather explains.

The shadowy impressions of two human faces appear in the front window of a nearby rondavel. Heather sees them and waves. "If you look to the left of that hut you will see two graves by the neighbouring dwelling with a large piece of roof missing on the corner, and the windows broken. I've just seen people in there. The water is pouring into that house. They are kids and they don't know how to cope, how to rebuild their house. They don't have the means, and there are no adults to show them. They are probably starving, and yet they're not even on our programme."

She sighs: "It's a crisis. South African society in the rural areas is imploding, but many people in other parts of the world don't yet grasp how serious it is, and many richer people in this country don't seem to think it's their problem."

Her first stop is to a child-led family that God's Golden Acre has been supporting for two years. The girl, now about 18, looks after four younger siblings, and her own baby — born before she was 16. Their rondavel was falling apart when a project run by God's Golden Acre, called Houses of Hope, received the funding to build the family a new home. "We built it just in time before the house collapsed. Now she's got a little garden, chickens, and receives a food parcel every month. It's barely sufficient to feed them all, but they get some help from neighbours and will soon be eating what they grow – as long as the rain keeps coming. She has to buy her water because she's so far away from the well, and we help her with that. We also pay the fees for two of the children to go to a school in the valley and they also get a uniform and stationery.

"It's a hard life for an 18-year-old child. Imagine if we weren't there. What would have happened to them? Their house would have collapsed. Where would this girl and her four siblings and infant child have gone? Where? What choices would she be forced to make?" Heather gazes ahead in silence into the arcing wipers as the rain lashes into the front of the vehicle.

The girl has hurriedly put on her best clothes. She smiles politely as she stands framed within the doorway of her candlelit home. There is a picture of Christ on the wall of the living room, a table and four chairs, and curtains given by the group of Dutch volunteers who helped to build this square concrete blockhouse with green corrugated iron roof, that has replaced the traditional rondavel.

There are two bedrooms, and all six members of the family share two beds, a double and a single, each covered with an old blanket. The girl keeps her home spotlessly clean. But she whispers to Heather in Zulu that they are hungry. They have no food in the house for Christmas. Heather explains: "She has been waiting and praying that I would bring food. She says, 'Oh Gogo! I didn't know whether you were going to come.'"

So the girl prays in thanks with Heather, whose supplies, as usual, include a sack of rice, mealie-meal, samp beans, soya, teabags, sugar, candles, matches, cooking oil, body soap and washing soap for clothes. She also gives the girl 20 Rand to buy water. Together they sing:

Haleluya Ameni (Hallelujah Amen)
Usithethelele (You paid...)
Usithetheleli izono (You paid for our sins)
Usithethelele baba (You paid, Father)
Usithethelele moya oyingcwele (You paid, Holy Spirit)
Jesu! (Jesus)
Usithethelele (You paid)

About a dozen children appear out of the mist with a hopeful look and there are cries of delight when Heather gives each of them a present wrapped in Christmas gift paper, and a fistful of sweets. Small faces, beaming with happiness, melt away into the mist as quickly as they came.

Heather drives on and provides the big picture: "There's no work here in the valley. Nothing. Absolutely nothing. So it makes no sense when white people say these girls should get a job and help themselves. Where? Where would they work? Who would look after their young siblings? Most of them have no support whatsoever apart from what a generous neighbour might provide. Ironically many of these girls are entitled to some form of basic government benefit but the bureaucratic rigmarole they have to go through to get it means they just don't know how. So it's down to NGOs – like us at God's Golden Acre – to do what we can to help them."

Most girls bringing up a family follow a predictable pattern, Heather explains. They fall pregnant around fifteen or sixteen, either in a relationship seeking emotional and financial support, or through more casual encounters – sex in exchange for favours. For them it is the only way of coping in a world without adults.

"Although things are beginning to change, thanks to government campaigns, many South African men will not tolerate condoms; they don't care about safe sex. This in turn vastly increases the risk of infection, and the prospect of yet another generation dying from the HIV/AIDS virus. It just repeats itself. Women in this rural and traditional Zulu society obey their menfolk. Then there are the children – whose parents have died – who go to live with older relations in the extended families. Here the young girls are often treated very badly; they become real-life cinderellas, and sometimes get sexually abused."

Heather drives across a hill along a rutted track to the home of a young woman, also about 18. Following the gang murder of her father, and the death of her mother, she looks after two younger siblings, and now also a baby of her own. Her hut had virtually disintegrated when rescue came just in time from volunteers and a team of young African men from God's Golden Acre. They had completed building her new house in Christmas week. Heather explains the girl's situation.

"She lost her father seven years ago when he was 'neck-laced'. She watched helplessly with her mother and two younger brothers, one about eight, the other around three, as the gang put a tyre around her father's neck, doused him in petrol and then set him alight. He was burned alive in front of them. The middle boy just started screaming and screaming. He was like that for hours, and by the end of it his mind had gone. Their mother died shortly afterwards, and the girl, the oldest child, was left to look after her brothers and bring them up for six years.

"When we found them they were still alive, but living in a hut which no longer kept out the wind and the rain. The walls of the shack had gaping holes, but she'd had the dignity to cover them with cloth. The support beams had been so eaten by white ants that you could almost blow them away. The girl was the mother figure, but to get food she needed to have a relationship with a man. By the age of fourteen she had her first baby. She had to use her body to get food for her younger siblings, and she did so.

"I prayed for someone to sponsor them, and their house, and their needs. Then unexpectedly someone did come forward from overseas, and we took her to see this little family. She immediately gave us the go-ahead to rebuild the house and she gave the family a substantial cash donation. She also provided fruit trees to plant, chickens for breeding, a coop, food and clothing. With that small gesture, the family has gone from rags to wearing decent clothes, and to look upon life as not so much a terrible ordeal, but with possibilities and promises.

"As for the brother who was emotionally damaged by his terrible experience, all I can say is that he may never again be normal. But he will look after and feed those chickens, and perhaps feel he has some purpose in life. He was never mad; he has just withdrawn into an inner consciousness for protection from a world he can't understand. We are praying for him, and maybe one day he will become well again."

The girl is slim, very attractive and smartly dressed. She is waiting when Heather's Land Rover pulls up. It is not a traditional round Zulu structure, but, like the previous family's new home, a square concrete blockhouse with two bedrooms, a kitchen and living room, with a corrugated iron roof, overlooking a small sloping garden. Many Zulus stopped building with thatch during the transitional years before 1994 when thousands of homes were set alight during rival political infighting between the African National Congress and the Inkatha Freedom Party.

"Oh thank you, Gogo!" the teenage girl cries in English, as a table and chairs are unloaded, with food sacks and presents for the children. Looks reveal joy and gratitude. There is no income earner here, just what the unemployed father of the baby brings when he is in work.

Heather whispers: "They said they prayed we would come in time for Christmas. There is no food in this house either. Nothing."

Soon over 30 Zulu children arrive at the back of the Land Rover and stand in a respectful queue, their hands cupped together, waiting politely for a present from Heather. The girls squeal as they unwrap the parcels to discover a doll. For the boys there is a plastic car kit. Sweets are then piled into out-stretched hands. The children and adults stand in a circle around Heather and pray. A beautiful child of about nine years of age, in a pressed pink party frock, and plaits, steps forward and leads the singing – a Zulu hymn of thanksgiving sung in harmony and with intense passion.

Siyabonga Baba (Thank You, Father)
Haleluya Ameni (Hallelujah Amen)
Siyabongo Jesu (Thank You, Jesus)
Haleluya Ameni (Hallelujah Amen)
Siyabongo Moya Oyingcwele (Thank You, Holy Spirit)

As she drives away Heather says: "It's an absolutely basic diet. Basic. Basic. Samp beans and rice, maize, cooking oil and soya gravy. Yet that song, *Siyabonga Baba*, means "Thank You, Father" for our blessings – and that's what is so humbling about the whole thing. They receive just £15 worth of food for each family for one month, and a few presents that I lugged over from the Netherlands.

"There's a dignity and standard among these young girls. You can drop in here any time and you will find them clean and tidy, and if they have been in the garden, or putting cow dung down on the floor, they'll quickly wash their hands and slip on a clean top. The Zulu people are incredibly polite too, and that's why they get angry with us when we teach their children different ways. They don't appreciate us showing their children how to do things Western style. Their kids are very, very respectful of adults, do not behave badly, or get out of hand."

The next two hours are spent visiting other Zulu families in Sankontshe, whose circumstances are all etched in tragedy; and which constitute a caseload of despair for the handful of community health workers who try to monitor their plight from within the valley. On a higher level in the management chain, a pitifully insufficient number of qualified social workers are either completely overwhelmed, or in some disgraceful cases, seemingly indifferent to the scale of the problem, and inertia has become apparent.

South Africa's government has a heavy burden to bear. In 2003 in some rural schools children were learning nothing about the virus, neither did many valley teenagers receive instruction about safe sex. Vital life-prolonging drugs have not – until recently – been available for AIDS patients in hospitals. Death certificates have never shown HIV as the cause of death. The majority of the rural black population has been in denial about the deadly illness that is gradually destroying their culture like a cancerous growth.

In one hut Heather visits, the children last saw their mother when she was taken to hospital suffering from tuberculosis fours years ago. No word since. They have no idea what happened to her body, where she is buried, or when she died. The oldest daughter has brought up her two young siblings since she was fourteen, and now more recently her own newborn baby. AIDS is not mentioned, out of respect. The word remains taboo, its ownership a terrible social stigma.

In another hut, its roof pitted with rust holes, the mother of the family, and her eldest son, were shot dead by her brother-in-law because she could not repay a debt of 20 Rand (£2). The oldest teenage daughter is now the mother of the family, and has been so since she was fourteen. Heather explains: "The whole family watched the uncle shoot their mother and older brother in front of their eyes. The oldest girl took over the household. Several years later we were called in as an emergency when the hut was collapsing all around them and the youngest baby was dying. One room at a time had fallen in, and they had retreated into the final room where there was a degree of shelter. We found a sponsor, built them a house, and gave them back their dignity. They now have a food parcel a month and the children are back at school."

A group of children smile and wave at Heather's Land Rover as she drives by. Then a pitiful-looking African *gogo* steps forward out of the shadows and flags her down on the track to plead for food. She tells Heather she and her grandchildren are starving. Heather gives the old woman what she can spare from the back of the Land Rover. Within moments, the *gogo* is joined by a group of children, and several teenage girls with babies. All need help. And so it goes on. One human tragedy confronts her after another.

"The old woman was crying about her home collapsing, and saying she needed some wire for the fence of her garden, and I told her I couldn't do all that. I just don't have the budget. I told her the government must help them. I can only do a little bit, what I can. We give our families on the project their food once a month, and we know that by the end of it they will have nothing. They are literally praying on their knees for us to come."

In another house – built by God's Golden Acre volunteers – a blind *gogo* looks after three grandchildren under the age of six. When Heather arrives they stare vacantly ahead. It is a listlessness that signifies despair. The blind *gogo* cannot manage her home. The chickens she has been given are nowhere to be seen, and the young trees she planted in the overgrown garden have died in the dry winter, parched without water. She is too weak to dig the soil, plant seeds, and then fetch water from the nearest well that is nearly half a mile away, and up a hill. By now the rain is lashing down across the hillside, blowing cascades of spray in random directions. Dark grey clouds race across the sky a few feet above the ridge in this magnificent African panorama.

Heather's hands continue to grasp the wheel, and she peers through the arcing wipers. "These roads are incredibly slippery but thankfully it's easy with this Land Rover. But if we were travelling in a small truck it could be very dangerous. A Land

Rover is one of the few vehicles that can cope with this, and much worse conditions."

At length, they come to the home of Gogo Beauty, the much-loved carer at God's Golden Acre. Her home, middle-class by African standards, consists of a small cluster of Zulu rondavels, and a modern square building. It is a meeting point for several families. A plate of chicken is provided for the two white visitors. Dozens of children are waiting and hoping for a present and a fistful of sweets. None are to be disappointed.

At length an African woman whispers in Heather's ear and she follows her to an *umuzi* less than 200 metres from the home of Gogo Beauty. The house is clean, and stands in a cluster of others, signifying an extended family group. The walls are painted lime green, and a rug covers the linoleum floor. There is a suite of red lounge chairs, a sideboard displaying porcelain birds, books on a shelf, and a portrait of Nelson Mandela on the wall.

There is also a framed photograph of a beautiful Zulu girl holding a smiling baby. On the single bed, in the corner of the dim room, lies the pathetic skeletal outline of this same person. Her name is Beth. She is 19 years old.

Heather and a group of African women quietly gather round the bed to sing and pray for the girl's life. They ask the white *gogo* to lead them in prayer. Heather sings. Beth has tuberculosis. A child about five years old lies tucked in beside Beth, lying with her face at the other end of the bed. A young chicken plucks at the fluff on the blanket that covers mother and child. The group, some weeping, pray in Zulu with such intensity and sorrow that the girl wakes from her light sleep, eyes huge on her shrunken face, and gazes around in bewilderment before finding the strength to brush the chicken off her bed. She listens to the prayers for a few moments, and then returns to her delirious world of intermittent slumber.

Before departing, Heather holds Beth's shrunken hand and whispers quietly to her in Zulu. An elderly African woman sobs in deep gasps as the white woman crouches down by the bed. Afterwards Heather says she had not met Beth before. The presence of Mawethu – it means "our mother" and is the name Heather has been given by the Zulus – had been requested to give Beth strength and faith, and to prepare her for Jesus.

Heather explains: "She was a bag of bones. The little hand that I held, and her tiny arm outstretched, was just down to nothing. Apparently they took her to hospital but she was soon discharged. Her family brought her home to die. She was showing all the signs of AIDS. Her bodyweight had diminished, she was vomiting all her food, and it was just a matter of time before she would be gone. Thank God, the little girl who was lying beside her is healthy, but Beth also has a baby and she is sick. Her mother died of AIDS, now Beth will die, and so will her baby. That's three generations of females in the same family. The woman who was leading the prayers was her aunt, and she was overcome with grief because there are other children in her immediate family who have been orphaned. This is just the latest tragedy to hit them."

What form had the prayers taken?

"There were many pleas to God for mercy, asking for help and strength, and for God to come back again and show himself – to alleviate the suffering and the pain being endured by the family. They really need him now to come and help them because they can't do it on their own. They prayed for God's strength and comfort. There were some really desperate pleas from the heart there, deep down.

"I whispered words of comfort to Beth and prayed that in her darkest moments in the time when she is suffering the most pain – when it's almost unbearable – that she will turn her eyes to Jesus. I told her he is the one who can help her to bear the pain. She should know that he is close to her, always close to her, and always will be. I told her to cling on to him right through anything that might seem too terrible to bear. I think this is very important for people when they are dying painfully. They can turn inwards. When you are dying you sometimes go into a coma, into semi-consciousness, and at that time you can hallucinate about God, and Jesus, which can bring a sense of peace about death, rather than struggling to keep going. It's easier to think of Jesus at a time like that and go to him at peace knowing you are in his care.

"I don't believe that I should create false expectations while doing my prayers of comfort in a situation where somebody is dying as a result of diseases caused by the HIV virus. We see such death all the time. So I am not going to give her and the family false hope. We know in the back of our minds that God can do a miracle, but we also know the realities of AIDS. That family has been hit hard and those old grannies are feeling the pain. They have lost a daughter, now a granddaughter, and soon her baby. They are a big family, but you could hear from the agony in their voices that they have gone through a lot of suffering."

Who's preparing the child for her mother's death? How will they do that in the family?

Heather shrugs: "They've got a philosophical way of looking at it. Death is something that the Zulu people have always lived with. They are warriors, and they believe the spirits of their ancestors live on among them. They know that God gives, and takes, gives, and takes again. So they will be teaching her that, and to be strong."

In fact Beth survives the festive season and over the following months her health improves. She puts on weight but remains frail and weak. Soon she is well enough to walk short distances in the valley and it is a precious reprieve from her illness. She died in June 2004.

The Land Rover heads back through the remote tracks in the dark valley towards God's Golden Acre at Cato Ridge, passing hundreds more graves and huts where Africans, who will never receive Heather's ministry, are dying in silence surrounded by terrified children. A ghastly paradox – the magnificent panorama of rural Africa, but one that has become a graveyard for the victims of a new plague; the horror film scenario.

How can you stand this, every day?

It is the question every visitor to God's Golden Acre asks Heather Reynolds.

5
CHRISTMAS EVE

Petrus Venter, a big-boned Afrikaaner in khaki shirt and shorts, picks up a small African child with his huge hands and hoists the delighted youngster into his pickup to take him for a joyride, while roaring with laughter at the question.

Five years ago might he have imagined – in his wildest dreams – spending Christmas in the company of dozens of Zulu orphans?

Petrus, in middle age, has the stern military air of a retired policeman, which is exactly what he is. "No – not by any stretch of the imagination!" he continues, chuckling. "I made it quite clear to Myrtle that there was no way we'd ever visit her sister Heather while she was involved with these black kids running all over the house and all over everybody. I made that quite clear. I was trained to fight African terrorists on our borders with Namibia and Zimbabwe, brainwashed to hate them with a passion, and to kill them whenever I saw them. I voted for the apartheid system, and that is where the hatred came from. I was brought up with it – yet I also believed I was a Christian. It was only later I realized that to be a real Christian you have to live it – like Heather does."

A few years before, when Heather brought baby Chummy, one of her orphans, to the home of her brother-in-law in Johannesburg, she was invited by Petrus to leave the child in the garage. It was only in a later incident, when Heather and a larger number of Zulu orphans were stranded in the city, that Petrus had little choice but to give them shelter and sanctuary in his home. It was an experience that started to change him. "I began to listen to what Heather had to say and realized that they were only kids, just like our own children. It's not their doing that they have been orphaned, or that some of them are HIV-positive. The big turning point came when I saw how committed she was to her mission. She was adamant that she was going to succeed. I asked myself why I was rejecting these little black children and turning my back on them."

At Christmas lunch Uncle Petrus will play a big part in the fun and games – and love every moment. On New Year's Eve he'll run the firework display. "It'll be like last year – they'll be jumping on me, and hanging from me, and singing my ears off," he chuckles. "I think in a way God spoke to me through Heather. I watched this woman driving through her incredible mission on her own, believing in what she was doing, determined to reach her goal come hell or high water, not worrying how, but having the faith that the Lord would provide. This convinced me that through Christianity the finest things can be achieved. Black and white men of my generation still have some way to go to reconcile the past, and only some of us are trying hard. One of my best friends now is a former ANC terrorist and we can laugh and joke together about the years when we would have tried to shoot one another had we met. But it's not that way for the majority, and I think South Africa can only be pushed forward by the young generation, those who have no personal memories of the recent past. The biggest hope is in the universities, where the black and white students are integrated, and youngsters from both ethnic groups are totally comfortable with that."

It is shortly before dusk on Christmas Eve and Petrus Venter is part of a group of around 30 people – children and adults – making their way to a quiet corner of God's Golden

Acre. They walk through long grass along a path skirted by gum trees. Heather and Patrick lead the group, each carrying a small child, followed by their dogs. Heather holds hands with a small Zulu girl in a pink frock. Behind them the orphans laugh and chat with the volunteers and caregivers, with whom they walk hand in hand, singing in harmony.

Siyabonga Baba,
Haleluya Ameni,
Siyabongo Jesu,
Haleluya Ameni.

The crickets also sing a familiar chorus, herbal aromas pervade the encroaching night air, and a giant fireball drifts slowly beneath the horizon. It is a hot evening and the children are tired after playing for hours in the pools and waterslide of the resort. At length they come to three graves, two marked with crosses, the third smaller, and freshly dug.

The marked crosses are where they buried Snenhlanhla, who died a week after her seventh birthday on 16th July 2003, and Manalisi, aged two-and-a-half, who went to Jesus on 26th July 2003. The unmarked grave is that of a baby boy who came to the hospice at God's Golden Acre two weeks before he died just a few days before. A small bunch of withering flowers marks his resting place.

Heather gathers the group of adults and children around their graves. "Snenhlanhla was a great fighter like Hope is now. She just fought and showed such courage. She was sick for two years and I tell you she was so full of life – even to the last days when Wendy would hold her when she couldn't sleep. She was so courageous. She would wake up out of a coma, laugh and try and tickle Wendy, and then fall back into her coma again.

"So we come here tonight just to remember all the little children of the world like Sne who through no fault of their own were taken. On the birth of Christ it's good to bring our minds back to our faith in God and to remember Thulani, Happiness, Manalisi, Sne, Megan and many other beautiful children, to pay tribute to them, and also to all the little children whom we don't know.

"We are here to serve little children who find themselves in dire circumstances. The real purpose comes home when we stand around these little graves and we know that we served them well. We were there for them in the worst, most painful, moments of dying. They had no tummies left and food dropped into their mouth and went right through them.

"It's not really a time for crying, or feeling sad, because they have moved on to their home in heaven with our Father. We are the ones that remember the pain and the suffering. We are the ones who cling to the happy memories and because we remember them we feel sad. There's a little song I wrote for the children that explains they are now in heaven and it's not an end for our children when they die, but a beginning."

There's a new star that shines, oh so bright,
A new star that lights up the night,
A new star has reached heaven's door,
She's home, she's home for evermore.
There's a new song she will sing
For her Saviour and her King,
A new life she's found there, in our Father's care.

The following is an extract from the journals of God's Golden Acre volunteer Susan Balfour, written in August 2003:

Snenhlanhla, who had just celebrated her seventh birthday, passed away during my visit. We all knew it was coming. At Christmas, Snenhlanhla was battling, and the doctors informed us that she only had two months to live. But Snenhlanhla never failed to surprise us. She joined preschool, and blew us away with her intelligence and her amazing sense of humour.

Then, three months ago, her condition deteriorated. She was oxygen-dependent all that time, and was cared for in the hospice. The day after her seventh birthday, she developed an abnormal (terminal) breathing pattern and was transferred to the high care room. Though clearly in pain, coughing up pus and blood continually and usually a very miserable little girl, there were windows of hope during the day, when she would laugh and giggle and joke and tease us.

"You're a fruit," her favourite volunteer, an Irish girl called Ruth, told her.

Both Sne and I were confused by this, until Ruth explained that in Ireland they call crazy people "fruits".

Snenhlanhla looked at Ruth and thought for a moment. "Then you're a banana!" she told Ruth, pointedly!

I can't even begin to tell you how her special little spirit touched us. Her humour, her resilience... she taught us so much. She inspired us to carry on bravely and cheerfully. In the darkest moments, when Snenhlanhla cried hoarsely that she couldn't breathe, Wendy, the hospice nurse, reassured her that she was doing really well, that she didn't have to fight.

I did a night shift with her once. She lay on her chest, as I sat propped against a beanbag. That was the only comfortable position for her. But Sne refused to sleep.

"I'm frightened," she told us, her eyes brimming with terror.

"It's all right baby." "It'll be better soon." "It's so nice in Heaven."

But all through the night, she fought. Her breathing was laboured, gasping, irregular, and every now and then she would sit bolt upright and search the room desperately to make sure that Ruth, Wendy and I were still there.

Every time she did it, my heart broke all over again. "It's OK, darling, no-one is going anywhere," we told her, over and over. We reassured her constantly that we all loved her, and that she was going to be with her mummy and Jesus in Heaven. Sne asked us to pray for her, so we did, and Wendy played some of the little girl's favourite praise and worship music.

Wendy and Ruth stayed with her day and night. They never left her. 24 hours a day, one of them sat with Sne. 24 hours a day, there was someone to hold her, rock her, read to her or stroke her forehead.

Heather and the Zulu *gogos* slipped into the tiny room one afternoon and sang for Sne, in gently layered harmonies. She was on morphine at that point, and in such a lot of pain, but the music soothed her troubled spirit, and Sne's breathing, though still laboured, became steady.

She was surrounded by an awesome measure of love and compassion. I just don't know how to describe to you all that I experienced in that room. It was phenomenal. I feel so privileged to have shared in it.

Over the days that followed, Snenhlanhla became unresponsive. Then, late one morning, in Wendy's arms, she looked up at a mural of Jesus on the wall, and then at Wendy.

"You will fly to Jesus," I had promised her. And in that moment, Sne knew it was true. She was filled with peace. She closed her eyes and breathed her last breath – a gentle death in the arms of someone who loved her. For that, I am thankful.

We all cried as we washed her – tears of sorrow and relief. I closed Sne's eyes and stroked her beautiful face. The tension had melted from it. The air in the room was now lighter: the sense of despair had lifted.

Already, we were preparing to accept another terminally ill child into our home – a two-year-old boy. It's not rare to us anymore, but it's always unthinkable somehow.

Lala ngoxola sisi omncane. Siyakuthanda Kakhulu. Sizokhumbula. (Rest in peace little sister. We love you so much. We will miss you. We will remember you.)

6
CHRISTMAS MORNING

As the sun climbs higher in the sky above the eucalyptus trees on Christmas morning, the orphans of God's Golden Acre are beginning to stir for their breakfast, having dreamed in anticipation of the joyous day that lies ahead. There will be a roast chicken lunch, a visit from Father Christmas, a carol service, sweets and of course presents, opened and enjoyed in the company of the carers, volunteers and other grown-ups who love them and make them feel special. It will be another hot day and the boisterous kids will rush around the waterslide, splashing one another and the volunteers in the resort's swimming pools... The dark shadows of terror and shame will be banished for these daylight hours.

Christmas Day at God's Golden Acre is always arranged and orchestrated by Heather. However, she has other children on her mind as she sits at the wheel of the familiar white Land Rover and heads down the rocky track out of the estate. Her destination this Christmas morning at sunrise, while most still slumber, is a remote cluster of homesteads high in the mountains, overlooking the valley of Sankontshe. The vehicle is loaded with food and provisions – and presents and sweets for children.

"There's one little group of families that I didn't get to before Christmas, and who to me are very important. They'll be wondering why I didn't get there, but it doesn't matter because this will be a lovely surprise for them. It's a visit that has a lot of significance for me because, of all the families that I have helped over the years, these have had the most impact. It's about how you can help to change people. I arrived at their small and remote community at the top of the mountain back in January 2000, having been advised by the community health worker that they needed help, and some of the children were sick. When I got to their homes, I discovered they were a group living on the fringe of rural African society. Local people disapproved of them.

"Many were just young teenagers of fourteen or fifteen, and it was clear that the girls were exchanging sex for favours, and the boys were surviving through crime. It shocked and saddened me to find the young girls living that way. You could see by the painted nails and the way their hair was styled and dyed, by the clothes they wore, and the sexual way they moved, that they were in the sex trade. They turned and stared at me with utter disinterest, and even animosity.

"Their faces revealed what they were thinking: 'What are you doing here? We don't need you and your kind.' It was as if they didn't want me there because they feared I was judging them. People like that don't want 'do-gooders'; they don't need to be told what they are, and what they should be. They had for sure already been told many a time – written off in contempt as bad by other Zulus in the valley. Promiscuity, drugs and alcohol abuse – it was all here in this group of outcasts. There is a Zulu song called *Ntombi Hlope*, and these girls would have been called that. It is a term used for people for whom there is no respect or honour in the Zulu culture. Their young faces, hard and mean, revealed a short lifetime of abuse.

"As for the young men, they had the shifty look of thieves about them, which is exactly what many of them were. It turned out later that some of these lads had been responsible for much of the pilfering and stealing around Cato Ridge, including some burglaries at God's Golden Acre, and in one case it was my evidence in court that put two of them in prison.

"However, these young teenagers all had kids, and not only did they have a lot of children, but among them were a large number of orphaned children – left behind by adults who had died of AIDS. Many of the children were riddled with tapeworm, ringworm, scabies, and they were covered in sores. The worst cases were brought back, after hospital treatment, to God's Golden Acre, for a period of recuperation before returning to the community.

"So there was this totally dishevelled bunch of people and children who were dirty, poor and totally disinterested in a society that had rejected them. They were not expecting anything except condemnation from me, the community health workers, and everybody else. So I would get there every month, hand out the food parcels, ignore the hostile looks in the eyes of the teenagers, and just focus on the children.

"The older ones had gone into a way of living that was totally unacceptable to society. This stand-off went on for about six months, and eventually I tried to get closer to the children – I said one day, 'Come on kids, let's have a song. Let's sing a song together.' They looked at me blankly. These kids didn't sing. They didn't know church songs. This was an outcast group of people. To give the children credit, they did try to sing, but it was no good, it didn't come from their heart. I decided not to pursue it. Years went by, and I would still go to their community each month with food parcels and sweets, and talk to the kids. At Christmas I would invite them all up to our parties to join our kids.

"Then one of their houses fell down – it literally collapsed. So I found a sponsor from England and we rebuilt the house for them – and at last they were really happy. It was the first time I saw these teenagers smile and laugh. I felt they were realizing, at last, that in the world there really were people who cared about them.

"Then an amazing thing happened. We were due to plant fruit trees on their land, but when I arrived they hadn't dug the holes for the trees to be planted in. That was part of the agreement. They were supposed to prepare for the planting, and we would bring the fruit trees for them. But they'd fallen down on their side of the deal and I got really mad. I felt the least they could have done was to dig the holes.

"So I told the community health worker, 'That's it! I'm leaving with the trees. They don't get any fruit trees.' I was fuming. These trees were worth 25 Rand each and there were plenty of people in the valley who wanted them and would look after them. But before I drove away, I had second thoughts. I realized that the whole community wasn't at fault. In fact it was the community health workers who should have checked that the digging had been done before we arrived.

Then all hell broke loose. Everybody in the community was offering to dig the holes, and by the time my anger expired, they'd dug all the holes so fast that the trees could be planted after all. I'd never seen holes dug so quickly! I relented.

"The next thing that happened was that a little wooden bench was brought over by the children for me to sit on. This had never happened before. So I sat down on the bench and all the kids started to crowd affectionately around me. They were now four years older than when I first came. So the ones who had been four were now eight, and the ones who had been eight were now twelve. They had got used to the white *gogo* coming around, and it was apparent now that they cared for me. They were all gathered around me. I said in Zulu: 'Shall Gogo teach you a song?'

"They all cried out 'Yes. Yes.' So I started singing, and they followed me, even though they spoke hardly any English.

This little light of mine,
I'm going to let it shine,
This little light of mine,
I'm going to make it shine.

"The next thing, the older girls, the mothers who were now 20 or so, all came out, and they were trying to catch the words too. At the end of it, a whole lot of us were singing, "This little light of mine", and we were all singing together. Suddenly I looked at the mothers properly for the first time in years – I'd always tried to avoid looking directly into their eyes because I hated their cold, hostile looks – but now I looked closely, and it dawned on me in a flash that they were no longer dressing and behaving like prostitutes. I suddenly realized this whole group of people had changed their lifestyle!

"We had built them a house, we were laying a water pipeline up to their settlement, and trying to raise money to get them connected, and we had given them food through the outreach programme. Their kids were now going to school, because we paid the fees, and they'd been given uniforms. As a consequence of all this, the young parents had got back their self-respect.

"Now here we were, singing Christian songs – a whole community of lovely people. In the end they had found God in their own way. I couldn't tell you the joy I felt, the warmth that enveloped me, when they were all singing and I looked at them, and the incredible change that had come over these girls. They were all dressed cleanly and were respectable young women. Now, each one of them could walk down the road, hold her head high, and be any ordinary girl. And the kiddies were singing from their heart.

"Over those years with all the good nutrition the children had received, they were normal, healthy youngsters. In fact they were beautiful – their skins were glowing, their eyes were bright, their hair was shining, and they were growing up in a healthy environment thanks to our rural outreach project. Not only that, when I go up there now I always find that all the plants and fruit trees are well tended. They are so proud, they keep some of the best and most beautiful gardens in the entire valley. If it turned out that this was the only group of people in Africa who had benefited from my help, then my whole life would have been worth it."

Part Two

7
LIFE ON THE
TRADING STATION

Heather Reynolds was born among the Zulus and spent the first nine years of her life living in their midst. Her parents ran two trading stations and the one where she lived stood on the summit of a small hill ten miles outside Mtubatuba in KwaZulu-Natal. It overlooked the rolling plains and foothills of the great African kingdom, and bordered the Umfolozi Game Reserve, home of the black and white rhino.

For months of the year the sky was a blue ocean with islands of white clouds on an endless horizon. Beneath this vastness, the bush was an exotic flora patchwork of shades from khaki brown to dark green. Hills and ridges rose and fell into valleys where great rivers tumbled towards the Indian Ocean.

The sights, sounds and smells of rural Africa, as they'd existed for thousands of years, were locked in a time warp. However, the end of an era, with its political upheaval, was approaching like a stalking leopard, unnoticed by ordinary men and women in the rural areas.

The white girl, who in later life would become known among the Zulus as Mawethu, "our mother", was a familiar figure among the Africans with her cropped hair, snub nose and enquiring brown eyes. She might have been mistaken for a boy, because she wore her older brother's hand-me-downs. Heather was born in January 1952, the second youngest in a family of five. John and Brenda McLellan were only unusual in that their oldest son Kenny, born in 1940, was severely handicapped, suffering from cerebral palsy. David came after Kenny in 1946. Myrtle was born in 1949, then Heather, and finally Basil in 1954.

Trading stations in the veldt were reminiscent of provision stores in Hollywood Wild West films. Africans and a few white farmers would purchase food, ironmongery, clothes, domestic items and stationery. Usually the families running the trading station were the only whites in the neighbourhood, so Heather's friends and contemporaries, apart from her brothers and sister, were black. Selina looked after the younger children while their parents worked, and Togo the cook was strict about hygiene and being tidy around the kitchen. Hands had to be clean before they could eat. The housekeeper, Maliya, was big and buxom, in the African mama style.

Heather's earliest memories are of playing with Selina's children around the trading post. She was bilingual, speaking fluent Zulu by the age of four. Myrtle remembers of her younger sister: "Heather used to read a lot in her bedroom, or she used to paint, and she kept to herself. She did not spend much time with me because I spent a lot of time with Mum, cooking and sewing. Then my dad got Heather into the garden and she became good at that. So although we grew up together, we were quite separate, different people. She had her thing and I had my thing. That's how we went through school days too."

In 1961 the family moved out of Zululand to Madada in Pondoland. Here the children helped to run the trading post managed by their parents. The African children used to come in with their parents and that was how Heather got to know them. She would walk barefoot down the track to meet them and bring with her a bag of sweets. They would all squat on their haunches under an acacia tree, out of the heat of the sun, sweating in the humidity, brushing away the flies and insects.

Heather would sit in the middle and tell stories about Africa, or tales and legends that she'd read. Other times she would tell them about her boarding school and adventures there. The African children wanted to hear about her life, and compare it with their own. They would listen wide-eyed as she told them about her school, the pranks and japes, and the sport.

"It wasn't really the done thing to spend time with black children, and so I used to sneak off out of my parents' way. The Africans did not own much furniture, and no one slept on a bed. Most families in the village had meagre belongings that might consist of a few tin plates and cups, three or four grass mats and blankets, wooden stools fashioned from planks, and an ancient metal pot that was usually dented from generations of use."

After work the family would have supper, as it was called, and then Kenny, who had been sitting in his wheelchair all day, would be lifted up and lain down on his bed. Brenda and Heather would wash him, and afterwards, they would all sit on the bed around the oldest son. John McLellan would turn on the radio, get into his own bed, and they would listen to the BBC World Service news. Outside, the crickets, frogs and other nocturnal creatures of Africa provided a symphonious hum in the background to the radio, along with the "pud-pud" of the generator that supplied the power for the lights. Some time around 10pm John McLellan would switch off the radio and go to sleep. The children would sit with their mother, and she'd hand out fruit or sweets. Their father was careful with money, so they were not allowed to keep the light on late, and he insisted the generator be shut down. This created a problem for Heather, who was an avid reader of novels. It meant using a torch under the bed covers until the early hours of the morning. Myrtle remembers: "She was the cleverest of all us children, a great thinker, who would sometimes surprise you with what she would come out with!"

8
CHILDREN IN
THE WILDERNESS

Holidays and camping expeditions are another vivid childhood memory. Settled by the Pondos in the north and Xhosas in the south, the Wild Coast was a black homeland virtually untouched by time. In the 1960s the white government did not regard it as worthy of development. In the vast wilderness, dotted with occasional villages of mud and thatch huts, cattle grazed on the grasslands, and Africans toiled by hand and with oxen to scratch a subsistence living, growing corn maize in small fields, and vegetables in their gardens. Transport was on foot, or horseback, except for occasional whites in their pickup trucks.

Inland, the McLellans explored rivers and estuaries winding through spectacular gorges and forested ravines. In wooded areas, they found prolific bird life, and on the coast, beyond the rocks at sea, fish eagles sometimes perched on the numerous shipwrecks. Heather and her brothers became expert at spotting and identifying the exotic birds that dived into the veldt grassland for insects, sang on the wing in the sky, or called to one another from acacia, white stinkwood, and Natal mahogany trees. In the valleys a dense thicket of evergreen species enveloped the landscape, providing an environment for insect- and seed-eating birds such as weavers, wild canaries and black-eyed bulbuls, whose dawn call resembles that of the European blackbird.

The children became aware of the rich varieties of plants, many of which they learned had been imported during Victorian times as ornamental species for the gardens of the wealthy, before migrating into the wild and becoming common weeds. It was the fishing, however, that most stirred the imagination of Heather's brothers. "I used to go off with David and Basil when I was eleven or twelve and we lived in the Transkei. We clambered from the main tracks down wild paths, watching out for snakes, and it was always a great adventure – kids alone in the wilds of Africa. Eventually we'd get down to the bottom of these valleys behind the Wild Coast in Pondoland, and spend the whole day fishing in the swirling pools of deep rivers like the Mzimhlava and Mthentu.

" I hated to kill anything. My brothers discovered one day that as fast as they were collecting their fish in the holding pond I was trying to set them free again. When I thought they were not looking I'd use my foot to push away the walls of the holding pond they'd built until the trapped fish could squeeze between the stones and dart back into the river. When they caught me they threatened to leave me behind the next time."

David told her: "You idiot, instead of mucking up our fishing have a go with this rod. Here – I'll show you how to cast the line and put the bait on the hook."

"I stood there praying not to have a bite. Somehow the fish always chose my bait and I had to drag several ashore to meet their fate. I was in tears and quietly asking the poor things to forgive me."

On their walking expeditions they would sometimes stop at a hut for water and talk with the local people. They were always welcomed, and Heather never felt threatened by the men. Within two decades the stirring of political activism was to make such informal social interaction in these same rural areas difficult.

As a child Heather looked up to her brother David. He was perhaps an inch under six feet tall and a sportsman like her father, exceptionally well built, a good rugby player and an all-round athlete. He always worked hard at school, although he was not academic like his younger sister. Basil, like David, was also an athlete, but slim and rangy.

"We had our love of nature in common but I do not think my brothers, David and Basil, really understood me. I was academic, bookish, and content to sit in my room, quietly absorbed. I was also an artist, always painting, and then slipping off quietly to spend time with the African children. I felt different from the boys, even though they were my heroes."

At the trading post there was a crisis for Heather when John McLellan had to slaughter a sheep or pigs. The girl could not bear the thought that a creature she knew was going to be killed. She would rush up to her room and put her head under the pillows so that she would not hear the sound of the pig squealing, and the gun going off. When they told her, laughing, that the sheep had not tried to resist but had lain on the ground passively, she could not bring herself to eat the meat.

Heather also soon developed a strong affection for the stray dogs from the African village. These were lean, mangy animals that would hang around the trading station hoping for food. One day a stray snarled at David when he tried to shoo him out of the store, and the McLellan guard dogs went berserk. They were going to kill the unfortunate creature when Heather intervened hysterically, screaming and screaming at them to stop. Another time, David went out to shoot a stray that was disturbing the chickens, trying to steal eggs. Heather pleaded with him not to kill the dog but he went out, and moments later the family heard a shotgun being fired. David had killed it and the next day Heather discovered it was a lactating bitch with puppies. She screamed at David: "I hate you! I'll never love you again!" She meant it.

The next day David walked down the path to where the Africans lived and went to every single kraal until he found the puppies, and then brought them back to Heather and her mother to look after. Animals played an important part in Heather and Brenda's life, and many years later at God's Golden Acre at Wartburg, and then Cato Ridge, stray dogs and cats would always find a home there. She has never been able to turn away any human being or animal, especially a sick one. A consequence of this has been that wherever Heather has lived, her home has resembled a zoo, with wild and domestic animals sometimes following her every step in the hope of food, or petting.

Myrtle recalls: "We all loved animals, but Heather was exceptional. If she saw something die she used to be sick for a whole week. A little pig came to live with us in the house and Dad eventually slaughtered it – since then she hasn't eaten pork. In fact it's only now and then that she'll eat meat, but otherwise not.

"Our love of animals came from our mother who had lots of them. As well as cats and dogs she would look after sick animals like owls and they would all come into the house – like that little pig. There were cows putting their heads through the window hoping for bread. Dad had no say in it – he used to get cross about the dogs coming in and lying on our mother's bed but she didn't take any notice. We all accepted that Mum was a special person."

Wild game was also close at hand in Heather's childhood. Africans would find sick animals in the bush and bring them back to Brenda and Heather to care for. "At the trading post near Mtubatuba when I was very small, animals would knock down the fencing around the Umfolozi Game Reserve. They were getting out all the time."

The Hluhuwe and Umfolozi reserves had been founded before the Boer War in 1895 and were the oldest sanctuaries in Africa. It was there that Operation Rhino was launched during Heather's childhood in the 1960s, successfully capturing and relocating white rhino to other havens within South

Africa. The reserve now holds a fifth of the world's black and white rhino population.

"One night this huge buck nyala appeared in our backyard," Heather remembers. "He seemed to look down his nose at us and appeared unperturbed, before galloping off down to the nearest lake."

However, the most dangerous animals were the rhinos. You'd look up and see one crossing your lawn! Everybody would scream 'Rhino!' and we'd scramble up the nearest tree. You certainly didn't want to be in their way. They would charge anything that moved. You didn't spend time making up your mind where to go – you just ran. A hut, a shed, preferably a tree – anything would do that obscured your scent, or made you invisible.

"Then there were the crocodiles. Dad would organize fishing expeditions and take us children with him. The family truck would arrive at rivers like the Nylazi or the Sombus to find a dozen crocodiles basking in the sun a few yards away. The crocodiles would slide off the near bank and cross the river to the far side. If we were lucky we might see a fish eagle and hear its distinctive cry as it rose from the water with a fish lifeless in the grip of its talons. Other times wading birds would take off in fright at the approaching vehicle. The humans would arrive – exit the crocs and the birds!

"The boys and I would march into the river, splashing about with our black dog Teddy, who used to swim and paddle alongside us. He must have known about the crocodiles but didn't show any fear. To this day I cannot understand how our dad allowed us go wading into a crocodile-infested river, but he did. He'd be totally absorbed with his fishing. We'd be paddling on one side of the river and the crocodiles would be on the opposite bank, basking in the sun, but we felt they were eyeing us up. We weren't scared, but we just made sure we kept away from the other side."

Camping has remained one of the passions of Heather's life.

"I can imagine no more awesome experience than sleeping under an African night sky – transfixed by the infinite number of stars blazing above, spread out in a colossal galaxy. On those early camping trips in the Transkei, we'd listen in wonder as dusk fell to the incredible orchestra of sound from insect to elephant. It was truly the call of the wild."

9
THE FAMILY HISTORY

The McLellans had originally come from Kirkcudbright in Scotland. Heather never met her grandfather, John McLellan, who was an engineer, and her father never talked later in life about him. John junior had been born in 1910 and was only nine years old when he lost his mother in the 1919 world flu epidemic. He was by far the youngest of four children and unable to fend for himself. John McLellan senior decided he could not look after his youngest son and placed him in a convent. He then went off to South America, possibly on an engineering contract. He didn't return to South Africa until he was an old man many years later. The son never saw the father again after he went into the convent, coming out only for holidays when he would go to stay with his cousins on a farm outside Stutterheim.

At the age of 16, John junior ran away from the convent and began to support himself, working in shops. He made his way in life successfully so that by the late 1930s, when he met Brenda May, he was a man with some prospects. John McLellan was a powerful, handsome man, over six feet tall and athletic, with brown hair and brown eyes; he met Brenda May, a piano teacher, at a tennis club. She was 18, six years younger than him, and a small, ordinary-looking girl, but also athletic. Part of their courtship was spent on the tennis court playing tournaments together. From where she stood, perhaps it was love at first sight. Brenda May was a Protestant of German descent and had grown up in a small town called Mt Ayliffe, in East Griqualand, between KwaZulu-Natal and the Cape, where her father was an ironmonger. She was a devout Christian and before the Second World War played the organ on Sundays at the Anglican church in Mt Ayliffe.

The couple married shortly before the war, and as soon as it broke out John rushed off to volunteer, leaving Brenda behind, despite the fact she had already become pregnant. Once he had embarked overseas, he did not see her again for nearly five years. Being a big and athletic man, he enlisted in the infantry, and after basic training was attached to the 8th Army in Egypt where he fought at the Battle of El Alamein and all the successive desert campaigns in Northern Africa. After the African campaign, he took part in the conquest of Sicily and then went on with his regiment to fight on the Italian mainland. Eventually his luck ran out and he was seriously wounded. A German shell exploded when it hit a tree where John McLellan and a section of soldiers were dug in. The shrapnel had a devastating effect and killed most of them. John was taken to the mortuary, his right foot severed. He was presumed to be dead because he had lost so much blood, then someone noticed him twitching and they realized he was still alive. He spent at least a year in Florence in convalescence before being repatriated back home in 1945, having had a series of operations in which the surgeons removed more of his right leg. John McLellan returned a very different man from the one who had departed in 1940.

Heather recounts: "He came home to South Africa expecting to find a childlike wife, barely out of her teens, waiting for him. While in hospital he had written Mum many touching and sensitive letters making it clear that all would be well, and he would soon be returning fit and well. He would come home and be able to look after both her and Kenny. These were letters of reassurance, of telling her not to worry about him. In fact he must have been enduring unimaginable pain.

"Perhaps he was expecting to be the centre of Mum's world, a man who had suffered a disability fighting for his country and who needed tender loving care to help him settle back into civilian life. Certainly Mum had kept herself for him; she was a virtuous and caring woman. However, by now, she was a mature adult in her twenties who had endured the hardship of being a single parent and looking after a disabled child – born while her husband was at war. Perhaps when he did at last return he found himself second on the list for affection."

There had been an accident with Kenny McLellan during a difficult birth. The doctor used instruments to extract the baby and inadvertently damaged his spine. He was paralyzed from his neck down, the accident had left him unable to speak, and his whole body was grotesque.

The child's face was not deformed, but his chest, hips and arms were twisted, his legs shrunken and thin, and his hands screwed up. People looked away from him in embarrassment. Tragically, he was a normal man trapped in a wasted body. There was nothing wrong with his brain. Kenny was Heather's first deep emotional attachment and from the age of six she regarded him as her personal responsibility.

"I helped Mum all I could to nurse and feed Kenny when I was home from school, and I would put him to bed. However, the brunt of the job of caring for him fell on her. I doubt whether Mum ever had a full night's sleep after Kenny was born because she had to turn and change him during the night. His weak lungs, in a distorted ribcage, left him highly susceptible to illnesses like bronchitis and pneumonia, and so he needed constant care. He did not get angry and never became depressed. He was always smiling and ready to listen."

Heather's relationship with her father, John McLellan, was more complex. It was loving, but distant, and also challenging. "Mum had a hard life, running a business, caring for a handicapped son, looking after four other children, and coping with a husband who had a serious drinking problem. She never, ever complained. I can remember only once when these hard circumstances nearly overwhelmed her. After a beating following one of Dad's drinking sessions, I found her crying. She told me she was going to end it all.

"I rushed off in a panic to fetch David and we eventually found her standing by a steep cliff at the back of our house. We talked her round, of course, and I think she realized that Kenny could not survive without her. She loved him dearly and this was her strength in putting up with Dad."

The family never discovered whether John McLellan brought his drinking habit back with him from Italy, as a result of his long period in convalescence, or whether it was because he found it difficult to come to terms with himself in peacetime South Africa. He would drink in binges, and these drinking sessions would last sometimes for several days, and then stop altogether for weeks. Drink could transform him from a quiet and serious man into a loud, boisterous and truculent bully. The violence engendered by the drinking cast a shadow over the family, bringing sadness and dread to them all. The drinking did not end with the school trips. He would start drinking after closing the shop early on a Saturday afternoon, having brought bottles of brandy back with him from town.

It became an ugly ritual. At first Brenda would drink with him, getting tipsy herself, and gradually they would both become louder. The children could see their father's expression turning to one of truculence. The arguments and the fighting would start. The other children would back off, fearful of their father's temper, but Heather would be defiant. "The rows would become violent and then he would beat my mother up. I remember one day something had gone wrong with the generator, or my brother had turned it off for the night. There were no electric lights. We were in my parents' bedroom – Kenny slept next to Mum, and Dad's bed was on the other side of the room. I don't know what provoked him but they began shrieking at one another. He took a burning kerosene lamp and flung it across the room. I dived to catch it. The glass was red hot but I held on to stop it falling to the floor, bursting into flames and spreading onto my paralyzed brother's bed. My hand was totally blistered from the glass. I was so frightened.

"When the rows started, my brothers and sisters would just leave the room, but I wanted to protect Mum and so I would always stay and listen to them fighting. Kenny couldn't leave, of course, and when the beating started he would howl with a mixture of rage and fear for Mum, but was helpless to inter-vene. So when Dad started beating Mum it was down to me to stop it. I would attack him from behind. Once, when I was very little, she was making cakes and had gone into the pantry to fetch some flour and he rushed in and came from behind to attack her. I dashed over to the fireplace, picked up a large piece of wood and hit him over the back with it several times as hard as I could.

"Other times I used to grab one of my shoes and hit him over and over on his back or neck. He'd get really mad with me and leave Mum, allowing her to escape, and start chasing me. However, with his artificial leg he never had a hope of catching me. Except once. He cornered me and placed his enormous hands around my neck. His face was red and con-torted. I thought he was going to strangle me. I was terrified, but instead of pleading for mercy, I screamed: 'Go on then, do it! Do it – kill me! Do it now!'"

It was a turning point in their relationship. The big man just stood there looking down at his tiny but defiant daughter and saying nothing. Slowly his face muscles relaxed, he looked puzzled, then bewildered, took his hands from around Heather's neck and walked away. Despite the drunken periods that demeaned her father, she looks back upon him with fond-ness. "He was a very positive man. I cannot, for example, remember him expressing self-pity about anything. He never complained about his artificial leg. He suffered from stump sores, but would take a mild painkiller, and get on with his life, walking without a stick and with just a slight limp. Unfortunately, I don't think Dad was able to express loving emotion. It was only when he had taken alcohol that he became affectionate and that was when we would reject him. He would get mad at us, starting the rows. He loved us dearly, but I don't think he knew how to express love, having never had a mother figure to care for him. It wasn't until much later that I understood how his own past had affected him."

10
THE ODD ONE OUT

The sound of the Tom Jones hit, "The Green, Green Grass Of Home", being sung by children accompanied by a slightly out-of-tune piano, wafted from an open window across the trading station. At the piano was a slim, dark-haired girl, Myrtle, and around it stood three other children with tearful faces. A large man with a slight limp marched into the room and his voice seemed louder than the singing and the music: "Come on now, enough! It's time to go. The bus will be here soon." In the South Africa of the 1950s and 1960s, it was not just the children of the rich who were packed off to boarding institutions. Trading station children had to be sent away for an education. The McLellan children regarded the approaching term with dread.

Nongoma School was a single-storey, colonial-style brick building, the classrooms surrounded by several levels of wooded terracing. The teachers' houses, and other buildings, were situated around the perimeter. The boarding houses were on the other side of the road, opposite the school, which was run by the headmaster, Mr Hattingh, and his wife. Heather can recall certain moments, flashbacks, of her childhood. She loved to paint whenever she had spare time, and remembers having a colouring-in book and spending the afternoon working away on a picture. She showed it to somebody older who said dismissively: "Don't tell lies, you couldn't

possibly have painted that. It must have been done by someone older than you."

In 1961 when the family moved to Madada, she followed
her older siblings to Kokstad High School and remained a
pupil there until 1969, when she was 16. She loved sport, particularly hockey, and was in the school team. However, she
could be absorbed for hours reading, painting or listening to
music. "I remember there was a teacher who sang very well,"
says Heather. "She had a beautiful soprano voice and I listened
enthralled by her."

There were both Afrikaaners and English children at
Kokstad High School. However, out of respect for the twin
cultures that made up the white minority of South Africa,
there were separate hostels and two parallel class streams. For
some reason, and Heather suspected it was because her father
had discovered it was cheaper, she was placed in the
Afrikaaner hostel – even though her language was English and
she was studying in that stream of the school. This increased
her sense of isolation, and as the years rolled by she retreated
further into herself.

What mattered to the teenage Heather were campaigns to
save the elephants from dying in Namibia because of the
drought, campaigns to save the rainforests of the Amazon,
campaigns to save the whales, to stop pollution, and to help
the poor. There were few allies to be found at the school.
"These were the things I saw as real – these were the things
that interested and also worried me. Politics was never discussed at home or in the classroom. Both my parents were
racist in the sense that they believed white people were
ordained to run society and that the given role of the blacks
was to serve them. They would not have been able to perceive
Africans on equal terms with the whites socially, but they
never displayed any hostility towards them and sincerely
believed it was their duty to treat black people fairly.

"Looking back, I believe that God did not intend for me to

develop radical political ideas at that stage of my life, because I might then have embarked on my struggle too early, and this would have diverted its subsequent direction. People were aware of my sense of kinship with the black people, but they did not care to discuss it with me. It used to enrage me to hear them talking about 'kaffirs' and referring to black people as inferior human beings, but I did not realize their views were abnormal. I thought I was the misfit.

"I had never travelled outside the world in which I had been brought up, and so it did not occur to me that the racist laws of South Africa, which discriminated against the black and mixed-race people, were any different from anywhere else. Our society was, after all, the only thing that young people like me had ever known."

As she grew older Heather became aware of religion and showed a precocious knowledge of the Bible that she would sometimes read at night, but the family did not go to church. "Mum would tell us, 'Never forget there is a God', and she would inspire us with how she treated people."

Heather progressed through the school always close to, if not top of the class, in all subjects except science. Her world was reading, reading and reading, painting and poetry, with hockey, netball and tennis thrown in to keep her fit and satisfy her strong competitive spirit. In class, as she went through the school, she was considered by some teachers to be a rebel because she often questioned the established order of things.

The teachers were aware that the classroom rebel was academic and they regarded young Heather McLellan as a star pupil who would matriculate and go on to take her place in higher education. It came as a shock to both them, and her family, when she decided at the age of 16 to leave school with her junior certificate of education, the equivalent of the British GCSE qualification. She took the decision to leave school because she doubted that her father would be prepared to pay for her fees through university.

"I had desperately wanted to go on to university, was a leading pupil in standard nine (lower sixth form), and was expecting to matriculate the following year and go to Durban University. My ambition was to become a geologist, or go into teaching. In retrospect I believe God was guiding me, even at this stage, and by steering me away from Durban University and a career as a geologist, he was keeping me for other ways in which to serve him."

Looking back, Heather recalls her childhood and adolescence as a time of loneliness, haunted by violence and shame. Her father's drinking, his violence towards her mother, and the ritual killing of animals either for food or because they supposedly posed a threat to food supplies, had left her in a state of depression. She longed for a peer group soulmate but never found one.

" I believed I was a misfit, which separated me from others. I felt awkward with people of my own age, and I could not explain to myself why was I so easily moved to tears. Then on top of that, there was this bizarre sense of experiencing the pain and grief of others. When I witnessed any kind of accident, like a fall or a cut, it would come on me as surely as though I had suffered it myself. I would get this numbness. At first I thought everyone experienced this sensation when others were hurt, then I discovered that I was the only one, and I felt a freak. It has remained with me through life. I have learned to deal with it now, but when I was younger it terrified me.

"To this day, I still get deeply affected by the lives and troubles of total strangers. I find myself going to absurd lengths to try to help people I don't even know. I know it's not how normal people react and I don't understand it. I don't choose to be an oddity, and I am not proud about it."

It was the end of Heather's childhood and the end of an era for the McLellan family. David and Myrtle had left home, and her parents were about to move on too. Later in 1969 they were forced to sell Madada to the Xhosa Development Corporation in the process of the black homeland being founded. By this time the McLellans had made enough money to buy a farm and supermarket 20 miles from Cathcart on the Thomas River in the Ciskei. Heather moved out of the home in the Transkei and went to stay with her aunt and uncle in Pietermaritzburg. She knew it was far too young to be leaving school but was excited by the new experiences that awaited her. She got a clerical job in an office, and had to learn how to type.

The head of the house was Brenda's younger brother, Uncle Vic May. He had always been a favourite with Heather. He was a lot younger than her mother, and his young lodger didn't feel there was a huge age gap between them. Vic and Rina, his wife, were ordinary working-class people and Heather felt safe at their house, living with her small cousins, one of whom was her godchild. After a few months, however, Heather felt an urge to move on and set her sights on moving to Durban.

The city is a major international port, with a cross-flow of young people from many parts of the world, and at that time it was in the full swing of the "flower power" era. Heather embraced the whole idea of this with a new excitement she hadn't encountered before. It all seemed to be about loving people and bringing peace – not war – to the world. She draped her now much longer hair with flowers at every opportunity, and embraced hippy make-up and hippy clothes. She started smoking and drinking but avoided the drugs scene. For the first time she felt a sense of total freedom. She was making the rules that governed her life, unconstrained by parental and institutional convention.

"I loved the songs of the Beatles and enjoyed the innocence of it all. I think I could have gone on enjoying the 'flower power' scene in Durban for longer, but after six months news came from home that Kenny was getting very ill, and was about to be admitted to hospital in Kokstad. I rushed home and I could see that he was sick. I remember looking at him and thinking: *He's going to die if he goes into hospital because he can't talk and no one will be able to understand him. Maybe I can go and work as a nurse at Kokstad Hospital. Then I can look after him and pull him through!* I was the only one, for example, who knew how to get the phlegm out of his throat.

"So I applied for a job and was accepted. I started nursing, and though I really enjoyed the caring side of the job, I still could not get rid of my phobia of blood, and other people's painful feelings somehow get transmitted through to me. It was really, really hard. On top of that, I had this whole thing about death. I had a fear about watching life leaving somebody's eyes. The staring eyes, the stiffness of the body, were not things that I could cope with emotionally. I also hated to see anybody cry – like when Mum used to weep when an animal died on the trading post."

Somehow, working in a hospital, she had to overcome those feelings, the fear of blood, and death. In the casualty ward, children would often be ambulanced in after a car crash, covered in blood. Heather hated it and was about to resign when she came up with an answer. She would swap duties with the other nurses. "Most of the other nurses could cope with blood, tragedy and death, but hated the smell and sight of clearing up when incontinent or sick people had made a mess of their clothes or bed linen. Now, here I had my chance! After all the years of looking after Kenny I was oblivious to the smell and sight of bodily fluids. So I used to swap duties with other nurses. I would do the things they hated and vice versa! It worked like a treat for a while. I was also allowed to look after Kenny in the hospital, and gradually we made him stronger."

Then something unfortunate happened. Heather still had not been able to overcome her emotional feelings, especially for sick babies and children. One night she was on duty in the paediatric ward when an 18-month-old baby with a heart defect died suddenly. His mother let out a long agonized and wounded cry. The young father collapsed in grief too. Then the grandparents also lost their self-control. Heather remembers: "I was crying and sobbing with them, and I realized with embarrassment that this was unprofessional. I was supposed to be strong for them, a shoulder for the baby's parents to cry on. I knew then that I could not cope with being a nurse. I was not cut out for it. So I resigned, and decided I would go back to office work or find something new."

It was at this time that Heather met the man who would have a profound effect upon her life for the next six years, bringing at first happiness, but later great sorrow and misery. She would marry him twice, and divorce him twice. Her first husband was a man who, perhaps without realizing it, would play a major role – as John McLellan had also done – in moulding the future Heather Reynolds.

She would become an atheist as a young woman, debunking Christianity, and doing her best to divert others away from religion too. The next six years of Heather's life would be painful and challenging.

11
LOVE AT FIRST SIGHT

He was a tall, dark, handsome stranger and he came into her life with a knock on the door at the small flat in Kokstad that Heather was renting while she worked at the hospital. He stood there with her neighbour, another girl, whom Heather knew quite well.

"Excuse me for disturbing you, but have you got any change? Sorry to bother you," he said, smiling. She was attracted immediately by his dark hair and smiling blue eyes. Barely over five feet three inches tall herself, she had to look up to his lean bronzed face. His name was Sarel Olivier, he was in his early twenties, and he literally swept her off her feet.

"Sarel and a male friend were visiting the girl next door and apparently he told her he liked the look of me. She came over shortly afterwards to ask if I wanted to join them on a night out. I politely declined that invitation, but two or three more followed in the next few days — and eventually I accepted. I soon fell completely in love with him. I was on fire with passion whenever he touched me."

It was, and remained while it lasted, an entirely physical relationship. They were opposites in every physical as well as spiritual sense: he a tall, dark man, and she a petite blonde. What clinched their relationship for Heather was that Sarel soon made it clear he was very happy to come with her to visit

Kenny in hospital. They would spend hours there, and she was extremely pleased to find that Sarel had great patience with Kenny. It was clear the two men were bonding despite her brother's handicap, and Sarel seemed to love her brother.

"For the first time, I was in a physical relationship and I couldn't think about much more than just this guy. I was in a vacuum with him; the other Heather, the thinker, the artist, and the conservationist, was put away. At first, I didn't seem to mind the fact we had nothing in common spiritually or intellectually. If I did try to talk about any of the many things that interested me, he would change the conversation. So I let it go. The major issues of life somehow became less important."

Looking back on those years in the late 1960s and early 1970s, she realizes that if she had stayed in Durban things might have been different. However, in East Griqualand, a rural backwater, the vast majority of young people knew and cared nothing of politics, or of the storm clouds looming on the horizon due to the apartheid system, and the growing international abhorrence of racism.

Sarel was Afrikaans and worked as a telephone technician, installing lines in the Kokstad area. This was a good job, although it meant a lot of travelling, and the couple felt that he could earn enough to keep both of them, allowing Heather time to look after Kenny during some months to give her mother a break. So they decided to get married after just eight months, and make their first home in an apartment in Winterton, Natal. Heather's mother and father didn't approve of the plans. "Perhaps they sensed that because I was a serious-minded person, it would not be a good match. I should have listened. This was indeed only my first affair, and there needed to be several of those before I got married. They didn't dislike Sarel at this stage – but they also thought we needed much more time.

"However, I must have started paying attention to their misgivings, or maybe Sarel's indifference to the things I held so dear began to sow seeds of doubt. The day before the wedding, I became very upset and felt we should not go through with it. I went to see Mum and confided in her. 'Mum, I want to call the wedding off. I want to cancel it. I don't want to be married,' I told her. She was horrified at the prospect of halting the whole bandwagon and said she thought everything had gone too far. She didn't think we should cancel it. I cried – but she said it was probably only wedding nerves. And so we were married early in 1972. I think it's significant that if you look at the photos of that day, you will not find one of me smiling. I had realized I was making a mistake. I still loved Sarel but felt we should not be making it so final. Mind you, there were lots of happy times in the following months."

They both enjoyed outdoor pursuits, and would travel long distances to stay in interesting places all over Natal and further into other provinces. In the summer they would camp in the nearby Drakensberg Mountains. The young couple would lie in their sleeping bags, watching a majestic sunrise, listening to the sounds of the bush, drinking in the intoxicating mountain air. "We loved our time together when we were camping in the mountains. Sarel also continued to enjoy his relationship with Kenny. I just wanted it to work for everyone."

However, an element of disillusionment began to undermine their relationship by the end of the second year. On the physical side, the passionate fires were ebbing away. There were none of the great heights that Heather had expected. She felt their bonding should have become closer in some spiritual way, but the opposite appeared to be the case. She did not understand what was absent. What she never realized was that what was missing was the intellectual core of their relationship. They were not kindred spirits; there was no meeting of minds. There were more and more silly arguments, which later on became more and more aggressive. Sarel really enjoyed provoking her and making her lose her temper. This really gave him a kick and she got to dread it when he got into that mood. She began to recognize the pattern but never learned how not to react. When he made her lose control she got so angry she felt she could almost hit him.

"For example," she recalls, "on one occasion I came into the kitchen and found a bowl covered over by a cloth. When I removed the cloth I was horrified to find a sheep's guts ladled into it with the head stuck on top. That was his idea of a joke because he knew I could not stand anything dead, especially staring eyes."

She once threw a plate at him and he so enjoyed that spectacle he laughed and laughed, and she felt for the first time that she hated him. She hated the way he would do certain things for no other reason except to get her really angry, and would then tell her that he loved her, and loved to see her fighting mad. At times like this she felt totally repulsed, she felt she could hit him, she felt so much anger and humiliation. She also felt utterly alone.

The problems in the marriage also began to manifest themselves as a result of the couple's long absences from one another. When Brenda began to develop a heart problem and needed to go into hospital, Heather would take charge of both Kenny and John, sometimes for a month. Mostly though, she would bring Kenny to stay with them for a while until her mother recovered. Meanwhile Sarel was frequently working outside the area.

At that time, they got involved enthusiastically with a new charismatic church. The pastor and the leading members of the church told them that if they had sufficient faith they could help Kenny to walk, despite the fact that he was severely crippled and deformed. Naively, Heather became convinced that this miracle could really happen. In church they used to undertake strident prayer sessions for Kenny in which they would exhort him to walk. "Get up, Kenny, get up, Kenny. Walk! Come on!" they used to pray aloud, with the pastor leading exhortations. The group aroused such expectations in Kenny that at first he really believed he would get up and walk. In his eyes there was hope.

To this day Heather feels deeply guilty about what they did to her oldest brother. "Now can you imagine this severely crippled young man, 30 years old and in a wheelchair all his life, with the pastor telling him he is going to walk? I look back and realize it was cruel — how could we have done that? Then, when he wasn't able to get out of his wheelchair, it was almost implied that his own faith might be inadequate — nothing was wrong with their prayers, the church leaders assured us. It just required more faith and effort on Kenny's part. We did these prayer sessions with Kenny several times, on each occasion building up his expectations, exhorting him to have another try."

One day Heather noticed a different look on her brother's face when they took him to prayers. She said: "Come on, Kenny, shall we try it again?" From his body language it was clear he did not want to go on. Heather will never forget that look in his eyes, realizing in a moment how insensitive and stupid they had been, and how disillusioned Kenny had become. It left her very distressed, and it widened the gulf between herself and Sarel. The marriage was clearly in trouble, and there was a disturbing distance between them spiritually.

12
BETRAYAL
AND DIVORCE

The couple moved to Escourt, an historic town in the foothills of the Central Drakensberg. One day Heather came back from a long spell at the farm looking after Kenny and found that some of the photographs from her camera film had been developed before she completed the roll. When Sarel got home she asked him why, and asked for the negatives. He said he'd lost them. Instinctively from his response, she knew he was lying. It became an issue with her because there were photos on it that she wanted. "Stop lying!" she demanded. "Where are those negatives?"

Sarel searched, and eventually found them. However, there were only 16 negatives. He tried to claim that the others had not come out. "But where are they? I want to see them. I'm not a fool!" she shouted.

"I was imagining all sorts of things," she now recalls. "It was the first time in our relationship that I'd suspected him of betrayal. I was still a young girl, not into this kind of behaviour, and I was ragingly jealous and upset. By now it had become an obsession, and I started to phone people to try to find out what was behind it all. Their reactions made me feel there was something going on."

Sarel had become friendly with the pastor and his wife, and someone suggested: "Why not ask the pastor's wife? She knows a lot about his business." So Heather phoned her, and the pastor's wife was clearly cagey. Heather thought immediately: *She knows something for sure!*

When Sarel came back home, Heather had had time to think through a strategy and she play-acted the whole thing. "Why didn't you tell me there was another woman?" she asked. "I have just spoken to Maria and she told me all about it." Sarel then confessed. He begged forgiveness, and said he had met a girl from Mooi River and they had gone away for a weekend. Heather demanded the photographs and he told her the girl had got them.

"OK," she replied. "We're going to drive to her place in Mooi River now, and I want those photographs." So they went over to Mooi River and knocked on her door. When she answered the door the girl was obviously shocked and guilty, but instead of anger Heather remembers feeling hurt. She was just a plain girl.

"There was nothing about her that I could fathom to justify his adultery. What did he see in her? If she had been a glamorous or sexy woman, I might have been able to understand more about why he had done this to me. I knew I was not beautiful, but I did not feel inferior to her. I was also in good shape because I was very active, loved mountain climbing, hiking and was a keen badminton player. 'How could he do this to me – prefer her to me?' I kept asking myself."

There were photographs of Sarel and the girl on the film spending a weekend on the South Coast. Later, a bombshell exploded in Heather's mind when she discovered that the adulterous couple had stayed with the pastor and his wife. "This shocked me to the roots of my being. How could a man of the church, a man of God, not only condone, but also encourage adultery in this way? I had gone away to be at my mum's bedside when she was having a heart attack and they had sanctioned Sarel's deception!"

It was an episode that knocked not only her confidence in herself, but also her faith in God, and it triggered a period of her life in which she began to move away from a strong belief in Christianity towards atheism. She began to meet, through her job, educated people who endorsed her views. Perhaps as a form of revenge, Heather actively sought every opportunity to dissuade people from religion.

"I wanted to leave Sarel, of course, but he phoned his mum and dad on the night of his confession and they came over and did some counselling. His mother said that she had had the same experience with her own husband, and that she had forgiven him, and they had made a go of the marriage. Sarel was pleading with me to stay and promised there was no longer any relationship with the girl from Mooi River. From then on, he swore to me, I would be the only woman in his life. So I agreed to give him a second chance."

The marriage continued for another year and the couple tried to compensate for this fracture in their intimate relationship, and in Heather's broken trust in him, by travelling. She also managed to get a good job with a well-known international company and found this both absorbing and challenging. At the weekends they would go to the beach, or camp in the mountains. They would hike into the foothills and mountains around Escourt. It was a beautiful town, and one with which Sir Winston Churchill had been familiar nearly 80 years before. A few miles to the north is the Armoured Train Cemetery, where the future British prime minister was "captured" by the Boers while working as a newspaperman.

The "Burg" mountains stretch for over 150 miles. Heather and Sarel trekked across parts of it, from the massive basalt cliffs in the northern reaches, to the awesome sandstone buttresses in the south. At the Amphitheatre, site of the great Tugela waterfall, they spent hours trying to work things out. Sometimes it felt that they had, and at times like this the couple were contented. However, Sarel was restless. He always needed to be visiting or inviting guests to stay, always needing to go somewhere or do something, or wanting to party. He seemed to suffer from an innate restlessness within himself. The idea of working on the house or relaxing with a book or entertaining himself with some sort of hobby was something he would not consider seriously.

Heather recalls: "He needed company and drinks so that everyone was having a grand time. This was how we spent every weekend. I craved for quiet peaceful weekends, to do some work in the garden, and spend time with our animals. We had four dogs, two cats and a budgie, and they needed to be taken care of.

"I think I still must have been in love with him. However, there was an abusive streak in his nature that possibly acted to prevent the scars from healing. I was never physically abused, but he always tried to make me feel negative about myself. In the end he succeeded in making me think that I wasn't capable of anything. I felt I was useless at everything. He would criticize me endlessly. It was a form of mental cruelty, and no matter how resilient you try to be, it eventually gets to you."

To make things worse, Sarel remained a compulsive adulterer. More affairs followed the first one, and every time Heather found out, he would beg, he would plead, and he would cry. She could not work out why he went to other women. She had never refused him, and she felt that their relationship was normal — although for her the images of the other woman were often in the background making her feel inadequate. As a woman she felt she had failed him. At first, after discovering he had been unfaithful she would leave him for a week or so, but he would always manage to persuade her to come back. Perhaps she could not imagine life without him.

Eventually however, in 1975, Heather divorced him and moved to an apartment of her own in Escourt. It made no difference to Sarel. He would not believe she had stopped loving him and he would visit her and plead with her, hoping to rekindle their relationship. Despite her ex-husband's behaviour, Heather was so softhearted that she continued to see him when he was behaving rationally. She argued to herself that since both of them were in secure jobs, and she was living in a comfortable apartment in a quiet town, it was just possible they might work things out eventually and become reunited. Looking back over the years, it astonishes her that she did not have the courage to force the break in the relationship by moving right out of his life. Perhaps it had something to do with Kenny, with whom Sarel continued to have a bonded relationship, and who was going to become increasingly dependent upon Heather, with her mother in ailing health.

Around this time, Heather discovered that she was pregnant, having conceived with Sarel during one of their periods of reconciliation. Heather was ecstatic. At last, her own baby! She would love and nurture it – build her life around this infant. Perhaps it would be the first real step in creating a family around Sarel so they could settle down. She did not tell him at that time because although she really hoped they might succeed in this latest attempt at forging a relationship, she wanted the option to stay free if he continued to look for sex elsewhere. Heather also did not tell the doctor, who was a friend of hers, feeling ashamed that she had conceived a baby when she was no longer married. She was convinced people would see her as immoral, but was excited and happy to be pregnant.

It was a hard job not to reveal the secret, but she was strong enough mentally to keep it from Sarel, and for the moment the rest of the family. The bombshell came a few weeks later when an angry man, a stranger, came knocking at her door. "Do you realize your husband is having an affair with my wife?" he snapped.

Heather was devastated. Here she was, pregnant. They were supposed to be starting all over again, but they were back to square one. Shortly after the angry husband left, her brother David and his wife Sherril arrived to stay for the weekend. She didn't want to talk about what she had just learned because she knew they all thought she was crazy to have become involved with Sarel again. So she suppressed it, and began to feel extremely unwell over the weekend. They could tell something was wrong and Heather's sister-in-law wanted to stay and look after her, but she sent them away.

No sooner had they gone than she started bleeding profusely. "I thought, *What shall I do?* I tried ringing Mum but my call coincided with visitors arriving at her home, and she could not talk to me. Then the bleeding became much worse and I lay on my bed wondering whether I should summon the doctor. It would mean revealing to him that I was pregnant but not married.

"I did not have the opportunity to call him. Suddenly there was this excruciating pain and in those moments I lost the baby, a living fetus that had died because of me. My stress and unhappiness had ended its life. This experience tipped me over the edge. I just remember thinking, *I don't want to be here!* I couldn't face another tomorrow, or any further part of this troubled life. I had no expectation of an afterlife because I was utterly disillusioned with God after what had happened at the church with Kenny, and then the pastor's encouragement of Sarel's adultery. My contempt for Christianity had, incidentally, increased further when it was discovered the pastor had embezzled money from the church. I just wanted to find peace, to remove myself from what I felt was an evil world.

"I did see everything in a gloomy light at that time. The forests were being destroyed, whole species of animals were becoming extinct largely because of the greed of humankind, there was fighting all over Africa, and many other parts of the world including Ireland. I was exhausted, too, by the mental condition that seemed to make me the world's conscience, and by feeling the physical pain of others.

"I remember being quite cold and calculating as I went about the apartment preparing to end it all. Those who know me well will understand that I am a thorough person, one who likes to do things correctly. I wanted to make absolutely sure that my suicide would not fail because I could not face the shame of having failed.

"Kenny's sleeping tablets were stored in the apartment. I got the pills, a bottle of water and a hosepipe, and drove my grey Beetle Volkswagen deep into the countryside. I knew a place in the foothills of some mountains around Escourt where nobody would find me. Just nobody. It was so remote, right off the dirt road, and in high grass. I went in and parked near a little stream that I had come to know in the dry season when the water was low. The previous summer I had camped by the river when the shallow pools were heaving with fish. Some were stranded on their sides in the few inches of water remaining. On that visit I had clambered into the shallows and worked all weekend, heaving out stones and rocks to make the pools deep enough for the fish to survive the drought. It was probably futile but I had felt I had to do something.

"I fixed the hosepipe over the exhaust, fed this into the car, took 50 sleeping pills, locked myself in, and finally turned on the engine. *If the pills don't kill me, the fumes will. There's no chance of failure!* I thought to myself. *There's no way anyone will find me here. Just no way!* I lay back and could feel this sense of total peace come over me. It was such a feeling of relief now that I had got this far, a wonderful feeling of being able to let go and never having to worry about anything any more, never having to deal with the continual realization that I was a failure.

"I was slipping happily away into unconsciousness, and knew I would never come back again. As I was falling deeper into this peace I suddenly thought of God. *What if he does exist? No*, I thought, *he doesn't. It's all hocus-pocus! But if you do exist, God, then I'm going to meet you now, it's not going to be long! And I will confront you and tell you that you're a liar, because in the Bible you said you wouldn't push anybody beyond what he or she could bear. And I know that you have pushed me beyond my point of endurance. You cannot be a loving God.*"

It was Heather's last conscious thought.

1 3
A FOOLISH DECISION

Heather woke up the following day in a bed in a hospital ward. "This is impossible!" she exclaimed angrily. "What am I doing in Escourt Hospital? The hospital where everybody knows me!"

She just couldn't believe it, and there was her doctor, an old friend, saying softly: "Why, Heather?"

She snapped: "Why am I here? How did this whole thing fail?" She was shocked and angry.

When the doctor saw how angry she was, and heard her strident demand for an immediate discharge, he replied: "No chance! You belong to the state. By law you're a criminal; suicide is a crime. You can be charged."

She replied: "Don't talk a load of nonsense to me. I'm leaving now." Then they forcibly held her down and sedated her.

She woke up the following day in a hospital in Pietermaritzburg, two-and-a-half hours away from Escourt by road. The doctors knew that if she had walked out of Escourt Hospital there and then, she would probably have gone straight back to the apartment and organized a second suicide attempt. She was in a state of total despair and mental collapse. She didn't want to see anybody, and she certainly didn't want to go through the whole thing and explain it. Heather didn't want visitors and was still angry.

The first person to come down was someone called Malcolm

Green, and he told her what had happened. Two teenage boys he knew had been walking early in the morning on a high ridge on his land, and looking down in the valley, they saw a bright light flashing in the sun. They figured out it must be poachers and that the sun was reflecting on the glass windshield of their vehicle. They ran down the hill as fast as they could to catch the poachers before they got away – and found the grey Beetle instead, with Heather unconscious and locked inside it. The older boy shouted: "My God! There's a woman in the car. She's locked herself in! We've got to smash in the side window. Quick, let's grab some rocks from the river and break it before the fumes kill her." Together, the boys smashed the side window, switched off the ignition, and frantically drove Heather up to Malcolm Green's homestead. She was then rushed to hospital just in time for the doctors to save her life.

Over the following days at Pietermaritzburg Hospital, flowers from friends – and other people Heather didn't realize cared about her – started to pour in. The ward was ablaze with colour. She was so ashamed, so embarrassed. All this love, all this attention – and what was she but a failed suicide? Once more she had failed!

Her boss, the managing director of the company she worked for, came to see her. He was full of compassion, saying: "Heather, you can take as much leave as you need, and it will all be fully paid. Just get well and don't worry about the time it takes. We'll be waiting for you when you come back."

She recalls: "It was like that from everybody. Whether I wanted to or not, I was not going to be allowed another suicide attempt, because now I was under close observation, and being overwhelmed with kindness and compassion. So the healing process started, and I went home to Mum, and later the Greens invited me to go and stay with them, instead of going back to the apartment in Escourt."

While she was at home with her mother Heather was strongly denying God. This worried Brenda McClellan. About six weeks later Heather's mother developed a huge boil under her arm; she was feeling incredibly tired, and her kidneys were failing. She was weak and it was clear she did not have long to live.

One evening Heather and her mother had a long conversation about faith. They agreed that when Brenda died she would return, to show Heather there was life after death. Their talk continued for several hours and Heather cried bitterly, telling her mother over and over again that if she was going to die, then there would be very little left in life for her. Three days later, Brenda McLellan died.

"A strange calm came over me, and it was as if my inner consciousness was making me strong because I had already said my farewells. I was able to cope with it. Despite the trauma of Mum's death I continued to grow stronger, and I think the realization that Kenny was going to need me even more gave me that vital inner strength. However, for the moment he continued to live with Dad and me on the farm, and then when I went back to work in Escourt he went on to live with my sister Myrtle and her family in Ladysmith."

Life began to get back to normal and Heather did eventually allow Sarel to re-enter it again. He seemed to be more reasonable now, and pleaded with her to come back to him for a fresh start. Few women who had been on the end of such mental cruelty from a partner, and endured so much misery that it engendered a suicide attempt, would have contemplated renewing the relationship. But Heather explains: "I had no close friend, family or familiar faces nearby and Sarel represented someone I could lean on, a comfortable shoulder. I certainly wasn't in love with him any more but I did have this lingering affection for him, and above all he still loved Kenny. I recall weighing all these things up, looking at the pros and cons, and coming to the conclusion that although ours was a deeply flawed relationship, there might be sufficient intent to make it work on both sides.

"My suicide experience had changed me. I was tougher than

before, more self-reliant, and believed the events of the past few months had had a positive effect upon me. I knew I should control my own life better. Others were beginning to rely upon me, and my new targets were based on practicality rather than emotion."

The priorities were clear. A proper home would have to be found for Kenny, and there was no one better qualified than Heather to provide it. Her mother had gone and John was alone, looking after himself – and running the business. The time was fast approaching when he would need to retire, and again, Heather felt she could look after him and provide him with a home. Her sister Myrtle had a young family and a relatively small home. Sarel appeared to fit well into the overall picture, and although Heather would never love him deeply again, she was moved by his pleading and apparent humility, and felt able to make a further commitment to him.

"What a fool I was!" she now admits.

Sarel and Heather were remarried in 1976. "We heard that a large house in Merrivale was on the market and we went to look for the owner, a man called Charles Kirton, who was chairman of the Natal Weightlifting Association. Charles owned a gym, so we went there and met him and he introduced us to a short, wiry guy with a beard in his early thirties called Patrick Reynolds. He was one of the Natal weightlifters with whom Charles was working out. We appeared to have interrupted an important training session, and it was clear from the way he scowled at me that this guy Patrick wasn't very pleased. He looked irritated, and was obviously wishing we would go away. Charles was happy to talk because he wanted to sell his house, but the scowl on Patrick's face deepened as the minutes went by. We eventually left and went to see the house."

They were introduced to Charles' wife who said half-jokingly: "OK. If you're taking over the house, how about taking over my job?"

"So what do you do?" asked Heather.

"I'm working in a local hospital as a secretary and typist. I also do some of the administration, and help the superintendent. It's a disability hospital actually," the woman explained.

"That could be just the answer to my problem," said Heather. "I have a brother with a disability who is living with me – so at the moment I am unable to work. If I could take over your job, and take Kenny with me when I go there, it would solve everything. Do you think they would let me take him to the hospital with me on a daily basis?"

"Oh, yes, surely. That wouldn't be a problem," the woman smiled.

So Heather contacted the Umgeni Waterfall Care and Rehabilitation Centre in Howick and was asked to go for a job interview with the secretary in charge of administration. And who should that be? Yes – Patrick Reynolds! He was the secretary at the hospital, the man who had clearly been so impatient at the gym. She thought: *Well, I've really blown this. I won't get the job. And to be fair I don't have very good typing skills, or much experience of the sort I think they require.*

However, fate was on Heather's side. She did get the job and she took Kenny with her each day. Patrick Reynolds turned out to be a good boss, considerate and loyal, but a total introvert. The following few months were a good period. Now she had a settled job, Kenny was happy, her father had moved in, and she was able to release her creative energies, especially in the garden. Patrick and his boss Cats Nelemans, the hospital superintendent, and Cats' wife Trisca, became good friends to Heather. She enrolled for painting classes, and who should be there? Yes, Patrick again! He turned out to be a highly talented sculptor in wood, and although he was still an amateur, his work was very highly regarded in the district.

"In a way he became my confidant," says Heather. "I started talking to him about personal things. He was a listener, he didn't talk much, but I found I could discuss any subject with him. I grew to love him as a friend."

Then, later in 1977, things began to unravel. To her great distress Heather discovered some grocery bills in Sarel's car that strongly suggested he had started cheating on her again. She confronted him and insisted that they move to separate rooms. Then she found out she was pregnant once more.

"Because of all the emotional upheaval, I started to have slight bleeding and due to the danger of miscarriage I was given sick leave. I managed to persuade Patrick to let me carry on working at home, and he used to come over with the typing that needed doing. I couldn't afford to lose my job now. I was a married woman, I had a home, I was pregnant, but I didn't want anything more to do with the man who was going to be the father of my child. This time I was much tougher than before." Heather desperately wanted the baby and was scared of losing it through fighting with Sarel, but she was determined now to resist him.

The atmosphere in the house grew tense because John McLellan, still physically powerful, saw himself as her natural protector, and he began to loathe Sarel. He made no effort to conceal his contempt for him. Heather had to confide in someone, and that person was Patrick Reynolds. However, the friendship was entirely platonic. In fact she had already made up her mind that if divorce from Sarel was coming, she would never, ever, ever have any kind of relationship with a man again. She was totally disillusioned.

Finally, one night there was a heated argument over some of Patrick's artwork that she had acquired. Sarel was suspicious that there was something between them and he raised it for the first time.

"What the hell are you wasting your money on this for?" Sarel demanded.

Heather replied angrily: "It's my money, and if I want to buy a couple of pieces of artwork, I can do that. I don't ask you why you waste half your money on booze and stuff like that!"

Sarel had acquired some workable wood while camping in

the forest and shortly afterwards in a telephone conversation Heather suggested he might give it to Patrick to create a sculpture. She recalls: "Sarel then went nuts, absolutely crazy, going on like a madman about Patrick. My father came into the room and told me to slam down the phone – which I did. Sarel rang back moments later, and my father let rip at him: 'Don't you dare accuse my daughter of doing something like that!' he shouted at him. 'She's seven months pregnant – she's hardly likely to be going out looking for a man, you idiot. She's not going to talk to you now, and if I had my way she'd never talk to you again.' Then he slammed the phone down.

" 'Right,' said my father. 'That's it. We're leaving. I'm going to go to town tomorrow and find us a place. We're getting out of here this week.' Frankly, I was nervous. I didn't want to fall back under my father's control, especially since he had started drinking again with his old service chums. Furthermore I was pregnant and in a very vulnerable condition that meant I could easily lose another baby. On the other hand, I was deeply insulted and wounded to have been accused of having an affair with Patrick. So, in many ways I did feel that I had had enough."

The next day Heather went to see Patrick at work, told him about the row, and asked for time off to move. He knew that the three of them – Heather, her father and their maid – would find it hard to lift heavy furniture, and he said: "Who's going to help you move?"

"Nobody. We'll manage on our own," said Heather.

"Well, would you like some help?" he asked. She accepted, thinking that being a weightlifter, he would be able to load up furniture that they could not possibly shift on their own.

The next day Patrick came, but the neighbour, who was a good friend of Sarel's, telephoned him to warn him Heather was moving out. After a couple of hours, Sarel arrived at the house and another serious confrontation developed. John McLellan warned Sarel to leave his daughter alone and not to approach her.

"I suspect he was quite prepared to use his crutch on him," says Heather. "He was still a formidably big man, and I think people around him always suspected that he was capable of inflicting considerable damage with it."

Sarel pointed to Patrick, who was quietly loading furniture onto a vehicle, and said accusingly to Heather: "And so what's with you and this guy?" Patrick just ignored Sarel's presence and went on moving the furniture onto the truck. When they'd finished they all drove off, leaving Sarel brooding in the house. Heather had taken just her personal belongings, a few inherited things from her mother, and they moved into the house that her father had found. She left nearly everything behind. "Frankly I didn't really care. I just wanted out – the time had come. Indeed, I never went back to that house," she recalls. It was a major turning point in her life. She was leaving behind years of heartbreak and frustration.

Sarel, however, still believed he could win her back. "Our departure didn't deter Sarel, of course, once he had found out where we were staying. He would come round and beg me to go back to him. He would plead and cry for hours. In a way I felt sorry for him, because he was a man who had desperately wanted a child, and was now going to be a father – but would not be in a position to enjoy a normal fatherhood. I think it was fate's cruel hand on this man's life and it chose to manifest itself at that critical moment. He desperately wanted a child, and now I had gone. The pleading, the cajoling, the threats, went on for several weeks but now I was determined not to succumb. One day I realized the only way to get Sarel out of my life was to move far away, possibly to Cape Town."

It was a fateful decision that would change her life for ever. Heather went into work the next morning and said to Patrick that she had had enough; she didn't think she could cope with Sarel any more. The only way to deal with it would be to leave the job, leave the town and move away. She said she thought she would go to Cape Town and make a clean break from Natal.

Once, a long time before, Heather had made a joke with Patrick, enquiring who cut his hair because there was a slight step in the cutting on one side of his scalp.

"Oh, it's the woman next door," he replied.

"Is she your girlfriend?" she asked.

"What's it to you?"

"Have you ever thought of getting married?" she asked.

"No, not really," he said.

"But have you ever wanted to get married?" she persisted.

"There's only one woman I've ever thought about getting married to," he said after a pause. And so she left it there, and never asked him again about his private life.

Now, some months later in his office, she was about to tender her immediate resignation. Patrick looked at her and said: "Do you remember asking me about ever wanting to get married?"

"Yes," said Heather.

"Do you remember me saying there was only one woman I ever wanted to marry?"

"Yes," she said.

"Well, now she's telling me she's going to Cape Town."

Heather laughed, thinking he wasn't being serious. "What? You're crazy!" she said, still laughing a little bewilderedly.

Heather recalls it was such a shock that she didn't have time to measure her response, or say something to avoid hurting his feelings – and later she realized her laughter had certainly done that. She hadn't handled it well, and went off to tea, leaving him in the office. They didn't really talk for the rest of the afternoon, and then it was time to go home in the evening. Just as it was time to leave, he stood in the doorway and asked: "Have you thought about what I said?"

She told him that she didn't consider there was anything further to be said. She didn't think it could possibly work, and she would certainly never, ever consider getting married again. She said that although she knew him as a friend, she didn't really know him on a personal level and so she couldn't consider it. She reminded him how she was (at that time) a heavy smoker, and he wasn't a smoker and would hate living with someone who was. She also reminded him that she was eight months pregnant and that her brother and father were living with her and that there would never be a chance of a relationship surviving under these circumstances.

Heather recalls she wasn't attracted to Patrick at that time. That's not to say he wasn't attractive, but she had been through something so horrific that she was not interested in any man. Patrick was just a good friend. They could talk for hours across a range of cerebral subjects, totally immersed in ideas and thoughts, and they shared many interests. But it never once occurred to her that this was exactly the kind of partner who could bring her fulfilment in every way. She had just never looked upon him as a man, a member of the opposite sex. Patrick Reynolds was a soulmate.

"So there it was. I had turned him down pretty bluntly, but I really didn't think there was much feeling on his part either. He had never indicated or demonstrated any affection or attraction for me, so I think I was reacting as though he had suggested this idea of marrying me off the top of his head — without thinking it through. There was no emotion involved." As far as Heather was concerned she had filed for divorce, was free, and intended to stay that way. She didn't even appease Patrick by saying she'd think about it. So she walked out and went home for the weekend.

On the Monday morning Patrick walked in to work and Heather was shocked by what she saw. She had never seen him looking so terrible. He was ashen, and appeared sick. "What's wrong?" she gasped.

"Don't ask me what happened," he snapped back, with a cold look in his eyes.

Then the realization hit her. This man cared about her, and she had broken him. She just could not believe it. There was this guy, usually so remote and aloof, and here he was, looking stricken, haggard and awful. She was appalled at what she had said and done, and realized too late the depth and extent of his feelings.

"I am so sorry," she blurted out.

"I really don't want to discuss it," he replied quietly.

Heather felt the full force of his hurt, and wanted to make it better. Her eyes welled with tears.

"Surely we can talk," she pleaded.

"I don't think there's much to be said," he replied.

"Look, you've put me in a predicament," said Heather. "I don't even know you. We've been friends for two years but on an entirely different level. Patrick, I can't bear you being hurt like this – why don't we go out to dinner, why don't we start getting to know one another? At least we can try?" She was somehow searching for a way to ease his misery, and now hers. "Let's go and have a coffee after work and talk about this," she suggested.

He agreed. So they met after work and it gave her an opportunity to explain why she had reacted in a negative and off-handed manner, and how she now regretted that and was sorry. She had not been able to accept that he loved her that deeply, but now realized his feelings were genuine.

"Why would I ask you to marry me if I didn't feel deeply for you?" he asked.

"Look," she said, "before yesterday you never gave me the slightest idea about how you felt. There was nothing to suggest it in what you said and did. How would I know you loved me so deeply?"

Patrick Reynolds, she was about to find out, is an incredibly honourable and moral man. He told her then that he would never have considered speaking to her about his feelings while she was married, and would not have done so before she was properly divorced – had she not announced her intention of moving out of his life. The two of them went into new and deep discussions. He argued that going to Cape Town would not help her because Sarel only needed to apply for a transfer and could follow her down there. She would be away from her friends and there would be less of a support system in the big city than in Merrivale. She listened to him and agreed. Patrick then suggested that he should move in to Heather and John's house as a paying guest with his own room because he could give her support in the pregnancy, taking her to hospital when she needed to go there nearer the birth, and also helping to look after Kenny when she had to go into hospital.

"But what will that look like?" she asked, worried what people might think, and about her reputation.

"Let's do what's best for us and not worry about that," he replied.

So Patrick moved in, and Heather met his family. Sarel, of course, was now convinced there was something going on between them. Heather was nine months pregnant with Brendan, but because that was the way Sarel's mind worked, he was convinced the new set-up was all about sex. He must have been shocked by the strength of her reaction. "I'm not having an affair with Patrick," Heather told Sarel, "but I've filed for divorce from you, and if I want to I *will* have an affair – either with him or a hundred others. I'm entitled now to live my own life without you and that's the way it's going to be!" Sarel had discovered to his cost that Heather now felt much more confident in dealing with him. Then it finally dawned on him that Patrick was going to be a feature in her life for ever. He had lost her.

Sarel arrived outside Heather's house, carrying a metal bar. She walked out towards him and he strode up with a threatening expression on his face. "I'm going to kill him. He's not taking you away from me!" he shouted.

She screamed back: "I don't belong to you any more! It's finished."

Heather was frightened now because Sarel was a big man. Her father was not around and she thought Patrick might be killed, or seriously injured, if Sarel lost control of himself. What made it so much worse was that Patrick was completely innocent. She ran into Patrick's room at the back of the house. He looked up calmly as she shouted: "Sarel's here, he's got a metal bar, and he says he's going to kill you!"

Heather was trying to find in her mind some way to appease Sarel and prevent the confrontation. She walked hurriedly around to the front of the house ahead of Patrick, but he gently took her by the shoulders, put her firmly aside and said quietly: "I'll deal with this."

He confronted Sarel, asking: "What exactly is this all about?"

"I'm not going to allow you to steal her from me. She's mine!" Sarel snarled.

Patrick's voice was quiet and assured. "She's certainly not yours. Face the truth, Sarel, you've never wanted her. You've always wanted someone else. You ruined her life, and you're still ruining her life. You treat her without any respect and dignity, any true affection and love, and you certainly don't deserve her. Now you are even putting her baby under threat."

He continued: "Heather is everything that I've ever wanted, and now I am going to look after her, care for her and the baby. I'll treat her properly, give her respect, and love, and everything that she deserves."

The quiet words had the power of ten sledgehammers upon Sarel as he realized the truth of what Patrick said, and that this time there would be no turning back of the clock. He seemed to crumple, to wilt before their eyes, with tears welling up. Heather recalls: "I'll never forget it. Patrick and I were on the veranda of the house by now, and we walked down the steps together. I felt so sorry for Sarel. He turned away, walked in a dejected manner down the drive, and drove off in his car. I was astonished. Here was this new man in my life that I still felt I hardly knew, who in a few quiet words — but words expressive of such strength and conviction — had charted a new way forward for me. He had shown total courage in the face of aggression from a man much larger than himself, and armed with a weapon that could have been lethal."

A few weeks later, Brendan was born and it caused some confusion in the hospital because Heather had two men visiting her, both playing the paternal role. She was determined to get Patrick involved with Brendan from the first moment. On the other hand, she couldn't say no to Sarel because Brendan was his son. "He would sit at my bedside and cry and cry. I think, somehow, Brendan must have felt the incredible tension. Then Patrick would come in and find me with a face swollen from tears. I could feel the incredible pain that Sarel was suffering, but I knew I just could not go there again. It was over. He loved his little son so much, and was so remorseful that, maybe, he would never have had an affair with a woman again, but this was now only part of the equation for me. I was through, for ever, with power struggles and provocation."

Heather had seen the harmony in Patrick's life. There was another path waiting for her.

14
A NEW LIFE
WITH PATRICK

The divorce began to go through, and in due course Patrick asked Heather to marry him. She resisted it and suggested they might just live together. She told Patrick she could never have an intimate relationship with a man again. Why didn't they just live together as friends, with no physical relationship?

"I've never asked you to have a physical relationship with me," he replied.

Heather looked at him and realized he was quite serious. "Then why don't we just live together?" she asked again.

"No, I want to marry you," he insisted. "I will be your husband. I will protect you, and love you for the rest of your life. But if you never want to sleep with me, then so be it."

A few months passed, and he would say to her with increasing frequency, "Well, have you thought about it?"

Eventually Heather thought to herself: *Look, this thing could possibly work. We get on very well together, share so much in common, and if he is prepared not to want anything from me, then perhaps we could get married. He puts up with my father's drinking, and my brother's illness. If I could still sleep in Kenny's room, then everything could be fine.*

So she said to Patrick: "OK. Let's take it a step closer. You know a lot about me. I don't really know anything about you — or your personal habits. Let's take a trip together overseas

to Europe, maybe about seven weeks on maximum leave."
This was a test. Heather reckoned that when companions
were travelling at that pace continually, and in close proximity physically, it would be hard to hide things away – not to see
one another in their worst light. Patrick might get on her
nerves, and if she also happened to be tired and hungry, it was
a recipe for conflict.

So they travelled from South Africa to England, to
Germany, Denmark, Switzerland, to Sweden, Norway,
Austria... and just kept moving – backwards and forwards,
always tailing back – to see the effects of this stressful trip
upon their relationship. It turned out to be the most memorable and romantic journey of their lives! The schedule was
irrelevant. Heather fell deeply in love with Patrick and then
was sorry that she had planned it so badly – because they were
having so much fun. "It was amazing," she recalls. "I had found
my soulmate! The trip was the most fantastic, wonderful time.
He was so considerate, so gentle, and so marvellous in everything. I told him one night I would give him my answer to his
marriage proposal when we arrived back home."

As soon as they got out of the airport and into his car, he
said: "Well, what's your answer?"

She looked at him, and smiled: "Yes. OK. Let's go for it!"

They had arrived back in South Africa just before the New
Year in 1979, and the divorce papers had already come
through. Now, Patrick's feet hardly touched the ground. That
very day he was on the telephone to the Methodist minister in
Howick and arranged the wedding in the minimum time permitted, which was three weeks.

Patrick and Heather were married at a quiet service for just
family and a few friends in January 1979. She was married for
the third time, and at the age of 27 had at last found happiness
and a solid family life with Patrick, her father, Kenny and
Brendan. Bronwen, their daughter, was born in 1980. They
moved from the house John McLellan had rented, to Umgeni

Waterfall Care and Rehabilitation Centre. The secretary's residence was a smart and spacious, double-storey house with a large garden.

Who was this man Patrick who had come into Heather's life and why was he important to her development as a person?

"He is a total introvert," she explains, "with really strong principles and values. He never compromises. You tend not to notice Patrick, because he is always in the background. He is a listener and seems to engender respect among all who know him. If he says anything, people normally listen. However, even though he may be an intellectual, he doesn't enjoy working on cars or doing maintenance; his skills lie elsewhere. Tell him to make a scale model of your house, make a model of a ship etc., or even a toy chainsaw, but don't ask him to cook and don't ask him to fix your car."

Patrick Reynolds has been a great reader of books all his life. He consumes them. Friends say that if there is nothing to hand published for him to look at, he'll read bits of paper on the desk. He loves literature, history, mythology, astronomy and the sciences. Heather had never explored this world and meeting him was the beginning of a long and intensive process of self-education. At school she had been in the top stream but life had been regimented, with sporting commitments. She recounts: "I got totally caught up in astronomy, and I literally devoured every book I could lay my hands upon. Soon, I came upon quantum physics and was fascinated by it. Patrick introduced me to Darwin and evolution. At school, we had not really discussed evolution. Now I was devouring everything I could find about it. At first, it reinforced my conviction that Christianity had been a blind alley. I read about scientific explanations for how the universe had started through the "Big Bang" and how human beings had evolved. Patrick and I together explored all these things but I became disillusioned when I had read every book about it.

"The Darwinian principle of survival of the fittest and its

concept of natural adaptation is unquestionable and very few people will argue with that conclusion. But I still needed to be convinced that everything came from one living cell and that random mutations were responsible for every major adaptation, and provided perfect DNA. For example, the perfect wing of a bird and its changed bone structure, the eye, the lungs, etc. – these are not adaptations but incredibly complex and sophisticated body organs, plus functions. That is where I found it easier to believe that a creator designed and masterminded everything – rather than that billions of random mutations just happened at various times."

Heather was also still deeply disillusioned with the church. She then started reading the ideas of many other scientists on evolution, such as Fred Hoyle. She discovered that there were others whose work remained ignored and unpublished in the mainstream. They were often denied a proper platform upon which to put forward their views and ideas. She realized then that there could be no sense of fulfilment in the quest for knowledge about the creation. So she moved on. "I then got involved with subatomic particles and found that here was a world in which I could blow my mind!"

However, the most inspiring quality of Patrick Reynolds was his talent as an artist. Heather was deeply impressed by the wooden sculptures – many depicting the human form – which he created in his spare time. She was convinced his work was the result of a natural gift, and it became an essential part of her programme to provide him with the maximum creative time and space to carry on his work. She began to feel they should move away from the hospital to give him more space and opportunity to develop his artistic work.

Before any decision could be made, there was news within the family concerning her father and it was sad news: "At this time my dad had gone back to live with Myrtle and some time later he went into hospital for heart treatment, and died after a short illness. I always regretted not having that final, definitive conversation with him because in later life I came to realize what had made him behave in the way he did, and why he took to drinking. He had never known love as a young, orphaned and abandoned child, and so he had found it difficult to give hugs and show affection when sober, although his heart was full of love for us. I now can see that when he was under the influence of alcohol his inhibitions dropped and he wanted to hug and cuddle us – but that was when we all rejected him. No child wants a drunken parent hugging and kissing her.

"Of course when we rejected him he would be hurt and angry and that was possibly the beginning of many of the misunderstandings that led to awful quarrels, with him chasing us all out of the house. These are some of the possible conclusions that I have reached when analyzing his behaviour now. There were things in his personality that were due to his awful childhood – perhaps he had not even understood that himself. Counselling would probably have sorted out all that unhappiness. I wanted to tell him that I understood, and that Mum and I forgave him. He had sometimes brought shame and sadness to our family through his drinking, but my overriding memories of him are fond ones.

"I admired his loyalty towards those he cared about, his honest and straightforward nature, and the way he tackled life without allowing his disabilities to sap his energy and resolve. Dad never complained about anything – except other members of the family spending money – and he set us a fine example. I loved him deeply."

It was now clear that Heather and Patrick needed less space than before, because her father would not be returning, and Kenny was staying with Myrtle, while Bronwen was still in her infancy. Soon the opportunity presented itself for them to buy their first home together, and they bought a family house in the nearby town of Merrivale. It was a beautiful home with a large garden and double garage, which they converted into a studio. Most weekends would be spent blissfully, with the children playing around them, as Patrick worked in his studio and Heather painted her landscapes or worked in the garden. She continued to enjoy her art, reading, gardening and badminton, and she also found time to respond to stiffer challenges that included mountain climbing and flying.

Heather was in her late twenties and at last, thanks entirely to Patrick's support and encouragement, able to enjoy the kind of self-fulfilment that had been missing during her first marriage. Her self-confidence increased in leaps and bounds. She remained an atheist, although she always wondered about her failed suicide attempt and questioned whether there was a remote possibility that it had failed through divine intervention. Then she had an important experience that would change her life profoundly and bring her back to God.

15
HEATHER RETURNS TO GOD

Dusk was approaching, and Heather was late for a badminton club committee meeting that was being held in Pietermaritzburg. She was driving fast along the motorway with Brendan, who was still a toddler. He was strapped into a baby-seat in the back. Ahead, she saw two trucks, one behind the other in the left-hand lane. She was expecting the second truck to pass the one ahead of it, so she slowed and waited for the driver to pull out. But he didn't.

"Come on, come on, get on with it," she muttered impatiently as she slowed down.

Still the second lorry driver held his position. Heather started to accelerate and was in the process of overtaking when the second lorry pulled out in front of her without any signal. She literally "stood" on the brakes, swerving to the right, leaving a cloud of blue smoke and missing the truck by inches. She was shaken but very relieved.

The road into Pietermaritzburg is long, steep and winding. Heather had to brake at each curve to control her speed and soon realized something was wrong with her brakes. They were spongy. She had to pump repeatedly to produce any effect. As she approached a stop sign at a major intersection, they failed completely. She wrote later:

Then I saw headlights approaching at speed. I knew that a collision was unavoidable! Brendan, my precious son, was directly in its path. In an instinctive attempt to avoid the collision I accelerated. The oncoming car struck the rear passenger door — close to where Brendan was sleeping — I remember vividly the terrible sound of the impact. The car spun several times and finally came to rest on the pavement. There was a deathly silence. I realized I was unhurt, just dazed and shocked. But what of my baby — was he alive? In frantic anxiety I jumped out and opened the rear door. With my heart filled with dread I fumbled in the dark interior for an interminable moment. I could not find him. I said: "God, if you are there, please let my son be safe. I ask for a miracle. If he is unhurt I'll search for you."

And then my hands found him, untouched, his eyes wide open. I shook him to make sure he was alive; his little mouth quivered as he began to cry. My heart filled with joy.

I turned towards the car that had hit me. I didn't know if anybody had been killed or injured. Perhaps someone had gone through the windscreen — my heart filled with dread once more! Two men were walking towards me, one of them a very big man. They were both dressed in tennis outfits.

I have always hated any kind of public humiliation, and now all these cars were stopping, and a crowd was gathering. I was responsible for this accident. I expected them to be furious and even abusive, but they didn't speak, they just kept walking towards me. I wondered again, had anyone been killed? The big man loomed over me; by now I was quite terrified. Was he going to assault me? But instead of shouting or cursing, he laid a hand on my shoulder, and asked in the gentlest voice, "Are you OK? Are you hurt?"

I had just wrecked his brand new silver Jaguar sports car, written if off — and yet this man's only concern was whether anyone had been injured. It was the last thing I expected him to say. I replied: "I'm fine."

"Anyone else in the car?" he asked.

"Just my son in the back and he's OK."

"Then let us thank God that no one was hurt."

He placed his other hand on the shoulder of his friend, and together we bowed our heads in prayer. Suddenly all the pain, and the hurt, and the anger of those former years dissolved. Here standing in front of me was what I had searched for in Christianity. This was the sort of person I had always hoped Christianity would produce. In some way, this big man had expunged all the earlier pain I had experienced as a young woman. I started to cry.

He probably thought I was crying because of the shock, and this may have been partly true. However, I was thinking, *This is how I would like to be. This is the sort of Christian I would like to become.*

I whispered to God: "From this day on I will seek you, in truth, and with an open heart and with an open mind."

When the police arrived, the big man said to them: "Her brakes failed. It was an act of God." They checked the car and confirmed this.

The next day he telephoned to see if I was OK.

The accident seemed to mark a turning point in the Reynolds' lives because within weeks things were to change for ever — and for the better.

Heather had taken a job that seemed to offer her a career path. She loved the challenges it presented, and although some might not necessarily see her in a corporate role, she had come across a project that excited her for two reasons. It would test her abilities as a good manager and organizer, and it would benefit the poorer members of society. This was a new innovative group insurance policy that was affordable and targeted the African market. Heather was fluent in both the Zulu and Xhosa languages. She worked with a team of enthusiastic young men, and as they travelled around KwaZulu-Natal they were extremely successful in developing the programmes from scratch. Unfortunately, the boss was one of those people who liked to socialize and was often in the canteen chatting with the guys. He also took the credit for the endeavour of others, and was disinclined to do much work himself. Looking back, Heather agrees that she had become rather ruthless with men who treated women without proper respect. She was not – and never had been – a feminist but having survived terrible ordeals with Sarel Olivier, men ceased to intimidate her.

"At that time South Africa was a chauvinistic world," recalls Heather, "and women accepted that. However, I had made up my mind that I was never going to be subjected to male dominance again. Men were no longer something to fear. I had won my freedom from that. I put up with my boss, provided he did not interfere with the way I ran things, but unfortunately he began to see me as a threat. People were coming to me for answers, and also for solutions to problems. Often he found himself out of the loop through his own loose management style." She realized it was only a matter of time before he would forfeit his job over this mismanagement, and she would be asked to take over the reins to manage the business properly. However, a shock was around the corner, and it came in 1983.

"When first recruited for the job, I had told the management that I would never be available to work on Saturdays because it was family time. I had promised to give 100 percent, five days a week, Monday to Friday, but also made it clear I could do no more than that. This had been accepted, and I had been hired."

Now, the boss called her into his office and announced that he wanted everyone on the team to work on Saturdays – because of the huge increase in business, which Heather's team had generated. Cunningly, he had worked out that she would not want to lose her weekends with Patrick and the children, and realized it was the only way he could get rid of

her. This came at a time during which Heather had been working a lot of overtime and seeing a lot less of her children than
she would have liked, coming home late and leaving early in
the mornings.

One previous Sunday afternoon, as Heather and her
mother-in-law Agnes were sitting chatting, Agnes had asked
her: "Do you know Bronwen took her first steps?" Heather
was stunned. Trying to hide her devastation, all she could
remember was a story she'd heard some years earlier, about a
friend who'd missed her child's first steps, and Heather could
recall feeling terribly sorry for her. Now she sat in the same
position, and nothing she could do could turn back the clock
to undo it. With this in mind, her priorities had been highlighted, and now, as the unfair call to work weekends came,
her resolve strengthened.

"I was so angry. I phoned head office and spoke to the man
who had jointly recruited me for the job. I said to him: 'Do
you remember that the day I went for my final interview, I
made it clear that I would not be prepared to work on
Saturdays?'

" 'No,' the man said, 'I don't.' "

Heather felt that was the end. She had no leg to stand on. If
the head office man could not remember their verbal agreement, she had no option but to resign – because it would be
the word of two managers against hers, and they were senior.

"OK. Then I'll resign," she told them – furious that she had
not asked for a clause to be written into her contract. That
night she went home really angry. She had put her heart and
soul into the job. She told Patrick what had happened and they
talked about it. Then she remembered that a friend, Rob
Wareing, a portrait artist who had recently painted Heather,
had told them a few months before how he had become a full-
time artist.

"I'd just wanted to get out of it," he'd said, referring to his
full-time job. An electrician, he had put down his tools and

announced: "That's it – I'm finished with this." Next day, he started life as an artist.

Although Heather treasured their weekends together, she used to loathe Sunday evenings when Patrick had to put down his tools in the studio, no matter how important the work, or how critical the stage he had reached, and close it down for another five days. She had come to realize he desperately needed the opportunity to operate as a full-time artist. He had a folder full of ideas that he wanted to sculpt, yet if he carried on working only at weekends he would face nothing but continuing frustration in the future. Very few of his wonderful ideas would ever be created. Patrick Reynolds' speciality is for the human figure, usually female and often in adolescent or child form.

Shortly after they met, Heather had bought one of Patrick's best, well-known pieces, *The Bicycle Girl*, which he originally sculpted in wood. It is now available to everyone in bronze, and is a great favourite. She says of her husband: "He has also done some outstanding work of animals. All of Patrick's work is intricate and finely detailed. There is a 'feel' in everything he touches with his chisel that I find unique."

Locally, around Pietermaritzburg, Patrick already had a substantial following – but his problem was in finding enough time to do the pieces people wanted. Heather relates: "I was by now deeply in love with Patrick, and regarded him as a truly great sculptor. It hurt me to see him so frustrated, even though he would never admit it to anyone. Patrick was rarely demonstrative with his emotions, but I could read his true mood. And so, when the altercation with my boss came out of the blue, instead of treating it as a disaster I decided to regard it as an opportunity for us to break free and move on together. Patrick would have his freedom to become a full-time professional artist, whatever the cost, and whatever the risk."

The couple had some savings, some income from pensions, and there would be money from the sale of the house.

Heather and Patrick calculated this would be sufficient to last them for two years until Patrick had completed sufficient pieces to attend a big exhibition in Pietermaritzburg. "Why don't we go off and do it?" she said to Patrick. Her recollection is that he didn't need much persuading! She was up at dawn to read the paper and find out if there were any properties in the "For rent" columns that might suit their plans. Once again fate intervened. There was an old farmhouse advertised, not far away, but in a direction that they had never travelled, in a place called Dalton.

It was set in the foothills about 30 miles from Pietermaritzburg. By six o'clock the next morning they were there. It turned out to be a remote, stand-alone property called Deep Valley that had fallen into a state of considerable dereliction. The homestead was midway up a hill, about four miles along a narrow road from the nearest shop, and nearly a mile from the nearest neighbour.

They fell in love with Deep Valley immediately. It was a German colonial farmhouse, built in cut stone. The white paintwork was peeling off both the wooden shuttered windows and the ornate trellis on the wide verandas. No matter! Here was the perfect setting for a couple of artists to go and hide – and do their thing! "So we signed up to rent the farmhouse, with the idea that one day we might have sufficient money to buy it," Heather recalls.

They agreed Patrick would take the leave owing to him at the hospital as soon as possible and tender his resignation. Heather, of course, had already resigned from her company and did not expect to hear from them again. That day they paid a few months' rent to the owner of Deep Valley, and went back home to Merrivale. As soon as they got back, the phone rang. It was the head office of Heather's former company. The managing director came on the line.

"Hello, Heather," he said. "We'd like you to reconsider your resignation. We want you to take over the office immediately."

She couldn't believe her ears. Patrick said immediately, "You have to take the position." She shook her head. Not for one moment was she tempted to say: "Yes! I'll come back!" The promotion was no longer important. They were artists. They were going to live as artists. They had just glimpsed paradise.

16
THE DEEP VALLEY YEARS

In the coming weeks Heather and Patrick could hardly wait for their move to Deep Valley. Patrick brought with him his chisels, a collection built up during his travels in Europe. They invested in a band saw, a circular saw and a planer. Later, when the local community discovered that a sculptor had come to live in the district, the local boys' school invited Patrick to go along once a week and teach woodwork.

They converted one of the front rooms off the veranda into Patrick's studio, while the other, which had been the lounge, became the bedroom. It meant that while Patrick was working, and Heather was with the children in the bedroom, they could still communicate, especially if he wanted to work late. She remembers: "Those were balmy days before the climate began to change. Now, in KwaZulu-Natal, the weather is not predictable. I would bring my easel out onto the veranda, painting in the shade of the hot sun, while Patrick worked in the studio. The hours would glide by in tranquil bliss. Even in the months of winter, from May until August, the weather was generally sunny, although some days it was freezing cold."

Heather has always been an organizer, and her skills extended to running a kitchen that most other women would envy. She learned to bake her own bread at Deep Valley, made jam from the garden fruit, chutney from the vegetables, and even found time to bake biscuits and cakes. The children remember elaborate icing on their birthday cakes. They would enjoy English-style birthday parties in the garden, when all their friends from school and the local farms around would be invited. Here in her piece of paradise, Heather was finally content with life.

One night, as she was lying in bed next to Patrick, the figure of her mother appeared. Heather still does not know whether it was a dream, or reality. Brenda McLellan stood at the foot of the bed. Heather relates: "I experienced this powerful rushing sound within my head, and it felt as if my mind was being sucked by a powerful vacuum cleaner. It was such a strong feeling – not scary – and it felt as though I would be swept across the universe in a moment. Part of me wanted to let go, and go with her, but the logical side of me was afraid of not being able to return. I remember saying in my mind, *No, no, Mum, I can't go with you. I don't want to leave Patrick, Kenny and the children. I am all right now. I am too scared to go with you, I am scared I will not come back. I cannot go with you.*"

Heather has never since been able to explain the visitation of her mother, but recalls the promise Brenda made to her before she died. She will never know whether it was a powerful dream or not!

In the first year at Deep Valley Kenny returned to live with them and together they made the garden a priority target, creating it in the English style with a lawn, roses, hydrangeas, and paths intertwining with herbaceous flowerbeds of exotic African flora. It was large, about an acre, and had become quite wild. There was plenty to do. The Africans who had worked for them at Merrivale soon found the travelling out to Deep Valley too much, and so they didn't stay long after helping to train replacements. New faces appeared. "Lena had come to Deep Valley to nurse my brother Kenny, and I was teaching her to understand him because he couldn't speak. One day she told me that her daughter Betty, who was still of school age, had become pregnant and would like an opportunity to work for us. I said OK, so Betty came with her baby, lived on the farm, and we got to love her dearly."

Sadly, as the months passed, Kenny's health began to deteriorate. The last few weeks of Kenny's life are a painful memory for Heather and it brings tears when she revisits them, but she takes comfort from the fact that at Deep Valley he was able to experience once again, in some form, the outdoor life he had enjoyed on John McLellan's farm. There he'd looked after the dairy, and maintained the fencing on the land.

"At Deep Valley," says Heather, "we built a chicken run and Kenny kept an eye on the chickens and the garden, making sure it was weeded and watered daily. However, he had major circulation problems by this time and his kidneys were not functioning well. He no longer had the energy to do the amount of work he'd once been capable of doing, but at least he found a form of fulfilment.

"One day in 1984, we took him for a treat to the Royal Show and on the way back he seemed to be in considerable pain. I gave him a painkiller but while I was talking to him he stopped responding. It was clear he was dying. I jumped into the back seat and tried to revive him. We drove as fast as we could to the nearby hospital, the same one where Brendan and Bronwen were born, but he was certified dead on arrival. A blood clot had lodged in his lung. I loved Kenny dearly and I find it hard even now, 20 or so years after he has left us, not to cry when I recall his life and his death. He was a normal man trapped inside a feeble body, imprisoned for his entire life within something from which he had no hope or chance of escape. And yet Kenny tackled his life with courage, usually with humour and without complaint. My oldest brother inspired me as a true hero."

Fortunately, Kenny's death came at a time when Heather's faith was growing stronger. She was starting to pray regularly, and this often seemed to help in bringing solutions to the family's problems. They were now towards the end of the second year at Deep Valley, and Patrick was completing more of his pieces. Heather was able to assist him in several ways. Soon after she had met Patrick she wanted to help him, and when she bought *The Cup Girl* when they were living at Howick, she asked if he would mind if she did a little more finishing work on it. "It was slightly rough in surface and its hardboard base was unsightly. Patrick is a creator rather than a finisher. So I took the sandpaper and spent hours and hours doing the finishing. It was almost as if I had been doing it all my life; my fingers knew just what to do. Soon I was picking up the knife and cleaning off bits and refining. I could not sculpt, but could help him by finishing his work. By the time we were living at Deep Valley I had learned how to wet and raise the burr, sand it once more, stain and polish."

Most of the figures for that first exhibition in Pietermaritzburg were about one-and-a-half feet tall and included *The Cup Girl*, *The Bicycle Girl*, *The Nude With A Towel*, and *The Girl On A Rock*. Heather and Patrick had attended the Pietermaritzburg exhibition when he was still working at the hospital but he had never been able to produce enough work to meet the potential demand. This time, they knew that if they could create a sufficient number of pieces, it would begin to establish his name beyond the locality. The exhibition attracted artists and dealers from all over the country and the sizeable stand exhibiting the work of Patrick Reynolds would now be noticed. So at least, Heather and Patrick felt, they were on the first rung of the ladder. Patrick's work was deemed to be of sufficient quality to stand alongside sculptors who were better known.

As the time approached, they managed to complete about twelve pieces and carefully wrapped them in blankets before packing them into the hand-made trailer they had recently bought. Ominously, on the day before the exhibition when they would have to travel to Pietermaritzburg, there were dark grey skies overhead that threatened heavy rain. Worse was to come. Shortly before they departed it began to drizzle. Heather explains: "Patrick's pieces have a polish on them, and if they get wet the polish goes white, and you have to start again to get the finish. Furthermore, this was an open-air exhibition and so we approached the coming day with a certain degree of trepidation."

Things went from bad to worse. They were halfway to Pietermaritzburg when the trailer cover blew off, exposing the very pieces it was supposed to be protecting. Patrick pulled up the vehicle and examined the frame. Worryingly, it had buckled beyond repair. They couldn't believe their terrible fortune. "Here we were with all this work standing in the drizzle, knowing it could start raining really hard at any moment. We had travelled beyond the point of no return, having already covered 20 kilometres – so we had no choice – we had to go on. We climbed back into the car, not saying much, but we were totally devastated. This could be the end. This could totally ruin everything. We would have to go back to office work after two years of using up our savings. I could hardly comprehend it. After so much creative effort, one downpour could ruin everything. Patrick was grim-faced as he drove, and I looked at him anxiously. I loved this man so dearly I just couldn't bear the thought of putting him back in an office again."

Then it started to rain heavily, and now they were in a critical position. As on so many occasions in Heather's life her simple faith motivated her to turn to God. "I started praying in my heart, saying, 'Dear Father God... I beg you – if you are out there – stop the rain. Please just stop the rain.' It didn't work. Then I did something that really embarrassed me in front of Patrick. I decided to sing my prayers aloud. I sang the Lord's Prayer: 'Our Father, who art in Heaven... for ever and ever, Amen.' As I finished the prayer we came round a corner, and there were blue skies ahead." The rain had stopped – just like that!

They arrived at the exhibition and to their huge relief discovered that the rain hadn't penetrated the blankets after all. They sold every piece to private buyers, on average for around 2,000 Rand each, which was not a fortune in 1984 but sufficient to justify two years' work, and to provide the Reynolds with the capital to carry on with their cherished lifestyle for a further twelve months.

Eventually the couple realized that Patrick would have to work in bronze and they discussed this with a friend, Dave Falconer, who wanted to start a foundry nearby. They realized that if Dave Falconer could cast and finish Patrick's work to the required standard, then the entire process of creating the figures in bronze would be possible. Gradually the two men began to collaborate. It turned out to be much more difficult than they envisaged, and it took longer than planned. As time went by, the Reynolds began to get into financial difficulties. Things went from bad to worse and eventually they faced financial ruin. But providence intervened.

For some years, Heather had been involved in growing bonsai miniature trees. She was by now chairperson of the Natal Midlands Bonsai Society, and the garden at Deep Valley was full of miniature trees. It had been difficult to find pots for bonsai trees and so a few months earlier they decided there might be a niche in the market, specializing in producing pots to grow them in. Showing great foresight, they decided to invest in a pottery and now it began to be successful, with a growing number of local customers. By the time of the financial crisis caused by the expense of Patrick's conversion to working in bronze, Heather was selling the trees and had opened the pottery.

"With guidance from Patrick, I had trained myself to make the pots, without having any classes. We were just learning as we went, and we found our way through. It was fascinating. I remember the first time we fired the kiln, which we put in our kitchen. We could hardly wait to open it to see what would come out. I prayed hard for good results. They were certainly good enough to encourage us to go on, and I started to make different shapes as I became more skilled. Within a year we were producing really fine pots in various sizes, some terracotta and others glazed in a variety of beautiful colours: shades of beige, blue, greens and earthy colours. Slowly our reputation began to spread throughout the entire country."

From the humble beginnings of the first pots coming out of Deep Valley, the Reynolds began to build a profitable business with customers all over South Africa; some pots were even exported to neighbouring Zimbabwe, during its transitional period from Rhodesia. However, net profit margins were low because higher productivity depended upon intensive recruitment of labour. Here were to be found the roots of the altruism which ultimately would take over Heather's life. All around them the Africans were living in miserable poverty, and now there was something she could do to alleviate that by employing Zulu women, who were more productive than the men. As she recalls: "We became even more labour intensive than perhaps we needed to, but we wanted to take in as many women as we could to give them work. It had become important to me to help the Zulu people and I began to feel within me that it was what God wanted me to do."

From here the idea of a community of needy people working at Deep Valley gradually evolved. Perhaps, during the latter part of the 1980s, this altruism became focussed as a mission for Heather. It was to move a step further forward when a pregnant Zulu child called Zodwa arrived out of the blue from the valley, looking for both a home and a job. She was only about fourteen years old and desperate. She had nowhere to go, and the baby was about to come. Zodwa knew that Heather gave people work tending the garden, and also in the pottery.

"You can't work; you're just a child," Heather told her at first. Zodwa burst into tears and said she was hungry and had to have food.

"Then you must go to your parents. I certainly can't employ you," said Heather.

"My mum and dad are dead; the whole family were killed in a car crash. I'm the only survivor. I've nowhere to go. Please help me," the girl implored Heather.

Heather and Patrick were horrified, and didn't know what to do. They realized that if Heather agreed to raise an African baby in her home, meaning that blacks would be using the family bathroom and kitchen, then the Reynolds could soon expect to become the focus of unwanted attention from other white people living in the community. Heather was trapped between her humanitarian instincts, all the things she and Patrick believed in, like equality between black and white, and her own family's social predicament.

The Reynolds knew they could not turn Zodwa away. "Come in," Heather said, and gave her food. Zodwa stayed and became the first resident helper in the new pottery. The young girl had her baby the following Christmas morning at Deep Valley, and they called her Gracie. Baby Gracie's birth signified a growing split between the lifestyle that Heather and Patrick had chosen, and that expected of them by the overwhelming majority of their white neighbours in the German community. The first to reject them were members of Heather's own family, one of whom told her he would not come to stay for Christmas with a black baby in the house.

The Reynolds had already made friends with several leading African artists. It was one area where, to a certain extent, people could be equal. At the annual art exhibition in Pietermaritzburg, their friend Mizriam Mazibuko, a popular African artist from Johannesburg, had a stand near the Reynolds. However, he parked his caravan outside the local camping ground in the car park and Heather asked him why. He looked at her with bewilderment and whispered: "Heather, where else would I park it?"

"At first I thought, *What on earth is he talking about, where would he park it?*" recalls Heather. "Suddenly, click, click, click, I realized he couldn't go to the caravan park because it was for whites only. Things fell into place." Earlier that day, the Reynolds had insisted he join them for a barbecue, and some of the other exhibitors around them had moved away. Now they knew why.

Despite incidents like the one involving Mizriam, Heather and Patrick continued to keep a low profile in the community and to steer well away from apartheid South Africa's notorious white-run police force. It was racist towards Africans, and highly intolerant of anyone, regardless of race, who set out to disturb the status quo. However, trouble with the local police was beckoning. It all started when Heather's maid Betty began to get seriously harassed by her drunken partner, the father of her child.

"The father of the baby had an alcohol problem and so Betty decided she wanted to break off her relationship, which is not easy in Zulu culture, because a man won't accept this from a woman after she has produced his child. I was part of the process of helping Betty to start off a new life with a new family outside the district. But because the man had made threats that he would kill her if she left him, I told her to report to the police that the threat had been made on her life.

"So I took Betty to the police station one morning to go and make a statement and have it filed, and told her I would pick her up later. By the evening they had still not attended to her. She had sat in the police station all day. So I phoned them and demanded to know why this young woman had not been attended to. I got some sarcastic response, and demanded to speak to the station commander.

"I would just like to know," I said, "why Betty was made to sit at your police station all day and no one attended to her..."

"He butted in: 'Look! I'm not here to nursemaid your black...'

"'I beg your pardon! I'm talking about simply taking a statement from somebody whose life has been threatened.' I was furious.

"As it happened I played badminton for some years with a

colonel in the police force, so I got hold of him. He was up in Pretoria doing senior security work for P W Botha. I rang him: 'Bob, I will not be spoken to like that by this commander on a matter as serious as this. I'm not going to stand for it. I want an apology from that man for the way he spoke to me. And I want an apology to Betty for not attending to her for the entire day. She has rights. She was not attended to because she's black.'

"I asked him who I should get hold of and he gave me the name of the colonel for the district, and agreed to phone him to tell him I would be contacting him. This second colonel then listened to what I had to say, and the net result of my complaint and demand was that the local acting commander was made to drive out to Deep Valley with another officer. They knocked at our door, and he introduced himself and said he had come to apologize to Betty and me. I must have needed my head examining to have done something like that, because I saw murder in his eyes. I knew it would be only a matter of time before he tried to get his revenge, and I was right. Two months later I was caught speeding in a radar speed trap on a freeway near Heidelberg and the magistrates sent notification of a fine by post. But I didn't send it back; in the rural areas like ours, usually an officer would come round with the summons, and then you'd pay the fine.

"It was the Friday afternoon before Christmas when they came and told me I was under arrest.

" 'What for?' I asked.

" 'You didn't go to court. You didn't pay your fine.'

" 'This is crazy,' I said. 'Why didn't you give me my summons?'

"They said: 'Oh. We didn't know where you lived.'

" I said: 'Of course you knew where I lived.'

" 'No,' they said, 'none of us knew where you lived. You are under arrest and you must come with us. You are to go to jail.'

"I was in a panic. I could see no way out. Because it was just before Christmas, and we were going into the weekend, there would have been no court to hear my case for at least a week. I faced the prospect of being in a prison cell for the entire Christmas holiday and possibly into the New Year for a stupid little offence.

" 'Can I go into the house?' I asked, trying to think of a way to delay them.

" 'No, get into the car now. You are wasting our time,' they insisted.

" 'Look, I'm a woman, and it's my time of the month, and I am going to get what I need,' I said angrily.

"I went into the house, locked the door, and got straight onto the phone. I said to the operator, 'Quickly, get me Heidelberg Magistrates Office as soon as you can.' Then I phoned Bob on a club call and told him they were arresting me: 'Please, Bob, you've got to get hold of the Magistrates Office and tell them I am coming in to pay before three o'clock.' I got a call back, and Bob said: 'Here's your number, quote the number, pay it at your local police station and quote my name and rank to those policemen.'

"By now they were banging on the door. I walked out of the house to the policemen and said, 'Gentlemen, I have just been given this reference number by the Heidelberg Magistrates Office, and I am now operating under the instructions of a very senior officer in the police. Here's his name, rank and number. It has been agreed between us, and the magistrate, that I should pay the fine at the police station before three o'clock. As instructed by this senior officer I will accompany you in my car, rather than travel in yours. I am sorry for all the trouble I have caused you – as you could have been preparing for Christmas this afternoon. I am so sorry.' I had foiled them, and they were very angry, but their set-up had failed. I kept my nose clean after that."

Heather and Patrick focused on trying to help people who needed it, and despite the deteriorating political situation the Deep Valley pottery continued to prosper. Heather employed more girls, most of them very young, unmarried, pregnant and homeless. The Reynolds converted the farm outbuildings where the young Zulu mothers could live with their babies. Within a year there were about seven girls staying at Deep Valley. Sometimes, they would just arrive and plead for help, and it was not in Heather's nature to turn anyone away. It was the same with animals. The farm became a menagerie of domesticated and wild animals, some sick, others just continually hungry and noisy.

There was very little employment for girls in the district, but at Deep Valley there were many jobs to do. Another important task was the mixing of the clay, the pouring, and the cutting, on the production line. Then there was the mould-making – and the African women, who had been totally unskilled, became expert potters under Heather's supervision.

More girls arrived and Heather offered them work in the garden with the bonsai trees. The Reynolds were also trying to be self-sufficient in vegetables, keeping chickens and looking after sick animals that they found or that were brought to Deep Valley. By now Heather was travelling all over the country – getting pots to Durban, and further to Cape Town, Johannesburg etc. She would pack the truck with the pots, usually pack in the kids, and just take off!

Deep Valley may have been a sanctuary for African girls, and Heather's animals, but it was also home to Heather's children, Brendan and Bronwen, whose upbringing turned out to be just as unconventional as their mother's had been. Bronwen recalls: "I think every child should grow up on a farm. It was amazing because my brother and I had the run of the place, riding our bikes and climbing trees, going to play in the cane fields, or whatever we wanted to do. It was idyllic. There was the barn where Mum did pottery and we would climb onto the roof, and draw on it with bits of hard clay. I loved the little babies of the women workers who lived in the outhouses. I used to be in their huts constantly, on the floor playing with the babies and children. As a child I wasn't conscious that they were anything different from us, that some of them may have been refugees or orphans, because they were always at Deep Valley growing up alongside us."

The active support of her children, Brendan and Bronwen, as they grew from childhood to adolescence, became a source of great reassurance to Heather. In 1988 she became the chair of the Bonsai Society, and this helped her to develop skills as a public speaker, overcoming a lack of confidence. Now, Heather was quietly drawing ever closer to God. She had grown up in the Anglican faith but as there was no Anglican church in Dalton, her young family joined the local Methodist church, and the children also joined the youth group who met every Friday evening.

Heather began to feel a developing sense of mission – a mission that God had planned, and one that she anticipated would require total dedication. For the moment, however, she was not sure where this lay. She felt she was being drawn along an unfamiliar path. Now was the time to express total dedication to God, to subjugate everything else in her life beneath his calling. "There were so many times when I really needed God and I needed miracles and I needed help." The night of her mother's visitation at the foot of her bed, Heather had vowed that she would serve God for the rest of her life. Now, as she lay in bed one night she remembers feeling very close to God. She reminded him that he needed to show her what it was that he wanted her to do. She told God that if she had to leave her family for him on her life's mission, then she would do that.

"I truly gave my entire life, every atom of my being to him that night. 'I just want to serve you, Father. Take my life and let it become a meaningful one,' I told him. I remember this warmth that filled my body, and tears of happiness were streaming down my cheeks. I felt so close to him, it was almost like he was touching me and enveloping me in his love. Next to me Patrick was sleeping while all this was happening.

He was totally unaware of it. That moment was so profound for me. I had always wanted to serve God since I was young but the intervening years and the strife I endured as a young married woman had created the doubts. Now, all those were resolved. I had proof in my own mind that God existed and I knew that for the rest of my life I was going to be a servant of the Lord."

Heather registered for a Bible diploma at the local Methodist church at Rosebank, where she could join the classes and study theology seriously. She found it hard doing assignments with the demands made by the factory, and the bonsai sales had also started to take off.

As the Reynolds invested greater time in their pottery, and more pregnant African girls arrived to live at Deep Valley, they became less involved socially with their neighbours. Most white people around Dalton regarded them as eccentric. By now, the white community was anticipating a bloodbath in the rural areas as the country moved through the transitional period to majority rule and a black government.

"I was very conscious of trying to avoid getting identified with one faction or another," says Heather. "We didn't know who was right or wrong between the black political groups, and we also took great care not to get involved in the crossfire between them. It was extremely dangerous for white people to become involved, and there were many violent attacks on whites, and even murders. We knew many of the victims."

Heather Reynolds, however, is not one to watch the world destroy itself for long. By 1989 she felt she had a role to play in helping the victims of violence. The white regime was gradually losing its grip as the world expressed its revulsion of apartheid. Militant political activism increased dramatically. South Africa was entering into the strife of the transitional years, the final phase of the apartheid era, and it was clear that majority rule was going to come at some time in the future.

In KwaZulu-Natal the Zulus split into several factions, but

mainly into two political groups: the Inkatha Freedom Party and the African National Congress. Tribal Africa, old Africa, lies just off the beaten track in every direction to the horizon in much of KwaZulu-Natal. It was in these vast tracts of land that the black-upon-black violence occurred. The Valley of a Thousand Hills at that time was inaccessible by anything more than dusty tracks and many of these became quagmires during the wet summer months. Danger lurked in many of those remote rural areas, as factions within it resisted the political creed of the African National Congress.

New socialist principles sought to remove the absolute power of the king, and break down traditional Zulu tribal structures to impose a more democratic system of local government through the election of councillors. Inkatha, or the IFP as it is known, at that time stood fiercely against the ANC. Serious conflict resulted, in which thousands died. Nowhere was the violence worse than in the valley of Swayimane. The Zulus had their own laws, their own king and their own *nkosis*. Many were violently opposed to change.

Fortunately, neither the ANC nor the IFP regarded Patrick and Heather's intervention in the valley as political. Fighting units did not stop the couple as they helped to support children, some of whom had been orphaned. On some occasions they brought bodies back from hospital to the valley for a Zulu burial. Heather recalls: "A house would be burned down, and we would be asked to go and help. Patrick would go to the Edendale Hospital mortuary to fetch the body, and try to get it back to the valley for burial. In the Zulu custom you must bury a dead person within a certain period, because it is important for the wellbeing of the soul, or spirit. There is still profound ancestral worship among the Zulus, and it has been integrated into their Christian faith.

"There were police roadblocks stopping people because it was very dangerous for strangers to drive in that area. However, we had got to know the valley so well that we knew which side roads to go down and where there wouldn't be a blockade. The police couldn't man every single entrance into the valley. You'd go from one zone – perhaps a river or a road or a hedge would delineate it as the ANC area – then the next moment you might cross into the IFP zone. You'd go through several of these pockets until you reached the house where you would drop off the body. You'd pray that nobody was going to shoot at you, because trigger-happy people might not have any idea whether you were friend or foe.

"We cultivated a network of informants who would let us know how and where to find the victims of the civil strife. We became known and also trusted by many of the people living there, who were terrified by what was going on. We were aware it was dangerous but we put our trust in God. You never really knew as you rounded a corner, or came to the crest of a hill, whether there might be huts on fire, an ambush prepared – if armed men would shoot first and ask questions afterwards. Some gangs and fighting groups did not know who we were. We were just white people in their land, which to them was justification to kill. There was terrible hatred – *umuzis* (homes) were coming under attack from armed groups who had identified a neighbour, often wrongly, as being on the other side. Thousands of homes were burned down and people killed summarily.

"The unrest didn't stop until Nelson Mandela's government took control and then the politicians and Zulu leaders worked out a peace formula that permitted a dual system of local government in which the Zulu *nkosi* and *induna* were able to work alongside the elected councillors."

One day in 1993, in the cold weather, a group of 38 destitute women and children arrived at Deep Valley, pleading for shelter and food. They had walked 20 kilometres from the Swayimane, in driving wind and rain, to find sanctuary with the Reynolds. After an attack upon their *umuzi*, they had been left with nothing but the clothes they were wearing. Heather opened up a big shed, and made a base on the floor from the newspapers used for wrapping the pots. Then she piled on underfelt and old carpeting obtained from the few friends who were still prepared to help her. They managed to find some old sheets, and then laid more newspaper over those. In fact she created a duvet of newspapers. The entire band of 38 people crawled in underneath it. They had nowhere else to go and stayed at Deep Valley for nearly two weeks.

Every morning the Zulus would sit under the same euca-lyptus tree in the garden as Heather walked past to go to the pottery. They looked upon her in silence, but in hope and expectation that she would help them. Heather had given her life to God, to serve his will, and she turned to him now. She said: "Father God, just show me how I can help these people."

Heather wept at their plight. "They had lost everything, absolutely everything. Their clothing and their few possessions were gone and only Deep Valley stood between them and star-vation. I telephoned the Red Cross, but they said they had been inundated, there was fighting going on in several locali-ties, and a state of emergency had been declared."

Heather said to Patrick: "I've got to see if I can start a self-help scheme and get these people to earn some money." She reckoned that with Patrick's studio work, her pottery and bonsai garden, and by encouraging the Zulus to learn craft-work and a variety of skills, they could jointly develop a com-plete business project. Heather prayed to God to help her get work again to earn sufficient funds to finance the project because it would take time to train the refugees, and this large new group of nearly 40 people would need food and clothes. She had been successful in the insurance business, and thought there might be something in sales, with good commission, that would earn the kind of big money they needed.

Heather didn't know what she was looking for but felt she would recognize it when she saw it. Help soon came, but from an unexpected source.

17
A LIFE-CHANGING JOURNEY

Myrtle rang from Johannesburg and said she had been working as a "temp" for a company called Roadfix. She explained they were selling a plant that manufactured asphalt for road repair projects. The company offered a total manufacturing kit or package, from crusher and mixer to conveyor belt, which was simple to operate, and the finished mix of gravel, asphalt and tar could be transported on the back of a truck in bags. It was extremely suitable for filling in potholes, and ideal for the pan-African market, where nearly all roads have gaping holes.

The cost of the entire package was just over 1 million Rand and, Myrtle said, the company was looking for salesmen to go to Northern and Central Africa and the Gulf.

"What's in it?" Heather asked.

"Ten percent commission on the million," Myrtle replied.

So I just have to sell one to some government, and get the European Union or something to fund it, and I'm home and dry, Heather thought to herself. It seemed just what she needed. God had answered her prayers! It was a one-off thing, she was looking for something big, and this was certainly the sort of solution they had envisaged.

So Heather went to Johannesburg to have an interview with the Roadfix management. She walked in and they thought it was a joke. In fact they all laughed. She was a woman, white, and the countries they wanted her to go to, like Uganda, were all very anti-South African. In fact many of these countries were providing training camps for guerrillas to fight the South African regime.

The problem for the Roadfix bosses was that no one else had asked for the job – they were stuck with Heather. So they came to an agreement that she would travel initially to both Kenya and Uganda, then on to Egypt and Dubai. They agreed to pay all of her travelling costs, but she would have to find and fund her own accommodation, and then she would receive her commission upon successful completion of the contract. Heather thought that was fair, and so she booked a ticket. Her brothers, and their families, then woke up to the fact that their sister was going off to Kenya and Uganda in Central Africa and they might not see her again. So they started trying to dissuade her from making the journey. They warned her that if she disappeared nobody would ever know what had happened to her. She looked at them and said: "Listen. I believe that this project is for God. If you think I am going alone, then you are wrong. He will be at my side."

On the face of it she now agrees that her family had good cause to be angry and scared for her, but she was convinced this was a journey God was calling upon her to make. She told them: "I trust that God will keep me safe, I'll be successful and I'll come back safely." Kenya was not dangerous, and it is not a difficult place for white South Africans. Uganda was a different proposition and presented all kinds of problems, involving both risk and logistics, for a sales expedition that was totally disorganized. Heather had no idea whom she was going to meet, who might be suitable contacts to approach, how to get in touch with the Transport Ministry, and how she was going to get about once she got there. On top of all this, she was a white woman – and a South African one at that.

She told her brothers: "The only person here who can stop me is Patrick, my husband, and if he is willing to let me go into this unknown country and raise the money we need, then there is no further argument. He could object, but he hasn't, so I'm going!" It was only then that her brothers realized just how radical she was. Her view had become both fatalistic and faithful. Even now, in the valleys where Heather goes to do her pastoral work, to help orphans for God's Golden Acre, or to set up foster homes for abandoned children, she is prepared to accept death. "I don't believe God allows his servants, his followers, or his children to be killed unless there is a reason for it. So off I went on my sales mission for Roadfix."

First, Heather flew to Nairobi, Kenya where she met government officials and gave them the plan. She then headed for Entebbe. She was late for the plane and rushed across the tarmac in the sweltering heat to the waiting aircraft. People on board were both hot and cross. They believed she'd kept them waiting on the ground needlessly. Heather got onto the plane and there was one seat left. She found herself next to another white woman; everyone else on board was black. She sat down, highly flustered, but after a while the two women started chatting.

The woman asked Heather what she was going to be doing in Uganda, and Heather told her she needed to speak to somebody in Parliament. "My first aim is to try to get somebody from the Department of Transport to have a look at this asphalt plant because they could produce the stuff, use it for their own roads, and sell the excess to Rwanda and Kenya and other neighbouring countries and make money. It could be a profitable concern," said Heather, her sales spiel rolling off her tongue.

Her travelling companion said: "Oh, that's very interesting, and it could be quite easy to arrange, because my husband is working in Parliament at the moment."

She added: "As a matter of fact, he's coming from Parliament to Entebbe to pick me up. I'm then going to drop him off back there and drive home. You must come and stay with us."

This was marvellous. Heather had only just arrived on the plane, and within a few minutes, she had a place to stay, and a route to members of the government. And so her new friend's husband picked them up from the airport. Heather met him, and he drove the two women to Parliament. They waited until there was a tea-break and then he introduced Heather to the deputy minister of transport, with whom she had a brief meeting and made arrangements to have a further meeting at the tennis club on the following Sunday.

That evening the host said to Heather: "Why don't you use one of my vehicles and a driver and have a look around Kampala?" This was just what Heather needed. They scouted around the provincial part of Uganda within striking distance of the capital, and went to see the source of the Nile, among many other features of the country. She did not get to see the famous gorillas, which was a great source of disappointment but the trip there was fully booked. However, everything she had read about Uganda, and its verdant beauty, was confirmed.

In the meantime Heather had the arranged meeting with the deputy transport minister at the all-African but nevertheless colonial-style tennis club, and discovered that it was exclusively male. She walked in, expecting to be laughed at again, or worse, but they were courteous and gave her lunch, and listened to her. "We talked through the whole procedure and they were very interested and suggested we might make the project possible by linking up with Chinese funding and investment. The minister and his team could see that the process was extremely relevant to Uganda where the road network is riddled with potholes. I came away with the distinct impression that the men had seen an opportunity and would come back to me in South Africa if they could secure the Chinese investors. If they were successful, they said they would send the Chinese team to South Africa to negotiate a deal on their behalf. They then provided me with a car to take me back to my friends' house."

The following day was the last of her visit. Heather and her driver bodyguard had by now visited all the interesting places to go locally. What would he like to do, she asked? He said he'd like to go and see his family. He was a resourceful man and soon produced a car and so they went off shortly after dawn. His village was incredibly far away. They went right up past Mbali, far into the bush along dusty track roads, and it was near there that they passed a small village. Heather relates: "There were children from the village all around. But I noticed that there was something about these youngsters that worried me – they weren't laughing. They were absolutely quiet. Normally, if children see a strange woman, they will at least talk among themselves. But there was this eerie silence. The children stared – but without expression. Eventually I couldn't stand it, so I asked the Ugandan driver: 'What's wrong with these kids?' "

The man said to her: "These are the AIDS orphans."

Heather asked: "What do you mean – orphaned by AIDS?"

He replied: "Well, the parents have died."

In an instant it became clear. Heather will remember it for the rest of her life. "Now you see, at that point, in South Africa in 1992/93, we were faced with political upheavals in the country and the change from apartheid. We'd heard about the HIV virus and AIDS-related diseases, but it was in San Francisco, in the gay community, or in Central Africa. I hadn't made the connection until that moment. With a start, I realized I was in Central Africa! I was just horrified. 'And so, who's going to look after them?' I asked.

" 'Nobody,' he said.

" 'But surely,' I insisted, 'there must be churches or somebody.'

"He said: 'Yes, there are. There are some Roman Catholic missions but not here.' "

Heather was stunned. She realized that Uganda was a vast country and that a few missionaries, here and there, were but a drop in the ocean. She decided to look inside one of the village huts. She was about to come face to face with the effects of possibly the world's greatest catastrophe since the bubonic plague.

"There were two children lying on the floor on a mat. One lay on her side, was completely motionless, and I think she was already dead. The other was so sick he had probably less than another day to live. His body was covered in a dirty cloth and his eyes were glazed. I came close to him and stared long and hard into his mournful eyes. I have seen many like him since, and know I will see many more in my lifetime. However, this was a first time for me. I thought to myself: *These children are starving to death*."

As Heather looked at the dying boy, who might have been three years old, she realized her journey to the hut had been no coincidence. God had guided her there to show her the way forward. It was the mission for which she had been waiting. The words of Jesus came into her mind: "Anything you did for one of my brothers here, however humble, you did for me." (Matthew 25:40, New English Bible)

"I made my pledge with God. I knew now that this was the work I was supposed to do. He had brought me here." She broke the silence in the hut as she said aloud: "God, from this day on, I will help every child in need, every child that needs a home, every child that needs food that crosses my path. I will see to it. I promise you."

Later she told Patrick: "I made that pledge easily and willingly as I looked at the poor child dying on the mat without the comfort of an adult. We were silent and didn't speak. There was no common language for us to communicate in."

What struck Heather hardest was that this was an unnecessary death. A child's life was being taken away because he was unable to get food. He was starving to death because he had no parents. Here was just a little person wasting away in front of her from malnutrition. Just alone in a room! In that moment her thoughts were like snapshot images. She was out-raged at what she saw as the total failure of Western society and the Christian church. She wrote later:

> We have reached the moon, we have a spaceship out in the solar system, past Neptune and Pluto, we have communications systems so fantastic that we can put encyclopedias on silicon chips, we can cut the cornea of an eye with a laser. We are incredibly advanced technologically – but we can't see to the feeding of starving children in the world. All over the Western world, people are getting on with their ordered and well-fed lives and they are oblivious, or worse, indifferent, to what is happening here.

It shocked Heather so much she felt sick. She felt ashamed for humankind. Then she looked at herself and thought: *I'm part of that society.* Her mind was racing: *There are a billion Christians in the world, and millions of those in the West are earning good salaries, enough surely to give substantially – and yet we can't come together to help the starving!*

She walked out of the hut, weeping in both grief and rage. Slowly, she composed herself and told the frightened body-guard driver that they could now go on and see his family. She didn't say anything to him about her experience, or her feelings. In fact, she doesn't recall much about meeting his family.

She vaguely remembers getting back to her hosts late that evening. They were cross and worried. She apologized that she would have to leave almost immediately to get to the airport. Heather was no longer at the dinner table in her mind. She was already on a mission. Something had happened inside her. She was struggling to cope with emotions and what she had discovered. "I left my hosts and I checked into a hotel. I had to be completely alone."

She telephoned Patrick and was crying down the phone as she said: "I've got to come back to Uganda. We've got work here. There are children starving and dying. And they've been left alone. It's the HIV virus."

He said: "Look, let's talk about it when you get home."

Next day, she took a flight back to Nairobi and checked into the Stanley Hotel. Once in her room she collapsed and cried for hours for the little children of Uganda. Over and over in her mind she thought to herself: *These young children are little more than babies and they are trying to cope, to stay alive, but their parents are dead. They have no support through their grief, and thousands of them are becoming sick, some with HIV. They have no food to eat.*

It was the awful fact that they were dying alone. The little boy she found would die alone. There was nobody to hold him, nobody to comfort him. There might have been an older brother or sister around, but there was nobody attending to him. Heather couldn't speak his language, so there had been no communication between them whatsoever. She felt helpless, hopeless and guilty that she had not been able to do anything to save him. She sat on the edge of the bed and thought. What, logically, could she do quickly? She recalls: "I thought to myself, *I can't wait until I get back to South Africa. I'm going crazy!*"

Then she thought – maybe she could write a letter to the *Natal Witness*, and tell them what she had seen, and hope and pray that there would be somebody out there who was not interested just in politics, and who would pick up the cost, maybe sponsor a trip for her to get back there. She didn't know whether it would work, but she understood she was doing God's work now. She knew nothing about fundraising, but she must, and would, succeed.

Then she thought: *I need a name for this project. It must be something African.* She thought of many African words and expressions, but then realized she was thinking in Zulu. Hopeless! Then, all of a sudden and from nowhere, "God's Golden Acre" came into her head – it just wafted in.

Heather immediately rejected it. "Can you imagine?" she says. "From a marketing point of view at that time it would be a crazy name to choose because people would think it was some kind of fundamentalist sect, perhaps like those crazy people who had all committed suicide in America."The name didn't reveal that it was about children, or suggest anything about her mission. Mentioning God's name would make it unacceptable for a donor who might not be "into" Christianity. So she tossed "God's Golden Acre" right out. It kept coming back – a bit like a tune someone can't get out of her head. Heather prayed: "God, are you trying to make this thing impossible for me, having been an atheist? Is this your way of making things hard for me?"

She told God: "Believe me, I know about marketing. This is the wrong way to market. This name is not right. Red Cross, Salvation Army... they tell us a little bit about what they are doing in your name. 'God's Golden Acre' doesn't tell us anything about children, about helping little children..." The name kept coming back. Eventually Heather said: "OK, Lord. If it's going to be 'God's Golden Acre', I will follow you."

Heather had never written a song in her life or created a tune. Now, with incredible speed, her head was filled with both. "I thought then, *God's Golden Acre, give a child a home project, don't let them die all alone.* This exact moment in my life became another great turning point. I will remember it vividly for ever. As I sat on the bed in that room in the Stanley Hotel, my world began to change course, and I believe God came to me. I can't even read music. But a song, music, a tune, came into my head, almost word perfect. I don't know how long it took, how long I sat there, but a song just came out from within."

Give a child a home, give a child a home,
don't let them die all alone,
on God's Golden Acre they'll get to know their maker,
give a child a home,
give to God on high,
give to God on high,
we'll meet him by and by,
on God's Golden Acre
we'll work for our creator,
give a child a home,
give a child a home,
give a child a home,
let them into your heart,
to God's Golden Acre,
that's where we are going to take her,
give a child a home,
to God's Golden Acre,
that's where we are going to take her,
give a child a home...

This song has since become the vehicle of Heather's simple faith in God. It is not a tune copied from any other in the world. It came to her in that moment in the Nairobi hotel, and to her was a miracle. When times were hard – and they would get agonizingly tough in the coming years – the song inspired her. She would sing it, or the orphans would sing it, and then she would feel reassurance. It underpinned her faith.

Since then Heather has written over 20 songs and this has provided her with the strength to believe that he would also give her every quality that she would need in her struggle. "So it was more than a song. It was also a promise to me, showing me God's way of how he can change you, and give you some gift like that. At that moment in the hotel room the song also took away the grief and depression that I was feeling."

Part Three

18
THE ESTABLISHMENT OF GOD'S GOLDEN ACRE

The next day, Heather flew back to South Africa and the first thing that she discovered when she got home was that the refugees had moved back to Swayimane. To everyone's relief, they had found support in their own community in the valley. The second thing she discovered was that the Reynolds' time at Deep Valley had come to an end. The landlord had notified them that he needed the homestead for his son, who was getting married. It was the end of a highly significant twelve years for the Reynolds family, of ups and downs, great happiness and joy, and sometimes despair. They were sorry to go, but realized that as one cycle was ending, another was just beginning. The Reynolds viewed the future with both determination and optimism.

The new home, and what was to become the first proper location for God's Golden Acre, was a farmhouse called Kort-Kraanzkloof, by a little gorge and in a beautiful setting, in the village of Wartburg. It was also within the German community, about 20 kilometres from Deep Valley. The Wartburg farm was a big settlement, and easily large enough to accommodate all the Africans in the community. It had a spacious farmhouse, lots of subsidiary buildings, and an outbuilding for cattle that the Reynolds converted into a pottery.

Meanwhile, anxious for the finance to get started on her project in Uganda, Heather followed up the lead she had made for Roadfix there to find out if the Chinese had come over and signed a contract with the company for 1 million Rand. It soon transpired that the Chinese had indeed come over to Johannesburg at the invitation of the Roadfix directors. Myrtle was in the office and knew about the meeting. Heather waited for her 10 percent but nothing happened. A month later she phoned up and was told: "Oh, the company has gone bankrupt." She made a few more enquiries about the people involved, but nobody seemed to know anything about anybody or anything and she reluctantly came to accept that she had lost her money.

A few weeks after their move to Wartburg, Heather and Patrick were sitting and talking, and watching TV. It was a Sunday night and a programme came on about AIDS. It explained that Acquired Immunity Deficiency Syndrome developed from a viral infection caused by the HIV-1 virus. This virus slowly killed off the autoimmune system with the result that immunity, and thus resistance to any normal infection, was drastically reduced. A paediatrician called Dr Neil McKerrow was being interviewed. He was talking about statistics and they were horrifying. He said that an estimated 2 million children were going to be orphaned in Southern Africa in the next decade, and people had already started dying.

Heather thought: *What!* The doctor was so sure of his facts; he was even talking about so many deaths a day, and about the figures peaking. These were horrendous statistics. Of course, Heather and Patrick had heard of AIDS, and had talked with the girls in the pottery in order to support AIDS awareness. They had stressed to them the importance of being careful. But the Reynolds didn't realize that the virus had moved into South Africa.

The programme credits revealed that Dr McKerrow was a well-known paediatrician at Edendale Hospital in Pietermaritzburg. The next morning Heather phoned him and told him she'd seen terrible things in Uganda, with a whole village full of children left without adults. Dr McKerrow said: "Yes, that's so, because people have been up there to study and see what is happening."

Heather said: "Well, I want to go and start an orphanage there and help the children."

There was a pause, then he said: "Heather, you would be better off to stay here, and help Zulu children. You tell me you live in a rural area. Go and find out what is happening. You'll find there are children who have been orphaned by AIDS within a few miles of where you are."

She said: "What?"

"Oh, sure," said the doctor. "Within a few years your valley – the one you are taking care of because of the civil war – is going to be affected. My advice to you is to stay exactly where you are, because you already know the people in those rural areas, and that will be a great help. You could help your own people."

He continued: "Listen, as hard as it may seem, forget about Uganda. Just stay where you are; we need people like you here. You speak Zulu. You know and understand the Zulu culture."

"But," Heather stammered, "where do I start? I haven't got a clue where to start."

He said: "Look, it's your vision. You and God."

"Yeah, but I need some practical advice."

He paused and then said: "OK. The first thing I would say is, make sure you tell everybody what you are going to do. Always, if you are going to do anything, let everybody know, because already many people in several organizations are doing good work."

He added: "They are looking after people who already have AIDS here in South Africa. Get hold of the AIDS Training Centre. Speak to Toni, and ask her to help you. Ask her to send invitations to key people. Then get them together and tell them where you are coming from so that they will know you – and know about God's Golden Acre. Then, people might trust you. But don't just start something and end up feeling isolated. If people aren't sure who you are, you probably won't get the support you need."

Heather thought that was good advice. "But nobody's going to come if they think I'm some eccentric or radical Christian woman who has just come from Uganda and..."

He interrupted: "Well, that's your problem..."

She said: "Neil, I need somebody like you to come and talk. If you were coming to that meeting, people would come."

"Well, you haven't asked me yet."

She asked: "Are you a Christian?"

"No," he replied.

Heather felt foolish suddenly. She'd being going on and on about how God had sent her to Uganda, how God had given her this and that, how God had guided her every step – and he was an atheist!

She persisted however: "Well, would you come?"

"Sure," he said.

"Would you chair the meeting?"

"Yes."

Neil ended the conversation with the following advice: "By the way, don't put all your energy into opening an orphanage. Consider the cluster foster care concept. That means creating small family units around a foster parent and giving that small nucleus, of perhaps six or seven people, all the help and support it needs to sustain itself."

The next day Heather contacted Toni, the secretary of the AIDS Training Centre, and they set up a meeting at the training centre in Pietermaritzburg. Toni helped Heather to build up her address book, and offered to send out all the invitations announcing that Neil was going to chair the meeting. Heather eventually met him on the day of the meeting. He was one of a very interesting group of people who attended. She didn't expect such a response, but to her astonishment the small hall was full. She recalls: "Neil chaired the meeting and introduced me and my concept of God's Golden Acre. I nervously got up to speak. However, being nervous is a stimulant. I suddenly felt fired up and off I went, straight into it. Afterwards I invited a smaller group – who I thought might be in a position to help me – to sit on the God's Golden Acre committee."

As far as the meeting went, Heather later realized that she had made a mistake. When she stood up to give her talk, her passion took over and indeed overwhelmed her. "I didn't just say that I wanted to start a cluster foster care centre. I jumped too far ahead, possibly because I had had time to think through my longer-term plans, about making the centre and its satellite community sustainable. So I told them how I planned to help the children, but then bring in life skills, resource centres – how we could earn money, as we do now, for instance, with the Young Zulu Warriors, and with art exhibitions – and how we would train these children to become skilled to do jobs, such as being motor mechanics and builders etc."

Heather sounded to them like a woman who had got nothing, but wanted to do a huge project, rather than start with something limited and nurture it into something bigger. They were asking themselves whether or not she was big on dreams but short on reality. Next day, Karen Stone, the lawyer, phoned her up. She said to Heather: "It was just overwhelming. You came across with so much passion about God's Golden Acre, and with so much stuff, that you overwhelmed me!"

Heather had learned a valuable lesson. If a person has got huge vision, others often can't get their heads around it. They won't just jump to it. Most people can accept one goal at a time. So give them small goals. Nowadays, she always reminds herself that while she might have the big picture, it is better to be cautious, and add on piece by piece, slowly, until the whole picture is finished.

Now, she had created doubts in the minds of some people.

Thanks to her extreme and wild enthusiasm, there were those who thought she was going to be a loose cannon, and not perhaps wholly reliable. A few days later, however, Professor Ron Nicholson agreed he would be chairman of God's Golden Acre, and a Dutch missionary doctor, Dr Gerrit Ter Haar, volunteered to be deputy chairman. Both subsequently turned out to be brilliant – wise, kind and gentle – and Heather numbers them both among her most special friends and mentors. Dr Ter Haar's background had been in medical missionary work in the Transkei where he had developed a hospital and community health service amongst the Xhosa people. He had come out fresh from the Netherlands as a young man in the 1960s and was a capable administrator in his field.

He recalls: "After retirement I moved to Pietermaritzburg and started a health programme for a local radio station and in the process interviewed all kinds of humanitarian people – amongst them Heather. I think we had an immediate rapport, a lot in common." Then he discovered to his astonishment that all the Reynolds' personal financial resources were being drawn into helping the children who were brought to Heather, and also those whom she helped in the valley. From that moment he became one of her closest supporters and admirers. "I planned to raise funds for her so that her personal income could be separated from the project funds," he wrote.

Heather recalls: "I started to put my management board into place, to create a proper constitution for God's Golden Acre, and to initiate policies that would give us goals and a procedural way to operate. None of it was an easy process – I even encountered problems with formulating a constitution, until a lawyer came to my rescue. I knew I would have to have an acceptable constitution in place if we wanted to raise money. The problem was, I'd never written a constitution in my life, and although my management board had said they were prepared to support me, they couldn't help me with a constitution."

At three o'clock one morning she was still struggling with it. She said: "God, I have done everything I can. I don't know what more to do about this constitution. I don't have the expertise to write one." She fell asleep with it still incomplete.

The next evening, Heather went to the local Wesleyan chapel to give a talk. Afterwards a man came up to her and said: "I don't know if I can be of any use, but if there is anything I can do for you let me know."

She said: "Well, what is your background?"

He said: "I'm a lawyer, an advocate."

So Heather confided: "Well, I've been up till three o'clock this morning trying to write a constitution and I have got the basic things done, but I have no idea how to finish it."

"Oh, no problem at all," he replied. "Come to my office tomorrow and if you don't mind waiting for a few minutes I'll stick it in my 'in' tray and work on it."

However, Heather's vision for God's Golden Acre, its aspirations, and her trust that God would help her in achieving her goals often received a sceptical reception from non-Christians involved in the fight against the AIDS pandemic. Heather acquired a reputation for being too reliant upon her faith. "It was extremely humiliating," she says. "I clearly remember one awful, awful moment. I was sitting in a CINDI (Children in Distress) meeting in Pietermaritzburg. I knew people were impatient with me and my thoughts. I had sat patiently, waiting for my turn to say something, and I started speaking, and then this woman with a sneer on her face – I'll never forget it – said, 'Oh Heather, Heather and her God... they're going to solve the entire AIDS problem.'

"I was no great speaker. I was crushed, and felt humiliated. She just put me down with her actions and her words, and sometimes with that particular woman, when I was speaking, you could almost feel her sneer, it was so obvious. And all I was trying to do was to make useful suggestions. My work would be at the coalface in the deep rural areas and they were working in the urban areas; sometimes our problems were not quite the same. I became extremely disillusioned with an organization I had supported from its inception.

"Even Gerrit himself had to defend me at times when I was speaking to somebody about my vision. Eventually, however, we were ready to take in orphans from the valley. We were in business. The first visible signs of the AIDS pandemic were already appearing in the valley. By 1995 you could see the familiar pattern of people losing a lot of weight, becoming weaker, and frightened people asking themselves: Is it AIDS?"

Heather had realized earlier that she should become more knowledgeable about AIDS-related diseases and the HIV virus, and learn about how it was going to impact on the local communities. So she joined every organization she could find in Pietermaritzburg that was concerned with it. "I went to every conference. I went to every seminar and every work-shop. There were all sorts of ideas being thrown around about the value of nutrition, high vitamin C intake, high antioxi-dants, and various medications. Patrick and I were really focussed on studying to find ways of helping the children to survive. For example, we spent quite a lot of money on get-ting things with high antioxidants in them to treat children that were very ill, to see if we could boost their immune sys-tems. We used powdered baby milk with a high fat content believing it might help to strengthen the babies. We didn't have a lot of success at that time, but then most of our little children were very ill.

"As I began to visit the valley I found there was a social stigma about the HIV/AIDS virus. This in turn was leading to isolation and rejection. Those who were afflicted experienced shame from contracting the virus – and usually rejection by family and friends." In those early days in the valley Heather was almost always entirely alone, the only white person for miles in a world where normal life had broken down for an increasing number of family groups – as the adults began to die.

Heather was in Swayimane one day at the homestead of the Jila family when a group of fourteen or so youngsters, who knew some of the girls at the pottery, approached her. They had heard about Heather's work helping the victims of the violence and then of AIDS, and so they asked her to take them on as their choirmaster. These youngsters, several of whom were related, it turned out, had been selected and trained initially by an old man who had been killed during the violence, and they wanted to carry on as a choir with a new master.

"At that time," says Heather, "I was quite shocked because I did not have a clue about music. I did not know what to say. I had no experience and wondered what I would do with them. I looked at this bunch of little people and thought, *What have I got here?* What could I do with a Zulu choir? These children had nothing. Some were orphans. The others came from families impoverished by the civil war. You could see the expectancy on their faces. I would have devastated them if I had made an excuse. They reasoned I would know exactly what to do with a choir, because in their minds I knew everything. To them, it just required me to say yes!

"Thoughts were racing through my mind: *What will be expected of me? What am I supposed to do?* I couldn't say no! I wouldn't have been able to get the word out of my mouth. Their passion and commitment made it impossible for me to refuse."

Heather's response was automatic, and later she would realize it was a defining moment. "Yes! Of course, I'd be delighted," she told them without much conviction. "Stand over there and let me hear how you sound." They formed into a group, and she sat on the one chair in the room. Then they started singing.

"The moment I heard them, I experienced an almost indescribable feeling. My spirits were soaring, yet I was choking

Heather as a baby in the garden of the trading station run by her parents near Mtubatuba in KwaZulu-Natal.

An early picture of the McLellan children taken at the trading station near Mtubatuba in KwaZulu-Natal in the 1950s. At the back is Heather's oldest brother Kenny, second row left to right, Myrtle and David, front row Basil and Heather. When they were older, the children roamed far and wide during their holidays – fishing expeditions to rivers like the Mtentu were especially popular.

Heather, born in 1952, with her older sister Myrtle, born 1949.

The family group pictured at Heather's first marriage to Sarel Olivier in 1972.

Heather's parents Brenda and John McLellan.

Sarel and Heather after their wedding. No photographs shot that day showed her smiling. A few days before, she had asked her mother to 'postpone' the marriage.

Heather and Patrick's wedding in 1979 was altogether a happier occasion for the bride – who knew she had met both her soul-mate for life, as well as a faithful husband.

Heather and Patrick found Deep Valley in a newspaper advertisement in 1983 when they decided as a young couple to give up office work and become artists. It was a rather ramshackle German-style farmhouse but they lovingly restored it into a comfortable home and created a pottery for bonsai pots.

The Deep Valley years in the 1980s are remembered for the 'English-style' tea parties for the children in the garden with homemade bread and cakes. This occasion was a birthday party for one of the children.

Moving in! Proud mother Heather shows her two toddlers Brendan and Bronwen round the gardens at Deep Valley in 1983. The family recalls the long hot summers and blue skies.

Brendan and Bronwen had the run of the glorious garden at Deep Valley which was redesigned by Heather.

Bronwen, born 1980, recalls her mother's strong Christian faith from a very young age.

Bronwen as a woman says of her mother....*there isn't a daughter alive as blessed as I am, and none loves her mum more than me.*

Building a business. The pottery at Deep Valley became a thriving business – Heather's pots for bonsai trees were being sold all over South Africa by 1988.

Heather became an expert self-taught potter, creating a wide range of pots for bonsai trees in a variety of shapes and glazed colours.

From a very young age Heather regarded her disabled oldest brother Kenny as her special responsibility. Even in childhood she took over the duties of looking after him from Brenda McLellan whenever possible. Towards the end of his life Kenny came to live at Deep Valley where he looked after the garden and the chickens. He died in 1984.

Wherever you find Heather you will find animals. She is a Good Samaritan to her fellow humans, but when it comes to four and two-legged creatures she will never turn one away.

Patrick and Brendan developed a strong bond over the years as father and son.

After the move to Wartburg and the establishment of God's Golden Acre in the mid-1990's, Mary Van der Leeuw became one of Heather's earliest supporters and a member of the board. When Heather decided Khayelihle should be the new home for GGA in 1998 it was Mary who said...*Heather, if it's your vision, we'll stand by you.*

Marianne Jenum and Vibeke Blaker from Norway were among the first volunteers to work at God's Golden Acre at Wartburg and over the years have become successful ambassadors and fund-raisers for GGA in their country.

The lively lads! Sbo, Siphamandla and Siyabonga, three young teenage boys who Heather brought from the valley to live at Wartburg in 1997. They slept in the back of an old 'combi' and became close to Marianne and Vibeke - after being caught spying on them in their bedroom.

A classic picture of Heather at Wartburg. She grew accustomed to sharing her bed with one of the baby orphans – and usually one of the dogs managed to sneak in as well.

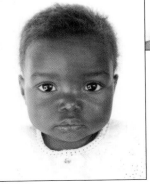

Megan's was a story of tragedy. She was found in the sugarcane with a twin sister who died shortly afterwards – but Megan survived into infancy. Heather loved Megan dearly and remembers her as the most beautiful baby she ever nursed.

Cheeky chappie! Marcus is one of the great characters at God's Golden Acre who delights visitors with his outward going and friendly manner. He came to GGA as a premature baby and was one of those who spent much of his infancy in Heather's bedroom at night.

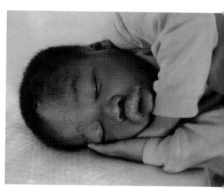

Chummy is one of the most popular children at God's Golden Acre with his handsome face and wise eyes. He has accompanied Heather on several trips abroad and his spellbinding treble voice, once heard, is an experience never forgotten.

The little angel sleeps. Susiwe has had a difficult infancy because of sickness, but the loving and caring manner of GGA nurses, and plenty of good nourishment since she was a small baby, has brought hope for Susiwe's future.

Lucy Foster, seen here holding Thabiso, was one of the first volunteers to arrive at God's Golden Acre, Khayelihle, near Cato Ridge, after it became the new HQ of GGA. She wrote...*you will find 97 happy children – Heather is responsible for most of them being alive!*

Practical help arrives. Volunteer Orin Wilson, who had been a longstanding friend of Bronwen, made a significant contribution in improving the standard of living for everyone at Khayelihle, Cato Ridge, in 1999 thanks to his building and electrical work.

The GGA building team and volunteers built the Hospice and this allowed the sick children to receive a higher level of professional nursing - and also acted as a sanctuary within a sanctuary for the new babies arriving.

Spick and span. When the refurbishment of Mons House at Khayelihle was completed in 1999 it became once more an imposing farmhouse. In the early years Mons House accommodated the children and later became an activity centre.

Gerrit and Anneke Mons from Holland mortgaged their home so that God's Golden Acre could buy Khayelihle, Cato Ridge in 1998. They visit regularly and are always received with joy by the children. Gerrit wrote... *the children call us Oupa and Ouma (grandfather and grandmother) and we love them so much that sometimes we can hardly speak.*

Muslim students were among those who built the pre-primary school at God's Golden Acre. It is now a well-equipped little centre staffed by volunteers where the toddlers and small children are prepared for local primary schools.

The housing and communal dining room projects at God's Golden Acre marked the beginning of a new era after the millennium. It became a cluster foster care community – with each house becoming home for a specific number of children living with African foster mothers and aunties.

Heather is determined that all the children at God's Golden Acre will grow up as Zulus, thoroughly familiar with their culture, customs, and food. Pictured are some of the gogos, foster mothers, and aunties who look after the 97 children living in the community.

Nearly finished! After several years sleeping in a bedroom behind the office, Heather and Patrick were able to move into their own magnificent home at God's Golden Acre Khayelihle in 2004 where they can enjoy – at least some – well-deserved privacy.

The view of the valley from Heather's new home in the grounds of GGA.

Making a splash! The resort at Khayelihle has been refurbished and is now the major play area for the children when they are home from school. It means that most have learned to swim from a young age and the toddlers soon become accustomed to the water.

Wholesome food. Gradually GGA is trying to become self-sustaining in its food production both in poultry and cultivation of fruit and vegetables.

The new dining room at GGA means that when cultural and sports events are organised visitors can be catered for. When all the community needs to come together – such as at Yuletide and Easter and other special occasions like birthday parties – the true Christian spirit of God's Golden Acre can be fostered in one room.

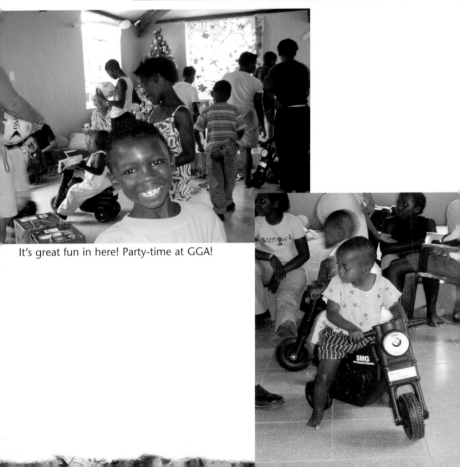

It's great fun in here! Party-time at GGA!

A joyful place to be. Despite the traumas and abuse that some of the children have suffered, God's Golden Acre is above all a joyful and happy place to be where the children smile and have lots of fun in a big family atmosphere.

Gogo Beauty is one of the legends of God's Golden Acre where she is loved by the children and regarded by the Reynolds as one of the family. She is pictured here with her daughter Zani who also works as a carer at GGA.

Gogo Beauty with Marcus who she has helped to bring up in the Zulu culture.

Heather is now a granny figure to the children of GGA. Mothering is the responsibility of the African foster mothers and aunties. At first this broke Heather's heart. Now she carries the responsibility for a more strategic role in the fight against the AIDS pandemic and so inevitably had to give up the day-to-day care of her babies. *Sometimes with all the sadness and tragedy I encounter in the valley, and when I am missing my babies at night, I feel like crying till I die.*

Death has stalked tens of thousands of families in the valley. The graves, created from stones, and usually marked by a wooden cross, are found in the gardens of the umuzi where the Zulu families live.

SNE.11-7-96-16-7-03

In a quiet corner of God's Golden Acre at Cato Ridge the young children who have died there are buried. They are not forgotten, and at Christmas and other religious festivals the children gather around and sing hymns led by Gogo Heather.

The famous white Landrover that for thousands of people in the Valley of a Thousand Hills has become a symbol of hope. Mawethu (our mother) is a familiar and much-loved figure to the Africans who live in the rural areas and she is almost always welcome wherever she goes.

This mother, only in her mid-20's, is HIV-positive and knows she is dying. She is among tens of thousands of young women in the rural areas of KwaZulu-Natal who are infected with the deadly virus. One small comfort for this mother is that her children will be safe with mawethu, who came to her in her moment of greatest need.

These orphans are among the luckier ones in the valley. Heather, working with government community welfare officers will ensure that either they are integrated into a granny-led family group - supported by an outreach programme – or brought into sanctuary at GGA Khayelihle, Cato Ridge.

In tens of thousands of cases, the mantle of motherhood falls upon the oldest daughter, usually a girl in her early teens. It is a hard and precarious existence just made possible by support from outreach programmes like those run by God's Golden Acre. The girls usually accept their role with courage and humour. Heather: *There is a dignity and standard among these young girls. You can drop in here any time and you will find them clean and tidy, and if they have been in the garden, or putting cow dung down on the floor, they'll quickly wash their hands and slip on a clean top.*

The child-led orphan families exist on a simple diet supplied largely by outreach programmes. Heather: *Imagine if we weren't there. What would have happened to them? Their house would have collapsed. Where would this girl and her four siblings have gone?*

Heather remains on excellent terms with King Zwelithini Goodwill kaBHEKUZULU, King of the Zulu Nation (below). A party of Japanese volunteers is pictured with Queen Buhle (left).

The Zulu Theatre, set in the grounds of God's Golden Acre, Khayelihle, was completed towards the end of 2004 and has become a cultural focus for the valley.

God's Golden Acre has become a leading cultural centre in the Valley of a Thousand Hills for traditional African song and dance. There are several choirs and dance groups. The child and adult members – drawn both from GGA Khayelihle and the valley – are now performing locally, regionally, nationally, and overseas. Varied sounds of continual rehearsal echo from the thatched Zulu Theatre and Mons House and are among the poignant memories that visitors carry away with them.

They are in rural Africa, their sense and intuitions sharpened by the air, the light, the sounds of the greatest continent on earth, and perhaps 50 metres away the throbbing drumbeat of the boys and girls in rehearsal for a concert. Are they dreaming? Why, no! It's real! It's part of the magic, mystique, and perhaps, the sheer witchcraft of Africa. They feel more alive, more aware, more excited, and perhaps closer to God than anywhere else.

Heather at the opening ceremony of the Zulu Theatre.

Trips to the seaside are an integral part of life at God's Golden Acre for the children and they are often led by Gogo Heather who takes charge for a weekend - or day trip - in one of the GGA vehicles.

THE LIFELINE. Orphaned families led by a granny figure – or a teenage girl – receive food supplies once a month that helps to sustain them but is rarely sufficient to meet all needs. The God's Golden Acre rural outreach programmes are now bringing food and clothing to hundreds of families - but much more remains to be done. There are tens of thousands in the Valley of the Thousand Hills who have not yet been reached.

It's lunchtime at God's Golden Acre and the children who are not away at school in the daytime eat communally in the new dining room which can also be used for catering at special events.

The new houses at God's Golden Acre were designed to make them feel like family homes to the children. The older boys and girls are segregated and each has a support team of adults and volunteers.

One day in 2003 Heather was in the huge Kwa Ximba valley and saw a group of boys loitering around and sniffing glue to alleviate their hunger. She took this as a message from God that she should take the lead role in creating a structure to enable the children to play organised league football to give them a better life. Through the author's friendship with Martin Edwards, President of Manchester United, Heather went on to meet several men and women at the top of British professional football, and also from the worldwide sports equipment company NIKE. Collectively they came to her assistance in what she regards as another miracle.

The God's Golden Acre Junior League Association was brought into being thanks to the help and co-operation of the local Thandanani League and Nkosi Mlaba. Soon thousands of youngsters – boys and girls - will be getting the chance to play for teams in organised leagues. Heather hopes the GGA Junior League will become a benchmark for other associations wishing to develop football for youth in the rural areas of South Africa.

In the same year Heather was invited to Old Trafford, the home of Manchester United, by club President Martin Edwards. She is seen with him holding the world famous FA Cup.

Heather at the Football Association in London in 2004 with (left to right) Ann Smith, Chief Fundraiser for GGA UK, Alastair Bennett, Director of External Relations Football Foundation, Dave Richards, Chairman of the F.A. Premier League, Heather Reynolds, David Davies, Executive Director, Football Association, Jane Bateman, Head of International Relations, Football Association.

Not often caught on camera! Patrick Reynolds is a retiring man of few words who prefers to work quietly in his studio at God's Golden Acre. He is regarded as one of South Africa's leading sculptors of the living form and in the early years of GGA his work largely subsidised it.

Oprah Winfrey has played an increasingly important role at God's Golden Acre since her first visit there in 2002. She is now a close friend and supporter of Heather and 'mother' figure to some of the orphans.

While many Western children cannot get out of their school uniform quickly enough when they get home, African children in the Valley of a Thousand Hills regard their school uniform with the highest level of pride. For many it is their most treasured possession because it gives them a sense of belonging and is a ticket for an education.

back tears. I thought to myself: *They are not just good, they are wonderfully good!* Somehow, at that moment, Heather knew that these young men and women were going to become an important part of her life. "I taught them phonetically because they couldn't read, or understand the English. They'd learn the songs by ear, picking up the words from me as I sang slowly, and going over the lines again and again. They were all very quick to learn. They would sing at funerals, they would sing at weddings, and other Zulu festivals and events."

One night the sky was darkening across the valley as Heather neared the last drop-off point for the members of the younger choir who had practised together that day. As she stopped the "bakkie", a woman made her way hurriedly towards the car. The desperation on her face was all too familiar. She knew of a family that was in dire need of help, and had a sick baby who would not last much longer without medical attention. Heather later wrote:

In response to my enquiry as to where or how far away the family lived, she pointed vaguely over the hill and assured me it wasn't far. Some older children climbed in the back of the bakkie to give directions and we set off to find them. Two hours later, along a treacherous path that seemed to be fading away altogether as the rocky hillside became more uneven, we came at last upon the broken hut.

As I climbed out of the vehicle, with the engine still running, as we'd had much trouble with the battery and I dared not turn it off, a little girl only about ten years old came out of the hut. She didn't falter, but walked straight into my arms and held onto me. I'll never forget it. Her simple trust – it was as if in some way she had been expecting me.

I said "hello" and asked her how she was. She led me to her younger siblings, a girl of six, a boy of four, and the youngest, a two-year-old girl. The baby girl was very ill, Sandisile explained, but she didn't know what to do to make her better. She handed me the child, and as my hands held her wet and sticky thighs and buttocks, my first thought was that she'd messed herself and wasn't wearing a nappy.

The bakkie's headlights pierced the growing darkness, and as I held the child closer to the light, I realised in horror that the stickiness was in fact a mass of wet, gaping sores. The other children huddled closer, and I saw that their clothing, old and caked with mud, barely covered their little bodies.

We took all four children home with us that night, and after treating the ringworm, scabies, sores and dehydration, they soon blossomed under the care and attention they received. The baby girl, Jabu, became very close to me. After some time, Sandisile told me that Jabu used to be left at home with their father when she took the other siblings to school. Their father had been sick for a long time, and was too weak to do very much except sit at home, largely unresponsive. One day, as she and the others got home from school, they found Jabu sitting next to her dead father's body, singing in her little baby voice the melody to the traditional song, *Bawelile ba Peshe ya* ("They've Gone Across the River").

Sandisile became a lead singer in the God's Golden Acre Singers Choir and received sponsored funding to attend a private Christian school in Pietermaritzburg, where she excelled. Heather's work with the choir, and her pastoral missions in the valley, took her into some of the most dangerous places in rural South Africa. More than once she was stopped by gangs of youths, and the menace of hijacking was always present. However, she relied upon her exuberant personality that often stretched to feigning anger, or even outrage. She seemed to possess an inner strength, and conviction, in potentially dangerous situations. She also discovered that Zulu men didn't quite know how to deal with her when she addressed them abruptly in their own language.

Then came a very narrow escape. One fog-ridden night

Heather dropped off the choir at the Jila homestead after a church service. Before she drove away she was told about a young girl, Wendy Zulu, who was struggling to bring up her siblings Ruth, Sikhumbuzo and Thandeka, alone. Heather had brought a missionary with her – he had been at the church service – but he was frightened about the dangers of driving into the night with no clear idea of how to find Wendy Zulu. Heather was adamant that all the children had to be rescued, and eventually they found the hut where Wendy and her siblings were living.

Wendy told her she had been trying to look after her three young siblings since her father had died. The children were loaded into the back of the truck, and the party was driving to Wartburg in the fog when Heather realized they were being followed. A group of young men in another combi came up alongside and tried to push her vehicle off the road. "They had seen me in the lights of their car and came straight after me. I thought that night was going to be it. They chased me along this narrow road, came up alongside, and tried to force me onto the side. My knees were shaking and the missionary sitting next to me was screaming."

"I told you not to come. I told you not to come," the man wailed. He was getting on Heather's nerves. His hysterical attitude was stopping her from thinking.

"Please shut up!" she shouted at him. She said quietly to God: "Please help me."

Heather slammed on the brakes and in an instant her fear was replaced by anger. She opened the car door, pulled herself up to her full five feet three inches, and glared at the group of youths in fury and indignation. Then she let them have it in Zulu: "How dare you worry an old woman who is rescuing a family? One you probably know! People told me of their plight and I am trying to help them. Go on, look in the truck – what do you see? Your people – the young Zulu family! Don't you realize I am trying to help you and your people? These children are orphans! I have permission from the *nkosi* to take them home. What do you think will happen to them if you take my truck? How dare you interfere! I'm trying to get them back for food and safety, and all you can do on a stormy night is jeopardize my life and yours!"

Suddenly the young men were all becoming apologetic: "We never wanted to harm you, Gogo. We just wanted to find out what you were doing in the middle of the night and see if we could help you." The ringleader added: "If you're ever in trouble, or anyone tries to harm you, just let me know!"

19
THE HORRORS OF
THE VALLEY

The community at Wartburg continued to grow, and Heather began to take in more sick babies and abused youngsters from the valley. Many were healthy, and just needed plenty of love, care and protection. The terminal cases needed somewhere to die with dignity and receive one-to-one nursing.

They converted the family TV room into a nursery. More than 24 babies and toddlers lived in a room that was perhaps 18 feet square. Every morning the Zulu girls from the pottery piled up the mattresses against the wall. They would put them down again on the floor at night. It created an astonishing picture that visitors found hard to believe. There, on the floor without cots, were two dozen babies and toddlers dependent for their survival upon Heather, and a group of African caregivers. The babies needed 24-hour nursing and included many heartbreaking cases.

As they worked tirelessly through the night, bottle-feeding and changing nappies, they knew some of their beloved infants would eventually succumb to the virus, whatever anyone did. Heather would sometimes weep, choking back her sobs so as not to disturb the infant, as the sick baby lay snuffling in her arms, losing its fight for life. Large tears would well up in her sad brown eyes, and stream down her face. Sometimes it seemed she was fighting alone against the world's worst catastrophe since the plague – without support from the rest of the world.

Efforts to raise finance to underpin God's Golden Acre had failed. She recalls all this was happening at the worst period of her life. By 1997 they had approximately 30 children and were feeding them, educating them, supplying nappies, medication, and bearing all living costs. Yet they had no money. The importance of her work was going largely unrecognized in the outside world. One day without warning, a workman from Eskom, the power company, was sent to cut off the electricity supply because the bill had not been paid quickly enough. She asked them to wait so she could boil a kettle for sterilized water for the babies' bottles. They refused.

The electricity was disconnected on several more occasions during the Wartburg years, putting the lives of the sick babies at great risk. "We had our electricity disconnected three times and the phone cut off frequently because we couldn't pay our bill. We even had our water cut off once. I didn't dare let our board of management know how bad things were."

Babies like Chummy, Susiwe, Tommy, Michael, Siyanda, Fikile, Nosipho, Thulani, Gadiga, Siswe, Nkosi, Scelo and Happiness found their way to God's Golden Acre at this time. Some were HIV-positive, and among these were Megan and her twin sister, who were found abandoned in the sugar cane. Basetsane, her twin, had died there, but Megan survived for nearly a year, before she too passed on to heaven.

Heather recalls the time with sadness: "The little girl, Megan, was three months old and the most beautiful child I had ever seen. Like a tiny doll, her perfect features were so delicate you felt you had to hold her very carefully, like glass. Even now, her face fills my mind, and I remember her funny disposition that endeared her to everyone who saw her. Being so young, there are few specific stories about her life, except to say that she was my baby, and in the year that I had her, she managed to touch my life so deeply that I carry her memory close to my heart, and cannot allow myself to think on her too deeply, as the tears come too quickly.

"She was brought to me with an enlarged spleen and swollen glands, and the rollercoaster ride of watching her fight the disease, having her good days and her bad days, close to death on many occasions, was heart-rending. Her vulnerability and innocence in the situation into which she was born broke me, and I hated the powerlessness I felt against this silent killer. A Canadian volunteer named Laura Harlos was with us at the time, teaching our preschool children, and she too fell in love with our precious little baby. Her parents baptized Megan and really bonded with her in the time that she was with us.

"Fifteen months after she had arrived at God's Golden Acre, Megan finally lost the battle and faded away. The worst of it was that after she went to Jesus we wanted to have the funeral. She was taken to the Pietermaritzburg mortuary but the staff there lost Megan's body, and we were never able to grieve properly. We spent weeks trying to find her body, but it was never recovered. This baby that we so loved was lost. We will never know why or how it happened. They have these pauper burials where two or three people are interred together. Maybe a mistake was made there. I don't think we'll ever know.

"Those are the most crushing experiences in this work. To have a child sleep in your bed with you, to watch her fight death almost daily, and to know that there are thousands more just like her is almost enough to make you lose hope altogether. But the miracles we witness almost daily at God's Golden Acre, and the success stories that are found in the lives of healthy, happy children who have overcome, is priceless, and keeps us all going. In ten years at God's Golden Acre, we have lost only twelve children in our residential care to HIV/AIDS. God has been good to us, and we pray daily for his hand upon all of the children he has entrusted to our care."

In the early days, God's Golden Acre linked in with Thuli Mzizi, a social worker from nearby Grey's Hospital, who started to send their most acute cases. Some were HIV-positive, others victims of cerebral palsy, and in all cases, it was impossible to find them foster parents.

"Sicelo Madikwa was among those first infant arrivals and is still with us today. He had an older sister, Ntombi, and a brother, Majola, and we took in all three of them. There were no medical records, but we know Sicelo's mother was run over by a taxi. He had developed cerebral palsy at eleven months of age, and this was something that I recognized from my brother Kenny's condition many years before. So my heart went out to this boy. 'You are not going to stay stiff like that, Sicelo Madikwa! As long as I live I'm going to get those arms of yours straight. I'm going to work on them,' I promised him, although, of course, at twelve months old he could not understand what I was saying to him.

"I used to cry when I pulled Sicelo's arms, they were so stiff. I'd pull them a little bit and he would scream and his poor sister must have thought I was being cruel to him. Can you imagine, me holding him, and this child screaming in agony? Ntombi would look at me with horror in her eyes, not understanding what I was trying to do. It must have been really hard for her. She didn't know that I had had a brother like hers."

Sicelo's arms loosened gradually and now his arms are straight again. He can even open his hands. A wonderful singer and dancer, Ntombi is now teaching the younger children, and is one of the leading members of the Young Zulu Warriors who made the UK tour in 2002.

Then there was Siyanda Vundla who was abandoned in a hut as a tiny baby. Heather remembers he bit her when she first tried to feed him. Siyanda was severely malnourished and his little body, from his feet upwards, was swollen with fluid. Heather nursed him back to health and now he is a healthy boy. Another of the children was Nondeka, who had been shot through the spine by her stepfather. She was about nine years old and in a dreadful state and in great pain when she arrived with an appalling sore on her foot.

Heather would weep for hours at every death, but exhorted her team of Zulu helpers to go on with their work. And grim, dedicated work it was. The number of sick babies being brought to them kept on increasing steadily as the scourge of the pandemic ravaged the valley. "Caring and nursing these sick children and babies took hours of our day. Those who turned the corner from apparent terminal sickness, and did survive, created enormous relief and joy within the community."

There are no more joyful stories than that of Thabani, who was born ten weeks prematurely near Ingwavuma, which lies on the border between South Africa and Swaziland. At birth, Thabani weighed maybe just over one kilogram. His mother, a thirteen-year-old girl with learning disabilities who had been raped by an older man, abandoned him at the local hospital less than a week later. Heather recalls: "Thabani arrived at God's Golden Acre in a banana box. Born premature, he was about a month old when we got him from the social workers at Ingwavuma. They were desperate for a place that could take him, as he was very ill. The first thing we noticed about Thabani were his enormous eyes. Slightly squint and seeming almost too big for his head, these dark pools seemed to hold an infinite wisdom beyond his infant age. There was just something about him that drew everyone to him, and we all knew without a doubt that this child would be destined for great things. Some of the volunteers there at the time formed an informal campaign for his presidency... this all at the tender age of four months!"

His health was no laughing matter. Rattling coughs shook his tiny body until he gagged and lost his breath, making every moment of the day a struggle for survival. His coughing made it impossible to keep any medication down, as he'd just vomit as soon as it went in. Tuberculosis ravaged him to the brink of death, and every night was a battle. Becoming so accustomed to his rattling breathing, Heather would jerk awake in shock every time he'd slip into deep sleep and she didn't hear the familiar sound of his heavy breathing. She would yell to Patrick: "He's dead, Patrick, he's not breathing!" Shining the torch on his sleeping face, her heart would settle in relief as she realised he was still alive. Those were long nights, and it eventually took Thabani twelve-and-a-half months to over-come the TB – twice as long as it should usually take.

Now four years old, he has become a firm favourite amongst staff and volunteers, and his deep eyes still command the same reverence. He walks around with a strange gait, cap-turing the hearts of all who meet him, and the caregivers all still speculate about his mysterious destiny, which might never have come to fruition had he not arrived in that little banana box. Heather wrote:

Many children came riddled with serious illness like tuberculo-sis, malnutrition, or problems with their lymph nodes, or spleens. It took 24-hour supervision and intervention to save them. We cared, prayed for, comforted and nurtured them all. God called many of the infants to heaven. That was how we saw it in our faith.

Happiness was the first child to pass away, and so it was the hardest, and also because she was not a baby. She was a little girl of six years old. She just wasted away. Being the first one, you question God's motives. This is a child. Why? Why give her this suffering? This beautiful little girl, who we had to watch just waste away.

Happiness had been brought to us by a social worker and she came from Swayimane. She had been born with full-blown AIDS, terrible sores in her mouth, thrush down below, and I felt the pain for this child. Unimaginable. I will remember, for ever, the long hours I spent with her. Happiness, my little girl, sitting on the toilet for hours, with me beside her for comfort – a skeleton of a child. I would sit on the edge of the bath too, and ask her what songs she wanted me to sing. Sometimes I'd sit there for an hour at a time, singing, and then carry her back to the room. She'd no sooner settle down than she was up again, sitting on the toilet. You had to be sitting with her because she would fall over, she was that weak. You couldn't leave her. She couldn't walk back to the room. You had to pick her up and carry her.

At the end it was really the songs that helped her, and the music, and the telling her about Jesus – the whisper in her ear that when she was ready, to just let Jesus come and take her, because she was going to go to this beautiful home and live with him there. "No more pain, darling, no more pain. Close your eyes now, and go…"

There's a beautiful song in Zulu and it goes like this:

When I meet him who I love,
I will then be with him who is my protector,
There's a new name for me,
I will sing my praises to him.

It's got the most beautiful Zulu words and has about six verses. It's the whole thing about when we reach heaven we get a new name, a new dress, and everything will be fine, there's no more pain, and all the bad things will be gone. And everything will be perfect.

Little Happiness went away from God's Golden Acre like the others. Closed her eyes and went to Jesus. That's the way it is, that's the way it happens. The deaths I was involved with were very peaceful.

It was hard to have so many funerals, even though the Zulu way of dealing with it is beautiful. The infant is laid out on the floor and we put a little candle beside the body, cover him or her up, and close the eyes. Everyone who loved that child comes in, sits around, talks and sings hymns. We spend at least three hours in the room. It's a farewell, and it helps to take away the hurt because we know we will all miss the child because we loved him or her. I tell the children we all have to die, and to die is not final, just passing from one world into the next world. For some reason God wants us to live in this world which is not perfect, where there is pain, and many imperfect things, but we love to live here because it is the only thing we know.

I explain to them there is a much better life on the other side, so we don't die, our spirit never dies. Everybody that we know and love is on the other side. That's the perfect place, and where we really want to be, but thank goodness, we all want to hang on to life here because it is all we know. Then I sing them a song I wrote to help ease the pain of parting.

There's a new star
That shines, oh surprise,
A new star that lights up the night,
Because a new soul has reached heaven's door,
She's home, she's home, for evermore,
There's a new song she will sing,
For her Saviour and her King,
A new life she's found there,
In her Father's care.

20
LOCAL HOSTILITY TO GOD'S GOLDEN ACRE

In **1996 a letter came through** the post informing Heather she was to receive an award from Archbishop Desmond Tutu for the work she had carried out during the transitional years. The reward was in recognition of the manner in which she had helped many people, including refugees, who were made homeless and had suffered during the fighting between various political factions in the valley. It was called the SANLAM Bridge-builder's Award and it exemplified Heather's humane and compassionate role during the unstable years when she set an example by remaining neutral and offering succour to all who needed it.

Locally, however, most white people were cynical about Heather's vision. Worse still as far as local whites were concerned, she was bringing sick and orphaned children out of the valley – creating a community they did not want to be there. The farm's unkempt appearance created further disapproval, with washing hanging on every available fence, and small children, dogs, cats and chickens running around unsupervised. To make matters worse, abandoned vehicles were strewn here and there among the farm buildings, and kids' toys and play equipment was piled high on the veranda.

"Looking back now at the kind of person I was at that time," says Heather, "I do have to admit that many 'normal' whites might have been justified in thinking I was eccentric. What were they to make of a white woman who goes to the valley several times a week to pray among the dead and the dying? Many people were privately saying that Heather and Patrick Reynolds were not quite normal. Stalwart members of the German community were asking why this woman was going to places she had no sane reason to go to, and interfering in the affairs of the Zulus. Had she got some kind of death wish? What was she doing bringing out these sick children who would probably die anyway? And if there really were healthy orphans starving in the valley, why weren't their extended family group caring for them? The Zulus were a proud and independent people, they'd always resented interference — why not leave them alone?"

Among the few Christians in Wartburg who sympathized with Heather was Pastor Hugo Fulter of Wartburg Lutheran Church, whose Bible studies group Patrick and Heather attended. The pastor recalls the day he first met Heather: "When I came into the area in 1995 I heard about Heather and that she was living on a farm, and wanted to start an orphanage. Then one day our Mission Committee went there and visited her. Immediately I thought that we as a church could help her to reach out to the community because the effects of the AIDS pandemic were beginning to escalate in our area."

Apart from the pastor himself, and a few friends from the Bible studies group, however, all the local churches in Wartburg left Heather to fend for herself at God's Golden Acre. Pastor Fulter recalls: "The key for me as a pastor was her strength in faith in standing alone. In the church we have support structures. We've got the organization, houses to live in, a salary, a congregation — but she just stood in faith and said, 'God will provide.' During those difficult times he opened doors, and closed doors, just to see if she would keep her faith. In the beginning, I must say I was a bit sceptical — will God really fulfil her vision? She was, for instance, in debt, and we could not see how she would get out of that, she didn't have transport, and many people were hostile to her. Through all this she trusted the Lord in everything.

"Eventually it was clear to us he was leading and guarding her. Many people were hostile to her because they still had not been reconciled with black people. They found it hard, and they were afraid that the orphanage would draw other Africans, and these in turn would be responsible for more crime, and possibly sickness, and things like that."

Heather understood some of their fears: "We were living in a conservative area and there was uncertainty and resentment among the white community for the political future of the country. They were wondering what kind of society the former terrorist Nelson Mandela, now president after 27 years of imprisonment, intended to create."

Perhaps Heather Reynolds appeared to them as yet another manifestation of the new Africa, a strange woman who seemed to have this intense faith in God and a troubling preference for spending her life among Africans. Displaced blacks, most of them babies and children, were all living in her home, which other white people thought was unthinkable.

Here and there people appeared who believed that what Heather was doing was right, and among them were Ilse Ceronio and her sister Lenthuen Smit, who were both devout Lutherans. Ilse recalls: "She told us about her vision of the black cloud that would fall over us if we didn't care for the AIDS orphans now. She used to say, 'A child that is uncared for, unloved and uneducated becomes a criminal.' She endured real hardship – sometimes on a Sunday she would phone and say, 'There's no food – can you gather some and bring it to me?' My sister Lenthuen usually had something in the garden that we could give. Then the Harburg congregation – a small town 22 kilometres from Wartburg – got to hear about Heather and they really were marvellous. They started by praying, then helped with gifts, and after that by supplying cars and trucks. She needed friends at that time."

However, if local people thought Heather eccentric, the family unit, the board, staff and caregivers at God's Golden Acre remained loyal to her vision. Mary Van der Leeuw and her husband Carl had come on the scene right at the beginning of the Wartburg years. Mary recalls: "Our maid's sister had died of AIDS-related diseases and her baby son was HIV-positive and we were looking after the child at our home. He was really very sick and I'd been phoning round several organizations looking for help – and then someone put me on to Heather. When I phoned her she was totally shocked that they had given us her name because although she had moved to Wartburg, she didn't have any sick children there at that time – only a vision. Anyway, I was so desperate I didn't know what to do with the little boy.

"She gave me some other numbers with the instruction that if they did not turn out to be OK, then I should contact her again. Eventually he went to a hospital in Greytown and Heather asked us to come to a meeting to find out more about her vision – soon afterwards I started working as her secretary."

During the mid-1990s, Heather's two children, Brendan and Bronwen, had been successful students at a small German school nearby and were fluent in both English and German. Brendan was accepted as a scholar at Pietermaritzburg College and became a promising tennis player on the junior Natal championship circuit before injury forced him to give it up. Bronwen recalls that the many trials and tribulations brought about during the momentous Wartburg years strengthened their family unit, but any thought of being a normal family was jettisoned: "As you've heard, the TV room was converted into a nursery. The floor at night would be one big bed. Babies were everywhere, you couldn't easily reach the TV – you'd have to pick your way across the room to turn it on – and then watch your programme quietly with this crowd of sleeping babies on the floor! How could you get angry about the loss of privacy when you realized what they had been through?

"I only went to the valley when I was working at God's Golden Acre quite recently and I just cried. So I think through our childhood Mum protected us from the awful things she saw and the heroic things she had to do. She would come back from the valley and she would be very tired and she wouldn't really talk about it. I think maybe this was because she knew I am also very sensitive and hated to see, or hear about, people being hurt. So I don't think she really off-loaded that much of what was happening. But we knew she had saved those babies in our living room.

"Did I ever rebel against it all? Well, like any teenager in high school you grow up and become more self-absorbed, and it's all 'about me'. And so in that respect Mum and I some- times had a difficult time just because I was your typical teenage girl — having to share a bathroom with hordes of chil- dren when there was only one bathroom. So, yes, I had my moments!

"I think we were brought up from a young age to be aware of God. I personally remember feeling his presence when I was very small and we were still living in Dalton, where we were involved in the Methodist church, and I used to go to the youth group. So I knew him from small, and later I never lost sight of the fact that it was God's calling on our life."

Among her activities with the choir at this time Heather became well known in the evangelical movement of the church; she worked with Bishop Sibiya who ran a training col- lege for priests and was also responsible for a group of affili- ated churches in various parts of KwaZulu-Natal. She travelled great distances in Zululand with the choir, often to very remote areas, to attend all-night services, but always felt safe with her Zulu boys beside her as protection. She recalls: "It was useful because black people got to know me through my evangelical work. Usually I was the only white woman in the congregation in these churches and I would get up on the stage with the choir and sing with them. It was of course unheard of in the rural areas for a white woman to be involved in that kind of church business. It was also a time of reconciliation and healing between millions of black and white people.

"On another occasion, after a big demonstration in a rugby stadium in Durban against violence being perpetrated upon white farmers, we had nowhere to sleep and so people of both races gathered around us impromptu, and we sang right through the night. It developed into a wonderful occasion with white and black people coming together. At about three o'clock in the morning I remember an Afrikaans man who broke down after he'd been singing with the choir. He confessed to having done horrible things and it was a cleansing process."

21
THE NORWEGIAN
VOLUNTEERS ARRIVE

Towards the end of the time that God's Golden Acre was at Wartburg, some of the pressure was taken off Heather, in her role as a day-to-day nurse, when her first overseas volunteers, Vibeke Blaker and Marianne Jenum, arrived from Norway. Both girls experienced severe culture shock.

Marianne Jenum: "Dr Ter Haar picked us up and he told us that the children slept in the garage and in mud huts. I had trouble picturing myself sleeping in a mud hut. When we arrived, I forgot my worries. Beautiful, smiling children gave us the warmest welcome. There were also dogs, cats, chickens, roosters, and a frog in the bathroom. I was relieved when I found out that we were sleeping in Bronwen's room, indoors. 'Chaotic' is the word that best describes the first evening. There were so many people and animals around and so many things happening at the same time, while I tried to fit as many children as possible on my lap and learn their names."

Vibeke Blaker: "One evening, it was dark outside, and I sat alone on the bed in our room. We had closed the curtains in front of the window, and I thought nobody could see me. Then I heard a loud, deep voice saying: 'Sugar!' It came from outside the window. I almost got a little scared. And then I again heard the voice saying, 'Sugar!' I did not understand who this was and I looked out of the window. The only thing I could see was an old combi-van that was parked on the grass. But after a while I heard laughter, and then three heads became visible from inside the combi. Then I understood that the curtains in our room were transparent. There were three boys living in the van, and it became clear that they had the perfect place to spy on us in our room, and they did! Marianne and I realized that they had probably seen some funny things during the first days we were at God's Golden Acre, for instance us putting lotion on our sunburned bodies before we went to bed at night.

"The three boys living in the combi were Sbo, Siphamandla and Siyabonga. They were all in the class we taught and we became really close to them during our stay. We could not help noticing that they often looked really tired in the mornings. They never fell asleep before we did, and often they made funny noises after we turned off the light, and we had a lot of laughs. Seeing that these children were actually cheerful children made me very happy. It didn't look like they were damaged from experiences in their past; it seemed like they were able to live full lives. Watching how much they enjoyed singing and dancing made me glow, as did the feeling that me coming to South Africa meant a lot to them.

"On the other hand, there were lots of things that made me sad too. All of the children had experienced horrible things before they came to God's Golden Acre, and I wept hearing their stories. I felt that it was 'unfair' that small, innocent children should have to be that sick, and that they all grew up with no parents. I kept thinking about their future; I worried about what chances they would have in life. The poverty was so extreme, and I analyzed my own life in Norway. I felt sort of guilty for living under such pampered conditions and for my love of material things."

Marianne: "At a closer sight, I saw that several of them were very thin and tiny, and one of them had ugly sores on his feet. I was prepared to meet sick babies, and deal with the low risk of being infected, so I tried not to let the sores scare me.

Heather didn't test all the children systematically, so we did not know who had HIV, but we could see that several children were obviously sick. Tiny Nonto was constantly crying and had chronic ear-infections. Gadiga and Thandeka had terrible sores that wouldn't heal, so we worried about them. Mavu and Goodman were skinny and wouldn't put on weight. It turned out they had TB, and after they got rid of that, they've turned into healthy young boys."

Vibeke: "Siyanda and Gadiga were a little bit older; they wanted to be held a lot. I was actually a bit scared of Gadiga. Since he had these open sores, I was afraid of being in physical contact with his blood. I was very afraid of that at the beginning of my stay at God's Golden Acre, but we all grew used to it. There was a girl called Happiness who had died of AIDS-related disease just before Marianne and I came to God's Golden Acre. Heather talked a lot about her, how they treated her at the end, how she died, how they let the other children see her after she died. It made a huge impression. To be honest, I was actually a bit relieved that I didn't stay at God's Golden Acre when Happiness died. I'm not sure how I would have handled it."

Marianne: "One little girl – Pume – was so tiny I was afraid she would break if I touched her. She was only eight or nine years old, but had been a prostitute together with her mum. Heather had made an exception and taken her in – although her mum was alive. The girl was just lying in a hut while men kept going in to abuse her. She was so scared of men that she got hysterical and broke into tears once when Brendan accidentally touched her, and she was so weak that she fell asleep everywhere. It broke my heart when Heather later told me that her mum took her back, and there was nothing she could do about it. I remember actually hoping she had AIDS and would die quickly. Life on earth must have been hell for her, poor thing. She didn't know English, but she usually calmed down when I had her on my lap and sang to her.

"Learning about Pume's life and other similar life stories were our saddest moments. We asked, and Heather told us, their life stories. Then later, we usually talked about these things in our bedroom at night, after the children had gone to sleep. Vibeke and I often cried. We took turns being 'the strong one' – we couldn't both cry and ask difficult existential questions – one of us had to 'pull' the other one up and help the other to see the bright side. This arrangement was our way to deal with the overwhelmingly tragic information."

Heather avoided exposing Vibeke and Marianne to the everyday horrors she herself experienced in the valley, on their first tour of duty. However, the arrival of the two European girls at Wartburg allowed her even greater opportunities to spend more time in the valley, where her presence was desperately needed. Eventually, there were 41 children at Wartburg. The babies still all lived in Heather's home, and the older ones lodged in outbuildings and garages, and of course that old motor-caravan, known as a "combi", outside the Norwegian girls' room, where three of the bigger boys slept. The strong Christian ethic within the community was expressed at mealtimes where there would be prayers before food. In the evening the orphans would wear their pyjamas and come into the lounge to sing, play games, and get their toothpaste and vitamins.

Marianne recalls: "They would fetch their toothbrushes and stand in line. I'd give them toothpaste, and they'd have to say 'thank you'. I don't really know why I loved this so much. Perhaps it was the normality about it: clean children in pyjamas, brushing their teeth at night. Maybe it was how they tried hard to pronounce the 'thank you' correctly, like they really wanted to be good. Maybe what made an impression was that they were in fact thankful for such a trivial thing like toothpaste. I guess I loved to be able to look each and every one in the eye, and give each attention."

One of the happiest moments for the Norwegian volunteers was finding out that the older girls they were teaching in their class in the little school at God's Golden Acre were not HIV-positive. "After having heard Heather talk about all the cases of sexual abuse, and seeing the girls' faces when Heather did her 'Sex can give you AIDS' speech, Vibeke and I had the impression that the girls thought they might be infected. We talked with Heather about testing them. We thought that if they were negative, the girls would be extremely grateful and protect themselves from then on. This was only an idea from our side, but Heather knew some of the girls had been abused and asked them if they wanted to get tested. And they did. Afterwards, a few more of the girls came, and it turned out they had been abused too. So suddenly, Vibeke and I found ourselves escorting five girls, aged eleven to fourteen, to the doctor to find out if they were going to die within a few years or not. It was horrible; we knew that our naïve idea might have a terrible impact on the lives of these girls. They were tested, and we had to wait some time for the results. It was tormenting. When the results finally came through, they were all negative. I've never felt more relieved, and the girls instantly started singing and dancing and jumping. Was it the right thing to do, to test them? I still don't know, but we are both grateful that it turned out the way it did."

22
BANKRUPTCY LOOMS

In the meantime, life at Wartburg remained difficult. In the farming community there remained scant sympathy for what Heather and Patrick were doing. When a local sawmill at Windy Hill decided to stop housing its workforce, the board of God's Golden Acre immediately applied to buy the houses – but the local farmers managed to stop them from doing it. Heather recalls: "The farmers' association decided they didn't want orphans there and that they were going to bulldoze the buildings we could have used. And that's exactly what they did."

The worst instance of racism Heather ever encountered came one day when she was in Pietermaritzburg at a printing company who were doing some free posters for God's Golden Acre. She had gone in to look at the proofs and was talking to the staff about some small adjustments. She noticed there was a man behind her in the queue and from his body language she knew he was becoming impatient. So she turned round and apologized for delaying him. "We're nearly done," she said politely.

"Well, what is it all about anyway?" he asked gruffly, looking at the proofs.

She said: "Oh! It's an exhibition, 'Flowers Through The Home', to raise money for our AIDS Orphans Project."

He hissed: "What do you mean? Black children?"

She replied, startled: "Yes."

"What! You mean you've been keeping me here waiting – and all this to try and save these bloody little black bastards? Look, do me a favour: why don't you stick the whole damn lot of them down a mineshaft. And then do me another favour – make doubly sure that it's sealed, so they can never get out."

She was devastated and shocked: "I'm just so sorry. I don't know what's caused your anger."

He fumed: "Don't feel sorry for me. Be sorry for those little black bastards."

Heather got out of there as fast as she could. "I was devastated at the force and depth of his hatred. It was so overpowering and when I got home I cried and cried. I cried for the man and his anger, and I cried for the children and for all this unnecessary hatred. From that awful incident I wrote a little song and dedicated it to the unknown racist man."

Have you asked the question,
Is life always fair?
Have you asked the question,
And do you really care?
Like a child born today,
They say that she has AIDS,
Victim of the dreaded HIV,
She's condemned at infancy,
A man-made situation,
An infant, the infant had no choice,
Will you ask the question,
Is life always fair?
For you ask the question,
And please, will you care?
And please, will you care?

In fact, the proofs the racist had seen were for a 'Flowers Through The Home' exhibition to raise funds for God's Golden

Acre organized by a close friend of Heather's who had come up with a plan to relocate the charity to an area north of Pietermaritzburg called the Karkloof. Heather remembers: "One day a dear friend of ours, Yvonne Shaw, who lived in a beautiful and wealthy farming and plantation area called the Karkloof, 60 miles from Wartburg, came to see us to look at Patrick's work, because she was interested in buying a sculpture. She saw some of the children and was impressed. I told her about my vision, and she went back to the Karkloof and spoke to her son William. He agreed to give us a piece of land, which was marvellous because we did not have much money at that time, and it would have meant all we had to do was raise enough money to put up some buildings and get things started. We were going to do a little craft village, and a gallery for Patrick's sculptures. At the back there would be a few dormitories for the children. It wasn't going to be anything too big but it would have catered for our needs at the time, and we would own it.

"Yvonne did the 'Flowers Through The Home' exhibition, which was very successful and a lot of people came. But somehow people had got to hear that William had offered us this land before he had actually spoken to the farmers himself. I got a phone call from a man who said that people wanted to know what was going on. He knew that we were to be given land – and he and his neighbours wanted some answers. So I agreed to set up a meeting and told them I was very willing to answer any questions that people would like to ask me. I did not ask Yvonne or William to come, because I did not want to involve them in any nastiness. They had been kind enough to offer us the land and I felt I was quite capable of answering the questions.

"The meeting was set up for the country club up in the Karkloof and I went there. I knew I was going to be facing some angry farmers because of what was happening at Wartburg. I asked the chairman to keep control and not allow anyone to get out of order because I didn't want to face being lynched. He assured me he'd keep order. Well, my goodness, did they have a go at me? Yes, they did – with everything. I had no chance. It was a lynch mob. I have never been so humiliated. I turned to the chairman and said, 'You are supposed to be keeping order.'

"Then I turned round and looked at the farmers and I said, 'You know, gentlemen, even if you offered to build me that place on that land, I wouldn't want to bring my children amongst the likes of you. I wouldn't actually like to bring my children up in this area. I think we're better off where we are.' I walked out. The meeting was adjourned and they invited me to go and have a drink, which I accepted, and some people came round who felt bad about the way they had behaved. Once again I had come across aggression because I was trying to help little black children. They did not want us in their area. So we abandoned the idea of moving there and remained at Wartburg – for the time being."

Meanwhile another much more serious dilemma presented itself. Heather had to manage the growing community at Wartburg, yet the crisis in the valley was escalating and she was needed to go there more often. There were no spare hours to go to the pottery. Soon, the pottery was in serious decline. Although Heather tried to delegate the creative work to the most experienced women, when she wasn't in the pottery keeping a direct eye on the process, quality control would quickly fall apart.

When they lost one of their biggest contracts because too many bonsai pots were sub-standard, Heather realized she was going to have to choose between the pottery and God's Golden Acre. She must revive the pottery and run it properly, or else close it down, put her faith in God, and run God's Golden Acre full-time. "It was a very hard decision to make – because if we abandoned the pottery, we risked going bankrupt. We were grinding along with 41 children, many of them sick. But the needs of the children, and the plight of those in the valley, had priority on my time – and so we prepared to take a desperate gamble by closing the pottery."

2 3
THE STREET PROTEST

eather and Patrick decided to apply to the Nelson Mandela Children's Fund for financial assistance. "I had the organization structured as best I could," she says. "We had a management board and a constitution, and I believed that we were now eligible for funding. We applied to the Fund thinking that what they had said about raising money to help underprivileged children would apply to our orphans. I was now living, waiting daily, for this funding proposal to come back. I saw it as a lifeline with the pottery closed. Then Patrick got sick with hepatitis and both Brendan and I had to have expensive hospital operations. I began to feel that God was throwing everything at us. Then came a further disaster – our vehicle was stolen and so we had no wheels except when the local Lutheran pastor, Hugo Fulter, was able to lend us his car.

"There were friends who tried to discourage us from going on. Among these was Dave Beyers, a bank manager, who shared our love of bonsai tree cultivation and had worked with us at Deep Valley many years before, building and staging a number of fantastic exhibitions.

" 'Look, Heather, you can't save the world,' he would tell us over and over again. 'You can't let yourself go bankrupt. You have neglected the pottery, and you have neglected your bonsai. It's not good business. You can't do that...'

"Meanwhile we were heading for real trouble. One day when we met Dave at a convention for bonsai growers he said, 'I'm sorry, Heather, I don't even want to sit and talk tonight, because you are crazy – you can't save the whole bloody world! Get that into your head.'

"Very shortly after that I told him, 'Dave, I need you as treasurer. You are a bank manager, and you would give us credibility because we want to register as an NGO. So I'm asking you, calling in a favour, since I shared with you all my knowledge of bonsai.' He was surprised at my request.

" 'You know I don't believe in this whole thing,' he said, 'because I don't believe in something that is going to bankrupt you. It doesn't make sense to me.'

"I was pleading now: 'Please, Dave. There's hardly any money, and it won't take up much of your time. I just need to have a treasurer and I need to have a small bank account – if people do donate funds to God's Golden Acre, everything must be properly handled... because up till now it has all been our own money.' Dave reluctantly agreed. It gave me a sense of some security to have him around, despite his doubts."

The stress was now getting to Heather... no money, no wheels and no support. Around this time, some close friends from the Lutheran church decorated a large basket with ribbons and put it in the local supermarket with information about God's Golden Acre, what it was trying to do, and asking for donations of food items. The result was a disaster and illustrated clearly what the local community thought of God's Golden Acre. As she recalls: "In six months we were given one loaf of bread and a few cents. Some of the richest farmers in South Africa lived around Wartburg, and the best they could do was one loaf of bread and a few cents. We agreed there was no point in keeping the basket there. There was deep anger within me when I got home that afternoon – but worse was to come. A letter delivered that day told us we had been rejected by the Nelson Mandela Children's Fund. They said sorry but they couldn't help us. It was such a disappointment and I was very angry.

" 'What the heck is this Nelson Mandela Children's Fund about?' I raged. 'Here we've got children who have been orphaned and abandoned. We are helping the vulnerable children in our community, supporting many of them in their extended families... What other criteria do we have to meet to be able to get this money?' I could not understand what else we would have to do to meet their requirements. I believed there could not be any organization in greater need than ours.

"I was devastated, angry, tired and at the end of my tether. I was near to my breaking point. Life was becoming impossible without a vehicle. Things were hectic. I had so much to do! I had to keep finding a car to borrow for this, and borrow a car for that, and it was driving me crazy. I picked up the phone and rang the office of the Nelson Mandela Children's Fund. A man answered the phone and I blasted him from all sides. I said, 'How can you reject this proposal? How is it possible that an organization that is caring for the most vulnerable children in its community does not qualify for your support? I just want to tell you something – don't you ever forget the name God's Golden Acre and don't you ever forget my name, Heather Reynolds.' I was furious and slammed the phone down."

"Some years after this," Heather admits, "things would be patched up and we did get funding, and the children got to meet Nelson Mandela – but that comes later...

"Next I phoned up the police station, the local commandant, and all my frustrations came pouring out in a strident torrent: 'Look, I'm just going to tell you that I'm going to stage a peaceful parade through town tomorrow. We're going to do a march. I want to walk around the streets and say: "Here I am with my children, these are the children orphaned because of AIDS-related diseases and violence. They exist and we love them." There won't be anything violent or anything but I want it so that no one will be able to say they don't know about God's Golden Acre, who we are, and for whom we are caring. I want them to understand that there are whites who love black people and who love black children too, and that you white people can hold children who have the HIV virus, and you won't catch it because it's not contagious. I want all this to be seen, and I want it heard too at a public meeting afterwards in the church hall.'

"So I took out with me a lot of little blackboards and I wrote all over them – slogans about caring about children, appropriate verses from the Bible, and so forth. I sent out word to the choir and others in the valley to come up to the taxi rank and prepare to sing.

" 'What's it all about, Gogo?' they asked.

" 'Just come up,' I said. 'I want people to know that God's Golden Acre exists, that we are providing a useful service to the community.'

"So I went into the town, with all the children. I parked the truck and put all the placards out. The choir from the valley arrived, and other supporters too, and I said, 'Sing, guys, sing... ' They looked at me sheepishly and I said again, 'Come on, let's sing!' And they did – right there in the taxi rank. Then we marched around the small area. Lots of people saw us and read the slogans on the blackboards. The evening came and a mystified Dr Ter Haar arrived to chair the meeting. I told him confidently, 'Oh, we're just letting the local people know about us.'

"We slipped over the road to the church hall for the meeting, and our friends attended – as did a number of local white people. I stood up and welcomed everybody and explained our difficulties in trying to do our work, in particular our lack of transport. I told them about the AIDS pandemic, and its impact, and how it was going to affect everybody and that we needed to take action and support each other – and they

needed to support us because we were actually doing something responsible which would benefit the community in the
years to come... I read in some people's eyes that I had lost
them; they had shut me out. I hadn't reached them. Then suddenly I got angry.

"I said, 'It would be better for us to leave this area – we are
never going to get this community to support us.'

"Suddenly a hand went up at the back of the hall and a man
stood up. We had never met him before. He was Ron Kusel, a
highly respected member of the local community, who came
from the nearby village of Harburg. He said: 'I think I could
take care of your transport problems.' There was a stunned
silence. I could hardly believe my ears. He added: 'I've got a
relatively new Toyota truck, and I think we could help.'

"Dr Ter Haar stood up and diplomatically took over where
I'd left off, thanking Ron and the rest of the audience for their
help. At the end of that meeting it was arranged that Ron
would deliver the vehicle to us in the morning. The Toyota
provided us many years of excellent service. It was the lifeline
we needed. Ron's act of generosity came at a very crucial time
when I was at breaking point. This act of kindness gave me the
courage to go on. Subsequently Ron was to help us in many
other ways with resources, like wood from his sawmill to
build our hospice and accommodation for our volunteers."

The desperate measures Heather had taken to win partial
support from the white community around Wartburg had met
with success. However, it wasn't only the white community
who failed to show compassion. Many black people resented
Heather. It became, for example, a humiliating experience for
her to get sell-by-date food from the supermarkets in
Pietermaritzburg.

"A large chain store nearby kindly agreed to give us the
daily sell-by-date foods. However, the young black assistants
employed there were the first generation to work in a South
Africa not ruled by whites. I would spend hours waiting in the

delivery section, waiting — sometimes with Brendan or Patrick — for the shop assistants to bring out the trolleys. They would be quite rude and shove the trolleys out so hard that they would tip over, and there would be cream cakes and doughnuts everywhere, all over the tarred surface. After clearing the trolleys, we had to clean up the mess. Can you imagine what it was like to have to go there and fetch this food, night after night, for nearly two years?

"We had to sit there from six o'clock and wait for the hatch doors to open, sometimes as late as nine o'clock. It was dark — there was no lighting. We were tired. We had children to go to who needed us. We were exhausted from the night before. Rats and cockroaches were everywhere.

The moment the hatch opened, and the food was pushed out on trolleys, the cockroaches rushed, like an advancing black shadow, for the food. We were competing with these repulsive creatures. I did not want to take them home with me and start an infestation there. We would salvage what we could, and then we had to scrape the cream off the tarmac. At any one moment I could have said: 'I'm not going to close the pottery. I'll just place the children in an institution, and go back to my normal life.' I didn't have to be there, kneeling on the tarmac in the dark with cockroaches all around me, scraping cream off the ground. There was nothing forcing me to do this. The only thing making me do it was that I knew our sick babies and children would probably starve to death back where they came from, so we had to push on.

"I knew that at any point I could give up. I could still salvage the pottery, turn things around, get old contracts back, and abandon God's Golden Acre. I could return to the art of growing bonsai trees, and to my painting. I could still change my mind! Perhaps Dave Beyers was right after all. There was no money coming in; the children needed clothing, medical care and schooling. My own children were being neglected. I could let it all go, and return to normality. As I scrabbled among the dirt outside the food store, night after night, can you imagine my dilemma?"

A volunteer, Susan Balfour, who worked at God's Golden Acre in the later years, expressed Heather's dilemma in her journals:

> There *are* moments of doubt, pain and discouragement for her. Resistance to the work has been enormous at times, some intensely painful instances of rejection by friends and family. The cruelty of strangers can be equally devastating. That is what I have seen in my time with her, and believe me, it cuts deep. Sometimes, when things have really built up, Heather has expressed thoughts that she would like to disappear, go back to her art and her bonsai. But somewhere in that pain, comes the realization that if she were gone, there would be no one to care for the children. You can see this awareness come upon her. It sends a shiver through her sometimes, and then she goes about the work just as she did before and as fiercely! This is human frailty. Although there *is* an almost superhuman quality in Heather's endurance, she is still human, and vulnerable.

The arrival of Vibeke and Marianne shortened the waiting time for food at night because the young assistants realized two beautiful European girls were hanging around outside. It aroused sufficient interest for the store assistants to open up earlier — but the two Norwegians nevertheless found the food run a repulsive experience. Marianne wrote:

> The worst part was the bread. Most of it was all right, but some of it was disgusting, all green with mould, and smelly. And they wouldn't let us throw it in the big container; for some reason we had to take "all or nothing", so we couldn't protest. A lot of it was unhealthy stuff, cakes and buns, not very suitable for bringing up children. I couldn't understand why we didn't get fresher stuff. In order to give us green mouldy bread, they must have

stored it for weeks to rot. I still don't understand what they were thinking."

Heather had also managed to get a contract with another food chain, to have the store's leftovers for free. This time there were none of the squalid goings-on, with food being literally thrown out of garage doors. Heather, Brendan, or one of the volunteers, would have to be there about 3.30pm. They would press a bell at the warehouse, go in, and be given what was available. It improved things a lot. They were supplied with some really classy food and lots of good meat and chicken, but never knew in advance what they were going to get, so it made meal planning a virtually impossible task. Sometimes the remnants consisted of all the same thing – on more than one occasion the menu at God's Golden Acre had a rather eccentric appearance. Marianne remembers the night of fish pâté: "We sat in the lounge and ate loads of really fine trout pâté. We had to eat it before the wonderful food turned into a major health risk."

However, it was the expense of the powdered milk, special foods, preparations for the sick babies, and the cost of disposable nappies that blew one of the biggest holes in the God's Golden Acre budget. They managed to find a Muslim company that supplied them with nappies when they had them. Nestlé supplied them with powdered milk. So for the moment there was enough for everybody – just. Heather's sister-in-law was working for a pharmaceutical company and they gave God's Golden Acre boxes and boxes of vitamins. It meant all the children could now have a proper baby formula, and even the older ones, who had been malnourished, benefited from that aid project.

The day came, however, when even the small change in coins had gone. Unfortunately, it was a date that coincided with a visit from deputy chairman Dr Gerrit Ter Haar. Heather was desperately anxious that he should not find out how bad things were. She did not want to scare him. Before he arrived she said, kneeling in a quiet prayer by her bedside: "God, now we stand absolutely alone, and only you can help us."

Halfway through the meeting an African girl who was helping to do the cooking came to Heather. "What are we cooking, for tonight, Gogo?" she asked.

Heather replied in an exaggerated tone of unconcern: "Oh. Don't worry about that. We'll deal with that later."

The look on the Zulu girl's face was one of total bewilderment, because she knew that Heather knew the kitchen staff needed to get started with the cooking – if everything was to be ready in time for the evening meal at 6pm. Heather tried to conceal the look of fear upon her face, and turned back to Gerrit to continue their discussions, but privately she was thinking, "What am I going to do, what am I going to do? I must not let on that the situation is so bad."

As in so many other moments in Heather's life, there appeared to be divine intervention. The next moment the phone rang and it was a young man, Sarel van der Merwe, from Family Favourites products. His boss in Johannesburg had read an article about God's Golden Acre in a magazine and decided to help with food supplies. Heather explains: "His company had decided to place 2,000 Rand each month on account at Metro, and we could buy food from there to that value, on the basis that most of it would be his branded foods. The account had been opened and we could start purchasing right away. We rushed out that afternoon to get food and came home with everything we would need for the month. God had provided."

Heather casually told the unsuspecting Dr Ter Haar: "Oh. Wonderful news. We've had someone give us 2,000 Rand of food every month!"

However, the act of generosity was only a temporary respite from the ongoing financial crisis – and just around the corner loomed what appeared at the time to be a disaster from which there could be no recovery. It came from an unexpected quarter.

Patrick was now planning to turn out exquisite saleable bronzes, and he was preparing to send them off to the 1998 annual exhibition in Pietermaritzburg. It would be the first group of bronzes, just as all those years before they had worked to create the first group of sculptures in wood. Patrick collected the waxes and took them to the foundry. Then came terrible news. They had a call from Dave Falconer: "I'm sorry, they haven't come out. We had a bad run with the metal and they all failed."

The men at the foundry poured them again, recast them, and cleaned them, but the foundry couldn't get them finished in time. It had failed to produce the bronzes in time for the exhibition. The collection was brought to Wartburg two days after the exhibition had started. There they were, all finished, sparkling and beautiful, and sitting on the lounge table when they should have been in Pietermaritzburg, being seen by thousands of people. Heather recalls: "Can you imagine? We were devastated. We had nowhere to sell them. This was our next year's income. We were in big trouble. That week we did not have enough money for food again because our credit card was taken away. I have never been a person to have much debt, but we depended upon the bank overdraft and credit facility. However, things were now out of my control. I owed money on the credit card. The First National Bank promised to give me until the 18th of the month to pay. Then a representative from the bank arrived at Wartburg the week before that date, and demanded my card. I had to give it to him."

Heather was exhausted. She would have to give up her babies and her children. The alternative was bankruptcy. One of the first people who would need to know this was her treasurer, Dave Beyers, and she went to his office to break the news. She spoke almost in a whisper.

"Dave, you know what? You were right. You were right. I should never have started this. Never done it. God hasn't offered anything. We've lost the credit card, and we've run ourselves into the ground. I'm just thinking now what I'm going to tell the committee."

Dave stood up with an angry look on his face. Heather could see he was really cross. "What's this?" he said. "I've just come to believe in you! I believe in you now! How can you tell me you've achieved nothing! You told me yourself that if you asked any one of those children what difference it's made to them they'd tell me... I believe in it now. I've seen those kids. We are not disbanding anything!"

At this moment Heather's life switched itself on again. She felt a surge of excitement, and her strength came flooding back. "I was so excited that Dave Beyers had made this whole turnaround in believing in us, and believing in God's Golden Acre. I walked out of that office with my troubles temporarily forgotten. I felt as if I'd won a million dollars!"

24
HEATHER'S
DESPERATE GAMBLE

When Heather got home triumphantly from the meeting with Dave Beyers she discovered that they'd sold one sculpture for 2,500 Rand — which was now all they had in the world. Suddenly, as she stood looking at the pieces in the lounge, her eye fell upon an arts magazine that had been left on a chair. Patrick had picked it up at the exhibition. She flicked through the magazine out of curiosity, and saw an advert listed: " 'Royal Birmingham Society of Artists international competition and exhibition. Prizes to be won for painting and sculpture.' The closing date for entry was that very day. The day I was reading the advert."

She thought to herself that with the 2,500 Rand, if she could get a ticket for about 2,200, she could fly to England and submit the artwork to the selection panel. Heather wondered: "Is this God?" She'd never sold Patrick's work in England but rushed out of the room and told him about it. She warned him they might not get the pieces into the competition because the selection panel could reject them — but maybe they should have a try anyway; they could just afford it!

Around that time, Harry Tomlinson from Greenwood Nursery in Nottingham, England had been out to South Africa as a guest speaker to the Bonsai Society and had stayed at Wartburg. Heather knew she could save on hotel bills by staying with him if she flew to England. Patrick, with his total faith in his extraordinary wife, said: "It's up to you — it's our last money."

Heather had made her mind up: "I phoned Birmingham, said what we had got, and the person replied: 'Sure, just fax us through the titles and give us a bank draft for the entry fee, and be here on the right day to hand the sculptures in — and then we will let you know whether you have made it.' Well, I did it. I sent in the bank draft, and phoned up the travel agent who found a ticket for me two weeks later — which was the time when I had to deposit the bronzes with the Society. I took the two sculptures we were entering, and other bronzes we hoped to sell, and packed them into my suitcase with my clothes in it, and the smaller ones into my shoulder bag.

"The luggage was very heavy and I was in despair at the airport at both ends — but my real problems began at New Street Station in Birmingham because I didn't have enough money for a taxi. I had no choice but to drag my suitcase and shoulder bag, both loaded with bronzes, up the hill to the art gallery. I also had a trolley with small wheels, upon which I had strapped the two biggest bronzes, The Curled Up Nude and The Chairgirl. The street outside was cobbled, and every few yards the heavy bronzes kept slipping off the wheels. I was under pressure because I knew I had to get up to the gallery before it closed, as this was the final day for exhibits to be entered. I had to make it up this hill before closing time.

"Now I reached breaking point. I just started crying. I couldn't go on. Then somebody put his arm around my shoulder and whispered, 'I'm so sorry.' I dried up my tears, bucked up my ideas, and just carried on. Somehow I managed to get up the hill to the gallery. I arrived dishevelled and out of breath and a young man helped me to get the bronzes up the top flight of steps. The pieces were all wrapped up in towels and paper etc. and once they were opened, they caused an immediate stir of interest because they were so beautiful. I left them there and headed over to the National Exhibition Centre."

There was a gardening exhibition going on at the NEC and Harry Tomlinson was exhibiting on a stand. So he and Heather spent part of the evening on the stand and then he drove her to his home in Nottingham. Next day they had to wait for the reply to find out if Patrick's work had been accepted. It was nerve-racking and soul-destroying. Heather could not bear thinking about it too much, yet she could think of nothing else. The future of God's Golden Acre depended upon the decision of a panel of strangers about Patrick's bronze sculptures!

When the letter came she could not open it — because if they had not made it, the consequences seemed unimaginable. Harry opened the envelope and smiled. Hurrah! Both of the entries had been accepted!

"We went to the opening of the exhibition and found even more wonderful news awaiting us. One of the pieces, a curled up nude, had won the Bryan Hyde Prize, and had been sold for £2,000! That was a huge amount of money in Rand."

The following day, Sir David Shepherd, the well-known artist, also bought a piece for over £1,000, and so did Harry Tomlinson. More commissions followed from people who had been impressed by Patrick's work at the exhibition. That night Heather prayed and thanked God for rescuing them. God's Golden Acre would stay in business.

The following week she flew back to South Africa, feeling happier than she could remember. Now they could carry on and develop God's Golden Acre in the way that they had always hoped. They had real, real money! They were able to deposit around £5,000 in their fund. The partnership between Patrick Reynolds and Dave Falconer of Birdman Foundry at Nottingham Road had at last paid wonderful dividends, bringing success and recognition to both men.

Dave Falconer recalls: "I just think it is amazing because in those very early days when we began to turn out good bronzes, all Patrick's money was going to support the orphans and I think it is marvellous that eventually the whole situation came round a full circle for him. He now has a tremendous market through the people he has contacts with in Europe and it is a fitting reward for a job well done. Patrick is now probably one of South Africa's leading sculptors in the human form, and the 'big five' animals *Elephant, Buffalo, Rhino, Lion And Leopard*, done for Coca-Cola in Johannesburg, reveal his extraordinary talent in creating the spirit of creatures too. Patrick is the only sculptor I have ever worked with who has always paid tribute to the foundry. Most people don't do that – they just forget the foundry and concentrate on their own egos – but Patrick at every opportunity mentions the foundry and makes us feel good."

25
HATRED AND
RESENTMENT GROWS

In **1998 the farmland** on the estate was sold to a near neighbour, and this neighbour's white foreman, who hated and resented Africans, began to behave in a way that threatened the lives of the children. At the time, some of the older orphans were using the roads because they were doing a running programme. If the foreman saw the orphans he would try to run them down in his truck. He was prepared to wipe out children he considered were on a par with wild game. After a couple of serious incidents, Heather contacted the new owner to express her disgust at his foreman's behaviour. She explained that the children had only escaped by running into the sugar cane.

"Please, the kids have just got the first decent clothes they've ever had, thanks to our friends in Norway. The clothes are now torn because the orphans ran into the sugar cane, some of them have been cut, and the others hurt their ankles. Please tell your foreman to stop doing this," she pleaded. It had little effect.

As 1999 approached, Heather and Patrick realized they would have to get out of Wartburg and find a new place. Dr Ter Haar was also becoming increasingly worried about the sanitation and hygiene at Wartburg. God's Golden Acre was close to saturation point with 41 children, and a further fifteen adults. He also realized that God's Golden Acre could only raise funds properly if it was registered as an NGO and that was the next step that had to be taken. Then there was more depressing news when the Chairman, Professor Ron Nicholson, resigned because of new commitments in the academic field. His departure meant they would go through the transitional period of any coming move without anyone at the helm.

The Reynolds became even more distressed when Cats and Trisca Nelemans, with whom they had been so close at Umgeni Waterfall Care and Rehabilitation Centre in Howick, passed away. However, their son Roland, who inherited the estate, gave God's Golden Acre 10,000 Rand, in an act of unsolicited generosity. At least they could now use this as a deposit and look for somewhere rundown, a derelict smallholding perhaps, that no one else wanted. Heather wrote later:

We found several suitable sites but they all seemed to be just beyond our price range and we never seemed to have quite enough deposit. Finally, when at last we found a property we felt we could afford, the bank would not help us with the loan. We had the deposit, but nothing for surety. It meant we had to pull out of the deal, and this was deeply humiliating because I felt guilty about letting down the vendors at the last moment. The whole business had depressed me deeply, and I told the board: "Look, for the moment, let's stop searching, getting excited, going through the hoop, and then being disappointed. Let's wait for God."

Heather was at home at Wartburg when Mary Van der Leeuw phoned to say she had seen an advert in a local newspaper for a little place that was going cheaply, 30 miles from Durban. Heather replied: "Mary, I really don't want to look at a place right now. I just don't feel like going through the whole business again with banks failing to support us."

Mary continued: "Heather, it's at a place at Cato Ridge and it's got some sort of resort on it." Bells suddenly started ringing in Heather's head. Right at the early stages, when she came back from Uganda, the Reynolds had been friendly with a young architectural engineer, Didier d'Hotman de Villiers, from Mauritius, whose wife Michelle had been the second secretary at God's Golden Acre. When Heather and Patrick were planning the future God's Golden Acre, Didier did a drawing of how it should look.

Heather had said at that time: "I'd like a little place at the back of the property where our choir could sing and perform. From what I have learned from exhibitions where Patrick's work is displayed, many adults are driven by their youngsters, who within minutes of arriving are pulling on their parents' arms shouting, 'Come on, Mum, or come on, Granny, let's go, let's go!' The problem with places grown-ups want to visit is that usually there is nothing for the children to do while the adults look round."

A new Water World had recently been opened just outside Durban, and every kid in Natal wanted to go there. "I felt we needed a place with a waterslide, or something like that, as an attraction for the children. Either they would encourage their parents or their grandparents to come to spend a day here, or else when they got here, they would be shooting off to play in the water while the adults looked round the galleries, or listened to singing etc. and hopefully became involved with our children and provided a donation."

That whole concept had gathered dust, years had gone by, and the Reynolds had more or less forgotten about it. Their budget, by this time, had also made it a pipe dream. Now Heather followed up the lead in the local paper. She phoned the number, but the man at the other end was extremely unforthcoming. She could hardly get anything out of him — there were no ancillary buildings and what there were had fallen down, he said. The man seemed very wary and unenthusiastic about telling Heather anything about the property, McPherson Farm, a former dairy and pig farm, at Cato Ridge. He was putting her off rather than trying to sell.

Finally, Heather said to him: "What is this resort? What do you have, what is it all about?"

He said: "Oh, we've got a waterslide."

There was a pause as Heather's thoughts were racing. She was excited, thinking to herself: *This place is in the middle of nowhere, four miles off the highway, with a waterslide, and water features!*

The man added: "Em... and there are also two swimming pools and another little paddling pool."

Trying to contain her excitement, Heather said: "I'd like to come and have a look at the place."

26
BUYING
MCPHERSON FARM

As Heather stood on the summit of the hill her memory stirred and returned to Mtubatuba in KwaZulu-Natal, and Madada in the Transkei, the settlements of her childhood more than 40 years before. Both had overlooked the rolling veldt and bush. There was a feeling within her that at last her journey with God had been defined. The wheel had turned a full circle.

McPherson Farm was a derelict, rusty, rundown place but in a wondrous position. The settlement, with its single-storey farmhouse, overlooked two valleys. This was rural Africa at its most magnificent. On the northern horizon lay the Valley of a Thousand Hills, and they could see the summits from the farm. The main house, about a hundred years old, was surrounded by gum trees and bougainvillea, and was an elegant wood-and-iron building – but in an advanced state of disrepair. Close to it was a wild fig tree, with branches sweeping in every direction. The iron roof was laid out in a pleasant design in several shapes, to enable the rainwater to run off effectively, and there were verandas on three sides of the house. The main front room, the dining room, had a large fireplace and high ceilings, but there were several leaks. When it rained, water poured into the room through the corrugated iron roof. The Reynolds knew it had the potential to be just what they required as their principal building – but the challenge would be in finding the funds to restore it properly.

As well as the large farmhouse, there were several small outbuildings, including an old dairy with milking bays. On the scrubland there was a gum tree plantation, and this, with its timber, would later provide a vital component for the God's Golden Acre building programme. Next to the farm was the resort, which although shabby, was landscaped, terraced and in working order.

On the downside, there were snakes: deadly green and black mambas, cobras, and worst of all, puff adders, which are small and aggressive. The Reynolds knew they would have to remove as many of the snakes as they could, and keep them under control, because the creatures would be a considerable threat to the smaller children. The snakes had moved in over the years, as human occupation had declined.

The owner, an engineer, had inherited the dairy and pig farm from his father, but had lost interest in the agricultural side and tried to convert it into a resort. He had funded the waterslide, swimming pools, trampolines and other landscaped features, including several reservoirs, before running out of money. He was now under tremendous pressure to sell up from his wife, who hated living in a semi-derelict property. His lack of enthusiasm on the telephone had been due to the fact that he didn't want to sell and was still hoping to find a backer or partner for the resort project.

When Heather stood on the waterslide, she knew. It was a defining moment. This was the place. There was no question about it in her mind – although there were, she correctly anticipated, going to be plenty of misgivings from the board about such a risky project. The charity had limited money, barely enough to pay the deposit, let alone carry out the vast amount of corrugated roofing repair work that was required. Some of the outbuildings had no roof and the others were like lacework. You looked through the holes at the sky. She knew her board would say: "Heather, it doesn't add up. We know you've got the deposit, but you'll need lots more money to do what's necessary here, and where are you going to get it from?"

Nevertheless, it would have to be a board decision because of the constitution. So, nervously, Heather called a meeting of the board at Cato Ridge, and they all stood under the 100-year-old fig tree by the main residence. As she had expected, half the members thought she was crazy. All they saw was a derelict heap. They looked at her as if she had totally lost her mind. Patrick, Mary and Carl, on the other hand, who understood her walk with God, were behind her. Mary said: "Heather, it's your vision. If you feel this is right, since we have come along this far, we'll go with what you want. We'll stand by you."

With Heather's vote, it was four against four. The others, who voted against, said they were sorry, but they wouldn't even dream of saying yes to something like that. It was now all down to the deputy chairman, Dr Gerrit Ter Haar, who was also acting as chairman, and so had two votes. Heather thought to herself: *He is a meticulous and precise man and I know he is going to be against it. There is no way this man is going to say yes to such a mess.* She looked at him frowning and said quietly to God: "This is your vision. I can't persuade this man. You know how difficult he is. You need to persuade him, because you know this is right."

Then she said to the acting chairman, quietly: "Gerrit, this is the place. I'll tell you the story of the waterslide another day. But you have got to trust me. This is the place. It might look dreadful and filthy and whatever, but this is it, Gerrit. I don't know how we are going to put a roof on the main house so the kids can be safe, warm and dry, but we have got to buy it."

He looked at her and after a pause said: "Well, I am just going to try one thing. If it works I can give the OK."

So the board agreed to take an option on the property for one week, and Dr Ter Haar went off to do what he said he had to do. Heather had no idea what he had got in his mind, or what he was working around. In fact she hadn't quite read her deputy chairman correctly. He had more faith in her judgement and intuition than she realized, but the canny doctor took good care not to tell her that.

Gerrit Ter Haar said long afterwards: "For six months we had looked around Pietermaritzburg to find a suitable place, and once, when we had nearly made a deal, Heather confided her bad gut feeling about the place, although the owners were committed Christians and were willing to meet us financially. She was right. It proved to be a false lead. A shebeen was hidden in the entrance, selling liquor and stolen goods. I have come to respect Heather's gut feelings."

Later that week the phone rang in Heather's office. She picked it up and found Gerrit on the other end, very excited. "You won't believe what's happened, Heather! I e-mailed a couple of my friends," he said. "Do you remember you met a Dutch couple a few years ago at Wartburg called Gerrit and Anneke Mons? They provided some money for a lawnmower and washing machine and then the wife, Anneke, came back again with her brother and they provided more support for the children?"

"Yes," she said, "I remember all three of them clearly."

He continued: "Well, the Mons went today to mortgage their house in Holland, and they are sending you all the money so that you can use it as a surety for the bank."

Heather and Patrick were astonished. She said to her husband: "How many people that anybody has met just twice in their life would mortgage their house so that some strange woman could go on helping kids in the middle of Africa? No, it doesn't happen in real life. This is fairytale stuff!" The Mons had mortgaged their house and deposited the money into the God's Golden Acre bank account without Heather and Patrick even having to sign a single piece of paper. There was nothing in writing that stipulated the charity had to repay the money at a certain time; there was no time limit on the loan.

Dr Ter Haar explained that his e-mail had informed the Mons that Heather had found the property she wanted for God's Golden Acre and that he believed in her judgement, but God's Golden Acre did not have any way of securing the property because it lacked fixed assets. The quick and astonishing response of this couple showed the sort of trust and Christian action that had kept Heather in her faith over the years. The Dutch couple were strangers; they didn't know her, apart from meeting her again one afternoon, when Gerrit and Anneke Mons had visited the Reynolds a couple of years later. That was the sum total of their knowledge of Heather, who she was, and the work of God's Golden Acre.

The Dutch couple's courageous generosity was also seen as final confirmation to Gerrit Ter Haar that God believed McPherson Farm at Cato Ridge was the correct home for God's Golden Acre. Far from being opposed to the concept of buying and converting the farm and resort, Gerrit had decided when he sent out the e-mails that if anyone responded with help, in answer to his questions, then he would say "yes" to Heather's plans. That's what he did. Within the week, the money was put into fixed deposit at the bank. The Reynolds bought McPherson Farm in August 1999.

Gerrit and Anneke Mons were not wealthy people – which made their intervention to help Heather and Dr Ter Haar even more astonishing. He had been a policeman based in Arnhem, and later a public relations executive. Anneke had been involved for many years with the Red Cross. They were an ordinary Dutch couple – members of the Baptist Church – with five children and twelve grandchildren. They met Dr Gerrit Ter Haar through their son Marcel who had done voluntary work at a hospital in Rietvlei, where the doctor was the director. The Mons went to South Africa to visit Marcel and soon became close friends with Gerrit Ter Haar. It was on a subsequent visit in 1997 that they met Heather.

They recall: "We saw a woman with a heart and a love as big as the whole of Africa, with a way of believing we had never encountered before. While the children were playing, she told us her life story, spoke about her dreams for God's Golden Acre, and her belief in the Lord. We are not people who give money away, because we are not rich. But after a final phone call from Gerrit Ter Haar about the situation, we asked ourselves: 'Shall we lend them what they need?' Anneke immediately said yes, so we mortgaged our house. When we mailed Gerrit about our decision, we got a reply saying that this was an answer to many prayers. We now go to Cato Ridge every year and every time we discover more children, new buildings, more staff, more volunteers, more help, more love and care – and more Heather!

"We go with the children to the shops, to the beach, to Shakaland, to Hluhluwe, and the children call us *Oupa* and *Ouma*, Grandfather and Grandmother, and we love them so much that sometimes we can hardly speak. To go with Heather to the valleys is a shocking experience. We think everybody should see the poverty, sickness, hunger, and the broken huts. We believe Heather's mission stands above disputes between tribes and politics. It is close to God. She can lose her temper, and sometimes she is so tired that she cannot argue, only shout. Then you had better get out of her way. She is not a saint, but a wonderful woman."

27
A MAN SHE COULD DO BUSINESS WITH

When a challenge or difficulty presents itself, Heather goes into overdrive to get a positive result — alone if necessary — when those close to her fear it may be impossible. Negative outcomes are not an option. She draws strength from her total trust in God. Dr Ter Haar says: "I think any record of her life should focus primarily not on her achievements but on the blind trust she has in God. He gave her a vision and empowered her to make it happen."

There are certainly no doubts in Heather's mind about the guiding hand of God in her life. She sees herself as an ordinary woman, and has never been quite sure why she was chosen for the task of saving thousands of lives in Africa. All she knows is that she does have that mission, and everything and everyone in her life must be subjugated to it.

People who meet Heather for the first time are struck by her softness of nature, good humour and concern for other people. She is easily moved to tears. Tell her a sad story, or of a personal tragedy or disaster, then this mother figure will weep in distress. On the other hand, she can flare up easily, and can be so stubborn that she sometimes fails to see the logic in an argument that appears to contradict her point of view. There is also a tough streak which some at first mistake for selfishness.

One of her greatest admirers, Hugh Evans, Young Australian of the Year 2004, summed it up succinctly: "She is a doer and great visionary and her whole life is in response to it. Every person she meets, she has to find some way that he or she can fit into the plan. It's not possible for her to meet someone and for that person not to be able to contribute something. Everybody has something to offer as far as Heather is concerned – and she has an innate ability to find out what that is. Then in a very short time she has the inspirational and persuasive ability to fire that person up. Sometimes, like many great visionaries, she can be erratic, and even make decisions that don't seem sensible. But this is partly because she is pushing herself so hard. She is always out there extending the territory."

Bronwen Reynolds wrote this moving testimony to her mother:

Many people ask me what it's like to be Heather's daughter. I know they're asking because of the impact she's had on their own lives, and I have wondered what it would be like to be like the volunteers or visitors she meets, to encounter this phenomenal woman it is so easy to admire.

I have come to realise that, as much as they do admire her, they'll never have more admiration than her own family, who know her – and her shortcomings. We can vouch for her human frailty, and because of that we stand in astonished wonder in the face of all she has accomplished through her faith.

My mum has become to me the definition of the word "capable". Nothing seems too much for her, no matter how impossible it may appear. She has this way of making things happen, and pulling them together in the last minute, just when the rest of us are losing the last shred of hope we may ever have had. I'll never forget the afternoon of my 21st birthday. We'd hired a large tent and I'd spent the day trying to get the decorations done, while still working in the office. With half an hour to go, and the tent far from finished, I was not dressed, and had hit absolute panic mode.

Mum arrived back from the valley, and as I sobbed my frustrations, she took control and sent me off to get ready. I remember thinking that even Mum couldn't fix this one, as guests would be arriving in the next 30 minutes.

Emerging from the house at the time we were supposed to start, I stood in the driveway, staring with unbelieving eyes at a perfectly decorated tent, with flower arrangements hanging that half an hour before had been bunches of blooms in buckets on the ground, hundreds of candles glowing a calm welcome, and everything in its place. A million-and-one stories like that are testimony to her uncanny ability to "make things happen".

Linked to her "nothing is too much" approach to life is her incredible empathy and boundless love for humanity at large. As far back as I can remember, Mum would stop the car along the road to pick up perfect strangers who did not have transport. Odd characters coloured my childhood as she reached out to anyone in need. As much as I resisted this impulse of hers, sometimes very vocally, as I entered my teenage years – not being able to bear being late for my activities as a result of unnecessary detours to take extra passengers to their destinations – I think it was because deep down I knew she was right, and admirable, in refusing to push those impulses aside like many of us do, as we justify our refusals to become involved.

When making the decision to work for my mum at God's Golden Acre in 2001, I remember a friend telling me that it would be a good decision, as I'd get to see a side of my mum I'd otherwise never know. He was right. In that year, I saw another aspect to her capability – as a good businesswoman, and having the strength of character to make difficult decisions and stick by them in the face of sometimes very hot-blooded opposition.

The blend of love and strength that characterises my mum has been a fascinating revelation to me, as I've realised that they are often the same thing. It is because of her love that she finds the strength to do the awe-inspiring things she does. Add to that the immense power of her faith, and you might begin to understand how she has come this far. But I doubt that anyone could ever understand.

My mum is by far the most inspirational person I have ever known or heard of. I have grown accustomed to the miraculous, as the unbelievable becomes fleshed out in daily life, through her unwavering faith in a living God who most certainly still answers prayer. I am grateful for this opportunity to let her know now, just how much she has changed and shaped my life in the most remarkable way, and how grateful I am to know her as a mother. There isn't a daughter alive as blessed as I am, and none loves her mum more than me."

On a slightly less endearing note, Heather is also a perfectionist who finds compromise difficult – which can make her hard to work with. That was certainly the case in finding a new chairman for God's Golden Acre in 1999. Following the widely anticipated failure of Heather to find anyone measuring up to her requirements, Dr Gerrit Ter Haar had set himself the challenge of seeking out a dynamic chairman for the charity. The board agreed a capable person was required, and he or she would need to be someone who could lead the charity into the next stage of its development. Heather knew the kind of person she wanted, but this did not always conform to what Dr Ter Haar, and some members of the board, thought would be the ideal choice.

Gerrit said to her: "Heather, you say you want this particular, fantastic person, who can guide us and support you in your faith and be a shrewd business person. You haven't found him, and so I'm going to look for a chairman. We can't run this organization without one. Apart from anything else, it doesn't read well on a funding proposal if we haven't got a respected chairman."

That night she prayed: "God, why don't you send me the

right man? You know that God's Golden Acre is a special organization. I need someone incredibly special to be able to head up the board of management." Nobody came, despite her prayers. No great man walked through the door. She wanted someone she felt would listen to Gerrit and her, whenever they met head-on, and give them a clear direction.

Finally, one day Gerrit walked into the office at God's Golden Acre, looking like the cat that had stolen all the cream. He said quietly: "I've found the right chairman."

Heather's heart sank. "I was worried that he might have found a wealthy businessman with lots of influence. But I wanted somebody who also knew about God and about stepping out in faith – about not always doing things according to the book. Jesus didn't do everything by the book, either. I needed somebody who would understand that sometimes you have to break, or bend, the rules."

Gerrit interrupted her thoughts: "Don't look so apprehensive, Heather!"

"I'm not looking apprehensive, Gerrit," she said. "Who is it?"

He said: "It's Mr Alan McCarthy."

She felt herself going ice cold, and said: "Gerrit, who did you say?"

"Mr Alan McCarthy," he repeated. Then he raised his voice defensively: "Heather, please don't get on your high horse! This man is a Christian, and he is chairman of this and chairman of that..."

She said quietly: "Gerrit, sit down. I have a long story to tell you." He looked puzzled and sat down opposite her. "Gerrit, 22 years ago I was driving down a hill and my brakes failed. A car hit me, nearly killing my son, and the man who drove that car and prayed at my side was Alan McCarthy."

The man who had changed her life 22 years before was about to come back into it to be her mentor, and God's Golden Acre's chairman. She had completely lost touch with him. However, when she had given her life to God one night at Deep Valley, she had phoned him the next day and said: "I just want you to know that I am the woman who crashed into you all those years ago, and I want to tell you that it was your Christian behaviour that turned me again to God."

Gerrit had been attending an African Enterprise Seminar, and Alan McCarthy was a speaker. The vice chairman was very impressed by his abilities as a speaker, his business credentials, and above all by his Christian faith. Knowing nothing of Alan McCarthy's shared experience with Heather, Gerrit had approached him about God's Golden Acre. He found he really didn't have to do a lot of persuading to get him to agree, in principle, to join God's Golden Acre. Alan McCarthy recalls: "My initial reaction was that I was exceedingly busy at that stage and that being such a small outfit it didn't really need a big support group. So I asked Gerrit to give me a couple of days while I prayed about this. I seemed to get a strong connection that I should do it."

Once again, Heather believed God had answered her prayers in an unexpected way. A meeting was arranged at Gerrit's house, and she was apprehensive about that because it had been a long time since she had met Alan McCarthy. She knew they would both have changed a lot in 20 years. So she went in, and there he was. She didn't recognize him. "Even at the time of the accident I wasn't really looking at his features, so now his face was not familiar. I just remembered he was a tall man. It was like meeting for the first time, and yet he was someone who had changed my life. It gave me an uncanny feeling."

They all sat down, and didn't have much to say. Both of them looked at each other like strangers. It was quite formal. He was reserved because he didn't know much about Heather. But it was a meeting he had wanted before he made up his mind about her.

Heather said later: "At least it was businesslike, and we

were able to explain about the work of God's Golden Acre, its finances, constitution and administration. When we had discussed everything on the agenda, he said he would go away and pray again, and talk to God. We waited for several days in a state of apprehension, and about a week later he told us he would accept the chairmanship. Shortly afterwards we had our first board meeting with Alan McCarthy in the chair, and now he was relaxed."

Alan McCarthy had been extremely impressed by that first meeting: "There was Heather, a capable, lovely lady, battling in rented premises, and the farmer wanted them out. Her love and care, even taking sick kids into bed with her, so they might die being loved and cared for, was amazing. She was and is a very capable woman with tremendous energy, foresight, and vision. If you added to that Dr Ter Haar's background and experience in founding and running hospitals it was clear God had put together an incredibly good team. My major function was to smooth the path between two very strong personalities, and keep the peace."

They all discovered they were on the same wavelength. That, according to Heather, has never changed. There is mutual trust.

28
MORE MIRACLES FOLLOW

The staff and children started moving to the farm at Cato Ridge with the Reynolds in late August 1999, and christened it Khayelihle which is Zulu for "beautiful home". Superhuman fundraising efforts would be needed to restore the settlement. Some of the older Zulu lads, who were part of the choir, and whom the Reynolds had helped to bring up, worked as labourers. They formed the backbone of the do-it-yourself team in the absence of funding to pay for professional builders. The young men worked with Patrick, Brendan and Heather on the removal operation from Wartburg, and began tidying up the new place, which was extremely overgrown. They took away loads of rotting corrugated iron, rusty wire and broken farm implements. Heather even hired a digger to bury some of the rubbish.

In the farmhouse there were cobwebs and choking dust everywhere, and many of the floorboards were rotten, so the boys had to lay makeshift planks across some of the rooms. The house appeared to be sinking into its own foundations. When they walked in, they felt they were going downhill. Nevertheless, out of necessity, Heather and the caregivers had taken 25 children with them to Cato Ridge, while friends looked after the fifteen tiniest babies until she was ready for them. This process took about four weeks.

"We had a bed in the middle of our bedroom," says Heather,

"and the rain poured in all around it, except on one dry spot. Five little children slept on the dry bed. We managed to find spaces out of the rain in other rooms too, so that all 25 children could sleep soundly. The pantry – also dry – became the clinic. It was touching at night to see the children lying there, not lengthwise, but in a line across the beds like little sausages. Nearly three years later, when we built the foster homes, each child had his or her own bed. They all got quite confused and tried to climb in sideways."

For the first few months there was no place to eat, and the entire community, which now numbered in the region of 70 people, ate their meals outside on the veranda. The Reynolds had a bedroom in the farmhouse and there was only one kitchen, bathroom and single toilet for the whole community. The lounge was a communal meeting room where the choir would sing, and it would double as a large family room for TV, and prayers in the colder evenings.

It was clear the first job should be to get what they had in the way of outbuildings fixed up. It was easier said than done – most of the buildings had no corrugated iron roof, or just the remains of one. Heather and Patrick were particularly worried that visitors might find their circumstances too shocking. Rather than provide them with donations, they might decide the charity was not fit to look after the children, and try to get God's Golden Acre closed down. To add to the problems when they arrived, Heather and Patrick had to meet the commitments – made by the former owner of the resort – to nine schools who had booked up to spend a day at the resort in September. It was up and running and the equipment was working, but some of the picnic shelters were derelict and required thatching, and the whole grassed area needed cutting to keep the snakes at bay. In the early days Patrick and Heather ran the resort. Later, the work was shared around, but at the beginning the Reynolds had to be everywhere.

As Christmas 1999 approached Heather found herself

facing a new dilemma. "The white Toyota that Ron Kuzel had given us and that had served us so faithfully started to boil on the long uphill stretches in the valley. It was so bad that by November I found I could no longer go to the valley because I was scared of seizing up the engine. We could only use it to take the children to and from hospital in Pietermaritzburg and to pick up supplies, and so forth. I did my last drop-off for food in the valley in the old truck in October, and November came without my being able to get there again. I was at my wits' end. Dr Ter Haar had sent away funding proposals to some organizations that he knew in Holland who might help us. He told them about our difficulties with delivering food to the valley.

"November went past, we were into December, and still I hadn't heard anything and there was no car. I hadn't been able to deliver any parcels. I felt terrible because I knew these people were getting desperate. I could just imagine how they would look up the road expecting me every day, and praying that I would come down it with the food parcels. I didn't know how they were surviving and I felt terrible. I was actually getting quite ill, and people started worrying about my health. It was the first time I had had real pains across the chest and all sorts of things were happening due to overwork and the consequences of not having had a break for so many years."

It was now the beginning of December and Heather went into town to get supplies. Everybody was rushing around doing Christmas shopping. She went into one of the supermarkets in Hayfields and saw dozens of loaded trolleys and people getting into the Christmas frenzy.

"All those trolleys, and so much food. It was almost as if there was going to be some famine or something, or the shops were going to be shut for a month. It was sheer greed and it upset me so much. All I could think about were the children in the valley a few miles away who were going hungry – or worse – and what was happening as these rich people stockpiled food. I went home angry and was physically sick with despair. I couldn't comprehend how this could happen in a civilized society."

Then Dr Ter Haar arrived at God's Golden Acre and brought with him some medicines with expired sell-by dates. Heather said to him: "Gerrit, I need a vehicle. I have got to get food to the people. They haven't had food parcels for two months."

He replied: "Heather, I know. I've done what I can. I have sent off the funding proposals."

He got up to leave and suddenly she again felt this anger shoot right through her and she thought: *No, it's not good enough. I can't go on with all those people buying that food, and me eating three meals a day, and all the money in the world, and the injustice of it…* She said: "You know what, Gerrit, people in the valley are starving. I'm not going to eat. I'm going to fast until I get a vehicle. I'll fast until God provides a vehicle."

Gerrit turned round and was really cross. "Don't be stupid. You'll ruin your health and you're really not well anyway."

Heather was adamant: "Gerrit, I tell you now I'm just not going to eat. How can I, when these people are starving and haven't got any food?"

So Dr Ter Haar walked back to the table. He realized Heather was absolutely serious. "I think we'd better pray about this, Heather." He sat down across the dining room table and put his hand over Heather's, and they prayed together: "God, you see the need, that Heather really needs a vehicle. God we urgently, urgently, urgently need a car. God, I put this in your hands. Amen." Then he left.

Half an hour later, when he had got back to his home in Pietermaritzburg, he phoned her. "Heather, you won't believe this! You are just not going to believe this – as I got home the phone was ringing while I was opening my front door. I got to it just in time and answered it, and Metter Daad, from Holland, was on the line saying they have approved the funds and issued a deposit today so we can go out and look for a vehicle."

Within a week, and well before Christmas Eve, Heather was back in the valley in her new vehicle, a second-hand Isuzu truck. Once again God had provided in her hour of need, and the desperate families were provided for. "We worked right into Christmas Day getting the sacks of food, and the donated presents for the children out to the valley. They were over-joyed to see us, so grateful and so relieved, and it was won-derful to watch the happiness on the faces of the children. They just glowed. That's what Christmas is all about – giving joy and happiness to the poor people."

Shortly after Christmas, in the New Year, a British team from the Soul Survivor Church in Watford, who had been working on a Durban street children's project, arrived virtu-ally unannounced at God's Golden Acre. The young Christians did a thorough job in clearing much of the site over their four-day visit, helping the Zulu lads to remove old corrugated iron roofing and rotted timber beams. They returned a week later to clear the final roofing, and presented Heather with a gen-erous donation from a collection they had made.

Meanwhile, another miracle solved the roofing problem, and came in the form of an elderly missionary doctor from America called Dr Hales. He was a Mormon from Salt Lake City, in Utah, and he was in Africa with his wife to carry out various medical projects. He had arrived at God's Golden Acre, Wartburg, earlier in 1999, and now visited the new headquarters for the first time with his wife to treat Nondeka, the little girl who had been shot through the spine by her step-father. Her leg was numb and she still had a nasty sore on her left foot. Dr Hales had a brace that he hoped might straighten the knee. Two operations had already helped to straighten Nondeka's leg, but more work was required. Dr Hales looked around the settlement, and exclaimed: "This is too awful; you can't live here like this! The roofs are collapsing!"

He contacted church friends in America and within a few months raised 70,000 Rand. On his last visit, before returning to the USA, he told Heather: "I want to see a proper new roof on all the old buildings when I return. I know you're going to use everything." The building supplies for the restoration work arrived, and the African lads got to work on the repairs at the beginning of winter 2000. Within a few months all of God's Golden Acre's collection of tumbledown buildings had a new corrugated iron roof.

Later that year, a team of Dutch volunteers, led by Ralph and Heidi Hekman from the charity Livingstone, were diverted from another project to Cato Ridge to do a month's work, much to Heather's delight. "It was just what we needed when there was so much work to be done, and they brought with them project money, but it was also a bit of a predicament for me because the children were really cramped in Mons House. So we juggled things around and then worked hard for a month refurbishing the farmhouse, sanding down, and repainting the iron cladding on the walls and cleaning the wooden beams. We repainted it white, and the place just looked so different.

"We also used the project money to put in a better bathroom in Mons House. The Dutch worked tirelessly, fingers to the bone, and when the work was all finished we decided to officially christen it Mons House, at a special ceremony in honour of Gerrit and Anneke Mons. They were there for the opening on Christmas night 2000."

Gerrit Mons recalls: "They kept it from us to make it a huge surprise. They tricked us into leaving the family's evening dinner. As we walked in, the orphans stood there with burning candles in the dark and sang for us. It was one of the very few times in my life that I've had tears in my eyes."

Dr Hales came back to visit God's Golden Acre two years later and could not believe his eyes at the incredible progress that the charity had made with all its building work, much of it done by the Zulu lads.

29
MORE VOLUNTEERS ARRIVE

Since their arrival at Cato Ridge, Patrick had been growing very concerned about the crippling workload upon Heather — the stress of it had already made her unwell late in 1999. The community was now nearly 80 strong and she was directing every aspect of its life, nursing the babies, organizing food and supplies, managing the fundraising, educating the orphans, and then finding time every day to make her journeys into the valley. She was often up during the night, awake by dawn, and sometimes did not return from the valley until long after dusk. The Zulu caregivers provided solid support with nursing, housekeeping and cooking, but Heather desperately needed specialized help, such as that provided the previous year by her Norwegians, Vibeke Blaker and Marianne Jenum. Once again, fate intervened. In January 2000 Heather received a call from Project Trust in England. They wanted to place two female volunteers with God's Golden Acre who had been working at Durban Boys' Town. The organizer of Project Trust said: "Could you use two volunteers for a year?"

"Oh, that would be marvellous!" Heather replied.

One of the new volunteers was Lucy Foster from Warwickshire, England, and the other Sarah Rodin from North London. Heather's life was immediately made easier by the arrival of the two British teenage girls. She told Patrick:

"They literally put down their suitcases and started work tonight changing nappies, feeding the babies, lifting toddlers out of the mud, and making sure they had something to eat at mealtimes."

In the following years hundreds of young people from many countries were to become volunteers at God's Golden Acre and most of them have remained ambassadors for it, raising funds and raising its profile in the world. Their presence enabled Heather to establish a hospice, a crèche, an infants' school, and various project teams for building and maintenance work. At any one time there may be more than 40 volunteers working at God's Golden Acre.

Shortly after the arrival of Lucy and Sarah, Project Trust contacted Heather again to say a young man, Sam, and another girl, Helen, were not happy at their placement in Swaziland. Would she have them too? So the two additional volunteers arrived at God's Golden Acre the following week.

Sarah Rodin took special care of Millie. This little girl was both disturbed and mentally challenged when she arrived at God's Golden Acre, at the age of twelve. She had severe learning difficulties and was aggressive towards the other children. A charity worker had found Millie wandering by the road in December 1999 and discovered that her mother was a prostitute and when her mum couldn't work she'd send Millie to "fetch water". The little girl would be taken away and sexually abused by men. The first thing Millie said to Heather, upon arrival at God's Golden Acre, was: "Please don't send me to fetch water for anyone." The charity worker had taken Millie round to several children's homes but none would have her because she was so retarded and disturbed that she needed one-on-one care. She pleaded with Heather: "Please take Millie, because if you don't, I'm going to have to take her back home to where I found her. No one else will take her on."

Heather took her in and at first, until Sarah arrived, she did not know how to cope with Millie. She did not play with the other children, was aggressive, swearing in Zulu, and would shuffle around mumbling and shaking. If Heather paid Millie any attention she would grab and squeeze her, and often bite. It was Millie's way of showing affection, but easily misunderstood. Sarah took on the job of calming Millie, gaining her trust, and working with her for two or three hours a day.

Heather wrote: "Sarah gradually turned her around, and she went from not being able to concentrate on anything, to becoming a pupil at a special school where she is learning maths and English. Millie is now tidily dressed, she can take care of herself, and gets along with the other children. They don't push her away any more."

Eighteen-year-old Susan Balfour, from Stirling in Scotland, arrived shortly after Sarah and Lucy. Susan soon started to focus on one of the sickest and weakest babies, Thulani, a blind HIV-positive baby, by caring for and cuddling him for hours. Thulani's was a shocking case that appalled other Zulus because it involved the betrayal of two daughters by a father — from whom they should have expected to receive protection. He raped Thulani's thirteen-year-old mother, who was his younger daughter. He was prosecuted for this offence, released on bail, and then returned home and turned his attentions to his older daughter — whom he also raped. It is a sickening fact that many African men believe the myth that they can be cured of AIDS by having sex with a virgin. The nearest virgin is usually a young female relative, and so there are many cases of sex abuse like that of Thulani's mother and her sister.

In the months after she arrived, Susan Balfour made sure that Thulani's last days, as AIDS gradually killed him, were spent in being loved and cared for. The following are extracts from her journals.

6th February 2000. My third day in Khayelihle. Starting tomorrow I have been assigned to work with the nursery children aged birth to six years. I am to establish a preschool class for the three-year-olds and Heather has also asked me to work one-on-one with one of the babies. His name is Thulani, he is eleven months old and he has full-blown AIDS and hydrocephalus, a build up of fluid on his brain. Because of this, he is blind and disabled.

"He just looks so lonely," Heather told me with a troubled countenance.

So at about 7:30 this evening, after the children had eaten and been bathed, I went into the nursery to spend some time with the little ones.

Absolute madness! There are children everywhere; sprawled across the beds, rolling all over the floor, on top of the wardrobe...

"Down from there *right now*," I shout across a din of squeals and shouts and laughter as a little body darts out in front of me from under a bed. And in the thick of it all, lying in a pram in the middle of the room – Thulani.

I bent over him. "Hello my little man," I crooned, "I'm Susan." Thulani's appearance is heartbreaking. Huge milky eyes deviated downward in a bulging skull. Thulani is obviously completely blind – his gaze is darting and completely unfocussed: quite spooky. He is tiny – more like eleven weeks than eleven months and there isn't a single ounce of flesh or muscle on his bony frame. He has twig limbs, I can trace every rib, his stomach is caved in and the skin around his knees is loose and wrinkled. He looks like a famine victim, like he is hanging on in this world by a thread.

There was a bottle in the pram beside him. He looked like he cold do with a good feed, so I picked him up. His skin was hot and dry to my touch and Thulani screeched as I lifted him into my arms. He was prostrate and burning.

Meningitis, the doctor told Heather over the phone. The hospital wouldn't treat this in a terminally ill child. Keep him at home and keep him comfortable, was the advice. These were difficult words to hear. My processing mechanisms slowed the path to realization, and I struggled to come to terms with this cruel aberration of nature. The death of a baby – surely not.

We gave Thulani paracetamol syrup and were sponging him with tepid water when Heather returned from the storeroom, clutching a medicine bottle in her hands.

"I don't know if this little one will make it through the night," she sighed quietly, "But he deserves a fighting chance." Heather explained that children with compromised immune systems were vulnerable to a rare form of meningitis caused by a fungus and that this extremely expensive antibiotic was effective against it.

Hope!

Thulani was too weak to suck from his bottle. Heather showed me how to feed him with a syringe. "Take it slowly," she instructed. "You'll have to feed him every hour. Give him as much as he will take."

Six international volunteers, Thulani and I were with Heather in her sitting room that night. Those of us who believed prayed. It was a beautiful time of fellowship. Thulani was surrounded by love.

7th February 2000. My Thulani did not die last night! He took two full bottles of his milk today, and two small servings of baby porridge. He is tired and lethargic, but he is here! He seems a little realer today: just a little more "here". God, what a victory! I am surprised that I have the courage to love a fatally ill child. I suppose at first I clutched the drop of hope Heather offered. Now I know Thulani is my little fighter. I'll fight with him.

24th February 2000. We celebrated Thulani's first birthday today!

I am so, so proud! Less than three weeks ago, we would never have dared to dream about this day. Now it has come! For the first fortnight, Thulani got better, then sicker, then better and then sicker again. I can't remember the day the fever broke for good, but at some point, Thulani moved from better, *to even* better. The last week or so just seems to have been up and up, and up again! I am still holding my breath! Is it my imagination or is this baby filling out? Is that a double chin? Is there flesh on those thighs? – Wishful thinking perhaps?

Maybe, but Andrea, German volunteer, says Thulani is definitely looking fatter and yesterday he smiled when I said "Good morning" to him. *I know* that was real! Then later, as I was outside doing preschool with my little boys in the yard, Lucy came out of the nursery.

"Your baby is very lively today!" she commented. I went in to find him cooing and babbling in his cot! So then I stroked him under the chin, kissed him, blew a raspberry on his tummy and Thulani laughed! Wow, so many firsts in one day! Here is my little man doing all this "proper baby stuff," and I feel so warm and fuzzy inside! I swear, I never knew what joy was until that moment!

And that's not the best of it – I have three small witnesses to all of this! Khethiwe, Zinhle and Mlu saw Thulani's response. They began to take turns entertaining him, and encouraged by his smiles and giggles, continued with this until someone rang the school bell out in the resort to signal the end of break time. Pure magic! Thulani has emerged from that cold dark place called despair. Gone is the little skeleton child. Thulani is all soft and sweet – too cute!

27th February 2000. It's official – Thulani's transformation is nothing short of miraculous – Heather says so! She has just recently returned from a trip in the Drakensberg mountains. I was cleaning Thulani up in the bathroom, feeling a little low as he had just projectile vomited his entire feed! Heather was with a guest in the living room. She asked to hold him and marvelled over how heavy he was, saying she had heard how bubbly he had become.

"See, Susan my girl," she told me, "God sent you across the

ocean to make a difference in the life of a child!" I turned red, but of course, I was very flattered. Heather continued to talk about how this transformation was all down to my gentle way with him, my care and attention. Of course, her praise is totally unwarranted, but her words meant so much to me. I have felt quite despondent at times. Heather has boosted my confidence today. She has achieved such a lot and she has a huge vision, and it's *amazing* to be noticed by her! I find that I'm really pondering her words on the impact basic care and tender loving care on Thulani's spirit. Was it really that simple? Is it really so easy? Surely there must be more to it? Yet Heather absolutely maintains there is not! If she's right, this miracle can be replicated and one person really can make a huge difference, step by step, one child at a time. And if this is what one person can do, imagine what we can do if we all get in on it!

30

THE DEATH OF THULANI AND THE INSPIRATION OF ELLIE

Lucy Foster and Sarah Rodin were still only teenagers, but the English girls were so well organized that in April 2000 Heather felt confident in leaving them in charge of the children and the eight senior caregivers while she was out of the country on a trip to Zambia. The other senior male staff, Pieter Nel, George and her son Brendan, were there to give them support. Heather has always put a priority on making sure her volunteers and visitors get the chance to experience the real Southern African wilderness and introducing them to a variety of countries.

Sadly one night while the party was out of the country, Thulani passed away and the two English girls who had been left to run Khayelihle had to take charge. They laid Thulani out, placed him in the coffin, and organized the funeral. Lucy Foster recalls: "His death was a big, fast lesson, and the most important thing that had happened to me while I was there. Sarah and I were woken very early one morning by one of the carers who was sleeping with Thulani, who said that he had passed away. We went into the nursery and found that he had gone. We checked him over, laid him out, and somehow coped with it, sort of going into autopilot. We phoned Dr Ter Haar as Heather had instructed we should do if we needed him, and he helped us get the death certificate and all the legal side of things sorted out. Thulani's body was taken to the mortuary.

"We just coped. We got things arranged, ordered the coffin. At the funeral Sarah and I were the only white people, and everyone stood in a circle around the grave. They had dug the grave in preparation, placed in the coffin, covered it with earth, and then built a mound of rocks over it.

"The Zulus took it in turns to start a song and then other mourners joined in. When each song ended there was a pause and you wondered what would happen next. Then someone else would start another song. It was very spontaneous and there was singing for the whole funeral really, lasting perhaps 40 minutes."

Susan Balfour went on to care for Ellie, who at the time was two-and-a-half years old and a victim of the HIV virus. The struggle to keep Ellie alive was eventually to succeed. Lucy Foster and Susan Balfour spent many hours each day pouring love and care into Ellie. They tried everything they could think of to make her smile and eventually came up with the answer. The Teletubbies! They would sit with her and watch the big beam of happiness appear on her face. Heather says: "It was wonderful to see. So, thank you, Teletubbies!" The nurses at God's Golden Acre placed Ellie on expensive vitamins and good nutrition, and she responded well. In time, Ellie grew into a healthy little girl and went on to attend preschool, where she became an excellent singer.

31
VOLUNTEERS AND
VISITORS
IN THE VALLEY

If life at God's Golden Acre, a sanctuary for the orphans, was witness to occasional tragedies like the death of Thulani, interspersed with joyful news like the recovery of Ellie, then new volunteers soon became aware that real horrors were to be found in the valley. Sophie Wong, a 25-year-old British volunteer worker at God's Golden Acre for several months, wrote on the Internet of her experience in the valley:

We went to Swayimane today, which is one of the valleys where God's Golden Acre delivers food parcels. We drove to the drop-off point where there were already quite a few people waiting. We spent some time with the children, who sang and danced to us. Heather gave a short talk and pointed out to us a couple of children who were the heads of their families, and looked after their younger brothers and sisters. One of these girls was perhaps 16 years old, and she cried when she was pointed out to us.

At first she did not want to speak to anyone who tried to comfort her. We found a Zulu speaker and asked her if we could pray for her. She agreed and a few of us just gathered around her, and her brothers and sisters. For a brief moment whilst we were praying, God gave me an insight into how she was feeling.

My heart ached with how she was hurting, how she felt so lost and in despair. I could not stop the tears from rolling down my cheeks. How could we in our comfortable lives imagine for a moment what she goes through every single day that she lives?

Just as we were packing up and ready to go I went over to say goodbye to her. We had a photo taken together and she smiled and gave me a hug. I was so touched how she had allowed us, complete strangers, to comfort her and to pray with her in the space of a few hours. While we were there, we obtained some profiles for the child sponsorship programme that is being set up. Some of the children had written that their happiest moments had been the day that Heather had brought them food. Their most difficult moments were when their mother died or when their parents "left and never came back".

I saw these children today and they were so friendly and loving. Not once did I hear any of them complain and they were so grateful for the food and clothes that they received. Being there today has been the most special day of my trip so far. I can only try to imagine how they all must feel – and pray that God will guide, help and protect all of them every day that they live, and remind us that we can do our bit to help, and together make a difference.

Volunteers like Sophie Wong who come to work at God's Golden Acre soon discover that things are run in a highly unusual manner. Heather is so swept up in the tidal wave of unplanned events that the only workable way of operating is to prioritize them as they happen. The casualties of this method of working are that important, long-term or strategic matters get shelved, appointments are missed, and even important people kept waiting.

Heather regrets this but is unrepentant because she believes the important things that need doing first usually concern a child's life. "I sometimes have to stand people up; when there is an emergency call I have to go. I am answering a call to a situation where a mother may be dying and I must reach the children to bond with them before she dies. I get in my Land

Rover and I shoot down to the valley. The ones I go to are usually those who have no family support. So I know it is going to be somebody passing on, and in need of help for the children. You can never be sure how bad the children are. The sufferers will always be incredibly thin, wasted and in terrible pain. It is very important for me to be able to make a bond with the children because these are such incredibly sad situations."

She e-mailed to a close circle of friends one night:

I have had a most dreadful, trying day and evening and feel so very upset. I was doing my rounds in the rural valleys, taking poverty relief parcels to the grannies, or child-headed households, and as we were approaching our last port of call – it was already getting quite dark by this time – we were stopped, and an old woman begged us to come to help her friend.

We turned around and went along the most appalling road that finally petered out, and so we parked the vehicle and took the last poverty food parcel and our first-aid kit. We walked the remaining kilometre down a mountain in the dark with a miserable flashlight. When we arrived at the little hovel it was in total darkness, with only a small portion still with any roof covering at all. We always put candles and matches into our food parcels, so we lit a candle and entered the tiny room.

There on the small bed lay a young woman, approximately 26 years old. As we entered, rats took off across the bed: they had been eating her feet. There were three little children aged 18 months to seven years. The dying woman was clinging to her babies, and by her sunken face and shrivelled body was obviously HIV-positive which was now full-blown AIDS.

There was not a single crumb of food or any medication. The children were in tatters and so cold and hungry. I spent a few hours sorting things out and I will arrange a small support team but this has really shaken me. I should be used to it, but I still find myself so emotionally involved.

It is so awful – how many other people are lying helplessly in the same way? I just wanted to share this with you all. It is 3am and I find sleep impossible.

Heather added later: "The people in the valley know I do not have endless money, but every dying mother wants me to take care of her children because she knows they will survive. I have often wondered how it must feel to be that dying woman, praying that I will come to her hut. For her, my arrival may be a miracle."

Ann Smith, treasurer of God's Golden Acre in the United Kingdom, who also heads the child sponsorship programme there, arrived for her first visit to Cato Ridge. On her first morning she was packed into the Land Rover, with other visitors, to distribute food and supplies to the valley. She wrote:

News comes that a girl of ten has suddenly died. She was at school the day before and seemingly well. The little girl had the "voice of an angel" and a promising future. The cause of death is probably meningitis. The parents would not be familiar with its symptoms or how to deal with it.

Our group makes its way to the mud hut where the body lies on a mattress. The mother and grandmother are there. The women mourners sit on one side of the door, and the men on the other. Gentle songs are sung in harmony, led by Heather. The grandmother is shattered. The child's mother sits silently, grief-stricken.

Our group moves on. Heather says she will now go to another hut to say prayers for a mother who has just lost her second son, just 18 years old, to AIDS-related diseases. We climb to the home and sit indoors while Heather prays with the family. Two mounds in the garden are the only remaining symbols of the existence of the mother's sons on Earth.

The girlfriend of the latest victim is 16 and banished to a tiny hut further up the hill where she will die alone without care. We walk quietly into the darkness where the girl lies; not a single candle burns. At first there is no sign of anything in the bed, but soon our eyes become accustomed to the darkness; the girl is so emaciated that there is not much left to see. Heather prays for the teenager. It is evident she will not need to visit again.

One more family is calling for Heather today. There are fifteen of them and they have no food. The Land Rover climbs higher and higher in the fog and drizzle until we get to a tiny path where we get out and walk to a hut. Darkness falls in a matter of minutes and there is no light. Inside, the father makes a fire in the middle of the floor – burning sprigs of wood and plastic bags. The smoke is overpowering, and we realize this family has no choice but to breathe these fumes every day. The family is touchingly grateful for the supplies of rice, beans, candles and tea. Only one candle is lit at any time. They are stockpiled in case Heather is unable to get through next time.

Susan Balfour wrote in her journals on her first visit to the valley, of her horror at observing the potential for child abuse in these rural areas:

We go to see a thirteen-year-old girl, Thandiwe, who tends to four younger children. These are her eight-year-old sister, a six-year-old nephew, a four-year-old girl, and her own baby. Thandiwe has headed this little household since their mother abandoned them two years ago. The children all have different fathers. Maybe the men are dead, maybe not, but they certainly are not here.

Thandiwe greets us at the gate with the warmest smile. She asks politely, in broken English, to please wait a few minutes before coming inside – she wants to wash the children first. Home is a cold and dark stick-and-clay hut with a dirt floor, no electricity or running water, a set of lopsided shelves and a bed. A campfire burns dimly in the centre and the acrid aroma of the smoke hangs in the air. I am gripped by an acute sense of gloom.

We have all seen the pictures of gaunt adults, the sick and dying, naked pot-bellied children with twig legs. Now reality.

As the sun rises every morning Thandiwe and her sisters set off on a walk of two-and-a-half miles to the river with empty plastic containers. They fill them there, and then return to the hut, with the containers balanced on their head. They sweep the dirt floor inside.

There will be no breakfast. They never eat in the mornings – the sacks of rice and mealie-meal and beans must be used sparingly if they are to last. Thandiwe unties the baby from her back and the oldest children make their way to school with empty stomachs. Four-year-old Nomosa is now in charge of the baby until the children come home. They will go to collect firewood, cook supper and then, off to bed. The children are beautiful but frail, and their thin arms are bare, even though it's winter. The baby scratches at a scaly rash on her bare buttocks.

Some of the orphans from God's Golden Acre are with us. "Last year," an eleven-year-old girl whispers, "I visited Thandiwe here." She describes how the children had run out of food and how, after scraping the burned starch from the bottom of the rice pot and eating it, they had lain down on the bed and cried as hunger pains racked their empty stomachs.

All the children join us outside the hut to sing with her. A drunken man in a blue boiler suit saunters up to the group, leering at a young girl, who is no older than twelve. I prickle with a new awareness. These children are open to abuse. They were born out of wedlock, and in the Zulu culture that means they are not recognized by their extended family, and there is no protection from within its traditional patriarchal structure. Child rape is rife here, and in this hut there are five children alone, with no way of securing their home at night. Anger inflates inside my chest. I have a lump in my throat. Visualize it as a rock in my hand... On the way back up the dirt road out of the valley, I simmer with rage. Orphans lose their childhood – and the breath of innocence around them disappears. Sickness, death, malnutrition, ostracism and rape... it is a shock that this reality exists for tens of thousands of children in the Valley of a Thousand Hills.

Many other volunteers ventured into the valley in the early years of God's Golden Acre — some reluctantly. The Norwegian girls Marianne Jenum and Vibeke Blaker travelled to the valley against their better judgement. Marianne recalls: "I remember Vibeke and I actually made the decision never to go to the valley. Heather told us horrific stories before we got a chance to go there — especially about white people being killed. The worst story was about a white nun who was raped and then got her throat cut. For me, the rape and murder of a nun symbolizes the dangers of the valley. Of course, Heather talked us into it. And as long as I was with her, I only experienced short moments of fear.

"But there have been other times when I've been very afraid. Heather always stressed how dangerous the highways were, how the breakdown of the car could lead to robbery, and sometimes death. In short — African men walking along the roads at night could be very dangerous. Then, one late evening we were driving home. It was pitch-dark and misty. There was a tall Zulu man walking along the road. And suddenly Heather stopped the car! She rolled down the window and asked him if he wanted a ride. I just froze as he climbed in. Nothing happened, but it was a very scary ride. Her explanation for picking him up, despite her own warnings, was simple: 'He needed a lift.'

"Heather always rushes to get out of the valley before dark. But sometimes there was too much work, and it got dark and misty before we could leave. It freaked me out when I noticed that Heather looked worried. One night we experienced the worst storm on the way back. I was sitting in the back of the 'bakkie', with no canopy, when the rain came pouring down. It was impossible to see more than one metre ahead, and there was lightning every five seconds. Trees were falling over the road. I've never experienced the violence of nature like that. Heather drove the first car, and she drove very fast to get back. I was sitting in the second car, and I was terrified that we would lose her, because we didn't know the route back. And if we'd been trapped by a big tree, or if the car had broken down, we'd have been all alone in the dark valley. So – as long as Heather was there and was in control – everything was fine. When she looked worried, the rest of us freaked out..."

3 2
PRACTICAL HANDS ARRIVE... AND MORE MIRACLES

With the arrival of the first volunteers, the workload in terms of nursing, and managing the community and its needs on a day-to-day basis, was shared around. However, there were serious problems of an entirely different nature to resolve at God's Golden Acre. The Reynolds remained desperately short of practical help. There were no electricians, mechanics, plumbers or carpenters within their little community. There was no one to take a lead with the Zulu lads and teach them how to develop their building skills.

One afternoon a car arrived at Cato Ridge and 20-year-old Orin Wilson stepped out. He had been a close friend of Bronwen for some years. Orin had a good job with an engineering company but told Heather he was fed up with the corporate world. Heather said they would be happy to have him there, especially since he spoke English and Zulu. She recalls: "Orin was brilliant for us, as was his cousin Taffy Lloyd who went on to become our driver. Orin wired Mons House and put up poles with lights around the pool and the yard to improve our security. He did many other practical things like tiling, plumbing, laying floors and keeping the equipment in the resort maintained."

Then the Reynolds came to an agreement with Les Young, an experienced local builder, who had been very generous to

them by donating reject concrete blocks for the various building projects. Les owned a neighbouring farm and could
also speak Zulu. He agreed to become head of works, and
organized training. The African lads mixed cement, pushed
wheelbarrows and gradually learned skills such as bricklaying
and plastering.

Around this time Patrick felt that he and Heather needed
some privacy away from the main house. He wanted to move
into one of the barns that were being converted by the building team. Unfortunately, the building materials were running
out fast and there was no budget to fund continuing construction work. There was no cash at all to buy building sand,
and despite two badgering phone calls by Heather to a local
building supplies company for a free load, none was forthcoming. One day a German volunteer, Ove Spreckelsen, who
was an atheist, and impatient to get on with the work, challenged Heather: "We need the sand to do the floor, so why
don't you ask your God to provide the sand if you have no
money to buy some? We need a miracle," he said.

"I was so cross at that moment," Heather recalls. "I said to
him, 'Please don't make jokes.'

" 'I'm not joking,' he replied. 'You're always telling me
about this God of yours.'

" 'Just go,' I said."

After Ove went, Heather sat down and said to herself:
"God, this young man is quite right. Why don't you answer
our prayers? Why don't you? What is it, Lord? God, if you
really want me to beg, I will make a third call to these guys."
She swallowed her pride, picked up the telephone, and rang
the local building supply company again, asking for a load of
sand as a donation.

The girl on the other end of the phone was both curt and
unsympathetic. She went to consult with her boss. A moment
later she was back and said impatiently. "The manager says,
please, please don't phone him again, please. He is not going

to give any more sand and that's that." (He hadn't actually given God's Golden Acre any before.)

Heather now prayed quietly: "God, what more can I do?"

She continued with her work in the office but after about half an hour was disturbed by loud laughter coming from outside. Volunteers Orin Wilson and Ove Spreckelsen were hooting with laughter.

"What's all this about?" asked Heather.

"It's your miracle," Ove told her. "You see that man walking through the gate over there? He's the driver of a ten-ton truck of sand, and he has just broken down at our driveway. He has asked our permission to tip all this sand so his company can tow the truck away – apparently the gearbox is broken!"

In fact the contractor offloaded half of the sand and tried to tow the truck away, but only got about 100 metres. The remaining load was then dumped by the side of the road. Ironically, it was the same company from which Heather had just asked for some sand.

Meanwhile, the Reynolds continued to lurch from one financial crisis to the next. The problem was that although God's Golden Acre was a registered charity and an NGO with a board and a proper constitution, it remained financially largely a one-man band, with Patrick's sculptures funding everything except for various small cash gifts, and donations of food, clothes and medical supplies. All through 2000, and for most of 2001, the familiar spectre of bankruptcy continued to present itself again and again. What were they going to do? The community was bulging at its "seams", and there were thousands more children out there in the valley, in desperate need of help, yet God's Golden Acre was chronically underfunded.

A new crisis emerged suddenly when there was no money to purchase powdered milk for the babies. Heather summoned a group of God's Golden Acre staff and volunteers for prayers. She explains: "What I do in a moment like this is say,

'Let us pray, and put it before the Lord.' Most people don't make a fuss or argue, and if they happen not to be a Christian, they just come and join in. I don't worry if someone is a Christian or not; they are there and people just stand around while I pray. On this occasion they stood and listened to me in prayer on the veranda of Mons House: 'Our dear heavenly Father, we thank you for this day, we thank you for our blessings, Lord. Father, right now we just come before you. You know the problem that we are having, Lord, you know the crisis, know what we are facing, Father. In your name, Lord, we will pray now that you may help us with this crisis. Give us a solution Father, if this is your will. We pray now that we need a miracle, and that you will answer this prayer, so, Jesus, we just thank you that you have brought us into your Kingdom, that we may know you, and that we may turn to you in a moment like this, Father. Dear Jesus, we love you and trust in you, and we ask this in your name. Amen.' "

Divine intervention came just a few days later as it had with the sand. This time it came in the form of a broken-down truck three miles away. The truck, laden with powdered milk, broke down on the highway just off the turning to Cato Ridge. It could not be towed away with a full load and so the transport company needed to get rid of the powdered milk. As soon as she heard about this, Heather thanked God, then she made a call to the manager of the company. He said: "You're welcome to it, but you'll have to get it off the truck yourself."

Again, Heather's little army came out with the small truck. It took a lot of work to bring in – but the powdered milk kept them in supplies for three months! Heather says: "I've had proof of the power of prayer – that it works when it is done unselfishly. We just can't be blasé about this."

33

THE YOUNG ZULU WARRIORS TOUR THE UK

Dance Link emerged out of the blue at God's Golden Acre. Some say it was another miracle. Dance Link is a forum of about twelve dance companies, directed by a woman called Lynne Maree. It decided to give free dance classes to underprivileged children, selected a charity, and arranged to send professional dance coaches to them every Saturday. Luckily for God's Golden Acre, the agreement with that charity fell through.

Lynne heard about Heather's charity from an article she'd read, and offered her the chance to get involved with Dance Link. She rang Heather: "Would you be interested in having some of your children trained in dance?"

"Oh! We'd love that, it would be absolutely wonderful," Heather replied. So every Saturday, Lynne Maree sent over a dance teacher, and the children started to receive professional training.

South Africa was chosen to host the World AIDS Conference in 2000 at the International Conference Centre in Durban, and the children of God's Golden Acre were invited to perform on the main stage. Thanks to Lynne, they were brilliant and full of confidence. They performed in front of former President Nelson Mandela, Madiba, and afterwards he asked the children to meet him. He waited for them as they came off the stage. Heather recalls: "It was a wonderful moment to go and meet him and shake his hand. I told him: 'Madiba, these are my children. I am not just their choirmaster, or choreographer."

When the Nelson Mandela Hospital was opened in Durban, he asked for the God's Golden Acre Children's Choir again. They sang at the opening ceremony. "He has a wonderful sense of humour," says Heather, "because when we met again on that occasion I stepped up and said, 'Hello, how are you, Madiba?'

"He replied: 'How wonderful that you remember me!' We both laughed."

Heather met Nelson Mandela on several further occasions but was unable to attend his 85th birthday celebrations in 2003 because of family commitments. She remains extremely impressed by his humility.

The tour to England of the Young Zulu Warriors was the idea of Howick Rotarian, John Tungay, who rang Heather just before she was due to be a speaker at a World AIDS Conference in Durban. They knew one another because Rotary has been supportive of God's Golden Acre on rural outreach projects. John said on the phone: "Rotary has done a lot for God's Golden Acre. There's a group here of young Rotarians from Britain; can I show them God's Golden Acre?"

Heather replied: "Sure, but if it's tomorrow we'll have to get someone else to show you round because I am a speaker at the conference in Durban."

He asked: "When do you speak?"

"I am due on at two o'clock," said Heather.

John responded: "How about we make the tour during the morning?"

Feeling pressured, Heather replied: "I am already in Durban at the conference." Somehow she felt that was not going to be accepted as an excuse. "OK, I'll come back if you want me to be there. I will drive all the way back to Cato Ridge, meet you, and then go back in time for my speech," she heard herself saying!

What a cheek! she thought to herself. She had reserved time to be in Durban because she wanted to hear all the main speakers. There was still so much to learn. Now she would miss two speakers. That evening she drove back to God's Golden Acre and told the children that they would be needed next day to perform in front of the visitors. "Let's do our best," she said.

She met the party the next day and showed them around, giving it her best shot. Then, just before the English party left, she decided on impulse that they ought to hear the whole works and said: "Would you like to hear our full choir?" The Zulu lads overheard this and were really angry because they had just mixed up cement, were covered in dirt and in their overalls. A quarter of an hour later, however, the choir appeared. The party from England listened in awe to the singing, and when the choir stopped there was silence.

John said: "Wow! This choir is really very good. Would you like to take them abroad?"

It had always been in Heather's mind to travel overseas with them and she jumped at it. "Yes! Yes! We'd love to tour," she exclaimed.

"OK, leave it with me then," he said.

Heather didn't hear one word from him again for three months. As the weeks went by she thought to herself: *Yes, a great idea, but talk is cheap!*

Suddenly in December John Tungay was on the telephone to God's Golden Acre: "Well, I've got Rotary on board and it all seems like it is going to be happening – and so have you got all your passports in order?"

Heather shouted down the phone: "What? Don't give me a heart attack! Most of them don't even have birth certificates, let alone a passport!"

John replied nonchalantly: "Then you'd better get on with it, hadn't you?"

The moral of the story for Heather is that it pays to walk the extra mile, to go to that extra bit of trouble for people, as she did in making herself available on that day.

For the next few months the team worked hard to create

the show. She was choreographer – a first time for her – and they got it together as the story of God's Golden Acre in song and dance. It was a challenge to integrate the talents of everybody in the group and come up with a blend that would work. The younger ones were now trained to dance and move on stage; the older ones could sing well, but had not been trained to professional standards in movement and stagecraft. Gradually they achieved a remarkable standard. Together, they told the story of the early days of violence, and the children being affected by that. Then followed the death and the dying, and finally God's Golden Acre creating hope for the future.

However, while the youngsters were literally "getting their act together" creatively, the tour organizers faced a nightmare with officialdom in getting the relevant papers in order to allow the party to leave the country. First there was the problem of the birth certificates, which they eventually managed to assemble, then there were the individual identity documents and finally the travel documents, or passports. The God's Golden Acre office worked night and day for over three months and just when they believed they had all the papers in order, and the permissions signed from guardians and foster parents … a bombshell. The Home Affairs Office in Pietermaritzburg advised God's Golden Acre that a computer had gone down, and all the files containing the IDs were lost.

The party would not be able to get passports without the documentation being recreated and signed. The horrified organizers of the tour realized they had less than 24 hours to do all the paperwork that had previously taken several weeks. Mandy de Vos and Kath Simms rushed down to the Home Affairs Office with a small team from the God's Golden Acre office. Plane tickets had been bought by now, concert venues and accommodation arranged in England. Financial disaster loomed on the horizon. Heather recounts: "I got a desperate phone call from Mandy late in the afternoon saying that all the necessary permissions were signed except for a handful from

Baba Jila, who lived in the Swayimane and was legal guardian to a small group of our leading performers. We would not give a credible performance on stage without them. Mandy pleaded with me: 'We have got to reach him and get him down to the office straightaway. Heather, you've got to go and find him.' I was an hour away from Swayimane. Even if I'd found Baba Jila immediately in the valley I would not get him to the office before it closed for the day.

"I said: 'Look, Mandy, there's no way I can get Baba Jila to you in time. It will take two hours and the office closes in an hour's time. We have got to put this in the hands of God. We must pray for a miracle. You pray where you are, and I will pray here.' So I got down on my knees and prayed for God to help us, to intervene in some way. I spoke on the telephone to Dr Gerrit Ter Haar, God's Golden Acre's deputy chairman, who was in bed. He had just had a serious back operation. We agreed that we needed a miracle. He said he would pray all afternoon. I then got on with a backlog of work and the next thing I remembered was Mandy walking through the door back at God's Golden Acre.

"She said: 'Oh, Heather, it's amazing – something extraordinary happened. Just as you said you would pray for a miracle and you put the phone down, I looked towards the doorway and, guess what? Baba Jila was standing there in the Home Affairs Office in Pietermaritzburg! We grabbed him and he signed all the guardian permissions. So it's OK.'

"We never found out how or why Baba Jila, who lives miles and miles away in a rural valley area, happened to be in Pietermaritzburg on that day, and why he appeared at the Home Affairs Office right at the moment we started to pray. Maybe we should just let it remain a mystery. The other extraordinary thing about it was that while all the fuss was going on about Baba Jila turning up, the cashier was being robbed in front of Mandy and Kath by an armed gang who stole all the money from the till. They were so excited they didn't even notice the robbery and couldn't give any descriptions to the police afterwards."

Each person on the tour, in which over £30,000 was raised, was sponsored by a different Rotary Club in England — hence the 30 performances and venues. The group travelled around on an English single-decker school bus that was given to them. The last night of the UK tour, staged in the Temple speech room at Rugby School, was its highlight and many former volunteers at God's Golden Acre came to see this show. There was a fantastic party atmosphere. Susan Balfour was in the audience, and the performance evoked both memories and emotions for her. She wrote:

> The hall seats 600 and is bursting at the seams. The atmosphere sizzles as my little ones give a spectacular performance: an effortlessly professional, stunningly choreographed blend of drama, music, songs and dance. Among them is a ten-year-old girl who sat on my lap almost three years ago and revealed a long-guarded and terrible secret. One night a man that she regarded as a brother took what wasn't his to take — he raped her. My little one wept bitterly as she recalled the events of that night in graphic detail, releasing a dam of emotion, and a cleansing balm of tears.
>
> Now she performs. She is far from broken. She looks out boldly, rejects the shackles of fear, dares to trust, to love and be loved. She is sweet and affectionate and her steps are full of energy and grace; she is one of our most accomplished dancers. I watch her with pride as she plays her part in the performance ... traditional Zulu harmonies and contemporary township dances alike, pulsating with pure African rhythm; the resonant drumbeat throbbing in her veins and through the dancers' perfectly synchronised, exuberant steps.
>
> A powerful display of resilience; the children rise against a past rooted in the wastelands of humanity. The audience is enraptured as their performance reaches its crescendo. It has been vibrant and haunting, with some spicy, mischievous twists. The applause is exhilarating; they receive a standing ovation.

Now I know that these children are the true stars in my life. Little ones, born in humble mud shacks, are rising from the wastes of human depravity and broken dreams, shining bright with a message of hope, a living expression of God's compassion, power and grace.

Heather had similar feelings by the end of the tour:

It was the last weekend and we were all attending a barbecue at the home of friends in Rugby, and I found myself sitting on a chair, watching my many children in incredulous wonder. It seemed for a moment that time had stopped, as I surveyed the scene before me in a kind of frozen clarity. The older members of the choir sat comfortably chatting with past volunteers who had formed friendships with them after many experiences together. The younger children ran with arms linked with those of their new British playmates, their giggling fervour heightening at the prospect of a second helping of ice cream.

It seemed to me that the days on which I had witnessed each child's arrival at God's Golden Acre were somewhere far in a distant past lifetime, out of reach of the happiness and restoration I saw before me now. It was difficult to reconcile the two pictures: children, formerly abused, broken and abandoned, now confident and happy, assuming their rightful place in society with seemingly effortless ability.

I knew the truth: I could tell you each and every tragic story behind the smiling faces I now gazed upon. Heartbreak, fear, desperation and hopelessness had coloured the features of faces too young to have to deal with such trials. But meet and overcome them they did, and I could only pour out the thankfulness that swelled in my heart, silently heavenward. Overwhelming pride for all they had accomplished, and gratitude for the opportunity to witness the second chances each of them had received and embraced, made me realize how truly blessed I am to be a part of what God is doing.

34
OPRAH WINFREY
COMES TO
GOD'S GOLDEN ACRE

The phone rang in the office at God's Golden Acre. It was someone working for one of the world's most respected television personalities, Oprah Winfrey. Heather was told the famous talk show host was planning to visit South Africa to build an academy for girls and to launch ChristmasKindness South Africa 2002, an initiative to create one day in the lives of underprivileged children that they could remember as a happy one. Oprah's team would organize 12 massive Christmas parties as well as local orphanage parties – in total involving 63 rural schools and three orphanages, reaching 50,000 children. Could one of these be held at God's Golden Acre?

"Yes, of course! We will welcome Oprah's help and attention, and feel deeply privileged by it," Heather told the Americans.

Later, Oprah sent out her researchers to Cato Ridge and they also travelled to the valley, where the rural outreach programme is active. Heather soon found herself closely involved with one of the ChristmasKindness South Africa 2002 orphanage parties. She went to Chicago with Hugh Evans of The Oak Tree Foundation and they spent several days with Oprah's organization, talking through the project, and agreeing Oprah's producers should film at God's Golden Acre later that year.

Oprah, accompanied by her team, which included a camera crew, arrived in South Africa before Christmas to host the pre-planned parties. Then came the day of Oprah's party at God's Golden Acre in a festively decorated marquee. Two hundred children, the orphans at God's Golden Acre and more than 100 youngsters from the valley, enjoyed the biggest party anyone locally had ever seen. "I have never witnessed such happiness and gratitude," said Heather. It was also part of an experience that changed Oprah Winfrey's life, and she wrote a moving account that was published on Oprah.com.

The miracle workers from HOPE*worldwide* and God's Golden Acre orphanage helped us gather some of the neediest children affected by AIDS – children with no food, no family, no home. It was a day of Christmas celebration that the children could always remember as happy. The children we were blessed to meet, and the people who care for them, changed our lives.

At each orphanage party, children whose lives had been devastated by AIDS were gathered together for a day of Christmas celebration. They were children who often had nothing, and no one. No school... no food... no family. Some did not even have a home. Many had to borrow clothes or shoes, just to be able to come.

As soon as I began to meet them, I knew, these were my children.

Children like 14-year-old Thanda, whose parents were dead and who, with her 8-year-old sister, lived at the mercy of a drunken uncle. When I asked Thanda what gift she wanted more than any other in the world, she asked not for a toy or clothes, but for a school uniform, so she could attend school, become a doctor, and return to care for her village. I promised her the future she dreamed of.

Children like Esona, whose only wish was to share her Christmas joy with her 29-year-old mother who lay dying in a nearby hospital. Esona hadn't seen her mother in two weeks. I took her to her mother that day. Their courage overwhelmed me.

We wanted to create a Christmas wonderland that would live in their memories forever. Games, jesters, lights, fairies, silver bubbles floating in the air, gifts piled high, shoes to fit each child, small and large, and all the food they could eat!

The children began to play, to laugh and sing, to feel a moment of connection. I watched as their eyes lit up, and their burdens seemed to melt away. Then it was time to gather around the Christmas tree. I called each child by name and handed each boy and girl a gift, individually chosen, wrapped and labelled just for him or her. I wanted each of them to know that on this day they were thought of and beloved.

They waited – so incredibly patiently – to open their gifts. Not even a whimper from the tiniest tot. I cannot describe the moment. "On the count of three you can all open your gifts together – ONE. TWO. THREE...OPEN YOUR GIFTS!" Many girls had never even seen a black baby doll. Now they each had one to love. One little one couldn't unwrap her doll fast enough, and furiously kissed it through the plastic! Trucks, soccer balls, solar-powered radios, and a big box of brand-new clothes for each child!

"Can I keep this?" one child innocently asked.

I know it wasn't the gifts that made these parties so huge. Even more than the gifts was the IDEA that someone thought of you, that someone wanted to make sure *you* were happy, even for one day. If you feel that, you can feel hope. You can imagine a possibility, a dream beyond this moment. *That* is a gift that will live longer than the toys, the clothes, and the shoes.

"I feel like flying," said a boy to my best friend Gayle, "but I don't have wings."

As we left the party, another little boy took my hand and wished me: "Go well." That was it for me.

"Mother Oprah," said a letter from a 12-year-old girl, "Thank you for making me feel human again. I am convinced that God provides." I am convinced that God provides, too. And the joy I felt from those children was a pure Christmas miracle.

Heather, deeply moved by the scenes from Oprah's day at God's Golden Acre, wrote:

> Imagine what impact that day must have had on the children – most of whom would have come from a falling-down hut with barely anything inside it, probably not running water, or electricity, and maybe not even enough food to go round the siblings.
>
> All were orphans. I would just love to have known what was going on inside their minds! They were so grateful and happy for what was happening to them.

During Oprah's time at God's Golden Acre, Heather suggested that in order to understand more about the lives of the children who had been at the party, Oprah should go to the valley herself to see how the people live. She recounts: "Now I could take the chance to get to know Oprah better. She is an admirable woman, highly intelligent, and well informed, good humoured, and with a sense of mission that she can help to make the world a better place, especially for children, and with girls a priority.

"She was already well aware that the magnificent Valley of a Thousand Hills was the setting of one of the world's worst black spots in the AIDS pandemic. But if you haven't experienced it, then of course you cannot really grasp the awful implications. I explained to Oprah that although we were hard at work with the rural outreach project in a few valleys, the overwhelming majority of them had not even been reached. Thousands of children were out there starving and dying – little kids abandoned and alone who hadn't asked to be in such a helpless situation. There was nobody out there to care, to hear the cries of children who have nobody to turn to.

"An entire orphan generation would be lost, I told her. The

evidence was all there for Oprah to see. This affected her profoundly. She saw mud huts that were falling apart because
there were no adults to repair them, untended and unculti-
vated land, long since abandoned and overgrown with weeds,
and the absence of farm animals to provide milk, or meat, or
poultry for eggs. I told her that in the vast valley areas that we
had not reached with our rural outreach project, there were
thousands of sick, weak children. On another visit we showed
Oprah the results of our work in those parts of the valley that
the rural outreach project reached and she met community
health workers who lived in the valley. Oprah was visibly
moved."

Oprah Winfrey's understanding was soon translated into
action and she subsequently helped to fund a very significant
increase in the number of families getting a monthly food parcel in one rural outreach project, sustaining hundreds of families in the valley of Sankontshe for twelve months – solely
from the resources of her private foundation.

Heather said: "These orphans owe so much to her. It hum-
bles me to think that what we do every day touches such a
famous and important person. We have made a significant
impact upon one of the most important communicators in
America and she publicly vowed in front of millions of
Americans to devote a large part of her life to the AIDS
orphans."

BBC correspondent Bill Hamilton, a distinguished international television journalist, arrived at God's Golden Acre a
few months later. Hamilton was on an assignment to make a
TV documentary called *Children of the Epidemic*. A Christian,
with long first-hand experience of acute human crisis,
Hamilton was curious to meet Heather and discover the
woman behind the legend:

I had read that her response to the AIDS orphans crisis was fired
by her religious beliefs, having experienced a dramatic conver-

sion to the Christian faith. Like the Apostle Paul, Heather's came whilst on the road – not to Damascus – but after her brakes failed at a stop sign and she ran straight into a brand new Jaguar sports car. Instead of berating her, the owner offered up a prayer with her. A clear sign, she thought, that there must be a God.

God's Golden Acre... sounds like heaven on earth... so would there be a Peter-type figure on the gate?

No, instead a young man called Andrew – the name of Saint Peter's brother – signals us inside the compound. Andrew is a volunteer worker from Toronto in Canada... one of many young people who'd heard through the grapevine what was going on in this remote part of the world and decided he had something to offer to the cause.

No sooner have we pulled our vehicle to a halt than we are surrounded by an excitable pack of dogs leaping at the open doors and licking our bare hands in an obvious show of affection. I guess they are probably from broken homes too.

Andrew leads us to the office where Heather is busily trying to sort out the latest problem to hit her desk... the refusal by the authorities to let one of the boys in her charge sit his school exams because he isn't able to pay. I have two contrasting visions in my head of Heather. One is of a resolute and assertive head-mistress whom you would cross at your peril. The other – totally the opposite – is a cherubic-type figure dressed in long, flowing robes whose posture and charm would melt the ice off even the most resolute opponent. I am completely wrong.

Here is a larger than life character, intensely loquacious and voluble with beaming face and an obvious capacity to cope with the multiplicity of challenges and quandaries that come to the fore here at almost every minute of every day. Her desk is piled high with papers and lists of important contacts with whom she must get in touch. The computer is playing up... the sweat pouring from her brow. She breaks off a hundred and one other conversations with volunteers, *gogos*, and helpers all clamouring for attention, to welcome us and hand over the keys to a house in the grounds that has been prepared for our needs, including a pot of chicken and rice placed on top of the oven.

Behind the office, her living room… a double bed is barely visible beneath a myriad of books, lamps, curtains, clothes, toys and every conceivable gadget and novelty necessary to look after the needs of 97 children for whom God's Golden Acre has become home.

She glances up at my blazer curious to know the origins of the badge that adorns my buttonhole. I explain that, like thousands of others, I have been a member of The Boys' Brigade that has been around for more than 110 years, and is part of the boyhood experience of many adults.

The Boys' Brigade is a Christian youth organization with over half a million members worldwide. It offers a wide range of activities, including games, crafts, sports, Christian teaching, music and holiday camps. It also embraces the Global Fellowship of Christian Youth whose object is the advancement of Christ's Kingdom, the promotion of education and the relief of poverty among the youth of the world.

It seems to me that the movement Sir William Alexander Smith founded in Glasgow all those years ago is just what Heather needs to help catch the energy and enthusiasm of youth and to channel it purposefully. She readily agrees.

When it comes to interviewing Heather for our BBC World documentary *Children of the Epidemic*, I find her oddly shy and diffident. It is as if the experience holds a terror for her. She understands the needs of the media but has been tricked in the past and now delivers her message in a way that leaves no room for misinterpretation.

Her relationships with Government – both national and regional – are nothing if not fiery. At first, it seems Pretoria took a dim view of her "cluster foster" experiment because it did not fit readily with their idea of *ubuntu* or care in the community. Indeed, some in authority went as far as accusing her of uprooting orphaned children from their own areas and engineering new families. But now they're softening their line... at first grudgingly and now enthusiastically supporting her idea of placing orphans in the care of foster mothers, many of them grandmothers.

The grants she receives, though, fall well short of what is needed to keep God's Golden Acre afloat. Some call Heather a maverick but then she willingly courts controversy in defence of her aims. She's also a great believer in chasing money from the private sector to ensure survival. Contrast the rather Spartan surroundings, where children spend much of their time, to the Zulu Theatre that is now rising from the dust where dignitaries, businessmen and celebrities will be lured to watch her local dance troupes perform.

There's method in this seeming madness... for these are the very people she wants to sponsor her cluster fostering project and they cannot fail to notice it.

Heather's relationship with the Zulu people in the villages that straddle the Valley of a Thousand Hills is perhaps the best indicator of her success. Traditional leaders, witchdoctors, ministers and countless families salute her missionary zeal. She speaks Zulu fluently and is accepted as one of their own. The Outreach Program she runs from God's Golden Acre supports 300 families and 4,500 children in the valley. Desperate that so many AIDS orphans here should not end up as a generation of street children, sucked in, through desperation, to a life of crime, desolation and abuse, she has started a local football league and is organizing educational and sporting challenges to engender team spirit and promote habits of obedience, discipline and self-respect.

Her relationship with her husband Patrick is an intriguing one. He has his own studio where he sculpts exotic and interesting pieces of art. Some attract notable buyers, and money helps to keep the Reynolds afloat and provide much-needed income for God's Golden Acre too. My visit is for but a couple of days... but it is long enough to get a feel of the place and of the people who run it. Chaotic, eccentric, vibrant and God-driven. My only concern would be whether it could function without her. Well, she has four project organizers now and things are moving forward apace. Whenever Heather feels low, she turns to read the slogans she's plastered across her office wall. One best encapsulates her single-minded determination: "Obstacles are those frightful things you see when you take your eyes off the goal."

OK, Heather, I've got the message. Come to think of it... so too, at last, have the Government.

35
THE CHILDREN OF GOD'S GOLDEN ACRE

Visitors to God's Golden Acre at Cato Ridge never forget sunrise and sunset. At the back of the farm there are tall gum trees, and below them a sheer descent into the valley, with stunning views. The sun, a huge ball of fire, drops swiftly into the trees and slides straight down below the horizon, enveloping everything around it with a crimson and golden sheen. The magnitude of the fireball, which people feel they can almost touch, is nothing but an optical illusion of course. The human eye and brain are fooled by the seeming proximity of the falling sun through the familiar perspective of the near horizon.

They are in rural Africa, their senses and intuitions sharpened by the air, the light, the sounds of the greatest continent on earth, and perhaps 50 metres away the throbbing drumbeat of the boys and girls at God's Golden Acre in rehearsal for a concert. Are they dreaming? Why, no! It's real! It's part of the magic, mystique, and perhaps, the sheer witchcraft of Africa. They feel more alive, more aware, more excited, and perhaps closer to God than anywhere else. The falling sun at dusk, and its rise at dawn, is a moment all the arriving volunteers and visitors at God's Golden Acre long to experience, and one they remember for ever.

The musical enchantment of God's Golden Acre also manifests itself time and again in the recollections of the young people who have been volunteers there. The Zulu orphans express themselves poignantly in their songs. They seem to know the words from four or five years of age. Long after a tour of duty, the sounds of God's Golden Acre – the beating drums, the harmonies, and the melodious lilting tones of singing voices inspired by faith and love – dwell in the sub-conscious. Among those who have experienced this breath of rural Africa is a young Australian volunteer called Hugh Evans.

The Oak Tree Foundation, founded by Hugh Evans when he was 19 years old, is Australia's first entirely youth-run and youth-driven aid and development agency. It is a movement of volunteers – all under the age of 25 – seeking to empower developing communities in South Africa through education. In 2004, at the age of 20, Hugh Evans was voted Young Australian of the Year, and in 2005 Young Person of the World. A tall, slim man with an engaging smile, he is one of many popular figures with the orphans at God's Golden Acre, taking them on field trips, spending time with them at play, and even learning to become a white Zulu dancer!

He says of them: "I think they are the most amazing children in the whole world. They know how to sing, they know how to dance, and they know how to express themselves well. Nowhere do you go in the world and get such a huge hug. Every time I come back to God's Golden Acre I get this nerv-ous feeling in my heart, and I get so excited, like I'm coming back home. They call me by my Zulu name, Echlantabo, ('stone of the mountain') which is from the song I like singing, and when I get there they are shouting it, and rushing up to give me huge hugs. The feeling of joy is indescribable.

"They have an extraordinary level of humility, politeness and grace – qualities that any parent would be delighted to find in their child. Yet they have all – almost without excep-tion – been through appalling times in earlier childhood and we do have to understand that there has been violence in their lives. One time two of the boys were having a fight and I tried to break it up. I was in the middle of it and one of the children pulled a steak knife out of a drawer and faced up to me with it in his hand. I'm sure he wouldn't have used it but his aggression really shocked me for three or four hours. I was literally speechless, and could not work out what had happened. Then I thought to myself – often these children have grown up in situations where all they have known is abuse, and sexual abuse, daily, sometimes for years. Violence is a natural response to threat."

Hugh's friend Esther Perenyi was 17, a pupil at Melbourne's Carey Baptist Grammar, and on her first visit to God's Golden Acre. She had never been to a funeral in her life, but arrived on a day when the children of God's Golden Acre were saying goodbye to a little boy who had just died in the hospice – after a brief period in the sanctuary – having been brought there from the valley by his relations. She describes the experience: "Because I'd never actually been to a funeral before – it is a shock. I walk in and the first thing I see is a tiny white coffin placed on two chairs, and all the little children are seated around the coffin. I am really unsettled by this because I didn't think there would be any children at the funeral. I sit down and wait, and suddenly this nine-year-old girl gets up and starts singing and leads the 95 orphans in song in a marvellous harmony to send this child off to heaven. At the end, they open up the coffin and everyone files past, looking at the child, and paying their last respects.

"I think what gets to me is that these children – who are so young – have seen this so many times and seem to understand it so much better than they should. I feel they shouldn't have to experience all this when they are so young. I didn't really know what to expect when I arrived at God's Golden Acre, but I certainly wasn't anticipating going to a funeral. This was something beyond any of my expectations.

"I shall go back to Australia feeling very different about

things. I want to share my experiences with others, motivate them, and get them involved. Young people in my country need to know and understand about what is happening in South Africa. Children will always be children, no matter where you are in the world, but with these children, in their eyes, you can see an underlying sadness that is very striking. I have played with them a lot and they are very boisterous and outgoing, but they have a constant need for affection – always wanting to hold your hand, and jump on your lap and give you hugs.

"A few days after I came here a little chap arrived and I took a liking to him instantly. Just this morning I went down to the hospice because I couldn't get him out of my mind, and he held my finger as I was sitting next to him. Suddenly his eyes glazed over, and the grip loosened, and I just got the biggest fright. I thought he had died. I know it sounds silly but I started shaking him – and he started screaming. Death has really gotten to me. They took him to a local hospital where he was found to have pneumonia. But he's going to be OK."

Zanele Jila is among the oldest from the first generation at God's Golden Acre, whose arrival there was more due to the poverty caused by the civil war than the later AIDS epidemic. Now, having grown up, she worked at God's Golden Acre as a caregiver, cleaner and teacher of Zulu song and dance, before going to college to train as a teacher and lecturer. At 21 she is still a virgin, has promised Heather not to rush into a relationship, and hopes to go on to study at university where she will prepare for a career in teaching. With her haunting beauty, grace, humility and consideration for the feelings of others, she personifies all the best qualities to be found in the children and young people of God's Golden Acre. She says: "I was eleven years old when I came to God's Golden Acre at Wartburg. If it had not been for Heather I would not have survived because life was really difficult. We came from a very poor family. My mother had seven children and three died.

"Sometimes there was not enough to eat and we went to bed hungry. I would probably have got a boyfriend some time in my early teens and then have become HIV-positive. Heather took me in, became a mother to me, and always warned me about the dangers that I faced. That's why I feel so good about God's Golden Acre – it gave me my childhood back and I was happy as I was growing up. Ten years have gone by and I have not passed away. Had I stayed in the valley I would probably have had three children or more by now, and be facing the risk of death. I have not had relationships with boys. Instead I am proud that I have stayed in control of my life and I have plans for the future.

"I am going through college and want to go to university so I can help my family. I have a mother, a big sister, a brother born in 1985, and Mavu born in 1990, who lives at God's Golden Acre. Mavu would also have died because he had tuberculosis and was really sick when he came here – but Gogo Heather made sure he had hospital treatment and over the years she has brought him back to health. He is OK now.

"When I am qualified I will go back to the valley because I will be able to help people who need it. I want to teach little kids because that is the time to start influencing them to live their lives in the right way. Education is so important to my people – yet so many of them did not have the money to go to school. This is where things must change. If you don't go to school you have no chance of getting a job. Many of the boys grow up with nothing to look forward to – except sex and drugs and joining a gang. They don't think about their lives because no one has taught them to think otherwise.

"As far as AIDS is concerned, a lot of people of my generation don't believe it. Another reason is they are ashamed of it. It is very embarrassing to tell people if you have lost members of your family because of AIDS. You keep it inside you. You don't tell anyone because you feel you will be laughed at and badly treated. My cousin died of AIDS last year. When I saw her she looked like she had AIDS but on the clinic cards they told her she had TB. But I knew the truth but no one wanted to say so. The other girls in my family have learned nothing from my cousin's death because they refuse to believe it was HIV – they think maybe it was just bad luck, or it was God calling her early. One of the things I want to do when I go back to the valley as a teacher is to sit down and talk with the kids, and make sure they know the truth so they will perhaps grow up and have a better life. I'm very proud to be a Zulu, it's very special for me, and I want to protect my people.

"Here at God's Golden Acre I stay in one of the foster homes with 22 girls up to the age of fifteen. I sleep with six of the older girls in one room and we talk a lot about our lives and the future. I tell them, 'Girls, you are really young and you have seen people who are sick in the valley. So don't go to bed with boys and if a boy comes to you and asks you to go to bed with him just say no – otherwise maybe you are going to get HIV, get sick, and are going to die.' They are really afraid about that. They have learned from me.

"I go back to the valley quite often and stay for perhaps three days or more with relatives, my uncles and their kids, but more often I stay with my mother who lives now in Pietermaritzburg with my 18-year-old brother. She is sick and the others look to me as the head of the family. I am strict with my brother and make him save money so that he can become a driver and have a future. I think he is listening to me.

"I believe that the special opportunities that the orphans have here at God's Golden Acre will mean that one day some will become leaders of the Zulu communities in the valley. Although people are sometimes jealous of what we have got, I think our education and Christian beliefs will help us to be people of influence."

3 6
SYMBOLS OF
RECONCILIATION

One evening as the sun was sliding behind
a mountain, Hugh Evans drove a van owned
by God's Golden Acre towards KwaNgcolozi, a valley where
the Oak Tree Foundation is sponsoring a $100,000 commu-
nity resource centre that will provide 1,000 students with the
opportunity to receive a primary and secondary education,
and also tertiary education in fields such as computer training.
The road twisted sharply downhill and eventually reached the
floor of the valley. The van followed the road for two miles
along the shore of a large reservoir. Cattle and goats grazed
peacefully on an abundance of bush grass.

"It can be extremely frightening here at the weekends,"
Hugh explained. "The tracks along the side of the road are full
of drunken men, most of them young and aggressive. I get
very frightened as a white person travelling alone here on
Saturdays, especially the evening, and try to avoid it if I can.
The young men drink, of course, because they have nothing
else to do. Nowhere to work and nowhere for recreation – the
options are drink, drugs, sex and crime. Those who are lucky
might have work in Durban, but for most it's a case of
scrounging and rooting around for some kind of existence in
what they see as a 'no hope' valley. I believe that education is
empowerment and so we are helping to finance a pilot project
that will be a non-residential community resource centre."

He pointed to a large plot of land. It looked out over a reservoir; grey-green mountains were its magnificent back-drop. "It has been given to us by the local *nkosi* who really believes in our project. And we've got just the right people to run it," he said.

The figures of a tall African, and an attractive white blonde woman in her early forties, appeared at the entrance to the site where clearance and some early construction work had already started. They both waved at the approaching van. Pastor Eric Shezi, of Thandanani Family Church, and his pro-fessional partner Debbie Wells, a social worker from Hillcrest (and social worker to God's Golden Acre) are heroic symbols of post-apartheid South Africa. They would be embarrassed to hear themselves described in such a way. However, they sym-bolize the spirit of reconciliation and selfless dedication that many middle-class people – both black and white – have so far failed to demonstrate in this young country. Eric and Debbie have worked together as a team since 1994, helping poor peo-ple whose lives have been shattered by the AIDS epidemic.

At first it was a soup kitchen at Embo, financed by Eric's church, and now they run a rural outreach project supporting 70 families and involving nearly 400 children in KwaNgcolozi, funded by God's Golden Acre. The new multipurpose hall provided by the Oak Tree Foundation will enable them to help people beyond the basic level of food and clothing, and spread a wider net over the community. How did it all begin?

"We were running the soup kitchen for about three or four years and we didn't get involved helping individual people or their families because we didn't have any resources to do that. Then we heard about a child in KwaNgcolozi whose father had died and who was believed to have great potential. He wasn't able to go back to school because there was no one to pay the fees. We came down to see the school, and pay the fees, and we met the headmaster who told us he had a lot more destitute children unable to go to school – could we help any of them? So I said, 'OK. Put their names down and give me a list and we'll see what we can do.' We had a list with the names of 16 children on it. We formed a profile on each one so that we could help in other ways as well. So our project started from that one child, to 16 children, and grew from there."

On the list scrutinized by Eric and Debbie was a child who had been raped by a neighbour in her own home. The man had been charged with the rape by the police but released on a bail – paid for by his family – and he was living at his home again. Meanwhile the girl was going to be summoned to court to give evidence against him. Eric felt her life was in real danger. Heather took in the little girl. Soon afterwards Eric and Debbie's rural outreach programme came under God's Golden Acre's umbrella where it remained until 2004.

Pastor Eric explained: "What usually happens is that far from rejecting Christianity, the adults come closer to Christ. They don't blame him for what has happened to them and what they are going through. Instead they grow closer to God because faith is their only hope. They find prayer a source of great comfort. We are also doing as much as we can to educate adolescents about safer sex. Twice a year we hold a camp and there we teach them a large range of life skills. We are fighting negative apathetic attitudes, however, in many young people, who say they don't care. They know about AIDS, but for some reason they don't seem to think they will be infected by it. Meanwhile, the epidemic spreads like wildfire. I feel this is just the beginning and I am very sorry to say that."

Every Saturday there are many funerals in Eric's parish. Around 150 people belong to his church, but when it comes to funerals he includes the close friends and relatives of his congregation, so he is really responsible for up to 600 people. The dead are nearly always victims of AIDS, in their mid-twenties or much younger. It is the most stressful thing the young pastor has experienced, because the grief is so intense when people die young. He cannot remember the last time he did not have a funeral on a Saturday and is desperate to be with his family so that he can relax – away from the intensive pressure and emotion of his ministry.

All over the country priests like Eric are gradually cracking under the strain. They cannot conduct more than one funeral in a day because Zulu custom dictates that the pastor is an important part of the ritual – which takes many hours. Eric has to assign his lay ministers on Saturdays to conduct funerals. It's a heavy emotional burden and what frightens him is that the scenario is getting worse all the time.

Rosetta Heunis, Cheryl Harris and Alta Collins are also responsible for separate elements of the rural outreach programmes at God's Golden Acre. By 2004, the furthest drop-off point was an hour's drive from Cato Ridge, and in the years to come it is hoped to extend programme boundaries to every corner of the Valley of a Thousand Hills. The God's Golden Acre team constantly witness deprivation and hopelessness in the valley but do what they can to alleviate it within the constraints of the funding available. The white members of the God's Golden Acre team have to be vigilant while working in the valley. Cheryl said: "We're not stupid. We've never been threatened but Zulu people we have worked with warn us that it is unusual we have never been hijacked. The sight of a white woman driving a 'bakkie' alone in the valley presents a target and so whenever possible I avoid that. Sometimes I'll nip down quickly but it would be in the daytime. There are some areas we don't go into. We lost a boy once from God's Golden Acre and Sandra and I went looking for him. We were about to go into one area with one of the *gogos*, and a security guy actually said to us, 'It's not a good idea to go in there because they shoot strangers.' It's a matter of judgement."

Most children who have no parents are redirected into extended families looked after by a granny figure, or older sister, within their own community in the valley. Food supplies, school uniforms, school fees, small livestock, seeds, soap and sapling fruit trees enable each family unit to be self-sustaining. Cheryl personally feels pity for many of the *gogos*. "You just look at their life and think, *It's so hard*. At a time when they should be sitting back and relaxing, they've now got their kids' kids to look after because their own kids have died – yet when they talk to you they have courage, spirit and a sense of duty that seems to be ingrained in them."

Getting the children back to school and providing them with school uniforms is recognized as a most effective way to help them regain their self-confidence; and it brings back a sense of order into their lives. Alta Collins is responsible for the stationery, uniforms and clothing for the children on the outreach projects. "The orphans would rather go without food than go to school looking shabby. Their appearance is everything and in actual fact I would say that the sad thing is that while most of the children who go to school in the valley are well dressed, some of them have not even had a cup of tea or slice of bread before going to school. I think it's a pride issue, because even as children the Zulus are very proud people. For instance when they attend any kind of function, they will put on their best clothes. They are always smiling, and so grateful and excited when we take the uniforms to them. They rush off and put them on – often over their old clothes! It's a fantastic feeling to be able to help them."

Cheryl continued: "The African women gather at the drop points and bring their wheelbarrows. We unload the right number of food parcels at each drop point. Once the food is unloaded, the community health workers get the women to line up behind their food and when that is done we take their card and click it, mark them off, and hand it back. It works really, really well. The people stay there, they are patient, and are extremely grateful for what we are doing. To miss a family by mistake could mean people going hungry.

"The women stroll off to their hut with the sacks and boxes

perched on their head. They are the lucky ones. A mile or so down the valley others may be hungry or even starving, but for the moment, they cannot be helped because of lack of funds. It seems cruel, and it can create tension, but most people appear to understand that God's Golden Acre cannot help everyone."

Some analysts in organizations like the United Nations believe that rural outreach projects – such as the one pioneered by God's Golden Acre in stricken areas of the valley – are capable of bringing back a measure of normality and are likely to be the most effective self-sustaining approach to take, in recreating family life in the wake of the AIDS pandemic in rural areas. It frustrates Heather to know that much of the infrastructure is now in place that could drive a massive expansion programme, not only in the field of rural outreach, but also in the provision of community resource centres. These would have a huge impact throughout the Valley of a Thousand Hills. Painstakingly, she has worked out all the statistics, the logistics and the final amounts of money that would be required to launch the rural outreach project there.

Heather explains: "We have the methodology – the process model as they call it – and could organize projects on a massive scale. We know how to get the food there; we've got the wholesalers who would be only too happy to be able to provide the food and deliver it – it's good business for them. We can employ more people to be rural outreach coordinators and service the areas – that would mean more employment.

"We also need to create self-sustaining craft industries with links to markets outside the valley. Training in craft skills is vitally important because adults who are skilled in them may die before they can hand on their expertise to the next generation. So we have got to set up the programmes to get craft education into the school curriculum. It means the children, as they grow up, will have a basic form of employment within their own community. As the pandemic begins to peak we are discovering that the stricken communities are not able to absorb the loss of loved ones and everywhere the impact of that is having devastating effects.

"There might be a self-sustaining extended family where perhaps a number of brothers and sisters are working. They have all got children, and a granny, and at this level it all works out. Then one will die, perhaps a sister leaving three children, then another sister will die leaving now her three children, that's six children, and so now a brother has to support his own, let's say, four children, plus those other six. Then he dies after a year. Suddenly Granny is faced with ten children. What does she do? Maybe she's too young to get a pension – because African women often have children at 16 or 17 – so she could be a grandmother by the time she's 40 years old. But she can't leave to go to work because she's now got at least three children who are under the age of three. She's got to cook and wash and try and help to keep this family together and get them off to school, and then after a certain period of time she's begging and borrowing from neighbours... so how does this granny survive with no income and ten children?

"One day I went with Councillor Shabalala – a councillor from Sankontshe – to look at a 'worst case' scenario. There was a community in his ward at Georgedale based around a working textile mill where people had moved to find work. He wanted to get me involved in that area. We were taken to see a granny and she came out in a very tatty dress; one breast was almost completely exposed because of the tears in it. She explained to us that she had had to farm her grandchildren out because there was no way she could keep them together because they were starving. I thought, *How amazing she is*. She stood there with all her dignity in this dress that revealed so much of her tired body – and she was so poor. But it took nothing away from her, and I felt so incredibly sorry for her.

"It's an amazing quality the Zulus, and other Africans, have. No matter how much sorrow, and how much pain, and how much poverty, and the things they have to bear, when you go down into the valley and you say in Zulu, *sawbona khungani*, 'Hello, how are you?', a big smile will always greet you and the person will nearly always reply, 'Oh, I'm fine, thank you.'

"In KwaXimba, there are 42 community health workers but their dedicated work falls far short of what is needed. There just are not enough of them to look after the 62,000 people who live there, 52 percent of whom are HIV-positive. KwaXimba is a spectacular setting. Sometimes the summits are above the line of the clouds, and the African sunlight illuminates the valleys in a myriad of changing shades. The birds are singing, tropical plants bloom, and there is tranquillity. Yet for many Zulus who live in its 26 traditional rural districts it is hell on earth. Families beyond our reach are starving to death.

"One day a group of the local councillors came to me and pleaded for help. It was hard for me to witness these grown men in such a state of despair. I had to tell them it would cost about two million Rand (£200,000) a year to launch an effective rural outreach project in KwaXimba, and we did not currently have that kind of money at our disposal. However, I promised them that when I went to Europe I would represent their cause, provided they were able to fulfil certain conditions to help me. I needed facts, figures and statistics from them. Nkosi Mlaba had sent the group of councillors to see me. However, I was still worried by the security problem. 'Your area is so big it is going to be a nightmare for me to try and roll out any programme, you are going to have to guarantee our security, and do this, that, and this...' I warned.

"The next day I received a phone call from Councillor Ngubane just as I was about to set off from God's Golden Acre to fly to England and he said: 'Heather, you've got to come down here now!'

" 'I can't, I'm flying today,' I replied.

" 'You've got to, you must,' he insisted.

"I was exhausted and tired from having been working seven days a week, and I hadn't even packed for my long journey to Europe, but I rushed down to KwaXimba knowing it was something that was very important to them. I discovered they had fulfilled every requirement that I had stipulated to the last letter at our previous meeting. All the names, the locations, the families, the amount of people who were HIV-positive, and the number of children who needed help to go to school etc. were listed. It was just as I'd asked. 'We wanted you to have this before you went overseas, so you can really go and fight for our area,' the community development officer Mr Mapunga told me.

"I was very heartened by what Nkosi Mlaba had done because it was the first manifestation of a return to the rule of law, and respect for the law, in a very large area of the valley. I felt like a jet of energy had been pumped into me. My exhaustion was replaced by a feeling of elation. KwaXimba was an area I had long wanted to get into – but had been put off by the enormity of the place and the scale of the problems I knew we would encounter. Now it would become a priority area for action. Perhaps unexpectedly, the first major project we would undertake there was to establish a football league for boys, through another miracle with the help of some of the top men in British professional football.

37

"I FEEL LIKE CRYING TILL I DIE..."

The community health worker's voice was tense with urgency over the phone line. She was adamant that Heather should leave what she was doing at the time and come to the valley. She gave Heather a brief outline of the little family she had identified in Sankontshe. It was to be a day Heather would remember for ever — despite the briefing, nothing could have prepared her for the heartbreak she would witness that morning.

"After a hurried descent into the valley, we arrived at the tiny mud hut around midday. Switching off the Land Rover's engine, I steeled myself against the familiar sense of trepidation that rose in my chest as we made our way to the entrance. Each time, I never know just how bad it will be on the other side of the door. As we entered, and our eyes grew accustomed to the dark, we saw a woman lying on a low bed, with her two babies in bundles next to her. Painfully thin, and powerless to move her lower limbs, this proud young Zulu woman could not stand to greet us. Too weak to draw herself up on her elbows, she simply lay on her back, while the community health worker introduced us.

"As I moved closer to her, I was stunned by the exquisite beauty of this dying mother. With high, elegant cheekbones that would have captivated the world of modern fashion, she lay before me, helpless. Her gaze met mine with a strange mix of uncertainty, hopelessness and hope, as I told her I'd heard about her and her triplet babies, and had come to offer my help. Her eyes moved slowly to the bundles beside her as I told her I'd heard that one of the three babies had already died, and that we knew the other two were also sick.

"With the HIV virus attacking her immune system, she had succumbed to one of the common ailments, dysentery, and being so weak, could not even move off the bed to relieve herself. The mattress was sodden and her body had developed sores from lying in her own excrement. Alone with her babies, and shunned by the community around her as the stigma of her disease took effect, she had no help and could only lie powerlessly watching her own body deteriorate and her three babies starve, as her body stopped producing breast milk.

"Now, as I stood before her, as a white woman she'd never met before in her life, she was faced with the most horrific decision a mother should have to make: to entrust her babies to a complete stranger, as their only hope for survival. Deciding at last to take the only chance to save their lives, she agreed to let us take them to hospital. Unwrapping the tiny bundles to change their nappies and give them some of the formula we had brought, I felt overwhelmingly powerless. I could not give this woman her life back; I couldn't tell her for certain that her babies would survive. We had sent for an ambulance to fetch her, but the babies were to be taken to a different hospital – one with the best paediatric facilities.

"The young mother said her goodbyes to her children as we carried them out of the door and rushed them into town. Despite our efforts, Thanda, the little boy, died in hospital after three days. The only remaining triplet, a little girl named Lina, managed to pull through, and we ensured that she had regular visits with her mother at the hospital to which she had been admitted. The beautiful young mother died in hospital, six weeks later. Lina grew up to be a healthy, happy little girl despite her difficult beginnings."

Heather's work at the coalface of the AIDS pandemic in South Africa continues at an unrelenting pace. The pressure upon her – both in the valley and at God's Golden Acre – had by 2004 continued at this relentless pace for nearly a decade. Often, Gogo Beauty, Heather's cook, would prepare three meals in a day, and then discover eight hours later that Heather had not even had time to eat any of them. At times it brought the unhappy Gogo Beauty close to the point of resignation. Living just behind the office for more than three years until 2004 made intrusions upon Heather's privacy even more inevitable. Lucy Foster tried to take some of the strain off in the mornings as early as 2000, but it proved impossible. She wrote:

A day in the life of Heather starts early in the morning, even before she has had the chance to get dressed, wash her face and comb her hair. She will be taking meetings from her bed, still wearing her nightdress. She doesn't have the time to get out of bed, get dressed, and ready for the day before people are knocking on her door. When I first worked for her I'd say, "Right, nobody's going to go into Heather's room until 9am, so she can wake up nicely, talk to her husband, and get dressed." We tried to keep up that regulation, but it lasted about a week! The important phone calls, some from abroad, would be coming in, and because we rely on donations, we just couldn't put people off when they were asking to talk to her."

Heather is held in awe by both her staff and volunteers, who fear her outbursts of anger. Staff and family at God's Golden Acre worry about the stress she faces, and the exhausting workload she places upon herself. In her journal Susan Balfour wrote of her disquiet at the stress Heather's pastoral work was having upon her boss physically, and also of Heather's practice of frequently going without food and warmth herself, so that she could better understand the feelings and pain of those who were deprived of it. Susan wrote the following account in her journals:

"Whosoever will come after me let him deny himself, and take up his cross, and follow me." (Mark 8:34)

A few nights ago, one of the Zulu caregivers knocked on my room door. "Gogo Heather is calling you." I reached for a jersey and my coat and made my way across to her house in the chilly night air. June is one of the coldest months in KwaZulu-Natal. I arrived to find the door and windows of Heather's rooms wide open, and her, in bed in a thin cotton nightdress with only a thin sheet. My eyebrows shot up. Heather caught my look, and went on to explain...

She had visited the Sankontshe valley the week before and found a sick old granny, caring for four grandchildren in a dilapidated mud hut that was almost caved in. They were living in desperate poverty, sleeping on the dirt floor, without a single blanket between them. "When I am cold, I remember that there are thousands of people in the valleys around us shivering in bed with empty stomachs, and it motivates me to work harder and faster," she said. There was a fierce determination in her eyes. I understood the desire but nevertheless, there was a flutter of anxiety below my ribs.

"You'll make yourself sick," I told her pointedly.

She has an unforgiving schedule of outreach visits in the valley, meetings, delivering talks, greeting visitors. She never sleeps for more than four hours per night – Heather is often up until 3am, handling a huge volume of e-mail correspondence or preparing funding proposals. Sometimes, if no one suitably qualified is available, she will care for a sick child around the clock. People often ask how much longer she can keep this up. But for as long as I have known Heather she has possessed a terrific energy and vitality. It persists despite a hectic schedule that precludes any sense of physical well-being.

She is fuelled by an awesome measure of compassion, in a desperate sprint towards a searing vision; "...focused beyond the horizon on a land of rich crops, where justice and peace prevails." (Isaiah 32:15–17)

"I am comprised of atoms," she says, "and atoms don't get sick." Her resolve is unshakeable. She prays, trusts in God, and keeps going. She is quite well.

What the volunteers did not realize, however, was that Heather's mental state of health was indeed deteriorating – but not through the burden of work. Her heart had been broken through physical separation from her babies. After moving to Cato Ridge she made a deliberate and difficult decision not to spend as much time at God's Golden Acre – as she had done for instance in the past at Wartburg – caring for, and nursing, the younger children now living in Mons House. This was something she explained to no one, apart from Patrick, because she was desperately anxious to maintain the equilibrium at God's Golden Acre, and to do nothing to dispel the happiness of the older children, and the high morale of both the volunteers and African staff.

"In the longer term the Lord was telling me that my role in fighting the AIDS pandemic would have to become more strategic. There were going to be millions of children in South Africa that needed my intervention in their lives – and I knew this was where God wanted me to be. Meanwhile, all the babies and children now being brought up at God's Golden Acre would need to be taken right the way through to adulthood, including education. They would each have to bond with a foster mother, a Zulu, who would bring them up in their culture. It meant heartbreak for me personally. I would have to let go of my little babies at God's Golden Acre. I didn't realize how painful it would be until the time came. Thank goodness I didn't know beforehand – because I think that if I had known, I would not have formed the close and very loving relationships with the children that I did."

Heather's first step in this direction came when she and Patrick moved out of the farmhouse and into accommodation at the back of the main office. The nursery-age children like Chummy, Fikile and Marcus had grown up in her bedroom, and the crying, sobbing and deep distress of these infants on the night she walked away will haunt her for the rest of her life. Many children had been abandoned in the valley and now seemed to imagine that it was happening to them all over again. "That first night was the worst, and even now I don't like going back to that memory, because I so very nearly cracked up and gave in. As I walked out of Mons House the toddlers were prevented from following me. They were phys-ically stopped from going with me. They realized I wasn't coming back. Instead of going to my own room in the house with them, I had shut the door and walked out. It was terri-ble, terrible. I walked away. I felt like a murderer. I couldn't explain to them that I had to do this, why I was leaving them, and sleeping in another house. They didn't understand because they were too small, just two- and three-year-olds. Fikile, Marcus and Chummy, they were the ones who were screaming.

"Marcus had slept in a pram by my bed until he was nearly two years old. How can you explain to a child of not yet three that you are letting go? That it was hurting me more than it was hurting him? I also felt particularly guilty about Fikile, who was adopted soon afterwards, because I will never have the chance to explain it all to her when she grows older. Gogo Beauty, Ida, the aunties and the caregivers – some of the older girls from the choir – they were there for them, but the babies had always been used to me nursing them. I had become their mother. It took months, months. I had to stop going to Mons House at night. I just couldn't stand it any more. I cut it out of my schedule, stopped going. And they didn't understand. I couldn't look at them, but sometimes I could hear their cry-ing. They would scream like wounded animals if they caught sight of me walking to my new house. I would just get in the car and drive out, heartbroken.

"I said to God, 'I couldn't do it again, God. Next time, I'll walk back to those kids, and I won't take care of anything else. I'll just walk straight back to them, and not walk away from them again.'

"Now I threw myself into the valley more than ever to compensate for my misery, and of course found so many terrible and shocking things there that I often could not sleep at night. So I was sleepless because of the terrible things I encountered in the valley – and sleepless because of my feelings of guilt for leaving the babies at God's Golden Acre. It made me very ill. I had an angina attack and people actually thought that I was going to die. It was then that the volunteers became more protective of me. But it was not the workload that was making me ill – it was the pain of separation from my babies. I could only share this with Patrick."

Heather's health had also been affected by her endless problems with the Department of Social Services. It seemed impossible to convince them that God's Golden Acre was not designed to be a residential institution, like an orphanage, but a community where African foster mothers would provide homes for extended families within a larger community providing support, education, and social welfare. The authorities saw God's Golden Acre as a throwback to the institutional orphanage or children's home, where the parental unit had been substituted for something less acceptable. Heather was perceived by many experts to be contravening national policy on orphans, even carrying out social engineering by removing children from their natural family groups and placing them in foster care. Over several years she had to stand up against so-called experts in child welfare, and their prevailing wisdom, to fight her case for the survival of God's Golden Acre. Being white did not make it any easier for her.

"They would not accept that we were not an institution.

They couldn't see that it was developing into a happy and successful community centre, where the children would be taught Zulu as their main language, and have the opportunity concurrently to be part of the community in the valley – going to funerals and weddings and festivals at weekends and holidays. At God's Golden Acre the children live in family units looked after by the African *gogos*, supported by white volunteers. I stand there as the big granny figure, a white *gogo*. What is wrong with that? South Africa is meant to be a multiracial country now, so I didn't see why we could not have a community centre as we envisaged it, with African *gogos* in charge, supported by largely European volunteers. Eventually they gave way, albeit reluctantly, conceding that cluster foster care – as practised at God's Golden Acre – did have an important role to play in bringing up orphaned children. The pandemic still has not peaked yet and I am sure cluster foster care – the vision of people like Dr Neil McKerrow – is going to become an essential response to the huge increase in the number of orphans."

The regulations dictated that the *gogos*, and the aunties, should become responsible as foster parents for a maximum number of six children, and each child had to be registered in the care of a specific adult. It was another strong reason why Heather had to take a step back from the babies. "Two or three years on, it is good to see that my babies have become totally integrated into their foster homes and they are growing up to be strong and healthy children, surrounded by happiness. I am a granny figure to them now, and I don't spend too much time around the smaller ones – because toddlers bond very quickly with me, and frankly it's just too hurtful. I can't go through that again. I spend small amounts of time with them, and then I break it up. I don't want them to get so close in their bonding with me that it then makes the inevitable separation distressing.

"I love those children so much – I think they just respond

to it very easily. It doesn't take long to bond with anybody when there is a mutual love. I feel overwhelming love for them, but if the children grow to sense that in me, it could delay the bonding with their *gogo* in the foster house. Sometimes with all the sadness and tragedy I encounter in the valley, and when I am missing my babies at night, I feel like crying till I die. If I let myself cry, I would just keep crying until I died."

38
A TREAT FOR THE ORPHANS

The white Land Rover was crowded with orphans and towed a battered trailer carrying luggage and food provisions. Heather engaged a low gear and the vehicle began the tortuous ascent of a steep hill with the trailer swaying precariously behind it. The latter performed better since having some air pumped in its tyres at Pietermaritzburg.

The Land Rover was in the foothills of the Drakensberg Mountains on the lonely R617 route, heading towards the small town of Underberg. It was well after midnight – we did not set off until 11pm, but at God's Golden Acre the unusual and the unpredictable are the norm.

It was a Saturday night in rural KwaZulu-Natal and in the moonlight the verges revealed shapes. A few of these had four legs, but most appeared and were gone in a flash – providing the split-second apparition of a man staggering in a drunken lurch along the roadside. This road was not a place to be a stranger and alone in the night on foot. Not a place to break down. Not a sensible time to be travelling with children – but we were. Every half hour Heather rang Patrick at God's Golden Acre from her mobile telephone to give him her location.

"It's best to be careful and stay in regular contact, because vehicle hijackings are not uncommon around here, and I don't

want us to lose this vehicle in such a lonely and remote location – especially with so many young girls on board," said
Heather without a trace of anxiety in her voice. "This is my
special time with the children – a time to be Mum again. This
little team bonded on the UK tour of the Young Zulu
Warriors," she said, pointing her thumb, over her shoulder, at
the youngsters sleeping in the back.

Behind them were another group in the covered rear compartment. All the children – Mavu, Goodman, Ruth,
Khetiwe, Majola, Mlungisi, Zinhle and Khanyisile – were aged
between eleven and thirteen, except for six-year-old
Chummy Mthalane and his eight-year-old brother Sizwe.
Their behaviour throughout the entire 48 hours would be
nothing short of exemplary. It was clear they adored their
"granny" but remained formally respectful to her in a manner
rarely seen in Western children. In the back of the vehicle
were Australians Hugh Evans and Alex Bryson of the Oak Tree
Foundation, and 21-year-old Zanele Jila, a caregiver at God's
Golden Acre and one of Heather's original children from long
ago.

The Land Rover headed for the famous Sani Pass in the
Drakensberg Mountains, which offered the only route by road
into Lesotho. The specific destination was a backpackers' hostel, from where the older boys and girls would take a trek
through the mountains with Hugh and Alex. A glorious weekend was in store. The vehicle pulled into a garage at
Underberg to refuel. Heather noticed a rusted blue "combi" at
the pumps with a forlorn man standing next to a teenage girl,
and a boy of about twelve, who was vomiting continuously.
Heather said quietly: "Things don't look right there at all. I'd
better see if they are OK and find out if I can help."

As Heather approached the combi she realized there was a
coffin in the back. The girl was stricken with grief. She discovered an old woman, exhausted and at her wits' end,
hunched in the front seat of the vehicle. Within a few

moments Heather was embracing both the young girl and grandmother and giving them comfort in their native language. Then, as a little group, they came together, holding hands, and prayed with Heather. They sang a Zulu song together. It all happened on a garage forecourt in the middle of the night in the space of a few moments.

She said afterwards: "They are from Durban. The mother has died of AIDS and the father is taking them back to the village for the funeral. The prayers and the song helped them in their grief. The father is sick too, which means the teenage girl will soon have to take over the family. They have nothing, not even enough fuel to reach the village, so I have given them money for diesel and for the funeral."

The following weekend Heather was travelling again. This time north east, along the N2 North Coast toll road towards St Lucia and the Hluhluwe and Umfolozi Game Reserves, for another of Heather's weekends. Now the group comprised younger orphans, all under the age of seven. Three of them were sick. There were nine little girls: Susiwe, Nosipho, Sibongile, Slindile, Noxolo, Thina, Nomvula, Nonjabula and Zinhle, and three boys: Chummy, Khanyisane and Siphamandla. Again the behaviour of the children was exemplary, even for such little ones. The single exception was a lapse from the mischievous Sibongile. She ate someone else's dinner, and left the table without asking. The child was sent to bed – loud sobs of shame wafted down the staircase. Later, Sibongile got an extra cuddle from the white *gogo* before going to sleep.

The next day the African children, the caregivers, and volunteers Gael Tremaux from France, and Peg Judge, a pensioner from England, were absorbed by the experience of seven hours in the drought-stricken Hluhluwe Game Reserve. Groups of baboons, elephants and rhinos strolled past the transit van, a family of warthogs crossed the track ahead, forcing it to halt, and two giraffes pruned the top of a Marula tree in front of them. No lions were visible – but the evidence of their most recent kill, the carcass of an impala, was lying by the side of the track. Vultures were still circling in the sky overhead. Children and adults also watched buffalo, nyala, and zebra grazing within 50 metres of the transit. Throughout the seven hours the children sat absorbed, sometimes squealing with delight, other times singing Zulu songs. It hurt to remember that some of them would never grow up.

Shortly before dusk the party from God's Golden Acre returned to the Tiger Lily Lodge run by Charles and Corrue. While the children staged an impromptu concert for their hosts, Charles spoke of his own concerns about the AIDS epidemic. Fifty-six children had been found the previous month living in the bush some miles from Mtubatuba without any adult supervision, he said. They were aged between two and fourteen and several of them were starving and sick when they were discovered. His own church was trying to provide them with homes. Even more seriously, 200 young people had taken over the Hluhluwe town dump, where they were living off its garbage. They were hostile to any outside approach, and were refusing to have anything to do with social workers. A local pastor, he said, was trying his best to find out if their number included many sick or dying. The story disturbed Heather who made a decision to work with the pastor – even though the district is over 150 miles from Cato Ridge. She wanted to approach the dump early the next morning to see what could be done for the young people – but was advised to speak to the pastor first.

On the return journey Heather was deep in thought about this new challenge, but found time to visit the Mpukenyoni trading station, ten miles from Mtubatuba, where she had spent the first nine years of her life. Some of the Zulu men she met walking near the old trading station appeared to remember her father John McLellan's name. However, as she gazed upon the station, after an absence of more than 40 years, there was sadness in her eyes. It had become semi-derelict and there was no longer any evidence of trading. Windows were broken, doors vandalized, hanging off their hinges, and there was an air of degeneration and decay. Dogs barked and children stared at the uninvited visitors. Heather said sadly: "Mum and Dad kept it beautifully. The window frames and doors were freshly painted and the garden was just a joy to behold – a blaze of colour. Our rooms were immaculate and clean. This brings back no fond memories at all. Now there's nothing but filth, litter, weeds and broken bricks. Thank God they're not here to see this."

39
THE LITTLE BOY
FROM UPPINGTON

Heather was relaxing later that evening, enjoying a few glasses of wine, now the children were asleep. "There is something about the beat and the heart of Africa that is in me," she says. "I feel I must go on searching and discovering the magic of Africa relentlessly. Inevitably God's Golden Acre will follow in my wake — for the AIDS pandemic haunts the entire continent. Although I go to rest, every time I visit another part of Africa I stumble upon a drama — I find people who are starving through drought, or devastated by the AIDS epidemic. God tells me I have to do something for them.

"I love Africa, and its countries. I haven't visited them all, of course, but those that I have been to leave a deep and lasting impression upon me. For example, I am overwhelmed by Namibia for its vastness, and Zambia for its great Zambezi River. Even the moon seems twice as big at night on the Zambezi, and the daytime sky is bigger and wider than any place in the world. It is so quiet and remote, and I go there to camp and gaze upon the stars, to recharge my own emotional batteries, to drink in the aromas, sounds and rhythms of Africa. No one can reach me. Wildlife is all around me in my camp, and there is no thrill in the world greater than the sound of a pride of lions in the bush. One day when we were returning from a trip to Namibia with a party of volunteers, an extraordinary thing happened in the town of Uppington, which I wrote about in my diary:

We stop off to get a burger after a long drive on the dusty roads. As I step down, three street urchins come up asking for food. So I give a volunteer some money and ask her to fetch them bread and fish. I ask the little urchins to look after my car until we come back from the café. Afterwards we start talking to this little boy of about eight who has a cherubic face. There is something pitiful and heart-rending about him. He climbs into my arms and just says: "Please take me with you."

"Look, I can't help you. I can't take you with me. I can't do anything for you. The laws wouldn't allow me to do that. You must stay here. Don't let the older boys teach you to go on drugs and glue and stuff. Just don't do it. Just don't land up on drugs. I can't do anything for you at the moment but I'll be back next year, I promise. Just don't get onto drugs, whatever you do."

The boy starts crying. He is cuddled up in my arms and holding me so very tight. Now I am crying too. All the volunteers with me are crying. All the while the child is pleading: "Take me. Take me with you. Please. Please. Don't leave me here."

"I can't take you. I can't take you. There are laws. I can't just take you, little fellow." I get so cross with God at that moment. Tears pour down my face. "God, what is the point of this whole exercise here if I can do nothing? What can I do? I feel so helpless, so guilty."

I hold this little boy for as long as I can. Finally I take my arms away and leave him – step away from him. I don't talk. None of us speak for at least 20 minutes in the bus. I just cry. *How do I help that child? How do I help these people?*

We drive on a few miles, and arrive at a backpackers' hostel. "I'm going to bed," I say to everybody.

The next morning we get up for breakfast and the manager there, who knows me, says: "You were quiet last night."

"Yes. I wasn't feeling too well. Do you people know that you have a street children problem here?"

"Well, yes, I know. It's dreadful."

"Well, what exactly are you doing about it?"

"What are we doing about it? Well, nothing!"

"Why not? Who's going to do something about it? What are you going to do in 20 years' time when those kids are all 30-year-olds slitting your throats? What are you going to do then? What are you going to do about your children then? You should be doing something about it now!"

That is the mood I am in that morning! The hostel manager looks shocked: "Well, I haven't even thought about it!"

"There are lots of things you people could do at this point because those kids are still innocent children. They might be sniffing glue, but they are not hardened criminals. They are still children. You could organize youth groups, you could organize soccer matches in the afternoons, music nights in church groups – there are seven churches here – and included in that, you could serve soup. Do something now and it won't be dangerous. Just do it for God – instead of asking God to do something for you, which is what most Christians do."

By now the hostel manager is looking startled. "Well, I don't know where we'd start."

"I'll tell you. Get the churches together, call a group together, and I'll come. I'll be happy to talk through any programme that you'd like to start. Any initiative – no matter how small, I'll come – ten hours' drive. No matter. I'll come up and talk you through anything for a weekend if necessary!"

I leave feeling a bit better because, although I have arraigned her, the manager is now committed. She'd like to do something, get people together. She'll give me a ring. So I feel at least some hope for that little boy, and all the others.

We get back home to KwaZulu-Natal, and all the volunteers are feeling a bit empty about the Uppington episode, and the boy there. Everybody feels the pain, a sense of frustration, that first night back at God's Golden Acre.

Shortly afterwards, the Rockefeller Foundation comes through with some money so that God's Golden Acre is able to advertise two posts, one of them for a rural outreach project coordinator. I have somebody earmarked called Rosetta Heunis. Rosetta is somebody I know, but she is running a project.

I ring her and say: "Look, Rosetta, the money has come through – are you still interested in the job?"

"Yes! But I'll have to resign and work out my notice on this project."

So she comes to God's Golden Acre and I am talking to her – and then Rosetta says something extraordinary. "You know, in my home town, Uppington, we've got to do something."

"What?"

"Yes! There's a big street children problem in Uppington."

I put my hand to my heart and shout: "Rosetta! I don't believe this!" Then I tell her the whole story about Uppington and this cherub.

"Well! It's my home town," she says, "and I know everybody, and I'm dying to get my hands onto a project there! I know exactly the right project leaders."

That's how God puts things together. I pray the Uppington project will happen.

40
A PROPHET IN
HER OWN LAND

In 2002 Heather attended a conference on AIDS and she was invited as one of the delegates to a reception afterwards in the premier's office in Pietermaritzburg. As she returned to her car in the car park and switched on her lights she noticed something lying on the road. She got out and picked it up and thought at first that it was her First National Bank chequebook. When she opened it, however, she found it wasn't hers – it belonged to a Mr T Blose, and had a telephone number in it.

"I was on my way to go and pick up a sick child that I had left in town," says Heather, "and when I got there I called the number. A man answered.

" 'Mr Blose, I've got your chequebook. You are obviously going to the conference tomorrow so I can return it. I'm one of the delegates, Heather Reynolds, from God's Golden Acre,' I said.

" 'Oh, thank you so much. Yes, I know all about you,' he replied.

" 'OK, I'll see you at the conference. I've got your chequebook; don't worry about it,' I told him."

The next day Heather had completely forgotten about the chequebook because she was there at the conference to look for new funding organizations, and in particular the Nelson Mandela Children's Fund, because now the board of God's

Golden Acre felt ready to send another submission. "We still needed money from them, and we were now more structured than before. The next thing, I saw this big chest in front of me, and I looked at the badge to see whose it was – and it said T Blose.

" 'Oh, it's you,' I said. 'Where are you from?'

" 'Oh, the Nelson Mandela Children's Fund,' he replied.

" 'You mean to say I've had the Nelson Mandela chequebook all night?' I joked.

"Neil McKerrow had overheard what I said and came up afterwards with a smile on his face: 'You mean you gave him back his chequebook?' Well, we had a good laugh about it at the conference and when I got home I mentioned it to Patrick.

" 'What did you say his name was?' asked Patrick.

" 'T Blose,' I said.

" 'Well, you do realize, don't you, that that was the very man whom you tore a strip off a couple or more years ago when they turned down your application?' So again we roared with laughter!

"In fact we did get funding some time later from the Nelson Mandela Children's Fund and we are extremely grateful that they continue to support us. Temba Blose also came to know us better in the course of his important work in KwaZulu-Natal for CINDI and was a respected figure there. I always remember him advising me about my refusal to back down on the controversial issue of cluster foster care: 'Heather, if people challenge your ideas, and make it more difficult for you – then go out there and prove them wrong!' I like to tell people he was absolutely right and I followed his advice."

Heather's model for cluster foster care has now been copied elsewhere. By 2003 there were fewer people in government and in voluntary organizations who disputed her vision. Heather has turned out to be correct in both her judgement and her faith. Cluster foster care is now being seen as an effective way to bring up orphaned children right the way through their childhood and education, without losing touch with their culture and communities.

Furthermore, the South African government, inspired by Nelson Mandela himself, has now accepted the link between HIV and AIDS, and has implemented a new programme making highly active anti-retroviral therapy (HAART) available to millions of South Africans. Some of the orphans at God's Golden Acre are now receiving anti-retroviral medication. The outcome of this treatment will be to slow down and lessen the effects of the illness, in combination with powerful painkilling drugs. The wider recognition of Heather's theories about cluster foster care has enabled God's Golden Acre to attract the sort of funding from international organizations that should underpin its future. After all the hard years of struggle this has come as a welcome relief to the Reynolds.

"However, funding organizations come and go. It will always be important to continue to seek ongoing financial support," Heather reminds us. "Now that we have proper support facilities, thanks to our wonderful benefactors like the Nelson Mandela Children's Fund, Starfish, HopeHIV, and the Rockefeller Brothers Foundation, it seems incredible that we ever managed to cope," she says. "Things have changed such a lot since the days when we were trying to do everything on our own, and had just about enough food to eat. Our dream for God's Golden Acre has become reality.

"It was not until 2002, when we began to become better known in South Africa and overseas, that we started to receive donations on a scale that would enable us to move forward. In fact we will never forget our first large donor, HopeHIV in London. It was the most wonderful feeling suddenly to have something in the bank. There was money now to pay the electricity bills, phone bills, and the many running costs. For a whole year we did not have to worry when utility bills arrived in the post. We felt we were getting there, even though we continued to rely upon finding new funding."

In the early years Marie Godlyman, a senior official from the government's Department of Housing, had arrived unexpectedly on a visit to look round, but not in her official capacity. Later, she told Heather: "I think the Department of Housing could help. These children are orphans, and that is part of our responsibility. The fact that the parents have died shows how calamitous the whole situation is becoming, with all these children having no homes."

She went back to Durban and actually adapted South African government policy to embrace the problem of housing thousands of orphans in need. Eventually, Marie Godlyman orchestrated a 1.2 million Rand scheme for God's Golden Acre that would transfer the orphans into the cluster foster homes that Heather had always envisaged. The project was the catalyst of all change at God's Golden Acre, and the basis upon which everything since has been able to develop. It was, as Sir Winston Churchill once famously said, the end of the beginning.

The Department of Housing brought in Paul Keenan, a consulting engineer, who remained with the charity as a member of the board, to head up the cluster foster homes project – and all this gave the Zulu youngsters a further chance to get an official training in the building trade, because they could use the project as the basis for developing their skills. Four single-storey rectangular houses were eventually built, designed to make them feel to the children like a family home. When the final house was completed, Heather felt the years of sacrifice had been totally vindicated. "The bedrooms are light and airy, there are modern bathrooms, and day rooms for the children to use in the evenings after school. There is also a communal dining room connected to the kitchen. The homes have properly equipped sanitation, modern kitchens, and facilities to wash clothes and bed linen."

A crèche and nursery school provide the first steps in education for the orphans before primary school, and when the

purpose-built hospice for the sick babies was completed
Heather wrote:

> Today has been a very, very special day. We opened our hospice.
> Everything went off wonderfully and the place looked beautiful.
> God has truly blessed us. It was a real team effort and the Dutch
> volunteers from Livingstone worked like Trojans. The children
> did several special dance routines and the choir sang. All the chil-
> dren are well and they now also have a beautiful jungle gym to
> play on. Things are really looking up!

41
OVER THE RAINBOW

In 2004, **Apple Studios** in England gave God's Golden Acre the rights to two songs, "Imagine" and "Let It Be", to use in its choir productions. This enabled Heather to use further the creativity and talent of the young Zulus – proved on their successful tour to England two years earlier – to play a larger role in fundraising for the charity. She wrote:

Rotarians from Rugby Dunsmore, from Warwickshire in the United Kingdom, offered to help us put a CD together and market it, if we could get a good quality recording of our choir singing the songs. In order to do this, we needed recording equipment and a sound engineer. However, after a number of phone calls we realized that purchasing the equipment was certainly beyond our means. Not knowing anyone in the music industry, the time drew nearer for us to have completed the recording. With only a week to go we still had no sign of hope.

While I sat discussing the dilemma with the office staff, a friend of ours, Frank Vurovecz, walked in. He had been installing cupboards in the various new buildings at God's Golden Acre. In desperation I looked up at him and asked: "Frank, you don't by any chance know anyone in the music industry that could help us record a CD?" Frank looked at me and smilingly pointed a finger at himself.

"I have a recording studio," he said.

"What? Since when?" I exclaimed in disbelief.

It turned out he'd always had an interest, and when his son became involved in a band, they had obtained the equipment. "Frank," I said earnestly, "*you* have got to help me. And not only that, you've got to do it for free... I have no money." He agreed.

Don Fardon, a well-known record producer and singer musician, arrived from England to help with the recording, and we rushed to set up the recording equipment in the still-uncompleted Community Theatre building. With the set-up complete, Don and Frank switched it all on, only to discover that one of the amplifiers was not working, and the replacement parts from Japan would take three weeks to arrive. They tried to repair it for the rest of the day, but to no avail. Don told us we'd have no option but to book a recording studio to get the tracks down, as there was no time left. I baulked at the idea of paying between 15,000 and 20,000 Rand for a studio, calculating how many families I could feed in the valley for that amount of money. With no other options presenting themselves, the mood was sombre as we each went off to bed. I spent the night praying, wondering what God was doing, as the provision of the equipment had seemed so miraculous.

The next morning, Don came through to our meeting to say that the equipment was still not working. I turned to the staff around the table and said: "We have to pray. We need a miracle." We joined hands round the table and asked God for a miracle: "Father God, we need a miracle. We need to have that equipment working. We don't need to understand how you do it, but we believe that you can. Jesus, you said that what we ask in your name, it shall be done. So in your name we pray this prayer. If it be your will, then we ask that you repair that equipment, please. You know the situation is desperate and we have no money and we have to do this thing. So in your name we pray this prayer. Amen."

After the prayers some of us walked over to the theatre

building. I was feeling light-hearted somehow, despite the weight of the problem. As we stepped through the door, Don and Frank switched the equipment on again. Suddenly I heard a voice cry, "Whoo-hoo! It's working!" Astonishment registered on the faces of everyone in the recording room. The equipment didn't give one more hitch throughout the entire recording process, and we were able to lay down the tracks for all eight songs in time to be sent off to England for final mixing and production. God had proved himself faithful once more.

The CD album, *Over the Rainbow*, is being sold over the internet and also being marketed via Rotary. Over the coming years the album will provide a substantial revenue source for the charity. It is one of a number of projects – including music albums, concert tours, plays, musicals and TV productions – produced at God's Golden Acre.

On 17th October 2004 Heather achieved another of her long-held dreams. The opening of the Young Zulu Warrior Theatre at God's Golden Acre was an important milestone in the development of the community because it opened up a range of new opportunities, not only for the children of Khayelihle, but also for those in the valley.

At last there was a professional stage to express the enormous range of talent in the field of music and dance that is so vividly expressed in Zulu culture – it was indeed the world's first Zulu theatre and would act as a magnet for talent throughout the Valley of a Thousand Hills... bringing revenue, opportunity and perhaps fame to God's Golden Acre. Talented young Zulus from the valley found themselves presented with exciting opportunities to work alongside professional actors and musicians from the international world of theatre and music.

Lynne Maree of KwaZulu-Natal Dance Link was among the old friends present at the opening night of the theatre and it was an evening when she was able to look back with nostalgia upon a long association with God's Golden Acre and its young dancers. She wrote:

In March 2000 I was told that the offer that KwaZulu-Natal Dance Link had made, to run weekly dance workshops "somewhere", had been looked on positively by someone called Heather Reynolds who lived out somewhere off the N3 along a dirt track, and that I should visit her.

I drove up past a beautiful tree into a ramshackle parking lot covered in bougainvillea, found an open door that went into a living-room-cum-warehouse full of mattresses and piles of clothes. A quietly spoken man (Patrick) was the only person to appear. He greeted me and suggested that I wait for Heather. That was then.

The warmth and immediacy and rampant readiness to grab opportunities for "her" children took me into her spell, as it does everyone, and four-and-a-half frustrating and incredibly positive years have produced a theatre, a performing arts company of accomplished singers and dancers who did an international tour to the UK, three annual performances of our Dance for Youth production on a specially built theatre in the open air, and a happy relationship between God's Golden Acre and a multitude of teachers and members of KZN Dance Link. Long may it last!"

Bronwen Reynolds was also among the guests and she recorded the poignancy of that memorable day in her diary:

It's a hot summer afternoon, and as I drive into the parking lot at God's Golden Acre and park in the shade of the enormous fig tree, I sit for a moment and watch the scene before me. Dogs chase each another playfully across the sand, two Zulu dancers in traditional dress carry a pile of chairs into the community dining room, and a group of children deep in conversation suddenly burst into peals of laughter and run off, to where I assume the distant sounds of singing are coming from.

The rhythmic beating of a drum pulsates in the sticky heat as I exit the car and catch sight of my father Patrick coming across the parking lot from his studio.

Entering the coolness of the double-storey thatch building, with its generous roof sloping in graceful curves almost to the ground, we find a seat and observe the final preparations while the crowds who have come for this momentous occasion enjoy a traditional meal in the dining room.

Here in the theatre, Thulabona, the artistic director, fiddles with the spotlights; a young boy carries in a rawhide drum and positions it behind the *inthingos* – stage props made of thin branches roped together. Two men with beads of perspiration on their foreheads carry in extra speakers and begin to connect them, as their companions who stand and watch the process give very vocal, if not entirely helpful, input in Zulu.

Mum arrives, and a cloud of activity trails her as she gives her attention to each of the voices that clamour for her attention, needing decisions and direction for the multitude of tasks that still need to be completed before the ceremony can begin. At last the moment arrives, and the simple, ethnic interior of the theatre is hidden by the 550 bodies who, seated and standing, form a buzz of anticipation, mindless of the summer heat.

Affectionate greetings abounded across the crowded room, as old friends reacquainted themselves, once more gathered in solidarity for the cause of the children touched by God's Golden Acre. Bronwen continues:

The lights are dimmed, and the explosive beating of several traditional drums suddenly resonates through the building, vibrating through the structure and into the very chests of the audience, as a line of Zulu men dressed in traditional animal skins bursts onto the stage in a vibrant and energetic dance. Lifting their shields in unity and moving in fluid solidarity, their bodies hammer out an expression of the passion and pride that resides in the soul of each member of the Zulu nation.

The audience bursts into loud applause and the ceremony begins as Heather welcomes the attending dignitaries, management board members, staff, supporters and old friends. Scrutinizing the faces before her as she attempts to express her gratitude to each one for their involvement in the story of God's Golden Acre, she is overcome, and is stilled for a moment by a wave of tears.

Looking at the faces of the audience, I see several knowing smiles match my own, as together we recognize the Heather we know: strong enough to command an army, yet so full of the emotion that drives her that tears are never far from her and may descend at a moment's notice.

Lynne Maree of Dance Link introduces the premiere of *Thula Sizwe*, the drama production written and produced by Heather that was inspired by her work in the valley. The opening scenes, in which a Zulu king and his wife are killed by a rival tribe, leaving his children orphaned and alone, are emotionally laden and close to the hearts of many present. The powerful performances of the actors and the ever-changing scenes – from deep rural locations to a modern urban setting complete with taxi drivers and gossiping domestic workers, keep the audience riveted until the end.

Emerging from the theatre building, and gathering on the grass outside, we find that the summer heat has been replaced by darkening skies and a cold wind that swiftly ascends the crest of the hill on which we stand. As the storm approaches, and people scurry to their cars, I am reminded that, like the shifting weather, change is inevitable. For all those involved at God's Golden Acre, change has been, and will continue to be, an integral part of the process, and certainly for all the children whose lives have been touched by the work here, it is a change worth welcoming.

Yet behind the scenes of joy, and the chance of progress and consolidation, the fundamental purpose and role of the sanctuary had again been underlined just a few days before the opening of the theatre. Both the staff and children were in mourning for the death of a much-loved infant of God's Golden Acre. The tragedy was recorded by Bronwen Reynolds:

As I sit reading through this manuscript, surrounded by visiting family, and my mother and father sitting on the bed, one of the caregivers, Gogo Elina, comes to let Mum know that four-year-old Sne has just passed away. We'd all known that her time was fast approaching. Now, as Mum gives instructions to have everyone gather together for prayers and songs, she and Gogo Elina begin to sing a hymn of praise for the life that has just ended. Their voices lift together spontaneously until Mum's voice cracks with emotion and she can't sing any more.

The low Zulu voice sings on steadily as Mum's face creases with grief... for a brief moment, the characteristic strength gives way to a threatening flood of sadness. And I wonder how she does it day after day. But then I realize this is *why* she does it. I see in her eyes the peace that comes from knowing that she has fulfilled in some small way the vow she made to her God, to "never let them die all alone". She knows that Sne has passed away surrounded by people who loved her, and that makes it somehow seem worthwhile.

While the staff members go to Cato Ridge to arrange the death certificate, I hear Mum dialling a phone number. She begins to chat, and I realize she's phoned my brother Brendan in Holland. Her voice, a little thin from the crying and singing, warms as she teases him about sleeping late. They talk for a while and Mum starts to sing a funny little song from a movie we'd watched many years ago. I have to smile, and sitting here in a blanket on the armchair, watching my family, I realize that I am truly blessed, and given the chance, I'd not change a thing. The reality of life – and death – reminds us to value the precious arbitrary moments that would otherwise pass us by.

42
THE FOOTBALL
MIRACLE

The world of show business was not the only one where Heather had ambitions for young Zulus, and not the only one where miracles would happen in 2004. She believed strongly that organized sport, and specifically football, could help to instil hope and a sense of direction in the thousands of youngsters in the valley who had no outlets for their energy and natural aggression.

Mr Mapanga of the Thandanani Football League was visiting God's Golden Acre one day when he heard for the first time that Heather had managed to develop a connection with Martin Edwards, the president of Manchester United Football Club, and through him Dave Richards, the chairman of the Premier League in England. He realized that both Edwards and Richards were in positions of power and influence and might be able to help the development of youth football in the valley beyond people's wildest dreams and imagination. It was incredible news.

In fact Mr Mapanga's eyes opened so wide it seemed they would consume his cheeks. He stared out of the window of the office – his mouth gaping. The mind of the man was obviously racing at the possibilities of a connection between his humble and largely impoverished organization, and in the first place, the president of the most famous football club in the world, and in the second, the world's top football league, the

English Premier League. At length he let out what seemed to be an enormous whistling sound and turned his gaze upon Heather, with a beaming smile upon his face.

It might possibly have been the best and most exciting piece of news that Mr Mapanga had ever received in his life – and yet it was so implausible nobody would have blamed him if he had dismissed it as a joke. Mr Mapanga, head of marketing and publicity of the Thandanani League, had been meeting Heather together with Nkosi Mlaba, honorary president of the God's Golden Acre Junior League Association. They were putting together a memorandum of agreement between the Association and the League. The former would be affiliated to the latter – and the League would organize the administration of, and arrange the fixtures for, the junior games. If ambitions were to be realized, there might be over 100 teams eventually – enabling boys from the age of twelve to 20 to play competitive football on a regular basis.

At the time, Heather still did not know whether her meetings with Martin Edwards and Dave Richards would take place – or if they would help God's Golden Acre. However, she was so excited at the prospect of a meeting with them that she could not resist telling both men about it. The logistics of maintaining and sustaining a successful youth football programme had been worrying Heather for some months. They had three grounds – that the clubs of the Thandanani League shared – and a number of "kick-abouts" for practice. However, there was every prospect that more than the initially agreed 68 Zulu youth teams, at various age levels, would – in fairness to all – have to be extended across the huge rural district of KwaXimba, and beyond into other valley areas.

All her life Heather had followed the English Football League and was a supporter of Manchester United. She felt at this time that she needed top-class outside help and advice, and also a greater level of funding than she could obtain from any local corporate sponsorship. Perhaps, she reasoned, the

answer lay in the English Premier League. BBC producer Bill
Hamilton, a qualified football referee, had warned her – while
filming at God's Golden Acre – that it would be very hard to
get direct access to any of Britain's top professional football
league clubs. He told Heather they were all besieged by charities looking for financial support or kit sponsorship. The only
way in – he advised – was if she could find someone who
could be persuaded that the God's Golden Acre Junior League
Association deserved priority treatment.

Within weeks, by sheer coincidence, at a meeting at God's
Golden Acre she found herself talking about football to a visitor who, it turned out, knew someone very important at
Manchester United. By 2004, Martin Edwards had retired
from the job of running the club as chairman, and had
divested his considerable shareholding. He was enjoying the
more honorary position as its president. However, he
remained a man of considerable status, importance and influence in European football. Heather was astonished at the
unexpected connection her friend was able to offer.

Martin Edwards had been a director of Manchester United
since 1970 and succeeded his father Louis as chairman in
1980. The following year he became the club's first chief
executive, a position he held for almost 20 years until August
2000. He ran the club during the most successful period in its
history. In the more than 30 years that Martin Edwards was a
member of the Board of Directors, Manchester United won
seven League titles, seven FA Cups, the European Cup, the
European Cup-Winners Cup, the League Cup, the UEFA
Super Cup, the Inter-Continental Cup, and seven Charity
Shields. It was an awesome record – probably unequalled in
the history of professional club administration at board level.

The prospect of meeting this very senior man in a world of
which she knew nothing made Heather nervous. It was
February 2004 when she and Patrick were driven up the M6
motorway in central England to the home of Martin and Sue

Edwards for Heather's first meeting with the couple. The latter had kindly agreed to meet the Reynolds to hear about God's Golden Acre and its proposed Junior Football League. Characteristically, Heather prayed aloud in the back of the car: "Oh dear heavenly Father, I wish to thank you for this day, Lord, and thank you for our many, many blessings. Father, today we ask you to be with us in this meeting. We ask you to guide us with wisdom, Lord, to say and do the things that need to be said and done, Father. We always trust in you, Lord, and your will of what the outcome will be; we shall accept that graciously, Father. So, Father, we ask you to be with Martin and Sue, to open their ears and their heart so they might hear and see the things I shall show to them today. Let them be an instrument of your will, that we may reach and serve these many, many, wonderful disadvantaged children, Father. Amen."

Soon the car was approaching the gates of the Edwards' house in Cheshire and the host himself was at the front door to usher the Reynolds into his home. They remained together for nearly three hours. Heather told Martin Edwards that financial help to kick-start the football league could change the face of the entire valley for the underprivileged children. Any youngster growing up in a normal society – being fed, clothed and educated – and then being put into disciplined sporting activities had a better chance of growing up to become a good citizen within his or her community. Children involved in sport were not so likely to be distracted into a harmful lifestyle.

"You don't find them sitting on the grass verges, forming gangs and using drugs. So it's that important to us. With positive things going on around them, our children can become not only good sportsmen but also hopefully be sent back to school to become the next generation of professionals, and business people – tomorrow's teachers, doctors, plumbers and electricians. It is vitally important that we are able to put them into a disciplined environment like sport, where they can grow up and develop a sense of responsibility. They deserve that chance," she said. Heather came away more than delighted with what the president of Manchester United said to her.

On the journey home she said to Patrick: "The problem is that people like the Edwards are bombarded with requests and pestered continually by people trying to use them. However, the moment Martin stepped out of that doorway I knew he wanted to meet us. His wife Sue was extremely warm and it was clear she is a Christian, and committed to many charities for children. So her heart was in the right place and she put me at ease."

Back in KwaXimba, influential people like Nkosi Mlaba and Mr Mapanga, who knew about the meeting, were praying for it to be successful. It was not every day that someone they knew had an opportunity to meet a person of the calibre and status of the man who has run Manchester United for three decades.

The new friendship with Martin Edwards began to bear fruit for Heather's football ambitions in the Valley of a Thousand Hills within a few months. In November 2004 she was back in England and this time was the president's guest at Old Trafford Stadium where she was thrilled to be conducted round the club's famous museum with its awesome collection of trophies and memorabilia of a hundred years of Manchester United. On this day Heather also met David Daly of Nike, who control the Manchester United kit and equipment brand. He was deeply moved by her presentation of the predicament and social exclusion facing thousands of children in the valley and pledged to help her in whatever way he could by referring her through the organization.

The following week, thanks to Martin Edwards, Heather was able to meet Dave Richards, the chairman of the Premier League and one of the most powerful figures in British football. He turned out to be a man with a compassionate interest in the safety and well-being of children, with strong links to the Football Foundation and also the National Society for the Prevention of Cruelty to Children. Fortunately for Heather he had also spent part of his professional life in South Africa and was well acquainted with the crisis facing the rural parts of the country. He was moved by what Heather had to say and was struck by her sincerity. It was a day he was flying out to Madrid to watch England play Spain but he found time to take her personally in his car to meet David Davies, the executive director of the Football Association; Jane Bateman, head of international relations at the FA; and Alastair Bennett, director of external relations at the Football Foundation. Further meetings followed with senior Nike executives in London and Holland, so that by Christmas 2004 Heather was able to look ahead to the future with confidence for making things happen in her very African world of football.

For her it was yet another miracle. God had once again answered her prayers. She now looks forward to the day – and she believes it will happen – when a steady stream of young men from the valley can establish themselves as international star players, thus feeding the dreams and aspirations of an even younger generation. She believes that with the help of funding from English football through the Premier League and the Football Association, the God's Golden Acre Junior Football Association and its academy can become a benchmark for youth football in the rural areas of southern Africa – laying down an infrastructure for other government-funded projects to follow.

By early 2005 Heather had asked the Premier League and the FA to help fund a project that would include a multi-sports AstroTurf stadium at God's Golden Acre with floodlights and modern changing facilities, and the introduction of FA coaches in KwaZulu-Natal to train African coaches. The stadium, she hopes, would be the home of the football academy for the Valley of a Thousand Hills and the source from which her Junior League would thrive with up to 30 full-size pitches equipped with changing rooms and toilets in the valley itself, plus dozens of kick-abouts for the children to play on – alongside valley schools. She was hoping Nike would also assist in the funding.

If this further miracle happens, then thousands of boys and girls who have previously faced social exclusion will have the chance to play organized sport for the first time.

43
THE PARABLE OF THE
GOOD SAMARITAN

Late one night, Heather was driving one of the God's Golden Acre vehicles along National Highway 3, the motorway that acts as the artery linking Durban on the south east coast to the north. National Highway 3 is imprinted upon the heart of rural South Africa and continues through Pietermaritzburg, Ladysmith, Harrismith and then Heidelberg, before reaching Johannesburg.

It was misty with torrents of rain, driven by high winds, lashing the front and sides of the vehicle, reducing visibility to a few yards in the watery haze. There were few cars on the road. She was travelling after a night out, with a group of volunteers, south from Pietermaritzburg, towards God's Golden Acre at Cato Ridge. They were sitting in the back, and most were asleep. At that moment, in the vehicle travelling on the national highway, came the appropriate ending to a book about the life of Heather Reynolds. It mirrored the parable of the Good Samaritan.

Suddenly in the corner of her eye, through lashing rain and the mist, Heather noticed a man walking on crutches along the side of the road. It was like an apparition. Many people in the same circumstances – stormy weather on a dark, wet night where it is dangerous to stop because of vehicle hijackings – would have driven on, assuming, or hoping, that it was just a figment of their imagination. Heather, however, made a decision instantly. She called out: "Sorry, guys, I've got to stop. I cannot go on. I think there is a man on crutches walking along the main highway back there."

She stopped the vehicle, gently reversed back in the dark, and suddenly an African in his forties appeared by the side of the passenger seat window. Heather told him quickly: "Come on, jump in." It was not an appropriate thing to say in the circumstances, but she did not want to remain parked on the side of the road for any longer than she had to be.

She said later: "I'll never forget the pain on his face when he tried with his one leg to get in beside us. In a flash I realized he was an amputee. I caught that look, and I was sucked into all the emotions that he was feeling. The pain. The frustration. The anger. The cold winds and the lashing rain. He had endured so much. We helped him into the passenger seat and I asked him where he had come from. He told me he was Mr Zungu and he was a diabetic and had had his leg amputated at Edendale Hospital. I was astonished.

"'The hospital is way on the other side of Pietermaritzburg – on the other side of town. How long have you been walking on your crutches?'

"'Nine hours,' he replied. 'I was discharged from hospital this afternoon at three o'clock. But I didn't have money to catch a local taxi or bus, so I just started walking.'"

It became clear that Mr Zungu had been sent away with no food, nothing to drink, with nobody to turn to for help. The only way he could get home was to take his crutches and walk. He'd been hobbling along for nine solid hours when she found him. Heather recalls: "It was amazing. My thoughts were racing and it brought me close to tears. Not one single person had stopped to offer him a lift. How many vehicles must have passed him that day? Thousands and thousands of cars and lorries! How could every single person have passed him? What's wrong with us?

"Imagine, you are driving along and you see a man trying to walk with crutches on one leg and you drive by; you do nothing. Surely, somebody could have stopped and picked him up. Even the police patrol cars must have gone along the N3 highway several times during those nine hours.

"I asked him where he was going to and I could not make out the area where he lived from what he told me, but I followed his directions and it turned out to be the main road down to KwaXimba, and of course I knew it well. If he had continued walking on his own it would have been another seven or eight hours before he reached home. I don't think he would have made it. He would have become delirious, either with cold and exhaustion, or sheer weakness. He might have died on that road.

"He sat hunched up beside me and he clearly was at the point of total exhaustion. I put the heater on full blast to warm him and eventually, after 40 minutes, we reached the point on the valley road nearest to his home. He was so grateful he was unable to express himself. I gave him some money, we said some prayers, and we sang a little song together in the vehicle before he left us. Looking back, I could not imagine where Mr Zungu's thoughts must have gone that day. What would have been the most dominant? Would it have been anger, frustration, sadness or despair? All those things must have crossed his feelings during those nine hours on crutches. The poor fellow had only just been amputated. He should have been lying down on his back.

"So were the hundreds, if not thousands of people who passed him by that day on National Highway 3 by definition uncaring or cruel? 'Judge not', the Bible tells us – but one answer to that question could be that it's always easier to find a reason, or excuse, for not doing something, not to help someone. It's easier not to take responsibility for, or not to get involved with, the problems and difficulties of our brothers and sisters.

"Self-justification can start at a personal level, like walking past a beggar on a street corner and turning our head away. It is an attitude of mind that is likely to lead to absence of community spirit, a detachment of responsibility for our obligations towards our fellow human beings. Is this the harvest of the nuclear age – the 'me' generation? The choice is ours. In the same way, if we don't respond to the desperate plight of a generation of children in Africa, and in the other AIDS hotspots in our world, we will be sowing the seeds ultimately of the destruction of those societies that have abandoned them.

"Nearly 5 million people in Africa are HIV-positive and by 2010 there could be up to 4.8 million maternal orphans. Without hope they will turn to crime, drugs and prostitution. Without help and guidance they will not be able to take their rightful place in society. The possibility of a feral society developing within our midst and the implications of that are too awful to contemplate. What would then be the solution to that problem? Shooting young criminals, as has been done in some other parts of the world?

"Are we going to secure the future of the orphans? Future generations will hold us responsible for the world we bequeath to them. Children will look back and ask us uncomprehendingly: 'Why did you not do something? How could you abandon all those children, allow so many to suffer and die?'

"Well, that scenario thankfully hasn't played itself out yet, and we still have enough time to make a difference. As Christians it's so important to remember the two greatest laws: 'Love the Lord your God,' and 'Love your neighbour'. Matthew 25 makes one think very deeply. When you call, 'Lord, Lord', will Jesus say, 'I know you not'? Did you feed him? Did you clothe him? Did you give him something to drink? Did you visit him in prison? This is a clear directive of what Jesus expects from us.

"My journey through life with God, serving him, has taught me the power of prayer, the power of love, and the incredible healing power of compassion and forgiveness. To every one of you who has travelled with me through the pages of this book, I pray that in some way my life has touched yours. Together let us reach out to enrich the lives of millions of little children who would otherwise face a life without hope.

"I truly believe that as brothers and sisters in Christ, humanitarians, people from all races, colour or creeds, we can combine our efforts to change this world into a better place. As a global nation let us take responsibility: what we invest in the future of a child, we invest in the future of our world. God bless."